American Government and Politics Today
2010–2011 Brief Edition

American Government and Politics Today

2010–2011 Brief Edition

Steffen W. Schmidt
Iowa State University

Mack C. Shelley II
Iowa State University

Barbara A. Bardes
University of Cincinnati

WADSWORTH
CENGAGE Learning

Australia • Brazil • Japan • Korea • Mexico • Singapore • Spain • United Kingdom • United States

WADSWORTH
CENGAGE Learning™

American Government and Politics Today
THE ESSENTIALS 2010–2011 Edition
Schmidt • Shelley • Bardes

Publisher: Suzanne Jeans

Executive Editor: Carolyn Merrill

Developmental Editor: Suzy Spivey

Assistant Editor: Katherine Hayes

Editorial Assistant: Angela Hodge

Associate Development Project Manager: Caitlin Holroyd

Senior Marketing Manager: Amy Whitaker

Marketing Communications Manager: Heather Baxley

Senior Content Production Manager: Ann Borman

Print Buyer: Rebecca Cross

Photo Research: Ann Hoffman

Copy Editor: Ann Conklin

Proofreaders: Pat Lewis, Judy Kiviat

Indexer: Terry Casey

Art Director: Linda Helcher

Interior Design: IRDG

Cover Design: Rokusek Design

Compositor: Parkwood Composition Service

For product information and technology assistance, contact us at
**Cengage Learning Academic Resource Center,
1-800-423-0563.**
For permission to use material from this text or product, submit all requests online at
www.cengage.com/permissions.
Further permissions questions can be emailed to
permissionrequest@cengage.com.

Library of Congress Control Number: 2009935789

Student Edition ISBN-13: 978-0-495-79713-5
Student Edition ISBN-10: 0-495-79713-8

Instructor's Edition ISBN-13: 978-1-4390-8314-7
Instructor's Edition ISBN-10: 1-4390-8314-2

Wadsworth Political Science
25 Thomson Place
Boston, MA 02210

Cengage Learning products are represented in Canada by Nelson Education, Ltd.

For your course and learning solutions, visit
www.cengage.com.
Purchase any of our products at your local college store or at our preferred online store at **www.ichapters.com.**

Printed in the United States of America
2 3 4 5 6 7 14 13 12 11 10

ContentsinBrief

Contents

Part I: The American System

Chapter 1 Features

(AP Photo/Toby Talbot)

CHAPTER 2: Forging a New Government: The Constitution 19

Chapter 2 Features

(The Granger Collection)

CHAPTER 3: Federalism 44

(Bettmann/Corbis)

Chapter 3 Features

CHAPTER 4: Civil Liberties 65

Chapter 4 Features

(AP Photo/Joel Andrews/*The Lufkin Daily News*)

CHAPTER 5: Civil Rights 91

Chapter 5 Features

The Politics of
Boom and Bust:
The Recession's Impact
on Immigration 106

making a difference
Dealing with Discrimination 112

(AP Photo)

Part II: The Politics of American Democracy

CHAPTER 6: Public Opinion, Political Socialization, and the Media 116

Chapter 6 Features

(AP Photo/Kristie Bull/Graylock.com)

(AP Photo/Tony Dejak)

Chapter 7 Features

At Issue:
Should Workers Forgo Secret
Ballots When Attempting to
Organize a Union? 147

making a difference
You Can Be a
Convention Delegate 169

(AP Photo/Elise Amendola)

CHAPTER 8: Campaigns, Elections, and Voting Behavior 173

Chapter 8 Features

making a difference
Registering and Voting 197

Part III: Institutions of American Government

(Todd Gipstein/Corbis)

Chapter 9 Features

CHAPTER 10:
The Presidency 228

Chapter 10 Features

(Darren McCollester/Getty Images)

CHAPTER 11 : The Bureaucracy 252

Chapter 11 Features

CHAPTER 12: The Judiciary 277

(AP Photo/Todd Goodrich)

Chapter 12 Features

making a difference
Changing the Legal System 298

Part IV: Policymaking

CHAPTER 13: Domestic and Economic Policy 301

(Win McNamee/Getty Images)

Chapter 13 Features

Chapter 14 Features

The Politics of
Boom and Bust:
Twenty-First-Century Pirates 345

making a difference
Working for Human Rights 355

(AP Photo/Nasser Nasser)

PREFACE

With Barack Obama in the White House, the great game of politics entered a new phase. The Democrats, now in control of the presidency as well as the U.S. House and Senate, faced an extraordinary series of challenges. What should the federal government do to steer the nation out of the greatest economic crisis in more than seventy years? How should the government address the issue of health-care reform? What should be done about global warming? How should we handle the issues posed by Afghanistan, Iran, Iraq, and other countries? Throughout this Brief Edition of *American Government and Politics Today,* you will read about how our government has responded to past issues and how these responses have shaped American government and politics.

This edition is basically a condensed and updated version of the larger editions of *American Government and Politics Today.* It has been created specifically for those of you who want a text that presents the fundamental components of the American political system while retaining the quality and readability of the larger editions. You will find that this edition is up to date in every respect. The text, figures, tables, and all pedagogical features reflect the latest available data. We have also included coverage of all recently issued laws, regulations, and court decisions that have—or will have—a significant impact on American society and our political system.

Like the larger editions, this volume places a major emphasis on political participation and involvement. This brief, fourteen-chapter text has been heralded by reviewers as the best essentials text for its affordability, conciseness, clarity, and readability.

- Getting straight to the point, this text helps pare down a wealth of material, focusing on the essential events, concepts, and topics of an American government course.
- Strong themes of informed and active participation along with a critical-thinking approach spark student interest in wanting to get involved and know more.
- *At Issue* feature boxes focus on a controversial topic to provoke discussion and conclude with a *For Critical Analysis* question to ignite critical thinking.
- *Making a Difference* boxes at the end of each chapter promote student participation by answering the questions "Why Should You Care?" and "What Can You Do?" offering practical ways for students to get involved in politics with online resources.

NEW TO THIS EDITION

This new edition has been thoroughly updated and revised to reflect the significant events and explosive changes that have occurred in the last year.

- A new design creates a visually appealing, user-friendly presentation that will engage students' interest while maintaining the affordable price.
- The text includes the very latest coverage on the Obama administration and legislative agenda, the banking crisis, and health-care reform.
- There are all new sections on immigration, including Obama's immigration proposals; energy and the environment, including new information on the Cap-and-Trade Program; the economy, including unemployment, inflation, monetary policy, and the tax system; and China's economic growth.
- New "Helpful Online Resources" sections at the end of each chapter foster further exploration and participation.

THE MOST COMPLETE WEB CONNECTION

While this edition may be physically brief, its scope is enlarged by numerous resources that are available on the Web. You can access these resources to gain a fuller understanding of the issues dominating today's politics. You can begin your journey by accessing a Web site specific to the Brief Edition:

academic.cengage.com/polisci/Schmidt/Brief6e

Features of the Web site include:

- Learning Objectives
- Chapter Glossary
- Flashcards
- Crossword Puzzles
- Internet Activities
- Tutorial Quizzes

HIGH-INTEREST FEATURES

In this edition, we have included special features designed to pique your interest. These features are interspersed throughout the text.

Topical Features

Each *At Issue* feature focuses on a controversial topic and concludes with a *For Critical Analysis* question to invite critical thinking. *The Politics of Boom and Bust,* a feature new to this edition, addresses current economic developments. Almost all features are new for this edition. They discuss the following topics:

At Issue Features:

- Should We Elect the President by Popular Vote? (Chapter 2)
- Should Same-Sex Marriages Be Recognized Everywhere? (Chapter 3)
- Should Muslims' Religious Needs Be Accommodated on Campus? (Chapter 4)
- Did the Stimulus Legislation Contain Too Much Pork? (Chapter 11)
- Should the Rich Pay Even More in Taxes? (Chapter 13)

The Politics of Boom and Bust features:

- Liberals—or Progressives? (Chapter 1)
- The Recession's Impact on Immigration (Chapter 5)
- Just What Is a Trillion Dollars, Anyway? (Chapter 6)
- Endless Federal Budget Deficits? (Chapter 9)
- The Audacity of Barack Obama (Chapter 10)
- What Should the Government Do about Troubled Banks? (Chapter 11)
- Bailouts and the Danger of Moral Hazard (Chapter 13)
- Twenty-First-Century Pirates (Chapter 14)

Making a Difference Features

At the end of every chapter, a feature entitled *Making a Difference* enhances our emphasis on participation. These features provide you with useful information for active citizenship. We give you tips on how to find information on issues, how to learn about your elected representatives, how to join and participate in advocacy organizations, how to protect your civil rights and liberties, and more.

OTHER SPECIAL PEDAGOGICAL AIDS

The 2010–2011 Brief Edition of *American Government and Politics Today* retains many of the pedagogical aids and features of the larger editions, including the following:

- **Key Terms**—Important terms that are boldfaced and defined in the text when they are first used. These terms are defined in the text margins, listed at the end of the chapter with the page numbers on which they appear, and included in the Glossary at the back of the book.
- **Chapter Summary**—A point-by-point summary of the chapter text.
- **Questions for Critical Analysis**—A series of questions at the end of each chapter designed to inspire creative thinking about the topics introduced in the chapter. Some questions also introduce new information.

APPENDICES

The Brief Edition of *American Government and Politics Today* includes, as appendices, both the Declaration of Independence (Appendix A) and the U.S. Constitution (Appendix B). The text of the Constitution has been annotated to help you understand the meaning and significance of the various provisions in this important document. Also, Appendix C presents *Federalist Papers* No. 10 and No. 51. These selections are also annotated to help you grasp their importance in understanding the American philosophy of government.

SUPPLEMENTS

For the Instructor

PowerLecture DVD with JoinIn™ and ExamView®

- Interactive **PowerPoint® Lectures,** a one-stop lecture and class preparation tool, makes it easy for you to assemble, edit, publish, and present custom lectures for your course. You will have access to a set of PowerPoint slides with outlines specific to each chapter of *American Government and Politics Today, Brief Edition,* as well as photos, figures, and tables found in the book. In addition, we provide media-enhanced PowerPoint slides for each chapter that can be used on their own or easily integrated with the book-specific outlines. Audio and video clips depicting both historic and current-day events; NEW animated learning modules illustrating key concepts; tables, statistical charts, and graphs; and photos from the book as well as outside sources are provided at the appropriate places in the chapter. You can also add your own materials—culminating in a powerful, personalized, media-enhanced presentation.
- A **Test Bank** in Microsoft® Word and in ExamView (computerized testing) offers a large array of well-crafted, multiple-choice and essay questions, along with their answers and page references.
- An **Instructor's Manual** includes learning objectives, chapter outlines, discussion questions, suggestions for stimulating class activities and projects, tips on integrating media into your class (including step-by-step instructions on how to create your own podcasts), suggested readings and Web resources, and a section specially designed to help teaching assistants and adjunct instructors.
- **JoinIn** offers book-specific "clicker" questions that test and track student comprehension of key concepts. Political Polling questions simulate voting, engage students,

foster dialogue on group behaviors and values, and add personal relevance; the results can be compared to national data, leading to lively discussions. Visual Literacy questions are tied to images from the book and add useful pedagogical tools and high-interest feedback during your lectures. Save the data from students' responses all semester—track their progress and show them how political science works by incorporating this exciting new tool into your classroom. It is available for college and university adopters only.

■ The *Resource Integration Guide* outlines the rich collection of resources available to instructors and students within the chapter-by-chapter framework of the book, suggesting how and when each supplement can be used to optimize learning.

Premium Web site with Infotrac® Instant Access Code

The Premium Web site for *American Government and Politics Today, Brief Edition,* offers a variety of rich online learning resources designed to enhance the student experience. These resources include podcasts, critical-thinking activities, simulations, animated learning modules, timelines, flashcards, and videos. Chapter resources are correlated with key chapter learning concepts, and users can browse or search for content in a variety of ways.

CL NewsNow

CL NewsNow brings the news right into your classroom with a combination of Associated Press news stories, videos, and images that bring current events to life. For students, a collection of news stories and accompanying videos are served up each week via the Premium Web site that accompanies *American Government and Politics Today, Brief Edition.* For instructors, an additional set of multimedia-rich PowerPoint slides are posted each week to the password-protected area of the text's companion. Instructors may use these slides to take a class poll or trigger a lively debate about the events that are shaping the world right now. And because this all-in-one presentation tool includes the text of the original newsfeed—along with videos, photos, and discussion questions—no Internet connection is required!

WebTutor™ on WebCT™, Blackboard®, and Angel®

Rich with content for your American government course, this Web-based teaching and learning tool includes course management, study/mastery, and communication tools. Use WebTutor to provide virtual office hours, post your syllabus, and track student progress with WebTutor's quizzing material. For students, WebTutor offers real-time access to interactive online tutorials and simulations, practice quizzes, and Web links—all correlated to *American Government and Politics Today, Brief Edition.*

Companion Web site

Students will find open access to learning objectives, tutorial quizzes, chapter glossaries, flashcards, and crossword puzzles, all correlated by chapter. Instructors also have access to the Instructor's Manual and PowerPoint slides at **www.cengage.com/politicalscience/ schmidt/agandptbrief6e**.

Political Theatre DVD 2.0

Bring politics home to students with Political Theatre 2.0, up-to-date through the 2008 election season. This is the second edition of this three-DVD series and includes real video clips that show American political thought throughout the public sector. Clips include both classic and contemporary political advertisements, speeches, interviews, and more.

Available to adopters of Cengage textbooks, version 2.0 provides lots of added functionality, such as critical-thinking questions and voiceover introductions.

JoinIn on Turning Point® for Political Theatre

For even more interaction, combine Political Theatre with the innovative teaching tool of a classroom response system through JoinIn. Poll your students with questions created for you or create your own questions. Built within the Microsoft PowerPoint software, JoinIn is easy to integrate into your current lectures in conjunction with the "clicker" hardware of your choice.

Wadsworth News Video for 2010 DVD

This collection of three- to six-minute video clips on relevant political issues serves as a great lecture or discussion launcher.

Great Speeches Collection

The Great Speeches Collection includes the full text of more than sixty memorable orations for you to incorporate into your course. Whether your interest is to examine speech structure, intent, or effect, you're sure to find an example that fits your needs. Speeches can be collated in a printed reader to supplement your existing course materials or even bound into a core textbook.

ABC Video: Speeches by President Barack Obama

This DVD contains nine famous speeches by President Barack Obama, from 2004 to the present day, including his speech at the 2004 Democratic National Convention; his 2008 speech on race, "A More Perfect Union"; and his 2009 inaugural address. Speeches are divided into short video segments for easy, time-efficient viewing. This instructor supplement also features critical-thinking questions and answers for each speech, designed to spark classroom discussion.

For the Students

Premium Web site with Infotrac® Instant Access Code

The Premium Web site for *American Government and Politics Today, Brief Edition,* offers a variety of rich online learning resources to enhance the learning experience. These resources include podcasts, critical-thinking activities, simulations, animated learning modules, timelines, flashcards, and videos. Chapter resources are correlated with key chapter learning concepts, allowing users to browse or search for content in a variety of ways.

CL NewsNow

CL NewsNow is a combination of Associated Press news stories, videos, and images that bring current events to life. Each week, a collection of news stories and accompanying videos are served up via the Premium Web site for *American Government and Politics Today, Brief Edition.* And because this all-in-one presentation tool includes the text of the original newsfeed—along with videos, photos, and discussion questions—no Internet connection is required!

Companion Web site

You will find open access to online study aids such as learning objectives, tutorial quizzes, chapter glossaries, flashcards, and crossword puzzles, all correlated by chapter, on this book's companion website at **www.cengage.com/politicalscience/schmidt/ agandptbrief6e**.

Election 2008: An American Government Supplement

The use of real examples in this election booklet, which addresses the 2008 presidential, congressional, and gubernatorial races, makes the concepts covered come alive.

The Handbook of Selected Court Cases

This handbook includes more than thirty United States Supreme Court cases.

The Handbook of Selected Legislation and Other Documents

This handbook features excerpts from laws passed by the U.S. Congress that have had a significant impact on American politics.

ACKNOWLEDGMENTS

In preparing *American Government and Politics Today,* 2010–2011 Brief Edition, we were the beneficiaries of the expert guidance of a skilled and dedicated team of publishers and editors. We have benefited greatly from the supervision and encouragement given by our executive editor, Carolyn Merrill.

We are grateful to our production editor, Ann Borman, for her ability to make this project as smooth-running and as perfect as is humanly possible. We are also indebted to our developmental editor, Suzy Spivey, for pushing us to be accurate with the manuscript and with the photos and their captions. We are indebted to the staff at Parkwood Composition. Their ability to generate the pages for this text quickly and accurately made it possible for us to meet our ambitious printing schedule. We also thank Ann Hoffman for her work on photo research and permissions, and Anne Sheroff for clearing rights. In addition, our gratitude goes to all of those who worked on the various supplements offered with this text, especially assistant editor Katherine Hayes, and to Caitlin Holroyd, who coordinates the Web site and other multimedia offerings. We would also like to thank Amy Whitaker, marketing manager, for her tremendous efforts in marketing the text.

Many other people helped during the research and editorial stages of this edition as well. Gregory Scott coordinated the authors' efforts and provided editorial and research assistance. Anne Kelley Conklin's and Pat Lewis's copyediting and proofreading abilities contributed greatly to the book. We also thank Roxie Lee for her assistance, and Sue Jasin of K&M Consulting for her contributions to the smooth running of the project. Finally, we are grateful for the proofreading services provided by Judy Kiviat.

Any errors, of course, remain our own. We welcome comments from instructors and students alike. Suggestions that we have received on previous editions have helped us to improve this text and to adapt it to the changing needs of instructors and students.

S.W.S.
M.C.S.
B.A.B.

ABOUT THE AUTHORS

Steffen W. Schmidt

Steffen W. Schmidt is a professor of political science at Iowa State University. He grew up in Colombia, South America and studied in Colombia, Switzerland, and France. He obtained his Ph.D. from Columbia University, New York, in public law and government.

Schmidt has published six books and more than 150 journal articles. He is also the recipient of numerous prestigious teaching prizes, including the Amoco Award for Lifetime Career Achievement in Teaching and the Teacher of the Year award. He is a pioneer in the use of Web-based and real-time video courses and is a member of the American Political Science Association's section on computers and multimedia. He is on the editorial board of the *Political Science Educator* and is the technology and teaching editor of the *Journal of Political Science Education.*

Schmidt has a political talk show on WOI radio, where he is known as Dr. Politics, streaming live once a week at **www.woi.org**. The show has been broadcast live from various U.S. and international venues. He is a frequent political commentator for *CNN en Español* and the British Broadcasting Corporation.

Schmidt likes to snow ski, ride hunter jumper horses, race sailboats, and scuba dive.

Mack C. Shelley II

Mack C. Shelley II is professor of political science, professor of statistics, and director of the Research Institute for Studies in Education at Iowa State University. After receiving his bachelor's degree from American University in Washington, D.C., he completed graduate studies at the University of Wisconsin at Madison, where he received a master's degree in economics and a Ph.D. in political science. He taught for two years at Mississippi State University before arriving at Iowa State in 1979.

Shelley has published numerous articles, books, and monographs on public policy. From 1993 to 2002, he served as elected coeditor of the *Policy Studies Journal.* His published books include *The Permanent Majority: The Conservative Coalition in the United States Congress; Biotechnology and the Research Enterprise* (with William F. Woodman and Brian J. Reichel); *American Public Policy: The Contemporary Agenda* (with Steven G. Koven and Bert E. Swanson); and *Redefining Family Policy: Implications for the 21st Century* (with Joyce M. Mercier and Steven Garasky). Other recent work has focused on electronic government and the "digital divide," learning communities, how to improve student life (especially in residence halls), and public health.

His leisure time includes traveling, working with students, and playing with the family dog and three cats.

Barbara A. Bardes

Barbara A. Bardes is a professor of political science at the University of Cincinnati. She received her bachelor of arts degree and master of arts degree from Kent State University. After completing her Ph.D. at the University of Cincinnati, she held faculty positions at Mississippi State University and Loyola University in Chicago. She returned to the University of Cincinnati as dean of one of its colleges. She has also worked as a political consultant and directed polling for a research center.

Bardes has written articles on public opinion and foreign policy, and on women and politics. She has authored *Thinking about Public Policy; Declarations of Independence: Women and Political Power in Nineteenth-Century American Fiction;* and *Public Opinion: Measuring the American Mind* (with Robert W. Oldendick). Her current research interests include public opinion on terrorism and homeland security and media effects on elections.

Bardes's home is located in a very small hamlet in Kentucky called Rabbit Hash, famous for its 150-year-old general store. Her hobbies include traveling, gardening, needlework, and antique collecting.

1

The Democratic Republic

These are students in a citizenship class in Yuma, Arizona. They are singing *God Bless America*. (AP Photo/ Jared Dort/*The Yuma Daily Sun*)

Politics, for many people, is the "great game." The stakes in the game are always high. After all, they involve vast sums and the very security of the nation. In 2008 and 2009, the stakes grew higher still. Following the 2008 elections, a Democratic Congress and the first African American president in United States history faced the worst economic crisis in eighty years. President Barack Obama, however, intended to do much more than merely combat what many now call the "Great Recession." In one of the most significant outpourings of government action ever seen, Obama sought to completely reform the nation's health-care and energy industries. Politics is crucial in determining whether Obama's ambitious plans succeed or fail.

Politics
The struggle over power or influence within organizations or informal groups that can grant or withhold benefits or privileges.

POLITICS AND GOVERNMENT

What is politics? **Politics** can be understood as the process of resolving conflicts and deciding, as political scientist Harold Lasswell put it in his classic definition, "who gets what, when, and how."[1] More specifically, politics is the struggle over power or influence within organizations or informal groups that can grant benefits or privileges.

We can identify many such groups and organizations. In families, all members may meet together to decide on values, priorities, and actions. Wherever there is a community that makes decisions through formal or informal rules, politics exists. For

1. Harold Lasswell, *Politics: Who Gets What, When, and How* (New York: McGraw-Hill, 1936).

1

Institution
An ongoing organization that performs certain functions for society.

Government
The preeminent institution within a society. Government has the ultimate authority to decide how conflicts will be resolved and how benefits and privileges will be allocated.

Order
A state of peace and security. Maintaining order by protecting members of society from violence and criminal activity is the oldest purpose of government.

example, when a church decides to construct a new building or hire a new minister, the decision may be made politically. Politics can be found in schools, social groups, and any other organized collection of individuals. Of all the organizations that are controlled by political activity, however, the most important is the government.

What is the government? Certainly, it is an **institution**—that is, an ongoing organization that performs certain functions for society and that has a life separate from the lives of the individuals who are part of it at any given moment in time. The **government** can be defined as an institution within which decisions are made that resolve conflicts and allocate benefits and privileges. The government is also the *preeminent* institution within society because it has the ultimate authority for making these decisions.

WHY IS GOVERNMENT NECESSARY?

Perhaps the best way to assess the need for government is to examine circumstances in which government, as we normally understand it, does not exist. What happens when multiple groups compete with each other for power within a society? There are places around the world where such circumstances exist. A current example is the African nation of Somalia. Since 1991, Somalia has not had a central government. The regions of the country are divided among several warlords and factions, each controlling a block of territory. When Somali warlords compete for the control of a particular locality, the result is war, generalized devastation, and famine. Normally, multiple armed forces compete by fighting, and the absence of a unified government is equivalent to civil war.

The Need for Security

As the example of Somalia shows, one of the original purposes of government is the maintenance of security, or **order.** By keeping the peace, the government protects the people from violence at the hands of private or foreign armies. It dispenses justice and protects the people from the violence of criminals. If order is not present, it is not possible for the government to provide any of the other benefits that people expect from it.

▼ **This Afghan soldier** stands guard, holding a rocket launcher. He is reacting to an ambush by Taliban militants on a police patrol in a providence south of Kabul, Afghanistan. How does this conflict show that government is necessary? (AP Photo/Allauddin Khan)

Consider the situation in Iraq. In March and April 2003, U.S. and British coalition forces entered that nation, which was governed by the dictator Saddam Hussein. The relatively small number of coalition troops had little trouble in defeating their military opponents, but they experienced serious difficulties in establishing order within Iraq when the war was over.

Once it became clear that Saddam Hussein was no longer in control of the country, widespread looting broke out. Ordinary citizens entered government buildings and made off with the furniture. Looters stole crucial supplies from hospitals, making it difficult to treat Iraqis injured during the war. Thieves stripped the copper from electrical power lines, which made it impossible to restore electrical power quickly. A lack of security bedeviled Iraq for years following the initial occupation. Only as security and order were restored was it possible to begin reconstructing Iraqi society. Order is a political value to which we will return later in this chapter.

Limiting Government Power

A complete collapse of order and security, as seen in Somalia, is actually an uncommon event. Much more common is the reverse—too much government control. In 2009, the human rights organization Freedom House judged that forty-two of the world's countries were "not free." These nations contain 34 percent of the world's population. Such countries may be controlled by individual dictators. Iraq's Saddam Hussein was one obvious example. Others include Libya's Muammar Qaddafi and Hosni Mubarak of Egypt. Alternatively, a political party, such as the Communist Party of China, may monopolize all the levers of power. The military may rule, as in Burma (also called Myanmar).

In all of these examples, the individual or group running the country cannot be removed by legal means. Freedom of speech and the right to a fair trial are typically absent. Dictatorial governments often torture or execute their opponents. Such regimes may also suppress freedom of religion.

Protection from the violence of domestic criminals or foreign armies is not enough. Citizens also need protection from abuses of power by their own government. To protect the liberties of the people, it is necessary to limit the powers of the government. **Liberty**—the greatest freedom of the individual consistent with the freedom of other individuals—is a second major political value, along with order. We discuss this value further later in this chapter.

Authority and Legitimacy

Every government must have **authority**—that is, the right and power to enforce its decisions. Ultimately, the government's authority rests on its control of the armed forces and the police. Almost no one in the United States, however, bases their day-to-day activities on fear of the government's enforcement powers. Most people, most of the time, obey the law because this is what they have always done. Also, if they did not obey the law, they would face the disapproval of friends and family. Consider an example: Do you avoid injuring your friends or stealing their possessions because you are afraid of the police—or because if you undertook these actions, you would no longer have friends?

Under normal circumstances, the government's authority has broad popular support. People accept the government's right to establish rules and laws. When authority is broadly accepted, we say that it has **legitimacy.** Authority without legitimacy is a recipe for trouble. Iraq can again serve as an example. After the end of Saddam Hussein's regime, many Iraqis, especially Sunni Arabs (the former politically dominant group in Iraq), did not accept the legitimacy of the U.S.-led Coalition Provisional Authority or the elected Iraqi government that followed it. For many years, terrorists were able to organize attacks on coalition troops or even on innocent civilians, knowing that their neighbors would not report their activities. Although the government of Iraq has since gained a greater degree of legitimacy, terrorism remains a problem.

Liberty
The greatest freedom of the individual that is consistent with the freedom of other individuals in the society.

Authority
The right and power of a government or other entity to enforce its decisions and compel obedience.

Legitimacy
Popular acceptance of the right and power of a government or other entity to exercise authority.

DEMOCRACY AND OTHER FORMS OF GOVERNMENT

Totalitarian Regime
A form of government that controls all aspects of the political and social life of a nation.

Authoritarianism
A type of regime in which only the government itself is fully controlled by the ruler. Social and economic institutions exist that are not under the government's control.

Aristocracy
Rule by the "best"; in reality, rule by an upper class.

Theocracy
Literally, rule by God or the gods; in practice, rule by religious leaders, typically self-appointed.

Oligarchy
Rule by a few.

Democracy
A system of government in which political authority is vested in the people.

Direct Democracy
A system of government in which political decisions are made by the people directly, rather than by their elected representatives.

Legislature
A governmental body primarily responsible for the making of laws.

Initiative
A procedure by which voters can propose a law or a constitutional amendment.

Referendum
An electoral device whereby legislative or constitutional measures are referred by the legislature to the voters for approval or disapproval.

There are a variety of types of government, which can be classified according to which person or group of people controls society through the government.

Types of Government

At one extreme is a society governed by a **totalitarian regime.** In such a political system, a small group of leaders or a single individual—a dictator—makes all political decisions for the society. Every aspect of political, social, and economic life is controlled by the government. The power of the ruler is total (thus, the term *totalitarianism*). A second type of system is authoritarian government. **Authoritarianism** differs from totalitarianism in that only the government itself is fully controlled by the ruler. Social and economic institutions, such as churches, businesses, and labor unions, exist that are not under the government's control.

Many of our terms for describing the distribution of political power are derived from the ancient Greeks, who were the first Western people to study politics systematically. One form of rule was known as **aristocracy,** literally meaning "rule by the best." In practice, this meant rule by wealthy members of ancient families. Another term from the Greeks is **theocracy,** which literally means "rule by God" (or the gods). In practice, theocracy means rule by self-appointed religious leaders. Iran is a rare example of a country in which supreme power is in the hands of a religious leader, the grand ayatollah Ali Khamenei. One of the most straightforward Greek terms is **oligarchy,** which simply means "rule by a few."

The Greek term for rule by the people was **democracy.** Within the limits of their culture, some of the Greek city-states operated as democracies. Today, in much of the world, the people will not grant legitimacy to a government unless it is based on democracy.

Direct Democracy as a Model

The Athenian system of government in ancient Greece is usually considered the purest model for **direct democracy** because the citizens of that community debated and voted directly on all laws, even those put forward by the ruling council of the city. The most important feature of Athenian democracy was that the **legislature** was composed of all of the citizens. (Women, resident foreigners, and slaves, however, were excluded because they were not citizens.) This form of government required a high level of participation from every citizen; that participation was seen as benefiting the individual and the city-state. The Athenians believed that although a high level of participation might lead to instability in government, citizens, if informed about the issues, could be trusted to make wise decisions.

Direct democracy also has been practiced at the local level in Switzerland and, in the United States, in New England town meetings. At these town meetings, which may include all of the voters who live in the town, important decisions—such as levying taxes, hiring city officials, and deciding local ordinances—are made by majority vote. Some states provide a modern adaptation of direct democracy for their citizens. In these states, representative democracy is supplemented by the **initiative** or the **referendum.** Both processes enable the people to vote directly on laws or constitutional amendments. The **recall** process, which is available in many states, allows the people to vote to remove an official from state office.

The Dangers of Direct Democracy

Although they were aware of the Athenian model, the framers of the U.S. Constitution were opposed to such a system. Democracy was considered to be dangerous and to lead to instability. But in the 1700s and 1800s, the idea of government based on the **consent of the people** gained increasing popularity. Such a government was the main aspiration of the American Revolution in 1775, the French Revolution in 1789, and many subsequent revolutions. At the time of the American Revolution, however, the masses were still considered to be too uneducated to govern themselves, too prone to the influence of demagogues (political leaders who manipulate popular prejudices), and too likely to subordinate minority rights to the tyranny of the majority.

▲ **These Woodbury, Vermont,** residents cast their ballots after a town meeting. They voted on the school budget and sales taxes. What type of political system does the town meeting best represent? (AP Photo/Toby Talbot)

James Madison, while defending the new scheme of government set forth in the U.S. Constitution, warned of the problems inherent in a "pure democracy":

> A common passion or interest will, in almost every case, be felt by a majority of the whole . . . and there is nothing to check the inducements to sacrifice the weaker party or an obnoxious individual. Hence it is that such democracies have ever been spectacles of turbulence and contention, and have ever been found incompatible with personal security or the rights of property; and have in general been as short in their lives as they have been violent in their deaths.[2]

Like other politicians of his time, Madison feared that pure, or direct, democracy would deteriorate into mob rule. What would keep the majority of the people, if given direct decision-making power, from abusing the rights of minority groups?

A Democratic Republic

The framers of the U.S. Constitution chose to craft a **republic,** meaning a government in which sovereign power rests with the people, rather than with a king or a monarch. A republic is based on **popular sovereignty.** To Americans of the 1700s, the idea of a republic also meant a government based on common beliefs and virtues that would be fostered within small communities. The rulers were to be amateurs—good citizens who would take turns representing their fellow citizens.

The U.S. Constitution created a form of republican government that we now call a **democratic republic.** The people hold the ultimate power over the government through the election process, but all national policy decisions are made by elected

Recall
A procedure allowing the people to vote to dismiss an elected official from office before his or her term has expired.

Consent of the People
The idea that governments and laws derive their legitimacy from the consent of the governed.

Republic
A form of government in which sovereign power rests with the people, rather than with a king or a monarch.

Popular Sovereignty
The concept that ultimate political authority is based on the will of the people.

Democratic Republic
A republic in which representatives elected by the people make and enforce laws and policies.

---

2. James Madison, in Alexander Hamilton, James Madison, and John Jay, *The Federalist Papers,* No. 10 (New York: Mentor Books, 1964), p. 81. See Appendix C of this book.

Representative Democracy
A form of government in which representatives elected by the people make and enforce laws and policies, but in which the monarchy may be retained in a ceremonial role.

Universal Suffrage
The right of all adults to vote for their representatives.

Majority
More than 50 percent.

Majority Rule
A basic principle of democracy asserting that the greatest number of citizens in any political unit should select officials and determine policies.

Limited Government
A government with powers that are limited either through a written document or through widely shared beliefs.

officials. For the founders, even this distance between the people and the government was not sufficient. The Constitution made sure that the Senate and the president would not be elected by a direct vote of the people, although later changes to the Constitution allowed the voters to elect members of the Senate directly.

Despite these limits, the new American system was unique in the amount of power it granted to the ordinary citizen. Over the course of the following two centuries, democratic values became more and more popular, at first in Western nations and then throughout the rest of the world. The spread of democratic principles gave rise to another name for our system of government—**representative democracy.** The term *representative democracy* has almost the same meaning as *democratic republic,* with one exception. Recall that in a republic, not only are the people sovereign, but there is no king. What if a nation develops into a democracy but preserves the monarchy as a largely ceremonial institution? That is exactly what happened in Britain. Not surprisingly, the British found the term *democratic republic* to be unacceptable, and they described their system as a representative democracy instead.

Principles of Democratic Government. All representative democracies rest on the rule of the people as expressed through the election of government officials. In the 1790s in the United States, only free white males were able to vote, and in some states they had to be property owners as well. Women in many states did not receive the right to vote in national elections until 1920, and the right to vote was not secured in all states by African Americans until the 1960s. Today, **universal suffrage** is the rule.

Because everyone's vote counts equally, the only way to make fair decisions is by some form of **majority** will. But to ensure that **majority rule** does not become oppressive, modern democracies also provide guarantees of minority rights. If political minorities were not protected, the majority might violate the fundamental rights of members of certain groups—especially groups that are unpopular or dissimilar to the majority population, such as racial minorities.

To guarantee the continued existence of a representative democracy, there must be free, competitive elections. Thus, the opposition always has the opportunity to win elective office. For such elections to be totally open, freedom of the press and speech must be preserved so that opposition candidates can present their criticisms of the government to the people.

Constitutional Democracy. Another key feature of Western representative democracy is that it is based on the principle of **limited government.** Not only is the government dependent on popular sovereignty, but the powers of the government are also clearly limited, either through

▼ **The U.S. Constitution** allows the people to hold the ultimate power over the government through the election process. This process does not work well, however, unless a large percentage of eligible Americans not only register to vote, but vote. This campaign worker at Davidson College in Davidson, North Carolina, explains the voter registration process to a student. What do we call the form of republican government created by the U.S. Constitution for this country? (AP Photo/Chuck Burton)

a written document or through widely shared beliefs. The U.S. Constitution sets down the fundamental structure of the government and the limits to its activities. Such limits are intended to prevent political decisions based on the whims or ambitions of individuals in government rather than on constitutional principles.

WHAT KIND OF DEMOCRACY DO WE HAVE?

Political scientists have developed a number of theories about American democracy, including *majoritarian* theory, *elite* theory, and theories of *pluralism*. Advocates of these theories use them to describe American democracy either as it actually is or as they believe it should be.

Some scholars argue that none of these three theories, which we discuss next, fully describes the workings of American democracy. These experts say that each theory captures a part of the true reality but that we need all three theories to gain a full understanding of American politics.

Democracy for Everyone

Many people believe that in a democracy, the government ought to do what the majority of the people want. This simple proposition is the heart of majoritarian theory. As a theory of what democracy should be like, **majoritarianism** is popular among both political scientists and ordinary citizens. Many scholars, however, consider majoritarianism to be a surprisingly poor description of how U.S. democracy actually works. They point to the low level of turnout for elections. Polling data have shown that many Americans are neither particularly interested in politics nor well informed. Few are able to name the persons running for Congress in their districts, and even fewer can discuss the candidates' positions.

Democracy for the Few

If ordinary citizens are not really making policy decisions with their votes, who is? One theory suggests that elites really govern the United States. **Elite theory** holds that society is ruled by a small number of people who exercise power to further their own self-interest. American democracy, in other words, is a sham democracy. Elite theory is usually used simply to describe the American system. Few people today believe it is a good idea for the country to be run by a privileged minority. In the past, however, many people believed that it was appropriate for the country to be governed by an elite. Consider the words of Alexander Hamilton, one of the framers of the Constitution:

> All communities divide themselves into the few and the many. The first are the rich and the wellborn, the other the mass of the people. . . . The people are turbulent and changing; they seldom judge or determine right. Give therefore to the first class a distinct, permanent share in the government. They will check the unsteadiness of the second, and as they cannot receive any advantage by a change, they therefore will ever maintain good government.[3]

Majoritarianism
A political theory holding that in a democracy, the government ought to do what the majority of the people want.

Elite Theory
A perspective holding that society is ruled by a small number of people who exercise power to further their self-interest.

---

3. Alexander Hamilton, "Speech in the Constitutional Convention on a Plan of Government," in *Writings,* ed. Joanne B. Freeman (New York: Library of America, 2001).

Pluralism
A theory that views politics as a conflict among interest groups. Political decision making is characterized by bargaining and compromise.

Political Culture
The patterned set of ideas, values, and ways of thinking about government and politics that characterizes a people.

Political Socialization
The process by which political beliefs and values are transmitted to immigrants and children in a society. The family and the educational system are two of the most important forces in the political socialization process.

Dominant Culture
The values, customs, and language established by the group or groups that traditionally have controlled politics and government in a society.

Some versions of elite theory posit a small, cohesive, elite class that makes almost all the important decisions for the nation,[4] whereas others suggest that voters choose among competing elites. New members of the elite are recruited through the educational system so that the brightest children of the masses allegedly have the opportunity to join the elite stratum.

Democracy for Groups

A different school of thought holds that our form of democracy is based on group interests. Even if the average citizen cannot keep up with political issues or cast a deciding vote in any election, the individual's interests will be protected by groups that represent her or him.

Theorists who subscribe to **pluralism** see politics as a struggle among groups to gain benefits for their members. Given the structure of the American political system, group conflicts tend to be settled by compromise and accommodation. Because there are a multitude of interests, no one group can dominate the political process. Furthermore, because most individuals have more than one interest, conflict among groups need not divide the nation into hostile camps.

Many political scientists believe that pluralism works very well as a descriptive theory. As a theory of how democracy *should* function, however, pluralism has problems. Poor citizens are rarely represented by interest groups. At the same time, rich citizens are often overrepresented. There are also serious doubts as to whether group decision making always reflects the best interests of the nation.

Indeed, critics see a danger that groups may become so powerful that all policies become compromises crafted to satisfy the interests of the largest groups. The interests of the public as a whole, then, are not considered. Critics of pluralism have suggested that a democratic system can be almost paralyzed by the struggle among interest groups. We will discuss interest groups at greater length in Chapter 7.

FUNDAMENTAL VALUES

The writers of the U.S. Constitution believed that the structures they had created would provide for both popular sovereignty and a stable political system. They also believed that the nation would be sustained by its **political culture**—the patterned set of ideas, values, and ways of thinking about government and politics that characterized its people. Even today, there is considerable consensus among American citizens about certain concepts—including the rights to liberty, equality, and property—that are deemed to be basic to the U.S. political system. Given that the vast majority of Americans are descendants of immigrants having diverse cultural and political backgrounds, how can we account for this consensus? Primarily, it is the result of **political socialization**—the process by which political beliefs and values are transmitted to new immigrants and to our children. The two most important sources of political socialization are the family and the educational system. (See Chapter 6 for a more detailed discussion of the political socialization process.)

The most fundamental concepts of the American political culture are those of the dominant culture. The term **dominant culture** refers to the values, customs, and language established by the groups that traditionally have controlled politics and

---

4. Michael Parenti, *Democracy for the Few,* 8th ed. (Belmont, Calif.: Wadsworth Publishing, 2007).

government in a society. The dominant culture in the United States has its roots in Western European civilization. From that civilization, American politics has inherited a bias in favor of individualism, private property, and Judeo-Christian ethics. Other cultural heritages honor community or family over individualism and sometimes place far less emphasis on materialism. Additionally, changes in our own society have brought about the breakdown of some values, such as the sanctity of the family structure, and the acceptance of other values, such as women's pursuit of careers in the workplace.

Liberty versus Order

In the United States, our **civil liberties** include religious freedom—both the right to practice whatever religion we choose and the right to be free from any state-imposed religion. Our civil liberties also include freedom of speech—the right to express our opinions freely on all matters, including government actions. Freedom of speech is perhaps one of our most prized liberties, because a democracy could not endure without it. These and many other basic guarantees of liberty are found in the **Bill of Rights,** the first ten amendments to the Constitution.

Liberty, however, is not the only value widely held by Americans. A substantial portion of the American electorate believes that certain kinds of liberty threaten the traditional social order. The right to privacy is a particularly controversial liberty. The United States Supreme Court has held that the right to privacy can be derived from other rights that are explicitly stated in the Bill of Rights. The Supreme Court has also held that under the right to privacy, the government cannot ban either abortion[5] or private homosexual behavior by consenting adults.[6] Some Americans believe that such rights threaten the sanctity of the family and the general cultural commitment to moral behavior. Of course, others disagree with this point of view.

Security is another issue. When Americans have felt particularly fearful or vulnerable, the government has emphasized national security over civil liberties. Such was the case after the Japanese attack on Pearl Harbor in 1941, which led to the U.S. entry into World War II. Thousands of Japanese Americans were held in internment camps, based on the assumption that their loyalty to this country was in question. More recently, the terrorist attacks on the Pentagon and the World Trade Center on September 11, 2001, renewed calls for greater security at the expense of some civil liberties.

▲ **The legality of** same-sex marriages remains a controversial issue. These two supporters of same-sex marriages demonstrate in San Francisco. What, if anything, does the Bill of Rights have to say about this topic? (AP Photo/George Nikitin)

Civil Liberties
Those personal freedoms, including freedom of religion and of speech, that are protected for all individuals in a society.

Bill of Rights
The first ten amendments to the U.S. Constitution.

5. *Roe v. Wade,* 410 U.S. 113 (1973).
6. *Lawrence v. Texas,* 539 U.S. 558 (2003).

▲ When Hillary Clinton and

Barack Obama became the front-runners for the Democratic presidential candidacy, history was made. At least on some level, equality had become more real in the United States. (AP Photo/John Raoux)

Equality
As a political value, the idea that all people are of equal worth.

Equality versus Liberty

The Declaration of Independence states, "All men are created equal." The proper meaning of equality, however, has been disputed by Americans since the Revolution.[7] Much of American history—and indeed, world history—is the story of how the value of **equality,** the idea that all people are of equal worth, has been extended and elaborated.

First, the right to vote was granted to all adult white males regardless of whether they owned property. The Civil War resulted in the end of slavery and established that, in principle at least, all citizens were equal before the law. The civil rights movement of the 1950s and 1960s sought to make that promise of equality a reality for African Americans. Other movements have sought equality for additional racial and ethnic groups, for women, for persons with disabilities, and for gay men and lesbians.

While many people believe that we have a ways yet to go in obtaining full equality for all of these groups, we clearly have come a long way already. No American in the nineteenth century could have imagined that the 2008 Democratic presidential primary elections would be closely fought contests between an African American man (Illinois senator Barack Obama) and a white woman (New York senator Hillary Rodham Clinton). The idea that same-sex marriage could even be open to debate would have been mind-boggling as well.

To promote equality, it is often necessary to place limits on the right to treat people unequally. In this sense, equality and liberty are conflicting values. Today, the right to refuse equal treatment to the members of a particular race has very few defenders. Yet as recently as fifty years ago, this right was a cultural norm.

Economic Equality. Equal treatment regardless of race, religion, gender, or other characteristics is a popular value today. Equal opportunity for individuals to develop their talents and skills is also a value with substantial support. Equality of economic status, however, is a controversial value.

For much of history, the idea that the government could do anything about the division of society between rich and poor was not something about which people even

---

7. Gary B. Nash, *The Unknown American Revolution: The Unruly Birth of Democracy and the Struggle to Create America* (New York: Viking, 2005).

thought. Most people assumed that such an effort was either impossible or undesirable. This assumption began to lose its force in the 1800s. As a result of the growing wealth of the Western world, and a visible increase in the ability of government to take on large projects, some people began to advocate the value of universal equality, or *egalitarianism.* Some radicals dreamed of a revolutionary transformation of society that would establish an egalitarian system—that is, a system in which wealth and power were redistributed more equally.

Many others rejected this vision but still came to endorse the values of eliminating poverty and at least reducing the degree of economic inequality in society. Antipoverty advocates believed then and believe now that such a program could prevent much suffering. In addition, they believed that reducing economic inequality would promote fairness and enhance the moral tone of society generally.

Property Rights and Capitalism. The value of reducing economic inequality is in conflict with the right to **property.** This is because reducing economic inequality typically involves the transfer of property (usually in the form of income) from some people to others. For many people, liberty and property are closely entwined. Our capitalist system is based on private property rights. Under **capitalism,** property consists not only of personal possessions but also of wealth-creating assets such as farms and factories. Capitalism is also typically characterized by considerable freedom to make binding contracts and by relatively unconstrained markets for goods, services, and investments.

Property—especially wealth-creating property—can be seen as giving its owner political power and the liberty to do whatever he or she wants. At the same time, the ownership of property immediately creates inequality in society. The desire to own property, however, is so widespread among all classes of Americans that radical egalitarian movements have had a difficult time securing a wide following here. Still, one consequence of the "Great Recession" of 2008 and 2009 was to substantially enhance the popularity of egalitarian ideas among the voters. With a Democratic president and Democrats in control of both chambers of Congress, that party is now in a position to enact some of the most egalitarian legislation in many years.

The Proper Size of Government

Opposition to "big government" has been a constant theme in American politics. Indeed, the belief that government is overreaching dates back to the years before the American Revolution. Tensions over the size and scope of government have plagued Americans ever since. Citizens often express contradictory opinions on the size of government and the role that it should play in their lives. For example, in a 2009 public opinion poll, 55 percent of the respondents agreed that "limited government is always better than big government," and 61 percent thought that "government spending is almost always wasteful and inefficient." Yet 69 percent agreed that "government has a responsibility to provide financial support for the poor, the sick, and the elderly," 73 percent favored "government regulations . . . to keep businesses in check and protect workers and consumers," and a full 79 percent supported "government investments in education, infrastructure, and science."[8]

Property
Anything that is or may be subject to ownership. As conceived by the political philosopher John Locke, the right to property is a natural right superior to human law (laws made by government).

Capitalism
An economic system characterized by the private ownership of wealth-creating assets, free markets, and freedom of contract.

---

8. John Halpin and Karl Agne, *State of American Political Ideology, 2009: A National Study of Political Values and Beliefs* (Washington, D.C.: Center for American Progress, 2009).

▲ **The auto industry** was one sector that suffered a dramatic decline during the Great Recession. These automobile industry leaders were called to Washington, D.C., to justify a bailout from the federal government. Who pays for federal bailouts? Who benefits from federal bailouts? (AP Photo/Susan Walsh)

Big Government in Times of Crisis. Americans are most likely to call for the benefits of big government when they are reacting to a crisis. No recent crisis has had a greater impact than the recession that began in December 2007, and that turned into a worldwide economic avalanche in mid-September 2008. Not surprisingly, Americans demanded that something be done. In February 2009, after Congress enacted into law a $787 billion economic "stimulus" package, a poll reported that 64 percent of the public supported the measure. A legislative package to help distressed homeowners received similar levels of support.[9] Poll respondents, however, also expressed concern over the size of the resulting federal budget deficit—indeed, the stimulus package was part of one of the most rapid run-ups in federal spending ever. Support for government action did not extend to bailing out the banking system or the Detroit automakers—about three-fifths of respondents were opposed to both measures.[10]

Big Government and Civil Liberties. No matter how Americans might feel about economic issues, they value limited government when it comes to their private lives and civil liberties, often to a greater degree than do people in other democratic countries. Americans prize freedom of speech and will not accept government restrictions on speech that are common elsewhere. For example, display of the Nazi swastika is banned so completely in democratic Germany that hobbyists may not affix historically accurate swastika decals to plastic models of World War II–era aircraft. Americans would find such a law to be absurd, not to mention unconstitutional. Many Americans worry about crime, but most would be even more concerned about possible miscarriages of justice if they learned that 99.8 percent of all criminal prosecutions result in a conviction. Yet that is exactly what happens in democratic Japan.

POLITICAL IDEOLOGIES

Political Ideology
A comprehensive set of beliefs about the nature of people and the role of government.

A **political ideology** is a closely linked set of beliefs about politics. Political ideologies offer their adherents well-organized theories that propose goals for the society and the means by which those goals can be achieved. At the core of every political ideology is a

9. ABC News/*Washington Post* Poll, February 23, 2009.
10. *USA Today*/Gallup Poll, February 24, 2009.

set of guiding values. The two ideologies most commonly referred to in discussions of American politics are *conservatism* and *liberalism*.

Conservatism versus Liberalism

The set of beliefs called **conservatism** includes the idea that government should play only a limited role in helping individuals. Conservatism also includes support for traditional values. These values usually include a strong sense of patriotism. Conservatives believe that the private sector probably can outperform the government in almost any activity. Believing that the individual is primarily responsible for her or his own well-being, conservatives typically oppose government programs to redistribute income or change the status of individuals. Conservatives occupy a dominant position in the Republican Party.

The set of beliefs called **liberalism** includes advocacy of government action to improve the welfare of individuals, support for civil rights, and tolerance for political and social change. American liberals believe that government should take positive action to reduce poverty, to redistribute income from wealthier classes to poorer ones, and to regulate the economy. Liberals are an influential force within the Democratic Party. In recent years, people traditionally known as liberals have, in large numbers, switched to an alternative label—*progressives*. We discuss the terminology change in this chapter's feature titled *The Politics of Boom and Bust: Liberals—or Progressives?* on the following page.

The Traditional Political Spectrum

A traditional method of comparing political ideologies is to array them on a continuum from left to right, based primarily on how much power the government should exercise to promote economic equality. Table 1–1 on page 15 shows how ideologies can be arrayed in a traditional political spectrum. In addition to liberalism and conservatism, this example includes the ideologies of socialism and libertarianism.

Socialism falls on the left side of the spectrum. Socialists play a minor role in the American political arena, although socialist parties and movements have been important in other countries around the world. In the past, socialists typically advocated replacing investor ownership of major businesses with either government ownership or ownership by employee cooperatives. Socialists believed that such steps would break the power of the very rich and lead to an egalitarian society. In more recent times, socialists in Western Europe have advocated more limited programs that redistribute income.

On the right side of the spectrum is **libertarianism,** a philosophy of skepticism toward most government activities. Libertarians strongly support property rights and typically oppose regulation of the economy and redistribution of income. Libertarians support *laissez-faire* capitalism. (*Laissez faire* is French for "let it be.") Libertarians also tend to oppose government attempts to regulate personal behavior and promote moral values.

Problems with the Traditional Political Spectrum

Many political scientists believe that the traditional left-to-right spectrum is not sufficiently complete. Take the example of libertarians. In Table 1–1 on page 15, libertarians are placed to the right of conservatives. If the only question is how much power the government should have over the economy, this is where they belong. Libertarians,

Conservatism
A set of beliefs that includes advocacy of a limited role for the national government in helping individuals, support for traditional values and lifestyles, and a cautious response to change.

Liberalism
A set of beliefs that includes advocacy of positive government action to improve the welfare of individuals, support for civil rights, and tolerance for political and social change.

Socialism
A political ideology based on strong support for economic and social equality. Socialists traditionally envisioned a society in which major businesses were taken over by the government or by employee cooperatives.

Libertarianism
A political ideology based on skepticism or opposition toward most government activities.

the politics of Boom and Bust:
Liberals—or Progressives?

During the first weeks of September 2008, many observers thought that Arizona senator John McCain, the Republican presidential candidate, had a real chance of winning the elections. The financial crisis that struck on September 15, however, doomed McCain's bid for the presidency, and in January 2009, Illinois senator Barack Obama was sworn in as president of the United States. Obama's politics have been widely described as liberal. Obama, however, does not use this label. Like most elected Democrats, he calls himself a *progressive*.

The Origins of Liberalism

Those on the political left have long complained about conservatives' ability to make the word *liberal* an embarrassment. Indeed, most Americans today associate liberalism with big government, which is not a popular concept. A hundred years ago, however, a *liberal* was a person who believed in limited government and who opposed religion in politics, a philosophy that in some ways resembles modern-day libertarianism.

How did the meaning of the word *liberal* change? In the 1800s, the Democratic Party was seen as the more liberal of the two parties. Democrats opposed big-government Republican projects such as building roads, freeing the slaves, and prohibiting the sale of alcoholic beverages. Over time, however, the Democrats' economic policies began to change. By the time of President Franklin Delano Roosevelt (1933–1945), the Democrats stood for positive government action to help the economy. Roosevelt's policies were new, but he kept the old language—as Democrats had long done, he called himself a *liberal*. Outside the United States and Canada, the meaning of the word *liberal* never changed. European liberals continue to support free market, small-government policies.

▲ Theodore Roosevelt

is shown here campaigning for president. He ran against Woodrow Wilson in 1912. Why did both candidates call themselves progressives? Does anyone use this term today? (Corbis)

The Origins of the Progressive Label

Progressivism, as an American political label, came into fashion in the early twentieth century to describe a growing belief—in both of the major political parties—that a strong government was essential to curb the excesses of big business. In the presidential elections of 1912, both leading candidates, Woodrow Wilson and Theodore Roosevelt, called themselves *progressives.* By the end of the 1940s, however, members of the radical left had hijacked the label, and Democrats avoided it. Today, few people remember or care who called themselves progressive in the distant past, and the label is once again usable by the Democrats.

The Return of Progressivism

If the word *liberal* has sunk beneath the weight of accumulated historical baggage, *progressive* is still going strong. A research organization called the Center for American Progress recently asked Americans not whether they were liberal or conservative, as is usually done, but whether they were liberal, progressive, conservative, or libertarian. The label *conservative* has long been far more popular than the label *liberal,* but when *progressive* is tossed into the mix, everything changes. Counting both strong and weak supporters, 47 percent of Americans identify themselves as liberal or progressive, and 48 percent as conservative or libertarian. It is no wonder that *progressive* has become the Democrats' label of choice.

FOR CRITICAL ANALYSIS

Are the labels with which politicians identify their philosophies and their desired political programs truly important? Why or why not?

TABLE 1–1: **The Traditional Political Spectrum**

	Socialism	Liberalism	Conservatism	Libertarianism
How much power should the government have over the economy?	Active government control of major economic sectors.	Positive government action in the economy.	Positive government action to support capitalism.	Almost no regulation of the economy.
What should the government promote?	Economic equality, community.	Economic security, equal opportunity, social liberty.	Economic liberty, morality, social order.	Total economic and social liberty.

however, advocate the most complete freedom possible in social matters. They oppose government action to promote traditional moral values, although such action is often favored by other groups on the political right. Their strong support for civil liberties seems to align them more closely with modern liberals than with conservatives.

Liberalism is often described as an ideology that supports "big government." If the objective is to promote equality, the description has some validity. In the moral sphere, however, conservatives tend to support more government regulation of social values and moral decisions than do liberals. Thus, conservatives tend to oppose gay rights legislation and propose stronger curbs on pornography. Liberals usually show greater tolerance for alternative life choices and oppose government attempts to regulate personal behavior and morals.

A Four-Cornered Ideological Grid

For a more sophisticated breakdown of recent American popular ideologies, many scholars use a four-cornered grid, as shown in Figure 1–1. The grid includes four possible ideologies. Each quadrant contains a substantial portion of the American electorate. Individual voters may fall anywhere on the grid, depending on the strength of their beliefs about economic and cultural issues.

Note that there is no generally accepted term for persons in the lower-left position, which we have labeled "economic liberals, cultural conservatives." Some scholars have used terms such as populist to describe this point of view, but these terms can be misleading.

Individuals who are economic liberals and cultural conservatives tend to support government action both to promote the values of economic equality and fairness and to defend traditional values, such as the family and marriage. These individuals may describe themselves as conservative or moderate. They are more likely to be Democrats than Republicans but often do not identify strongly with any party.

Libertarian, as a position on our two-way grid, does not refer to the small Libertarian Party, which has only a minor role in the American political arena. Rather, libertarians more typically support the Republican Party. They are more likely than conservatives to vote for a compatible Democrat, however.

FIGURE 1–1: A Four-Cornered Ideological Grid

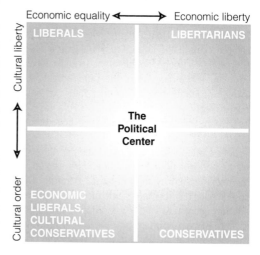

making a difference

SEEING DEMOCRACY IN ACTION

One way to begin to understand the American political system is to observe a legislative body in action. By "legislative body," we don't mean only the U.S. Congress and the various state legislatures—there are thousands of elected legislatures in the United States at all levels of government. You might choose to visit a city council, a school board, or a township board of trustees.

Why Should You Care? Local legislative bodies can have a direct impact on your life. For example, city councils or county commissions typically oversee the police or the sheriff's department, and the behavior of the police is a matter of interest even if you live on-campus. If you live off-campus, local authorities are responsible for an even greater number of issues that affect you directly. Are there items that the sanitation department refuses to pick up, for example? You might be able to change its policies by lobbying your councilperson.

Even if there are no local issues that concern you, there are still benefits to be gained from observing a local legislative session. You may discover that local government works rather differently than you expected. You might learn, for example, that the representatives of your political party do not serve your interests as well as you thought—or that the other party is much more sensible than you had presumed.

What Can You Do? To find out when and where local legislative bodies meet, look up the number of the city hall or county building in the telephone directory, and call the clerk of the council. If you live in a state capital such as Baton Rouge, Louisiana, or Santa Fe, New Mexico, you can view a meeting of the state legislature instead. In many communities, city council meetings and county board meetings can be seen on public-access TV channels. Many cities and almost all state governments have Internet Web sites.

Before attending a business session of the legislature, try to find out how the members are elected. Are the members chosen by the "at-large" method of election, so that each member represents the whole community, or are they chosen by specific geographic districts or wards? Is there a chairperson or official leader who controls the meetings? What are the responsibilities of this body?

▲ **Newark, New Jersey, mayor**
Cory Booker is shown with members of the city council behind him. He announced cuts in salaries for high-paid city employees, including himself. The budget problem facing his city was mirrored in most major cities throughout the United States. If you were a resident of Newark, could you actively participate in the city's decision-making process? If so, how? (AP Photo/Mike Derer)

When you visit, keep in mind the theory of representative democracy. The commissioners or council members are elected to represent their constituents (those who voted them into office). Observe how often the members refer to their constituents or to the special needs of their community or electoral district. Listen for sources of conflict within a community. If there is a debate, for example, over a zoning proposal that involves the issue of land use, try to figure out why some members oppose the proposal.

If you want to follow up on your visit, try to get a brief interview with one of the members of the council or board. In general, legislators are very willing to talk to students, particularly students who also are voters. Ask the member how he or she sees the job of representative. How can the wishes of the constituents be identified? How does the representative balance the needs of the particular ward or district that she or he represents with the good of the entire community? You can write to many legislators via e-mail. You might ask how much e-mail they receive and who actually answers it.

key terms

aristocracy 4	dominant culture 8	limited government 6	popular sovereignty 5
authoritarianism 4	elite theory 7	majoritarianism 7	property 11
authority 3	equality 10	majority 6	recall 5
Bill of Rights 9	government 2	majority rule 6	referendum 4
capitalism 11	initiative 4	oligarchy 4	representative
civil liberties 9	institution 2	order 2	democracy 6
consent of the people 5	legislature 4	pluralism 8	republic 5
conservatism 13	legitimacy 3	political culture 8	socialism 13
democracy 4	liberalism 13	political ideology 12	theocracy 4
democratic republic 5	libertarianism 13	political socialization 8	totalitarian regime 4
direct democracy 4	liberty 3	politics 1	universal suffrage 6

chapter summary

1   Politics is the process by which people decide which members of society receive certain benefits or privileges and which members do not. It is the struggle over power or influence within institutions or organizations that can grant benefits or privileges. Government is an institution within which decisions are made that resolve conflicts and allocate benefits and privileges. It is the predominant institution within society because it has the ultimate decision-making authority.

2   Two fundamental political values are order, which includes security against violence, and liberty, the greatest freedom of the individual consistent with the freedom of other individuals. To be effective, government authority must be backed by legitimacy.

3   Many of our terms for describing forms of government came from the ancient Greeks. In a direct democracy, such as ancient Athens, the people themselves make the important political decisions.

The United States is a representative democracy, in which the people elect representatives to make the decisions.

4   Theories of American democracy include majoritarianism, in which the government does what the majority wants; elite theory, in which the real power lies with one or more elites; and pluralism, in which organized interest groups contend for power.

5   Fundamental American values include liberty, order, equality, and property. Not all of these values are fully compatible. The value of order often competes with civil liberties, and economic equality competes with property rights.

6   Popular political ideologies can be arrayed from left (liberal) to right (conservative). We can also analyze economic liberalism and conservatism separately from cultural liberalism and conservatism.

QUESTIONS FOR

discussion**and**analysis

1   In Australia and Belgium, citizens are legally required to vote in elections. Would such a requirement be a good idea in the United States? What changes might take place if such a rule were in effect?

2   How well does the elite theory work as a description of American democracy? Can you provide evidence that suggests elites truly do rule on their own behalf? Is there evidence that contradicts the theory?

3   In your own life, what factors have contributed to your political socialization? To what extent were your political values shaped by your family, by school experiences, by friends, and by the media?

4   Following the terrorist attacks of September 11, 2001, the U.S. government imposed various restrictions, notably on airline passengers, in the belief that these measures would enhance our national security. How effective do you think these measures have been? In general, what limits on liberty should we accept in return for security?

5   We have discussed various fundamental political values in this chapter—liberty, order or security, equality, and property. How were these values reflected in the attempts by the George W. Bush and Obama administrations to bail out the banking industry? How were they reflected in the Obama administration's health-care proposals?

helpful online **Resources**

CONNECTING TO AMERICAN GOVERNMENT AND POLITICS

For a "front door" to federal, state, and international government Web sites, go to:
www.lib.umich.edu/govdocs/govweb.html

For access to federal government offices and agencies, go to the U.S. government's official Web site at:
www.usa.gov

To learn about political science as a profession, visit the American Political Science Association at:
www.apsanet.org

a special WebSite

FOR YOUR TEXT

Go to this book's special Web site at academic.cengage.com/polisci/Schmidt/Brief6e. Choose "For Students." Then click on Chapter 1, where you will find an online quiz and other helpful study aids. If your professor is using CengageNOW: *American Government and Politics Today, Brief Edition,* log in and go to Chapter 1 for additional online study aids.

2

Forging a New Government: The Constitution

The United States Constitution is the oldest living constitution in the world today. It has been used as the basis for constitutions in other nations. (Shutterstock)

We the People of the United States, in Order to form a more perfect Union, establish Justice, insure domestic Tranquility, provide for the common defence, promote the general Welfare, and secure the Blessings of Liberty to ourselves and our Posterity, do ordain and establish this Constitution for the United States of America.

Every schoolchild in America has at one time or another been exposed to these famous words from the Preamble to the U.S. Constitution. The document itself is remarkable. The U.S. Constitution, compared with others in the fifty states and in the world, is relatively short. Because amending it is difficult, it also has relatively few amendments. The Constitution has remained largely intact for over two hundred years. To a great extent, this is because the principles set forth in the Constitution are sufficiently broad that they can be adapted to meet the needs of a changing society.

How and why the U.S. Constitution was created is a story that has been told and retold. It is worth repeating, because knowing the historical and political context in which this country's governmental machinery was formed is essential to understanding American government and politics today. The Constitution did not result just from creative thinking. Many of its provisions were grounded in the political philosophy of the time. The delegates to the Constitutional Convention in 1787 brought with them two important sets of influences: their political culture and their political experience. In the years between the first settlements in the New World and the writing of the

Representative
Assembly
A legislature composed of
individuals who represent
the population.

Constitution, Americans had developed a political philosophy about how people should be governed and had tried out several forms of government. These experiences gave the founders the tools with which they constructed the Constitution.

THE COLONIAL BACKGROUND

In 1607, a company chartered by the English government sent a group of farmers to establish a trading post, Jamestown, in what is now Virginia. Jamestown was the first permanent English colony in the Americas. The king of England gave the backers of this colony a charter granting them "full power and authority" to make laws "for the good and welfare" of the settlement. The colonists at Jamestown instituted a **representative assembly,** a legislature composed of individuals who represented the population, thus setting a precedent in government that was to be observed in later colonial adventures.

Separatists, the *Mayflower,* and the Compact

The first New England colony was established in 1620. A group made up in large part of extreme Separatists, who wished to break with the Church of England, came over on the ship *Mayflower* to the New World, landing at Plymouth (Massachusetts). Before going onshore, the adult males—women were not considered to have any political status—drew up the Mayflower Compact, which was signed by forty-one of the forty-four men aboard the ship on November 21, 1620. The reason for the compact was obvious. This group was outside the jurisdiction of the Virginia Company of London, which had chartered its settlement in Virginia, not Massachusetts. The Separatist leaders feared that some of the *Mayflower* passengers might conclude that they were no longer under any obligations of civil obedience. Therefore, some form of public authority was imperative. As William Bradford (one of the Separatist leaders) recalled in his accounts, there were "discontented and mutinous speeches that some of the strangers [non-Separatists] amongst them had let fall from them in the ship; That when they came ashore they would use their owne libertie; for none had power to command them."[1]

The compact was not a constitution. It was a political statement in which the signers agreed to create and submit to the authority of a government, pending the receipt of a royal charter. The Mayflower Compact's historical and political significance is twofold: it depended on the consent of the

▼ **The Mayflower Compact** was signed off the coast of Provincetown, Massachusetts, in 1620. Was it a constitution? Why or why not?
(The Granger Collection)

1. John Camp, *Out of the Wilderness: The Emergence of an American Identity in Colonial New England* (Middleton, Conn.: Wesleyan University Press, 1990).

affected individuals, and it served as a prototype for similar compacts in American history. By the time of the American Revolution, the compact was well on its way toward mythic status. In 1802, John Quincy Adams, son of the second American president, spoke these words at a founders' day celebration in Plymouth: "This is perhaps the only instance in human history of that positive, original social compact, which speculative philosophers have imagined as the only legitimate source of government."[2]

More Colonies, More Government

Another outpost in New England was set up by the Massachusetts Bay Colony in 1630. Then followed Rhode Island, Connecticut, New Hampshire, and others. By 1732, the last of the thirteen colonies, Georgia, was established. During the colonial period, Americans developed a concept of limited government, which followed from the establishment of the first colonies under Crown charters. Theoretically, London governed the colonies. In practice, owing partly to the colonies' distance from London, the colonists exercised a large measure of self-government. The colonists were able to make their own laws, as in the Fundamental Orders of Connecticut in 1639. The Massachusetts Body of Liberties in 1641 supported the protection of individual rights and was made a part of colonial law. In 1682, the Pennsylvania Frame of Government was passed. Along with the Pennsylvania Charter of Privileges of 1701, it foreshadowed our modern Constitution and Bill of Rights. All of this legislation enabled the colonists to acquire crucial political experience. After independence was declared in 1776, the states quickly set up their own new constitutions.

BRITISH RESTRICTIONS AND COLONIAL GRIEVANCES

The conflict between Britain and the American colonies, which ultimately led to the Revolutionary War, began in the 1760s when the British government decided to raise revenues by imposing taxes on the American colonies. Policy advisers to Britain's King George III, who ascended the throne in 1760, decided that it was only logical to require the American colonists to help pay the costs of Britain's defending them during the French and Indian War (1756–1763). The colonists, who had grown accustomed to a large degree of self-government and independence from the British Crown, viewed the matter differently.

In 1764, the British Parliament passed the Sugar Act. Many colonists were unwilling to pay the tax imposed by the act. Further regulatory legislation was to come. In 1765, Parliament passed the Stamp Act, providing for internal taxation of legal documents and even newspapers—or, as the colonists' Stamp Act Congress, assembled in 1765, called it, "taxation without representation." The colonists boycotted the purchase of English commodities in return. The success of the boycott (the Stamp Act was repealed a year later) generated a feeling of unity within the colonies. The British, however, continued to try to raise revenues in the colonies. When Parliament passed duties on glass, lead, paint, and other items in 1767, the colonists again boycotted British goods. The colonists' fury over taxation climaxed in the Boston Tea Party: colonists dressed as Mohawk Indians dumped almost 350 chests of British tea into Boston Harbor as a gesture of tax protest. In retaliation, Parliament passed the Coercive Acts

---

2. Nathaniel Philbrick, *Mayflower: A Story of Courage, Community, and War* (New York: Penguin, 2007), p. 352.

(the "Intolerable Acts") in 1774, which closed Boston Harbor and placed the government of Massachusetts under direct British control. The colonists were outraged—and they responded.

THE COLONIAL RESPONSE: THE CONTINENTAL CONGRESSES

New York, Pennsylvania, and Rhode Island proposed the convening of a colonial congress. The Massachusetts House of Representatives requested that all colonies hold conventions to select delegates to be sent to Philadelphia for such a congress.

The First Continental Congress

The First Continental Congress was held in Philadelphia at Carpenter's Hall on September 5, 1774. It was a gathering of delegates from twelve of the thirteen colonies (delegates from Georgia did not attend until 1775). At that meeting, there was little talk of independence. The Congress passed a resolution requesting that the colonies send a petition to King George III expressing their grievances. Resolutions were also passed requiring that the colonies raise their own troops and boycott British trade. The British government condemned the Congress's actions, treating them as open acts of rebellion.

The Second Continental Congress

By the time the Second Continental Congress met in May 1775 (this time all of the colonies were represented), fighting had already broken out between the British and the colonists. One of the main actions of the Second Congress was to establish an army. It did this by declaring the militia that had gathered around Boston an army and naming George Washington as commander in chief. The participants in that Congress still attempted to reach a peaceful settlement with the British Parliament. One declaration of the Congress stated explicitly that "we have not raised armies with ambitious designs of separating from Great Britain, and establishing independent states." But by the beginning of 1776, military encounters had become increasingly frequent.

Public debate was acrimonious. Then Thomas Paine's *Common Sense* appeared in Philadelphia bookstores. The pamphlet was a colonial best seller. (To do relatively as well today, a book would have to sell between 9 million and 11 million copies in its first year of publication.) Many agreed that Paine did make common sense when he argued that

> a government of our own is our natural right: and when a man seriously reflects on the precariousness [instability, unpredictability] of human affairs, he will become convinced, that it is infinitely wiser and safer, to form a constitution of our own in a cool and deliberate manner, while we have it in our power, than to trust such an interesting event to time and chance.[3]

Paine further argued that "nothing can settle our affairs so expeditiously as an open and determined declaration for Independence."[4]

---

3. *The Political Writings of Thomas Paine,* Vol. 1 (Boston: J. P. Mendum Investigator Office, 1870), p. 46.
4. *Ibid.,* p. 54.

Students of Paine's pamphlet point out that his arguments were not new—they were common in tavern debates throughout the land. Rather, it was the near poetry of his words—which were at the same time as plain as the alphabet—that struck his readers.

DECLARING INDEPENDENCE

On April 6, 1776, the Second Continental Congress voted for free trade at all American ports with all countries except Britain. This act could be interpreted as an implicit declaration of independence. The next month, the Congress suggested that each of the colonies establish a state government unconnected to Britain. Finally, in July, the colonists declared their independence from Britain.

The Resolution of Independence

On July 2, the Resolution of Independence was adopted by the Second Continental Congress:

> RESOLVED, That these United Colonies are, and of right ought to be free and independent States, that they are absolved from allegiance to the British Crown, and that all political connection between them and the state of Great Britain is, and ought to be, totally dissolved.

In June 1776, Thomas Jefferson was already writing drafts of the Declaration of Independence in the second-floor parlor of a bricklayer's house in Philadelphia. When the Resolution of Independence was adopted on July 2, Jefferson argued that a declaration clearly putting forth the causes that compelled the colonies to separate from Britain was necessary. The Second Congress assigned the task to him.

July 4, 1776—The Declaration of Independence

Jefferson's version of the declaration was amended to gain unanimous acceptance (for example, his condemnation of the slave trade was eliminated to satisfy Georgia and North Carolina), but the bulk of it was passed intact on July 4, 1776. On July 19, the modified draft became "the unanimous declaration of the thirteen United States of America." On August 2, it was signed by the members of the Second Continental Congress.

Universal Truths. The Declaration of Independence has become one of the world's most renowned and significant documents. The words opening the second paragraph of the Declaration indicate why this is so:

> We hold these Truths to be self-evident, that all Men are created equal, that they are endowed by their Creator with certain unalienable Rights, that among these are Life, Liberty, and the Pursuit of Happiness—That to secure these Rights, Governments are instituted among Men, deriving their just Powers from the Consent of the Governed, that whenever any Form of Government becomes destructive of these Ends, it is the Right of the People to alter or abolish it, and to institute new Government.

▲ **King George III** ruled over the British colonies from the time he ascended to the throne in 1760 until the colonies declared their independence in 1776. Do you think there were any benefits of being colonies of Britain during this time period? What might they have been? (Ann Ronan Picture Library/ Heritage-Images [Britannica Elementary Encyclopedia])

Natural Rights

Rights held to be inherent in natural law, not dependent on governments. John Locke stated that natural law, being superior to human law, specifies certain rights of "life, liberty, and property." These rights, altered to become "life, liberty, and the pursuit of happiness," are asserted in the Declaration of Independence.

Social Contract

A voluntary agreement among individuals to secure their rights and welfare by creating a government and abiding by its rules.

Natural Rights and Social Contracts. The assumption that people have **natural rights** ("unalienable Rights"), including the rights to "Life, Liberty, and the Pursuit of Happiness," was a revolutionary concept at that time. Its use by Jefferson reveals the influence of the English philosopher John Locke (1632–1704), whose writings were familiar to educated American colonists, including Jefferson. In his *Two Treatises on Government,* published in 1690, Locke had argued that all people possess certain natural rights, including the rights to life, liberty, and property, and that the primary purpose of government was to protect these rights. Furthermore, government was established by the people through a **social contract**—an agreement among the people to form a government and abide by its rules. As you read earlier, such contracts, or compacts, were not new to Americans. The Mayflower Compact was the first of several documents that established governments or governing rules based on the consent of the governed.

After setting forth these basic principles of government, the Declaration of Independence goes on to justify the colonists' revolt against Britain. Much of the remainder of the document is a list of what "He" (King George III) had done to deprive the colonists of their rights. (See Appendix A at the end of this book for the complete text of the Declaration of Independence.)

The Significance of the Declaration. The concepts of universal truths, natural rights, and government established through a social contract were to have a lasting impact on American life. The Declaration of Independence set forth ideals that have since become a fundamental part of our national identity. The Declaration also became a model for use by other nations around the world.

Certainly, most Americans are familiar with the words of the Declaration. Yet, as Harvard historian David Armitage noted in his study of the Declaration of Independence in the international context,[5] few Americans ponder the obvious question: What did these assertions in the Declaration have to do with independence? Clearly, independence could have been declared without these words. Even as late as 1857, Abraham Lincoln admitted, "The assertion that 'all men are created equal' was of no practical use in effecting our separation from Great Britain; and it was placed in the Declaration, not for that, but for future use."[6]

Essentially, the immediate significance of the Declaration of Independence, in 1776, was that it established the legitimacy of the new nation in the eyes of foreign governments, as well as in the eyes of the colonists themselves. What the new nation needed most were supplies for its armies and a commitment of foreign military aid. Unless the United States appeared to the world as a political entity separate and independent from Britain, no foreign government would enter into an agreement with its leaders. Once the Declaration had fulfilled its purpose of legitimizing the American

▶ **John Locke** (1632–1704).
English philosopher. (The Granger Collection)

5. David Armitage, *The Declaration of Independence: A Global History* (Cambridge, Mass.: Harvard University Press, 2007).
6. As cited in Armitage, *The Declaration of Independence,* p. 26.

Revolution, the document suffered relative neglect for many years. The lasting significance of the Declaration—as a founding document setting forth American ideals—came much later.

THE RISE OF REPUBLICANISM

Although the colonists had formally declared independence from Britain, the fight to gain actual independence continued for five more years, until British general Cornwallis surrendered at Yorktown in 1781. In 1783, after Britain formally recognized the independence of the United States in the Treaty of Paris, Washington disbanded the army. During these years of military struggles, the states faced the additional challenge of creating a system of self-government for an independent United States.

Some colonists in the middle and lower South had demanded that independence be preceded by the formation of a strong central government. But the anti-Royalists in New England and Virginia, who called themselves Republicans (not to be confused with today's Republican Party), were against a strong central government. They opposed monarchy, executive authority, and virtually any form of restraint on the power of local groups. These Republicans were a major political force from 1776 to 1780. Indeed, they almost prevented victory over the British by their unwillingness to cooperate with any central authority.

During this time, all of the states adopted written constitutions. Eleven of the constitutions were completely new. Two of them—those of Connecticut and Rhode Island—were old royal charters with minor modifications. Republican sentiment led to increased power for the legislatures. In Georgia and Pennsylvania, **unicameral** (one-body) **legislatures** were unchecked by executive or judicial authority. Basically, the Republicans attempted to maintain the politics of 1776. In almost all states, the legislature was predominant.

THE ARTICLES OF CONFEDERATION: OUR FIRST FORM OF GOVERNMENT

The fear of a powerful central government led to the passage of the Articles of Confederation, which created a weak central government. The term **confederation** is important; it means a voluntary association of independent **states,** in which the member states agree to only limited restraints on their freedom of action. As a result, confederations seldom have an effective executive authority.

In June 1776, the Second Continental Congress began the process of drafting what would become the Articles of Confederation and Perpetual Union, more commonly known as the Articles of Confederation. The final draft had been completed by November 15, 1777, but not until March 1, 1781, did the last state, Maryland, agree to ratify the Articles. Well before the final ratification, however, many of the articles were implemented: the Continental Congress and the thirteen states conducted American military, economic, and political affairs according to the standards and the form specified by the Articles.[7]

---

7. Keith L. Dougherty, *Collective Action under the Articles of Confederation* (New York: Cambridge University Press, 2006).

Unicameral Legislature
A legislature with only one legislative chamber, as opposed to a bicameral (two-chamber) legislature, such as the U.S. Congress. Today, Nebraska is the only state in the Union with a unicameral legislature.

Confederation
A political system in which states or regional governments retain ultimate authority except for those powers they expressly delegate to a central government.

State
A group of people occupying a specific area and organized under one government; may be either a nation or a subunit of a nation.

The Articles Establish a Government

Under the Articles, the thirteen original colonies, now states, established on March 1, 1781, a government of the states—the Congress of the Confederation. The Congress was a unicameral assembly of so-called ambassadors from each state, with every state possessing a single vote. Each year, the Congress would choose one of its members as its president, but the Articles did not provide for a president of the United States.

The Congress was authorized in Article X to appoint an executive committee of the states "to execute in the recess of Congress, such of the powers of Congress as the United States, in Congress assembled, by the consent of nine [of the thirteen] states, shall from time to time think expedient to vest with them." The Congress was also allowed to appoint other committees and civil officers necessary for managing the general affairs of the United States. In addition, the Congress could regulate foreign affairs and establish coinage and weights and measures. But it lacked an independent source of revenue and the necessary executive machinery to enforce its decisions throughout the land. Article II of the Articles of Confederation guaranteed that each state would retain its sovereignty. Table 2–1 summarizes the powers—and the lack of powers—of Congress under the Articles of Confederation.

Accomplishments under the Articles

The new government had some accomplishments during its eight years of existence under the Articles of Confederation. Certain states' claims to western lands were settled. Maryland had objected to the claims of the Carolinas, Connecticut, Georgia, Massachusetts, New York, and Virginia. It was only after these states consented to give up their land claims to the United States as a whole that Maryland signed the Articles of Confederation. Another accomplishment under the Articles was the passage of the Northwest Ordinance of 1787, which established a basic pattern of government for new territories north of the Ohio River. All in all, the Articles represented the first real pooling of resources by the American states.

TABLE 2–1: Powers of the Congress of the Confederation

Congress Had Power to	Congress Lacked Power to
<ul><li>Declare war and make peace.</li><li>Enter into treaties and alliances.</li><li>Establish and control armed forces.</li><li>Requisition men and funds from states.</li><li>Regulate coinage.</li><li>Borrow funds and issue bills of credit.</li><li>Fix uniform standards of weight and measurement.</li><li>Create admiralty courts.</li><li>Create a postal system.</li><li>Regulate Indian affairs.</li><li>Guarantee citizens of each state the rights and privileges of citizens in the several states when in another state.</li><li>Adjudicate disputes between states on state petition.</li></ul>	<ul><li>Provide for effective treaties and control foreign relations; it could not compel states to respect treaties.</li><li>Compel states to meet military quotas; it could not draft soldiers.</li><li>Regulate interstate and foreign commerce; it left each state free to set up its own tariff system.</li><li>Collect taxes directly from the people; it had to rely on states to collect and forward taxes.</li><li>Compel states to pay their share of government costs.</li><li>Provide and maintain a sound monetary system or issue paper money; this was left up to the states, and monies in circulation differed tremendously in purchasing power.</li></ul>

Weaknesses of the Articles

In spite of these accomplishments, the Articles of Confederation had many defects. Although Congress had the legal right to declare war and to conduct foreign policy, it did not have the right to demand revenues from the states. It could only ask for them. Additionally, the actions of Congress required the consent of nine states. Any amendments to the Articles required the unanimous consent of the Congress and confirmation by every state legislature. Furthermore, the Articles did not create a national system of courts.

Basically, the functioning of the government under the Articles depended on the goodwill of the states. Article III of the Articles simply established a "league of friendship" among the states—no national government was intended.

Probably the most fundamental weakness of the Articles, and the most basic cause of their eventual replacement by the Constitution, was the lack of power to raise funds for the militia. The Articles contained no language giving Congress coercive power to raise revenue (by levying taxes) to provide adequate support for the military forces controlled by Congress. Due to a lack of resources, the Continental Congress was forced to disband the army after the Revolutionary War, even in the face of serious Spanish and British military threats.

Shays' Rebellion and the Need for Revision of the Articles

Because of the weaknesses of the Articles of Confederation, the central government could do little to maintain peace and order in the new nation. The states bickered among themselves and increasingly taxed each other's goods. At times they prevented trade altogether. By 1784, the country faced a serious economic depression. Banks were calling in old loans and refusing to give new ones. People who could not pay their debts were often thrown into debtors' prison.

In August 1786, mobs of musket-bearing farmers led by former revolutionary captain Daniel Shays seized county courthouses and disrupted the trials of debtors in Springfield, Massachusetts. Shays and his men then launched an attack on the federal arsenal at Springfield, but they were repulsed. Shays' Rebellion demonstrated that the central government could not protect the citizenry from armed rebellion or provide adequately for the public welfare. The rebellion spurred the nation's political leaders to action.

DRAFTING THE CONSTITUTION

The Virginia legislature called for a meeting of all the states to be held at Annapolis, Maryland, on September 11, 1786—ostensibly to discuss commercial problems only. It was evident to those in attendance (including Alexander Hamilton and James Madison) that the national government had serious weaknesses that had to be addressed if it was to survive. Among the important problems to be solved were the relationship between the states and the central government, the powers of the national legislature, the need for executive leadership, and the establishment of policies for economic stability. The result of this meeting was a petition to the Continental Congress for a general convention to meet in Philadelphia in May 1787 "to consider the exigencies [needs] of the union."

▲ **George Washington** presided over the Constitutional Convention of 1787. It formally opened in the East Room of the Pennsylvania State House (later named Independence Hall) on May 25. Only Rhode Island did not send any delegates. (Virginia Museum of Fine Arts, Richmond. Gift of Edgar William and Bernice Chrysler Garbisch. Courtesy U.S. Department of State)

The designated date for the opening of the convention at Philadelphia, now known as the Constitutional Convention, was May 14, 1787. Few of the delegates had actually arrived in Philadelphia by that time, however, so the opening was delayed. The convention formally began in the East Room of the Pennsylvania State House on May 25.[8] Fifty-five of the seventy-four delegates chosen for the convention actually attended. (Of those fifty-five, only about forty played active roles at the convention.) Rhode Island was the only state that refused to send delegates.

Factions among the Delegates

We know much about the proceedings at the convention because James Madison kept a daily, detailed personal journal. A majority of the delegates were strong nationalists—they wanted a central government with real power, unlike the central government under the Articles of Confederation. George Washington and Benjamin Franklin were among those who sought a stronger government.

Among the nationalists, some—including Alexander Hamilton—went as far as to support monarchy. Another important group of nationalists were of a more democratic stripe. Led by James Madison of Virginia and James Wilson of Pennsylvania, these democratic nationalists wanted a central government founded on popular support.

Other factions included a group of delegates who were totally against a national authority. Two of the three delegates from New York quit the convention when they saw the nationalist direction of its proceedings.

Politicking and Compromises

The debates at the convention started on the first day. James Madison had spent months reviewing European political theory. When his Virginia delegation arrived ahead of most of the others, it got to work immediately. By the time George Washington opened the convention, Governor Edmund Randolph of Virginia was prepared to present fifteen resolutions proposing fundamental changes in the nation's government. In retrospect, this was a masterful stroke on the part of the Virginia delegation. It set the agenda for the remainder of the convention—even though, in principle, the

8. This was the same room in which the Declaration of Independence had been signed eleven years earlier. The State House was later named Independence Hall.

delegates had been sent to Philadelphia for the sole purpose of amending the Articles of Confederation and not to write a new constitution.

The Virginia Plan. Randolph's fifteen resolutions proposed an entirely new national government under a constitution. Basically, the plan called for the following:

- A **bicameral** (two-chamber) **legislature,** with the lower chamber chosen by the people and the smaller upper chamber chosen by the lower chamber from nominees selected by state legislatures. The number of representatives would be proportional to a state's population, thus favoring the large states, including Virginia. The legislature could void any state laws.
- The creation of an unspecified national executive, elected by the legislature.
- The creation of a national judiciary, appointed by the legislature.

It did not take long for the smaller states to realize they would fare poorly under the Virginia Plan, which would enable Massachusetts, Pennsylvania, and Virginia to form a majority in the national legislature. The debate on the plan dragged on for a number of weeks. It was time for the small states to come up with their own plan.

The New Jersey Plan. On June 15, lawyer William Paterson of New Jersey offered an alternative plan. After all, argued Paterson, under the Articles of Confederation all states had equality; therefore, the convention had no power to change this arrangement. He proposed the following:

- The fundamental principle of the Articles of Confederation—one state, one vote— would be retained.
- Congress would be able to regulate trade and impose taxes.
- All acts of Congress would be the supreme law of the land.
- Several people would be elected by Congress to form an executive office.
- The executive office would appoint a Supreme Court.

Basically, the New Jersey Plan was simply an amendment of the Articles of Confederation. Its only notable feature was its reference to the **supremacy doctrine,** which was later included in the Constitution.

The "Great Compromise." The delegates were at an impasse. Most wanted a strong national government and were unwilling even to consider the New Jersey Plan. But when the Virginia Plan was brought up again, the small states threatened to leave. It was not until July 16 that a compromise was achieved. Roger Sherman of Connecticut proposed the following:

- A bicameral legislature in which the lower chamber, the House of Representatives, would be apportioned according to the number of free inhabitants in each state, plus three-fifths of the slaves.
- An upper chamber, the Senate, which would have two members from each state elected by the state legislatures.

This plan, known as the **Great Compromise,** broke the deadlock. (The plan is also called the Connecticut Compromise because of the role of the Connecticut delegates in the proposal.) It did exact a political price, however, because it permitted each state to have equal representation in the Senate. Having two senators represent each state in effect diluted the voting power of citizens living in more heavily

Bicameral Legislature
A legislature made up of two parts, called chambers. The U.S. Congress, composed of the House of Representatives and the Senate, is a bicameral legislature.

Supremacy Doctrine
A doctrine that asserts the priority of national law over state laws. This principle is rooted in Article VI of the Constitution.

Great Compromise
The compromise between the New Jersey and Virginia plans that created one chamber of the Congress based on population and one chamber representing each state equally; also called the Connecticut Compromise.

populated states and gave the smaller states disproportionate political power. But the Connecticut Compromise resolved the controversy between small and large states. In addition, the Senate would act as a check on the House, which many feared would be dominated by, and too responsive to, the masses.

The Three-Fifths Compromise. The Great Compromise also settled another major issue—how to deal with slaves in the representational scheme. Slavery was still legal in many northern states, but it was concentrated in the South. Many delegates were opposed to slavery and wanted it banned entirely in the United States. Charles Pinckney of South Carolina led strong southern opposition to a ban on slavery. Furthermore, the South wanted slaves to be counted along with free persons in determining representation in Congress. Delegates from the northern states objected. Sherman's three-fifths proposal was a compromise between northerners who did not want the slaves counted at all and southerners who wanted them counted in the same way as free whites. Actually, Sherman's Connecticut plan spoke of three-fifths of "all other persons" (and that is the language of the Constitution itself). It is not hard to figure out, though, who those other persons were. The three-fifths compromise illustrates the power of the southern states at the convention.[9]

The three-fifths compromise did not completely settle the slavery issue. There was also the question of the slave trade. Eventually, the delegates agreed that Congress could not ban the importation of slaves until after 1808. The compromise meant that the matter of slavery itself was never addressed directly. The South won twenty years of unrestricted slave trade and a requirement that escaped slaves in free states be returned to their owners in slave states.

Clearly, many delegates, including slave owners such as George Washington and James Madison, had serious objections to slavery. Why, then, did they allow slavery to continue? Historians have long maintained that the framers had no choice—that without a slavery compromise, the delegates from the South would have abandoned the convention. Indeed, this was the fear of a number of antislavery delegates to the convention. Madison, for example, said, "Great as the evil is, a dismemberment of the Union would be even worse."[10] Other scholars, however, contend that not only would it have been possible for the founders to ban slavery, but by doing so they would have achieved greater unity for the new nation.[11]

Other Issues. The South also worried that the northern majority in Congress would pass legislation unfavorable to its economic interests. Because the South depended on agricultural exports, it feared the imposition of export taxes. In return for acceding to the northern demand that Congress be able to regulate commerce among the states and with other nations, the South obtained a promise that export taxes would not be imposed. As a result, the United States is among the few countries that do not tax their exports.

---

9. See Garry Wills, *"Negro President": Jefferson and the Slave Power* (New York: Houghton Mifflin, 2003)
10. Speech before the Virginia ratifying convention on June 17, 1788, as cited in Bruno Leone, ed., *The Creation of the Constitution* (San Diego: Greenhaven Press, 1995), p. 159.
11. See, for example, Paul Finkelman, *Slavery and the Founders: Race and Liberty in the Age of Jefferson,* 2d ed. (Armonk, N.Y.: M. E. Sharpe, 2001); and Gary B. Nash, *The Forgotten Fifth: African Americans in the Age of Revolution* (Cambridge, Mass.: Harvard University Press, 2006).

There were other disagreements. The delegates could not decide whether to establish only a Supreme Court or to create lower courts as well. They deferred the issue by mandating a Supreme Court and allowing Congress to establish lower courts. They also disagreed over whether the president or the Senate would choose the Supreme Court justices. A compromise was reached with the agreement that the president would nominate the justices and the Senate would confirm the nominations.

These compromises, as well as others, resulted from the recognition that if one group of states refused to ratify the Constitution, it was doomed.

Working toward Final Agreement

The Connecticut Compromise was reached by mid-July. The makeup of the executive branch and the judiciary, however, was left unsettled. The remaining work of the convention was turned over to a five-man Committee of Detail, which presented a rough draft of the Constitution on August 6. It made the executive and judicial branches subordinate to the legislative branch.

The Madisonian Model—Separation of Powers. The major issue of **separation of powers** had not yet been resolved. The delegates were concerned with structuring the government to prevent the imposition of tyranny—either by the majority or by a minority. It was Madison who proposed a governmental scheme—sometimes called the **Madisonian model**—to achieve this: the executive, legislative, and judicial powers of government were to be separated so that no one branch had enough power to dominate the others. The separation of powers was by function, as well as by personnel, with Congress passing laws, the president enforcing and administering laws, and the courts interpreting laws in individual circumstances.

Each of the three branches of government would be independent of the others, but they would have to cooperate to govern. According to Madison, in *Federalist Paper No. 51* (see Appendix C), "the great security against a gradual concentration of the several powers in the same department consists in giving to those who administer each department the necessary constitutional means and personal motives to resist encroachments of the others."

The Madisonian Model—Checks and Balances. The "constitutional means" Madison referred to is a system of **checks and balances** through which each branch of the government can check the actions of the others. For example, Congress can enact laws, but the president has veto power over congressional acts. The Supreme Court has the power to declare acts of Congress and of the executive unconstitutional, but the president appoints the justices of the Supreme Court, with the advice and consent of the Senate. (The Supreme Court's power to declare acts unconstitutional was not mentioned in the Constitution, although arguably the framers assumed that the Court would have this power—see the discussion of *judicial review* later in this chapter.) Figure 2–1 on the following page outlines these checks and balances.

In the years since the Constitution was ratified, the checks and balances built into it have evolved into a sometimes complex give-and-take among the branches of government. Generally, for nearly every check that one branch has over another, the branch that has been checked has found a way of getting around it. For example, suppose that the president checks Congress by vetoing a bill. Congress can override the presidential veto by a two-thirds vote. Additionally, Congress holds the "power of the purse."

Separation of Powers
The principle of dividing governmental powers among different branches of government.

Madisonian Model
A structure of government proposed by James Madison in which the powers of the government are separated into three branches: executive, legislative, and judicial.

Checks and Balances
A major principle of the American system of government whereby each branch of the government can check the actions of the others.

FIGURE 2–1: Checks and Balances

The major checks and balances among the three branches are illustrated here. The Constitution does not mention some of these checks, such as judicial review—the power of the courts to declare federal or state acts unconstitutional—and the president's ability to refuse to enforce judicial decisions or congressional legislation. Checks and balances can be thought of as a confrontation of powers or responsibilities. Each branch checks the actions of the others; two branches in conflict have powers that can result in balances or stalemates, requiring one branch to give in or both to reach a compromise.

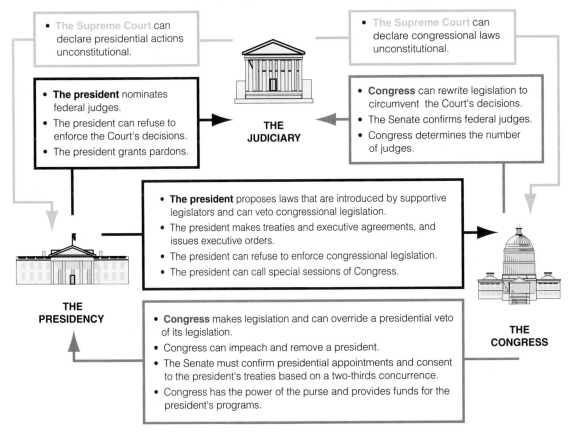

- The Supreme Court can declare presidential actions unconstitutional.

- The Supreme Court can declare congressional laws unconstitutional.

THE JUDICIARY

- **The president** nominates federal judges.
- The president can refuse to enforce the Court's decisions.
- The president grants pardons.

- **Congress** can rewrite legislation to circumvent the Court's decisions.
- The Senate confirms federal judges.
- Congress determines the number of judges.

- **The president** proposes laws that are introduced by supportive legislators and can veto congressional legislation.
- The president makes treaties and executive agreements, and issues executive orders.
- The president can refuse to enforce congressional legislation.
- The president can call special sessions of Congress.

THE PRESIDENCY

THE CONGRESS

- **Congress** makes legislation and can override a presidential veto of its legislation.
- Congress can impeach and remove a president.
- The Senate must confirm presidential appointments and consent to the president's treaties based on a two-thirds concurrence.
- Congress has the power of the purse and provides funds for the president's programs.

If it disagrees with a program endorsed by the executive branch, it can simply refuse to appropriate the funds necessary to operate that program. Similarly, the president can impose a countercheck on Congress if the Senate refuses to confirm a presidential appointment, such as a judicial appointment. The president can simply wait until Congress is in recess and then make what is called a "recess appointment," which does not require the Senate's approval.

The Executive. Delegates also had to settle disputes about the nature of the executive. Some delegates favored a plural executive made up of representatives from the various regions. This idea was abandoned in favor of a single chief executive. The seven-year single term that some delegates had proposed was replaced by a four-year term and the possibility of reelection.

A key issue was how the executive would be chosen. Some argued that Congress should choose the executive. To make the presidency completely independent of

Congress, however, an **electoral college** was adopted. This group would be made up of electors chosen by the states, and each state would have as many electors as it had members of Congress. The electoral college created a cumbersome presidential election process, but it supported the separation of powers while insulating the presidency from *direct* popular control. Proposals to replace the electoral college with a popular vote system have grown more frequent in recent years. The presidential elections of 2000, in which Democrat Al Gore carried the popular vote but lost in the electoral college to Republican George W. Bush, helped to motivate this cause. (See this chapter's feature titled *At Issue: Should We Elect the President by Popular Vote?* on the following page.)

The Final Document

On September 17, 1787, the Constitution was approved by thirty-nine delegates. Of the fifty-five who had attended originally, only forty-two remained. Three delegates refused to sign the Constitution. Others disapproved of at least parts of it but signed anyway to begin the ratification debate.

The Constitution that was to be ratified established the following fundamental principles:

- Popular sovereignty, or control by the people.
- A republican government in which the people choose representatives to make decisions for them.
- Limited government with written laws, in contrast to the powerful British government against which the colonists had rebelled.
- Separation of powers, with checks and balances among branches to prevent any one branch from gaining too much power.
- A federal system that allows for states' rights, because the states feared too much centralized control.

THE DIFFICULT ROAD TO RATIFICATION

The founders knew that **ratification** of the Constitution was far from certain. Indeed, because it was almost guaranteed that many state legislatures would not ratify it, the delegates agreed that each state should hold a special convention. Elected delegates to these conventions would discuss and vote on the Constitution. Further departing from the Articles of Confederation, the delegates agreed that as soon as nine states (rather than all thirteen) approved the Constitution, it would take effect, and Congress could begin to organize the new government.

The Federalists Push for Ratification

The two opposing forces in the battle over ratification were the Federalists and the Anti-Federalists. The **Federalists** favored a strong central government and the new Constitution. Their opponents, the **Anti-Federalists,** wanted to prevent the Constitution as drafted from being ratified.[12]

Electoral College
The group that officially elects the president and vice president of the United States. Today, the electors who make up this group are selected by the voters in each state and the District of Columbia.

Ratification
Formal approval.

Federalist
An individual who was in favor of the adoption of the U.S. Constitution and the creation of a federal union with a strong central government.

Anti-Federalist
An individual who opposed the ratification of the new Constitution in 1787. The Anti-Federalists were opposed to a strong central government.

---

12. There is some irony here. At the Constitutional Convention, those opposed to a strong central government pushed for a federal system because such a system would allow the states to retain some of their sovereign rights. The label *Anti-Federalists* thus contradicted their essential views.

atIssue: Should We Elect the President by Popular Vote?

▲ President-elect George Bush

meets with Vice President Al Gore at Gore's official residence in Washington, Tuesday, Dec. 19, 2000. (AP Photo/J. Scott Applewhite)

With the electoral college system, it is possible for a presidential candidate to win the majority of the popular votes but lose the election. This has happened on a few occasions, the latest being in the 2000 presidential elections. Although Democratic candidate Al Gore received 540,000 more votes than Republican George W. Bush, the Republican candidate won enough electoral college votes to become president. Some citizens believe that the electoral college should be abolished.

Normally, that would require a constitutional amendment, and the process of amending the Constitution is extremely difficult. As an alternative, some states have endorsed an interstate compact that would allow presidents to be elected by popular vote without abolishing the electoral college. Under the proposal, participating states would award their electoral votes to the candidate who wins the *national* popular vote. The proposal would go into effect when there were enough participating states to control a majority of votes in the electoral college.

The Popular Vote Should Determine the Winner

Today, voters in two-thirds of the states are effectively disenfranchised because they do not live in battleground states. Under the system used today, in all but two small states, the winner takes all of the state's electoral votes. Consequently, presidential candidates have little reason to campaign in states where they are certain to lose or win. In the 2008 presidential elections, the two major campaigns ended up focusing on approximately ten key states, including Colorado, Florida, Ohio, Pennsylvania, and Virginia. Partway through the campaign, Republican John McCain was forced to pull out of Michigan because he could not afford to run there, and Barack Obama was forced to close his operations in Georgia. These two states thus joined the "spectator" states, which also included some of the nation's most populous—California, Illinois, New Jersey, New York, and Texas.

It also seems absurd that the candidate winning the most popular votes can lose the election. In 2004, if Ohio had shifted 60,000 votes in favor of Democratic candidate John F. Kerry, he would have received all of that state's electoral votes and won the election, despite President Bush's 3.5 million–vote lead in the popular vote. If the popular vote determined the election results, presidential candidates would have to campaign in all fifty states. That would be democracy.

The Electoral College Works, Despite Its Faults

Electoral college supporters claim that under a popular vote system, small states would be ignored. Also, under the recent proposal for bypassing the electoral college, a state's electors would be forced to cast their electoral votes for a candidate who did not win the popular vote in that state. In 2008, that might have meant that all of Texas's electoral votes would have gone to Obama even though McCain won handily in that state. What would Texans think of that?

The electoral college system reflects a compromise reached by the framers of the Constitution, designed to satisfy those who wanted the president to be elected by popular vote and those who wanted Congress to elect the president. The electoral college has been part of our system ever since, and we should keep it.

FOR CRITICAL ANALYSIS

In many presidential elections, a strong third-party contender has kept both of the two major-party candidates from winning a majority of the popular vote. For example, in 1992, when businessman H. Ross Perot was a popular third-party candidate, Democrat Bill Clinton won only 43 percent of the popular vote, but carried the electoral college by more than two to one. Why might electing a president with a minority of the vote be more controversial under a popular vote system than under the electoral college system?

The *Federalist Papers.* In New York, opponents of the Constitution were quick to attack it. Alexander Hamilton answered their attacks under a pseudonym in newspaper columns and secured two collaborators—John Jay and James Madison. In a very short time, those three political figures wrote a series of eighty-five essays in defense of the Constitution and of a republican form of government.

These widely read essays, called the *Federalist Papers,* appeared in New York newspapers from October 1787 to August 1788 and were reprinted in the newspapers of other states. Although we do not know for certain who wrote every one, it is apparent that Hamilton was responsible for about two-thirds of the essays. These included the most important ones interpreting the Constitution, explaining the various powers of the three branches, and presenting a theory of *judicial review*—to be discussed later in this chapter. Madison's *Federalist Paper* No. 10 (see Appendix C), however, is considered a classic in political theory; it deals with the nature of groups—or factions, as he called them. In spite of the rapidity with which the *Federalist Papers* were written, they are considered by many to be perhaps the best example of political theorizing ever produced in the United States.[13]

The Anti-Federalist Response. Many of the Anti-Federalists' attacks on the Constitution were also brilliant. The Anti-Federalists claimed that the Constitution was written by aristocrats and would lead to aristocratic tyranny. More important, the Anti-Federalists believed that the Constitution would create an overbearing and overburdening central government hostile to personal liberty. (The Constitution said nothing about freedom of the press, freedom of religion, or any other individual liberty.) They wanted to include a list of guaranteed liberties, or a bill of rights. Finally, the Anti-Federalists decried the weakened power of the states.[14]

The Anti-Federalists cannot be dismissed as unpatriotic extremists. They included such patriots as Patrick Henry and Samuel Adams. They were arguing what had been the most prevalent view in that era. This view derived from the French political philosopher Baron de Montesquieu (1689–1755), an influential political theorist. Montesquieu believed that a republic was possible only in relatively small societies governed by direct democracy or by a large legislature with small districts. The Madisonian view favoring a large republic, particularly as expressed in *Federalist Papers* No. 10 and No. 51 (see Appendix C), was actually an exceptional view in those years. Indeed, some researchers believe it was mainly the bitter experiences with the Articles of Confederation, rather than Madison's arguments, that persuaded the state conventions to ratify the Constitution.

The March to the Finish

The struggle for ratification continued. Strong majorities were procured in Connecticut, Delaware, Georgia, New Jersey, and Pennsylvania. After a bitter struggle in Massachusetts, that state ratified the Constitution by a narrow margin on February 6, 1788. By the spring, Maryland and South Carolina had ratified by sizable majorities.

---

13. Some scholars believe that the *Federalist Papers* played only a minor role in securing ratification of the Constitution. Even if this is true, they still have lasting value as an authoritative explanation of the Constitution.
14. Herbert J. Storing edited seven volumes of Anti-Federalist writings and released them in 1981 as *The Anti-Federalist*. Political science professor Murray Dry has prepared a more manageable, one-volume version of this collection: Herbert J. Storing, ed., *The Anti-Federalist: An Abridgment of The Complete Anti-Federalist* (Chicago: University of Chicago Press, 2006).

Then on June 21 of that year, New Hampshire became the ninth state to ratify the Constitution. Although the Constitution was formally in effect, this meant little without Virginia and New York—the latter did not ratify for another month.

THE BILL OF RIGHTS

The U.S. Constitution would not have been ratified in several important states if the Federalists had not assured the states that amendments to the Constitution would be passed to protect individual liberties against incursions by the national government. Many of the recommendations of the state ratifying conventions included specific rights that were considered later by James Madison as he labored to draft what became the Bill of Rights.

Madison had to cull through more than two hundred state recommendations. It was no small task, and in retrospect he chose remarkably well. One of the rights appropriate for constitutional protection that he left out was equal protection under the laws—but that was not commonly regarded as a basic right at that time. Not until 1868 did the states ratify an amendment guaranteeing that no state shall deny equal protection to any person.

▼ **James Madison** is known as the "father" of the Bill of Rights. Why weren't they included in the final version of the U.S. Constitution? (Bettmann/Corbis)

On December 15, 1791, the national Bill of Rights was adopted when Virginia agreed to ratify the ten amendments. On ratification, the Bill of Rights became part of the U.S. Constitution. The basic structure of American government had already been established. Now the fundamental rights and liberties of individuals were protected, at least in theory, at the national level. The proposed amendment that Madison characterized as "the most valuable amendment in the whole lot"—which would have prohibited the states from infringing on the freedoms of conscience, press, and jury trial—had been eliminated by the Senate. Thus, the Bill of Rights as adopted did not limit state power, and individual citizens had to rely on the guarantees contained in a particular state constitution or state bill of rights. The country had to wait until the violence of the Civil War before significant limitations on state power in the form of the Fourteenth Amendment became part of the national Constitution.[15]

ALTERING THE CONSTITUTION: THE FORMAL AMENDMENT PROCESS

The U.S. Constitution consists of about 7,000 words. It is shorter than any state constitution except that of Vermont, which has 6,880 words. One of the reasons the federal Constitution is short is that the founders intended it to be only a framework for the new government, to be interpreted by succeeding generations. One of the reasons it has remained short is that the formal amending procedure does not allow for changes to be made easily. Article V of the Constitution outlines the ways in which amendments may be proposed and ratified.

---

15. For perspectives on these events, see Richard E. Labunski, *James Madison and the Struggle for the Bill of Rights* (New York: Oxford University Press, 2008), and Steven Waldman, *Founding Faith: How Our Founding Fathers Forged a Radical New Approach to Religious Liberty* (New York: Random House Trade Paperbacks, 2009).

Two formal methods of proposing an amendment to the Constitution are available: (1) a two-thirds vote in each chamber of Congress or (2) a national convention that is called by Congress at the request of two-thirds of the state legislatures (the second method has never been used).

Ratification can occur by one of two methods: (1) by a positive vote in three-fourths of the legislatures of the various states or (2) by special conventions called in the states and a positive vote in three-fourths of them. The second method has been used only once, to repeal Prohibition (the ban on the production and sale of alcoholic beverages). That situation was exceptional because prohibitionist forces were in control of the legislatures in many states where a majority of the population actually supported repeal.

Congress has considered more than eleven thousand amendments to the Constitution. Only thirty-three amendments have been submitted to the states after having been approved by the required two-thirds vote in each chamber of Congress, and only twenty-seven have been ratified—see Table 2–2. It should be clear that the amendment process is very difficult. Because of competing social and economic interests, the requirement that two-thirds of both the House and Senate approve the amendments is hard to achieve.

TABLE 2–2: **Amendments to the Constitution**

Amendment	Subject	Year Adopted	Time Required for Ratification
1st–10th	The Bill of Rights	1791	2 years, 2 months, 20 days
11th	Immunity of states from certain suits	1795	11 months, 3 days
12th	Changes in electoral college procedure	1804	6 months, 3 days
13th	Prohibition of slavery	1865	10 months, 3 days
14th	Citizenship, due process, and equal protection	1868	2 years, 26 days
15th	No denial of vote because of race, color, or previous condition of servitude	1870	11 months, 8 days
16th	Power of Congress to tax income	1913	3 years, 6 months, 22 days
17th	Direct election of U.S. senators	1913	10 months, 26 days
18th	National (liquor) prohibition	1919	1 year, 29 days
19th	Women's right to vote	1920	1 year, 2 months, 14 days
20th	Change of dates for congressional and presidential terms	1933	10 months, 21 days
21st	Repeal of the Eighteenth Amendment	1933	9 months, 15 days
22d	Limit on presidential tenure	1951	3 years, 11 months, 3 days
23d	District of Columbia electoral vote	1961	9 months, 13 days
24th	Prohibition of tax payment as a qualification to vote in federal elections	1964	1 year, 4 months, 9 days
25th	Procedures for determining presidential disability and presidential succession and for filling a vice-presidential vacancy	1967	1 year, 7 months, 4 days
26th	Prohibition of setting the minimum voting age above eighteen in any election	1971	3 months, 7 days
27th	Prohibition of Congress's voting itself a raise that takes effect before the next election	1992	203 years

Executive Agreement
An international agreement between chiefs of state that does not require legislative approval.

After an amendment has been approved by Congress, the process becomes even more arduous. Three-fourths of the state legislatures must approve the amendment. Only those amendments that have wide popular support across parties and in all regions of the country are likely to be approved.

Why was the amendment process made so difficult? The framers feared that a simple amendment process could lead to a tyranny of the majority, which could pass amendments to oppress disfavored individuals and groups. The cumbersome amendment process does not seem to stem the number of amendments that are proposed in Congress, however, particularly in recent years.

INFORMAL METHODS OF CONSTITUTIONAL CHANGE

Looking at the sparse number of formal constitutional amendments gives us an incomplete view of constitutional change. The brevity and ambiguity of the original document have permitted great alterations in the Constitution by way of varying interpretations over time. As the United States grew, both in population and territory, new social and political realities emerged. Congress, presidents, and the courts found it necessary to interpret the Constitution's provisions in light of these new realities. The Constitution has proved to be a remarkably flexible document, adapting itself time and again to new events and concerns.

Congressional Legislation

The Constitution gives Congress broad powers to carry out its duties as the nation's legislative body. For example, Article I, Section 8, of the Constitution gives Congress the power to regulate foreign and interstate commerce. Although there is no clear definition of foreign commerce or interstate commerce in the Constitution, Congress has cited the commerce clause as the basis for passing thousands of laws. Similarly, Article III, Section 1, states that the national judiciary shall consist of one supreme court and "such inferior courts, as Congress may from time to time ordain and establish." Through a series of acts, Congress has used this broad provision to establish the federal court system of today.

Presidential Actions

Even though the Constitution does not expressly authorize the president to propose bills or even budgets to Congress,[16] presidents since the time of Woodrow Wilson (1913–1921) have proposed hundreds of bills to Congress each year that are introduced by the president's supporters in Congress. Presidents have also relied on their Article II authority as commander in chief of the nation's armed forces to send American troops abroad into combat, although the Constitution provides that Congress has the power to declare war. Presidents have also conducted foreign affairs by the use of **executive agreements,** which are legally binding agreements between the president and a foreign head of state. The Constitution does not mention such agreements.

16. Note, though, that the Constitution, in Article II, Section 3, does state that the president "shall from time to time . . . recommend to [Congress's] consideration such measures as he shall judge necessary and expedient." Some scholars interpret this phrase to mean that the president has the constitutional authority to propose bills and budgets to Congress for consideration.

▲ **Supreme Court Justices (as of late 2009)**
With the addition of the Supreme Court's newest member, Justice Sonia Sotomayor, top row, right, the high court sits for a new group photograph, Tuesday, Sept. 29, 2009, at the Supreme Court in Washington. Seated, from left are: Associate Justice Anthony M. Kennedy, Associate Justice John Paul Stevens, Chief Justice John G. Roberts, Associate Justice Antonin Scalia, and Associate Justice Clarence Thomas. Standing, from left are: Associate Justice Samuel Alito Jr., Associate Justice Ruth Bader Ginsburg, Associate Justice Stephen Breyer, and Associate Justice Sonia Sotomayor. (AP Photo/Charles Dharapak)

Judicial Review

Judicial Review
The power of the Supreme Court or any court to declare unconstitutional federal or state laws and other acts of government.

Another way of changing the Constitution—or of making it more flexible—is through the power of judicial review. **Judicial review** refers to the power of U.S. courts to examine the constitutionality of actions undertaken by the legislative and executive branches of government. A state court, for example, may rule that a statute enacted by the state legislature violates the state constitution. Federal courts (and ultimately, the United States Supreme Court) may rule unconstitutional not only acts of Congress and decisions of the national executive branch but also state statutes, state executive actions, and even provisions of state constitutions.

The Constitution does not specifically mention the power of judicial review. In 1803, the Supreme Court claimed this power for itself in *Marbury v. Madison*,[17] in which the Court ruled that a particular provision of an act of Congress was unconstitutional.

Through the process of judicial review, the Supreme Court adapts the Constitution to modern situations. Electronic technology, for example, did not exist when the

---

17. 5 U.S. 137 (1803).

Constitution was ratified. Nonetheless, the Supreme Court has used the Fourth Amendment guarantees against unreasonable searches and seizures to place limits on the use of wiretapping and other electronic eavesdropping methods by government officials. Additionally, the Supreme Court has changed its interpretation of the Constitution in accordance with changing values. It ruled in 1896 that "separate-but-equal" public facilities for African Americans were constitutional; but by 1954 the times had changed, and the Supreme Court reversed that decision.[18] Woodrow Wilson summarized the Supreme Court's work when he described it as "a constitutional convention in continuous session." Basically, the law is what the Supreme Court says it is at any point in time.

Interpretation, Custom, and Usage

The Constitution has also been changed through interpretation by both Congress and the president. Originally, the president had a staff consisting of personal secretaries and a few others. Today, because Congress delegates specific tasks to the president and the chief executive assumes political leadership, the executive office staff alone has increased to several thousand persons. The executive branch provides legislative leadership far beyond the expectations of the founders.

Changes in ways of doing political business have also altered the Constitution. The Constitution does not mention political parties, yet these informal, "extraconstitutional" organizations make the nominations for offices, run the campaigns, organize the members of Congress, and in fact change the election system from time to time. Perhaps most striking, the Constitution has been adapted from serving the needs of a small, rural republic to providing a framework of government for an industrial giant with vast geographic, natural, and human resources.

18. *Brown v. Board of Education of Topeka*, 347 U.S. 483 (1954).

making a difference

HOW CAN YOU AFFECT THE U.S. CONSTITUTION?

The Constitution is an enduring document that has survived more than two hundred years of turbulent history. It is also an evolving document, however. Twenty-seven amendments have been added to the original Constitution. How can you, as an individual, actively help to rewrite the Constitution?

Why Should You Care? The laws of the nation have a direct impact on your life, and none more so than the Constitution—the supreme law of the land. The most important issues in society are often settled by the Constitution. For example, for the first seventy-five years of the republic, the Constitution implicitly protected the institution of slavery. If the Constitution had never been changed through the amendment process, the process of abolishing slavery would have been much different and might have involved revolutionary measures.

Since the passage of the Fourteenth Amendment in 1868, the Constitution has defined who is a citizen and who is entitled to the protections the Constitution provides. Constitutional provisions define our liberties. The First Amendment protects our freedom of speech more thoroughly than do the laws of many other nations. Few other countries have constitutional provisions governing the right to own firearms (the Second Amendment). Disputes involving these rights are among the most fundamental issues we face.

What Can You Do? Consider how one person decided to affect the Constitution. Shirley Breeze, head of the Missouri Women's Network, decided to bring the Equal Rights Amendment (ERA) back to life after its "death" in 1982. She spearheaded a movement that has gained significant support. Today, bills to ratify the ERA have been introduced not only in Missouri but also in other states that did not ratify it earlier, including Illinois, Oklahoma, and Virginia.

At the time of this writing, national coalitions of interest groups are supporting or opposing a number of proposed amendments. One hotly debated proposed amendment concerns abortion. If you are interested in this issue and would like to make a difference, you can contact one of several groups.

An organization whose primary goal is to secure the passage of the Human Life Amendment is:

American Life League
P.O. Box 1350
Stafford, VA 22555
540-659-4171
www.all.org

The Human Life Amendment would recognize in law the "personhood" of the unborn, secure human rights protections for an unborn child from the time of fertilization, and prohibit abortion under any circumstances.

A political action and information organization working on behalf of "pro-choice" issues—that is, the right of women to have control over reproduction—is:

NARAL Pro-Choice America (formerly the National Abortion and Reproductive Rights Action League)
1156 15th St., Suite 700
Washington, DC 20005
202-973-3000
www.naral.org

There is also another way that you can affect the Constitution—by protecting your existing rights and liberties under it. In the wake of the 9/11 attacks, a number of new laws have been enacted that some believe go too far in curbing our constitutional rights. If you agree and want to join with others who are concerned about this issue, a good starting point is the Web site of the American Civil Liberties Union (ACLU) at:

www.aclu.org

◀ **The controversy** over abortion rights has never died down in American politics. These pro- and anti-abortion demonstrators make their presence known in front of the United States Supreme Court building in Washington, D.C. Is it possible to pass legislation that satisfies both sides of this issue? Why or why not? (AP Photo/Joe Marquette)

key terms

Anti-Federalist 33	executive agreement 38	natural rights 24	social contract 24
bicameral legislature 29	Federalist 33	ratification 33	state 25
checks and balances 31	Great Compromise 29	representative	supremacy doctrine 29
confederation 25	judicial review 39	assembly 20	unicameral
electoral college 33	Madisonian model 31	separation of powers 31	legislature 25

chapter summary

1 The first permanent English colonies were established at Jamestown in 1607 and Plymouth in 1620. The Mayflower Compact created the first formal government in New England. By the mid-1700s, a total of thirteen British colonies had been established along the Atlantic seaboard.

2 In the 1760s, the British began to impose on their increasingly independent-minded colonies a series of taxes and legislative acts. The colonists responded with protests and boycotts of British products. Representatives of the colonies formed the First Continental Congress in 1774. The delegates sent a petition to the British king expressing their grievances. The Second Continental Congress established an army in 1775 to defend colonists against attacks by British soldiers.

3 On July 4, 1776, the Second Continental Congress approved the Declaration of Independence. Perhaps the most revolutionary aspects of the Declaration were its assumptions that people have natural rights to life, liberty, and the pursuit of happiness; that governments derive their power from the consent of the governed; and that people have a right to overthrow oppressive governments. During the Revolutionary War, the colonies adopted written constitutions that severely curtailed the power of executives, thus giving their legislatures predominant powers. By the end of the Revolutionary War, the states had signed the Articles of Confederation, creating a weak central government with few powers. The Articles proved to be unworkable because the national government had no way to ensure compliance by the states with such measures as securing tax revenues.

4 General dissatisfaction with the Articles of Confederation prompted the call for a convention at Philadelphia in 1787. Although the delegates ostensibly convened to amend the Articles, the discussions soon focused on creating a constitution for a new form of government. The Virginia Plan and the New Jersey Plan did not garner widespread support. A compromise offered by Connecticut helped to break the large-state/small-state disputes dividing the delegates. The final version of the Constitution provided for the separation of powers, checks and balances, and a federal form of government.

5 Fears of a strong central government prompted the addition of the Bill of Rights to the Constitution. The Bill of Rights secured for Americans a wide variety of freedoms, including the freedoms of religion, speech, and assembly. It was initially applied only to the federal government, but amendments to the Constitution following the Civil War were interpreted to ensure that the Bill of Rights would apply to the states as well.

6 An amendment to the Constitution may be proposed either by a two-thirds vote in each house of Congress or by a national convention called by Congress at the request of two-thirds of the state legislatures. Ratification can occur either by a positive vote in three-fourths of the legislatures of the various states or by special conventions called in the states for the specific purpose of ratifying the proposed amendment and a positive vote in three-fourths of these state conventions. Informal methods of constitutional change include reinterpretation through congressional legislation, presidential actions, and judicial review.

QUESTIONS FOR
discussionandanalysis

1 Naturalized citizens—immigrants—have almost all the rights of natural-born citizens, but under the Constitution they cannot be elected president. If the Constitution were changed to allow an immigrant to become president, do you think that today's voters would vote for such an individual? Why might a naturalized leader be more nationalistic than a natural-born one?

2 Historian Charles Beard argued that the Constitution was produced primarily by wealthy property owners who wanted a stronger government that could protect their property rights. Do you see any provisions in the text of the Constitution that would support Beard's argument? Even if Beard is right, is this in any way a problem?

3 If Georgia and the Carolinas had stayed out of the Union because of a desire to protect slavery, what would subsequent American history have been like? Would the eventual freedom of the slaves have been delayed—or advanced?

4 A result of the Great Compromise is that representation in the Senate dramatically departs from the one-person, one-vote rule. The almost 40 million people who live in California elect two senators, as do the half-million people living in Wyoming. In other words, the citizens of small states are much better represented in the Senate than the citizens of large ones. What political results would you expect this unequal representation to have? Do you see any evidence that your expectations are correct?

helpfulonline**Resources**

CONNECTING TO AMERICAN GOVERNMENT AND POLITICS

For U.S. founding documents, including the Declaration of Independence, scanned originals of the U.S. Constitution, and the *Federalist Papers*, go to Emory University School of Law's Web site at:
www.law.emory.edu/index.php?id=3130

The National Constitution Center provides information on the Constitution—including its

history, current debates over constitutional provisions, and news articles—at:
www.constitutioncenter.org

To look at state constitutions, go to:
www.findlaw.com/casecode/state.html

aspecialWebSite

FOR YOUR TEXT

Go to this book's special Web site at academic.cengage.com/polisci/Schmidt/Brief6e. Choose "For Students." Then click on Chapter 2, where you will find an online quiz and other helpful study aids. If your professor is using CengageNOW: *American Government and Politics Today, Brief Edition,* log in and go to Chapter 2 for additional online study aids.

3

Federalism

In the United States, rights and powers are reserved to the states by the Tenth Amendment. It may appear that since the terrorist attacks of September 11, 2001, the federal government, sometimes called the national or central government, predominates. Nevertheless, that might be a temporary exaggeration, for there are 87,525 separate governmental units in this nation.

Visitors from France or Spain are often awestruck by the complexity of our system of government. Consider that a criminal action can be defined by state law, by national law, or by both. Thus, a criminal suspect can be prosecuted in the state court system or in the federal court system (or both). Often, economic regulation covering exactly the same issues exists at the local level, the state level, and the national level—generating multiple forms to be completed, multiple procedures to be followed, and multiple laws to be obeyed. Many programs are funded by the national government but administered by state and local governments.

Relations between central governments and local units are structured in various ways. *Federalism* is one of these ways. Understanding federalism and how it differs from other forms of government is important in understanding the American political system. Indeed, many political issues today would not arise if we did not have a federal form of government in which governmental authority is divided between the central government and various subunits.

THREE SYSTEMS OF GOVERNMENT

There are almost two hundred independent nations in the world today. Each of these nations has its own system of government. Generally, though, we can describe how nations structure relations between central governments and local units in terms of three models: (1) the unitary system, (2) the confederal system, and (3) the federal system. The most popular, both historically and today, is the unitary system.

A Unitary System

A **unitary system** of government is the easiest to define. Unitary systems place ultimate governmental authority in the hands of the national, or central, government. Consider a typical unitary system—France. There are regions, departments, and municipalities (communes) in France. The regions, departments, and communes have elected and appointed officials. So far, the French system appears to be very similar to the U.S. system, but the similarity is only superficial. Under the unitary French system, the decisions of the lower levels of government can be overruled by the national government. The national government also can cut off the funding for many local government activities. Moreover, in a unitary system such as that in France, all questions of education, police, the use of land, and welfare are handled by the national government. Britain, Egypt, Ghana, Israel, Japan, the Philippines, and Sweden—in fact, most countries today—have unitary systems of government.[1]

A Confederal System

You were introduced to the elements of a **confederal system** of government in Chapter 2, when we examined the Articles of Confederation. A confederation is the opposite of a unitary governing system. It is a league of independent states in which a central government or administration handles only those matters of common concern expressly delegated to it by the member states. The central government has no ability to make laws directly applicable to member states unless the members explicitly support such laws. The United States under the Articles of Confederation was a confederal system.

Few, if any, confederations of this kind exist. One possible exception is the European Union (EU), a league of countries that has developed a large body of Europe-wide laws that all members must observe. Many members even share a common currency, the euro. Not all members of the EU use the euro, however, which demonstrates the limits of a confederal system. Nations have also formed organizations with one another for limited purposes, such as military or peacekeeping cooperation. Examples are the North Atlantic Treaty Organization (NATO) and the United Nations (UN). These organizations, however, are not true confederations.

A Federal System

The federal system lies between the unitary and confederal forms of government. As mentioned in Chapter 2, in a *federal system,* authority is divided, usually by a written constitution, between a central government and regional, or subdivisional,

Unitary System
A centralized governmental system in which ultimate governmental authority rests in the hands of the national, or central, government.

Confederal System
A system consisting of a league of independent states, each having essentially sovereign powers. The central government created by such a league has only limited powers over the states.

---

1. Recent legislation has altered somewhat the unitary character of the French political system. In Britain, the unitary nature of the government has been modified by the creation of the Scottish Parliament.

governments (often called *constituent governments*). The central government and the constituent governments both act directly on the people through laws and through the actions of elected and appointed governmental officials. Within each government's sphere of authority, each is supreme, in theory. Thus, a federal system differs sharply from a unitary one, in which the central government is supreme and the constituent governments derive their authority from it. Australia, Brazil, Canada, Germany, India, and Mexico are examples of other nations with federal systems. See Figure 3–1 for a comparison of the three systems.

WHY FEDERALISM?

Why did the United States develop in a federal direction? We look here at that question, as well as at some of the arguments for and against a federal form of government.

A Practical Solution

As you saw in Chapter 2, the historical basis of our federal system was laid down in Philadelphia at the Constitutional Convention, where advocates of a strong national government opposed states' rights advocates. This conflict continued through to the ratifying conventions in the several states. The resulting federal system was a compromise. The supporters of the new Constitution were political pragmatists—they realized that without a federal arrangement, there would be no ratification of the new Constitution. The appeal of federalism was that it retained state traditions and local power while establishing a strong national government capable of handling common problems.

Even if the founders had agreed on the desirability of a unitary system, size and regional isolation would have made such a system difficult operationally. At the time of the Constitutional Convention, the thirteen states taken together were much

FIGURE 3–1: The Flow of Power in Three Systems of Government

In a unitary system, power flows from the central government to the local and state governments. In a confederal system, power flows in the opposite direction—from the state governments to the central government. In a federal system, the flow of power, in principle, goes both ways.

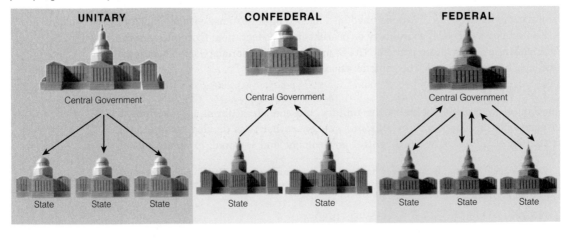

The Golden Gate Bridge in San Francisco forms part of America's massive transportation system. Because of our federal form of government, transportation is paid for in part by Washington, D.C., as well as by state and local governments. Would this be the case in a country with a unitary system? (AP Photo/Eric Risberg)

larger geographically than England or France. Slow travel and communication, combined with geographic spread, contributed to the isolation of many regions within the states. It could take several weeks for all of the states to be informed about a particular political decision.

Other Arguments for Federalism

The arguments for federalism in the United States and elsewhere involve a complex set of factors, some of which we already have noted. Even with modern transportation and communications systems, the large area or population of some nations makes it impractical to locate all political authority in one place. Federalism brings government closer to the people. It allows more direct access to, and influence on, government agencies and policies, rather than leaving the population restive and dissatisfied with a remote, faceless, all-powerful central authority.

Benefits for the United States. In the United States, federalism historically has yielded many benefits. State governments long have been a training ground for future national leaders. Many presidents made their political mark as state governors. The states themselves have been testing grounds for new government initiatives. As United States Supreme Court justice Louis Brandeis once observed:

> It is one of the happy incidents of the federal system that a single courageous state may, if its citizens choose, serve as a laboratory and try novel social and economic experiments without risk to the rest of the country.[2]

Examples of programs pioneered at the state level include unemployment compensation, which began in Wisconsin, and air-pollution control, which was initiated in California. Today, states are experimenting with policies ranging from educational reforms to homeland security defense strategies. Since the passage of the 1996 welfare reform legislation—which gave more control over welfare programs to state governments—states have also been experimenting with different methods of delivering welfare assistance.

Federalism Allows for Many Political Subcultures. The American way of life always has been characterized by a number of political subcultures, which divide along

---

2. *New State Ice Co. v. Liebmann*, 285 U.S. 262 (1932).

the lines of race and ethnic origin, region, wealth, education, and, more recently, degree of religious fundamentalism and sexual preference. The existence of diverse political subcultures would appear to be incompatible with a political authority concentrated solely in a central government. Had the United States developed into a unitary system, various political subcultures certainly would have been less able to influence government behavior than they have been, and continue to be, in our federal system.

Arguments against Federalism

Not everyone thinks federalism is such a good idea. Some see it as a way for powerful state and local interests to block progress and impede national plans. Smaller political units are more likely to be dominated by a single political group. (This was essentially the argument that James Madison put forth in *Federalist Paper* No. 10, which you can read in Appendix C of this text.) The dominant groups in some cities and states have resisted implementing equal rights for minority groups. Some argue, however, that the dominant factions in other states have been more progressive than the national government in many areas, such as in environmental protection.

Critics also feel that there is too much inequity among the states, so they call for increased federal oversight of various programs. Others, however, see dangers in the expansion of national powers at the expense of the states. President Ronald Reagan (1981–1989) said, "The Founding Fathers saw the federalist system as constructed something like a masonry wall. The States are the bricks, the national government is the mortar. . . . Unfortunately, over the years, many people have increasingly come to believe that Washington is the whole wall."[3]

THE CONSTITUTIONAL BASIS FOR AMERICAN FEDERALISM

The term *federal system* cannot be found in the U.S. Constitution. Nor is it possible to find a systematic division of governmental authority between the national and state governments in that document. Rather, the Constitution sets out different types of powers. These powers can be classified as (1) the powers of the national government, (2) the powers of the states, and (3) prohibited powers. The Constitution also makes it clear that if a state or local law conflicts with a national law, the national law will prevail.

Powers of the National Government

The powers delegated to the national government include both expressed and implied powers, as well as the special category of inherent powers. Most of the powers expressly delegated to the national government are found in the first seventeen clauses of Article I, Section 8, of the Constitution. These **enumerated powers,** also called *expressed powers,* include coining money, setting standards for weights and measures, making uniform naturalization laws, admitting new states, establishing post offices, and declaring war. Another important enumerated power is the power to regulate commerce among the states—a topic we deal with later in this chapter.

3. Text of the address by the president to the National Conference of State Legislatures, Atlanta, Georgia (Washington, D.C.: The White House, Office of the Press Secretary, July 30, 1981), as quoted in Edward Millican, *One United People: The Federalist Papers and the National Idea* (Lexington: The University Press of Kentucky, 1990).

The Necessary and Proper Clause. The implied powers of the national government are also based on Article I, Section 8, which states that the Congress shall have the power

> [t]o make all Laws which shall be necessary and proper for carrying into Execution the foregoing Powers, and all other Powers vested by this Constitution in the Government of the United States, or in any Department or Officer thereof.

This clause is sometimes called the **elastic clause,** or the **necessary and proper clause,** because it provides flexibility to our constitutional system. It gives Congress the power to do whatever is necessary to execute its specifically delegated powers. The clause was first used in the Supreme Court decision of *McCulloch v. Maryland*[4] (discussed later in this chapter) to develop the concept of implied powers. Through this concept, the national government has succeeded in strengthening the scope of its authority to meet the many problems that the framers of the Constitution did not, and could not, anticipate.

Inherent Powers. A special category of national powers that is not implied by the necessary and proper clause consists of what have been labeled the inherent powers of the national government. These powers derive from the fact that the United States is a sovereign power among nations, and so its national government must be the only government that deals with other nations. Under international law, it is assumed that all nation-states, regardless of their size or power, have an inherent right to ensure their own survival. To do this, each nation must have the ability to act in its own interest among and with the community of nations—by, for instance, making treaties, waging war, seeking trade, and acquiring territory. Note that no specific clause in the Constitution says anything about the acquisition of additional land. Nonetheless, through the federal government's inherent powers, we made the Louisiana Purchase in 1803 and then went on to acquire Florida, Texas, Oregon, Alaska, Hawaii, and other lands. The United States grew from a mere thirteen states to fifty states, plus several territories.

Powers of the State Governments

The Tenth Amendment states that the powers not delegated to the United States by the Constitution, nor prohibited by it to the states, are reserved to the states, or to the people. These are the reserved powers that the national government cannot deny to the states. Because these powers are not expressly listed—and because they are not limited to powers that are expressly listed—there is sometimes a question as to whether a certain power is delegated to the national government or reserved to the states.

State powers have been held to include each state's right to regulate commerce within its borders and to provide for a state militia. States also have the reserved power to make laws on all matters not prohibited to the

Elastic Clause, or Necessary and Proper Clause

The clause in Article I, Section 8, that grants Congress the power to do whatever is necessary to execute its specifically delegated powers.

"Sorry, but all my power's been turned back to the states."
(The *New Yorker* Collection, 2008. Lee Lorenz, from cartoonbank.com. All rights reserved.)

4. 17 U.S. 316 (1819).

Police Power
The authority to legislate for the protection of the health, morals, safety, and welfare of the people. In the United States, most police power is reserved to the states.

Concurrent Powers
Powers held jointly by the national and state governments.

Supremacy Clause
The constitutional provision that makes the Constitution and federal laws superior to all conflicting state and local laws.

states by the U.S. Constitution or state constitutions and not expressly, or by implication, delegated to the national government. Furthermore, the states have **police power**—the authority to legislate for the protection of the health, morals, safety, and welfare of the people. Their police power enables states to pass laws governing such activities as crimes, marriage, contracts, education, intrastate transportation, and land use.

The ambiguity of the Tenth Amendment has allowed the reserved powers of the states to be defined differently at different times in our history. When there is widespread support for increased regulation by the national government, the Tenth Amendment tends to recede into the background. When the tide turns the other way (in favor of states' rights), the Tenth Amendment is resurrected to justify arguments supporting increased states' rights.

Concurrent Powers

In certain areas, the states share **concurrent powers** with the national government. Most concurrent powers are not specifically listed in the Constitution; they are only implied. An example of a concurrent power is the power to tax. The types of taxation are divided between the levels of government. For example, states may not levy a tariff (a set of taxes on imported goods); only the national government may do this. Neither government may tax the facilities of the other. If the state governments did not have the power to tax, they would not be able to function other than on a ceremonial basis. Additional concurrent powers include the power to borrow funds, to establish courts, and to charter banks and corporations. To a limited extent, the national government exercises police power, and to the extent that it does, police power is also a concurrent power. Concurrent powers exercised by the states are normally limited to the geographic area of each state and to those functions not granted by the Constitution exclusively to the national government. Examples of functions exclusive to the national government are the coinage of money and the negotiation of treaties.

Prohibited Powers

The Constitution prohibits or denies a number of powers to the national government. For example, the national government has expressly been denied the power to impose taxes on goods sold to other countries (exports). Moreover, any power not granted expressly or implicitly to the federal government by the Constitution is prohibited to it. For example, many legal experts believe that the national government could not create a national divorce law system without a constitutional amendment. The states are also denied certain powers. For example, no state is allowed to enter into a treaty on its own with another country.

The Supremacy Clause

The supremacy of the national constitution over subnational laws and actions is established in the **supremacy clause** of the Constitution. The supremacy clause (Article VI, Clause 2) states the following:

> This Constitution, and the Laws of the United States which shall be made in Pursuance thereof; and all Treaties made ... under the Authority of the United States, shall be the supreme Law of the Land; and the Judges in every State shall be bound thereby, any Thing in the Constitution or Laws of any State to the Contrary notwithstanding.

In other words, states cannot use their reserved or concurrent powers to thwart national policies. All national and state officers, including judges, must be bound by oath to support the Constitution. Hence, any legitimate exercise of national governmental power supersedes any conflicting state action.[5] Of course, deciding whether a conflict actually exists is a judicial matter, as you will soon learn when we discuss the case of *McCulloch v. Maryland.*

National government legislation in a concurrent area is said to preempt (take precedence over) conflicting state or local laws or regulations in that area. One of the ways in which the national government has extended its powers, particularly since 1900, is through the preemption of state and local laws by national legislation. In the first decade of the twentieth century, fewer than twenty national laws preempted laws and regulations issued by state and local governments. By the beginning of the twenty-first century, the number had grown into the hundreds.

Interstate Relations

So far we have examined only the relationship between central and state governmental units. The states, however, have constant commercial, social, and other dealings among themselves. The national Constitution imposes certain "rules of the road" on interstate relations. These rules have had the effect of preventing any one state from setting itself apart from the other states. The three most important clauses governing interstate relations in the Constitution, all taken from the Articles of Confederation, require each state to do the following:

- Give full faith and credit to every other state's public acts, records, and judicial proceedings (Article IV, Section 1).
- Extend to every other state's citizens the privileges and immunities of its own citizens (Article IV, Section 2).
- Agree to return persons who are fleeing from justice in another state back to their home state when requested to do so (Article IV, Section 2).

Following these constitutional mandates is not always easy for the states. For example, one question that has arisen in recent years is whether states will be constitutionally obligated to recognize same-sex marriages performed in other states. We consider that question in this chapter's *At Issue* feature on the next page.

States may also enter into agreements with each other, called *interstate compacts,* so long as the compacts do not increase the power of the contracting states relative to other states or to the federal government. An example is the Port Authority of New York and New Jersey, established by an agreement between those states in 1921.

DEFINING CONSTITUTIONAL POWERS—THE EARLY YEARS

Recall from Chapter 2 that constitutional language, to be effective and to endure, must have some degree of ambiguity. Certainly, the powers delegated to the national government and the powers reserved to the states contain elements of ambiguity, thus leaving

---

5. An example of this is President Dwight Eisenhower's disciplining of Arkansas governor Orval Faubus in 1957 by federalizing the National Guard to enforce the court-ordered desegregation of Little Rock High School.

at Issue: Should Same-Sex Marriages Be Recognized Everywhere?

In November 2003, the Massachusetts Supreme Judicial Court ruled that same-sex couples have a right to civil marriage under the state constitution.* The California Supreme Court legalized same-sex marriages in May 2008, but California voters overturned the ruling in November by amending the state constitution.† By 2009, however, Connecticut, Iowa, New Hampshire, Maine, and Vermont had all accepted same-sex marriage.

The U.S. Constitution requires that each state give full faith and credit to every other state's public acts. If a man and woman are married under the laws of Nevada, the other forty-nine states must recognize that marriage. But what if one state recognizes same-sex marriages? Does that mean that all other states must recognize such marriages and give each partner the benefits accorded to partners in opposite-sex marriages?

In 1996, Congress attempted to prevent such a result through the Defense of Marriage Act, which allows state governments to ignore same-sex marriages performed in other states. But what if the United States Supreme Court ruled the Defense of Marriage Act unconstitutional? If this happened, then all state laws that refuse to recognize same-sex marriages performed in another state would be unconstitutional as well, because the U.S. Constitution is the supreme law of the land. Furthermore, the federal government itself would presumably have to accept all state-defined marriages, and a same-sex marriage in a state that allowed such unions would entitle the couple to federal benefits.

Same-Sex Marriages Should Be Recognized Nationwide

Most advocates of same-sex marriage believe that the Defense of Marriage Act should be repealed or ruled unconstitutional. They argue that all couples should have the right to marry. Why should a couple be denied the many benefits of marriage just because of their sexual orientation? Same-sex marriages do not interfere with traditional unions in any way—indeed, gay and lesbian couples strengthen the institution of marriage by their attachment to it. Same-sex marriages will promote healthier lifestyles and discourage promiscuity.

The key argument in favor of nationwide recognition, however, is that banning same-sex marriage is unfair discrimination against a minority group. Our constitution and laws are designed to protect minority rights even when a majority of the voters oppose such rights. Therefore, all states should accept same-sex marriages performed elsewhere, even if a state does not itself authorize such marriages.

The States Should Be Able to Make Their Own Decisions

A majority of the American electorate is opposed to same-sex marriages. Either by statute or by constitutional amendment, twenty-nine states explicitly ban same-sex marriages, and these marriages remain illegal in an additional fifteen states. Opponents of same-sex marriage contend that marriage between a man and a woman is the basis for creating and defining a family. All major world religions reject same-sex marriage, and the legalization of same-sex marriages will lead to an attack against religious institutions and values.

One of the strongest arguments in favor of the Defense of Marriage Act, however, is that it reflects the American federal system. If same-sex marriage is such a good idea, why not prove this by allowing it in a limited number of jurisdictions—and then see what happens? That will truly allow the individual states to serve as "laboratories of democracy." Attempts to force same-sex marriage on states where the overwhelming majority of the people oppose such a step are likely to have unfortunate results.

FOR CRITICAL ANALYSIS

If same-sex marriage became common, what impact would this have on American culture generally?

WE ALL DESERVE THE FREEDOM TO MARRY

▼ **This replica of President Abraham Lincoln** was used at a protest rally in favor of legally recognizing same-sex marriages. Currently, only a few states recognize same-sex unions. (Frederic Larson/Corbis/San Francisco Chronicle)

*Goodridge v. Department of Public Health, 798 N.E.2d 941 (Mass. 2003).
†In re Marriage Cases, 183 P.3d 384 (Cal. 2008).

the door open for different interpretations of federalism. Disputes over the boundaries of national versus state powers have characterized this nation from the beginning. In the early 1800s, the most significant disputes arose over differing interpretations of the implied powers of the national government under the necessary and proper clause and over the respective powers of the national government and the states to regulate commerce.

Although political bodies at all levels of government play important roles in the process of settling such disputes, ultimately it is the Supreme Court that casts the final vote. As might be expected, the character of the referee will have an impact on the ultimate outcome of any dispute. From 1801 to 1835, the Supreme Court was headed by Chief Justice John Marshall, a Federalist who advocated a strong central government. We look here at two cases decided by the Marshall Court: *McCulloch v. Maryland*[6] and *Gibbons v. Ogden.*[7] Both cases are considered milestones in the movement toward national government supremacy.

McCulloch v. Maryland (1819)

The U.S. Constitution says nothing about establishing a national bank. Nonetheless, at different times Congress chartered two banks—the First and Second Banks of the United States—and provided part of their initial capital; thus, they were national banks. The government of Maryland imposed a tax on the Second Bank's Baltimore branch in an attempt to put that branch out of business. The branch's cashier, James William McCulloch, refused to pay the Maryland tax. When Maryland took McCulloch to its state court, the state of Maryland won. The national government appealed the case to the Supreme Court.

One of the issues before the Court was whether the national government had the implied power, under the necessary and proper clause, to charter a bank and contribute capital to it. The other important question before the Court was the following: If the bank was constitutional, could a state tax it? In other words, was a state action that conflicted with a national government action invalid under the supremacy clause?

Chief Justice Marshall held that if establishing a national bank aided the national government in the exercise of its designated powers, then the authority to set up such a bank could be implied. Having established this doctrine of implied powers, Marshall then answered the other important question before the Court and established the doctrine of national supremacy. Marshall ruled that no state could use its taxing power to tax an arm of the national government. If it could, "the declaration that the Constitution . . . shall be the supreme law of the land, is [an] empty and unmeaning [statement]."

▼ **John Marshall** (1755–1835) was the fourth chief justice of the Supreme Court. Some scholars have declared that Marshall is the true architect of the American constitutional system. (Library of Congress)

Marshall's decision enabled the national government to grow and to meet problems that the Constitution's framers were unable to foresee. Today, practically every expressed power of the national government has been expanded in one way or another by use of the necessary and proper clause.

6. 17 U.S. 316 (1819).
7. 22 U.S. 1 (1824).

Commerce Clause
The section of the Constitution in which Congress is given the power to regulate trade among the states and with foreign countries.

Gibbons v. Ogden (1824)

One of the most important parts of the Constitution, included in Article I, Section 8, is the so-called **commerce clause,** in which Congress is given the power "[t]o regulate Commerce with foreign Nations, and among the several States, and with the Indian Tribes." The meaning of this clause was at issue in *Gibbons v. Ogden*.

The Background of the Case. Robert Fulton and Robert Livingston secured a monopoly on steam navigation on the waters in New York State from the New York legislature in 1803. They licensed Aaron Ogden to operate steam-powered ferryboats between New York and New Jersey. Thomas Gibbons, who had obtained a license from the U.S. government to operate boats in interstate waters, decided to compete with Ogden, but he did so without New York's permission. Ogden sued Gibbons. The New York state courts prohibited Gibbons from operating in New York waters. Gibbons appealed to the Supreme Court.

There were actually several issues before the Court in this case. The first issue was how the term *commerce* should be defined. New York's highest court had defined the term narrowly to mean only the shipment of goods, or the interchange of commodities, not navigation or the transport of people. The second issue was whether the national government's power to regulate interstate commerce extended to commerce within a state (*intrastate* commerce) or was limited strictly to commerce among the states (*interstate* commerce). The third issue was whether the power to regulate interstate commerce was a concurrent power (as the New York court had concluded) or an exclusive national power.

Marshall's Ruling. Marshall defined *commerce* as *all* commercial intercourse—all business dealings—including navigation and the transport of people. Marshall also held that the commerce power of the national government could be exercised in state jurisdictions, even though it could not reach *solely* intrastate commerce. Finally, Marshall emphasized that the power to regulate interstate commerce was an *exclusive* national power. Marshall held that because Gibbons was duly authorized by the national government to navigate in interstate waters, he could not be prohibited from doing so by a state court.

Marshall's expansive interpretation of the commerce clause in *Gibbons v. Ogden* allowed the national government to exercise increasing authority over economic affairs throughout the land. Congress did not immediately exploit this broad grant of power. In the 1930s and subsequent decades, however, the commerce clause became the primary constitutional basis for national government regulation—as you will read later in this chapter.

STATES' RIGHTS AND THE RESORT TO CIVIL WAR

The controversy over slavery that led to the Civil War took the form of a dispute over national government supremacy versus the rights of the separate states. Essentially, the Civil War brought to an ultimate and violent climax the ideological debate that had been outlined by the Federalist and Anti-Federalist parties even before the Constitution was ratified.

The Shift Back to States' Rights

As we have seen, while John Marshall was chief justice of the Supreme Court, he did much to increase the power of the national government and to reduce that of the states. During the Jacksonian era (1829–1837), however, a shift back to states' rights began. The question of the regulation of commerce became one of the major issues in federal-state relations. When Congress passed a tariff in 1828, the state of South Carolina unsuccessfully attempted to nullify the tariff (render it void), claiming that in cases of conflict between a state and the national government, the state should have the ultimate authority over its citizens.

Over the next three decades, the North and South became even more sharply divided—over tariffs that mostly benefited northern industries and over the slavery issue. On December 20, 1860, South Carolina formally repealed its ratification of the Constitution and withdrew from the Union. On February 4, 1861, representatives from six southern states met at Montgomery, Alabama, to form a new government called the Confederate States of America.

War and the Growth of the National Government

The ultimate defeat of the South in 1865 permanently ended the idea that a state could successfully claim the right to secede, or withdraw, from the Union. Ironically, the Civil War—brought about in large part because of the South's desire for increased states' rights—resulted in the opposite: an increase in the political power of the national government.

Thousands of new employees were hired to run the Union war effort and to deal with the social and economic problems that had to be handled in the aftermath of the war. A billion-dollar ($1.3 billion, which is about $17.4 billion in today's dollars) national government budget was passed for the first time in 1865 to cover the increased government expenditures. The first (temporary) income tax was imposed on citizens to help pay for the war. This tax and the increased national government spending were precursors of the expanded future role of the national government in the American federal system. Many scholars contend that the North's victory set the nation on the path to a modern industrial economy and society.

▲ **President Lincoln** meets with some of his generals and other troops on October 3, 1862. While the Civil War was fought over the issue of slavery, it was also a battle over the supremacy of the national government. Once the North won the war, what happened to the size and power of our national government? (Bettmann/Corbis)

THE CONTINUING DISPUTE OVER THE DIVISION OF POWER

Although the outcome of the Civil War firmly established the supremacy of the national government and put to rest the idea that a state could secede from the Union, the war by no means ended the debate over the division of powers between the national

Dual Federalism
A model of federalism that looks on national and state governments as co-equal sovereign powers. Neither the state government nor the national government should interfere in the other's sphere.

government and the states. The debate over the division of powers in our federal system can be viewed as progressing through at least two general stages since the Civil War: dual federalism and cooperative federalism.

Dual Federalism

During the decades following the Civil War, the prevailing model was what political scientists have called **dual federalism**—a doctrine that emphasizes a distinction between federal and state spheres of government authority. Various images have been used to describe different configurations of federalism over time. Dual federalism is commonly depicted as a layer cake, because the state governments and the national government are viewed as separate entities, like separate layers in a cake. Under the doctrine of dual federalism, national and state governments are co-equal sovereign powers, and neither level of government should interfere in the other's sphere. The doctrine represented a revival of states' rights following the expansion of national authority during the Civil War. Many people viewed this change as a return to normal—that is, to the conditions that had existed before the war.

The Civil War crisis drastically reduced the influence of the United States Supreme Court, which had supported the institution of slavery in the years leading up to the war. Over time, however, the Court reestablished itself as the legitimate constitutional umpire. For the Court, dual federalism meant that the national government could intervene in state activities through grants and subsidies, but in most cases it was barred from regulating matters that the Court considered to be purely local. The Court generally limited the exercise of police power to the states. For example, in 1918, the Court ruled that a 1916 national law banning child labor was unconstitutional because it attempted to regulate a local problem.[8] In effect, the Court placed severe limits on the ability of Congress to legislate under the commerce clause of the Constitution.

▼ **The Works Progress Administration (WPA)** was part of the federal government's attempt to put people back to work during the Great Depression. In what way did the Great Depression increase the powers of the federal government?
(AP Photo/Works Progress Administration)

The New Deal and Cooperative Federalism

The doctrine of dual federalism receded into the background in the 1930s as the nation attempted to deal with the Great Depression. Franklin D. Roosevelt was inaugurated as president on March 4, 1933. In the previous year, nearly 1,500 banks had failed (and 4,000 more would fail in 1933). Thirty-two thousand businesses had closed down, and almost one-fourth of the labor force was unemployed. The public expected the national government to do something about the disastrous state of the economy. For the first three years of the Great Depression (1930–1932), the national government did very little. Roosevelt, however,

8. *Hammer v. Dagenhart,* 247 U.S. 251 (1918). This decision was overruled in *United States v. Darby,* 312 U.S. 100 (1940).

energetically intervened in the economy. Roosevelt's "New Deal" included large-scale emergency antipoverty programs and introduced major new laws regulating economic activity. Initially, the Supreme Court blocked many of Roosevelt's initiatives. Beginning in 1937, however, the Court, responding to political pressure, ceased to limit the federal government's actions. An expansive interpretation of the commerce clause became dominant.

Some political scientists have described national-state relations since 1937 as **cooperative federalism,** in which the states and the national government cooperate in solving complex common problems. Roosevelt's New Deal programs, for example, often involved joint action between the national government and the states. The pattern of national-state relationships during these years gave rise to a new metaphor for federalism—that of a marble cake. Unlike a layer cake, in a marble cake the two types of cake are intermingled, and any bite contains cake of both flavors.

▲ **President Franklin Delano Roosevelt** (1933–1945). Roosevelt's national approach to addressing the effects of the Great Depression was overwhelmingly popular, although many of his specific initiatives were controversial. How did the Great Depression change the political beliefs of many ordinary Americans? (Bettmann/Corbis)

The 1960s and 1970s were a time of even greater expansion of the national government's role in domestic policy. Today, few activities are beyond the reach of the regulatory arm of the national government.

The Politics of Federalism

In determining the allocation of powers between the state and national governments, conservatives traditionally have favored the states, and liberals have favored the federal government. In much of American history, after all, national authority has been an agent of change. The expansion of national authority during the Civil War freed the slaves, and beginning in the 1960s, the federal government was likewise responsible for extending civil rights such as the right to vote to African Americans.

For much of American history, conservative southern Democrats were the major advocates of states' rights. Under Republican presidents Richard Nixon (1969–1974) and Ronald Reagan (1981–1989), however, **devolution,** or the transfer of power from the national government to state governments, became a major theme for the Republican Party. In recent decades, competing theories of federalism no longer seem to divide the two parties in practice. While the Republicans continue to advocate devolution in theory, they do not follow it at all in reality.

Consider that the passage of welfare reform legislation in 1996, which involved transferring significant control over welfare programs to the states, took place under Democratic president Bill Clinton (1993–2001). In contrast, under Republican president George W. Bush (2001–2009), Congress enacted the No Child Left Behind Act of

Cooperative Federalism
A model of federalism in which the states and the national government cooperate in solving problems.

Devolution
The transfer of powers from a national or central government to a state or local government.

Categorical Grants
Federal grants to states or local governments for specific programs or projects.

2001. This act increased federal control over education, which had traditionally been under the purview of state governments. Indeed, the Bush administration expanded federal control in several areas—such as health, safety, and the environment—that traditionally had been the preserve of the states.

Methods of Implementing Cooperative Federalism

One means of implementing cooperative federalism is through grants. Even before the Constitution was adopted, the national government gave grants to the states in the form of land to finance education. The national government also provided land grants for canals, railroads, and roads. In the twentieth century, federal grants increased significantly, especially during the Great Depression and again in the 1960s, when the dollar amount of these grants quadrupled. These funds were used for improvements in education, pollution control, recreation, and highways. With this increase in grants, however, came a bewildering number of restrictions and regulations.

Categorical Grants. By 1985, **categorical grants** amounted to more than $100 billion a year. They were spread out across four hundred separate programs, but the largest five accounted for more than 50 percent of the revenues spent. These five programs were Medicaid (health care for the poor), highway construction, unemployment benefits, housing assistance, and welfare programs to assist mothers with dependent children and people with disabilities. For fiscal year 2009, the national government gave approximately $498.6 billion to the states. On the basis of President Obama's proposed 2010 budget, the 2010 figure was predicted to reach $516.4 billion. In both 2009 and 2010, Obama's stimulus plan, passed by Congress in February 2009, funneled large new federal resources to the states.

Federal grants to the states have increased significantly. One reason is that Congress has decided to offload some programs to the states and provide a major part of the funding for them. Also, Congress continues to use grants to persuade states and cities to operate programs devised by the federal government. Finally, states often are happy to apply for grants because they are relatively "free," requiring only that the state match a small portion of each grant.

▼ **These first-grade students** attend a school in a "failing" school district, which was penalized by the federal No Child Left Behind Act. How does that act represent recent developments in federalism? (AP Photo/Damian Dovarganes)

Feeling the Pressure—The Strings Attached to Federal Grants. No dollars sent to the states are completely free of "strings," however; all funds come with requirements that must be met by the states. Often, through the use of grants, the national government has been able to exercise substantial control over matters that traditionally have been under the purview of state governments. When the federal government gives federal funds for highway improvements, for example, it may condition the funds on the state's cooperation with a federal policy. This is exactly what the federal government did in the 1980s and 1990s to force the states to raise their minimum drinking age to twenty-one.

Block Grants. **Block grants** lessen the restrictions on federal grants given to state and local governments by grouping a number of categorical grants under one broad heading. Governors and mayors generally prefer block grants because such grants give state and local governments more flexibility in how the funds are spent. In contrast, Congress generally favors categorical grants because the expenditures can be targeted according to congressional priorities.

One major set of block grants provides aid to state welfare programs. The Personal Responsibility and Work Opportunity Reconciliation Act of 1996 ended the previously existing welfare program and substituted for it a block grant to each state. Each grant has an annual cap. According to some, this is one of the most successful block grant programs.

Federal Mandates. For years, the federal government has passed legislation requiring that states improve environmental conditions or the civil rights of various groups. Since the 1970s, the national government has enacted hundreds of **federal mandates** requiring the states to take some action in areas ranging from voter registration, to ocean-dumping restrictions, to the education of persons with disabilities. The Unfunded Mandates Reform Act of 1995 requires the Congressional Budget Office to identify mandates that cost state and local governments more than $50 million to implement. Nonetheless, the federal government routinely continues to pass mandates for state and local governments that cost more than that to put into place.

Block Grants
Federal grants that provide funds to state and local governments for general functional areas, such as criminal justice or mental-health programs.

Federal Mandate
A requirement in federal legislation that forces states and municipalities to comply with certain rules.

FEDERALISM AND TODAY'S SUPREME COURT

The United States Supreme Court, which normally has the final say on constitutional issues, plays a major role in determining where the line is drawn between federal and state powers. Consider the decisions rendered by Chief Justice John Marshall in the cases discussed earlier in this chapter. Since the 1930s, Marshall's broad interpretation of the commerce clause has made it possible for the national government to justify its regulation of almost any activity, even when the activity appears to be completely local in character. In the 1990s and early 2000s, however, the Court evidenced a willingness to impose some limits on the national government's authority under the commerce clause and other constitutional provisions. As a result, it is difficult to predict how today's Court might rule on a particular case involving federalism.

A Trend toward States' Rights?

Since the mid-1990s, the Supreme Court has tended to give greater weight to states' rights than it did during previous decades. In a widely publicized 1995 case, *United States v. Lopez,*[9] the Supreme Court held that Congress had exceeded its constitutional authority under the commerce clause when it passed the Gun-Free School Zones Act in 1990. The Court stated that the act, which banned the possession of guns within one thousand feet of any school, was unconstitutional because it attempted to regulate an area that had "nothing to do with commerce, or any sort of economic enterprise." This

---

9. 514 U.S. 549 (1995).

marked the first time in sixty years that the Supreme Court had placed a limit on the national government's authority under the commerce clause.

In 1999 and the early 2000s, the Court also issued decisions that bolstered the authority of state governments under the Eleventh Amendment to the Constitution. The cases involved employees and others who sought redress for state-government violations of federal laws regulating employment. The Court held that the Eleventh Amendment, in most circumstances, precludes lawsuits against state governments for violations of rights established by federal laws unless the states consent to be sued.[10] Additionally, the Court supported states' rights under the Tenth Amendment when it invalidated, in 1997, provisions of a federal law that required state employees to check the backgrounds of prospective handgun purchasers.[11]

The Court Sends Mixed Messages

Although the Court has tended to favor states' rights in some decisions, in other decisions it has backed the federal government's position. For example, in two cases decided in 2003 and 2004, the Court, in contrast to its earlier rulings involving the Eleventh Amendment, ruled that the amendment could *not* shield states from suits

---

10. See, for example, *Alden v. Maine,* 527 U.S. 706 (1999); *Kimel v. Florida Board of Regents,* 528 U.S. 62 (2000).
11. *Printz v. United States,* 521 U.S. 898 (1997).

▼ **California Governor Arnold Schwarzenegger** is shown signing a state executive order that established low-carbon fuel standards. California has often led the nation in environmental rules and legislation. Could new federal laws and regulations preempt California's? (AP Photo/Rich Pedroncelli)

by individuals complaining of discrimination based on gender and disability, respectively.[12] In 2005, the Court held that the federal government's power to seize and destroy illegal drugs superseded California's law legalizing the use of marijuana for medical treatment.[13] Yet less than a year later, the Court favored states' rights when it upheld Oregon's controversial "death with dignity" law, which allows patients with terminal illnesses to choose to end their lives early and thus avoid suffering.[14]

The Supreme Court also supported state claims in a 2007 case, *Massachusetts v. EPA*.[15] This case, which many have since hailed as the most significant decision on environmental law for decades, was brought against the Environmental Protection Agency (EPA) by Massachusetts and several other states, cities, and environmental groups. The groups claimed that the EPA, which administers the Clean Air Act, had the authority to—and should—regulate carbon dioxide and other greenhouse gases that promote global warming. The EPA maintained that it lacked the authority to do so, arguing that members of Congress, when passing the Clean Air Act, did not envision a massive greenhouse-gas control program. The Court, however, held that the EPA *did* have such regulatory authority and could choose *not* to regulate greenhouse gases only if it could provide a scientific basis for its refusal. The five-to-four decision was a strong rebuke to the Bush administration, which had refused to regulate carbon dioxide and other greenhouse gases under the Clean Air Act.

One year after this Supreme Court ruling, Massachusetts and the other states were back in federal court, suing the EPA for dragging its feet on issuing a carbon dioxide recommendation. The Obama administration's attitude toward greenhouse gases, however, was quite different from that of the Bush team. In March 2009, the EPA took a first step toward regulating greenhouse gases by proposing a national system for reporting emissions of carbon dioxide and other greenhouse gases.

12. *Nevada v. Hibbs,* 538 U.S. 721 (2003); *Tennessee v. Lane,* 541 U.S. 509 (2004).
13. *Gonzales v. Raich,* 545 U.S. 1 (2005).
14. *Gonzales v. Oregon,* 546 U.S. 243 (2006).
15. 549 U.S. 497 (2007).

making a difference

WRITING LETTERS TO THE EDITOR

Our federal system encourages debate over whether a particular issue should be a national, state, or local question. Many questions are, in fact, state or local ones, and it is easier for you to make a significant contribution to the discussion on these issues. Even in the largest states, there are many fewer people to persuade than in the nation as a whole. Attempts to influence your fellow citizens can therefore be more effective.

Why Should You Care? In this chapter, we have mentioned a variety of issues arising from our federal system that may concern you directly. Although the national government provides aid to educational programs, education is still primarily a state and local responsibility. The total amount of money spent on education is determined by state and local governments. Therefore, you can address this issue at the state or local level. Gambling laws are another state responsibility. Do you enjoy gambling—or do you believe that the effects of gambling make it a social disaster? State law—or state negotiations with Native American tribes—determines the availability of gambling.

What Can You Do? In our modern era, the number of ways in which you can communicate your opinion is vast. You can post a response on any of thousands of blogs. You could develop your own mini-video and post it on YouTube. Politicians use Facebook and MySpace to organize their supporters and often have thousands of online "friends." This can provide you with the opportunity to press your views upon someone who might be able to act on them.

If you want to effect policy change at the state or local level, however, the local newspaper, in both its paper and online formats, continues to be essential. Blogs, YouTube, and other new venues tend to be nationally and even internationally oriented. Most newspapers, however, are resolutely local and are the natural hub for discussions of local issues. Most papers allow blog responses on their sites, and you can make a point by contributing in that fashion. Nothing, however, will win you a wider audience than an old-fashioned letter to the editor. Use the following rules to compose an effective communication:

1. Use a computer, and double-space the lines. Use a spelling checker and grammar checker.
2. Include a lead topic sentence that is short, to the point, and powerful.
3. Keep your thoughts on target—choose only one topic to discuss. Make sure it is newsworthy and timely.
4. Make sure your communication is concise; never let it exceed a page and a half in length (double-spaced).
5. If you know that facts were misstated or left out in current news stories about your topic, supply the facts. The public wants to know.
6. Don't be afraid to express moral judgments. You can go a long way by appealing to readers' sense of justice.
7. Personalize the communication by bringing in your own experiences, if possible.
8. If you are writing a letter, sign it and give your address (including your e-mail address) and your telephone number. Blog entries and other communications may have their own rules on identifying yourself; follow them.
9. If writing a letter, send or e-mail it to the editorial office of the newspaper of your choice. Almost all publications now have e-mail addresses. Their Web sites usually give information on where you can send mail.

▲ **Facebook and MySpace** are now used by politicians to organize their supporters.
(Screen capture from www.facebook.com)

key terms

block grant 59	confederal system 45	dual federalism 56	federal mandate 59
categorical grant 58	cooperative	elastic clause, or necessary	police power 50
commerce clause 54	federalism 57	and proper clause 49	supremacy clause 50
concurrent powers 50	devolution 57	enumerated powers 48	unitary system 45

chapter summary

1 There are three basic models for ordering relations between central governments and local units: (a) a unitary system (in which ultimate power is held by the national government), (b) a confederal system (in which ultimate power is retained by the states), and (c) a federal system (in which governmental powers are divided between the national government and the states). A major reason for the creation of a federal system in the United States is that it reflected a compromise between the views of the Federalists (who wanted a strong national government) and those of the Anti-Federalists (who wanted the states to retain their sovereignty).

2 The Constitution expressly delegated certain powers to the national government in Article I, Section 8. In addition to these enumerated powers, the national government has implied and inherent powers. Implied powers are those that are reasonably necessary to carry out the powers expressly delegated to the national government. Inherent powers are those that the national government holds by virtue of being a sovereign state with the right to preserve itself.

3 The Tenth Amendment to the Constitution states that powers not delegated to the United States by the Constitution, nor prohibited by it to the states, are reserved to the states, or to the people. In certain areas, the Constitution provides for concurrent powers (such as the power to tax), which are powers that are held jointly by the national and state governments. The Constitution also denies certain powers to both the national government and the states.

4 The supremacy clause of the Constitution states that the Constitution, congressional laws, and national treaties are the supreme law of the land. States cannot use their reserved or concurrent powers to override national policies.

5 The three most important clauses in the Constitution on interstate relations require that (a) each state give full faith and credit to every other state's public acts, records, and judicial proceedings; (b) each state extend to every other state's citizens the privileges and immunities of its own citizens; and (c) each state agree to return persons who are fleeing from justice back to their home state when requested to do so.

6 Two landmark Supreme Court cases expanded the constitutional powers of the national government. Chief Justice John Marshall's expansive interpretation of the necessary and proper clause of the Constitution in *McCulloch v. Maryland* (1819), and his affirmation of the supremacy clause, enhanced the power of the national government. Marshall's broad interpretation of the commerce clause in *Gibbons v. Ogden* (1824) further extended the constitutional regulatory powers of the national government.

7 The controversy over slavery that led to the Civil War took the form of a fight over national government supremacy versus the rights of the separate states. Ultimately, the South's desire for increased states' rights and the subsequent Civil War had the effect of increasing the political power of the national government.

8 Since the Civil War, federalism has evolved through at least two general phases: dual federalism and cooperative federalism. In dual federalism, each of the states and the federal government remain supreme within their own spheres. The era since the Great Depression has sometimes been labeled one of cooperative federalism, in which states and the national government cooperate in solving complex common problems.

9 Categorical grants from the federal government to state governments help finance many projects, such as Medicaid, highway construction, unemployment benefits, and welfare programs. By attaching special conditions to the receipt of federal grants, the national government can effect policy changes

in areas typically governed by the states. Block grants, which group a number of categorical grants together, usually have fewer strings attached, thus giving state and local governments more flexibility in using funds. Federal mandates—laws requiring states to implement certain policies, such as policies to protect the environment—have generated controversy because of their cost.

10   The United States Supreme Court plays a significant role in determining the line between state and federal powers. Since the mid-1990s, there has been a trend on the part of the Court to support states' rights. Yet the Court has also issued several rulings in support of the federal government, making it difficult to predict how the Court will rule in a particular case involving issues of federalism.

QUESTIONS FOR
discussionandanalysis

1   While federal funding of primary and secondary education and federal influence on local schools have both grown considerably in recent years, K–12 education is still largely under the control of state and local governments. How might U.S. public schools be different if, like France, the United States had a unitary system of government?

2   The United States Supreme Court has interpreted the Fourteenth Amendment to the Constitution, adopted after the Civil War, to mean that most provisions of the Bill of Rights apply to state governments. If the First Amendment, with its guarantees of freedom of speech and religion, did not apply to the states, might some states seek to abridge these rights? If so, how might they do this?

3   Traditionally, conservatives have favored states' rights and liberals have favored national authority. Can you think of modern-day issues in which these long-standing preferences might be reversed, with conservatives favoring national authority and liberals favoring states' rights? Explain.

helpfulonlineResources

CONNECTING TO AMERICAN GOVERNMENT AND POLITICS

The Council of State Governments is a good source of information on state responses to federalism. Go to:
www.csg.org

The National Conference of State Legislatures is a similar source:
www.ncsl.org

Wikipedia, the online encyclopedia edited by volunteers, is a vast source of information on almost any topic, federalism included. For example, consider Wiki's in-depth analysis of the No Child Left Behind Act at:
en.wikipedia.org/wiki/No_Child_Left_Behind_Act

aspecialWebSite

FOR YOUR TEXT

Go to this book's special Web site at academic.cengage.com/polisci/Schmidt/ Brief6e. Choose "For Students." Then click on Chapter 3, where you will find an online quiz and other helpful study aids. If your professor is using CengageNOW: *American Government and Politics Today, Brief Edition,* log in and go to Chapter 3 for additional online study aids.

4

Civil Liberties

These residents of Alabama are reciting the Pledge of Allegiance at the state capitol. They came to support keeping a monument of the Ten Commandments on public display inside the state judiciary building. As you will see in this chapter, there is sometimes a tension between religion and government.
(AP Photo/Dave Martin)

"The land of the free." When asked what makes the United States distinctive, Americans will commonly say that it is a free country. Americans have long believed that limits on the power of government are an essential part of what makes this country free. Recall from Chapter 1 that restraints on the actions of government against individuals generally are referred to as *civil liberties*. The first ten amendments to the U.S. Constitution—the Bill of Rights—place such restraints on the national government. Of these amendments, none is more famous than the First Amendment, which guarantees freedom of religion, speech, and the press, along with many additional rights.

Most other democratic nations have laws to protect these and other civil liberties, but none of the laws is quite like the First Amendment. Take the issue of "hate speech." What if someone makes statements that stir up hatred toward a particular race or other group of people? In Germany, where memories of Nazi anti-Semitism remain alive, such speech is unquestionably illegal. In the United States, the issue is not so clear. The courts have often extended constitutional protection to this kind of speech.

In this chapter, we describe the civil liberties provided by the Bill of Rights and some of the controversies that surround them. In addition to First Amendment liberties, we look at the right to privacy and the rights of defendants in criminal prosecutions.

THE BILL OF RIGHTS

As you read through this chapter, bear in mind that the Bill of Rights, like the rest of the Constitution, is relatively brief. The framers set forth broad guidelines, leaving it up to the courts to interpret these constitutional mandates and apply them to specific situations. Thus, judicial interpretations shape the true nature of the civil liberties and rights that we possess. Because judicial interpretations change over time, so do our liberties and rights. As you will read in the following pages, there have been many conflicts over the meaning of such simple phrases as *freedom of religion* and *freedom of the press*. To understand what freedoms we actually have, we need to examine how the courts—and particularly the United States Supreme Court—have resolved some of those conflicts. One important conflict was over the issue of whether the Bill of Rights in the federal Constitution limited state governments as well as the national government.

Extending the Bill of Rights to State Governments

Many citizens do not realize that, as originally intended, the Bill of Rights limited the powers of only the national government. At the time the Bill of Rights was ratified, there was little concern over the potential of state governments to curb civil liberties. For one thing, state governments were closer to home and easier to control. For another, most state constitutions already had bills of rights. Rather, the fear was of the potential tyranny of the national government. The Bill of Rights begins with the words, "Congress shall make no law . . . ." It says nothing about *states* making laws that might abridge citizens' civil liberties. In 1833, in *Barron v. Baltimore,*[1] the United States Supreme Court held that the Bill of Rights did not apply to state laws.

We mentioned that most states had bills of rights. These bills of rights were similar to the national one, but there were some differences. Furthermore, each state's judicial system interpreted the rights differently. Citizens in different states, therefore, effectively had different sets of civil rights. It was not until after the Fourteenth Amendment was ratified in 1868 that civil liberties guaranteed by the national Constitution began to be applied to the states. Section 1 of that amendment provides, in part, as follows:

> No State shall . . . deprive any person of life, liberty, or property, without due process of law.

Incorporation of the Fourteenth Amendment

There was no question that the Fourteenth Amendment applied to state governments. For decades, however, the courts were reluctant to define the liberties spelled out in the national Bill of Rights as constituting "due process of law," which was protected under the Fourteenth Amendment. Not until 1925, in *Gitlow v. New York,*[2] did the United States Supreme Court hold that the Fourteenth Amendment protected the freedom of speech guaranteed by the First Amendment to the Constitution.

Only gradually, and never completely, did the Supreme Court accept the **incorporation theory**—the view that most of the protections of the Bill of Rights are incorporated into the Fourteenth Amendment's protection against state government actions. Table 4–1 shows the rights that the Court has incorporated into the

Incorporation Theory
The view that most of the protections of the Bill of Rights apply to state governments through the Fourteenth Amendment's due process clause.

---

1. 32 U.S. 243 (1833).
2. 268 U.S. 652 (1925).

TABLE 4–1: **Incorporating the Bill of Rights into the Fourteenth Amendment**

Year	Issue	Amendment Involved	Court Case
1925	Freedom of speech	I	*Gitlow v. New York*, 268 U.S. 652.
1931	Freedom of the press	I	*Near v. Minnesota*, 283 U.S. 697.
1932	Right to a lawyer in capital punishment cases	VI	*Powell v. Alabama*, 287 U.S. 45.
1937	Freedom of assembly and right to petition	I	*De Jonge v. Oregon*, 299 U.S. 353.
1940	Freedom of religion	I	*Cantwell v. Connecticut*, 310 U.S. 296.
1947	Separation of church and state	I	*Everson v. Board of Education*, 330 U.S. 1.
1948	Right to a public trial	VI	*In re Oliver*, 333 U.S. 257.
1949	No unreasonable searches and seizures	IV	*Wolf v. Colorado*, 338 U.S. 25.
1961	Exclusionary rule	IV	*Mapp v. Ohio*, 367 U.S. 643.
1962	No cruel and unusual punishment	VIII	*Robinson v. California*, 370 U.S. 660.
1963	Right to a lawyer in all criminal felony cases	VI	*Gideon v. Wainwright*, 372 U.S. 335.
1964	No compulsory self-incrimination	V	*Malloy v. Hogan*, 378 U.S. 1.
1965	Right to privacy	I, III, IV, V, IX	*Griswold v. Connecticut*, 381 U.S. 479.
1966	Right to an impartial jury	VI	*Parker v. Gladden*, 385 U.S. 363.
1967	Right to a speedy trial	VI	*Klopfer v. North Carolina*, 386 U.S. 213.
1969	No double jeopardy	V	*Benton v. Maryland*, 395 U.S. 784.

Fourteenth Amendment and the case in which it first applied each protection. As you can see in that table, in the fifteen years following the *Gitlow* decision, the Supreme Court incorporated into the Fourteenth Amendment the other basic freedoms (of the press, assembly, the right to petition, and religion) guaranteed by the First Amendment. These and the later Supreme Court decisions listed in Table 4–1 have bound the fifty states to accept for their citizens most of the rights and freedoms that are set forth in the U.S. Bill of Rights. We now look at some of those rights and freedoms, beginning with freedom of religion.

FREEDOM OF RELIGION

In the United States, freedom of religion consists of two principal precepts as they are presented in the First Amendment. The first precept guarantees the separation of church and state, and the second guarantees the free exercise of religion.

The Separation of Church and State—The Establishment Clause

The First Amendment to the Constitution states, in part, that "Congress shall make no law respecting an establishment of religion." In the words of Thomas Jefferson, the **establishment clause** was designed to create a "wall of separation of Church and State." Perhaps Jefferson was thinking about the religious intolerance that characterized the first colonies. Many of the American colonies were founded by groups pursuing religious freedom. Nonetheless, the early colonists were quite intolerant of religious

Establishment Clause
The part of the First Amendment prohibiting the establishment of a church officially supported by the national government.

beliefs that did not conform to those held by the majority of citizens within their own communities. Jefferson undoubtedly was also aware that state churches were the rule; among the original thirteen American colonies, nine had official churches.

As interpreted by the Supreme Court, the establishment clause in the First Amendment means at least the following:

> Neither a state nor the federal government can set up a church. Neither can pass laws which aid one religion, aid all religions, or prefer one religion over another. Neither can force nor influence a person to go to or to remain away from church against his will or force him to profess a belief or disbelief in any religion. No person can be punished for entertaining or professing religious beliefs or disbeliefs, for church attendance or nonattendance. No tax in any amount, large or small, can be levied to support any religious activities or institutions, whatever they may be called, or whatever form they may adopt to teach or practice religion. Neither a state nor the federal government can, openly or secretly, participate in the affairs of any religious organizations or groups and vice versa.[3]

The establishment clause covers all conflicts about such matters as the legality of giving state and local government aid to religious organizations and schools, allowing or requiring school prayers, teaching evolution versus creationist theories that reject evolution, placing religious displays in schools or public places, and discriminating against religious groups in publicly operated institutions.

Aid to Church-Related Schools. In the United States, almost 11 percent of school-aged children attend private schools, of which about 80 percent have religious affiliations. The United States Supreme Court has tried to draw a fine line between permissible public aid to students in church-related schools and impermissible public aid to religion. These issues have arisen most often at the elementary and secondary levels.

In 1971, in *Lemon v. Kurtzman,*[4] the Court ruled that direct state aid could not be used to subsidize religious instruction. The Court in the *Lemon* case gave its most general pronouncement on the constitutionality of government aid to religious schools, stating (1) that the aid had to be secular (nonreligious) in aim, (2) that it could not have the primary effect of advancing or inhibiting religion, and (3) that the government must avoid "an excessive government entanglement with religion." All laws that raise issues under the establishment clause are now subject to the three-part *Lemon* test. How the test is applied, however, has varied over the years.

In a number of cases, the Supreme Court has held that state programs helping church-related schools are unconstitutional. The Court also has denied state reimbursements to religious schools for field trips and for developing achievement tests. In a series of other cases, however, the Supreme Court has allowed states to use tax funds for lunches, textbooks, diagnostic services for speech and hearing problems, standardized tests, and transportation for students attending church-operated elementary and secondary schools, as well as for special educational services for disadvantaged students attending religious schools.

School Vouchers. An ongoing controversy concerning the establishment clause has to do with school vouchers. Many people believe that the public schools are failing to

---

3. *Everson v. Board of Education,* 330 U.S. 1 (1947).
4. 403 U.S. 602 (1971).

educate our children adequately. One proposed solution to the problem has been for state and local governments to issue school vouchers, representing state-issued funds that can be used to purchase education at any school, public or private. At issue is whether voucher programs violate the establishment clause.

In 2002, the United States Supreme Court held that a voucher program in Cleveland, Ohio, did not violate the establishment clause. The Court concluded that because the vouchers could be used for public as well as private schools, the program did not unconstitutionally entangle church and state.[5] The Court's 2002 decision was encouraging to those who support school choice, whether it takes the form of school vouchers or tuition tax credits to offset educational expenses in private schools.

Today, ten states allow public funds to be used for private education. Four states have small-scale voucher programs for a limited number of students, and seven states offer tuition tax-subsidy programs. At the national level, President George W. Bush strongly supported the use of public funds for private education, but with little success. Indeed, voucher programs have been killed in several jurisdictions. In 2005, the Florida Supreme Court ruled that vouchers violated the Florida state constitution. In 2007, Utah voters rejected a voucher plan that was created earlier that year by the state legislature. In March 2009, the U.S. Congress voted to halt a voucher program in the District of Columbia. President Barack Obama has opposed voucher systems, and new ones are unlikely to be established in the immediate future.

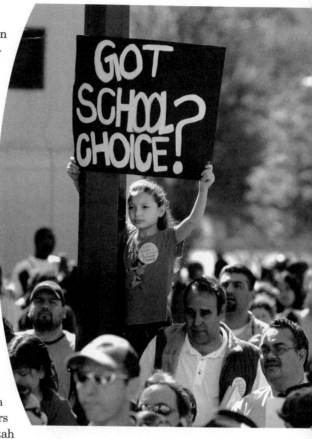

▲ **These advocates of school vouchers** are attending a rally in Austin, Texas. Some of those who oppose school vouchers argue that government funds might be used to support religious education. What are the arguments for and against school voucher programs? (AP Photo/L. M. Otero)

The Issue of School Prayer—*Engel v. Vitale*. Do the states have the right to promote religion in general, without making any attempt to establish a particular religion? That is the question raised by school prayer and was the precise issue presented in 1962 in *Engel v. Vitale*,[6] the so-called Regents' Prayer case in New York. The State Board of Regents of New York had suggested that a prayer be spoken aloud in the public schools at the beginning of each day. The recommended prayer was as follows:

> Almighty God, we acknowledge our dependence upon Thee, And we beg Thy blessings upon us, our parents, our teachers, and our Country.

Such a prayer was implemented in many New York public schools.

The parents of a number of students challenged the action of the regents, maintaining that it violated the establishment clause of the First Amendment. At trial,

---

5. *Zelman v. Simmons-Harris,* 536 U.S. 639 (2002).
6. 370 U.S. 421 (1962).

▲ **These high school students pray** around the school flagpole before classes in Lufkin, Texas. Do their actions violate the separation of church and state? (AP Photo/Joel Andrews/*The Lufkin Daily News*)

the parents lost. The Supreme Court, however, ruled that the regents' action was unconstitutional because "the constitutional prohibition against laws respecting an establishment of a religion must mean at least that in this country it is no part of the business of government to compose official prayers for any group of the American people to recite as part of a religious program carried on by any government."

The Debate over School Prayer Continued. Although the Supreme Court has ruled repeatedly against officially sponsored prayer and Bible-reading sessions in public schools, other means for bringing some form of religious expression into public education have been attempted. In *Wallace v. Jaffree*[7] (1985), the Supreme Court struck down as unconstitutional an Alabama law authorizing one minute of silence for prayer or meditation in all public schools. The Court concluded that the law violated the establishment clause because it was "an endorsement of religion lacking any clearly secular purpose." Since then, the lower courts have interpreted the Supreme Court's decision to mean that states can require a moment of silence in the schools as long as they make it clear that the purpose of the law is secular, not religious.

Forbidding the Teaching of Evolution. For many decades, certain religious groups have opposed the teaching of evolution in the schools. To these groups, evolutionary theory directly counters their religious belief that human beings did not evolve but were created fully formed, as described in the biblical story of the creation. State and local attempts to forbid the teaching of evolution, however, have not passed constitutional muster in the eyes of the United States Supreme Court. For example, in 1968 the Supreme Court held, in *Epperson v. Arkansas,*[8] that an Arkansas law prohibiting the teaching of evolution violated the establishment clause, because it imposed religious beliefs on students. The Louisiana legislature passed a law requiring the

7. 472 U.S. 38 (1985).
8. 393 U.S. 97 (1968).

teaching of the biblical story of the creation alongside the teaching of evolution. In 1987, in *Edwards v. Aguillard,*[9] the Supreme Court declared that this law was unconstitutional, in part because it had as its primary purpose the promotion of a particular religious belief.

Nonetheless, state and local groups around the country continue their efforts against the teaching of evolution. Some school districts have considered teaching "intelligent design" as an alternative explanation of the origin of life. Proponents of intelligent design contend that evolutionary theory has "gaps" that can be explained only by the existence of an intelligent creative force (God).

The federal courts took up the issue of intelligent design in 2005. The previous year, the Dover Area Board of Education in Pennsylvania had voted to require the presentation of intelligent design as an explanation of the origin of life. In December 2005, a U.S. district court ruled that the Dover mandate was unconstitutional. Judge John E. Jones III issued a 139-page decision that criticized the intelligent design theory in depth.[10] All of the school board members who endorsed intelligent design were voted out of office, and the new school board declined to appeal the decision.

Some school officials who oppose the theory of evolution have avoided lawsuits by employing ambiguous language. For example, until 2009, the statewide Texas Board of Education required public school students to discuss the "strengths and weaknesses" of evolution. Biology teachers who believed there were no "weaknesses" largely ignored this requirement. As of 2009, the Board encourages students to examine "all sides" of scientific explanations, an even more ambiguous standard.

Religious Displays on Public Property. On a regular basis, the courts are asked to determine whether religious symbols placed on public property violate the establishment clause. A frequent source of controversy is the placement of a crèche, or nativity scene, on public property during the Christmas season. The Supreme Court has allowed some displays but prohibited others. In general, a nativity scene is acceptable if it is part of a broader display that contains secular objects such as lights, Christmas trees, Santa Claus figures, and reindeer. A stand-alone crèche is not acceptable.[11] A related issue is whether the Ten Commandments may be displayed on public property. As with nativity displays, acceptability turns on whether the Ten Commandments are part of a larger secular display or whether the context is overtly religious.

In a new twist on the Ten Commandments controversy, the Supreme Court ruled in 2009 that the city of Pleasant Grove, Utah, was not required to accept a monument from Summum, a small religious group, and place it in a city park. A variety of donated monuments were already installed in the park, including one that displayed the Ten Commandments. Summum based its argument on freedom-of-speech grounds, not the establishment clause. In response, the Court ruled that by accepting monuments, the city was exercising its own freedom of speech, rather than regulating the speech of others. When New York accepted the Statue of Liberty from France, it was under no obligation also to accept a "statue of autocracy" from somewhere else.[12]

---

9. 482 U.S. 578 (1987).
10. *Kitzmiller v. Dover Area School District,* 400 F.Supp.2d 707 (M.D.Pa. 2005).
11. *Lynch v. Donnelly,* 465 U.S. 668 (1984).
12. *Pleasant Grove City v. Summum,* __ S.Ct. __ (2009).

The Free Exercise Clause

The First Amendment constrains Congress from prohibiting the free exercise of religion. Does this **free exercise clause** mean that no type of religious practice can be prohibited or restricted by government? Certainly, a person can hold any religious belief that he or she wants, or a person can have no religious belief. When, however, religious *practices* work against public policy and the public welfare, the government can act. For example, regardless of a child's or parent's religious beliefs, the government can require certain types of vaccinations. Additionally, public school students can be required to study from textbooks chosen by school authorities.

Churches and other religious organizations are tax-exempt bodies, and as a result they are not allowed to endorse candidates for office or make contributions to candidates' campaigns. Churches are allowed to take positions on ballot proposals, however, and may even contribute to referendum campaigns. For example, both the Church of Latter-Day Saints (the Mormons) and the Catholic Church were able to fund the campaign for California's 2008 Proposition 8, a measure to ban same-sex marriage.

The Internal Revenue Service (IRS) rarely bothers to threaten the tax-exempt status of a church based on simple candidate endorsements, however. For example, in September 2008, thirty-three ministers collectively endorsed Republican presidential candidate John McCain in a deliberate challenge to the 1954 law that prohibits such endorsements. So far, the IRS has not responded. In 1995, however, the IRS did revoke the tax-exempt status of Branch Ministries, Inc., and in 2000 a federal district court supported the revocation.[13] Branch Ministries went far beyond simply endorsing a candidate from the pulpit. The church had used tax-exempt income to buy newspaper advertisements denouncing Democratic presidential candidate Bill Clinton.

A fascinating recent issue involving the accommodation of religion is to what extent public colleges and universities ought to accommodate the religious practices of Muslim students. We look at this controversial topic in this chapter's feature *At Issue: Should Muslims' Religious Needs Be Accommodated on Campus?*

FREEDOM OF EXPRESSION

Perhaps the most frequently invoked freedom that Americans have is the right to free speech and a free press. Each of us has the right to have our say, and all of us have the right to hear what others say. For the most part, Americans can criticize public officials and their actions without fear of reprisal by any branch of our government.

No Prior Restraint

Restraining an activity before that activity has actually occurred is called **prior restraint.** When expression is involved, prior restraint means censorship, as opposed to subsequent punishment. Prior restraint of expression would require, for example, that a permit be obtained before a speech could be made, a newspaper published, or a movie or TV show exhibited. Most, if not all, Supreme Court justices have been very critical of any governmental action that imposes prior restraint on expression.

One of the most famous cases concerning prior restraint was *New York Times v. United States*[14] (1971), the so-called Pentagon Papers case. The *Times* and the

---

13. *Branch Ministries v. Rossetti,* 211 F.3d 137 (D.C.Cir. 2000).
14. 403 U.S. 713 (1971).

at**Issue**: Should Muslims' Religious Needs Be Accommodated on Campus?

The United States is known as a land of religious tolerance. Americans practice many minority religions in addition to the major faiths. So long as religious practices do not interfere with the rights of others, they are legally acceptable. The courts have drawn the line, though, when religious practices involve illegal activities, such as leaving beheaded animals on the side of the road or using prohibited drugs.

Recently, college campuses have been asked to accommodate the religious needs of Muslim students. Observant Muslims seek to wash their feet before they pray. Should universities build footbaths that Muslim students can then use? The Dearborn campus of the University of Michigan, where 16 percent of the students are Muslim, decided to do just that, in part to keep students from washing their feet in the restroom sinks. The university spent more than $25,000 to install footwashing stations in a number of restrooms.

And what about separate prayer rooms for Muslim students in public schools? There is also the issue of whether food in cafeterias conforms to Muslims' religious requirements. Finally, what about religious holidays? School calendars already accommodate Christians with vacations around Easter and Christmas. Why not also Muslim holidays?

Campus Officials Should Be Tolerant

While providing footbaths for Muslims on college campuses may seem strange, that is only because most students are not used to having Muslims around them. Just because America is basically a nation whose major religions are based on Judeo-Christian doctrines does not mean that we can't accommodate a growing alternative religion. One of the fastest-growing religions in the United States is indeed Islam. We should consider most Muslim student requests for accommodation on campuses as simply part of those students' right to practice their religion.

Campus authorities are going to have to face the issue of accommodating Muslim religious practices sooner or later anyway. In addition to the University of Michigan, dozens of other universities have installed footbaths in new buildings. The footbaths can be used by anyone, including sweaty athletes and janitors who fill buckets. They are not for the exclusive use of Muslim students. Such footbaths have no symbolic value; they are not designed in a religious manner.

What about Separation of Church and State?

Those who oppose religious accommodation for Muslims argue that, at least on public college campuses, the funding of such actions necessarily violates the constitutionally mandated separation of church and state. Footbaths are essentially structures for a particular religious tradition. The Constitution prohibits the government from endorsing any particular religion. On college campuses, the footbaths are being financed out of building-maintenance fees paid by students. Students are not given any voice in the decision, and that is wrong. Many colleges no longer sponsor Christmas music on campus, so why would those universities behave any differently when it comes to accommodating Muslims? The Constitution should be our guide.

FOR CRITICAL ANALYSIS

To what extent should college campuses accommodate the religious needs of students? Does installing footbaths that especially benefit Muslims (although the footbaths can be used by anyone) go too far? Why or why not?

These members of the Johns Hopkins University Student Muslim Association gather for prayer during one of their weekly meetings. To what extent should universities accommodate the needs of devout Muslim students? When does such accommodation violate the separation of church and state? (AP Photo/John Gillis)

Washington Post were about to publish the Pentagon Papers, an elaborate secret history of the U.S. government's involvement in the Vietnam War (1964–1975). The secret documents had been obtained illegally by a disillusioned former Pentagon official. The government wanted a court order to bar publication of the documents, arguing that national security was threatened and that the documents had been stolen. The newspapers argued that the public had a right to know the information contained in the papers and that the press had the right to inform the public. The Supreme Court ruled six to three in favor of the newspapers' right to publish the information. This case affirmed the no-prior-restraint doctrine.

The Protection of Symbolic Speech

Not all expression is in words or in writing. Articles of clothing, gestures, movements, and other forms of nonverbal expressive conduct are considered **symbolic speech.** Such speech is given substantial protection today by our courts. For example, in 1989, in *Texas v. Johnson*,[15] the Supreme Court ruled that state laws that prohibited the burning of the American flag as part of a peaceful protest also violated the freedom of expression protected by the First Amendment. Congress responded by passing the Flag Protection Act of 1989, which was ruled unconstitutional by the Supreme Court in June 1990.[16] Congress and President George H. W. Bush immediately pledged to work for a constitutional amendment to "protect our flag"—an effort that has yet to be successful.

▲ **These antiwar protesters** carry banners on Market Street in San Francisco. Is this symbolic speech? (Peter Maiden/Sygma/Corbis)

In 2003, however, the Supreme Court held that a Virginia statute prohibiting the burning of a cross with "an intent to intimidate" did not violate the First Amendment. The Court concluded that a burning cross is an instrument of racial terror so threatening that it overshadows free speech concerns.[17]

The Protection of Commercial Speech

Commercial speech usually is defined as advertising statements. Can advertisers use their First Amendment rights to prevent restrictions on the content of commercial advertising? Until the 1970s, the Supreme Court held that such speech was not protected at all by the First Amendment. By the mid-1970s, however, more and more commercial speech had been brought under First Amendment protection. According to Justice Harry A. Blackmun, "Advertising, however tasteless and excessive it sometimes may seem, is nonetheless dissemination of information as to who is producing and

15. 488 U.S. 884 (1989).
16. *United States v. Eichman*, 496 U.S. 310 (1990).
17. *Virginia v. Black*, 538 U.S. 343 (2003).

selling what product for what reason and at what price."[18] Nevertheless, the Supreme Court will consider a restriction on commercial speech valid as long as it (1) seeks to implement a substantial government interest, (2) directly advances that interest, and (3) goes no further than necessary to accomplish its objective. In particular, a business engaging in commercial speech can be subject to liability for factual inaccuracies in ways that do not apply to noncommercial speech.

Permitted Restrictions on Expression

At various times, restrictions on expression have been permitted. A description of several such restrictions follows.

Clear and Present Danger. When a person's remarks present a clear and present danger to the peace or public order, they can be curtailed constitutionally. Justice Oliver Wendell Holmes used this reasoning in 1919 when examining the case of a socialist who had been convicted for violating the Espionage Act by distributing a leaflet that opposed the military draft. Holmes stated:

> The question in every case is whether the words are used in such circumstances and are of such a nature as to create a *clear and present danger* that they will bring about the substantive evils that Congress has a right to prevent. It is a question of proximity and degree. [Emphasis added.][19]

The conviction was upheld. According to the **clear and present danger test,** then, expression may be restricted if evidence exists that such expression would cause a dangerous condition, actual or imminent, that Congress has the power to prevent.

Modifications to the Clear and Present Danger Rule. Over the course of the twentieth century, the United States Supreme Court modified the clear and present danger rule, limiting the constitutional protection of free speech in 1925 and 1951, and then broadening it substantially in 1969. In *Gitlow v. New York,*[20] the Court reintroduced an earlier *bad tendency rule,* which placed greater restrictions on speech than Justice Holmes's formulation. According to this rule, speech and other First Amendment freedoms may be curtailed if there is a possibility that such expression might lead to some "evil." In the *Gitlow* case, a member of a left-wing group was convicted of violating New York State's criminal anarchy statute when he published and distributed a pamphlet urging the violent overthrow of the U.S. government. In its majority opinion, the Supreme Court held that the First Amendment afforded protection against state incursions on freedom of expression—the first time that the First Amendment was ever invoked against a state government (see the discussion of incorporation on page 66). Nevertheless, Gitlow could be punished legally in this particular instance because his expression would tend to bring about evils that the state had a right to prevent.

Some claim that the United States did not achieve true freedom of political speech until 1969. In that year, in *Brandenburg v. Ohio,*[21] the Supreme Court overturned the conviction of a Ku Klux Klan leader for violating a state statute. The statute prohibited

Clear and Present Danger Test
The test proposed by Justice Oliver Wendell Holmes for determining when government may restrict free speech. Restrictions are permissible only when speech presents a "clear and present danger" to the public order.

---

18. *Virginia State Board of Pharmacy v. Virginia Citizens Consumer Council, Inc.,* 425 U.S. 748 (1976).
19. *Schenck v. United States,* 249 U.S. 47 (1919).
20. 268 U.S. 652 (1925).
21. 395 U.S. 444 (1969).

Obscenity
Sexually offensive
material. Obscenity can
be illegal if it is found to
violate a four-part test
established by the United
States Supreme Court.

anyone from advocating "the duty, necessity, or propriety of sabotage, violence, or unlawful methods of terrorism as a means of accomplishing industrial or political reform." The Court held that the guarantee of free speech does not permit a state "to forbid or proscribe advocacy of the use of force or of law violation except where such advocacy is directed to inciting or producing imminent lawless actions and is likely to incite or produce such action." The *incitement test* enunciated by the Court in this case is a difficult one for prosecutors to meet. As a result, the Court's decision significantly broadened the protection given to advocacy speech.

Unprotected Speech: Obscenity

A large number of state and federal statutes make it a crime to disseminate obscene materials. Generally, the courts have not been willing to extend constitutional protections of free speech to what they consider obscene materials. But what is obscenity? Justice Potter Stewart once stated that even though he could not define *obscenity,* "I know it when I see it."

Definitional Problems. The Supreme Court has grappled from time to time with the difficulty of specifying an operationally effective definition of **obscenity.** In 1973, in *Miller v. California,*[22] Chief Justice Warren Burger created a formal list of requirements that must be met for material to be legally obscene. Material is obscene if (1) the average person finds that it violates contemporary community standards; (2) the work taken as a whole appeals to a prurient interest in sex; (3) the work shows patently offensive sexual conduct; and (4) the work lacks serious redeeming literary, artistic, political, or scientific merit. The problem, of course, is that one person's prurient interest is another person's medical interest or artistic pleasure. The Court went on to state that the definition of *prurient interest* would be determined by the community's standards. The Court avoided presenting a definition of *obscenity,* leaving this determination to local and state authorities. Consequently, the *Miller* case has been applied in a widely inconsistent manner.

Protecting Children. The Supreme Court has upheld state laws making it illegal to sell materials showing sexual performance by minors. In 1990, in *Osborne v. Ohio,*[23] the Court ruled that states can outlaw the possession of child pornography in the home. The Court reasoned that the ban on private possession is justified because owning the material perpetuates commercial demand for it and for the exploitation of the children involved. At the federal level, the Child Protection Act of 1984 made it a crime to receive knowingly through the mail sexually explicit depictions of children. In 2008, the Court upheld the legality of a 2003 federal law that made it a crime to offer child pornography, even if the pornography in question does not actually exist.[24] The Court, however, has invalidated a 1996 law banning virtual pornography, which involves only digitally rendered images and no actual children. The Court concluded that the law was overbroad and thus unconstitutional.[25]

---

22. 413 U.S. 5 (1973).
23. 495 U.S. 103 (1990).
24. *United States v. Williams,* 128 S.Ct. 1830 (2008).
25. *Ashcroft v. Free Speech Coalition,* 535 U.S. 234 (2002).

Pornography on the Internet. A significant problem facing Americans and their lawmakers today is how to prevent young children from exposure to pornography that is disseminated by way of the Internet. In 1996, Congress first attempted to protect minors from pornographic materials on the Internet by passing the Communications Decency Act (CDA). The act made it a crime to make available to minors online any "obscene or indecent" message that "depicts or describes, in terms patently offensive as measured by contemporary community standards, sexual or excretory activities or organs." The act was immediately challenged in court as an unconstitutional infringement on free speech. The Supreme Court held that the act imposed unconstitutional restraints on free speech and was therefore invalid.[26] In the eyes of the Court, the terms *indecent* and *patently offensive* covered large amounts of nonpornographic material with serious educational or other value.

A second attempt to protect children from online obscenity, the Child Online Protection Act (COPA) of 1998, met with a similar fate. Although the COPA was more narrowly tailored than its predecessor, the CDA, it still used "contemporary community standards" to define which material was obscene and harmful to minors. Ultimately, in 2004 the Supreme Court concluded that it was likely that the COPA did violate the right to free speech, and so the Court prevented enforcement of the act.[27]

In 2000, Congress enacted the Children's Internet Protection Act (CIPA), which requires public schools and libraries to install filtering software to prevent children from viewing Web sites with "adult" content. The CIPA was also challenged on constitutional grounds, but in 2003 the Supreme Court held that the act did not violate the First Amendment. The Court concluded that because libraries can disable the filters for any patrons who ask, the system does not burden free speech to an unconstitutional extent.[28]

Unprotected Speech: Slander

Can you say anything you want about someone else? Not really. Individuals are protected from **defamation of character,** which is defined as wrongfully hurting a person's good reputation. The law imposes a general duty on all persons to refrain from making false, defamatory statements about others. Breaching this duty orally is the wrongdoing called **slander.** Breaching it in writing is the wrongdoing called *libel,* which we discuss later. The government itself does not bring charges of slander or libel. Rather, the defamed person may bring a civil (as opposed to criminal) suit for damages.

Legally, slander is the public uttering of a false statement that harms the good reputation of another. "Public uttering" means that the defamatory statement is made to, or within the hearing of, a person other than the defamed party. If one person calls another dishonest, manipulative, and incompetent to his or her face when no one else is around, that does not constitute slander. The message is not communicated to a third party. If, however, a third party accidentally overhears defamatory statements, the courts have generally held that this constitutes a public uttering and therefore slander, which is prohibited.

Defamation of Character
Wrongfully hurting a person's good reputation.

Slander
The public uttering of a false statement that harms the good reputation of another. The statement must be made to, or within the hearing of, someone other than the defamed party.

---

26. *Reno v. American Civil Liberties Union,* 521 U.S. 844 (1997).
27. *American Civil Liberties Union v. Ashcroft,* 542 U.S. 646 (2004).
28. *United States v. American Library Association,* 539 U.S. 194 (2003).

Student Speech

In recent years, high school and university students at public institutions have faced a variety of free speech challenges. Court rulings on these issues have varied by the level of school involved. Elementary schools, in particular, have great latitude in determining what kinds of speech are appropriate for their students. High school students have greater free speech rights, and college students have the most speech rights of all.

Rights of Public School Students. High schools can impose restrictions on speech that would not be allowed in a college setting or in the general society. For example, high school officials may censor publications such as newspapers and yearbooks produced by the school's students. Courts have argued that a school newspaper is an extension of the school's educational mission, and thus subject to control by the school administration. One of the most striking rulings to illustrate the power of school officials was handed down by the United States Supreme Court in 2007. An Alaska high school student had displayed a banner reading "Bong Hits 4 Jesus" on private property across from the school as students on the school grounds watched the Winter Olympics torch relay. The school principal crossed the street, seized the banner, and suspended the student from school. The Supreme Court later held that the school had an "important—indeed, perhaps compelling—interest" in combating drug use that allowed it to suppress the banner.[29] The Court's decision was widely criticized.

College Student Activity Fees. Should a college student have to subsidize, through student activity fees, organizations that promote causes that the student finds objectionable? In 2000, this question came before the United States Supreme Court in a case brought by several University of Wisconsin students. The students argued that their mandatory student activity fees—which helped to fund liberal causes with which they disagreed, including gay rights—violated their First Amendment rights of free speech, free association, and free exercise of religion. They contended that they should have the right to choose whether to fund organizations that promoted political and ideological views that were offensive to their personal beliefs.

To the surprise of many, the Supreme Court rejected the students' claim and ruled in favor of the university. The Court stated that "the university may determine that its mission is well served if students have the means to engage in dynamic discussions of philosophical, religious, scientific, social, and political subjects in their extracurricular life. If the university reaches this conclusion, it is entitled to impose a mandatory fee to sustain an open dialogue to these ends."[30]

▼ **Makenzie Hatfield,** a high school student in Charleston, West Virginia, holds up two books by well-known author Pat Conroy. *The Prince of Tides* and *Beach Music* were banned from Nitro High School English classes after the parents of two students complained about depictions of violence, suicide, and sexual assault. Should high school students have the same rights as college students? As adults? (AP Photo/Jeff Gentner)

---

29. *Morse v. Frederick,* 551 U.S. 393 (2007).
30. *Board of Regents of the University of Wisconsin System v. Southworth,* 529 U.S. 217 (2000).

Campus Speech and Behavior Codes. Another free speech issue is the legitimacy of campus speech and behavior codes. Some state universities have established codes that challenge the boundaries of the protection of free speech provided by the First Amendment. These codes are designed to prohibit so-called hate speech—abusive speech attacking persons on the basis of their ethnicity, race, or other criteria. For example, a University of Michigan code banned "any behavior, verbal or physical, that stigmatizes or victimizes an individual on the basis of race, ethnicity, religion, sex, sexual orientation, creed, national origin, ancestry, age, marital status, handicap" or Vietnam-veteran status. A federal court found that the code violated students' First Amendment rights.[31] Although the courts generally have held, as in the *University of Michigan* case, that campus speech codes are unconstitutional restrictions on the right to free speech, such codes continue to exist.

FREEDOM OF THE PRESS

Freedom of the press can be regarded as a special instance of freedom of speech. Of course, at the time of the framing of the Constitution, the press meant only newspapers, magazines, and books. As technology has modified the ways in which we disseminate information, the laws touching on freedom of the press have been modified. What can and cannot be printed still occupies an important place in constitutional law, however.

Defamation in Writing

Libel is defamation in writing (or in pictures, signs, films, or any other communication that has the potentially harmful qualities of written or printed words). As with slander, libel occurs only if the defamatory statements are observed by a third party. If Jane Smith writes a private letter to John Jones wrongfully accusing him of embezzling funds, that does not constitute libel. It is interesting that the courts have generally held that dictating a letter to a secretary constitutes communication of the letter's contents to a third party. Therefore, if defamation has occurred, the wrongdoer can be sued.

The case of *New York Times Co. v. Sullivan*[32] (1964) explored an important question regarding libelous statements made about public officials. The Supreme Court held that only when a statement against a public official is made with **actual malice**—that is, with either knowledge of its falsity or a reckless disregard for the truth—can damages be obtained.

The standard set by the Court in the *New York Times* case has since been applied to **public figures** generally. Public figures include not only public officials but also public employees who exercise substantial governmental power and any persons, such as movie stars, who are generally in the public limelight. Statements made about public figures, especially when they are made through a public medium, usually are related to matters of general public interest; they are made about people who substantially affect all of us. Furthermore, public figures generally have some access to a public medium for answering disparaging falsehoods about themselves, whereas private individuals do not. For these reasons, public figures have a greater burden of proof

Libel
A written defamation of a person's character, reputation, business, or property rights.

Actual Malice
Either knowledge of a defamatory statement's falsity or a reckless disregard for the truth.

Public Figures
Public officials, movie stars, and other persons known to the public because of their positions or activities.

---

31. *Doe v. University of Michigan,* 721 F.Supp. 852 (1989).
32. 376 U.S. 254 (1964).

Gag Order
An order issued by a judge restricting the publication of news about a trial or a pretrial hearing to protect the accused's right to a fair trial.

(they must prove that the statements were made with actual malice) in defamation cases than do private individuals.

A Free Press versus a Fair Trial: Gag Orders

Another major issue relating to freedom of the press concerns media coverage of criminal trials. The Sixth Amendment to the Constitution guarantees the right of criminal suspects to a fair trial. In other words, the accused have rights. The First Amendment guarantees freedom of the press. What if the two rights appear to be in conflict? Which one prevails?

Jurors certainly may be influenced by reading news stories about the trial in which they are participating. In the 1970s, judges increasingly issued **gag orders**—orders that restricted the publication of news about a trial in progress or even a pretrial hearing to protect the accused's right to a fair trial. In a landmark 1976 case, *Nebraska Press Association v. Stuart*,[33] the Supreme Court unanimously ruled that a Nebraska judge's gag order had violated the First Amendment's guarantee of freedom of the press. Despite the *Nebraska Press Association* ruling, the Court has upheld gag orders when it believed that publicity was likely to harm a defendant's right to a fair trial.

▼ **Rush Limbaugh** is perhaps one of the most listened to talk radio hosts in America. At times, he has been considered the spokesperson for American conservatives. Should the Federal Communications Commission regulate what he says? (AP Photo/Jeff Chiu)

Films, Radio, and TV

As we have noted, in only a few cases has the Supreme Court upheld prior restraint of published materials. The Court's reluctance to accept prior restraint is less evident with respect to motion pictures. In the first half of the twentieth century, films were routinely submitted to local censorship boards. In 1968, the Supreme Court ruled that a film can be banned only under a law that provides for a prompt hearing at which the film is shown to be obscene. Today, few local censorship boards exist. Instead, the film industry regulates itself primarily through the industry's rating system.

Radio and television broadcasting has the least First Amendment protection. In 1934, the national government established the Federal Communications Commission (FCC) to regulate electromagnetic wave frequencies. This was done to keep stations from interfering with each other's broadcasts—the number of airwave frequencies is limited. No one has a right to use the airwaves without a license granted by the FCC. The FCC grants licenses for limited periods, and, because broadcasts take place under a federal license, it imposes a variety of regulations on broadcasters. For example, the FCC can impose sanctions on radio or TV stations that broadcast "filthy words," even if the words are not legally obscene.

THE RIGHT TO PRIVACY

No explicit reference is made anywhere in the Constitution to a person's right to privacy. Until relatively recently, the courts did not take a very positive approach toward this right. In 1965, however, in *Griswold v. Connecticut*,[34] the Supreme Court overthrew a

33. 427 U.S. 539 (1976).
34. 381 U.S. 479 (1965).

Connecticut law that effectively prohibited the use of contraceptives, holding that the law violated the right to privacy. Justice William O. Douglas formulated a unique way of reading this right into the Bill of Rights. He claimed that the First, Third, Fourth, Fifth, and Ninth Amendments created "penumbras [shadows], formed by emanations (that which flows from) from those guarantees that help give them life and substance," and he went on to describe zones of privacy that are guaranteed by these rights. When we read the Ninth Amendment, we can see the foundation for his reasoning: "The enumeration in the Constitution, of certain rights, shall not be construed to deny or disparage others retained by the people." In other words, the fact that the Constitution, including its amendments, does not specifically talk about the right to privacy does not mean that this right is denied to the people.

Privacy Rights and Abortion

Historically, abortion was not a criminal offense before the "quickening" of the fetus (the first movement of the fetus in the uterus, usually between the sixteenth and eighteenth weeks of pregnancy). During the last half of the nineteenth century, however, state laws became more severe. By 1973, performing an abortion at any time during pregnancy was a criminal offense in a majority of the states.

Roe v. Wade. In *Roe v. Wade*[35] (1973), the United States Supreme Court accepted the argument that the laws against abortion violated "Jane Roe's" right to privacy under the Constitution. The Court held that during the first trimester (three months) of pregnancy, abortion was an issue solely between a woman and her physician. The state could not limit abortions except to require that they be performed by licensed physicians. During the second trimester, to protect the health of the mother, the state was allowed to specify the conditions under which an abortion could be performed. During the final trimester, the state could regulate or even outlaw abortions except when necessary to preserve the life or health of the mother.

After the *Roe* case, the Supreme Court issued decisions in a number of cases defining and redefining the boundaries of state regulation of abortion. During the 1980s, the Court twice struck down laws that required a woman who wished to have an abortion to undergo counseling designed to discourage abortions. In the late 1980s and early 1990s, however, the Court took a more conservative approach. For example, in *Webster v. Reproductive Health Services*,[36] the Court upheld a Missouri statute that, among other things, banned the use of public hospitals or other taxpayer-supported facilities for performing abortions. And, in *Planned Parenthood v. Casey*,[37] the Court upheld a Pennsylvania law that required preabortion counseling, a waiting period of twenty-four hours, and, for girls under the age of eighteen, parental or judicial permission. As a result, abortions are more difficult to obtain in some states than others.

The Controversy Continues. Abortion continues to be a divisive issue. Groups opposed to abortion continue to push for laws banning abortion, to endorse political candidates who support their views, and to organize protests. Because of several episodes of violence attending protests at abortion clinics, in 1994 Congress passed the

---

35. 410 U.S. 113 (1973). Jane Roe was not the real name of the woman in this case. It is a common legal pseudonym used to protect a person's privacy.
36. 492 U.S. 490 (1989).
37. 505 U.S. 833 (1992).

Freedom of Access to Clinic Entrances Act. The act prohibits protesters from blocking entrances to such clinics.

In recent years, abortion opponents have concentrated on state ballot proposals that could lay the groundwork for an eventual challenge to *Roe*. In 2008, for example, Colorado voters rejected a measure that would have granted full constitutional rights to a fertilized egg. The Colorado proposal failed by a margin of almost three to one. Also in 2008, South Dakota voters refused to ban most abortions in that state. Two years earlier, in 2006, South Dakotans rejected a measure that would have banned all abortions, even in cases of incest or rape, or when the mother's life or health is endangered.

"Partial-Birth" Abortion. In 2000, the Supreme Court again addressed the abortion issue directly when it reviewed a Nebraska law banning "partial-birth" abortions. Similar laws have been passed by at least twenty-seven states. A partial-birth abortion, which physicians call intact dilation and extraction, is a procedure that can be used during the second trimester of pregnancy. Abortion rights advocates claim that in limited circumstances the procedure is the safest way to perform an abortion and that the government should never outlaw specific medical procedures. Opponents argue that the procedure has no medical merit and that it ends the life of a fetus that might be able to live outside the womb. The Supreme Court invalidated the Nebraska law on the ground that the law could be used to ban other abortion procedures and contained no provisions for protecting the health of the pregnant woman.[38]

In 2003, legislation similar to the Nebraska statute was passed by the U.S. Congress and signed into law by President George W. Bush. In 2007, the Supreme Court, with several changes in membership since the 2000 ruling, upheld the federal law in a five-to-four vote, effectively reversing its position on partial-birth abortions.[39] The Court stated that "government has a legitimate and substantial interest in preserving and promoting fetal life." The Court noted that there was an alternative (though less safe, according to the act's opponents) abortion procedure that could be used in the second trimester. Also, the Court emphasized that the law allowed partial-birth abortion to be performed when a woman's life was in jeopardy.

Privacy Rights and the "Right to Die"

A 1976 case involving Karen Ann Quinlan was one of the first publicized right-to-die cases.[40] The parents of Quinlan, a young woman who had been in a coma for nearly a year and who had been kept alive during that time by a respirator, wanted her respirator removed. In 1976, the New Jersey Supreme Court ruled that the right to privacy includes the right of a patient to refuse treatment and that patients unable to speak can exercise that right through a family member or guardian. In 1990, the Supreme Court took up the issue. In *Cruzan v. Director, Missouri Department of Health*,[41] the Court stated that a patient's life-sustaining treatment can be withdrawn at the request of a family member only if there is "clear and convincing evidence" that the patient did not want such treatment.

---

38. *Stenberg v. Carhart*, 530 U.S. 914 (2000).
39. *Gonzales v. Carhart*, 550 U.S. 124 (2007).
40. *In re Quinlan*, 70 N.J. 10 (1976).
41. 497 U.S. 261 (1990).

What If There Is No Living Will?

Since the 1976 *Quinlan* decision, most states have enacted laws permitting people to designate their wishes concerning life-sustaining procedures in "living wills" or durable health-care powers of attorney. These laws and the Supreme Court's *Cruzan* decision have resolved the right-to-die controversy for cases in which a living will has been drafted. Disputes are still possible if there is no living will. An example is the case of Terri Schiavo. After the Florida woman had been in a persistent vegetative state for over a decade, her husband sought to have her feeding tube removed on the basis of oral statements that she would not want her life prolonged in such circumstances. Schiavo's parents fought this move in court but lost on the ground that a spouse, not a

▲ **Physician-assisted suicide** is supported by many Americans, such as this woman in Eugene, Oregon. So far, assisted suicide is legal only in Montana, Oregon, and Washington. Such laws have been upheld by the Supreme Court. Supporters of these laws argue that they are legal because of what right? (AP Photo/Charles Dharapak)

parent, is the appropriate legal guardian for a married person. Although the Florida legislature passed a law allowing then governor Jeb Bush to overrule the courts, the state supreme court held that the law violated the state constitution.[42]

In March 2005, the U.S. Congress intervened and passed a law allowing Schiavo's case to be heard in the federal court system. The federal courts, however, essentially agreed with the Florida state courts and refused to order the reconnection of the feeding tube, which had been disconnected a few days earlier. After appeals to the United States Supreme Court met with no success, the parents gave up hope, and Schiavo died shortly thereafter.

Physician-Assisted Suicide. In the 1990s, another issue surfaced: Do privacy rights include the right of terminally ill people to end their lives through physician-assisted suicide? Until 1996, the courts consistently upheld state laws that prohibited this practice, either through specific statutes or under their general homicide statutes. In 1996, after two federal appellate courts ruled that state laws banning assisted suicide (in Washington and New York) were unconstitutional, the issue reached the United States Supreme Court. In 1997, in *Washington v. Glucksberg*,[43] the Court stated, clearly and categorically, that the liberty interest protected by the Constitution does not include a right to commit suicide, with or without assistance. The Court left the decision in the hands of the states. Since then, assisted suicide has been allowed in only three states—Montana, Oregon, and Washington. In 2006, the Supreme Court upheld Oregon's physician-assisted suicide law against a challenge from the Bush administration.[44]

---

42. *Bush v. Schiavo*, 885 So.2d 321 (Fla. 2004).
43. 521 U.S. 702 (1997).
44. *Gonzales v. Oregon*, 546 U.S. 243 (2006).

CIVIL LIBERTIES VERSUS SECURITY ISSUES

As former Supreme Court justice Thurgood Marshall once said, "Grave threats to liberty often come in times of urgency, when constitutional rights seem too extravagant to endure." Not surprisingly, antiterrorist legislation since the attacks on September 11, 2001, has eroded certain basic rights, in particular the Fourth Amendment protections against unreasonable searches and seizures.

"Roving" Wiretaps

One Fourth Amendment issue involves legislation that allows the government to conduct "roving" wiretaps. Previously, only specific telephone numbers, cell phone numbers, or computers could be tapped. Now a person under suspicion can be monitored electronically no matter what form of electronic communication he or she uses. Such roving wiretaps contravene the Supreme Court's interpretation of the Fourth Amendment, which requires a judicial warrant to describe the *place* to be searched, not just the person. One of the goals of the framers was to avoid *general* searches. Further, once a judge approves an application for a roving wiretap, when, how, and where the monitoring occurs will be left to the discretion of law enforcement agents. As an unavoidable result, a third party may have access to the conversations and e-mails of hundreds of people who falsely believe them to be private.

The USA Patriot Act

The most significant piece of antiterrorism legislation, the USA Patriot Act, was originally passed in October 2001. In 2006, when the act was renewed, a heated debate emerged. While many Americans believe that the Patriot Act is a necessary safety measure to prevent future terrorist attacks, others argue that the act endangers long-established civil liberties guaranteed by the Constitution.

Much of the blame for the government's failure to anticipate the 9/11 attacks was assigned to a lack of cooperation among government agencies. A major goal of the Patriot Act was to lift interagency barriers to cooperation, especially between the Federal Bureau of Investigation and the Central Intelligence Agency. The Patriot Act also eased restrictions on the government's authority to investigate and arrest suspected terrorists. Law enforcement officials can secretly search a suspect's home and monitor a suspect's Internet activities, phone conversations, financial records, and book purchases. For the first time in American history, the government can open a suspect's mail.

National Security Agency Surveillance

Shortly after September 11, 2001, President George W. Bush issued an executive order authorizing the National Security Agency (NSA) to conduct secret surveillance without court warrants, even from special security courts. The NSA was to monitor phone calls and other communications between foreign parties and persons within the United States when one of the parties had suspected links to terrorist organizations. News of the secret program came out only in December 2005. The program was intensely criticized by civil liberties groups, which called for the immediate termination of the allegedly illegal surveillance.

In 2007, Congress passed a law to authorize the warrantless NSA wiretaps. The law expired in 2008, however, and its reauthorization was held up by a dispute between Congress and the Bush administration as to whether telephone companies should receive blanket immunity from lawsuits stemming from their past cooperation with the wiretaps. When it finally passed, the reauthorization protected the telephone companies, as Bush had wanted. The law was supported by, among others, then Illinois senator Barack Obama, who received criticism from fellow Democrats for his vote.

Writ of Habeas Corpus
Habeas corpus means, literally, "you have the body." A writ of habeas corpus is an order that requires jailers to bring a prisoner before a court or judge and explain why the person is being held.

Arraignment
The first act in a criminal proceeding, in which the defendant is brought before a court to hear the charges against him or her and enter a plea of guilty or not guilty.

THE GREAT BALANCING ACT: THE RIGHTS OF THE ACCUSED VERSUS THE RIGHTS OF SOCIETY

The United States has one of the highest murder rates in the industrialized world. It is not surprising, therefore, that many citizens have extremely strong opinions about the rights of those accused of violent crimes. When an accused person, especially one who has confessed to some criminal act, is set free because of an apparent legal "technicality," many people believe that the rights of the accused are being given more weight than the rights of society and of potential or actual victims. Why, then, give criminal suspects rights? The answer is partly to avoid convicting innocent people but mostly because due process of law and fair treatment benefit everyone who comes into contact with law enforcement or the courts.

The courts and the police must constantly engage in a balancing act of competing rights. At the basis of all discussions about the appropriate balance is, of course, the U.S. Bill of Rights. The Fourth, Fifth, Sixth, and Eighth Amendments deal specifically with the rights of criminal defendants.

Rights of the Accused

The basic rights of criminal defendants are outlined below. When appropriate, the specific constitutional provision or amendment on which a right is based also is given.

Limits on the Conduct of Police Officers and Prosecutors

- No unreasonable or unwarranted searches and seizures (Amendment IV).
- No arrest except on probable cause (Amendment IV).
- No coerced confessions or illegal interrogation (Amendment V).
- No entrapment.
- On questioning, a suspect must be informed of her or his rights if being placed under arrest.

Defendant's Pretrial Rights

- **Writ of *habeas corpus*** (Article I, Section 9).
- Prompt **arraignment** (Amendment VI).
- Legal counsel (Amendment VI).
- Reasonable bail (Amendment VIII).
- To be informed of charges (Amendment VI).
- To remain silent (Amendment V).

Trial Rights

- Speedy and public trial before a jury (Amendment VI).
- Impartial jury selected from a cross section of the community (Amendment VI).
- Trial atmosphere free of prejudice, fear, and outside interference.
- No compulsory self-incrimination (Amendment V).
- Adequate counsel (Amendment VI).
- No cruel and unusual punishment (Amendment VIII).
- Appeal of convictions.
- No double jeopardy (Amendment V).

Extending the Rights of the Accused

During the 1960s, the Supreme Court, under Chief Justice Earl Warren, significantly expanded the rights of accused persons. In a case decided in 1963, *Gideon v. Wainwright*,[45] the Court held that if a person is accused of a felony and cannot afford an attorney, an attorney must be made available to the accused person at the government's expense. Although the Sixth Amendment to the Constitution provides for the right to counsel, the Supreme Court had previously held that only criminal defendants in capital cases automatically had a right to free legal counsel.

Miranda v. Arizona. In 1966, the Court issued its decision in *Miranda v. Arizona*.[46] The case involved Ernesto Miranda, who was arrested and charged with the kidnapping and rape of a young woman. After two hours of questioning, Miranda confessed and was later convicted. Miranda's lawyer appealed his conviction, arguing that the police had never informed Miranda that he had a right to remain silent and a right to be represented by counsel. The Court, in ruling in Miranda's favor, enunciated the *Miranda* rights that are now familiar to virtually all Americans:

> Prior to any questioning, the person must be warned that he has a right to remain silent, that any statement he does make may be used against him, and that he has a right to the presence of an attorney, either retained or appointed.

Exceptions to the Miranda Rule. As part of a continuing attempt to balance the rights of accused persons against the rights of society, the Supreme Court has made a number of exceptions to the *Miranda* rule. In an important 1991 decision, the Court stated that a suspect's conviction will not be automatically overturned if the suspect was coerced into making a confession. If the other evidence admitted at trial is strong enough to justify the conviction without the confession, then the fact that the confession was obtained illegally can, in effect, be ignored.[47] In another case, in 1994, the Supreme Court ruled that suspects must unequivocally and assertively state their right to counsel in order to stop police questioning. Saying, "Maybe I should talk to a lawyer" during an interrogation after being taken into custody is not enough. The Court held that police officers are not required to decipher the suspect's intentions in such situations.[48]

---

45. 372 U.S. 335 (1963).
46. 384 U.S. 436 (1966).
47. *Arizona v. Fulminante,* 499 U.S. 279 (1991).
48. *Davis v. United States,* 512 U.S. 452 (1994).

The Exclusionary Rule

At least since 1914, judicial policy has prohibited the admission of illegally seized evidence at trials in federal courts. This is the so-called **exclusionary rule.** Improperly obtained evidence, no matter how telling, cannot be used by prosecutors. This includes evidence obtained by police in violation of a suspect's *Miranda* rights or of the Fourth Amendment. The Fourth Amendment protects against unreasonable searches and seizures and provides that a judge may issue a search warrant to a police officer only on probable cause (a demonstration of facts that permit a reasonable belief that a crime has been committed). The courts must determine what constitutes an "unreasonable" search and seizure.

The reasoning behind the exclusionary rule is that it forces police officers to gather evidence properly, in which case their due diligence will be rewarded by a conviction. Nevertheless, the exclusionary rule has always had critics who argue that it permits guilty persons to be freed because of innocent police procedural errors.

This rule was first extended to state court proceedings in a 1961 United States Supreme Court decision, *Mapp v. Ohio.*[49] In this case, the Court overturned the conviction of Dollree Mapp for the possession of obscene materials. Police found pornographic books in her apartment after searching it without a search warrant and despite her refusal to let them in. Under the Fourth Amendment, search warrants must describe the persons or things to be seized. In addition, however, officers are entitled to seize items not mentioned in the search warrant if the materials are in "plain view" and reasonably appear to be contraband or evidence of a crime.[50]

Over the last several decades, the Supreme Court has diminished the scope of the exclusionary rule by creating some exceptions to its applicability. For example, in 1984 the Court held that illegally obtained evidence could be admitted at trial if law enforcement personnel could prove that they would have obtained the evidence legally anyway.[51] The Court has also created a "good faith" exception to the exclusionary rule. In 2009, for example, the Court found that the good faith exception applies when an officer makes an arrest based on an outstanding warrant in another jurisdiction, even if the warrant in question was based on a clerical error.[52]

Exclusionary Rule
A judicial policy prohibiting the admission at trial of illegally seized evidence.

---

49. 367 U.S. 643 (1961).
50. *Texas v. Brown,* 460 U.S. 730 (1983); and *Horton v. California,* 496 U.S. 128 (1990).
51. *Nix v. Williams,* 467 U.S. 431 (1984).
52. *Herring v. United States,* __ U.S. __ (2009).

making a difference

YOUR CIVIL LIBERTIES: SEARCHES AND SEIZURES

Our civil liberties include numerous provisions, many of them listed in the Bill of Rights, that protect persons who are suspected of criminal activity. Among these are limits on how the police—as agents of the government—can conduct searches and seizures.

Why Should You Care? You may be the most law-abiding person in the world, but that does not guarantee that you will never be stopped, arrested, or searched by the police. Sooner or later, the great majority of all citizens will have some kind of interaction with the police. People who do not understand their rights or how to behave toward law enforcement officers can find themselves in serious trouble.

What Are Your Rights? How should you behave if you are stopped by police officers? Your civil liberties protect you from having to provide information other than your name and address. Normally, even if you have not been placed under arrest, the officers have the right to frisk you for weapons, and you must let them proceed. The officers cannot, however, check your person or your clothing further if, in their judgment, no weaponlike object is produced.

The officers may search you only if they have a search warrant or probable cause to believe that a search will

▼ **This person was arrested** on suspicion of shooting his estranged wife and his mother-in-law. Can the police legally search him without a warrant? (AP Photo/Sharon Cekada/Post-Crescent)

likely produce incriminating evidence. What if the officers do not have probable cause or a warrant? Physically resisting their attempt to search you can lead to disastrous results. You can simply refuse orally to give permission for the search, preferably in the presence of a witness. Being polite is better than acting out of anger and making the officers irritable.

If you are in your car and are stopped by the police, the same fundamental rules apply. Always be ready to show your driver's license and car registration. You may be asked to get out of the car. The officers may use a flashlight to peer inside if it is too dark to see otherwise. None of this constitutes a search. A true search requires either a warrant or probable cause. No officer has the legal right to search your car simply to find out if you may have committed a crime.

If you are in your home and a police officer with a search warrant appears, you can ask to examine the warrant before granting entry. A warrant that is correctly made out will state the place or persons to be searched, the object sought, and the date of the warrant (which should be no more than ten days old), and it will bear the signature of a judge or magistrate. If you believe the warrant to be invalid, or if no warrant is produced, you should make it clear orally that you have not consented to the search, preferably in the presence of a witness.

Officers who attempt to enter your home without a search warrant can do so only if they are pursuing a suspected felon into the house. Rarely is it advisable to give permission for a warrantless search. You, as the resident, must be the one to give permission if any evidence obtained is to be considered legal. The landlord, manager, or head of a college dormitory cannot give legal permission. A roommate, however, can give permission for a search of his or her room, which may allow the police to search areas where you have belongings.

If you would like to find out more about your rights and obligations under the laws of searches and seizures, you might want to contact the following organization:

American Civil Liberties Union
125 Broad St., 18th Floor
New York, NY 10004-2400
212-549-2500
www.aclu.org

keyterms

actual malice 79

arraignment 85

clear and present
  danger test 75

commercial speech 74

defamation of
  character 77

establishment clause 67

exclusionary rule 87

free exercise clause 72

gag order 80

incorporation theory 66

libel 79

obscenity 76

prior restraint 72

public figures 79

slander 77

symbolic speech 74

writ of *habeas corpus* 85

chaptersummary

1   Originally, the Bill of Rights limited only the power of the national government, not that of the states. Gradually and selectively, however, the Supreme Court accepted the incorporation theory, under which no state can violate most provisions of the Bill of Rights.

2   The First Amendment protects against government interference with freedom of religion by requiring a separation of church and state (under the establishment clause) and by guaranteeing the free exercise of religion. Controversial issues that arise under the establishment clause include aid to church-related schools, school vouchers, school prayers, the teaching of evolution, and discrimination against religious speech. The government can interfere with the free exercise of religion only when religious practices work against public policy or the public welfare.

3   The First Amendment protects against government interference with freedom of speech, which includes symbolic speech (expressive conduct). The Supreme Court has been especially critical of government actions that impose prior restraint on expression. Commercial speech (advertising) by businesses has received limited First Amendment protection. Restrictions on expression are permitted when the expression may incite immediate lawless action. Other speech that has not received First Amendment protection includes expression judged to be obscene or slanderous.

4   The First Amendment protects against government interference with the freedom of the press, which can be regarded as a special instance of freedom of speech. Speech by the press that does not receive protection includes libelous statements.

Publication of news about a criminal trial may be restricted by a gag order in some circumstances.

5   Under the Ninth Amendment, people's rights are not limited to those specifically mentioned in the Constitution. Among the unspecified rights protected by the courts is a right to privacy, which has been inferred from the First, Third, Fourth, Fifth, and Ninth Amendments. Whether an individual's privacy rights include a right to an abortion or a "right to die" continues to provoke controversy. Another major challenge concerns the extent to which Americans must forfeit civil liberties to control terrorism.

6   The Constitution includes protections for the rights of persons accused of crimes. Under the Fourth Amendment, no one may be subject to an unreasonable search or seizure or be arrested except on probable cause. Under the Fifth Amendment, an accused person has the right to remain silent. Under the Sixth Amendment, an accused person must be informed of the reason for his or her arrest. The accused also has the right to adequate counsel, even if he or she cannot afford an attorney, and the right to a prompt arraignment and a speedy and public trial before an impartial jury selected from a cross section of the community.

7   In *Miranda v. Arizona* (1966), the Supreme Court held that criminal suspects, before interrogation by law enforcement personnel, must be informed of certain constitutional rights, including the right to remain silent and the right to counsel.

8   The exclusionary rule forbids the admission in court of illegally seized evidence. There is a "good faith exception" to the exclusionary rule: evidence need not be thrown out due to, for example, a clerical error in a database.

QUESTIONS FOR

discussion and analysis

1 If freedom of speech were not a constitutional right, but merely a matter of tradition and custom, in what ways might the government be tempted to limit it?

2 France has banned symbols and garments that express religious sentiments from the public schools. This includes headscarves worn by Muslim girls. Would a ban of this type be constitutional in the United States? If constitutional, would it be a good idea?

3 The courts have never held that the provision of military chaplains by the armed forces is unconstitutional, despite the fact that chaplains are religious leaders who are employed by and under the authority of the U.S. government. What arguments might the courts use to defend the military chaplain system?

4 The courts have banned the teaching of the theory of creation by intelligent design in public school biology classes, arguing that the theory is based on religion, not science. Indeed, it is not hard to detect a religious basis in the classroom materials recently disseminated by the intelligent design movement. Is it possible to make an argument in favor of intelligent design that would not promote a religious belief?

5 In a surprisingly large number of cases, arrested individuals choose not to exercise their right to remain silent. Why might a person not exercise his or her *Miranda* rights?

helpful online Resources

CONNECTING TO AMERICAN GOVERNMENT AND POLITICS

Summaries and the full text of Supreme Court decisions concerning constitutional law, plus a virtual tour of the Supreme Court, are available at:
www.oyez.org

The American Civil Liberties Union (ACLU), the nation's leading civil liberties organization, provides much information on civil liberties issues at:
www.aclu.org

The Liberty Counsel takes a politically conservative "family values" position on civil liberties issues. You can visit its Web site at:
www.lc.org

a special Web Site

FOR YOUR TEXT   Go to this book's special Web site at academic.cengage.com/polisci/Schmidt/ Brief6e. Choose "For Students." Then click on Chapter 4, where you will find an online quiz and other helpful study aids. If your professor is using CengageNOW: *American Government and Politics Today, Brief Edition,* log in and go to Chapter 4 for additional online study aids.

Civil Rights

These women were part of a class-action federal discrimination lawsuit against the clothing retailer Abercrombie & Fitch. Ultimately, that company agreed to pay $40 million to black, Hispanic, and Asian employees as well as to job applicants to settle the discrimination suit. (AP Photo/ Ric Francis)

Equality is at the heart of the concept of civil rights. Generally, the term **civil rights** refers to the rights of all Americans to equal protection under the law, as provided for by the Fourteenth Amendment to the Constitution. Although the terms *civil rights* and *civil liberties* are sometimes used interchangeably, scholars make a distinction between the two. As discussed in Chapter 4, civil liberties are basically *limitations* on government; they specify what the government *cannot* do. Civil rights, in contrast, specify what the government *must* do—to ensure equal protection and freedom from discrimination.

Essentially, the history of civil rights in America is the story of the struggle of various groups to be free from discriminatory treatment. In this chapter, we first look at two movements that had significant consequences for the history of civil rights in America: the civil rights movement of the 1950s and 1960s and the women's movement, which began in the mid-1800s and continues today. Each of these movements resulted in legislation that secured important basic rights for all Americans—the right to vote and the right to equal protection under the laws. We then explore a question with serious implications for today's voters and policymakers: What should the government's responsibility be when equal protection under the law is not enough to ensure truly equal opportunities for Americans?

Civil Rights
Generally, all rights rooted in the Fourteenth Amendment's guarantee of equal protection under the law.

91

Note that most minorities in this nation have suffered—and some continue to suffer—from discrimination. These include such groups as older Americans and persons with disabilities. The fact that some groups are not singled out for special attention in the following pages should not be construed to mean that their struggle for equality is any less significant than the struggles of those groups that we do discuss.

AFRICAN AMERICANS AND THE CONSEQUENCES OF SLAVERY IN THE UNITED STATES

Before 1863, the Constitution protected slavery and made equality impossible in the sense in which we use the word today. The constitutionality of slavery was confirmed just a few years before the outbreak of the Civil War in the infamous *Dred Scott v. Sandford*[1] case of 1857. The Supreme Court held that slaves were not citizens of the United States, nor were they entitled to the rights and privileges of citizenship. The *Dred Scott* decision had grave consequences. Many historians contend that the ruling contributed to making the Civil War inevitable.

Ending Servitude

With the emancipation of the slaves by President Lincoln's Emancipation Proclamation in 1863 and the passage of the Thirteenth, Fourteenth, and Fifteenth Amendments during the Reconstruction period (1865–1877) following the Civil War, constitutional inequality was ended.

The Thirteenth Amendment (1865) states that neither slavery nor involuntary servitude shall exist within the United States. The Fourteenth Amendment (1868) tells us that *all* persons born or naturalized in the United States are citizens of the United States. It states, furthermore, that "[n]o State shall make or enforce any law which shall abridge the privileges or immunities of citizens of the United States; nor shall any State deprive any person of life, liberty, or property, without due process of law; nor deny to any person within its jurisdiction the equal protection of the laws." Note the use of the terms *citizen* and *person* in this amendment. *Citizens* have political rights, such as the right to vote and run for political office. Citizens also have certain privileges or immunities (see Chapter 3). All *persons,* however, including noncitizen immigrants, have a right to due process of law and equal protection under the law. Finally, the Fifteenth Amendment (1870) reads as follows: "The right of citizens of the United States to vote shall not be denied or abridged by the United States or by any State on account of race, color, or previous condition of servitude."

The Civil Rights Acts of 1865 to 1875

In 1865, southern state legislatures responded to the freeing of the African American slaves by enacting "Black Codes" to regulate the former slaves. The codes were so severe that they almost amounted to a new form of slavery. Typically, African Americans were required to enter into annual labor contracts and were subject to close regulation by their employers. Corporal punishment was permitted. In 1866, however, the U.S.

---

1. 60 U.S. 393 (1857).

Congress placed all the rebellious states except Tennessee under military rule, and the Black Codes were revoked.

From 1865 to 1875, Congress passed a series of civil rights acts to negate the Black Codes and enforce the Thirteenth, Fourteenth, and Fifteenth Amendments. The Civil Rights Act of 1866 implemented the extension of citizenship to anyone born in the United States and gave African Americans full equality before the law. The act further authorized the president to enforce the law with the national armed forces. The Enforcement Act of 1870 set out specific criminal sanctions for interfering with the right to vote as protected by the Fifteenth Amendment and by the Civil Rights Act of 1866. Equally important was the Civil Rights Act of 1872, known as the Anti–Ku Klux Klan Act. This act made it a federal crime for anyone to use law or custom to deprive an individual of rights, privileges, and immunities secured by the Constitution or by any federal law. The Second Civil Rights Act, passed in 1875, declared that everyone is entitled to full and equal enjoyment of public accommodations, theaters, and other places of public amusement, and it imposed penalties on violators.

The Ineffectiveness of the Early Civil Rights Laws

The Reconstruction statutes, or civil rights acts, ultimately did little to secure equality for African Americans. Both the *Civil Rights Cases* and the case of *Plessy v. Ferguson* (discussed next) effectively nullified these acts. Additionally, various barriers were erected that prevented African Americans from exercising their right to vote.

The *Civil Rights Cases*. The United States Supreme Court invalidated the 1875 Second Civil Rights Act when it held, in the *Civil Rights Cases*[2] of 1883, that the enforcement clause of the Fourteenth Amendment (which states that "[n]o State shall make or enforce any law which shall abridge the privileges or immunities of citizens") was limited to correcting *official* actions taken by states; thus, the discriminatory acts of private citizens were not illegal. ("Individual invasion of individual rights is not the subject matter of the Amendment.") The 1883 Supreme Court decision met with widespread approval throughout most of the United States.

Twenty years after the Civil War, the white majority was all too willing to forget about the Civil War amendments to the U.S. Constitution and the civil rights legislation of the 1860s and 1870s. The other civil rights laws that the Court did not specifically invalidate became dead letters in the statute books, although they were never officially repealed by Congress. At the same time, many former proslavery secessionists had regained political power in the southern states.

Plessy v. Ferguson: Separate but Equal. A key decision during this period concerned Homer Plessy, a Louisiana resident who was one-eighth African American. In 1892, he boarded a train in New Orleans. The conductor made him leave the car, which was restricted to whites, and directed him to a car for nonwhites. At that time, Louisiana had a statute providing for separate railway cars for whites and African Americans.

Plessy went to court, claiming that such a statute was contrary to the Fourteenth Amendment's equal protection clause. In 1896, the United States Supreme Court

---

2. 109 U.S. 3 (1883).

rejected Plessy's contention. The Court concluded that the Fourteenth Amendment "could not have been intended to abolish distinctions based upon color, or to enforce social . . . equality." The Court stated that segregation alone did not violate the Constitution: "Laws permitting, and even requiring, their separation in places where they are liable to be brought into contact do not necessarily imply the inferiority of either race to the other."[3] So was born the **separate-but-equal doctrine.**

Plessy v. Ferguson became the judicial cornerstone of racial discrimination throughout the United States. Even though *Plessy* upheld segregated facilities in railway cars only, it was assumed that the Supreme Court was upholding segregation everywhere as long as the separate facilities were equal. The result was a system of racial segregation, particularly in the South—supported by laws collectively known as Jim Crow laws—that required separate drinking fountains; separate seats in theaters, restaurants, and hotels; separate public toilets; and separate waiting rooms for the two races. "Separate" was indeed the rule, but "equal" was never enforced, nor was it a reality.

Voting Barriers. The brief voting enfranchisement of African Americans ended after 1877, when the federal troops that occupied the South during the Reconstruction era were withdrawn. Southern politicians regained control of state governments and, using everything except race as a formal criterion, passed laws that effectively deprived African Americans of the right to vote. By using the ruse that political parties were private entities, the Democratic Party managed to keep black voters from its primaries. The **white primary** was upheld by the Supreme Court until 1944 when, in *Smith v. Allwright*,[4] the Court ruled it a violation of the Fifteenth Amendment.

Another barrier to African American voting was the **grandfather clause,** which restricted voting to those who could prove that their grandfathers had voted before 1867. **Poll taxes** required the payment of a fee to vote; thus, poor African Americans—as well as poor whites—who could not afford to pay the tax were excluded from voting. Not until the Twenty-fourth Amendment to the Constitution was ratified in 1964 was the poll tax eliminated as a precondition to voting. **Literacy tests** were also used to deny the vote to African Americans. Such tests asked potential voters to read, recite, or interpret complicated texts, such as a section of the state constitution, to the satisfaction of local registrars—who were, of course, never satisfied with the responses of African Americans.

Extralegal Methods of Enforcing White Supremacy. The second-class status of African Americans was also a matter of social custom, especially in the South. In their interactions with southern whites, African Americans were expected to observe an informal but detailed code of behavior that confirmed their inferiority. The most serious violation of the informal code was "familiarity" toward a white woman by an African American man. The code was backed up by the common practice of *lynching*—mob action to murder an accused individual, usually by hanging and sometimes accompanied by torture. Of course, lynching was illegal, but southern authorities rarely prosecuted these cases, and white juries would not convict.

---

3. *Plessy v. Ferguson,* 163 U.S. 537 (1896).
4. 321 U.S. 649 (1944).

The End of the Separate-but-Equal Doctrine

As early as the 1930s, several court rulings began to chip away at the separate-but-equal doctrine. The United States Supreme Court did not explicitly over-turn *Plessy v. Ferguson* until 1954, however, when it issued one of the most famous judicial decisions in history.

In 1951, Oliver Brown decided that his eight-year-old daughter, Linda Carol Brown, should not have to go to an all-nonwhite elementary school twenty-one blocks from her home, when there was a white school only seven blocks away. The National Association for the Advancement of Colored People (NAACP), formed in 1909, decided to support Oliver Brown. The outcome would have a monumental impact on American society.

Brown v. Board of Education of Topeka. The 1954 unanimous decision of the United States Supreme Court in *Brown v. Board of Education of Topeka*[5] established that segregation of races in the public schools violates the equal protection clause of the Fourteenth Amendment. Chief Justice Earl Warren said that separation implied inferiority, whereas the majority opinion in *Plessy v. Ferguson* had said the opposite.

"With All Deliberate Speed." The following year, in *Brown v. Board of Education*[6] (sometimes called the second *Brown* decision), the Court declared that the lower courts needed to ensure that African Americans would be admitted to schools on a nondiscriminatory basis "with all deliberate speed." The district courts were to consider devices in their desegregation orders that might include "the school transportation system, personnel, [and] revision of school districts and attendance areas into compact units to achieve a system of determining admission to the public schools on a nonracial basis."

▲ **When Oliver Brown** wanted his daughter Linda to attend a white school close to their home, he took his case all the way to the Supreme Court. The outcome of that case is considered a landmark decision. Why? (AP Photo)

Reactions to School Integration

The white South did not let the Supreme Court ruling go unchallenged. Governor Orval Faubus of Arkansas used the state's National Guard to block the integration of Central High School in Little Rock in September 1957. The federal court demanded that the troops be withdrawn. Finally, President Dwight Eisenhower had to federalize the Arkansas National Guard and send in the Army's 101st Airborne Division to quell the violence. Central High became integrated.

The universities in the South, however, remained segregated. When James Meredith, an African American student, attempted to enroll at the University of Mississippi in Oxford in 1962, violence flared there, as it had in Little Rock. The white riot at Oxford was so intense that President John Kennedy was forced to send in 30,000 U.S. combat troops, a larger force than the one then stationed in Korea. There were 375 military and civilian injuries, many from gunfire, and two bystanders were killed. Ultimately, peace was restored, and Meredith began attending classes.[7]

---

5. 347 U.S. 483 (1954).
6. 349 U.S. 294 (1955).
7. William Doyle, *An American Insurrection: James Meredith and the Battle of Oxford, Mississippi, 1962* (New York: Anchor, 2003).

De Facto Segregation
Racial segregation that occurs because of patterns of racial residence and similar social conditions.

De Jure Segregation
Racial segregation that occurs because of laws or administrative decisions by public agencies.

Busing
In the context of civil rights, the transportation of public school students from areas where they live to schools in other areas to eliminate school segregation based on residential patterns.

An Integrationist Attempt at a Cure: Busing

In most parts of the United States, residential concentrations by race have made it difficult to achieve racial balance in schools. Although it is true that a number of school boards in northern districts created segregated schools by drawing school district lines arbitrarily, the residential concentration of African Americans and other minorities in well-defined geographic locations has contributed to the difficulty of achieving racial balance. This concentration results in *de facto* **segregation,** as distinct from *de jure* **segregation,** which results from laws or administrative decisions.

Court-Ordered Busing. The obvious solution to both *de facto* and *de jure* segregation seemed to be transporting some African American schoolchildren to white schools and some white schoolchildren to African American schools. Increasingly, the courts ordered school districts to engage in such **busing** across neighborhoods. Busing led to violence in some northern cities, such as in south Boston, where African American students were bused into blue-collar Irish Catholic neighborhoods. Indeed, busing was unpopular with many groups. In the mid-1970s, almost 50 percent of African Americans interviewed were opposed to busing, and approximately three-fourths of the whites interviewed held the same opinion. Nonetheless, through the next decade, the Supreme Court fairly consistently upheld busing plans in the cases it decided.

The End of Integration? During the 1980s and the early 1990s, the Supreme Court tended to back away from its earlier commitment to busing and other methods of desegregation. By the late 1990s and early 2000s, the federal courts were increasingly unwilling to uphold race-conscious policies designed to further school integration and diversity—outcomes that are not mandated by the Constitution. For example, in 2001, a federal appellate court held that the Charlotte-Mecklenburg school district in North Carolina had achieved the goal of integration,[8] meaning that race-based admission quotas could no longer be imposed constitutionally.

The Resurgence of Minority Schools. Today, schools around the country are becoming segregated again, in large part because of *de facto* segregation. A rapid decline in the relative proportion of whites who live in large cities, along with high minority birthrates, has increased the minority presence in those urban areas. Today, one out of every three African American and Latino students goes to a school with a minority student enrollment of more than 90 percent. In the largest U.S. cities, fifteen out of sixteen African American and Hispanic students go to schools with almost no non-Hispanic whites.

Generally, Americans are now taking another look at what desegregation means. The goal of racially balanced schools envisioned in the 1954 *Brown v. Board of Education of Topeka* decision is giving way to the goal of better education for all children, even if that means educating them in schools in which students are of the same race or in which race is not considered.

THE CIVIL RIGHTS MOVEMENT

The *Brown* decision applied only to public schools. Not much else in the structure of existing segregation was affected. In December 1955, a forty-three-year-old African American woman, Rosa Parks, boarded a public bus in Montgomery, Alabama. When

8. *Belk v. Charlotte-Mecklenburg Board of Education,* 269 F.3d 305 (4th Cir. 2001).

the bus became crowded and several white people stepped aboard, Parks was asked to move to the rear of the bus, the "colored" section. She refused, was arrested, and was fined $10; but that was not the end of the matter. For an entire year, African Americans boycotted the Montgomery bus line. The protest was headed by a twenty-seven-year-old Baptist minister, Dr. Martin Luther King, Jr. In the face of overwhelming odds, the protesters won. In 1956, a federal district court issued an injunction prohibiting the segregation of buses in Montgomery. The era of civil rights protests had begun.

King's Philosophy of Nonviolence

The following year, in 1957, King formed the Southern Christian Leadership Conference (SCLC). King advocated nonviolent **civil disobedience** as a means to achieve racial justice. The SCLC used tactics such as demonstrations and marches, as well as nonviolent, public disobedience of unjust laws. King's followers successfully used these methods to gain wider public acceptance of their cause.

For the next decade, African Americans and sympathetic whites engaged in sit-ins, freedom rides, and freedom marches. In the beginning, such demonstrations were often met with violence, and the contrasting image of nonviolent African Americans and violent, hostile whites created strong public support for the civil rights movement.

The March on Washington

In August 1963, African American leaders A. Philip Randolph and Bayard Rustin organized the massive March on Washington for Jobs and Freedom. Before nearly a quarter-million white and African American spectators and millions watching on television, Martin Luther King told the world his dream: "I have a dream that my four little children will one day live in a nation where they will not be judged by the color of their skin but by the content of their character."

MODERN CIVIL RIGHTS LEGISLATION

Attacks on demonstrators using police dogs, cattle prods, high-pressure water hoses, beatings, and bombings—plus the March on Washington—all led to an environment in which Congress felt compelled to act on behalf of African Americans. The second era of civil rights acts, sometimes referred to as the second Reconstruction period, was under way.

▲ **This is a police** photo of Rosa Parks after her arrest for not moving to the back of the bus. Why was her protest so important? (AP Photo/Montgomery County Sheriff's office)

Civil Disobedience
A nonviolent, public refusal to obey allegedly unjust laws.

▶ **Martin Luther King, Jr.'s** speech at the Washington Monument was watched by millions of Americans on television. What were those famous words? (AP Photo)

The Civil Rights Act of 1964

The Civil Rights Act of 1964, the most far-reaching bill on civil rights in modern times, forbade discrimination on the basis of race, color, religion, gender, or national origin. The major provisions of the act were as follows:

- It outlawed arbitrary discrimination in voter registration.
- It barred discrimination in public accommodations, such as hotels and restaurants, which have operations that affect interstate commerce.
- It authorized the federal government to sue to desegregate public schools and facilities.
- It expanded the power of the Civil Rights Commission, which had been created in 1957, and extended its life.
- It provided for the withholding of federal funds from programs administered in a discriminatory manner.
- It established the right to equality of opportunity in employment.

Title VII of the Civil Rights Act of 1964 is the cornerstone of employment-discrimination law. It prohibits discrimination in employment based on race, color, religion, gender, or national origin. Under Title VII, executive orders were issued that banned employment discrimination by firms that received any federal funding. The 1964 Civil Rights Act created a five-member commission, the Equal Employment Opportunity Commission (EEOC), to administer Title VII. It was not until 1972, however, that Congress gave the EEOC the right to sue employers, unions, and employment agencies. Thereafter, litigation became an important activity for the agency.

The Voting Rights Act of 1965

As late as 1960, only 29.1 percent of African Americans of voting age were registered in the southern states, in stark contrast to 61.1 percent of whites. The Voting Rights Act of 1965 addressed this issue. The act had two major provisions. The first one outlawed discriminatory voter-registration tests. The second authorized federal registration of voters and federally administered voting procedures in any political subdivision or state that discriminated electorally against a particular group. The act also provided that certain political subdivisions could not change their voting procedures and election laws without federal approval. The act targeted counties, mostly in the South, in which less than 50 percent of the eligible population was registered to vote. Federal voter registrars were sent to those areas to register African Americans who had been kept from voting by local registrars. Within one week after the act was passed, forty-five federal examiners were sent to the South. A massive voter-registration drive covered the country.

The Civil Rights Act of 1968 and Other Housing Reform Legislation

The Civil Rights Act of 1968 forbade discrimination in most housing and provided penalties for those attempting to interfere with individual civil rights (giving protection to civil rights workers, among others). Subsequent legislation added enforcement provisions to the federal government's rules against discriminatory mortgage-lending practices. Today, all lenders must report to the federal government the race, gender, and income of all mortgage-loan seekers, along with the final decision on their loan applications.

Consequences of Civil Rights Legislation

As a result of the Voting Rights Act of 1965 and its amendments, and the large-scale voter-registration drives in the South, the number of African Americans registered to vote climbed dramatically. By 1980, 55.8 percent of African Americans of voting age in the South were registered. In recent national elections, turnout by African American voters has come very close to the white turnout. In 2008, with an African American on the presidential ballot, African American turnout exceeded that of whites for the first time in history.

▲ **President Barack Obama** was uniformly the candidate of choice among African Americans in the 2008 presidential elections. Indeed, the first African American candidate pushed African American voter participation to a new high, exceeding that of whites for the first time in history. Why was African American voter participation so low in previous decades? (AP Photo/ Pablo Martinez Monsivais)

Political Participation by African Americans. Today, there are more than ten thousand African American elected officials in the United States. The movement of African American citizens into high elected office has been sure, if exceedingly slow. Notably, recent polling data show that most Americans do not consider race a significant factor in choosing a president. In 1958, when a Gallup poll first asked whether respondents would be willing to vote for an African American as president, only 38 percent of the public said yes. By 2008, this number had reached 94 percent. This high figure may have been attained, at least in part, because of the emergence of African Americans of presidential caliber. Of course, Barack Obama, elected president in 2008 on the Democratic ticket, is African American. Two Republican African Americans have also been mentioned in the past as presidential possibilities: Colin Powell, formerly chair of the Joint Chiefs of Staff and later secretary of state under President George W. Bush, and Condoleezza Rice, who succeeded Powell at the State Department.

Political Participation by Other Minorities. The civil rights movement focused primarily on the rights of African Americans. Yet the legislation resulting from the movement ultimately benefited almost all minority groups. The Civil Rights Act of 1964, for example, prohibits discrimination against any person because of race, color, or national origin. Subsequent amendments to the Voting Rights Act of 1965 extended its protections to other minorities, including Hispanic Americans (or Latinos), Asian Americans, Native Americans, and Native Alaskans.

The political participation of non–African American minority groups has increased in recent years. Hispanics, for example, have gained political power in several states. Hispanics do not vote at the same rate as African Americans, in large part because

Suffrage
The right to vote; a vote given in favor of a proposed measure, candidate, or the like.

many Hispanics are immigrants who are not yet citizens. Still, there are now about five thousand Hispanic elected officials in the United States. In 2004, Hispanics were 8 percent of the voters in Colorado, 10 percent in Nevada, and 32 percent in New Mexico. In 2008, these figures were 13 percent, 15 percent, and 41 percent, respectively. Election analysts have concluded that even if 2008 Republican presidential candidate John McCain had established a 1 percent lead in the national popular vote, Hispanics in these three states still would have tipped the election to Obama. The impact of immigration will be discussed in greater detail later in this chapter.

WOMEN'S STRUGGLE FOR EQUAL RIGHTS

Like African Americans and other minorities, women have had to struggle for equality. During the first phase of this struggle, the primary goal of women was to obtain **suffrage,** or the right to vote. Some women had hoped that the founders would provide such a right in the Constitution. The Constitution did not include a provision guaranteeing women the right to vote, but neither did it deny to women—or to any others—this right. Rather, the founders left it up to the states to decide such issues, and by and large, as mentioned earlier, the states limited the franchise to adult white males who owned property.

Early Women's Political Movements

In 1848, Lucretia Mott and Elizabeth Cady Stanton organized the first women's rights convention in Seneca Falls, New York. The three hundred people who attended approved a Declaration of Sentiments: "We hold these truths to be self-evident: that all men *and women* are created equal." In the following twelve years, groups that supported women's rights held seven conventions in different cities in the Midwest and East. With the outbreak of the Civil War, however, advocates of women's rights were urged to put their support behind the war effort, and most agreed.

Susan B. Anthony and Elizabeth Cady Stanton formed the National Woman Suffrage Association in 1869, after the war. In their view, women's suffrage was a means to achieve major improvements in the economic and social situation of women in the United States. In other words, the vote was to be used to seek broader goals. Lucy Stone, however, a key founder of the rival American Woman Suffrage Association, believed that the vote was the only major issue. In 1880, the two organizations joined forces. The resulting National American Woman Suffrage Association had just one goal—the enfranchisement of women—but it made little progress.

The Congressional Union, founded in the early 1900s by Alice Paul, adopted a national strategy of obtaining an amendment to the U.S. Constitution. The Union employed militant tactics. It sponsored large-scale marches and civil disobedience—which resulted in hunger strikes, arrests, and jailings. Finally, in 1920, the Nineteenth Amendment was passed: "The right of citizens of the United States to vote shall not be denied or abridged by the United States or by any State on account of sex." (Today, the word *gender* is typically used instead of *sex*.) Women now had the right to vote in all states. Although it may seem that the United States was slow to give women the vote, it was really not too far behind the rest of the world (see Table 5–1).

TABLE 5-1: **Years, by Country, in Which Women Gained the Right to Vote**

1893: New Zealand	1919: Germany	1945: Italy	1953: Mexico
1902: Australia	1920: United States	1945: Japan	1956: Egypt
1913: Norway	1930: South Africa	1947: Argentina	1963: Kenya
1918: Britain	1932: Brazil	1950: India	1971: Switzerland
1918: Canada	1944: France	1952: Greece	1984: Yemen

Source: Center for the American Woman and Politics.

The Modern Women's Movement

Historian Nancy Cott contends that the word *feminism* first began to be used around 1910. At that time **feminism** meant, as it does today, political, social, and economic equality for women—a radical notion that gained little support among members of the suffrage movement.

After gaining the right to vote in 1920, women engaged in little independent political activity until the 1960s. The civil rights movement of that decade resulted in a growing awareness of rights for all groups, including women. Increased participation in the workforce gave many women greater self-confidence. Additionally, the publication of Betty Friedan's *The Feminine Mystique* in 1963 focused national attention on the unequal status of women in American life.

In 1966, Friedan and others formed the National Organization for Women (NOW). NOW's goal was "to bring women into full participation in the mainstream of American society *now,* exercising all the privileges and responsibilities thereof in truly equal partnership with men."

Feminism gained additional impetus from young women who entered politics to support the civil rights movement or to oppose the Vietnam War. In the late 1960s, "women's liberation" organizations began to spring up on college campuses. Women also began organizing independent "consciousness-raising groups" in which they discussed how gender issues affected their lives. The new women's movement experienced explosive growth, and by 1970 it had emerged as a major social force.

The Equal Rights Amendment. The initial focus of the modern women's movement was to eradicate gender inequality through a constitutional amendment. The proposed Equal Rights Amendment (ERA), which was first introduced in Congress in 1923, states as follows: "Equality of rights under the law shall not be denied or abridged by the United States or by any state on account of sex." For years the amendment was not even given a hearing in Congress, but finally it was approved by both chambers and sent to the state legislatures for ratification in 1972. The necessary thirty-eight states failed to ratify the ERA within the seven-year period specified by Congress, however. To date, efforts to reintroduce the amendment have failed.

Challenging Gender Discrimination in the Courts. When ratification of the ERA did not take place, women's rights organizations began a campaign to win national and state laws that would guarantee the equality of women. This more

Feminism
The movement that supports political, economic, and social equality for women.

▲ **This female member** of the Marine Corps is stationed in Jacksonville, North Carolina. She is a firefighter and an emergency medical technician. Who decides whether women can participate in military combat? (AP Photo/John Althouse/*The Daily News*)

limited campaign met with much success. Women's rights organizations also challenged discriminatory statutes and policies in the federal courts, contending that **gender discrimination** violated the Fourteenth Amendment's equal protection clause. Since the 1970s, the United States Supreme Court has tended to scrutinize gender classifications closely and has invalidated a number of such statutes and policies. For example, in 1977 the Court held that police and firefighting units cannot establish arbitrary rules, such as height and weight requirements, that tend to keep women from participating in those occupations.[9] In 1983, the Court ruled that life insurance companies cannot charge different rates for women and men.[10]

A question that the Supreme Court has not ruled on is whether women should be allowed to participate in military combat. Generally, the Court has left this decision up to Congress and the Department of Defense. Recently, women have been allowed to serve as combat pilots and on naval warships. To date, however, they have not been allowed to join infantry direct-combat units, although they are now permitted to serve in combat-support units.

Women in Politics Today

The efforts of women's rights advocates have helped to increase the number of women holding political offices at all levels of government. Although a "men's club" atmosphere still prevails in Congress, the number of women holding congressional seats has increased significantly in recent years. Elections during the 1990s brought more women to Congress than either the Senate or the House had seen before. In 2001, for the first time, a woman was elected to a leadership post in Congress—Nancy Pelosi of California became the Democrats' minority whip in the U.S. House of Representatives. In 2002, Pelosi was elected minority leader; and in 2006, she became the first woman to be Speaker of the House. In all, 133 women ran for Congress in 2008 on major-party tickets, and in 2009, the House contained 75 women. Following the 2008 elections, the Senate included 17 women, an all-time record.

In 1984, for the first time, a woman, Geraldine Ferraro, became the Democratic nominee for vice president. Another woman, Elizabeth Dole, made a serious run for the Republican presidential nomination in the 2000 campaigns. In 2008, Hillary Clinton mounted a major campaign for the presidency, and Sarah Palin became the Republican nominee for vice president. Recent Gallup polls show that close to 90 percent of Americans said they would vote for a qualified woman for president if she was nominated by their party.

Increasing numbers of women are also being appointed to cabinet posts. President George W. Bush appointed several women to cabinet positions, including Condoleezza Rice as his secretary of state in 2005. President Barack Obama named his former rival

Gender Discrimination

Any practice, policy, or procedure that denies equality of treatment to an individual or to a group because of gender.

9. *Dothard v. Rawlinson,* 433 U.S. 321 (1977).
10. *Arizona v. Norris,* 463 U.S. 1073 (1983).

Hillary Clinton to be secretary of state and added six other women to his cabinet. Increasing numbers of women are sitting on federal judicial benches as well. President Ronald Reagan (1981–1989) was credited with a historic first when he appointed Sandra Day O'Connor to the United States Supreme Court in 1981. (O'Connor retired in 2005.) President Clinton appointed a second woman, Ruth Bader Ginsburg, to the Court. In 2009, President Obama named Sonia Sotomayor to the Court, the first Hispanic and third woman to serve.

Gender-Based Discrimination in the Workplace

Traditional cultural beliefs concerning the proper role of women in society continue to be evident not only in the political arena but also in the workplace. Since the 1960s, however, women have gained substantial protection against discrimination through laws mandating equal employment opportunities and equal pay.

Title VII of the Civil Rights Act of 1964. Title VII of the Civil Rights Act of 1964 prohibits gender discrimination in employment and has been used to strike down employment policies that discriminate against employees on the basis of gender. In 1978, Congress amended Title VII to expand the definition of gender discrimination to include discrimination based on pregnancy.

▲ **Hillary Clinton**
was appointed secretary of state by President Obama. She is the third female to hold that office. Clinton almost became the Democratic presidential candidate in the 2008 elections. (AP Photo/J. Scott Applewhite)

Sexual Harassment. The United States Supreme Court has also held that Title VII's prohibition of gender-based discrimination extends to **sexual harassment** in the workplace. One form of sexual harassment occurs when job opportunities, promotions, salary increases, and other benefits are given in return for sexual favors. Another form of sexual harassment, called *hostile-environment harassment,* occurs when an employee is subjected to sexual conduct or comments that interfere with the employee's job performance or are so pervasive or severe as to create an intimidating, hostile, or offensive environment.

Wage Discrimination. As of 2010, women constitute a majority of U.S. workers. Although Title VII and other legislation since the 1960s have mandated equal employment opportunities for men and women, women continue to earn less, on average, than men do.

The issue of wage discrimination was first addressed during World War II (1939–1945), when the War Labor Board issued an "equal pay for women" policy. In implementing the policy, the board often evaluated jobs for their comparability and required equal pay for comparable jobs. The board's authority ended with the war. Although it was supported by the next three presidential administrations, the Equal Pay Act was not enacted until 1963 as an amendment to the Fair Labor Standards Act of 1938.

Basically, the Equal Pay Act requires employers to provide equal pay for substantially equal work. In other words, males cannot legally be paid more than females who perform essentially the same job. The Equal Pay Act did not address the fact that certain types of jobs traditionally held by women pay lower wages than the jobs usually held by men. For example, more women than men are salesclerks and nurses, whereas more men than women are construction workers and truck drivers. Even if all clerks

Sexual Harassment Unwanted physical or verbal conduct or abuse of a sexual nature that interferes with a recipient's job performance, creates a hostile work environment, or carries with it an implicit or explicit threat of adverse employment consequences.

performing substantially similar jobs for a company earned the same salaries, they typically would still be earning less than the company's truck drivers.

IMMIGRATION, LATINOS, AND CIVIL RIGHTS

A century ago, most immigrants to the United States came from Europe. Today, however, most come from Latin America and Asia. The large number of new immigrants from Spanish-speaking countries increases the Hispanic proportion of the U.S. population. The number of persons who identify themselves as multiracial is also growing due to interracial marriages.

Hispanic versus Latino

To the U.S. Census Bureau, **Hispanics** can be of any race. They can be new immigrants or members of families that have lived in the United States for centuries. Hispanics may come from any of about twenty primarily Spanish-speaking countries and, as a result, are a highly diverse population. The three largest Hispanic groups are Mexican Americans, at 63.9 percent of all Hispanics; Puerto Ricans (all of whom are U.S. citizens), at 9.1 percent of the total; and Cuban Americans, at 3.5 percent. The term *Hispanic* itself, although used by the government, is not particularly popular among Hispanic Americans. Many prefer the terms **Latino** or Latina.

The Changing Face of America

As a result of immigration, the ethnic makeup of the United States is changing. Yet immigration is not the only factor contributing to changes in the American ethnic mosaic. Another factor is ethnic differences in the **fertility rate.** The fertility rate measures the average number of children that women in a given group are expected to have over the course of a lifetime. A rate of 2.1 is the "long-term replacement rate." In other words, if a nation or group maintains a fertility rate of 2.1, its population will eventually stabilize. This can take many years, however.

Hispanic
Someone who can claim a heritage from a Spanish-speaking country. Hispanics may be of any race.

Latino
An alternative to the term *Hispanic* that is preferred by many.

Fertility Rate
A statistic that measures the average number of children that women in a given group are expected to have over the course of a lifetime.

▶ **These immigrants** swear their allegiance to the United States during citizenship ceremonies on Ellis Island. Why are immigrants and their children changing the makeup of the U.S. population? (Michael S. Yamashita/Corbis)

Today, the United States actually has a fertility rate of 2.1 children per woman. Hispanic Americans, however, have a current fertility rate of 2.9. African Americans have a fertility rate of 2.1. Non-Hispanic white Americans have a fertility rate of 1.86. Figure 5–1 shows the projected changes in the U.S. ethnic distribution in future years. These estimates could change if immigration rates fall, as is typical during a recession. We look at the impact of the current economic crisis on immigrants in this chapter's feature *The Politics of Boom and Bust: The Recession's Impact on Immigration* on the following page.

The Civil Rights of Immigrants

The law recognizes that Latinos have been subjected to many of the same forms of ill treatment as African Americans, so Latinos are usually grouped with African Americans and Native Americans in laws and programs that seek to protect minorities from discrimination or to address the results of past discrimination. Such programs often cover Asian Americans as well.

Immigrants who are not yet citizens, however, possess fewer civil rights than any other identifiable group in the United States. The rights of unauthorized immigrants are fewer still. The terrorist attacks on September 11, 2001, reinforced the belief that the rights of noncitizens should be limited. Among the most obvious characteristics of the terrorists who perpetrated the 9/11 attacks is that they were all foreign citizens.

The Constitutional Rights of Noncitizens. The Bill of Rights contains no language that limits its protections to citizens. The Fourteenth Amendment specifies that all *persons* (as opposed to citizens) shall enjoy "due process of law." In decisions spanning more than a century, the United States Supreme Court has ruled that there are constitutional guarantees that apply to every person within our borders, including "aliens whose presence in this country is unlawful."

FIGURE 5–1: Percentage Changes in U.S. Ethnic Distribution

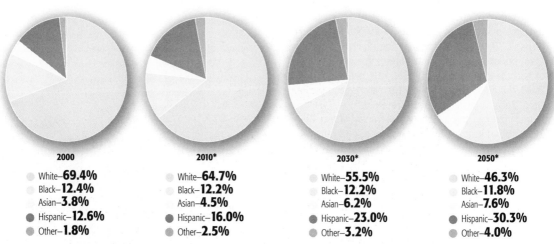

2000
- White–**69.4%**
- Black–**12.4%**
- Asian–**3.8%**
- Hispanic–**12.6%**
- Other–**1.8%**

2010*
- White–**64.7%**
- Black–**12.2%**
- Asian–**4.5%**
- Hispanic–**16.0%**
- Other–**2.5%**

2030*
- White–**55.5%**
- Black–**12.2%**
- Asian–**6.2%**
- Hispanic–**23.0%**
- Other–**3.2%**

2050*
- White–**46.3%**
- Black–**11.8%**
- Asian–**7.6%**
- Hispanic–**30.3%**
- Other–**4.0%**

*Data for 2010, 2030, and 2050 are projections. Numbers may not sum to 100% due to rounding.
Hispanics may be of any race. The chart categories *White, Black, Asian,* and *Other* are limited to non-Hispanics.
Other consists of the following non-Hispanic groups: *American Indian, Native Alaskan, Native Hawaiian, Other Pacific Islander,* and *Two or more races.*

Source: U.S. Bureau of the Census and authors' calculations.

the politics of Boom and Bust:
The Recession's Impact on Immigration

In recent years, a large number of unauthorized immigrants have entered the United States. The majority of these people, who are also called illegal immigrants or undocumented workers, came to the United States from Latin America. More than half are from Mexico. Most illegal immigrants come here to work.

How to respond to unauthorized immigration has been a controversial issue in American politics. Some politicians, including most Democrats, want to let illegal immigrants regularize their status and eventually become citizens. Most Republicans in Congress oppose this, although several prominent Republicans, such as former president George W. Bush and former presidential candidate John McCain, have supported such proposals. With the onset of the "Great Recession," however, immigration reform ceased to be one of the nation's priorities. Instead, many now ask: Can we afford to let immigrants compete for jobs in the United States when unemployment is high?

The (Temporary) End of Illegal Immigration

Undocumented workers are heavily concentrated in construction and in low-paying businesses such as agriculture, meatpacking plants, hotels, and restaurants. In 2008, employment in several of these industries was in a state of collapse. How did undocumented workers respond to unemployment? While many of these people were waiting out the recession, others simply went home.

Already in 2007, the return home of Mexicans from the United States was up by about 25 percent. The Pew Hispanic Center estimates that the unauthorized immigrant population in the United States, measured in March of each year, peaked in 2007 at 12.4 million. By March 2008, the figure had fallen to 11.9 million—and the latest Great Recession was just getting started.

According to the Mexican government, from August 2007 to August 2008, the combined legal *and* illegal outflow from Mexico to the United States fell from an annual rate of 455,000 to 204,000—and *legal* Mexican immigration has remained steady at about 175,000 per year. These figures suggest that by late 2008, the number of illegal immigrants headed north out of Mexico was a small fraction of what it had been one year earlier, and that flow was overwhelmed by the number of people returning south.

Both legal and illegal immigrants often send part of their earnings back to relatives in their home countries. In Mexico, these remittances are the second-largest source of foreign income, exceeded only by oil exports. From January 2008 to January 2009, however, the number of Mexican households receiving funds from relatives in the United States fell from 1.41 million to 1.16 million. This is one example of how the return of workers from the United States may place pressure on Mexico's fragile economic and political system, already stressed by a collapse in exports to the United States and by the horrific violence of domestic drug cartels.

U.S. Immigration Policy

Recent changes in American immigration policy have been inconsistent, driven more by domestic pressures than any overarching goal. For example, the economic stimulus bill passed in February 2009 banned companies that receive bailouts from hiring well-educated, high-tech foreign staff. At the same time, the bill failed to require that employers benefiting from the stimulus spending use the government's E-Verify program to check workers' immigration status. Leaving E-Verify optional makes it easier for employers to hire undocumented workers for low-wage positions. Senator Barbara Mikulski (D., Md.) even introduced legislation to triple the number of people admitted legally under a visa program for unskilled workers.

FOR CRITICAL ANALYSIS

Why might Congress be more willing to keep highly educated immigrants out of the workforce than persons with little or no training? Could it be that the Americans who might lose high-tech jobs to foreigners have more political clout than the working poor, who compete with unskilled immigrants? What effect are such policies likely to have on our international competitiveness?

▶ **Immigration law reform** has been controversial for years. These mostly Latino demonstrators in Los Angeles argue for reform. What are the arguments for and against legalizing the status of illegal immigrants? (AP Photo/Reed Saxon)

Immigrants who are not here legally may be deported. In 1903, however, the Supreme Court ruled that the government could not deport someone without a hearing that meets constitutional due process standards.[11] Today, most people facing deportation are entitled to a hearing before an immigration judge, to representation by a lawyer, and to the right to see the evidence presented against them. The government must prove that its grounds for deportation are valid.

Limits to the Rights of Deportees. Despite the language of the Fourteenth Amendment, the courts have often deferred to government assertions that noncitizens cannot make constitutional claims. The Supreme Court has stated, "In exercise of its broad power over naturalization and immigration, Congress may make rules as to aliens that would be unacceptable if applied to citizens."[12] Immigration and antiterrorism laws passed by Congress in 1996 were especially restrictive. As one example, the government was given the right to deport noncitizens in cases of alleged terrorism without any court review of the deportation order. In other words, with a simple allegation of terrorism that need not be proved, the government can suspend the Fourteenth Amendment deportation rights of noncitizens, even if they are in the country legally.

CIVIL RIGHTS: EXTENDING EQUAL PROTECTION

As noted earlier in this chapter, the Civil Rights Act of 1964 prohibited discrimination against any person on the basis of race, color, national origin, religion, or gender. The act also established the right to equal opportunity in employment. A basic problem remained, however: minority groups and women, because of past discrimination, often lacked the education and skills to compete effectively in the marketplace. In 1965, the federal government attempted to remedy this problem by implementing the concept of affirmative action. **Affirmative action** policies attempt to "level the playing field" by giving special preferences in educational admissions and employment decisions to groups that have been discriminated against in the past. These policies go beyond a strict interpretation of the equal protection clause of the Fourteenth Amendment. So do a number of other laws and programs established by the government during and since the 1960s.

Affirmative Action

In 1965, President Lyndon Johnson issued Executive Order 11246, which mandated affirmative action policies to remedy the effects of past discrimination. All government agencies, including those of state and local governments, were required to implement such policies. Additionally, affirmative action requirements were imposed on companies that sell goods or services to the federal government and on institutions that receive federal funds, such as universities. Affirmative action policies were also required whenever an employer had been ordered to develop such a plan by a court or by the Equal Employment Opportunity Commission because of evidence of past discrimination. Finally, labor unions that had been found to discriminate against women or minorities in the past were required to establish and follow affirmative action plans.

Affirmative Action
A policy in educational admissions or job hiring that gives special attention or compensatory treatment to traditionally disadvantaged groups in an effort to overcome present effects of past discrimination.

---

11. *Yamataya v. Fisher,* 189 U.S. 86 (1903).
12. *Demore v. Hyung Joon Kim,* 538 U.S. 510 (2003).

Reverse Discrimination
Discrimination against members of a majority group.

Affirmative action programs have been controversial because they allegedly result in discrimination against majority groups, such as white males (or discrimination against other minority groups that may not be given preferential treatment under a particular affirmative action program). At issue in the current debate over affirmative action programs is whether such programs, because of their discriminatory nature, violate the equal protection clause of the Fourteenth Amendment to the Constitution.

The *Bakke* Case

The first United States Supreme Court case addressing the constitutionality of affirmative action plans examined a program implemented by the University of California at Davis. Allan Bakke, a white student who had been turned down for medical school at the Davis campus, discovered that his academic record was better than those of some of the minority applicants who had been admitted to the program. He sued the University of California regents, alleging **reverse discrimination.** The UC-Davis Medical School had held sixteen places out of one hundred for educationally "disadvantaged students" each year, and the administrators at that campus admitted to using race as a criterion for admission for these particular minority slots.

In 1978, the Supreme Court handed down its decision in *Regents of the University of California v. Bakke.*[13] The Court did not rule against affirmative action programs. Rather, it held that Bakke had to be admitted to the UC-Davis Medical School because its admissions policy had used race as the sole criterion for the sixteen "minority" positions. Justice Lewis Powell, speaking for the Court, indicated that while race can be considered "as a factor" among others in admissions (and presumably hiring) decisions, race cannot be the sole factor. So affirmative action programs, but not specific quota systems, were upheld as constitutional.

Additional Limits on Affirmative Action

A number of cases decided during the 1980s and 1990s placed further limits on affirmative action programs. In a landmark decision in 1995, *Adarand Constructors, Inc. v. Peña,*[14] the United States Supreme Court held that any federal, state, or local affirmative action program that uses racial or ethnic classifications as the basis for making decisions is subject to "strict scrutiny" by the courts. Under a strict-scrutiny analysis, to be constitutional, a discriminatory law or action must be narrowly tailored to meet a *compelling* government interest. In effect, the Court's opinion in *Adarand* means that an affirmative action program cannot make use of quotas or preferences for unqualified persons. In addition, once the program has succeeded in achieving the purpose it was tailored to meet, the program must be changed or dropped.

In 2003, in two cases involving the University of Michigan, the Supreme Court indicated that limited affirmative action programs continued to be acceptable and that diversity was a legitimate goal. The Court struck down the affirmative action plan used for undergraduate admissions at the university, which automatically awarded a substantial number of points to applicants based on minority status. At the same time, it approved the admissions plan used by the law school, which took race into consideration as part of a complete examination of each applicant's background.[15]

---

13. 438 U.S. 265 (1978).
14. 515 U.S. 200 (1995).
15. *Gratz v. Bollinger,* 539 U.S. 244 (2003); and *Grutter v. Bollinger,* 539 U.S. 306 (2003).

The End of Affirmative Action?

Although in 2003 the United States Supreme Court upheld the admissions plan used by the University of Michigan Law School, a Michigan ballot initiative passed in 2006 prohibited affirmative action programs in all public universities and for state government positions. In addition to Michigan, other states, including California, Florida, Nebraska, and Washington, have banned all state-sponsored affirmative action programs. In 2008, however, Colorado voters rejected such a ban.

In 2007, the United States Supreme Court heard a case involving voluntary integration plans in school districts in Seattle, Washington, and in Louisville, Kentucky. The schools' racial-integration guidelines permitted race to be a deciding factor if, say, two students sought to be admitted to the school and there was space for only one. The schools' policies were challenged by parents of students, most of them white, who were denied admission because of their race. In a close (five-to-four) decision, the Court ruled that the schools' policies violated the Constitution's equal protection clause. (The Court did not, however, go so far as to invalidate the use of race as a factor in university admissions policies.)[16]

THE RIGHTS AND STATUS OF GAY MALES AND LESBIANS

On June 27, 1969, patrons of the Stonewall Inn, a New York City bar popular with gay men and lesbians, responded to a police raid by throwing beer cans and bottles because they were angry at what they felt was unrelenting police harassment. In the ensuing riot, which lasted two nights, hundreds of gay men and lesbians fought with police. Before Stonewall, the stigma attached to homosexuality and the resulting fear of exposure had tended to keep most gay men and lesbians quiescent. In the months immediately after Stonewall, however, "gay power" graffiti began to appear in New York City. The Gay Liberation Front and the Gay Activist Alliance were formed, and similar groups sprang up in other parts of the country. Thus, Stonewall has been called "the shot heard round the homosexual world."

Growth in the Gay Male and Lesbian Rights Movement

The Stonewall incident marked the beginning of the movement for gay and lesbian rights. Since then, gay men and lesbians have formed thousands of organizations to exert pressure on legislatures, the media, schools, churches, and other organizations to recognize their right to equal treatment.

To a great extent, lesbian and gay groups have succeeded in changing public opinion—and state and local laws that pertain to their status and rights. Nevertheless, they continue to struggle against age-old biases against homosexuality, often rooted in deeply held religious beliefs, and the rights of gay men and lesbians remain an extremely divisive issue in American society.

---

16. *Parents Involved in Community Schools v. Seattle School District No. 1*, 551 U.S. 701 (2007).

State and Local Laws Targeting Gay Men and Lesbians

Before the Stonewall incident, forty-nine states had sodomy laws that made various kinds of sexual acts, including homosexual acts, illegal (Illinois, which had repealed its sodomy law in 1962, was the only exception). During the 1970s and 1980s, more than half of these laws were either repealed or struck down by the courts.

The trend toward repealing state antigay laws was suspended in 1986 with the Supreme Court's decision in *Bowers v. Hardwick*.[17] In that case, the Court upheld, by a five-to-four vote, a Georgia law that made homosexual conduct between two adults a crime. But in 2003, the Court reversed its earlier position on sodomy with its decision in *Lawrence v. Texas*.[18] In this case, the Court held that laws against sodomy violate the due process clause of the Fourteenth Amendment. The Court stated: "The liberty protected by the Constitution allows homosexual persons the right to choose to enter upon relationships in the confines of their homes and their own private lives and still retain their dignity as free persons." The result of *Lawrence v. Texas* was to invalidate all remaining sodomy laws throughout the country.

Today, twenty states, the District of Columbia, and more than 140 cities and counties have enacted laws protecting lesbians and gay men from discrimination in employment. Many of these laws also ban discrimination in housing, in public accommodation, and in other contexts. In contrast, Colorado adopted a constitutional amendment in 1992 to invalidate all state and local laws protecting homosexuals from discrimination. Ultimately, however, the Supreme Court, in *Romer v. Evans*,[19] ruled against the amendment because it violated the equal protection clause of the U.S. Constitution by denying to homosexuals in Colorado—but to no other Colorado residents—"the right to seek specific protection of the law." Several laws at the national level have also been changed over the past two decades. Among other things, the government has lifted a ban on hiring gay men and lesbians and voided a 1952 law prohibiting gay men and lesbians from immigrating to the United States. The Obama administration has stated that it intends to allow gay men and lesbians to serve openly in the armed forces, and it is preparing plans to implement this policy.

Same-Sex Marriage

Perhaps one of the hottest political issues concerning the rights of gay and lesbian couples is whether they should be allowed to marry, just as heterosexual couples are. Controversy over this issue flared up in 1993 when the Hawaii Supreme Court ruled that denying marriage licenses to gay couples might violate the equal protection clause of the Hawaii constitution.[20] In response, the U.S. Congress passed the Defense of Marriage Act of 1996, which bans federal recognition of lesbian and gay couples and allows state governments to ignore same-sex marriages performed in other states. Ironically, the Hawaii court decision that gave rise to these concerns has largely come to naught. In 1998, residents in that state voted for a state constitutional

---

17. 478 U.S. 186 (1986).
18. 539 U.S. 558 (2003).
19. 517 U.S. 620 (1996).
20. *Baehr v. Lewin*, 852 P.2d 44 (Hawaii 1993).

amendment that allows the Hawaii legislature to ban same-sex marriage. (Chapter 3's *At Issue* feature discussed the Defense of Marriage Act in greater depth—see page 52.)

The controversy over gay marriage was further fueled by developments in the state of Vermont. In 1999, the Vermont Supreme Court ruled that gay couples are entitled to the same benefits of marriage as opposite-sex couples.[21] Subsequently, in April 2000, the Vermont legislature passed a law permitting gay and lesbian couples to form "civil unions." The law entitled partners forming civil unions to receive some three hundred state benefits available to married couples, including the rights to inherit a partner's property and to decide on medical treatment for an incapacitated partner. It did not, however, entitle those partners to receive any benefits allowed to married couples under federal law, such as spousal Social Security benefits.

Massachusetts was the first state to recognize gay marriage. In November 2003, the Massachusetts Supreme Judicial Court ruled that same-sex couples have a right to civil marriage under the Massachusetts state constitution.[22] The court also ruled that civil unions would not suffice. In 2005, the Massachusetts legislature voted down a proposed ballot initiative that would have amended the state constitution to explicitly state that marriage could only be between one man and one woman (but would have extended civil union status to same-sex couples).

In 2008, the Connecticut Supreme Court legalized same-sex marriage in that state, and New York, which does not perform same-sex marriages, began recognizing such marriages when they were performed in other states. Also in 2008, the California state legislature attempted to legalize gay marriage, but Governor Arnold Schwarzenegger vetoed the bill. Later that year, the California Supreme Court legalized same-sex marriage, in effect overruling the governor. The court's ruling, however, was overturned by a state constitutional amendment banning the marriages (Proposition 8) that voters approved in the November 2008 elections.

In 2009, the Iowa Supreme Court overturned a law against same-sex marriage in that state. The legislature of Vermont legalized same-sex marriage in 2009, overriding a veto by the governor. Shortly thereafter, Maine and New Hampshire legalized same-sex marriage, also by legislative action.

▲ **In most states,** there is no legally sanctioned way that same-sex couples can marry. Those in favor of such marriages gather outside City Hall in San Francisco to express their views. How have some states precluded the legality of same-sex marriages? (AP Photo/Marcio Jose Sanchez)

---

21. *Baker v. Vermont,* 744 A.2d 864 (Vt. 1999).
22. *Goodridge v. Department of Public Health,* 798 N.E.2d 941 (Mass. 2003).

making a difference

DEALING WITH DISCRIMINATION

Anyone applying for a job may be subjected to a variety of potentially discriminatory practices. There may be tests, some of which could have a discriminatory effect. At both the state and federal levels, the government continues to examine the fairness and validity of criteria used in job-applicant screening, and as a result, there are ways of addressing the problem of discrimination.

Why Should You Care? Some people may think that discrimination is only a problem for members of racial or ethnic minorities. Actually, almost anyone can be affected. Consider that in some instances, white men have actually experienced "reverse discrimination"—and have obtained redress for it. Also, discrimination against women is common, and women constitute half the population. Even if you are male, you probably have female friends and relatives whose well-being is of interest to you. Therefore, the knowledge of how to proceed when you suspect discrimination is another useful tool to have when living in the modern world.

What Can You Do? If you believe that you have been discriminated against by a potential employer, consider the following steps:

1. Evaluate your own capabilities, and determine if you are truly qualified for the position.
2. Analyze the reasons why you were turned down. Would others agree with you that you have been the object of discrimination, or would they uphold the employer's claim?

3. If you still believe that you have been treated unfairly, you have recourse to several agencies and services.

You should first speak to the personnel director of the company and explain politely that you believe you have not been evaluated adequately. If asked, explain your concerns clearly. If necessary, go into explicit detail, and indicate that you may have been discriminated against.

If a second evaluation is not forthcoming, contact your local state employment agency. If you still do not obtain adequate help, contact one or more of the following state agencies, usually listed in your telephone directory under "State Government."

1. If a government entity is involved, a state ombudsperson or citizen aide may be available to mediate.
2. You can contact the state civil rights commission, which at least will give you advice even if it does not wish to take up your case.
3. The state attorney general's office normally has a division dealing with discrimination and civil rights.
4. There may be a special commission or department specifically set up to help people in your position, such as a women's status commission or a commission on Hispanics or Asian Americans. If so, contact this commission.

Finally, at the national level, you can contact:

American Civil Liberties Union
125 Broad St.
New York, NY 10004-2400
212-549-2500
www.aclu.org

You can also contact the following organization:

Equal Employment Opportunity Commission
131 M St. N.E.
Washington, DC 20507
202-663-4900
www.eeoc.gov

▲ **The American Civil Liberties Union (ACLU)** often supports those involved with immigration problems. This young man was held for 15 days at a border immigration center in spite of the fact that he is a U.S. citizen. ACLU lawyers proved to federal authorities that he was a citizen by presenting his birth certificate. (AP Photo/Reed Saxon)

keyterms

affirmative action 107
busing 96
civil disobedience 97
civil rights 91
de facto segregation 96
de jure segregation 96

feminism 101
fertility rate 104
gender
  discrimination 102
grandfather clause 94
Hispanic 104

Latino 104
literacy test 94
poll tax 94
reverse
  discrimination 108

separate-but-equal
  doctrine 94
sexual harassment 103
suffrage 100
white primary 94

chaptersummary

1 The civil rights movement started with the struggle by African Americans for equality. Before the Civil War, most African Americans were slaves, and slavery was protected by the Constitution and the Supreme Court. Constitutional amendments after the Civil War legally ended slavery, and African Americans gained citizenship, the right to vote, and other rights through legislation. This legal protection was largely a dead letter by the 1880s, however, and politically and socially African American inequality continued.

2 Legal segregation was declared unconstitutional by the Supreme Court in *Brown v. Board of Education of Topeka* (1954), in which the Court stated that separation implied inferiority. In *Brown v. Board of Education* (1955), the Supreme Court ordered federal courts to ensure that public schools were desegregated "with all deliberate speed." Also in 1955, the modern civil rights movement began with a boycott of segregated public transportation in Montgomery, Alabama. Of particular impact was the Civil Rights Act of 1964. The act bans discrimination in employment and public accommodations on the basis of race, color, religion, gender, or national origin. The act created the Equal Employment Opportunity Commission to administer the legislation's provisions.

3 The Voting Rights Act of 1965 outlawed discriminatory voter-registration tests and authorized federal registration of persons and federally administered procedures in any state or political subdivision evidencing electoral discrimination or low registration rates. The Voting Rights Act and other protective legislation passed during and since the 1960s apply not only to African

Americans but to other ethnic groups as well. Minorities have been increasingly represented in national and state politics, although they have yet to gain representation proportionate to their numbers in the U.S. population.

4 In the early history of the United States, women by and large had no political rights. After the first women's rights convention in 1848, the women's movement gained momentum. Not until 1920, when the Nineteenth Amendment was ratified, did women finally obtain the right to vote in all states. The National Organization for Women was formed in 1966 to bring about complete equality for women in all walks of life. Efforts to secure the ratification of the Equal Rights Amendment failed, but the women's movement was successful in obtaining new laws, changes in social customs, and increased political representation of women.

5 Although women have found it difficult to gain positions of political leadership, their numbers in Congress and in other government bodies increased significantly in the 1990s and early 2000s. Women continue to struggle against gender discrimination in employment. Federal government efforts to eliminate gender discrimination in the workplace include Title VII of the Civil Rights Act of 1964, which prohibits, among other things, gender-based discrimination, including sexual harassment on the job. Wage discrimination also continues to be a problem for women.

6 Today, most immigrants come from Latin America and Asia. The Bureau of the Census refers to immigrants and citizens who can claim a heritage from a Spanish-speaking country as *Hispanics,* although many Hispanics prefer the term *Latino.* High levels of immigration combined with high fertility rates among Hispanic Americans mean that the proportion of Hispanics in the U.S. population will grow in future years. By 2050, non-Hispanic whites will be a minority of the total population. Hispanic American citizens receive many of the same protections against discrimination as African Americans. Noncitizen immigrants, however, have very few rights. The Fourteenth Amendment to the Constitution states that all *persons,* as opposed to citizens, shall enjoy due process of law. The Supreme Court, however, has allowed the government to suspend the due process rights of immigrants who face deportation on suspicion of terrorism.

7   Affirmative action programs have been controversial because they can lead to reverse discrimination against majority groups or even other minority groups. Supreme Court decisions have limited affirmative action programs, and voters in several states have passed initiatives banning state-sponsored affirmative action. Two

Supreme Court decisions in cases brought against the University of Michigan confirmed the principle that limited affirmative action programs are constitutional.

8   Gay and lesbian rights groups became commonplace after 1969 and now number in the thousands. These groups work to promote laws protecting gay men and lesbians from discrimination and to repeal antigay laws. After 1969, sodomy laws that criminalized specific sexual practices were repealed or struck down by the courts in more than half of the forty-nine states that had such laws, and in 2003, a Supreme Court decision effectively invalidated all remaining sodomy laws nationwide. Twenty states and more than 140 cities and counties now have laws prohibiting discrimination based on sexual orientation. Gay men and lesbians are no longer barred from federal employment or from immigrating to this country. The issue of same-sex marriage has fueled extensive controversy.

QUESTIONS FOR
discussionandanalysis

1   Not all African Americans agreed with the philosophy of nonviolence espoused by Dr. Martin Luther King, Jr. Advocates of Black Power called for a more militant approach. Can militancy make a movement more effective (possibly by making a more moderate approach seem like a reasonable compromise), or is it typically counterproductive? Either way, why?

2   Women in the military are currently barred from assignments that are likely to place them in active combat. (Of course, the nature of war is such that support units sometimes find themselves in combat, regardless of assignment.) Such barriers can keep female officers from advancing to the highest levels within the armed services. Are these barriers appropriate? Why or why not?

3   While polls of military personnel suggest that rank-and-file soldiers are more accepting of gay

men and lesbians than in years past, the current policy, known as "don't ask, don't tell," continues to result in the discharge of large numbers of military personnel on the basis of their sexual orientation. Is the current policy appropriate, or should it be liberalized? Either way, why? If a different policy were adopted, what should it be?

4   The prevention of terrorist acts committed by adherents of radical Islamism is a major policy objective today. Can we defend ourselves against such acts without abridging the civil rights and liberties of American Muslims and immigrants from predominantly Muslim countries? What measures that might be undertaken by the authorities are legitimate, and which are not?

helpful online **Resources**

CONNECTING TO AMERICAN GOVERNMENT AND POLITICS

You can find information on issues facing African Americans at the Web site of the National Association for the Advancement of Colored People:

www.naacp.org

The National Organization for Women offers information on the status of women's rights at:

www.now.org

The Human Rights Campaign, the nation's largest gay and lesbian political organization, provides information at:

www.hrc.org

a special WebSite

FOR YOUR TEXT

Go to this book's special Web site at academic.cengage.com/polisci/Schmidt/Brief6e. Choose "For Students." Then click on Chapter 5, where you will find an online quiz and other helpful study aids. If your professor is using CengageNOW: *American Government and Politics Today, Brief Edition,* log in and go to Chapter 5 for additional online study aids.

6

Public Opinion, Political Socialization, and the Media

These photographers work in Washington, D.C. Here they are photographing Treasury secretary Timothy Geithner as he testifies before a House Financial Services Committee hearing. (AP Photo/Susan Walsh)

In a democracy, the ability of the people to freely express their opinions is fundamental. Americans can express their opinions in many ways. They can write letters to newspapers. They can share their ideas in online forums. They can organize politically. They can vote. They can respond to opinion polls.

President Barack Obama and his administration found out how important public opinion can be in March 2009, when the giant insurance corporation AIG announced bonuses for executives in its financial unit amounting to as much as $450 million. Only days before, AIG admitted that it lost $61.7 billion in the final three months of 2008, the largest corporate loss for a three-month period in world history. The losses were due almost entirely to bad judgment by AIG's financial unit, the very same group receiving $450 million in bonuses. In 2008 and 2009, the federal government pumped $185 billion into AIG out of a fear that its collapse would bring down the rest of the financial system. The obvious conclusion: AIG was using taxpayer funds to reward the very people who had caused the catastrophe.

The resulting public outrage was severe. Senator Chuck Grassley (R., Iowa) actually suggested that AIG executives consider Japanese-style ritual suicide. The House quickly passed a measure to tax the bonuses out of existence (which the Senate quietly ignored). In the wake of this scandal, it was almost impossible for the Obama administration to get any more bailouts for financial institutions through Congress. Treasury secretary Timothy Geithner was left scrambling to find ways to prop up troubled banks that did not involve congressional action.

There is no doubt that public opinion can be powerful. The extent to which public opinion affects policymaking is not always so clear, however. For example, suppose that public opinion strongly supports a certain policy. If political leaders adopt that position, is it because they are responding to public opinion or because they share the public's beliefs? Also, political leaders themselves can shape public opinion to a degree.

DEFINING PUBLIC OPINION

There is no single public opinion, because there are many different "publics." In a nation of more than 300 million people, there may be innumerable gradations of opinion on an issue. What we do is describe the distribution of opinions about a particular question. Thus, we define **public opinion** as the aggregate of individual attitudes or beliefs shared by some portion of the adult population.

Typically, public opinion is distributed among several different positions, and the distribution of opinion can tell us how divided the public is on an issue and whether compromise is possible. When polls show that a large proportion of the American public appears to express the same view on an issue, we say that a **consensus** exists, at least at the moment the poll was taken. Figure 6–1 shows a pattern of opinion that might be called consensual. Issues on which the public holds widely differing attitudes result in **divided opinion** (see Figure 6–2). Sometimes, a poll shows a distribution of

Public Opinion
The aggregate of individual attitudes or beliefs shared by some portion of the adult population.

Consensus
General agreement among the citizenry on an issue.

Divided Opinion
Public opinion that is polarized between two quite different positions.

FIGURE 6–1: Consensus Opinion

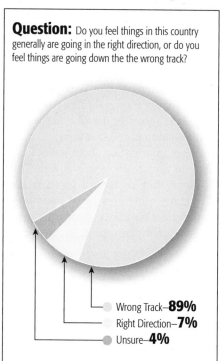

Question: Do you feel things in this country generally are going in the right direction, or do you feel things are going down the the wrong track?

Wrong Track–**89%**
Right Direction–**7%**
Unsure–**4%**

Source: CBS News/*New York Times* Poll, October 10–13, 2008.

FIGURE 6–2: Divided Opinion

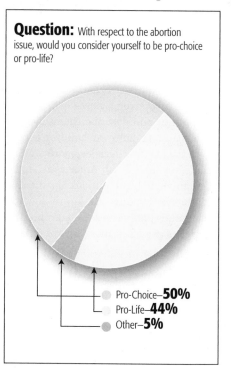

Question: With respect to the abortion issue, would you consider yourself to be pro-choice or pro-life?

Pro-Choice–**50%**
Pro-Life–**44%**
Other–**5%**

Source: The Gallup Poll, May 8–11, 2008.

Political Socialization
The process by which people acquire political beliefs and values.

opinion indicating that most Americans either have no information about the issue or are not interested enough in the issue to formulate a position. Politicians may believe that the lack of public knowledge of an issue gives them more room to maneuver, or they may be wary of taking any action for fear that opinion will crystallize after a crisis.

An interesting question arises as to when *private* opinion becomes *public* opinion. Everyone probably has a private opinion about the competence of the president, as well as private opinions about more personal concerns, such as the state of a neighbor's lawn. We say that private opinion becomes public opinion when the opinion is publicly expressed and concerns public issues. When someone's private opinion becomes so strong that the individual is willing to go to the polls to vote for or against a candidate or an issue—or is willing to participate in a demonstration, discuss the issue at work, speak out online, or participate in the political process in any one of a dozen other ways—then the opinion becomes public opinion.

HOW PUBLIC OPINION IS FORMED: POLITICAL SOCIALIZATION

Most Americans are willing to express opinions on political issues when asked. How do people acquire these opinions and attitudes? Typically, views that are expressed as political opinions are acquired through the process of **political socialization.** By this we mean that people acquire their political beliefs and values, often including their party identification, through relationships with their families, friends, and co-workers.

Models of Political Socialization

The most important early sources of political socialization are the family and the schools. Individuals' basic political orientations are formed in the family if family members hold strong views. When the adults in a family view politics as relatively unimportant and describe themselves as independent voters or disaffected from the political system, however, children receive very little political socialization.

In the last few decades, more and more sources of information about politics have become available to all Americans, and especially to young people on the Web. Thus, although their basic outlook on the political system may be formed by early family influences, young people are now exposed to many other sources of information about issues and values. This greater access to information may explain why young Americans are often more liberal than their parents on certain social issues such as gay rights.

The Family and the Social Environment

Not only do our parents' political beliefs, values, and actions affect our opinions, but the family also links us to other factors that affect opinion, such as race, social class, educational environment, and religious beliefs. How do parents transmit their political values to their offspring?

Studies suggest that the influence of parents is due to two factors: communication and receptivity. Parents communicate their feelings and preferences to children constantly. Because children have such a strong need for parental approval, they are very receptive to their parents' views.

Children are less likely to influence their parents, because parents expect deference from their children.[1] Nevertheless, other studies show that if children are exposed to political ideas at school and in the media, they will share these ideas with their parents, giving the parents what some scholars call a "second chance" at political socialization.[2]

Education as a Source of Political Socialization.
From the early days of the republic, schools were perceived to be important transmitters of political information and attitudes. Children in the primary grades learn about their country mostly in patriotic ways. They learn about the Pilgrims, the flag, and some of the nation's presidents. They also learn to celebrate national holidays. In the middle grades, children learn additional historical facts and come to understand the structure of government and the functions of the president, judges, and Congress. By high school, students have a more complex understanding of the political system, may identify with a political party, and may take positions on issues.

Generally, education is closely linked to political participation. The more education a person receives, the more likely it is that the person will be interested in politics, be confident in his or her ability to understand political issues, and be an active participant in the political process.

Peers and Peer Group Influence.
Once a child enters school, the child's friends become an important influence on behavior and attitudes. For children and for adults, friendships and associations in **peer groups** affect political attitudes. We must, however, separate the effects of peer group pressure on opinions and attitudes in general from the effects of peer group pressure on political opinions. For the most part, associations among peers are nonpolitical. Political attitudes are more likely to be shaped by peer groups when the peer groups are involved directly in political activities.

Individuals who join an interest group based on ethnic identity may find, for example, a common political bond through working for the group's civil liberties and rights. African American activist groups may consist of individuals who join together to support government programs that will aid the African American population. Members of a labor union may be strongly influenced to support certain pro-labor candidates.

Opinion Leaders' Influence.
We are all influenced by those with whom we are closely associated or whom we hold in high regard—friends at school, family members and other relatives, and teachers. In a sense, these people are **opinion leaders**, but on an *informal* level; that is, their influence on our political views is not necessarily intentional or deliberate. We are also influenced by *formal* opinion leaders, such as presidents, lobbyists, congresspersons, news commentators, and religious leaders, who have as part of their jobs the task of swaying people's views.

Peer Group
A group consisting of members sharing common social characteristics. Such groups play an important part in the socialization process, helping to shape attitudes and beliefs.

Opinion Leader
One who is able to influence the opinions of others because of position, expertise, or personality.

---

1. Barbara A. Bardes and Robert W. Oldendick, *Public Opinion: Measuring the American Mind,* 3d ed. (Belmont, Calif.: Wadsworth Publishing Co., 2007), p. 73.
2. See Michael McDevitt and Steven H. Chaffee, "Second Chance Political Socialization: 'Trickle-up' Effects of Children on Parents," in Thomas J. Johnson *et al.,* eds., *Engaging the Public: How Government and the Media Can Reinvigorate American Democracy* (Lanham, Md.: Rowman & Littlefield Publishers, 1998), pp. 57–66.

The Impact of the Media

Clearly, the **media**—newspapers, television, radio, and Internet sources—strongly influence public opinion. This is because the media inform the public about the issues and events of our times and thus have an **agenda-setting** effect. In other words, to borrow from Bernard Cohen's classic statement about the media and public opinion, the media may not be successful in telling people what to think, but they are "stunningly successful in telling their audience what to think about."[3]

Today, many contend that the media's influence on public opinion has grown to equal that of the family. For example, in her analysis of the role played by the media in American politics,[4] media scholar Doris A. Graber points out

▲ **As a presidential candidate, Barack Obama** (shown with his wife) invited Oprah Winfrey to a rally very early in his campaign. Why would he ask a TV personality to join him? (AP Photo/Kristie Bull/Graylock.com)

that high school students, when asked where they obtain the information on which they base their views, mention the mass media far more than they mention their families, friends, and teachers. This trend, combined with the increasing popularity of such information sources as talk shows and the Internet, may significantly alter the nature of the media's influence on public debate in the future. The media's influence will be discussed in more detail later in this chapter.

The Influence of Political Events

It is somewhat surprising that a person's chronological age has little consistent effect on political beliefs. In some years, young people have tended to favor the Republicans, and in other years they have tended to favor the Democrats. It is true that young adults are somewhat more liberal than older people on such issues as same-sex marriage, civil disobedience, and racial and gender equality. Nevertheless, a more important factor than a person's age is the impact of momentous political events that shape the political attitudes of an entire generation. When events produce such a long-lasting result, we refer to it as a **generational effect** (also called the *cohort effect*).

Voters who grew up in the 1930s during the Great Depression were likely to form lifelong attachments to the Democratic Party, the party of Franklin D. Roosevelt. In the 1960s and 1970s, the war in Vietnam, the **Watergate break-in,** and the subsequent presidential cover-up fostered widespread cynicism toward government. There

Media
The channels of mass communication.

Agenda Setting
Determining which public-policy questions will be debated or considered.

Generational Effect
A long-lasting effect of the events of a particular time on the political opinions of those who came of political age at that time.

Watergate Break-In
The 1972 illegal entry into the Democratic National Committee offices by participants in President Richard Nixon's reelection campaign.

3. *The Press and Foreign Policy* (Princeton, N.J.: Princeton University Press, 1963), p. 81.
4. Doris A. Graber, *Mass Media and American Politics,* 7th ed. (Chicago: University of Chicago Press, 2005).

is evidence that the years of economic prosperity under President Ronald Reagan during the 1980s led many young people to identify with the Republican Party. The very high levels of support that younger voters gave to Barack Obama during his presidential campaign may be good news for the Democratic Party in years to come.

The Influence of Economic Status

Family income is a strong predictor of economic liberalism or conservatism. Those with low incomes tend to favor government action to benefit the poor or to promote economic equality. Those with high incomes tend to oppose government intervention in the economy or to support it only when it benefits business. The rich often tend toward the right; the poor often tend toward the left.

If we examine cultural as well as economic issues, however, the four-cornered ideological grid discussed in Chapter 1 becomes important. It happens that upper-class voters are more likely to endorse cultural liberalism, and lower-class individuals are more likely to favor cultural conservatism. Support for the right to have an abortion, for example, rises with income. It follows that libertarians—those who oppose government action on both economic and social issues—are concentrated among the wealthier members of the population. (Libertarians constitute the upper-right-hand corner of the grid in Figure 1–1 on page 15 in Chapter 1.) Those who favor government action both to promote traditional moral values and to promote economic equality—economic liberals, cultural conservatives—are concentrated among groups that are less well off. (This group fills up the lower-left-hand corner of the grid.)

▼ **What impact** does religion have on political attitudes? (Ariel Skelley/Corbis)

Religious Influence: Denomination

Traditionally, scholars have examined the impact of religion on political attitudes by dividing the population into such categories as Protestant, Catholic, and Jewish. In recent decades, however, such a breakdown has become less valuable as a means of predicting someone's political preferences. It is true that, as they were in the past, Jewish voters are notably more liberal than members of other groups on both economic and cultural issues. Persons reporting no religion are very liberal on social issues but have mixed economic views. Protestants and Catholics, however, have grown closer to each other politically in recent years. This represents something of a change—in the late 1800s and early 1900s, northern Protestants were distinctly more likely to vote Republican, and northern Catholics were more likely to vote Democratic. Even today, in a few parts of the country, Protestants and Catholics tend to line up against each other when choosing a political party.

Nevertheless, two factors do turn out to be major predictors of political attitudes among members of the various Christian denominations. One is the degree of religious commitment, as measured by such actions as regular churchgoing. The other is the degree to which the voter adheres to religious

Gender Gap
The difference between
the percentage of women
who vote for a particular
candidate and the
percentage of men who
vote for the candidate.

Opinion Poll
A method of
systematically
questioning a small,
selected sample of
respondents who are
deemed representative of
the total population.

beliefs that (depending on the denomination) can be called conservative, evangelical, or fundamentalist. High scores on either factor are associated with cultural conservatism on political issues—that is, with beliefs that place a high value on social order. (See Chapter 1 for a discussion of the contrasting values of order and liberty.) An important exception to these trends is that African Americans of all religious backgrounds are highly likely to support liberal candidates.

The Gender Gap

Until the 1980s, there was little evidence that men's and women's political attitudes were very different. Following the election of Ronald Reagan in 1980, however, scholars began to detect a **gender gap.** A May 1983 Gallup poll revealed that men were more likely than women to approve of Reagan's job performance. The gender gap has reappeared in subsequent elections, with women being more likely than men to support Democratic candidates. In the 2000 presidential elections, 54 percent of women voted for Democrat Al Gore, compared with 42 percent of men. The gender gap closed somewhat in 2004, when only 51 percent of women voted for Democrat John F. Kerry, as opposed to 44 percent of men. The gap stayed at about 7 percentage points in 2008, when 56 percent of women voted for Democrat Barack Obama, compared with 49 percent of men. (Due to third-party candidates, Obama's 49 percent was still enough to carry the male vote.)

Women's attitudes also appear to differ from those of their male counterparts on a range of issues other than presidential preferences. They are much more likely than men to oppose capital punishment and the use of force abroad. Studies also have shown that women are more concerned about risks to the environment, more supportive of social welfare, and more in agreement with extending civil rights to gay men and lesbians than are men. In contrast, women were also more concerned than men about the security issues raised by the events of 9/11. This last fact may have pushed women in a more conservative direction, at least for a time.

Geographic Region

Finally, where you live can influence your political attitudes. In one way, regional differences may be less important today than in recent years. Although Barack Obama failed to carry the South, which has supported Republican presidential candidates for decades, he was still able to carry the southern states of Florida, North Carolina, and Virginia, and he was competitive in other southern states as well.

There is a tendency today, at least in national elections, for the South, the Great Plains, and several of the the Rocky Mountain states to favor the Republicans and for the West Coast and the Northeast to favor the Democrats. Perhaps more important than region is residence—urban, suburban, or rural. People in large cities tend to be liberal and Democratic. Those who live in smaller communities tend to be conservative and Republican.

MEASURING PUBLIC OPINION

In a democracy, people express their opinions in a variety of ways, as mentioned in this chapter's introduction. One of the most common means of gathering and measuring public opinion on specific issues is, of course, through the use of **opinion polls.**

The History of Opinion Polls

During the 1800s, certain American newspapers and magazines spiced up their political coverage by conducting face-to-face polls or mail surveys of their readers' opinions. In the early twentieth century, the magazine *Literary Digest* further developed the technique of opinion polling by mailing large numbers of questionnaires to individuals, many of whom were its own subscribers, to determine their political opinions. From 1916 to 1936, more than 70 percent of the magazine's election predictions were accurate. In 1936, however, the magazine predicted that Republican Alfred Landon would defeat Democrat Franklin D. Roosevelt in the presidential race. Landon ultimately won in only two states. A major problem was that in 1936, at the peak of the Great Depression, the *Digest*'s subscribers were considerably wealthier than the average American. In other words, they did not accurately represent all of the voters in the U.S. population.

Several newcomers to the public opinion poll industry accurately predicted Roosevelt's landslide victory. These newcomers are still active in the poll-taking industry today: the Gallup poll of George Gallup and the Roper poll, founded by Elmo Roper. Gallup and Roper, along with Archibald Crossley, developed the modern polling techniques of market research. Using personal interviews with small samples of selected voters (fewer than two thousand), they showed that they could predict with relative accuracy the behavior of the total voting population.

Sampling Techniques

How can interviewing fewer than two thousand voters tell us what tens of millions of voters will do? Clearly, it is necessary that the sample of individuals be representative of all voters in the population.

The most important principle in sampling, or poll taking, is randomness. Every person should have a known chance, and especially an *equal chance,* of being sampled. If sampling follows this principle, then a small sample should be representative of the whole group, both in demographic characteristics (age, religion, race, region, and the like) and in opinions. The ideal way to sample the voting population of the United States would be to put all voter names into a jar—or a computer hard drive—and randomly sample, say, two thousand of them. Because this is too costly and inefficient, pollsters have developed other ways to obtain good samples. One technique is simply to choose a random selection of telephone numbers and interview the respective households. This technique produces a relatively accurate sample at a low cost.

To ensure that the random samples include respondents from relevant segments of the population—rural, urban, northeastern, southern, and the like—most survey organizations randomly choose, say, urban areas that they will consider as representative of all urban areas. Then they randomly select their respondents within those areas. A generally less accurate technique is known as *quota sampling*. Here, survey researchers decide how many persons of certain types they need in the survey—such as minorities, women, or farmers—and then send out interviewers to find the necessary number of these types. Not only is this method often less accurate, but it may also be biased if, say, the interviewer refuses to go into certain neighborhoods or will not interview after dark.

Generally, the national survey organizations take great care to select their samples randomly, because their reputations rest on the accuracy of their results. The

Sampling Error
The difference between a sample result and the true result if the entire population had been interviewed.

Gallup and Roper polls usually interview about 1,500 individuals, and their results have a very high probability of being correct—within a margin of 3 percentage points.

Problems with Polls

Public opinion polls are snapshots of the opinions and preferences of the people at a specific moment in time and as expressed in response to a specific question. Given that definition, it is fairly easy to understand situations in which the polls are wrong. For example, opinion polls leading up to the 1980 presidential elections showed President Jimmy Carter defeating challenger Ronald Reagan. Only a few analysts noted the large number of "undecided" respondents a week before the election. Those voters shifted massively to Reagan at the last minute, and Reagan won the election. The famous photo of Harry Truman showing the front page that declared his defeat in the 1948 presidential elections is another tribute to the weakness of polling. Again, the poll that predicted his defeat was taken more than a week before Election Day.

Sampling Errors. Polls may also report erroneous results because the pool of respondents was not chosen in a scientific manner. **Sampling error** is the difference between the sample result and the true result if the entire population had been interviewed. Sampling error can generally be controlled by taking a large enough random sample, although the cost of doing so may be prohibitive. Other forms of sampling bias are possible. A sample would be biased, for example, if the poll interviewed people by telephone and did not correct for the fact that more women than men answer the telephone and that some populations (college students and very poor individuals, for example) cannot be found so easily by telephone.

Poll Questions. It makes sense to expect that the results of a poll will reflect the questions that are asked. Depending on what question is asked, voters could be said either to support a particular proposal or to oppose it. One of the problems with many polls is the yes/no answer format. For example, suppose that a poll question asks, "Do you favor the war in Iraq?" A respondent who has a complicated attitude toward the war, as many people do, has no way of indicating this view because "yes" and "no" are the only possible answers.

▼ **Harry Truman** won the presidential election in 1948 despite the prediction of all opinion polls that he would lose. Why were the polls so wrong? (AP Photo/Byron Rollins)

How a question is phrased can change the polling outcome dramatically. The Roper polling organization once asked a double-negative question that was very hard to understand: "Does it seem possible or does it seem impossible to you that the Nazi extermination of the Jews never happened?" The survey results showed that 20 percent of Americans seemed to doubt that the Holocaust ever occurred. When the Roper organization rephrased the question more clearly, the percentage of doubters dropped to less than 1 percent. Polling outcomes can also be affected if the participants do not fully grasp the meaning of various terms used in the questions. A *trillion,* for example, is a hard quantity for most people to grasp. We provide help in this chapter's feature *The Politics of Boom and Bust: Just What Is a Trillion Dollars, Anyway?* on the next page.

Respondents' answers are also influenced by the order in which questions are asked, by the possible answers from which the respondents are allowed to choose, and, in some cases, by their interactions with the interviewer. To a certain extent, people try to please the interviewer.

Unscientific and Fraudulent Polls. A perennial issue is the promotion of surveys that are unscientific or even fraudulent. All too often, a magazine or Web site asks its readers to respond to a question—and then publishes the answers as if they were based on a scientifically chosen random sample. Other news media may then publicize the survey as if it were a poll taken by such reliable teams as Gallup, CBS and the *New York Times,* or the *Wall Street Journal* and NBC. Critical consumers should watch out for surveys with self-selected respondents and other types of skewed samples. These so-called polls may be used to deliberately mislead the public.

PUBLIC OPINION AND THE POLITICAL PROCESS

Public opinion affects the political process in many ways. Politicians, whether in office or in the midst of a campaign, see public opinion as important to their careers. The president, members of Congress, governors, and other elected officials realize that strong support by the public as expressed in opinion polls is a source of power in dealing with other politicians. It is far more difficult for a senator to say no to the president if the president is immensely popular and if polls show approval of the president's policies. Public opinion also helps political candidates identify the most important concerns among the people and may help them shape their campaigns successfully.

Political Culture and Public Opinion

Americans are divided into a multitude of ethnic, religious, regional, and political subgroups. Given the diversity of American society and the wide range of opinions contained within it, how is it that the political process continues to function without being stalemated by conflict and dissension? One explanation is rooted in the concept of the American political culture, which can be described as a set of attitudes and ideas about the nation and the government. As discussed in Chapter 1, our political culture is widely shared by Americans of many different backgrounds.

▼ **This student** at Franklin & Marshall College in Lancaster, Pennsylvania, prepares for an online post-presidential debate. Why do you think young people today show more interest in politics than they did 20 years ago? (AP Photo/ Daniel Shanken)

the politics of Boom and Bust:
Just What Is a Trillion Dollars, Anyway?

"A billion here, a billion there, pretty soon, you're talking real money." This remark has been attributed to Everett Dirksen, who represented Illinois in the U.S. Senate from 1950 to 1969. If Dirksen were alive today, he might quip instead: "A trillion dollars here, a trillion dollars there . . ." Since the beginning of the latest economic crisis, references to trillions of dollars have been tossed around in the press, by the president, and certainly by Congress. People's opinions about political developments—and the answers they give to polltakers—depend on their understanding key terms such as *1 trillion*.

A Trillion Is Big, but How Big?

Yet even trained economists have a hard time "getting their arms around" a trillion dollars. The sum is far out of the range of ordinary experience. Consider the following ways of viewing $1 trillion: If you lay a trillion one-dollar bills end to end, you'll have a chain that stretches from the earth to the moon and back about 200 times. It would take a jet flying at the speed of sound, reeling out a roll of dollar bills behind it, 14 years to reel out a trillion dollars.

More to the point, the total cost of the various stimuli and bailouts approved by the U.S. Congress in 2008 and 2009 easily exceeds $1 trillion. Total government spending at all levels reached $4 trillion in fiscal year 2009. The federal budget deficit (spending in excess of revenues) has been estimated as $1.84 trillion for 2009 and $1.25 trillion for 2010. The value of the U.S. Treasury notes and other U.S. bonds owned by the government of China is about $1 trillion.

Relating $1 Trillion to the Economy

One way to make sense of $1 trillion is to divide it among every man, woman, and child in the United States. Each person would get about $3,270. The total annual income of the entire nation (called gross domestic product, or GDP) is around $14 trillion, so $1 trillion is about 7 percent of that. How long would it take $14 trillion in national income to increase by $1 trillion if the economy grew at a healthy rate of 3 percent a year? About two and one-third years. From the beginning of the current recession in December 2007 through March 2009, stock values on Wall Street dropped by more than $11 trillion, so $1 trillion is less than 10 percent of what investors lost in the economic crisis.

What Do Trillions in Government Spending Mean to You?

Even if $1 trillion seems abstract, the consequences of $1 trillion in additional government spending, whether on stimulus projects or bank bailouts, does affect you. We cannot fund government expenditures with resources that come from Mars. Rather, additional government spending must eventually be paid back either through future taxes or through inflation. You may think that your share of additional taxes will be small, but don't be so sure. As of 2010, the average family's share of the federal government's debt was about $144,500. As the saying goes, someday we all must pay the piper.

FOR CRITICAL ANALYSIS

The economic stimulus bill passed by Congress in February 2009 amounted to $787 billion, to be paid out over at least two years. With future interest charges, the total cost of this bill alone may exceed $1 trillion. How could you determine whether that additional federal spending is good or bad for you? For the nation? For the world economy?

▲ **Can you imagine** what a trillion dollars looks like?
(Shutterstock)

To some extent, it consists of symbols, such as the American flag, the Liberty Bell, and the Statue of Liberty. The elements of our political culture also include certain shared beliefs about the most important values in the American political system, including liberty, equality, and property.

The political culture provides a general environment of support for the political system. If the people share certain beliefs about the system and a reservoir of good feeling exists toward the institutions of government, the nation will be better able to weather periods of crisis.

The political culture also helps Americans evaluate their government's performance. At times in our history, **political trust** in government has reached relatively high levels. A poll taken two weeks after the 9/11 attacks found that trust in government was 64 percent—higher than it had been for more than three decades. At other times, political trust in government has fallen to low levels. For example, during the 1960s and 1970s, during the Vietnam War and the Watergate scandals, surveys showed that the overall level of political trust in government had declined from the 60 percent range to a low of 25 percent in 1980. A considerable proportion of Americans seemed to feel that they could not trust government officials and that they could not count on officials to care about the ordinary person. This index of political trust reached an all-time low of 20 percent in 1994 but then climbed steadily until 2001, after which the level of trust again declined to the 30 percent to 40 percent range.

Political Trust
The degree to which individuals express trust in the government and political institutions, usually measured through a specific series of survey questions.

Public Opinion about Government

A vital component of public opinion in the United States is the considerable ambivalence with which the public regards many major national institutions. Table 6–1 shows trends from 1989 to 2009 in opinion polls asking respondents, at regularly spaced intervals, how much confidence they had in the institutions listed. Over the years,

TABLE 6–1 : Confidence in Institutions Trend

Question: I am going to read a list of institutions in American society. Would you please tell me how much confidence you, yourself, have in each one—a great deal, quite a lot, some, or very little?

| | Percentage Saying "A Great Deal" or "Quite a Lot" | | | | | | | | | | | | | | |
	1989	1991	1993	1995	1997	1999	2001	2002	2003	2004	2005	2006	2007	2008	2009
Military	63	69	67	64	60	68	66	79	82	75	74	73	69	71	82
Church or organized religion	52	56	53	57	56	58	60	45	50	53	53	52	46	48	52
Banks and banking	42	30	38	43	41	43	44	47	50	53	49	49	41	32	22
U.S. Supreme Court	46	39	43	44	50	49	50	50	47	46	41	40	34	32	39
Public schools	43	35	39	40	40	36	38	38	40	41	37	37	33	33	38
Television news	NA	24	21	33	34	34	34	35	35	30	28	31	23	24	23
Newspapers	NA	32	31	30	35	33	36	35	33	30	28	30	22	24	25
Congress	32	18	19	21	22	26	26	29	29	30	22	19	14	12	17
Organized labor	NA	22	26	26	23	28	26	26	28	31	24	24	19	20	19
Big business	NA	22	23	21	28	30	28	20	22	24	22	18	18	20	16

NA = Not asked.
Source: Gallup polls.

military and religious organizations have ranked highest. Note, however, the decline in confidence in churches in 2002 following sex-abuse allegations against a number of Catholic priests. Note also the somewhat heightened regard for the military after the first Gulf War in 1991. Since that time, the public has consistently had more confidence in the military than in any of the other institutions shown in Table 6–1. In 2002 and 2003, confidence in the military soared even higher, most likely because of the military's role in the war on terrorism, but it has declined somewhat since then.

The United States Supreme Court and the banking industry have scored well over time, although banking suffered an abrupt collapse by 2009. Less confidence is expressed in newspapers, television, big business, and organized labor. In 2008, confidence in Congress plummeted to a record low of 12 percent, reflecting what many believed to be a growing disillusionment with overall representation in Washington, D.C. In 2009, with the new administration, Congress recovered slightly to 17 percent. At times, popular confidence in all institutions may rise or fall, reflecting optimism or pessimism about the general state of the nation.

Although people may not have much confidence in government institutions, they nonetheless turn to government to solve what they perceive to be the major problems facing the country. Table 6–2, which is based on various polls conducted from 1980 to 2009, shows that the most important problems have changed over time. The public tends to emphasize problems that are immediate. It is not at all unusual to see fairly sudden, and even apparently contradictory, shifts in public perceptions of what government should do. In recent years, the war in Iraq and the economic crisis have reached the top of the problems list.

TABLE 6–2: **Most Important Problem Trend, 1980 to Present**

Each year, one or two major issues are most on people's minds. Here you can see some issues reoccur years later.

Year	Problem	Year	Problem
1980	High cost of living, unemployment	1995	Crime, violence
1981	High cost of living, unemployment	1996	Budget deficit
1982	Unemployment, high cost of living	1997	Crime, violence
1983	Unemployment, high cost of living	1998	Crime, violence
1984	Unemployment, fear of war	1999	Crime, violence
1985	Fear of war, unemployment	2000	Morals, family decline
1986	Unemployment, budget deficit	2001	Economy, education
1987	Unemployment, economy	2002	Terrorism, economy
1988	Economy, budget deficit	2003	Terrorism, economy
1989	War on drugs	2004	War in Iraq, economy
1990	War in Middle East	2005	War in Iraq
1991	Economy	2006	War in Iraq, terrorism
1992	Unemployment, budget deficit	2007	War in Iraq, health care
1993	Health care, budget deficit	2008	Economy, war in Iraq
1994	Crime, violence, health care	2009	Economy

Sources: *New York Times*/CBS News poll, January 1996; Gallup polls, 2000 through 2009.

Policymakers cannot always be guided by opinion polls. In the end, politicians must make their own choices. When they do so, their choices necessarily involve trade-offs. If politicians vote for increased spending to improve education, for example, by necessity fewer resources are available for other worthy projects. Individuals who are polled do not have to make such trade-offs when they respond to questions. Indeed, survey respondents usually are not even given a choice of trade-offs in their policy opinions. Moreover, to make an informed policy choice requires an understanding not only of the policy area but also of the consequences of any given choice. Very rarely do public opinion polls make sure that those polled have such information.

Finally, government decisions cannot be made simply by adding up individual desires. Politicians engage in "horse trading" with each other. Politicians also know that they cannot satisfy every desire of every constituent. Therefore, each politician attempts to maximize the net benefits to his or her constituents, while keeping within the limits of whatever the politician believes the government can afford.

THE MEDIA AND POLITICS

The study of people and politics must take into account the role played by the media. Historically, the print media played the most important role in informing public debate. The print media developed, for the most part, our understanding of how news is to be reported. Today, however, more than 90 percent of Americans use television news as their primary source of information. In addition, the Internet has become a major source for news, political communication, and fund-raising. The Internet is now the second most widely used source of information, displacing newspapers. As Internet use grows, the system of gathering and sharing news and information is changing from one in which the media have a primary role to one in which the individual citizen may play a greater part.

The mass media perform a number of different functions in any country. In the United States, we can list at least six. Almost all of them can have political implications, and some are essential to the democratic process. These functions are as follows: (1) entertainment, (2) reporting the news, (3) identifying public problems, (4) socializing new generations, (5) providing a political forum, and (6) making profits.

Entertainment

By far the greatest number of radio and television hours are dedicated to entertaining the public. The battle for prime-time ratings indicates how important successful entertainment is to the survival of networks and individual stations.

Although there is no direct link between entertainment and politics, network dramas often

▼ **As a presidential candidate,** Barack Obama appeared on a number of popular TV shows, such as NBC's *Tonight Show with Jay Leno.* Why do political candidates make every attempt to appear in the mass media? (Margaret Norton/NBCU Photo Bank via AP Images)

Public Agenda
Issues that are perceived by the political community as meriting public attention and governmental action.

introduce material that may be politically controversial and that may stimulate public discussion. An example is *The West Wing,* a TV series (1999–2006) that many people believe promoted liberal political values. Made-for-TV movies have focused on a number of controversial topics, including AIDS, incest, and wife battering.

Reporting the News

A primary function of the mass media in all their forms is the reporting of news. The media provide words and pictures about events, facts, personalities, and ideas. The protections of the First Amendment are intended to keep the flow of news as free as possible, because it is an essential part of the democratic process. If citizens cannot obtain unbiased information about the state of their communities and their leaders' actions, how can they make voting decisions? One of the most incisive comments about the importance of the media was made by James Madison, who said, "A people who mean to be their own governors must arm themselves with the power knowledge gives. A popular government without popular information or the means of acquiring it, is but a prologue to a farce or a tragedy or perhaps both." [5]

Identifying Public Problems

The power of the media is important not only in revealing what the government is doing but also in determining what the government ought to do—in other words, in setting the **public agenda.** As we noted earlier in this chapter, the mass media identify public issues. An example is the release of convicted sex offenders to residential neighborhoods after the end of their prison terms. The media have influenced the passage of legislation, such as "Megan's Law," which requires police to notify neighbors about the release and/or resettlement of certain sex offenders. American journalists also work in a long tradition of uncovering public wrongdoing, corruption, and bribery and of bringing such wrongdoing to the public's attention.

Closely related to this investigative function is that of presenting policy alternatives. Public policy is often complex and difficult to make entertaining, but programs devoted to public policy are frequently scheduled for prime-time television, especially on cable networks. Network shows with a "news magazine" format sometimes include segments on policy issues as well.

Socializing New Generations

As mentioned earlier in this chapter, the media strongly influence the beliefs and opinions of Americans. Because of this influence, the media play a significant role in the political socialization of the younger generation, as well as immigrants to this country. Through the transmission of historical information (sometimes fictionalized), the presentation of American culture, and the portrayal of the diverse regions and groups in the United States, the media teach young people and immigrants about what it means to be an American. TV talk shows, such as the *Oprah Winfrey Show,* sometimes focus on controversial issues (such as abortion or assisted suicide). Many children's shows are designed not only to entertain young viewers but also to instruct them in the moral values of American society.

---

5. James Madison, "Letter to W. T. Barry" (August 4, 1822), in Gaillard P. Hunt, ed., *The Writings of James Madison,* Vol. 9 (1910), p. 103.

Providing a Political Forum

As part of their news function, the media also provide a political forum for leaders and the public. Candidates for office use news reporting to sustain interest in their campaigns, while officeholders use the media to gain support for their policies or to present an image of leadership. Presidential trips abroad are an important way for the chief executive to get colorful, positive, and exciting news coverage that makes the president look "presidential." The media also offer ways for citizens to participate in public debate through letters to the editor, blog posts, and other channels.

Making Profits

Most of the news media in the United States are private, for-profit corporate enterprises. One of their goals is to make profits for expansion and for dividends to the stockholders who own the companies. In general, profits are made as a result of charging for advertising. Advertising revenues usually are related directly to circulation or to listener/viewer ratings.

Several well-known media outlets, in contrast, are publicly owned—public television stations in many communities and National Public Radio. These outlets operate without extensive commercials, are locally supported, and are often subsidized by the government and corporations.

For the most part, however, the media depend on advertisers for their revenues. Consequently, reporters may feel pressure from media owners and from advertisers. Media owners may take their cues from what advertisers want. If an important advertiser does not like the political bent of a particular reporter, the reporter could be asked to alter his or her "style" of writing. According to the Pew Research Center's Project for Excellence in Journalism, 38 percent of local print and broadcast journalists know of instances in which their newsrooms were encouraged to do a story because it related to an owner, advertiser, or sponsor.[6]

Lately, newspapers have found it increasingly difficult to make a profit. Newspaper revenues have fallen because online services have taken over a greater share of classified advertising. The recent economic crisis, which depressed all forms of advertising spending, pushed many large daily newspapers over the edge. Newspapers in Chicago, Denver, and Seattle went out of business. Even some of the most famous papers, such as the *New York Times* and the *Boston Globe,* were in serious financial trouble.

THE PRIMACY OF TELEVISION

Television is the most influential medium. It is also big business. National news TV personalities such as Katie Couric and Brian Williams may earn millions of dollars per year from their TV contracts alone. They are paid so much because they command large audiences, and large audiences command high prices for advertising on national news shows. Indeed, news *per se* has become a major factor in the profitability of TV stations.

---

6. Pew Research Center for the People and the Press and the Project for Excellence in Journalism, *The State of the News Media 2007: An Annual Report on American Journalism.*

Sound Bite
A brief, memorable comment that can easily be fit into news broadcasts.

The Increase in News-Type Programming

In 1963, the major networks—ABC, CBS, and NBC—devoted only eleven minutes daily to national news. A twenty-four-hour-a-day news cable channel—CNN—started operating in 1980. With the addition of CNN Headline News, CNBC, MSNBC, Fox News, and other news-format cable and satellite channels since the 1980s, the amount of news-type programming has continued to increase. By 2009, the amount of time on the networks devoted to news-type programming had increased to about three hours per day. In recent years, all of the major networks have also added Internet sites, but they face thousands of competitors on the Web.

Television's Influence on the Political Process

Television's influence on the political process today is recognized by all who engage in that process. Television news is often criticized for being superficial, particularly compared with the detailed coverage available in newspapers and magazines. In fact, television news is constrained by its technical characteristics, the most important being the limitations of time—stories must be reported in only a few minutes.

The most interesting aspect of television is, of course, the fact that it relies on pictures rather than words to attract the viewer's attention. Therefore, the video that is chosen for a particular political story has exaggerated importance. Viewers do not know what other photos may have been taken or what other events may have been recorded—they see only those appearing on their screens. Television news can also use well-constructed stories to exploit the potential for drama. Some critics suggest that there is pressure to produce television news that has a "story line," like a novel or movie. The story should be short, with exciting pictures and a clear plot. In the extreme case, the news media are satisfied with a **sound bite,** a several-second comment selected or crafted for its immediate impact on the viewer.

It has been suggested that these formatting characteristics—or necessities—of television increase its influence on political events. As you are aware, real life is usually not dramatic, nor do all events have a plot that is neat or easily understood. Political campaigns are continuing events, lasting perhaps as long as two years. The significance of their daily turns and twists is only apparent later. The "drama" of Congress, with its 535 players and dozens of important committees and meetings, is also difficult for the media to present. Television requires, instead, dozens of daily three-minute stories.

▼ **Actress America Ferrera** shows her support for Hillary Clinton. How might the TV star of "Ugly Betty" influence voters? (Gilbert Carrasquillo/FilmMagic/Getty Images)

THE MEDIA AND POLITICAL CAMPAIGNS

All forms of the media—television, newspapers, radio, magazines, and online services—have a significant political impact on American society. Media influence is most obvious during political campaigns. Because television is the primary news source for the majority of Americans, candidates and their consultants spend much of their time devising strategies that use television to their benefit. Three types of TV coverage are generally employed in campaigns for the presidency and other offices: advertising, management of news coverage, and campaign debates.

Advertising

Political advertising has become increasingly important for the profitability of television station owners. Hearst Argyle Television, for example, obtains well over 10 percent of its revenues from political ads during an election year. During the 2008 elections, total spending on the media by candidates at all levels totaled close to $3 billion.

Perhaps one of the most effective political ads of all time was a thirty-second spot created by President Lyndon Johnson's media adviser in 1964. Johnson's opponent in the campaign was Barry Goldwater, a conservative Republican candidate known for his expansive views on the role of the U.S. military. In the ad, a little girl stood in a field of daisies. As she held a daisy, she pulled the petals off and quietly counted to herself. Suddenly, when she reached number ten, a deep bass voice cut in and began a countdown: "10, 9, 8, 7, 6 . . . ." When the voice intoned "zero," the mushroom cloud of an atomic bomb began to fill the screen. Then President Johnson's voice was heard: "These are the stakes. To make a world in which all of God's children can live, or to go into the dark. We must either love each other or we must die." At the end of the commercial, the message read, "Vote for President Johnson on November 3."

▼ **President Lyndon Johnson's "Daisy Girl" ad** contrasted the innocence of childhood with the horror of an atomic attack. Would such a campaign ad be effective today? (Doyle, Dane, Bernbach)

VOTE FOR PRESIDENT JOHNSON
ON NOVEMBER 3.

Spin
An interpretation of political events that is favorable to a candidate or officeholder.

Spin Doctor
A political adviser who tries to convince journalists of the truth of a particular interpretation of events.

Since the "Daisy Girl" advertisement, negative advertising has come into its own. In recent elections, an ever-increasing share of political ads have been negative in nature. The public claims not to like negative advertising, but as one consultant put it, "Negative advertising works." Negative ads can backfire, though, when there are three or more candidates in the race, a typical state of affairs in the early presidential primaries. If one candidate attacks another, the attacker as well as the candidate who is attacked may come to be viewed negatively by the public. A candidate who "goes negative" may thus unintentionally boost the chances of a third candidate who is not part of the exchange.

Management of News Coverage

Using political advertising to get a message across to the public is a very expensive tactic. Coverage by the news media, however, is free; it simply demands that the campaign ensure that coverage takes place. In recent years, campaign managers have shown increasing sophistication in creating newsworthy events for journalists to cover.

The campaign staff uses several methods to try to influence the quantity and type of coverage the campaign receives. First, the staff understands the technical aspects of media coverage—camera angles, necessary equipment, timing, and deadlines—and plans political events to accommodate the press. Second, the campaign organization is aware that political reporters and their sponsors—networks, newspapers, or blogs—are in competition for the best stories and can be manipulated through the granting of favors, such as a personal interview with the candidate. Third, the scheduler in the campaign has the important task of planning events that will be photogenic and interesting enough for the evening news.

A related goal, although one that is more difficult to attain, is to convince reporters that a particular interpretation of an event is true. Today, the art of putting the appropriate **spin** on a story or event is highly developed. Press advisers, often referred to as **spin doctors,** try to convince journalists that their interpretations of political events are correct. For example, the Obama administration and the Republicans engaged in a major spinning duel over the spending package passed by Congress in February 2009. The administration called the bill essential to stimulate the economy; the Republicans described it as a dangerous increase in the size of government. Journalists have begun to report on the different spins placed on events and on how candidates and officeholders try to manipulate news coverage.

Going for the Knockout Punch—Presidential Debates

In presidential elections, perhaps just as important as political advertisements and general news coverage is the performance of the candidates in televised presidential debates. After the first such debate in 1960, in which John Kennedy, the young senator from Massachusetts, took on the vice president of the United States, Richard Nixon, candidates became aware of the great potential of television for changing the momentum of a campaign. In general, challengers have much more to gain from debating than do incumbents. Challengers hope that the incumbent will make a mistake in the debate and undermine the "presidential" image. Incumbent presidents are loath to debate their challengers, because it puts their opponents on an equal footing with them, but the debates have become so widely anticipated that it is difficult for an incumbent to refuse.

Debates can affect the outcome of a race. In 2008, the three presidential debates may have given Democrat Barack Obama an added edge over Republican John McCain. Obama posted a small positive bump in the polls after each debate. More important, the debates gave Obama a chance to let the voters become more comfortable with him. His calm demeanor helped; McCain, in contrast, may have hurt himself in the third debate by being too aggressive.

Although debates are justified publicly as an opportunity for the voters to find out how candidates differ on the issues, what the candidates want is to capitalize on the power of television to project an image. They view the debates as a strategic opportunity to improve their own images or to point out the failures of their opponents. Candidates also know that the morning-after interpretation of a debate by the news media may play a crucial role in what the public thinks.

Political Campaigns and the Internet

Without a doubt, the Internet has become an important vehicle for campaign advertising and news coverage, as well as for soliciting campaign contributions. The Internet became even more important during the 2008 election cycle, when Democrat Barack Obama's fund-raising operation obliterated every political fund-raising and spending record in history. By mid-October, Obama had raised more than $650 million from about 3 million donors, in large part over the Internet. While about half of the funds came from people giving less than $200, larger donors were also generous. Obama was able to obtain this financing without extensive use of in-person fund-raising parties.

One highly effective characteristic of Obama's fund-raising machine was its decentralization, which was powerfully assisted by the nature of the Web. Obama was able to rely on thousands of individual fund-raising activists who solicited their friends and acquaintances, often for relatively small sums. No campaign had ever had so many volunteer fund-raisers. Obama's site, MyBarackObama.com, was a major social-networking hub.[7]

Today, the campaign staff of almost every candidate running for a significant political office includes an Internet campaign strategist—a professional hired to create and maintain the campaign Web site. The work of this strategist includes designing a user-friendly and attractive Web site for the candidate, managing the candidate's e-mail communications, tracking campaign contributions made through the site, hiring bloggers to promote the candidate's agenda on the Web, and monitoring Web sites for favorable or unfavorable comments or video clips about the candidate. Additionally, major interest groups in the United States use the Internet to promote their causes. Prior to elections, various groups engage in issue advocacy from their Web sites. At little or no cost, they can promote positions taken by favored candidates and solicit contributions.

Are Candidates Losing Control of Their Campaigns?

Blogs and Internet sites such as YouTube are making it difficult for candidates to manage the news coverage of their campaigns. Short video clips of candidates' bloopers can be propagated with lightning speed—all it takes is an onlooker's camcorder or smart cell phone and an Internet connection. Candidates have discovered that apparent slurs

7. Joshua Green, "The Amazing Money Machine," *The Atlantic,* June 2008, p. 52.

and other offensive statements soon find their way onto YouTube or other Web sites. For example, at a private fund-raiser during the Democratic primaries, Barack Obama stated that small-town voters bitter over their economic circumstances "cling to guns or religion or antipathy to people who aren't like them" as a way to explain their frustrations. Four days later a blogger reported the comment, and Obama's opponents immediately accused him of contempt for ordinary people.

Another problem for candidates is attempting to control their "Netroots" supporters. A candidate's supporters may engage in activities that are at odds with the candidate's own agenda or ethics. The supporter may become the story, not the candidate. Obama certainly experienced this difficulty when ABC News obtained a "greatest hits" collection of controversial sermons from the Web site of Obama's church in Chicago. In one sermon, Jeremiah Wright, at that time Obama's personal pastor, cried out, "The government . . . wants us to sing 'God Bless America.' No, no, no, not God bless America. God damn America . . ." Obama eventually broke with Wright, but the controversy dogged Obama throughout his campaign.

Republican John McCain began to have problems with his supporters toward the end of his presidential campaign. One of McCain's themes was that Obama was a dangerous radical with unsavory associates. Some of McCain's supporters in the blogosphere and elsewhere took this line to the outer limits. Statements shouted by crowd members at Republican rallies became so heated that at one point they touched off a Secret Service investigation into possible threats against Obama's life. McCain, after much criticism, finally made attempts to calm his audiences.

▼ **This U.S. Marine** walks by a media van in central Baghdad, Iraq. Media coverage of events throughout the world continues to fascinate Americans. What alternative sources of information are available today? (AP Photo/Dusan Vranic)

GOVERNMENT REGULATION OF THE MEDIA

The United States has one of the freest presses in the world. Nonetheless, regulation of the media, particularly of the electronic media, does exist. We discussed many aspects of this regulation in Chapter 4, when we examined First Amendment rights and the press.

The First Amendment does not mention electronic media, which of course did not exist when the Bill of Rights was written. For many reasons, the government has much greater control over the electronic media than it does over printed media. Through the Federal Communications Commission (FCC), which regulates communications by radio, television, wire, and cable, the number of radio stations has been controlled for many years, even though technologically we could have many more radio stations than now exist. Also, the FCC created an environment in which for many decades the three major TV networks (ABC, CBS, and NBC) dominated broadcasting.

Controlling Ownership of the Media

Many FCC rules have dealt with ownership of news media, such as how many stations a network can own. In 1996, Congress passed legislation that had far-reaching implications for the communications industry—the Telecommunications Act. The act ended the rule that kept telephone companies from entering the cable business and other communications markets. What this means is that a single corporation—whether Time Warner or Disney—can offer long-distance and local telephone services, cable television, satellite television, and Internet services, as well as libraries of films and entertainment. The act opened the door to competition and led to more options for consumers, who now can choose among multiple competitors for all of these services. At the same time, it launched a race among competing companies to control media ownership.

Many media outlets are now owned by corporate conglomerates. A single entity may own a television network; the studios that produce shows, news, and movies; and the means to deliver that content to the home via cable, satellite, or the Internet. The question to be faced in the future is how to ensure competition in the delivery of news so that citizens have access to multiple points of view from the media.

Today, all of the prime-time television networks are owned by major American corporations and are part of corporate conglomerates. The Turner Broadcasting/CNN network was purchased by a major corporation, Time Warner. Fox Television has always been a part of Rupert Murdoch's publishing and media empire. Many of these companies have also formed partnerships with computer software makers, such as Microsoft, for joint electronic publishing ventures.

Government Control of Content

On the face of it, the First Amendment would seem to apply to all media. In fact, the United States Supreme Court has often been slow to extend free speech and free press guarantees to new media as they became technically feasible. For example, in 1915, the Court held that "as a matter of common sense," free speech protections did not apply to cinema. Only in 1952 did the Court find that motion pictures were covered by the First Amendment.[8] In contrast, the Court extended full protection to the Internet almost immediately by striking down provisions of the 1996 Telecommunications Act.[9] Cable TV received broad protection in 2000.[10]

While the Court has held that the First Amendment is relevant to radio and television, it has never extended full protection to these media. The Court has used a number of arguments to justify this stand—initially, the scarcity of broadcast frequencies. The Court later held that the government could restrict "indecent" programming based on the "pervasive" presence of broadcasting in the home.[11] On this basis, the FCC has the authority to fine broadcasters for indecency or profanity. We discussed this issue in more detail in Chapter 4 on page 77.

---

8. *Joseph Burstyn, Inc. v. Wilson*, 343 U.S. 495 (1952).
9. *Reno v. American Civil Liberties Union*, 521 U.S. 844 (1997).
10. *United States v. Playboy Entertainment Group*, 529 U.S. 803 (2000).
11. *FCC v. Pacifica Foundation*, 438 U.S. 726 (1978). In this case, the Court banned seven swear words (famously used by the late comedian George Carlin) during hours when children could hear them.

Bias

An inclination or preference that interferes with impartial judgment.

BIAS IN THE MEDIA

For decades, the contention that the mainstream media have a liberal **bias** has been repeated time and again. Bernard Goldberg, formerly a CBS broadcaster and now a commentator for Fox News, is among the most prominent of these critics. Goldberg argues that liberal bias, which "comes naturally to most reporters," has given viewers reason to distrust the big news networks.[12] Some progressives, however, believe that conservatives find liberal bias even in reporting that is scrupulously accurate. In the words of humorist Stephen Colbert: "Reality has a well-known liberal bias."

Other observers claim that, on the whole, the media actually have a conservative bias, especially in their coverage of economic issues. In an analysis of visual images on television news, political scientist Maria Elizabeth Grabe has concluded that "image bites" (as opposed to sound bites) more often favor the Republicans.[13] Certainly, the almost complete dominance of talk radio by conservatives has given the political right an outlet that the political left cannot counter. The rise of the blogosphere and other online outlets has complicated the picture of media bias considerably. Neither the left nor the right clearly dominates in this arena.

Other Theories of Media Bias

Some writers have concluded that the mainstream media are really biased toward stories that involve conflict and drama, the better to attract viewers. Still others contend the media are biased against "losers," and when a candidate falls behind in a race, his or her press quickly becomes negative. Coverage of the 2008 presidential campaigns suggests that the "loser" theory may have merit. The Center for Media and Public Affairs at George Mason University found that in July and August of 2008, the media were actually more critical of Barack Obama than of the Republican candidate, John McCain. In these months, McCain gained support, slowly but continuously, until the race was a dead heat. Thereafter, the media were far more critical of McCain, whose poll numbers dropped steadily until the general elections in November. Did the press cost McCain the election? Not even Goldberg believes that. It is possible that the economic crisis turned both the press *and* the voters against the Republicans.

A Scientific Test for Bias?

Communications professor Tim Groeling has devised a test for media bias that may provide accurate results regardless of whether political events favor the Democrats or the Republicans. He has examined how ABC, CBS, NBC, and Fox News reported public opinion polls that assessed the job performance of Democratic president Bill Clinton and Republican president George W. Bush. Confirming what many suspect, Groeling found that ABC, CBS, and NBC gave Clinton more favorable coverage than Bush—and that Fox gave Bush more favorable coverage than Clinton.[14]

---

12. Goldberg's most recent book provides criticisms, widespread among conservatives, of the media's coverage of the Obama campaign. See Bernard Goldberg, *A Slobbering Love Affair: The True (and Pathetic) Story of the Torrid Romance between Barack Obama and the Mainstream Media* (Washington: Regnery Publishing, 2009).
13. Maria Elizabeth Grabe and Erik Page Bucy, *Image Bite Politics: News and the Visual Framing of Elections* (New York: Oxford University Press, 2009).
14. Tim Groeling, "Who's the Fairest of Them All? An Empirical Test for Partisan Bias on ABC, CBS, NBC, and Fox News," *Presidential Studies Quarterly,* December 2008, p. 631.

making a difference

BEING A CRITICAL CONSUMER OF THE NEWS

Television, print media, and the Internet provide a wide range of choices for Americans who want to stay informed. Still, critics of the media argue that a substantial amount of what you read and see is colored either by the subjectivity of editors and bloggers or by the demands of profit making. Few Americans take the time to become critical consumers of the news.

Why Should You Care? Even if you do not plan to engage in political activism, you have a stake in ensuring that your beliefs are truly your own and that they represent your values and interests. To guarantee this result, you need to obtain accurate information from the media and avoid being swayed by subliminal appeals, loaded terms, or outright bias. If you do not take care, you could find yourself voting for a candidate who is opposed to what you believe in or voting against measures that are in your interest.

Even when journalists themselves are relatively successful at remaining objective, they will of necessity give publicity to politicians and interest group representatives who are far from impartial. You need the ability to determine what motivates the players in the political game and how much they are "shading" the news or even propagating outright lies. You also need to determine which news outlets are reliable.

What Can You Do? To become a critical news consumer, you must develop a critical eye and ear. Ask yourself what stories are given prominence at the top of a newspaper Web site. For a contrast to most daily papers, visit the sites of publications with explicit points of view, such as the *National Review* (www.nationalreview.com) or the *New Republic* (www.tnr.com/politics). Take note of how they handle stories.

Sources such as blogs often have strong political preferences, and you should try to determine what these are. Does a blog merely give opinions, or does it back up its arguments with data? It is possible to select anecdotes to support almost any argument—does an anecdote represent typical circumstances, or is it a rare occurrence highlighted to make a point?

Watching the evening news can be far more rewarding if you look at how much the news depends on video effects. You will note that stories on the evening news tend to be no more than three minutes long, that stories with excellent videotape get more attention, and that considerable time is taken up with "happy talk" or human interest stories.

Another way to critically evaluate news coverage is to compare how the news is covered by different outlets. For example, you might compare the coverage of events on Fox News with the presentation on MSNBC, or compare the radio commentary of Rush Limbaugh with that of National Public Radio's *All Things Considered*. When does a show cross the line between news and opinion?

A variety of organizations try to monitor news sources for accuracy and bias. Consider visiting the following sites:

The American Journalism Review covers a wide variety of journalistic issues, including the migration from print media to online sources. See it at:

www.ajr.org

The Committee of Concerned Journalists is a professional organization concerned with journalistic ethics. Its site is at:

www.concernedjournalists.org

Fairness and Accuracy in Reporting is a media watchdog with a strong liberal viewpoint. Visit it at:

www.fair.org

Accuracy in Media takes a combative conservative position on media issues. View it at:

www.aim.org

▼ **The *National Review* Online.**

keyterms

agenda setting 120

bias 138

consensus 117

divided opinion 117

gender gap 122

generational effect 120

media 120

opinion leader 119

opinion poll 122

peer group 119

political
   socialization 118

political trust 127

public agenda 130

public opinion 117

sampling error 124

sound bite 132

spin 134

spin doctor 134

Watergate break-in 120

chaptersummary

1   Public opinion is the aggregate of individual attitudes or beliefs shared by some portion of the adult population. A consensus exists when a large proportion of the public appears to express the same view on an issue. Divided opinion exists when the public holds widely different attitudes on an issue.

2   People's opinions are formed through the political socialization process. Important factors in this process are the family, educational experiences, peer groups, opinion leaders, the media, and political events. The influence of the media as a socialization factor may be growing relative to that of the family. Voting behavior is also influenced by demographic factors such as education, economic status, religion, gender, and region.

3   Most descriptions of public opinion are based on the results of opinion polls. The accuracy of polls depends on the sampling techniques used. The sample should be representative of the population being polled and should be randomly selected.

4   Problems with polls include sampling errors (which may occur when the pool of respondents is not chosen in a scientific manner), the difficulty of knowing the degree to which responses are influenced by the type and order of questions asked, the use of a yes/no format for answers to the questions, and sometimes the respondents' interactions with the interviewer. "Polls" that rely on self-selected respondents are inherently inaccurate and should be discounted.

5   The political culture provides a general environment of support for the political system, allowing the nation to weather periods of crisis. The political culture also helps Americans to evaluate their government's performance. At times, the level

of trust in government has been relatively high; at other times, the level of trust has declined steeply. Similarly, Americans' confidence in government institutions varies over time, depending on a number of circumstances. Generally, though, Americans turn to government to solve what they perceive to be the major problems facing the country.

6   Public opinion also plays an important role in policymaking. Politicians cannot always be guided by opinion polls, however. This is because respondents often do not understand the costs and consequences of policy decisions or the trade-offs involved in making such decisions.

7   The media are enormously important in American politics today. They perform a number of functions, including (a) entertainment, (b) news reporting, (c) identifying public problems, (d) socializing new generations, (e) providing a political forum, and (f) making profits.

8   The political influence of the media is most obvious during political campaigns. Today's campaigns use advertising and expert management of news coverage. For presidential candidates, how they appear in campaign debates is of major importance. Internet blogs and sites such as YouTube are transforming today's political campaigns and making it more difficult for candidates to control their campaigns.

9   The electronic media are subject to government regulation. Many Federal Communications Commission rules have dealt with ownership of TV and radio stations. Legislation has removed some rules about co-ownership of several forms of media, although the most recent steps taken by Congress have halted further deregulation.

10 Frequently, the mainstream media have been accused of liberal bias, although some observers contend that these accusations result from true stories that offend conservatives. Other possible media biases include a bias against political "losers."

QUESTIONS FOR
discussion**and**analysis

1 In the 2000 presidential elections, Arab American votes were split almost evenly between the two major parties. By 2004 and 2006, the Arab American vote was heavily Democratic. Why, in the past, might Arab Americans have been more favorable to the Republicans than members of many other minority groups were? Why might Republican Arab Americans have switched their allegiance?

2 In recent years, more and more Americans have begun refusing to talk to poll takers. Also, many people now rely on cell phones, which have numbers that are not available to telephone pollsters. What problems could these two developments pose for polling organizations? How might they bias polling results?

3 Why do you think the American people express a relatively high degree of confidence in the military as an institution? Why do people express less confidence in Congress than in other major institutions? Could people be holding various institutions to different standards, and if so, what might these standards be?

4 Conservatives have long accused traditional media outlets of having a liberal bias. Are they correct? If so, to what degree? What other kinds of bias might affect the reporting of prominent journalists? To the extent that the press exhibits political bias, what factors might cause this bias?

helpful online **Resources**

CONNECTING TO AMERICAN GOVERNMENT AND POLITICS

The Gallup organization is one of the nation's oldest and most respected polling companies. Check it out at:
www.gallup.com

You can access polls conducted by a wide variety of organizations at:
www.pollingreport.com

Real Clear Politics is known for its "poll of polls," which aggregates results from leading pollsters in the run-up to elections. The site also aggregates polls on the president's job approval rating and other indicators. While the site is run by conservatives, it offers opinion pieces from multiple media sources on its home page. See it at:
www.realclearpolitics.com

The Pew Research Center, a major public opinion research group, sponsors projects on journalism, the Internet, and other topics. Its sites include:
pewresearch.org, people-press.org, and journalism.org

a special WebSite

FOR YOUR TEXT

Go to this book's special Web site at academic.cengage.com/polisci/Schmidt/Brief6e. Choose "For Students." Then click on Chapter 6, where you will find an online quiz and other helpful study aids. If your professor is using CengageNOW: *American Government and Politics Today, Brief Edition,* log in and go to Chapter 6 for additional online study aids.

7

Interest Groups and Political Parties

These California members of AARP listen to their governor propose health-care reform during a speech in Sacramento. (AP Photo/Rich Pedroncelli)

Interest Group
An organized group of individuals sharing common objectives who actively attempt to influence policymakers.

The structure of American government invites the participation of **interest groups** at various stages of the policymaking process. Americans can form groups in their neighborhoods or cities and lobby the city council or their state government. They can join statewide groups or national groups and try to influence government policy through Congress or through one of the executive agencies or cabinet departments. Representatives of large corporations may seek to influence the president personally at social events or fund-raisers. When attempts to influence government through the executive and legislative branches fail, interest groups can turn to the courts, filing suits in state or federal courts to achieve their political objectives.

The large number of "pressure points" for interest group activity in American government helps to explain why there are so many—more than one hundred thousand—interest groups at work in our society. Another reason for the multitude of interest groups is that the right to join a group is protected by the First Amendment to the U.S. Constitution (see Chapter 4). Not only are all people guaranteed the right "peaceably to assemble," but they are also guaranteed the right "to petition the Government for a redress of grievances." This constitutional provision encourages Americans to form groups and to express their opinions to the government and to their elected representatives as group members. Representatives are far more likely to pay attention to a group than to a single individual.

Another way to influence policymaking is to become an active member of a political party and participate in the selection of political candidates, who, if elected, will hold government positions. A **political party** might be formally defined as a group of political activists who organize to win elections, operate the government, and determine public policy. This definition explains the difference between an interest group and a political party. Interest groups do not want to operate the government, and they do not put forth political candidates—even though they support candidates who will promote their interests if elected or reelected.

In this chapter, we define interest groups, describe how they try to affect the government, and summarize the legal restrictions on **lobbyists,** people or groups who try to affect legislation and government administrative decisions. We also describe the major political parties, their history, and their organization. Finally, we explain why the two-party system has prevailed in the United States.

A NATION OF JOINERS

▲ **Former Senate Majority Leader** Tom Daschle worked for a Washington, D.C., lobbying firm. His clients included large health-care providers. In 2009, he had to withdraw his name from consideration as President Obama's secretary of health and human services because of tax problems. Why would such firms want to hire Daschle? (AP Photo/Susan Walsh)

Political Party
A group of political activists who organize to win elections, operate the government, and determine public policy.

Lobbyist
An organization or individual that attempts to influence the passage, defeat, or content of legislation and the government's administrative decisions.

Alexis de Tocqueville observed in the early 1830s that "in no country of the world has the principle of association been more successfully used or applied to a greater multitude of objectives than in America."[1] The French traveler was amazed at the degree to which Americans formed groups to solve civic problems, establish social relationships, and speak for their economic or political interests. Perhaps James Madison, when he wrote *Federalist Paper* No. 10 (see Appendix C), had already judged the character of his country's citizens similarly. He supported the creation of a large republic with many states to encourage the formation of multiple interests. The multitude of interests, in Madison's view, would work to discourage the formation of an oppressive majority interest.

Poll data show that more than two-thirds of all Americans belong to at least one group or association. While the majority of these affiliations could not be classified as "interest groups" in the political sense, Americans certainly understand the principles of working in groups.

Today, interest groups range from the elementary school parent-teacher association and the local "Stop the Sewer Plant Association" to the statewide association of insurance agents. They include small groups such as local environmental organizations and national groups such as the Boy Scouts of America, the American Civil Liberties Union, the National Education Association, and the American League of Lobbyists.

---

1. Alexis de Tocqueville, *Democracy in America,* Vol. 1 [1835], ed. Phillips Bradley (New York: Knopf, 1980), p. 191.

Interest Groups and Social Movements

Social Movement
A movement that represents the demands of a large segment of the public for political, economic, or social change.

Interest groups are often spawned by mass **social movements.** Such movements represent demands by a large segment of the population for change in the political, economic, or social system. A social movement is often the first expression of latent discontent with the existing system. It may be the authentic voice of weaker or oppressed groups in society that do not have the means or standing to organize as interest groups. For example, the women's movement of the early 1800s suffered disapproval from most mainstream political and social leaders. Because women were unable to vote or take an active part in the political system, it was difficult for women who desired greater freedoms to organize formal groups. After the Civil War, when more women became active in professional life, the first women's rights groups came into being.

African Americans found themselves in an even more disadvantaged situation after the end of the Reconstruction period. They were unable to exercise political rights in many southern and border states, and their participation in any form of organization could lead to economic ruin, physical harassment, or even death. The civil rights movement of the 1950s and 1960s was clearly a social movement. To be sure, several formal organizations worked to support the movement—including the Southern Christian Leadership Conference, the National Association for the Advancement of Colored People, and the Urban League—but only a social movement could generate the kinds of civil disobedience that took place in hundreds of towns and cities across the country.

Social movements are often precursors of interest groups. They may generate interest groups with specific goals that successfully recruit members by offering certain incentives. In the example of the women's movement of the 1960s, the National Organization for Women was formed in part out of a demand to end gender-segregated job advertising in newspapers.

TYPES OF INTEREST GROUPS

Thousands of groups exist to influence government. Among the major types of interest groups are those that represent the main sectors of the economy. In addition, a number of public-interest organizations have been formed to represent the needs of the general citizenry, including many single-issue groups. The interests of foreign governments and foreign businesses are represented in the American political arena as well.

Economic Interest Groups

More interest groups are formed to represent economic interests than any other set of interests. The variety of economic interest groups mirrors the complexity of the American economy. The major sectors that seek influence in Washington, D.C., include business, agriculture, labor unions, government workers, and professionals.

Business Interest Groups. Thousands of business groups and trade associations work to influence government policies that affect their respective industries. "Umbrella groups" represent collections of businesses or other entities. The U.S. Chamber of Commerce, for example, is an umbrella group that represents a wide variety of businesses, while the National Association of Manufacturers is an umbrella group that represents only manufacturing concerns.

Some business groups are decidedly more powerful than others. The U.S. Chamber of Commerce, which represents about 3 million member companies, can bring constituent influence to bear on every member of Congress. The National Association of Manufacturers is another powerful group. With a staff of about 150 people in Washington, D.C., the organization can mobilize dozens of well-educated, articulate lobbyists to work the corridors of Congress on issues of concern to its members.

Agricultural Interest Groups. American farmers and their employees represent less than 1 percent of the U.S. population. In spite of this, farmers' influence on legislation beneficial to their interests has been significant. Farmers have succeeded in their aims because they have very strong interest groups. They are geographically dispersed and therefore have many representatives and senators to speak for them.

The American Farm Bureau Federation, or Farm Bureau, established in 1919, represents more than 5.5 million families (a majority of whom are not actually farm families) and is usually seen as conservative. It was instrumental in getting government guarantees of "fair" prices during the Great Depression in the 1930s.[2]

In recent years, agricultural interest groups have become active on many new issues. Among other things, they have opposed immigration restrictions and are very involved in international trade matters as they seek new markets. One of the newest agricultural groups is the American Farmland Trust, which supports policies to conserve farmland and protect natural resources.

Agricultural interest groups have probably been more successful than any other groups in obtaining subsidies from American taxpayers. U.S. farm subsidies cost taxpayers at least $20 billion a year directly and another $12 billion a year in higher food prices. Republicans and Democrats alike have supported agricultural subsidy legislation, showing the success of agricultural lobbying groups. The latest legislation, passed in 2008, created the most expensive agricultural subsidy program ever.

Labor Interest Groups. Interest groups representing the **labor movement** date back to at least 1886, when the American Federation of Labor (AFL) was formed. In 1955, the AFL joined forces with the Congress of Industrial Organizations (CIO). The AFL-CIO experienced discord within its ranks during 2005, however, as four key unions left the federation and formed the Change to Win Coalition. Today, the Change to Win Coalition has a membership of about 6 million workers, while the AFL-CIO's membership is about 10 million. Many labor advocates fear that the split will reduce

Labor Movement
Generally, the economic and political expression of working-class interests; politically, the organization of working-class interests.

▼ **At Goodyear Tire and Rubber Company** headquarters in Akron, Ohio, this employee is on strike along with his fellow workers. Unions remain a powerful interest group in the United States. What are some of the reasons that Goodyear's 12,000 workers would choose to strike? (AP Photo/Tony Dejak)

2. The Agricultural Adjustment Act of 1933 (declared unconstitutional) was replaced by the 1937 Agricultural Adjustment Act and later amended several times.

Service Sector
The sector of the economy that provides services—such as health care, banking, and education—in contrast to the sector that produces goods.

organized labor's influence, and in 2009 leaders of the two federations met to discuss the possibility of reunification.

Even before the split, the role of unions in American society had been waning, as witnessed by a decline in union membership (see Figure 7–1). This decline has reduced labor's political influence. In the age of automation and with the rise of the **service sector,** blue-collar workers in basic industries (autos, steel, and the like) represent a smaller and smaller percentage of the total working population. Because of this decline in the industrial sector of the economy, national unions are looking to nontraditional areas for their membership, including migrant farmworkers, service workers, and, especially, public employees—such as police officers, firefighting personnel, and teachers, including college professors and even graduate assistants. Indeed, public-sector unions are the fastest-growing labor organizations.

Today, labor unions are pushing members of Congress to pass legislation that would make it easier for employees to join unions—and thus boost union membership. For a discussion of the controversy surrounding this effort, see this chapter's feature *At Issue: Should Workers Forgo Secret Ballots When Attempting to Organize a Union?*

Public Employee Unions. The degree of unionization in the private sector has declined over the past fifty years, but this has been partially offset by growth in the unionization of public employees. With a total membership of more than 7.5 million, public-sector unions are likely to continue expanding. Over the years, public employee unions have become quite militant and are often involved in strikes. Most of these strikes are illegal, because almost no public employees have the right to strike.

FIGURE 7–1: Decline in Union Membership, 1948 to Present

The percentage of the total workforce that consists of labor union members has declined precipitously over the last forty years. The percentage of government workers who are union members, however, increased significantly in the 1960s and 1970s and has remained stable since.

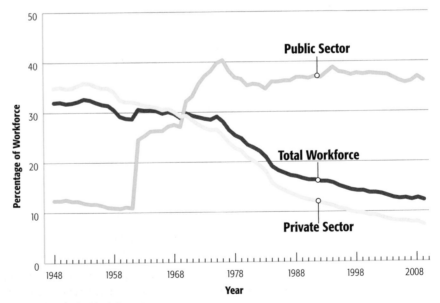

Source: Bureau of Labor Statistics.

atIssue: Should Workers Forgo Secret Ballots When Attempting to Organize a Union?

Several years ago, with union membership waning, union leaders began putting pressure on Congress to pass legislation that would help promote new membership. That legislation would allow for "card checks," which would permit a union to become the bargaining agent for a workplace if a majority of the workers signed cards indicating their support. Currently, companies do not have to recognize a union unless workers vote by a secret ballot in favor of union representation. Under existing law, companies can *voluntarily* agree to a card check, but they are not required to do so, and the method is rarely used. Under the new law, unions would be the ones to decide whether to employ a card check or a secret ballot, and they would probably choose the card-check system in most instances. Now that America has a Democratic president and Democratic control of Congress, we can expect a serious attempt to pass legislation that allows card checks to replace secret ballots.

Making the Environment More Prounion

Those who support enacting card-check legislation, such as Senator Ted Kennedy (D., Mass.), claim that this legislation would level the playing field between union members and management. It would do so by removing "large loopholes" in today's labor laws that allow employers to purportedly intimidate workers in the period leading up to a secret-ballot election.

Moreover, say proponents of the card-check bill, the decline of unionism does not bode well for the status of workers. Workers in general should do everything possible to strengthen their negotiating positions and to expand the choices available to them. When unions are strong, even nonunion workers benefit, because companies will improve wages and working conditions to avoid unionization. Former Democratic vice-presidential candidate John

Edwards said: "If you can join the Republican Party by just signing a card, you should be able to join a union by just signing a card."

Secret Ballots Are the Backbone of Democracy

In 2006, the Opinion Research Corporation surveyed a variety of Americans and found that 75 percent chose secret-ballot elections as the most democratic method of unionization. In 1991, the District of Columbia Circuit Court stated that "freedom of choice is a matter at the very center of our national labor relations policy, and a secret election is the preferred method of gauging choice." Back in 2001, many members of Congress, including Representatives Barney Frank (D., Mass.), George Miller (D., Calif.), and Bernie Sanders (Ind., Vt.), wrote to Mexican officials stating that "we are writing to encourage you to use the secret ballot in all union recognition elections. . . . We feel that the secret ballot is absolutely necessary in order to ensure that workers are not intimidated into voting for a union they might not otherwise choose."

In accord with all these views, opponents of the card-check bill claim that secret ballots are the only path to true democracy. Furthermore, they argue, even assuming that companies do intimidate workers before union elections, there is no guarantee that union organizers won't intimidate workers in attempts to convince them to sign union cards.

FOR CRITICAL ANALYSIS

Under what circumstances, if any, would a simple card-check system to establish union representation be legitimate? Do you see any essential differences between union representation contests and elections to choose public officials?

A powerful interest group lobbying on behalf of public employees is the National Education Association (NEA), a nationwide organization of about 3.2 million teachers and others connected with education. Most NEA locals function as labor unions. The NEA lobbies intensively for increased public funding of education.

Interest Groups of Professionals. Many professional organizations exist, including the American Bar Association, the Association of General Contractors of America, the Institute of Electrical and Electronic Engineers, and others. Some professional groups, such as those representing lawyers and physicians, are more influential than others because of their ability to restrict entry into their professions. Lawyers have a unique advantage—a large number of members of Congress share their profession. In terms of funds spent on lobbying, however, one professional organization for many years stood head and shoulders above the rest—the American Medical Association (AMA). Founded in 1847, it is affiliated with more than 1,000 local and state medical societies and has a total membership of about 250,000.

The Unorganized Poor. Some have argued that the system of interest group politics leaves out poor Americans and U.S. residents who are not citizens and cannot vote. Americans who are disadvantaged economically typically do not join interest groups; if they are members of the working poor, they may hold two or more jobs just to survive, leaving them no time to participate in interest groups. Other groups in the population—including non-English-speaking groups, resident aliens, single parents, Americans with disabilities, and younger voters—may not have the time or expertise even to find out what group might represent them. Consequently, some scholars suggest that interest groups and lobbyists are the privilege of upper-middle-class Americans and those who belong to unions or other special groups.

Environmental Groups

Environmental interest groups are not new. The National Audubon Society was founded in 1905 to protect the snowy egret from the commercial demand for hat decorations. The patron of the Sierra Club, John Muir, worked for the creation of national parks more than a century ago. But the blossoming of national environmental groups with mass memberships did not occur until the 1970s. Since the first Earth Day, organized in 1972, many interest groups have sprung up to protect the environment in general or unique ecological niches. The groups range from the National Wildlife Federation, with a membership of more than 4 million and an emphasis on education, to the more elite Environmental Defense Fund, with a membership of 500,000 and a focus on influencing federal policy. Other groups include the Nature Conservancy, which uses members' contributions to buy up threatened natural areas and then either gives them to state or local governments or manages them itself, and the more radical Greenpeace Society and Earth First.

▶ **The American Bar Association** (ABA) frequently has conferences in Washington, D.C. Why is the ABA such a powerful lobbying group? (AP Photo/Jose Luis Magana)

Public-Interest Groups

Public interest is a difficult term to define because, as we noted in Chapter 6, there are many publics in our nation of more than 300 million. It is almost impossible for one particular public policy to benefit everybody, which makes it practically impossible to define the public interest. Nonetheless, over the past few decades, a variety of lobbying organizations have been formed "in the public interest."

Nader Organizations. The best-known and perhaps the most effective public-interest groups are those founded under the leadership of consumer activist Ralph Nader. Nader's rise to the top began after the publication, in 1965, of his book *Unsafe at Any Speed,* a lambasting critique of the purported attempt by General Motors (GM) to keep from the public negative information about its rear-engine Corvair. Partly as a result of Nader's book, Congress began to consider an automobile safety bill. GM made a clumsy attempt to discredit Nader. Nader sued, the media exploited the story, and when GM settled out of court for $425,000, Nader became a recognized champion of consumer interests. Since then, Nader has turned over much of his income to the more than sixty public-interest groups that he has formed or sponsored. Nader ran for president in 2000 on the Green Party ticket and again in 2004 and 2008 as an independent.

Other Public-Interest Groups. Partly in response to the Nader organizations, several conservative public-interest legal foundations have sprung up and are often pitted against the liberal groups in court. Some of these are the Pacific Legal Foundation, the National Right-to-Work Legal Defense Foundation, the Institute for Justice, and the Mid-Atlantic Legal Foundation.

One of the largest public-interest groups is Common Cause, founded in 1968. Its goal is to reorder national priorities toward "the public" and to make governmental institutions more responsive to the needs of the public. Anyone willing to pay dues of $40 a year can become a member. Members are polled regularly to obtain information about local and national issues requiring reassessment. Other public-interest groups include the League of Women Voters, founded in 1920. Although officially nonpartisan, it has lobbied for the Equal Rights Amendment and for government reform. The Consumer Federation of America is an alliance of about three hundred nonprofit organizations interested in consumer protection.

Additional Types of Interest Groups

Single-interest groups, being narrowly focused, may be able to call attention to their causes because they have simple and straightforward goals and because their members tend to care intensely about the issues. Thus, such groups can easily motivate their members to contact legislators or to organize demonstrations in support of their policy goals.

A number of interest groups focus on just one issue. The abortion debate has created groups opposed to abortion (such as the National Right to Life Committee) and groups in favor of abortion rights (such as NARAL Pro-Choice America). Further examples of single-issue groups are the National Rifle Association, the Right to Work Committee (an antiunion group), and the American Israel Public Affairs Committee (a pro-Israel group).

Still other groups represent Americans who share a common characteristic, such as age or ethnicity. Such interest groups may lobby for legislation that enhances the rights of their members or may just represent a viewpoint.

Public Interest
The best interests of the overall community; the national good, rather than the narrow interests of a particular group.

▲ **Presidential candidates** frequently speak before interest groups, as did Barack Obama, shown here with the head of the American Israel Public Affairs Committee (AIPAC). (www.aipac.com)

AARP (formerly called the American Association of Retired Persons) is one of the most powerful interest groups in Washington, D.C., and, according to some, the strongest lobbying group in the United States. It is certainly the nation's largest interest group, with a membership of about 40 million. AARP has accomplished much for its members over the years. It played a significant role in the creation of Medicare and Medicaid, as well as in obtaining cost-of-living increases in Social Security payments. In 2003, AARP supported President George W. Bush's proposal to add prescription drug coverage to Medicare. Some observers believe that AARP's support tipped the balance and allowed Congress to pass the measure on a closely divided vote. In 2005, however, AARP was one of the leading opponents of President Bush's plan to reform Social Security.

Foreign Governments

Homegrown interest groups are not the only players in the game. Washington, D.C., is also the center for lobbying by foreign governments as well as private foreign interests. The governments of the largest U.S. trading partners, such as Japan, South Korea, Canada, and the European Union (EU) countries, maintain substantial research and lobbying staffs. Even smaller nations, such as those in the Caribbean, engage lobbyists when vital legislation affecting their trade interests is considered. Frequently, these foreign interests hire former members of Congress to promote their positions on Capitol Hill.

INTEREST GROUP STRATEGIES

Interest groups employ a wide range of techniques and strategies to promote their policy goals. Although few groups are successful at persuading Congress and the president to endorse their programs completely, many are able to block—or at least weaken—legislation injurious to their members. The key to success for interest groups is access to government officials. To gain such access, interest groups and their representatives try to cultivate long-term relationships with legislators and government officials. The best of these relationships are based on mutual respect and cooperation. The interest group provides the official with sources of information and assistance, and the official in turn gives the group opportunities to express its views.

The techniques used by interest groups can be divided into direct and indirect techniques. With **direct techniques,** the interest group and its lobbyists approach officials personally to present their case. With **indirect techniques,** in contrast, the interest group uses the general public or individual constituents to influence the government on behalf of the interest group.

Direct Techniques

Lobbying, publicizing ratings of legislative behavior, and providing campaign assistance are three main direct techniques used by interest groups.

Lobbying Techniques. As might be guessed, the term *lobbying* comes from the activities of private citizens regularly congregating in the lobbies of legislative chambers before a session to petition legislators. In the latter part of the 1800s, railroad and industrial groups openly bribed state legislators to pass legislation beneficial to their interests, giving lobbying a well-deserved bad name. Most lobbyists today are professionals. They are either consultants to a company or interest group or members of one of the Washington, D.C., law firms that specialize in providing lobbying services. Such firms employ hundreds of former members of Congress and former government officials. Lobbyists are valued for their network of contacts in Washington.

Lobbyists engage in an array of activities to influence legislation and government policy. These include the following:

- Meeting privately with public officials, including the president's advisers, to make known the interests of the lobbyists' clients. Although acting on behalf of their clients, lobbyists often furnish needed information to senators and representatives (and government agency appointees) that these officials could not easily obtain on their own. It is to the lobbyists' advantage to provide accurate information so that policymakers will trust them in the future.
- Testifying before congressional committees for or against proposed legislation.
- Testifying before executive rulemaking agencies—such as the Federal Trade Commission or the Consumer Product Safety Commission—for or against proposed rules.
- Assisting legislators or bureaucrats in drafting legislation or regulations. Often, lobbyists furnish advice on the specific details of legislation.
- Inviting legislators to social occasions, such as cocktail parties, boating expeditions, and other events, including conferences at exotic locations. Most lobbyists believe that meeting legislators in a relaxed social setting is effective.
- Providing political information to legislators and other government officials. Sometimes, lobbyists have better information than the party leadership about how other legislators are going to vote. In this case, the political information they furnish may be a key to legislative success.
- Suggesting nominations for federal appointments to the executive branch.

The Ratings Game. Many interest groups attempt to influence the overall behavior of legislators through their rating systems. Each year, these interest groups identify the legislation that they consider most important to their goals and then monitor how legislators vote on it. Legislators receive scores based on their votes. The usual scheme ranges from 0 to 100 percent. In the ratings scheme of the liberal Americans

Direct Technique
An interest group technique that uses direct interaction with government officials to further the group's goals.

Indirect Technique
An interest group technique that uses third parties to influence government officials.

for Democratic Action, for example, a rating of 100 means that a member of Congress voted with the group on every issue and is, by that measure, very liberal.

Ratings are a shorthand way of describing members' voting records for interested citizens. They can also be used to embarrass members. For example, an environmental group identifies the twelve representatives who the group believes have the worst voting records on environmental issues and labels them "the Dirty Dozen."

Campaign Assistance. Interest groups have additional strategies to use in their attempts to influence government policies. Groups recognize that the greatest concern of legislators is to be reelected, so they focus on the legislators' campaign needs. Associations with large memberships, such as labor unions, are able to provide workers for political campaigns, including precinct workers to get out the vote, volunteers to put up posters and pass out literature, and people to staff telephone banks for campaign headquarters.

In many states where certain interest groups have large memberships, candidates vie for the groups' endorsements in a campaign. Gaining those endorsements may be automatic, or it may require that the candidates participate in debates or interviews with the interest groups. Endorsements are important because an interest group usually publicizes its choices in its membership publication and because the candidate can use the endorsement in her or his campaign literature. Traditionally, labor unions have endorsed Democratic Party candidates. Republican candidates, however, often try to persuade union locals at least to refrain from any endorsement. Making no endorsement can then be perceived as disapproval of the Democratic Party candidate.

Indirect Techniques

Interest groups can also try to influence government policy by working through others, who may be constituents or the general public. Indirect techniques mask the interest group's own activities and make the effort appear to be spontaneous. Furthermore, legislators and government officials are often more impressed by contacts from constituents than from an interest group's lobbyist.

Generating Public Pressure. In some instances, interest groups try to produce a "groundswell" of public pressure to influence the government. Such efforts may include advertisements in national magazines and newspapers, mass mailings, television publicity, and demonstrations. The Internet and satellite links make communication efforts even more effective. Interest groups may commission polls to find out what the public's sentiments are and then publicize the results. The intent of this activity is to convince policymakers that public opinion supports the group's position.

Using Constituents as Lobbyists. An interest group may also use constituents of elected officials to lobby for the group's goals. In the "shotgun" approach, the interest group tries to mobilize large numbers of constituents to write, phone, or send e-mails to their legislators or the president. Often, the group provides postcards or form letters for constituents to fill out and mail. These efforts are effective on Capitol Hill only when the number of responses is very large, however, because legislators know that the voters did not initiate the communications on their own. Artificially manufactured grassroots activity has been aptly labeled *Astroturf lobbying.*

A more powerful variation of this technique uses only important constituents. With this approach, known as the "rifle" technique or the "Utah plant manager theory," the interest group might, for example, ask the manager of a local plant in Utah to contact the senator from Utah. Because the constituent is seen as responsible for many jobs or other resources, the legislator is more likely to listen carefully to the constituent's concerns about legislation than to a paid lobbyist.

REGULATING LOBBYISTS

Congress made its first attempt to control lobbyists and lobbying activities through Title III of the Legislative Reorganization Act of 1946, otherwise known as the Federal Regulation of Lobbying Act. The law actually provided for public disclosure more than for regulation, and it neglected to specify which agency would enforce its provisions. The 1946 legislation defined a *lobbyist* as any person or organization that received funds to be used principally to influence legislation before Congress. Such persons and individuals were supposed to "register" their clients and the purposes of their efforts and to report quarterly on their activities.

The Lobbying Disclosure Act

The reform-minded Congress of 1995–1996 overhauled the lobbying legislation, fundamentally changing the ground rules for those who seek to influence the federal government. The Lobbying Disclosure Act (LDA) passed in 1995 included the following provisions:

- A *lobbyist* is defined as anyone who spends at least 20 percent of his or her time lobbying members of Congress, their staffs, or executive-branch officials.
- Lobbyists must register with the clerk of the House and the secretary of the Senate.
- Semiannual reports must disclose the general nature of the lobbying effort.

Also in 1995, both the House and the Senate adopted new rules on gifts and travel expenses provided by lobbyists. The House adopted a flat ban on gifts, while the Senate established limits: senators were prohibited from accepting any gift with a value of more than $50 and from accepting gifts worth more than $100 from a single source in a given year. These gift rules stopped the broad practice of taking members of Congress to lunch or dinner, but the various exemptions and exceptions have allowed much gift-giving to continue.

Recent Legislation

The regulation of lobbying resurfaced as an issue in 2005 after a number of scandals came to light. When the Democrats took control of Congress in January 2007, one of their initial undertakings was ethics and lobbying reform. In the first one hundred hours of the session, the House tightened its rules on gifts and on travel funded by lobbyists. The Senate followed shortly thereafter.

In September 2007, President George W. Bush signed the Honest Leadership and Open Government Act. Under the new law, lobbyists must report quarterly, and the registration threshold becomes $10,000 per quarter in spending. Organizations must report coalition activities if they contribute more than $5,000 to a coalition. The House and Senate must now post lobbying information in a searchable file on the Internet. In a significant alteration to legislative practices, "earmarked" expenditures, commonly called "pork," must now be identified and made public. This last change may not have

Independent
A voter or candidate who does not identify with a political party.

Faction
A group or bloc in a legislature or political party acting in pursuit of some special interest or position.

its intended effect of reducing earmarks, however, because it turns out that many legislators are actually proud of their "pork" and happy to tell the folks back home all about it.

WHAT IS A POLITICAL PARTY?

Every two years, usually starting in early fall, the media concentrate on the state of the political parties. Prior to an election, a typical poll usually asks the following question: "Do you consider yourself to be a Republican, a Democrat, or an independent?" For many years, Americans divided fairly evenly among these three choices, with more than one-third describing themselves as **independents.**

In the United States, being a member of a political party does not require paying dues, passing an examination, or swearing an oath of allegiance. If nothing is really required to be a member of a political party, what, then, is a political party? As discussed earlier in this chapter, a political party is a group that seeks to win elections, operate the government, and determine public policy. Political parties are thus quite different from interest groups, which, as mentioned, seek to influence, not run, the government. Political parties also differ from **factions,** which are smaller groups that are trying to obtain power or benefits.[3] Factions preceded the formation of political parties in American history, and the term is still used to refer to groups within parties that follow a particular leader or share a regional identification or an ideological viewpoint. For example, until fairly recently, the Democratic Party was seen as containing a southern faction that was much more conservative than the rest of the party. Factions are subgroups within parties that may try to capture a nomination or get a position adopted by the party. A key difference between factions and parties is that factions do not have a permanent organization, whereas political parties do.

FUNCTIONS OF POLITICAL PARTIES IN THE UNITED STATES

Political parties in the United States engage in a wide variety of activities, many of which are discussed in this chapter. Through these activities, parties perform a number of functions for the political system. These functions include the following:

1. *Recruiting candidates for public office.* Because it is the goal of parties to gain control of government, they must work to recruit candidates for all elective offices. Often, this means recruiting candidates to run against powerful incumbents. If parties did not search out and encourage political hopefuls, far more offices would be uncontested, and voters would have limited choices.

2. *Organizing and running elections.* Although elections are a government activity, political parties actually organize the voter-registration drives, recruit the volunteers to work at the polls, provide much of the campaign activity to stimulate interest in the election, and work to increase voter participation.

3. *Presenting alternative policies to the electorate.* In contrast to factions, which are often centered on individual politicians or regions, parties are focused on a set of political positions. The Democrats or Republicans in Congress who vote together do so because they represent constituencies that have similar expectations and demands.

3. See James Madison's comments on factions in Chapter 2.

4. *Accepting responsibility for operating the government.* When a party elects the president or governor and members of the legislature, it accepts the responsibility for running the government. This includes staffing the executive branch with loyal party supporters and developing linkages among the elected officials to gain support for policies and their implementation.

5. *Acting as the organized opposition to the party in power.* The "out" party, or the one that does not control the government, is expected to articulate its own policies and oppose the winning party when appropriate. By organizing the opposition to the "in" party, the opposition party forces debate on the policy alternatives.

The major functions of American political parties are carried out by a small, relatively loose-knit nucleus of party activists. This arrangement is quite different from the more highly structured, mass-membership party organization typical of many European parties. American parties concentrate on winning elections rather than on signing up large numbers of deeply committed, dues-paying members who believe passionately in the party's program.

Two-Party System
A political system in which only two parties have a reasonable chance of winning.

A HISTORY OF POLITICAL PARTIES IN THE UNITED STATES

The United States has a **two-party system,** and that system has been around since about 1800. The function and character of the political parties, as well as the emergence of the two-party system itself, have much to do with the unique historical forces operating from this country's beginning as an independent nation. Indeed, James Madison (1751–1836) linked the emergence of political parties to the form of government created by our Constitution.

Generally, we can divide the evolution of our nation's political parties into seven periods:

1. The creation and formation of parties, from 1789 to 1816.
2. The era of one-party rule, or personal politics, from 1816 to 1828.
3. The period from Andrew Jackson's presidency to just before the Civil War, from 1828 to 1856.
4. The Civil War and post–Civil War period, from 1856 to 1896.
5. The Republican ascendancy and the progressive period, from 1896 to 1932.
6. The New Deal period, from 1932 to about 1968.
7. The modern period, from approximately 1968 to the present.

The Formative Years: Federalists and Anti-Federalists

The first partisan political division in the United States occurred before the adoption of the Constitution. As you will recall from Chapter 2, the Federalists were those who pushed for the adoption of the Constitution, whereas the Anti-Federalists were against ratification.

In September 1796, George Washington, who had served as president for almost two full terms, decided not to run again. In his farewell address, he made a somber assessment of the nation's future. Washington felt that the country might be destroyed by the "baneful [harmful] effects of the spirit of party." He viewed parties as a threat to both national unity and the concept of popular government. Nevertheless, in the years after the ratification of the Constitution, Americans came to realize that something more permanent than a faction would be necessary to identify candidates for office and represent political differences among the people. The result was two political parties.

One party was the Federalists, which included John Adams, the second president (1797–1801). The Federalists represented commercial interests such as merchants and large planters. They supported a strong national government.

Thomas Jefferson led the other party, which came to be called the Republicans. These Republicans should not be confused with the later Republican Party of Abraham Lincoln. (To avoid confusion, some scholars refer to Jefferson's party as the Democratic Republicans, but this name was never used during the time that the party existed.) Jefferson's Republicans represented artisans and farmers. They strongly supported states' rights. In 1800, when Jefferson defeated Adams in the presidential contest, one of the world's first peaceful transfers of power from one party to another was achieved.

▲ **Thomas Jefferson,** founder of the first Republican Party. His election to the presidency in 1800 was one of the world's first peaceful transfers of power from one party to another through a free election. (Library of Congress)

The Era of Good Feelings

From 1800 to 1820, a majority of U.S. voters regularly elected Republicans to the presidency and to Congress. By 1816, the Federalist Party had virtually collapsed, and two-party competition did not really exist. Although during elections the Republicans opposed the Federalists' call for a stronger, more active central government, they undertook such active government policies as acquiring the Louisiana Territory and Florida and establishing a national bank. Because there was no real political opposition to the Republicans and thus little political debate, the administration of James Monroe (1817–1825) came to be known as the **era of good feelings.** Because political competition now took place among individual Republican aspirants, this period can also be called the *era of personal politics.*

National Two-Party Rule: Democrats and Whigs

Organized two-party politics returned in 1824. With the election of John Quincy Adams as president, the Republican Party split in two. The followers of Adams called themselves National Republicans. The followers of Andrew Jackson, who defeated Adams in 1828, formed the **Democratic Party.** Later, the National Republicans took the name **Whig Party,** which had been a traditional name for British liberals. The Whigs stood for, among other things, federal spending on "internal improvements," such as roads. The Democrats opposed this policy. The Democrats, who were the stronger of the two parties, favored personal liberty and opportunity for the "common man."

Era of Good Feelings
The years from 1817 to 1825, when James Monroe was president and there was, in effect, no political opposition.

Democratic Party
One of the two major American political parties evolving out of the Republican Party of Thomas Jefferson.

Whig Party
A major party in the United States during the first half of the nineteenth century, formally established in 1836. The Whig Party was anti-Jackson and represented a variety of regional interests.

▲ **Andrew Jackson** earned the name "Old Hickory" for exploits during the War of 1812. In 1828, Jackson was elected president as the candidate of the new Democratic Party. (Library of Congress)

It was understood implicitly that the "common man" was a white man—hostility toward African Americans was an important force holding the disparate Democratic groups together.[4]

The Civil War Crisis

In the 1850s, hostility between the North and South over the issue of slavery divided both parties. The Whigs were the first to split in two. The Whigs had been the party of an active federal government, but southerners had come to believe that "a government strong enough to build roads is a government strong enough to free your slaves." The southern Whigs therefore ceased to exist as an organized party. In 1854, the northern Whigs united with antislavery Democrats and members of the radical antislavery Free Soil Party to found the modern **Republican Party.**

The Post–Civil War Period

After the Civil War, the Democratic Party was able to heal its divisions. Southern resentment of the Republicans' role in defeating the South and fears that the federal government would intervene on behalf of African Americans ensured that the Democrats would dominate the white South for the next century. Northern Democrats feared a strong government for other reasons. The Republicans thought that the government should promote business and economic growth, but many Republicans also wanted to use the power of government to impose evangelical Protestant moral values on society. Democrats opposed what they saw as culturally coercive measures. Many Republicans wanted to limit or even prohibit the sale of alcohol. They favored the establishment of public schools—with a Protestant curriculum. As a result, Catholics were strongly Democratic. In this period, the parties were very evenly matched in strength.

In the 1890s, however, the Republicans gained a decisive edge. In that decade, the populist movement emerged in the West and South to champion the interests of small farmers, who were often greatly in debt. Populists supported inflation, which benefited debtors by reducing the value of outstanding debts. In 1896, when William Jennings Bryan became the Democratic candidate for president, the Democrats embraced populism. As it turned out, the few western farmers who were drawn to the Democrats by this step were greatly outnumbered by urban working-class voters who believed that inflation would reduce the value of their paychecks and who therefore became Republicans. From 1896 until 1932, the Republicans were successful at presenting themselves as the party that knew how to manage the economy.

Republican Party
One of the two major American political parties. It emerged in the 1850s as an antislavery party and consisted of former northern Whigs and antislavery Democrats.

---

4. Edward Pessen, *Jacksonian America: Society, Personality, and Politics* (Homewood, Ill.: Dorsey Press, 1969). See especially pages 246–247. The small number of free blacks who could vote were overwhelmingly Whig.

The Progressive Interlude

In the early 1900s, a spirit of political reform arose in both major parties. Called *progressivism,* this spirit was compounded of a fear of the growing power of large corporations and a belief that honest, impartial government could regulate the economy effectively. In 1912, the Republican Party temporarily split as former Republican president Theodore Roosevelt campaigned for the presidency on a third-party Progressive ticket. The Republican split permitted the election of Woodrow Wilson, the Democratic candidate, along with a Democratic Congress.

Like Roosevelt, Wilson considered himself a progressive, although he and Roosevelt did not agree on how progressivism ought to be implemented. Wilson's progressivism marked the beginning of a radical change in Democratic policies. Dating back to its very foundation, the Democratic Party had been the party of limited government. Under Wilson, the Democrats became for the first time at least as receptive as the Republicans to government action in the economy. (Wilson's progressivism did not extend to race relations—for African Americans, the Wilson administration was something of a disaster.)

The New Deal Era

The Republican ascendancy resumed after Wilson left office. It ended with the election of 1932, in the depths of the Great Depression. Republican Herbert Hoover was president when the Depression began in 1929. While Hoover took some measures to fight the Depression, they fell far short of what the public demanded. Significantly, Hoover opposed federal relief for the unemployed and the destitute. In 1932, Democrat Franklin D. Roosevelt was elected president by an overwhelming margin.

The Great Depression shattered the working-class belief in Republican economic competence. Under Roosevelt, the Democrats began to make major interventions in the economy in an attempt to combat the Depression and to relieve the suffering of the unemployed. Roosevelt's New Deal relief programs were open to all citizens, both black and white. As a result, African Americans began to support the Democratic Party in large numbers—a development that would have stunned any American politician of the 1800s.

Roosevelt's political coalition was broad enough to establish the Democrats as the new majority party, in place of the Republicans. In the 1950s, Republican Dwight D. Eisenhower, the leading U.S. general during World War II, won two terms as president. Otherwise, with minor interruptions, the Democratic ascendancy lasted until about 1968.

An Era of Divided Government

The New Deal coalition managed the unlikely feat of including both African Americans and whites who were hostile to African American advancement. This balancing act came to an end in the 1960s, a decade that was marked by the civil rights movement, by several years of "race riots" in major cities, and by increasingly heated protests against the Vietnam War (1964–1975). For many economically liberal, socially conservative voters, especially in the South, social issues had become more important than economic ones, and these individuals left the Democrats. These voters outnumbered the new voters who joined the Democrats—newly enfranchised African Americans and former liberal Republicans in New England and the upper Midwest.

The Parties in Balance. The result, after 1968, was a nation almost evenly divided in politics. In presidential elections, the Republicans had more success than the Democrats. Until the 1990s, Congress remained Democratic, but official party labels can be misleading. Some of the Democrats were southern conservatives who normally voted with the Republicans on issues. As these conservative Democrats retired, they were largely replaced by Republicans.

In the forty years between 1968 and 2008, there were only ten years when one of the two major parties controlled the presidency, the House of Representatives, and the Senate. The Democrats controlled all three institutions during the presidency of Jimmy Carter (1977–1981) and during the first two years of the presidency of Bill Clinton (1993–2001). The Republicans controlled all three institutions during the third and fourth years of George W. Bush's first term and the first two years of his second term.[5]

Red State, Blue State. Nothing demonstrated the nation's close political divisions more clearly than the 2000 presidential elections. Democratic presidential candidate Al Gore would have won if he had received 538 more popular votes in Florida. George W. Bush actually lost the nationwide popular vote count by more than half a million votes, but he carried the electoral college (which coincidentally has 538 members) by five votes. The extreme closeness of the vote in the electoral college led the press to repeatedly publish maps showing state-by-state results. Commentators discussed at length the supposed differences between the Republican "red states" and the Democratic "blue states."

An interesting characteristic of the red state–blue state division is that it is an almost exact reversal of the results of the presidential elections of 1896, which established the Republican ascendancy that lasted until the Great Depression. Except for the state of Washington, every state that supported Democrat William Jennings Bryan in 1896 supported Republican George W. Bush in 2000 and 2004. This reversal parallels the transformation of the Democrats from an anti–civil rights to a pro–civil rights party and from a party that supported limited government to a party that favors positive government action.

The Parties Today

Although George W. Bush won the popular vote in the presidential elections of 2004 by a margin of more than 3 million votes, only three states changed hands. Bush picked up New Mexico and Iowa, which had voted Democratic in 2000, and lost New Hampshire to Democrat John F. Kerry. Clearly, the parties continued to be closely matched. (See Figure 7–2 on the following page.)

By 2006, however, the Republicans were in trouble. The war in Iraq was increasingly unpopular, and voters blamed the Republicans for involving the nation in a conflict that seemed to be endless. In the 2006 midterm elections, the Democrats picked up thirty seats in the House, enough for control. The Democrats also picked up six Senate seats, giving them a one-vote margin.[6]

---

5. The Republicans also were in control of all three institutions for the first four months after Bush's 2001 inauguration. This initial period of control came to an end when Senator James Jeffords of Vermont left the Republican Party, giving the Democrats control of the Senate.
6. The margin included two independents who caucus with the Democrats, Joe Lieberman of Connecticut and Bernie Sanders of Vermont.

FIGURE 7–2: The 2004 Presidential Election Results by State

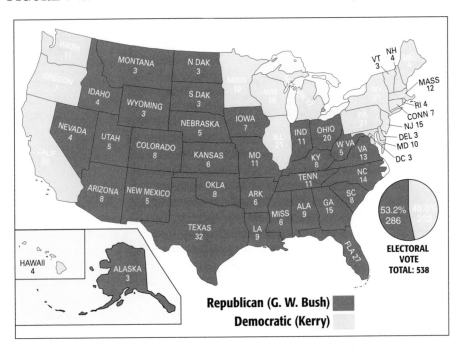

The Elections of 2008. By the 2008 elections season, Bush's popularity figures were among the lowest ever recorded for a president. Apparently, many voters were coming to view the Iraq conflict as an example of deeper problems within the Republican Party. Polls suggested that voters were even becoming more liberal on issues that had nothing to do with Iraq, such as support for antipoverty measures. The shocking collapse of the financial system that began on September 15 sealed the fate of the Republicans. In November, Democratic presidential candidate Barack Obama won the clearest electoral mandate seen in many years. (See Figure 7–3.) The Democrats also made additional gains in the House and the Senate.

An Opportunity for the Democrats? By 2009, more than half of the voters considered themselves to be either Democrats or independents leaning toward the Democrats. More ominously for the Republicans, Obama carried the 18- to 29-year-old vote by 66 percent to 32 percent. The Republicans were at risk of losing tomorrow's voters. The Democrats were also winning increased support from Hispanics and educated professionals.

Is it possible that someday we will look back at the elections of 2008 and see them as a turning point, similar to the elections of 1896 and 1932? The answer may depend on whether Obama's presidency is a success. If the recession of 2008–2010 lifts in a timely fashion, and if legislative initiatives such as the Democrats' plan for universal health insurance are passed and prove to be popular, the Democratic Party could remain in power for years. If Obama's policies should fail, however, the nation may again be closely divided, and the Republicans will have a chance to win future elections.

FIGURE 7–3: The 2008 Presidential Election Results by State

In the 2008 presidential elections, Democrat Barack Obama received a majority of the electoral college votes, outdoing Republican John McCain by a large margin. Although Obama won nine more states than Democrat John Kerry had won in the 2004 presidential elections, the regional political preferences remained similar to those of previous elections. Note that Obama carried Nebraska's second congressional district.

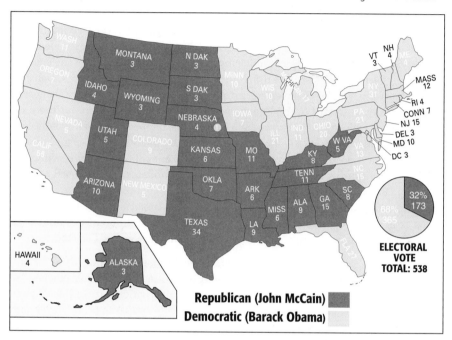

PARTY ORGANIZATION

Each of the American political parties is often seen as having a pyramid-shaped organization, with the national chairperson and committee at the top and the local precinct chairperson on the bottom. This structure, however, does not accurately reflect the relative power of the individual components of the **party organization.** If it did, the national chairperson of the Democratic Party or the Republican Party, along with the national committee, could simply dictate how the organization was to be run, just as if it were ExxonMobil Corporation or Microsoft Corporation. In reality, the political parties have a confederal structure, in which each unit has significant autonomy and is linked only loosely to the other units.

The National Party Organization

Each party has a national organization, the most conspicuous part of which is the **national convention,** held every four years. The convention is used to nominate the presidential and vice-presidential candidates. In addition, the **party platform** is developed at the national convention. The platform sets forth the party's position on the issues and makes promises to initiate certain policies if the party wins the presidency.

After the convention, the platform sometimes is neglected or ignored when party candidates disagree with it. Because candidates are trying to win votes from a wide

Party Organization
The formal structure and leadership of a political party, including election committees; local, state, and national executives; and paid professional staff.

National Convention
The meeting held every four years by each major party to select presidential and vice-presidential candidates, write a platform, choose a national committee, and conduct party business.

Party Platform
A document drawn up at each national convention, outlining the policies, positions, and principles of the party.

National Committee
A standing committee of a national political party established to direct and coordinate party activities between national party conventions.

State Central Committee
The principal organized structure of each political party within each state. This committee is responsible for carrying out policy decisions of the party's state convention.

Patronage
The practice of rewarding faithful party workers and followers with government employment and contracts.

spectrum of voters, it can be counterproductive to emphasize the fairly narrow and sometimes controversial goals set forth in the platform. Political scientist Gerald M. Pomper discovered decades ago, however, that once elected, the parties do try to carry out platform promises and that roughly three-fourths of the promises eventually become law.[7] Of course, some general goals, such as economic prosperity, are included in the platforms of both parties.

Convention Delegates. The party convention provides the most striking illustration of the difference between the ordinary members of a party, or party identifiers, and party activists. As a series of studies by the *New York Times* shows, delegates to the national party conventions are different from ordinary party identifiers. Delegates to the Democratic National Convention are far more liberal than ordinary Democratic voters. Typically, delegates to the Republican National Convention are far more conservative than ordinary Republicans. Why does this happen? In part, it is because a person, to become a delegate, must be appointed by party leaders or gather votes in a primary election from party members who care enough to vote in a primary. In addition, the primaries generally pit presidential candidates against each other on intraparty issues. Competition within each party tends to pull candidates away from the center, and delegates even more so. Often, the most important activity for the convention is making peace among the delegates who support different candidates and helping them accept a party platform that will appeal to the general electorate.

The National Committee. At the national convention, each of the parties formally chooses a national standing committee, elected by the individual state parties. This **national committee** directs and coordinates party activities during the following four years. One of the jobs of the national committee is to ratify the presidential nominee's choice of a national chairperson, who in principle acts as the spokesperson for the party. The national chairperson and the national committee plan the next campaign and the next convention, obtain financial contributions, and publicize the national party. The fact, though, is that the real strength and power of the party is at the state level.

The State Party Organization

Because every state party is unique, it is impossible to describe what an "average" state political party is like. Nonetheless, state parties have several organizational features in common. Each state party has a chairperson, a committee, and a number of local organizations. In theory, the role of the **state central committee**—the principal organized structure of each political party within each state—is similar in the various states. The committee has responsibility for carrying out the policy decisions of the party's state convention. The committee also has control over the use of party campaign funds during political campaigns. Usually, the state central committee has little, if any, influence on party candidates once they are elected.

Local Party Machinery: The Grassroots

The lowest layer of party machinery is the local organization, supported by district leaders, precinct or ward captains, and party workers. In the 1800s, the institution of **patronage**—rewarding the party faithful with government jobs or contracts—held

---

7. Gerald M. Pomper and Susan S. Lederman, *Elections in America: Control and Influence in Democratic Politics,* 2d ed. (New York: Longman, 1980).

the local organization together. For immigrants and the poor, the political machine often furnished important services and protections.

The last big-city local political machine to exercise substantial power was run by Chicago mayor Richard J. Daley, who was also an important figure in national Democratic politics. The current mayor of Chicago, Richard M. Daley, son of the former mayor, does not have the kind of machine that his father had. City machines are now dead, mostly because their function of providing social services (and reaping the reward of votes) has been taken over by state and national agencies.

Local political organizations provide the foot soldiers of politics—individuals who pass out literature and get out the vote on Election Day, which can be crucial in local elections. In many regions, local Democratic and Republican organizations still exercise some patronage, such as awarding courthouse jobs, contracts for street repair, and other lucrative construction contracts. The constitutionality of awarding—or not awarding—contracts on the basis of political affiliation has been subject to challenge, however. The Supreme Court has ruled that failing to hire or firing individuals because of their political affiliation is an infringement of these individuals' First Amendment rights to free expression.[8] Local party organizations are also the most important vehicles for recruiting young adults into political work, because political involvement at the local level offers activists many opportunities to gain experience.

The Party-in-Government

After the election is over and the winners are announced, the focus of party activity shifts from getting out the vote to organizing and controlling the government. As you will see in Chapter 9, party membership plays an important role in the day-to-day operations of Congress, with partisanship determining everything from office space to committee assignments and power on Capitol Hill. For the president, the political party furnishes a pool of qualified applicants for political appointments to run the government. (Presidents can, and occasionally do, appoint executive personnel, such as cabinet members, from the opposition party, but it is uncommon to do so.) As we note in Chapter 11, there are not as many appointed positions as presidents might like, and presidential power is limited by the permanent bureaucracy.[9] Judicial appointments also offer a great opportunity to the winning party. For the most part, presidents are likely to appoint federal judges from their own party.

All of these party appointments suggest that the winning political party, whether at the national, state, or local level, has a great deal of control in the American system. At the national level, the Republicans may have had such control from 2003 to 2006 because they controlled the presidency and both the U.S. House and the Senate, and the Democrats may have such control today. Because of the checks and balances and the relative lack of cohesion in American parties, however, such control is the exception rather than the rule. One reason is that Americans have often seemed to prefer a **divided government,** with the executive and legislative branches controlled by different parties. The trend toward **ticket splitting**—splitting votes between the president and members of Congress—may indicate a lack of trust in government or the relative weakness of party identification among many voters.

Divided Government
A situation in which one major political party controls the presidency and the other controls Congress or in which one party controls a state governorship and the other controls the state legislature.

Ticket Splitting
Voting for candidates of two or more parties for different offices. For example, a voter splits her ticket if she votes for a Republican presidential candidate and for a Democratic congressional candidate.

---

8. *Rutan v. Republican Party of Illinois,* 497 U.S. 62 (1990).
9. In 2007, President George W. Bush tried to gain more influence over the bureaucracy by establishing a Regulatory Policy Office (RPO) in each agency of the federal government. Each of these offices was headed by a political appointee.

WHY HAS THE TWO-PARTY SYSTEM ENDURED?

There are several reasons why two major parties have dominated the political landscape in the United States for almost two centuries. These reasons have to do with (1) the historical foundations of the system, (2) political socialization and practical considerations, (3) the winner-take-all electoral system, and (4) state and federal laws favoring the two-party system.

The Historical Foundations of the Two-Party System

As we have seen, at many times in American history one preeminent issue or dispute has divided the nation politically. In the beginning, Americans were at odds over ratifying the Constitution. After the Constitution went into effect, the power of the federal government became the major national issue. Thereafter, the dispute over slavery divided the nation, North versus South. At times—for example, in the North after the Civil War—cultural differences have been important, with advocates of government-sponsored morality (such as banning alcoholic beverages) pitted against advocates of personal liberty. During much of the twentieth century, economic differences were preeminent. In the New Deal period, the Democrats became known as the party of the working class, while the Republicans became known as the party of the middle and upper classes and commercial interests.

In situations like these, when politics is based on an argument between two opposing points of view, advocates of each viewpoint can mobilize most effectively by forming a single, unified party. The result is a two-party system, and when such a system has been in existence for almost two centuries, it becomes difficult to imagine an alternative.

Political Socialization and Practical Considerations

Given that the majority of Americans identify with one of the two major political parties, it is not surprising that most children learn at a fairly young age to think of themselves as either Democrats or Republicans. This generates a built-in mechanism to perpetuate a two-party system. Also, most politically oriented people who aspire to work for change consider that the only realistic way to capture political power in this country is to be either a Republican or a Democrat.

The Winner-Take-All Electoral System

At nearly every level of government in the United States, the outcome of elections is based on the **plurality**, winner-take-all principle. In a plurality system, the winner is the person who obtains the most votes, even if that person does not receive a majority (over 50 percent) of the votes. Whoever gets the most votes gets everything. Most legislators in the United States are elected from single-member districts in which only one person represents the constituency, and the candidate who finishes second in such an election receives nothing for the effort.

Presidential Voting. The winner-take-all system also operates in the election of the U.S president. Recall that the voters in each state do not vote for a president directly

Plurality
A number of votes cast for a candidate that is greater than the number of votes for any other candidate but not necessarily a majority.

but vote for **electoral college** delegates who are committed to the various presidential candidates. These delegates are called *electors*.

In all but two states (Maine and Nebraska), if a presidential candidate wins a plurality in the state, then *all* of the state's electoral votes go to that candidate. This is known as the **unit rule.** For example, suppose that the electors pledged to a particular presidential candidate receive a plurality of 40 percent of the votes in a state. That presidential candidate will receive all of the state's votes in the electoral college. Minor parties have a difficult time competing under such a system. Because voters know that minor parties cannot win any electoral votes, they often will not vote for minor-party candidates, even if the candidates are in tune with them ideologically.

Electoral College
A group of persons, called electors, who are selected by the voters in each state. This group officially elects the president and the vice president of the United States.

Unit Rule
A rule by which all of a state's electoral votes are cast for the presidential candidate who receives a plurality of the votes in that state.

Popular Election of the Governors and the President. In most of Europe, the chief executive (usually called the prime minister) is elected by the legislature, or parliament. If the parliament contains three or more parties, as is usually the situation, two or more of the parties can join together in a coalition to choose the prime minister and the other leaders of the government. In the United States, however, the people elect the president and the governors of all fifty states. There is no opportunity for two or more parties to negotiate a coalition. Here, too, the winner-take-all principle discriminates powerfully against any third party.

Proportional Representation. Many other nations use a system of proportional representation with multimember districts. If, during the national election, party X obtains 12 percent of the vote, party Y gets 43 percent of the vote, and party Z gets the remaining 45 percent of the vote, then party X gets 12 percent of the seats in the legislature, party Y gets 43 percent of the seats, and party Z gets 45 percent of the seats. Because even a minor party may still obtain at least a few seats in the legislature, smaller parties have a greater incentive to organize under such electoral systems than they do in the United States.

State and Federal Laws Favoring the Two Parties

Many state and federal election laws offer a clear advantage to the two major parties. In some states, the established major parties need to gather fewer signatures to place their candidates on the ballot than minor parties or independent candidates do. The criterion for determining how many signatures will be required is often based on the total party vote in the last general election, thus penalizing a new political party that did not compete in that election.

At the national level, minor parties face different obstacles. All of the rules and procedures of both houses of Congress divide committee seats, staff members, and other privileges on the basis of party membership. A legislator who is elected on a minor-party ticket, such as the Conservative Party of New York, must choose to be counted with one of the major parties to obtain a committee assignment. The Federal Election Commission (FEC) rules for campaign financing also place restrictions on minor-party candidates. Such candidates are not eligible for federal matching funds in either the primary or the general election. In the 1980 elections, John Anderson, running for president as an independent, sued the FEC for campaign funds. The commission finally agreed to repay part of his campaign costs after the election in proportion to the votes he received. Giving funds to a candidate when the campaign is over is, of course, much less helpful than providing funds while the campaign is still under way.

Third Party
A political party other than the two major political parties (Republican and Democratic).

THE ROLE OF MINOR PARTIES IN U.S. POLITICS

For the reasons just discussed, minor parties have a difficult, if not impossible, time competing within the American two-party political system. Nonetheless, minor parties have played an important role in our political life. Parties other than the Republicans or Democrats are usually called **third parties.** (Technically, of course, there could be fourth, fifth, or sixth parties as well, but we use the term *third party* because it has endured.) Third parties can come into existence in a number of ways. They may be founded from scratch by individuals or groups who are committed to a particular interest, issue, or ideology. They can split off from one of the major parties when a group becomes dissatisfied with the major party's policies. Finally, they can be organized around a particular charismatic leader and serve as that person's vehicle for contesting elections.

Frequently, third parties have acted as barometers of changes in the political mood. Such barometric indicators have forced the major parties to recognize new issues or trends in the thinking of Americans. Political scientists also believe that third parties have acted as safety valves for dissident groups, perhaps preventing major confrontations and political unrest.

Ideological Third Parties

The longest-lived third parties have been those with strong ideological foundations that are typically at odds with the majority mind-set. Ideology has at least two functions in such parties. First, the members of the party regard themselves as outsiders and look to one another for support; ideology provides great psychological cohesiveness. Second, because the rewards of ideological commitment are partly psychological, these parties do not think in terms of immediate electoral success. A poor showing at the polls therefore does not dissuade either the leadership or the grassroots participants from continuing their quest for change in American government (and, ultimately, American society).

Today's active ideological parties include the Libertarian Party and the Green Party. As you learned in Chapter 1, the Libertarian Party supports a *laissez-faire* ("let it be") capitalist economic program, together with a hands-off policy on regulating matters of moral conduct. The Green Party began as a grassroots environmentalist organization with affiliated political parties across North America and Western Europe. It was established in the United States as a national party in

▼ **Presidential candidate Ralph Nader**
campaigns during the last election cycle. He has run once as a candidate for the Green Party and twice as an independent. Why were his chances of becoming president very small? (AP Photo/Lisa Poole)

1996 and nominated Ralph Nader to run for president in 2000. Nader campaigned against what he called "corporate greed," advocated universal health insurance, and promoted environmental concerns.[10] He ran again for president as an independent in 2004 and 2008.

Splinter Parties

Some of the most successful minor parties have been those that split from major parties. The impetus for these **splinter parties,** or factions, has usually been a situation in which a particular personality was at odds with the major party. The most successful of the splinter parties was the Bull Moose Progressive Party, formed in 1912 to support Theodore Roosevelt for president. The Republican national convention of that year denied Roosevelt the nomination, despite the fact that he had won most of the primaries. He therefore left the Republicans and ran against Republican "regular" William Howard Taft in the general election. Although Roosevelt did not win the election, he did split the Republican vote so that Democrat Woodrow Wilson became president.

Third parties have also been formed to back individual candidates who were not rebelling against a particular party. H. Ross Perot, for example, who challenged Republican George H. W. Bush and Democrat Bill Clinton in 1992, had not previously been active in a major party. Perot's supporters probably would have split their votes between Bush and Clinton had Perot not been in the race. In theory, Perot ran in 1992 as a nonparty independent; in practice, he had to create a campaign organization. By 1996, Perot's organization was formalized as the Reform Party.

The Impact of Minor Parties

Third parties have rarely been able to affect American politics by actually winning elections. (One exception is that third-party and independent candidates have occasionally won races for state governorships—for example, Jesse Ventura was elected governor of Minnesota on the Reform Party ticket in 1998.) Instead, the impact of third parties has taken two forms. First, third parties can influence one of the major parties to take up one or more issues. Second, third parties can determine the outcome of a particular election by pulling votes from one of the major-party candidates in what is called the "spoiler effect."

The presidential elections of 2000 were one instance in which a minor party may have altered the outcome. Green candidate Ralph Nader received almost 100,000 votes in Florida, a majority of which would probably have gone to Democrat Al Gore if Nader had not been in the race. The real question, however, is not whether Nader's vote had an effect—clearly, it did—but whether the effect was important. The problem is that in an election as close as the presidential elections of 2000, *any* factor with an impact on the outcome can be said to have determined the results of the election.

THE RISE OF THE INDEPENDENTS

Polls that track **party identification** show increasing numbers of voters who identify themselves as independents. (See Figure 7–4 on the following page.) This trend extends back as far as the middle of the twentieth century. Not only has the number of

Splinter Party
A new party formed by a dissident faction within a major political party. Often, splinter parties have emerged when a particular personality was at odds with the major party.

Party Identification
Linking oneself to a particular political party.

---

10. Ralph Nader offers his own entertaining account of his run for the presidency in 2000 in *Crashing the Party: How to Tell the Truth and Still Run for President* (New York: St. Martin's Press, 2002).

FIGURE 7–4: Party Identification from 1944 to the Present

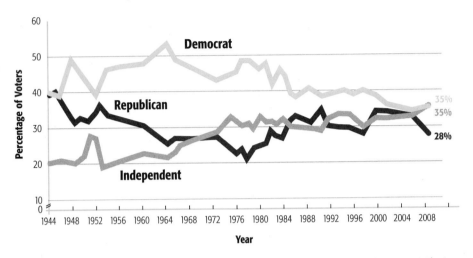

Sources: *Gallup Report,* August 1995; *New York Times*/CBS poll, June 1996; *Gallup Report,* February 1998; The Pew Research Center for the People and the Press, November 2003; Gallup polls, 2004 through 2009.

Straight-Ticket
Voting
Voting exclusively for the
candidates of one party.

independents grown, but voters are also less willing to vote a straight ticket—that is, to vote for all the candidates of one party. In the early twentieth century, **straight-ticket voting** was nearly universal. By midcentury, 12 percent of voters engaged in ticket splitting. By the 1970s and 1980s, 25 to 30 percent of all ballots cast in presidential election years were split-ticket. A major reason was that many voters, especially in the South, were pairing a Republican for president with a conservative Democrat for Congress. In recent years, conservative Democrats have become scarce, and the incidence of split-ticket voting has ranged only from 17 to 19 percent.

While the number of voters who identify as independents has never been greater, many voters who call themselves independents actually lean toward one or the other of the two major parties. In polls taken in early 2009, for example, about 52 percent of all voters reported either that they were Democrats or that they were independents who leaned toward the Democratic Party. The corresponding figure for the Republicans was just 38 percent. Leaving aside respondents who were unable to answer the question, true independents were less than 10 percent of the polling sample.

making a difference

YOU CAN BE A CONVENTION DELEGATE

The most exciting political party event, staged every four years, is the national convention. State conventions also take place on a regular basis. Surprising as it might seem, there are opportunities for the individual voter to become involved in nominating delegates to a state or national convention or to become a delegate.

Why Should You Care? How would you like to exercise a small amount of real political power yourself—power that goes beyond simply voting in an election? You might be able to become a delegate to a county, district, or even state party convention. Many of these conventions nominate candidates for various offices. For example, in Michigan, the state party conventions nominate the candidates for the Board of Regents of the state's three top public universities. The regents set university policies, so these are nominations in which students have an obvious interest. In Michigan, if you are elected as a party precinct delegate, you can attend your party's state convention.

In much of the country, there are more openings for party precinct delegates than there are people willing to serve. In such circumstances, almost anyone can become a delegate by collecting a handful of signatures on a nominating petition or by mounting a small-scale write-in campaign. You are then eligible to take part in one of the most educational political experiences available to an ordinary citizen. You will get a firsthand look at how political persuasion takes place, how resolutions are written and passed, and how candidates seek out support among their fellow party members.

What Can You Do? When the parties choose delegates for the national convention, the process begins at the local level—either the congressional district or the state legislative district. District delegates may be elected in party primary elections or chosen in neighborhood or precinct caucuses. If the delegates are elected in a primary, persons who want to run for these positions must file petitions with the board of elections. If you are interested in committing yourself to a particular presidential candidate and running for the delegate position, check with the local county committee or with the party's national committee about the rules you must follow.

It is even easier to get involved in the grassroots politics of presidential caucuses. In some states—Iowa being the earliest and most famous one—delegates are first nominated at the local precinct caucus. These caucuses, in addition to being the focus of national media attention in January or February, select delegates to the county conventions who are pledged to specific presidential candidates. This is the first step toward the national convention. At both the county caucus and the convention levels, both parties often try to find younger members to fill some of the seats.

For further information about these opportunities (some states hold caucuses and state conventions in every election year), contact the state party office or your local state legislator for specific dates and regulations. Or write to the national committee for its informational brochures on how to become a delegate.

Republican National Committee
310 First St. S.E.
Washington, DC 20003
(202) 863-8500
www.rnc.org

Democratic National Committee
430 Capital St. S.E.
Washington, DC 20003
(202) 863-8000
www.democrats.org/index.html

▼ **These delegates** to the Democratic National Convention in Denver in the summer of 2008 show their support for Barack Obama. (AP Photo/Jae C. Hong)

key terms

Democratic Party 156

direct technique 151

divided government 163

electoral college 165

era of good feelings 156

faction 154

independent 154

indirect technique 151

interest group 142

labor movement 145

lobbyist 143

national committee 162

national convention 161

party identification 167

party organization 161

party platform 161

patronage 162

plurality 164

political party 143

public interest 149

Republican Party 157

service sector 146

social movement 144

splinter party 167

state central
committee 162

straight-ticket
voting 168

third party 166

ticket splitting 163

two-party system 155

unit rule 165

Whig Party 156

chapter summary

1   An interest group is an organization whose members share common objectives and actively attempt to influence government policy. Interest groups proliferate in the United States because they can influence government at many points in the political structure. A political party is a group of political activists who organize to win elections, operate the government, and determine public policy.

2   Major types of interest groups include business, agricultural, labor, public employee, professional, and environmental groups. Other important groups include public-interest groups. In addition, single-issue interest groups and foreign governments lobby the government.

3   Interest groups use direct and indirect techniques to influence government. Direct techniques include testifying before committees and rulemaking agencies, providing information to legislators, rating legislators' voting records, and aiding in political campaigns. Indirect techniques include conducting campaigns to rally public sentiment and using constituents to lobby for the group's interests.

4   The 1946 Legislative Reorganization Act was the first attempt to control lobbyists and their activities through registration requirements. In 1995, Congress approved the Lobbying Disclosure Act, which more clearly defined lobbyists and their reporting requirements. In 2007, the Honest Leadership and Open Government Act increased the frequency of reports to four times a year, required reports on coalition activity, and created a searchable Internet file on lobbying activity.

5   Political parties perform a number of functions for the political system. These functions include recruiting candidates for public office, organizing and running elections, presenting alternative policies to voters, assuming responsibility for operating the government, and acting as the opposition to the party in power.

6   The evolution of our nation's political parties can be divided into seven periods: (a) the creation and formation of political parties from 1789 to 1816; (b) the era of one-party rule, or personal politics, from 1816 to 1828; (c) the period from Andrew Jackson's presidency to the eve of the Civil War, from 1828 to 1856; (d) the Civil War and post–Civil War period, from 1856 to 1896; (e) the Republican ascendancy and progressive period, from 1896 to 1932; (f) the New Deal period, from 1932 to about 1968; and (g) the modern period, from approximately 1968 to the present. Throughout most of the modern period, the parties have been closely matched in strength.

7 A political party consists of three components: the voters who identify with the party, the party organization, and the party-in-government. Each party component maintains linkages to the others to keep the party strong. Each level of the party—local, state, and national—has considerable autonomy. The national party organization is responsible for holding the national convention in presidential election years, writing the party platform, choosing the national committee, and conducting party business.

8 Two major parties have dominated the political landscape in the United States for almost two centuries. The reasons for this include (a) the historical foundations of the system, (b) political socialization and practical considerations, (c) the winner-take-all electoral system, and (d) state and federal laws favoring the two-party system. For these reasons, minor parties have found it extremely difficult to win elections. Minor, or third, parties have emerged from time to time, sometimes as dissatisfied splinter groups from within major parties, and have acted as barometers of changes in the political mood. Third parties can affect the political process (even if they do not win) if major parties adopt their issues or if they determine which major party wins an election.

9 From the 1940s to the present, independent voters have formed an increasing proportion of the electorate, with a consequent decline in Democratic and Republican party identification. Nevertheless, many independent voters lean toward one major party or the other.

QUESTIONS FOR

discussionandanalysis

1 Some interest groups are much more influential than others. Interest groups famous for their clout include the National Rifle Association, AARP, the National Federation of Independent Business, the American Israel Public Affairs Committee, and the American Association for Justice (formerly the Association of Trial Lawyers of America). What factors might make each of these groups powerful?

2 About half of the paid lobbyists in Washington are former government staff members or former members of Congress. Why would interest groups employ such people? Why might some reformers want to limit the ability of interest groups to employ them? On what basis might an interest group argue that such limits are unconstitutional?

3 In America, party candidates for national office are typically chosen through primary elections. In some other countries, a party's central committee might pick the party's candidates. How might primary elections limit the ability of a political party to present a united front on the issues?

4 Do you support (or lean toward) one of the major political parties today? If so, would you have supported the same party a hundred years ago—or would you have supported a different party? Explain your reasoning.

5 During 2008, what political developments had an impact on voters' support for the Republican and Democratic parties?

helpful online **Resources**

CONNECTING TO AMERICAN GOVERNMENT AND POLITICS

Every important interest group sponsors a Web site with information for supporters and the general public. Check out the National Rifle Association at:
www.nra.org

the American Farm Bureau at:
www.fb.org

and AARP (formerly the American Association of Retired Persons) at:
www.aarp.org

The American Presidency Project of the University of California at Santa Barbara collects political party platforms along with a host of other documents. Go to:
www.presidency.ucsb.edu/platforms.php

Ron Gunzburger's Politics1 site provides information on political parties, including an amazingly large number of third parties. Visit it at:
www.politics1.com/parties.htm

a special WebSite

FOR YOUR TEXT

Go to this book's special Web site at academic.cengage.com/polisci/Schmidt/ Brief6e. Choose "For Students." Then click on Chapter 7, where you will find an online quiz and other helpful study aids. If your professor is using CengageNOW: *American Government and Politics Today, Brief Edition,* log in and go to Chapter 7 for additional online study aids.

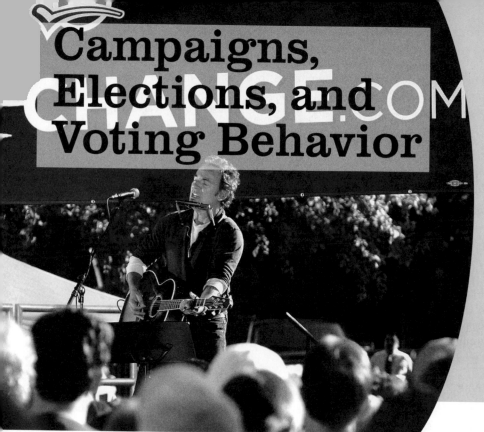

Campaigns, Elections, and Voting Behavior

8

Free elections are the cornerstone of the American political system. By casting ballots in local, state, and federal elections, voters choose one candidate over another to hold political office. There are thousands of elective offices in the United States—and consequently, thousands of elections. Although the major political parties strive to provide a slate of candidates for every election, recruiting candidates is easier for some offices than for others. Political parties may have difficulty finding candidates for the board of the local water control district, for example, but they generally find a sufficient number of candidates for county commissioner or sheriff. The higher the office and the more prestige attached to it, the more candidates are likely to want to run. In many areas of the country, however, one political party may be considerably stronger than another. In those situations, the minority party may have more difficulty finding nominees for elections in which victory is unlikely.

Presidential Primary
A statewide primary election of delegates to a political party's national convention, held to determine a party's presidential nominee.

THE PEOPLE WHO RUN FOR OFFICE

The presidential campaign provides the most colorful and exciting look at candidates and how they prepare to compete for office—in this instance, the highest office in the land. The men and women who wanted to be candidates in the 2008 presidential campaign faced a long and obstacle-filled path. First, they needed to raise enough funds to tour the nation, particularly the states with early **presidential primaries,** to see if they had enough local supporters. They needed funds to create an organization and

173

to win primary votes. Finally, if nominated as their respective party's candidate, they required funds to finance a successful campaign for president. Always, at every turn, there was the question of whether they had enough funds to effectively compete with their opponents.

Who Is Eligible?

There are few constitutional restrictions on who can be elected to national office in the United States. As detailed in the Constitution, the formal requirements are as follows:

1. *President.* Must be a natural-born citizen, have attained the age of thirty-five years, and be a resident of the country for fourteen years by the time of inauguration.
2. *Vice president.* Must meet the same requirements as the president and also not be a resident of the same state as the president.[1]
3. *Senator.* Must be a citizen for at least nine years, have attained the age of thirty by the time of taking office, and be a resident of the state from which elected.
4. *Representative.* Must be a citizen for at least seven years, have attained the age of twenty-five by the time of taking office, and be a resident of the state from which elected.

The qualifications for state legislators are set by the state constitutions and likewise include age, place of residence, and citizenship. (Usually, the requirements for the upper chamber of a legislature are somewhat higher than those for the lower chamber.) The legal qualifications for serving as governor or other state office are similar.

Who Runs?

In spite of these minimal legal qualifications for office at both the national and state levels, a quick look at the slate of candidates in any election—or at the current members of Congress—will reveal that not all segments of the population take advantage of these opportunities. Holders of political office in the United States are predominantly white and male. Until the twentieth century, presidential candidates were exclusively of northern European origin and of Protestant heritage.[2] Laws that effectively denied voting rights made it impossible to elect African American public officials in many areas in which African Americans constituted a significant portion of the population. As a result of the passage of major civil

▼ **The Republican primaries** had many hopefuls, soon reduced to three main ones. From left to right, former Massachusetts Governor Mitt Romney, Senator John McCain, and former Arkansas governor Mike Huckabee. What motivates individuals to run for high office? (AP Photo/Mary Ann Chastain)

1. Technically, a presidential and vice-presidential candidate can be from the same state, but if they are, one of the two must forfeit the electoral votes of their home state.
2. A number of early presidents were Unitarian. The Unitarian Church is not Protestant, but it is historically rooted in the Protestant tradition.

rights legislation in the 1960s, however, the number of African American public officials has increased throughout the United States, and in a groundbreaking vote, the nation elected an African American president in 2008.

Women as Candidates. Until recently, women generally were considered to be appropriate candidates only for lower-level offices, such as state legislator or school board member. The last twenty years have seen a tremendous increase in the number of women who run for office, not only at the state level but for the U.S. Congress as well. In 2008, 141 women ran for Congress on major-party tickets, and 78 were elected. Today, a majority of Americans say they would vote for a qualified woman for president of the United States. Indeed, Hillary Clinton came close to winning the Democratic presidential nomination in 2008, a year in which the eventual Democratic nominee was heavily favored to win the general election.

Professional Status. Candidates are likely to be professionals, particularly lawyers. Political campaigning and officeholding are simply easier for some occupational groups than for others, and political involvement can make a valuable contribution to certain careers. Lawyers, for example, have more flexible schedules than do many other professionals, can take time off for campaigning, and can leave their jobs to hold public office full-time. Furthermore, holding political office is good publicity for their professional practice. Perhaps most important, many jobs that lawyers aspire to—federal or state judgeships, state's attorneys offices, or work in a federal agency—can be attained by political appointment.

THE TWENTY-FIRST-CENTURY CAMPAIGN

After the candidates have been nominated, typically through a **primary election,** the most exhausting and expensive part of the election process begins—the **general election** campaign, which actually fills the offices at stake. Political campaigns are becoming more complex and more sophisticated with every election. Even with the most appealing of candidates, today's campaigns require a strong organization; expertise in political polling and marketing; professional assistance in fund-raising, accounting, and financial management; and technological capabilities in every aspect of the campaign.

The Changing Campaign

The goal is the same for all campaigns—to convince voters to choose a candidate or a slate of candidates for office. Part of the reason for the increased intensity of campaigns in recent decades is that they are no longer centered on the party but are centered on the candidate. The candidate-centered

Primary Election
An election in which political parties choose their candidates for the general election.

General Election
An election, normally held on the first Tuesday in November, that determines who will fill various elected positions.

▼ **Two major contenders** for the Democratic presidential nomination were of historic importance. Had Hillary Rodham Clinton won that nomination, she would have been the first female to do so. Barack Obama, of course, did win and was the first African American candidate for president. Clinton went on to become Obama's secretary of state. Have gender and race disappeared as impediments to political participation? (AP Photo/Elise Amendola)

Political Consultant
A paid professional hired to devise a campaign strategy and manage a campaign.

campaign emerged in response to changes in the electoral system, the increased importance of television in campaigns, technological innovations such as computers, and the increased cost of campaigning.

To run a successful and persuasive campaign, the candidate's organization must be able to raise funds for the effort, obtain coverage from the media, produce and pay for political commercials and advertising, schedule the candidate's time effectively, convey the candidate's position on the issues to the voters, conduct research on the opposing candidate, and get the voters to go to the polls. When party identification was greater among voters and before the advent of television campaigning, a strong party organization at the local, state, or national level could furnish most of the services and expertise that the candidate needed. Parties used their precinct organizations to distribute literature, register voters, and get out the vote on Election Day. Less effort was spent on advertising each candidate's positions and character, because the party label presumably communicated that information to many voters.

One of the reasons that campaigns no longer depend on parties is that fewer people identify with them, as is evident from the increased number of political independents. In 1954, less than 20 percent of adults identified themselves as independents, whereas today that share is about 35 percent.

The Professional Campaign

Whether the candidate is running for the state legislature, for the governor's office, for the U.S. Congress, or for the presidency, every campaign has some fundamental tasks to accomplish. Today, in national elections, most of these tasks are handled by paid professionals rather than volunteers or amateur politicians.

The most sought-after and possibly the most criticized campaign expert is the **political consultant,** who, for a large fee, takes charge of the candidate's campaign. Paid political consultants began to displace volunteer campaign managers in the 1960s, about the same time that television became a force in campaigns. The paid consultant devises a campaign strategy, thinks up a campaign theme, oversees campaign advertising, and possibly chooses campaign colors and the candidate's official portrait. The consultant monitors the campaign's progress, plans media appearances, and coaches the candidate for debates. Consultants and the firms they represent are not politically neutral; most will work only for candidates from one party.

▼ **The major parties** fielded two strong candidates, Senators John McCain and Barack Obama. As it turned out, Obama more effectively used the Internet to raise campaign funds and to organize supporters. (AP Photo/Dennis Cook)

The Strategy of Winning

In the United States, unlike some European countries, there are no rewards for a candidate who comes in second; the winner takes all. The campaign organization must plan a strategy

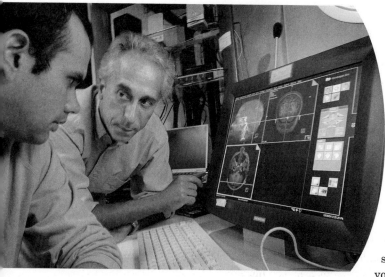

◀ **These two researchers** are viewing magnetic resonance imaging (MRI) scans of a volunteer's brain. Such MRI technology was used on behalf of political consultants during the last election cycle. Such consultants hope to discover how potential voters think while they view candidates' messages. Why wouldn't consultants simply ask potential voters about their reactions? (AP Photo/Reed Saxon)

that maximizes the candidate's chances of winning. Candidates seek to capture all the votes of their party's supporters, to convince a majority of the independent voters to vote for them, and to gain a few votes from supporters of the other party. To accomplish these goals, candidates must consider their visibility, their message, and their campaign strategy.

Candidate Visibility and Appeal. One of the most important concerns is how well known the candidate is. If she or he is a highly visible incumbent, there may be little need for campaigning except to remind the voters of the officeholder's good deeds. If, however, the candidate is an unknown challenger or a largely unfamiliar character attacking a well-known public figure, the campaign requires a strategy to get the candidate before the public.

In the case of the independent candidate or the candidate representing a minor party, name recognition is a serious problem. Such candidates must present an overwhelming case for the voter to reject the major-party candidate. Both Democratic and Republican candidates will label third-party candidates as "not serious" and therefore not worth the voter's time.

The Use of Opinion Polls. One of the major sources of information for both the media and the candidates is opinion polls. Poll taking is widespread during the primaries. Presidential hopefuls have private polls taken to make sure that there is at least some chance they could be nominated and, if nominated, elected. During the presidential campaign itself, polling is even more frequent. Polls are taken not only by the regular pollsters—Roper, Harris, Gallup, and others—but also privately by each candidate's campaign organization. These private polls are for the exclusive and secret use of the candidate and his or her campaign organization. As the election approaches, many candidates use **tracking polls,** which are taken almost every day, to find out how well they are competing for votes. Tracking polls enable consultants to fine-tune the advertising and the candidate's speeches in the last days of the campaign.

Focus Groups. Another tactic is to use a **focus group** to gain insights into public perceptions of the candidate. Professional consultants organize a discussion of the candidate or of certain political issues among ten to fifteen ordinary citizens. The citizens are selected from specific target groups in the population—for example, working

Tracking Poll
A poll taken for the candidate on a nearly daily basis as Election Day approaches.

Focus Group
A small group of individuals who are led in discussion by a professional consultant to gather opinions on, and responses to, candidates and issues.

Corrupt Practices Acts
A series of acts passed by Congress in an attempt to limit and regulate the size and sources of contributions and expenditures in political campaigns.

Hatch Act
An act passed in 1939 that restricted the political activities of government employees. It also prohibited a political group from spending more than $3 million in any campaign and limited individual contributions to a campaign committee to $5,000.

women, blue-collar men, senior citizens, or young voters. Recent campaigns have tried to reach groups such as "soccer moms" or "NASCAR dads."[3] The group discusses personality traits of the candidate, political advertising, and other candidate-related issues. Focus groups can reveal emotional responses to candidates or the deeper anxieties of voters—feelings that consultants believe often are not tapped by more impersonal telephone surveys. The campaign then can shape its messages to respond to those feelings and perceptions.

FINANCING THE CAMPAIGN

In a book published in 1932 entitled *Money in Elections,* Louise Overacker said the following about campaign financing:

> The financing of elections in a democracy is a problem which is arousing increasing concern. Many are beginning to wonder if present-day methods of raising and spending campaign funds do not clog the wheels of our elaborately constructed mechanism of popular control, and if democracies do not inevitably become [governments ruled by small groups].[4]

Although writing more than seventy-five years ago, Overacker touched on a sensitive issue in American political campaigns—the connection between money and elections. It is estimated that more than $3.5 billion was spent at all levels of campaigning in the 2003–2004 election cycle, and spending reached unprecedented heights during the 2007–2008 election cycle. Total spending for the presidential candidates alone in 2008 reached $2.4 billion. For the presidential campaigns, some of these funds come from the federal government. All of the rest has to be provided by the candidates and their families, borrowed, or raised by contributions from individuals or *political action committees.*

Regulating Campaign Financing

The way campaigns are financed has changed dramatically in the last several decades. Today, candidates and political parties must operate within the constraints imposed by complicated laws regulating campaign financing.

A variety of federal **corrupt practices acts** have been designed to regulate campaign financing. The first, passed in 1925, contained many loopholes and proved to be ineffective. The **Hatch Act** (Political Activities Act) of 1939 is best known for restricting the political activities of civil servants. The act also, however, made it unlawful for a political group to spend more than $3 million in any campaign and limited individual contributions to a political group to $5,000. Of course, such restrictions were easily circumvented by creating additional political groups.

The Federal Election Campaign Act

The Federal Election Campaign Act (FECA) of 1971, which became effective in 1972, essentially replaced all past laws. The act placed no limit on overall spending but restricted the amount that could be spent on mass media advertising, including television. It limited the amount that candidates could contribute to their own campaigns (a limit later ruled unconstitutional) and required disclosure of all contributions and

---

3. NASCAR stands for the National Association of Stock Car Auto Racing.
4. Louise Overacker, *Money in Elections* (New York: Macmillan, 1932), p. vii.

expenditures over $100. In principle, the FECA limited the role of labor unions and corporations in political campaigns. Another act provided for a voluntary $1 check-off on federal income tax returns to create a general campaign fund to be used by major-party presidential candidates.

Further Reforms in 1974 and 1976. For many, the 1971 act did not go far enough. Amendments to the FECA passed in 1974 did the following:

- *Created the Federal Election Commission (FEC).* This commission consists of six nonpartisan administrators whose duty is to enforce compliance with the requirements of the act. (The FEC, however, is conspicuously ineffective and typically does not rule that a campaign has violated the rules until the elections are over.)
- *Provided public financing for presidential primaries and general elections.* Any candidate running for president who is able to obtain sufficient contributions in at least twenty states can obtain a subsidy from the U.S. Treasury to help pay for his or her campaign. Candidates who accept federal financing for the general elections are limited to spending what the government provides and cannot raise funds privately. The system began to break down after 2000, when many candidates rejected public funding in the belief that they could raise larger sums privately. George W. Bush opted out of primary financing in 2000, as did John Kerry in 2004. In the 2008 primaries, most of the major candidates refused public financing, and Barack Obama became the first candidate since the program was founded to opt out of federal funding for the general elections as well. As a result, he was able to raise unprecedented sums.
- *Limited presidential campaign spending.* Any candidate accepting federal support must agree to limit campaign expenditures to the amount prescribed by federal law.
- *Limited contributions.* Under the 1974 amendments, citizens could contribute up to $1,000 to each candidate in each federal election or primary; the total limit on all contributions from an individual to all candidates was $25,000 per year. Groups could contribute up to a maximum of $5,000 to a candidate in any election. (As you will read later in the chapter, some of these limits were changed by the 2002 campaign-reform legislation.)
- *Required disclosure.* Each candidate must file periodic reports with the Federal Election Commission, listing who contributed, how much was spent, and for what the money was spent.

Buckley v. Valeo. The original FECA of 1971 had limited the amount that each individual could spend on his or her own behalf. The Supreme Court declared the provision unconstitutional in 1976, in *Buckley v. Valeo*,[5] stating that it was unconstitutional to restrict in any way the amount congressional candidates could spend on their own behalf: "The candidate, no less than any other person, has a First Amendment right to engage in the discussion of public issues and vigorously and tirelessly to advocate his own election." In 2006, the Court reaffirmed *Buckley v. Valeo* and extended its reach to candidates for state offices. The Court did so by holding unconstitutional a 1997 Vermont law that limited the amount that candidates for Vermont state offices could spend on their own campaigns.[6]

---

5. 424 U.S. 1 (1976).
6. *Randall v. Sorrell*, 548 U.S. 230 (2006).

Political Action Committee (PAC)
A committee set up by and representing a corporation, labor union, or special interest group. PACs raise campaign donations.

Soft Money
Campaign contributions unregulated by federal or state law, usually given to parties and party committees to help fund general party activities.

Interest Groups and Campaign Funds

The 1974 and 1976 changes to the FECA established tight limits on contributions to campaigns. The rules facilitated the growth of *political action committees*.

Political Action Committees. The 1974 and 1976 changes to the FECA allow corporations, labor unions, and other interest groups to set up **political action committees (PACs)** to raise funds for candidates. For a federal PAC to be legitimate, the funds must be raised from at least fifty volunteer donors and must be given to at least five candidates in the federal election. PACs can contribute up to $5,000 to each candidate in each election. Each corporation or each union is limited to one PAC.

The number of PACs grew significantly after 1976, as did the amounts that they spent on elections. There were about 1,000 PACs in 1976; today, there are more than 4,500. Since the 1990s, however, the number of PACs has leveled off because interest groups and activists have found alternate mechanisms for funneling resources into campaigns. Total spending by PACs exceeded $900 million in the 2003–2004 election cycle, when about 44 percent of all campaign funds raised by House candidates came from PACs. In subsequent years, the share of election financing provided by PACs fell even as the dollar amount of PAC contributions continued to climb.

Interest groups funnel PAC funds to the candidates they think can do them the most good. Frequently, they contribute to candidates who face little or no opposition. The great bulk of campaign contributions goes to incumbent candidates rather than to challengers. Many PACs give most of their contributions to candidates of one party. Other PACs, particularly corporate PACs, tend to give funds to Democrats in Congress as well as to Republicans. Interest groups see PAC contributions as a way to ensure access to powerful legislators, even though the groups may disagree with the legislators some of the time.

Soft Money. In the years after 1976, interest groups and PACs hit upon the strategy of generating **soft money**—that is, campaign contributions to political parties that escaped the limits of federal election law. Although legislation limited contributions that could be spent on elections, there were no limits on contributions to political parties for activities such as voter education and voter-registration drives. This loophole enabled the parties to raise millions of dollars from corporations and individuals. Soft money contributions to the national parties were outlawed after Election Day 2002.

The Bipartisan Campaign Reform Act of 2002

Campaign reform had been in the air for so long that it was almost anticlimactic when President George W. Bush signed the Bipartisan Campaign Reform Act in 2002. This act, also known as the McCain-Feingold Act after its chief sponsors in the Senate, amended the 1971 FECA. The act took effect on the day after the congressional elections were held on November 5, 2002.

Key Elements of the 2002 Law. The 2002 law bans the large, unlimited contributions to national political parties that are known as soft money. It places curbs on, but does not entirely eliminate, the use of campaign ads by outside special interest groups advocating the election or defeat of specific candidates. Such ads are allowed up to sixty days before a general election and up to thirty days before a primary election.

In 1974, contributions by individuals to federal candidates were limited to $1,000 per individual. The McCain-Feingold Act increased this to $2,000. Also, the maximum amount that an individual can give to all federal candidates was raised from $25,000 per year to $95,000 over a two-year election cycle. The act did not ban soft money contributions to state and local parties, which can accept such contributions as long as they are limited to $10,000 per year per individual.

The constitutionality of the 2002 act was immediately challenged by groups negatively affected. In December 2003, the Supreme Court upheld almost all of the clauses of the act.[7] In 2007, however, the Court eased the restrictions on advocacy ads when it ruled that only those ads "susceptible of no reasonable interpretation other than as an appeal to vote for or against a specific candidate" could be restricted prior to an election.[8] In 2008, the Court found another provision of the act to be unconstitutional— one that penalized wealthy candidates by exempting their opponents from various campaign-finance rules.[9]

Interest Groups and Campaign Funds since 2002

Soon after soft money was banned, business corporations, labor unions, and other interest groups discovered that it was legal to make **independent expenditures** in an election campaign so long as the expenditures were not coordinated with those of a candidate or political party. These groups began setting up new organizations outside the parties, called 527 organizations after the section of the tax code that provides for them. These tax-exempt organizations first made a major impact during the 2003–2004 election cycle. The groups focus on encouraging voter registration and running issue ads aimed at energizing supporters. These groups continue to be active up to the present day.

New Types of Independent Committees. In the 2007–2008 election cycle, campaign-finance lawyers began recommending a new type of independent group— the 501(c)4 organization, which, like the 527 committee, is named after the relevant provision of the tax code. A 501(c)4 is ostensibly a "social welfare" group, and, unlike a 527, is not required to disclose the identity of its donors or report spending to the FEC.

Independent Expenditures
Unregulated political expenditures by PACs, organizations, and individuals that are not coordinated with candidate campaigns or political parties.

---

7. *McConnell v. Federal Election Commission,* 540 U.S. 93 (2003).
8. *Federal Election Commission v. Wisconsin Right to Life,* 127 S.Ct. 2652 (2007).
9. *Davis v. Federal Election Commission,* 128 S.Ct. 2759 (2008).

PRICKLY CITY ©2007 Scott Stantis. Distributed by Universal Press Syndicate. Reprinted with permission. All rights reserved.

Issue Advocacy
Advertising
Advertising paid for
by interest groups that
support or oppose
a candidate or a
candidate's position
on an issue without
mentioning voting or
elections.

"Beauty Contest"
A presidential primary
in which contending
candidates compete for
popular votes but the
results do not control the
selection of delegates to
the national convention.

Lawyers then began suggesting that 501(c)4 organizations claim a special exemption that would allow the organization to ask people to vote for or against specific candidates as long as a majority of the group's effort was devoted to issues. Only those funds spent directly to support candidates had to be reported to the FEC, and the 501(c)4 could continue to conceal its donors.

One result of the 501(c)4 was to make it all but impossible to determine exactly how much was spent by independent groups on the 2007–2008 elections. Critics claimed that 501(c)4s were being used illegally. The FEC was unable to rule on their validity in 2008, however, because a partisan deadlock in the Senate had left the commission with only two members, two short of the number it needed to make a ruling.

Issue Advocacy Advertising. A common tactic in recent years is **issue advocacy advertising,** which promotes positions on issues rather than candidates. Interest groups routinely wage their own issue campaigns. For example, the Christian Coalition, which is incorporated, annually raises millions of dollars to produce and distribute voter guidelines and other direct-mail literature to describe candidates' positions on various issues and to promote its agenda. Before the 2008 elections, AARP, which represents older Americans, aired a series of ads showcasing people who had been ruined by health-care costs. Ostensibly bipartisan, the campaign in fact benefited the Democrats.

Although promoting issue positions is very close to promoting candidates who support those positions, the courts repeatedly have held that interest groups have a First Amendment right to advocate their positions. Political parties may also make independent expenditures on behalf of candidates—as long as the parties do so *independently* of the candidates. In other words, the parties must not coordinate such expenditures with the candidates' campaigns.

RUNNING FOR PRESIDENT: THE LONGEST CAMPAIGN

The American presidential election is the culmination of two different campaigns: the presidential primary campaign and the general election campaign following the party's national convention. Traditionally, both the primary campaigns and the final campaigns take place during the first ten months of an election year. Increasingly, though, the states are holding their primaries earlier in the year, which has motivated the candidates to begin their campaigns earlier as well. Indeed, candidates in the 2008 presidential races began campaigning in early 2007, thus launching the longest presidential campaign to date in U.S. history.

Primary elections were first mandated in 1903 in Wisconsin. The purpose of the primary was to open the nomination process to ordinary party members and to weaken the influence of party bosses. Until 1968, however, there were fewer than twenty primary elections for the presidency. They were often **"beauty contests"** in which the candidates competed for popular votes but the results had no impact on the selection of delegates to the national convention. National conventions were meetings of the party elite—legislators, mayors, county chairpersons, and loyal party workers—who were mostly appointed to their delegations. The leaders of large blocs of delegates could direct their delegates to support a favorite candidate.

Reforming the Primaries

In recent decades, the character of the primary process and the makeup of the national convention have changed dramatically. The public, rather than party elites, now generally controls the nomination process. After the disruptive riots outside the doors of the 1968 Democratic convention in Chicago, many party leaders pushed for serious reforms of the convention system. They saw the general dissatisfaction with the convention, and the riots in particular, as being caused by the inability of the average party member to influence the nomination process.

The Democratic National Committee appointed a special commission to study the problems of the primary system. During the next several years, the group—called the McGovern-Fraser Commission—formulated new rules for delegate selection that had to be followed by state Democratic parties.

The reforms instituted by the Democratic Party, which were imitated in most states by the Republicans, revolutionized the nomination process for the presidency. The most important changes require that a majority of the convention delegates be elected by the voters in primary elections, in **caucuses** held by local parties, or at state conventions. Delegates are normally pledged to a particular candidate, although the pledge is not always formally binding at the convention. The delegation from each state must also include a proportion of women, younger party members, and representatives of the minority groups within the party. At first, virtually no special privileges were given to elected party officials, such as senators and governors. In 1984, however, many of these officials returned to the Democratic convention as **superdelegates.**

Primaries and Caucuses

A variety of types of primaries are used by the states. One notable difference is between proportional and winner-take-all primaries. Another important consideration is whether independent voters can take part in a primary, as we will explain shortly. Some states also use caucuses and conventions to choose candidates for various offices.

Direct and Indirect Primaries. A **direct primary** is one in which voters decide party nominations by voting directly for candidates. In an **indirect primary,** voters instead choose convention delegates, and the delegates determine the party's candidate in the general election. Delegates may be pledged to a particular candidate. Indirect primaries are used almost exclusively in presidential elections. Most candidates in state and local elections are chosen by direct primaries.

Proportional and Winner-Take-All Primaries. Most primaries are winner-take-all. Proportional primaries are used mostly to elect delegates to the national conventions of the two major parties—delegates who are pledged to one or another candidate for president. In 2008, all Democratic Party presidential primaries and caucuses allocated delegates on a proportional basis. This meant that if one candidate for president won 40 percent of the vote in a primary, that candidate would receive about 40 percent of the pledged delegates. If a candidate won 60 percent of the vote, she or he would obtain about 60 percent of the delegates. In contrast, the Republicans used the winner-take-all primary system in most, but not all, states. Under this system, the candidate who received the most votes won all of the state's delegates, no matter how narrow the margin of victory.

Caucus
A meeting of party members designed to select candidates and propose policies.

Superdelegate
A party leader or elected official who is given the right to vote at the party's national convention. Superdelegates are not elected at the state level.

Direct Primary
A primary election in which voters decide party nominations by voting directly for candidates.

Indirect Primary
A primary election in which voters choose convention delegates, and the delegates determine the party's candidate in the general election.

Closed Primary
A type of primary in which the voter is limited to choosing candidates of the party of which he or she is a member.

Open Primary
A primary in which any registered voter can vote (but must vote for candidates of only one party).

Because the Democratic contest between Barack Obama and Hillary Clinton in 2008 was so close, the proportional distribution of delegates ensured that the winner was not established until June. On the Republican side, the winner-take-all system allowed John McCain to sew up his party's nomination by March 4.

Closed Primary. A closed primary is one of several types of primaries distinguished by how independent voters are handled. In a **closed primary,** only avowed or declared members of a party can vote in that party's primary. In other words, voters must declare their party affiliation, either when they register to vote or at the primary election. In a closed-party system, registered voters cannot cross over into the other party's primary in order to nominate the weakest candidate of the opposing party or to affect the ideological direction of that party.

Open Primary. In an **open primary** system, any voter can vote in either party primary without declaring a party affiliation. Basically, the voter makes the choice in the privacy of the voting booth. The voter must, however, choose one party's list from which to select candidates.

Blanket Primary. A *blanket primary* is one in which the voter can vote for candidates of more than one party. Until 2000, a few states, including Alaska, California, and Washington, had blanket primaries. In 2000, however, the United States Supreme Court effectively invalidated the use of the blanket primary. The Court ruled that the blanket primary violated political parties' First Amendment right of association. Because the nominees represent the party, party members—not the general electorate—should have the right to choose the party's nominee.[10]

Run-Off Primary. Some states have a two-primary system. If no candidate receives a majority of the votes in the first primary, the top two candidates must compete in another primary, called a *run-off primary.*

Conventions and Caucuses. While primary elections are the most common way in which a party's candidates are selected, there are other procedures in use. State party conventions may nominate candidates for various offices. Those who attend meetings below the statewide level may participate in nominating candidates as well. The most famous of such meetings are the caucuses that help nominate a party's candidate for president of the United States.

In 2008, twelve states relied entirely on the caucus system for choosing delegates to the Republican and Democratic national conventions. Several other states used a combined system. Strictly speaking, the caucus system is a caucus/convention system. In North Dakota, for example, local citizens gather in party meetings, called caucuses, at the precinct level. They choose delegates to district conventions. The district conventions elect delegates to the state convention, and the state convention actually chooses the delegates to the national convention. The national delegates, however, are pledged to reflect the presidential preferences that voters expressed at the caucus level.

---

10. *California Democratic Party v. Jones,* 530 U.S. 567 (2000).

Front-Loading the Primaries

As soon as politicians and potential presidential candidates realized that winning as many primary elections as possible guaranteed them the party's nomination for president, their tactics changed dramatically. Candidates concentrated on building organizations in states that held early, important primary elections. By the 1970s, candidates recognized that the winner of an early contest, such as the Iowa caucuses or the New Hampshire primary election (both now held in January), would instantly become seen as the **front-runner,** increasing the candidate's media exposure and escalating the pace of contributions to his or her campaign.

The Rush to Be First. The state political parties began to see that early primaries had a much greater effect on the outcome of the presidential elections. Accordingly, in every successive presidential election, more and more states moved their primaries into the first months of the year, a process known as **front-loading** the primaries. One result was a series of "Super Tuesdays" when multiple states held simultaneous primaries. In 2008, twenty-four states held their primaries or caucuses on February 5, making it the largest Super Tuesday ever. The compressed primary schedule troubled many observers, who feared that a front-runner might wrap up the nomination before the voters were able to make a thorough assessment of the candidate. In the many months between the early primaries and the general election, the voters might come to regret their decision.

The National Parties Try to Regain Control of the Process. To keep primary dates from slipping into 2007, the national Republican and Democratic parties agreed that no state could hold a primary or caucus before February 5 without special permission. (This was the reason that so many states selected their delegates on that exact date.) The national parties let the traditional lead-off states, Iowa and New Hampshire, go first, and also allowed Nevada and South Carolina to hold their contests in January, giving the early primaries a national flavor.

Unfortunately, state officials in Florida and Michigan refused to obey the rules and also scheduled primaries in January. The Republicans penalized the two state delegations by cutting their representation at the national convention in half. After threatening even more severe penalties, the Democrats did likewise. (In the end, at the convention, the Democrats allowed Florida and Michigan to cast a full vote.)

The Consequences of Early Primaries. In 2008, so many states were in play on February 5 that it was impossible for the candidates to campaign strongly in all of them. Rather than winning more attention, many Super Tuesday states found that they were ignored. Because the Democratic race was not decided until the very end, the later Democratic primaries, such as those in Indiana, North Carolina, Ohio, Pennsylvania, and Texas, were hotly contested.

Front-loading, in short, had become counterproductive. As a result, it may be easier for the national parties to persuade states not to front-load the process so severely in 2012. Some have even suggested taking the power to set primary dates away from the states and replacing the current system with a series of nationally scheduled regional primaries.

Front-Runner
The presidential candidate who appears to be ahead at a given time in the primary season.

Front-Loading
The practice of moving presidential primary elections to the early part of the campaign to maximize the impact of these primaries on the nomination.

Credentials Committee
A committee used by political parties at their national conventions to determine which delegates may participate. The committee inspects the claim of each prospective delegate to be seated as a legitimate representative of his or her state.

Elector
A member of the electoral college, which selects the president and vice president. Each state's electors are chosen in each presidential election year according to state laws.

On to the National Convention

Presidential candidates have been nominated by the convention method in every election since 1832. Extra delegates are allowed from states that had voting majorities for the party in the preceding elections. Parties also accept delegates from the District of Columbia, the territories, and U.S. citizens living abroad.

Seating the Delegates. At the convention, each political party uses a **credentials committee** to determine which delegates may participate. The credentials committee usually prepares a roll of all delegates entitled to be seated. Controversy may arise when rival groups claim to be the official party organization for a county, district, or state. The Mississippi Democratic Party split along racial lines in 1964 at the height of the civil rights movement in the Deep South. Two separate sets of delegates were selected at the state level—one made up of white delegates and the other including both whites and African Americans—and both factions showed up at the national convention. After much debate on party rules, the committee decided to seat the pro–civil rights delegates and exclude those who represented the traditional "white" party.

Convention Activities. Most delegates arrive at the convention committed to a presidential candidate. No convention since 1952 has required more than one ballot to choose a nominee. Conventions normally last four days. On each night, featured speakers seek to rally the party faithful and to draw in uncommitted voters who are watching on television. In 2008, more than 42 million people watched Democrat Barack Obama address an audience of 85,000 in Denver's Mile High Stadium. A week later, at least 37 million people tuned in to see the Republican vice-presidential candidate, Alaska governor Sarah Palin. For most viewers (and Republican delegates), this was their first introduction to Palin, who was previously little known outside Alaska. The next night, John McCain's ratings matched or beat Obama's.

The Electoral College

Some people who vote for the president and vice president think that they are voting directly for a candidate. In actuality, they are voting for **electors** who will cast their ballots in the electoral college. Article II, Section 1, of the Constitution outlines in detail the method of choosing electors for president and vice president. The framers of the Constitution did not want the president and vice president to be selected by the "excitable masses." Rather, they wished the choice to be made by a few supposedly dispassionate, reasonable men (but not women).

The Choice of Electors. Electors are selected during each presidential election year. The selection is governed by state laws. After the national party convention, the electors are pledged to the candidates chosen. The total number of electors today is 538, equal to 100 senators, 435 members of the House, and 3 electors for the District of Columbia. (The Twenty-third Amendment, ratified in 1961, added electors for the District of Columbia.) Each state's number of electors equals that state's number of senators (two) plus its number of representatives.

The Electors' Commitment. When a plurality of voters in a state chooses a slate of electors, those electors are pledged to cast their ballots on the first Monday after the second Wednesday in December in the state capital for the presidential and vice-presidential candidates of their party.[11] The Constitution does not, however, *require* the electors to cast their ballots for the candidates of their party, and on rare occasions so-called *faithless electors* have voted for a candidate to whom they were not pledged.

The ballots are counted and certified before a joint session of Congress early in January. The candidates who receive a majority of the electoral votes (270) are certified as president-elect and vice president–elect. According to the Constitution, if no candidate receives a majority of the electoral votes, the election of the president is decided in the House from among the candidates with the three highest numbers of votes, with each state having one vote (decided by a plurality of each state delegation). The selection of the vice president is determined by the Senate in a choice between the two candidates with the most votes, each senator having one vote. The House was required to choose the president in 1801 (Thomas Jefferson), and again in 1825 (John Quincy Adams).[12]

It is possible for a candidate to become president without obtaining a majority of the popular vote. There have been many minority presidents in our history, who did not win a majority of the popular vote, including Abraham Lincoln, Woodrow Wilson, Harry Truman, John F. Kennedy, Richard Nixon (in 1968), and Bill Clinton. Such an event becomes more likely when there are important third-party candidates.

Perhaps more distressing is the possibility of a candidate's being elected when an opposing candidate receives a plurality of the popular vote. This has occurred on four occasions—in the elections of John Quincy Adams in 1824, Rutherford B. Hayes in 1876, Benjamin Harrison in 1888, and George W. Bush in 2000, all of whom won elections in which an opponent received a plurality of the popular vote. Such results have led to calls for replacing the electoral college with a popular vote system. We described this controversy in Chapter 2 in the *At Issue* feature on page 34.

HOW ARE ELECTIONS CONDUCTED?

The United States uses the **Australian ballot**—a secret ballot that is prepared, distributed, and counted by government officials at public expense. Since 1888, all states have used the Australian ballot. Before that, many states used oral voting or differently colored ballots prepared by the parties. Obviously, knowing which way a person was voting made it easy to apply pressure on the person to change his or her vote, and vote buying was common.

Office-Block and Party-Column Ballots

Two types of Australian ballots are used in the United States in general elections. The first, called an **office-block ballot,** or sometimes a **Massachusetts ballot,** groups all the candidates for a particular elective office under the title of that office. Parties dislike the office-block ballot because it places more emphasis on the office than on the party; it discourages straight-ticket voting and encourages split-ticket voting.

A **party-column ballot** is a form of general election ballot in which all of a party's candidates are arranged in one column under the party's label and symbol. It is also called the **Indiana ballot.** In some states, it allows voters to vote for all of a party's

Australian Ballot
A secret ballot prepared, distributed, and tabulated by government officials at public expense. Since 1888, all states have used the Australian ballot rather than an open, public ballot.

Office-Block, or Massachusetts, Ballot
A form of general election ballot in which candidates for elective office are grouped together under the title of each office. It emphasizes voting for the office and the individual candidate, rather than for the party.

Party-Column, or Indiana, Ballot
A form of general election ballot in which all of a party's candidates for elective office are arranged in one column under the party's label and symbol. It emphasizes voting for the party, rather than for the office or individual.

11. In Maine and Nebraska, electoral votes are based on congressional districts. Each district chooses one elector. The remaining two electors are chosen statewide.
12. For details, see Robert W. Bennett, *Taming the Electoral College* (Stanford, Calif.: Stanford Law and Politics, 2006).

Coattail Effect
The influence of a popular candidate on the electoral success of other candidates on the same party ticket. The effect is increased by the party-column ballot, which encourages straight-ticket voting.

candidates for local, state, and national offices by simply marking a single "X" or pulling a single lever. Most states use this type of ballot. As it encourages straight-ticket voting, the two major parties favor this form. When a party has an exceptionally strong presidential or gubernatorial candidate to head the ticket, the use of the party-column ballot increases the **coattail effect** (the influence of a popular candidate on the success of other candidates on the same party ticket).

Voting by Mail

Voting by mail has been accepted for absentee ballots for many decades (for example, for individuals who are doing business away from home or for members of the armed forces). Recently, several states have offered mail ballots to all of their voters. The rationale for using the mail ballot is to make voting easier and increase turnout. Oregon has gone one step further: since 1998, that state has employed postal ballots exclusively, and there are no polling places. (Voters who do not prepare their ballots in time for the U.S. Postal Service to deliver them can drop off their ballots at drop boxes on Election Day.) By national standards, Oregon voter turnout has been high, but not exceptionally so.

Voting Fraud and Mistakes

Voting fraud is something regularly suspected but seldom proved. Voting in the 1800s, when secret ballots were rare and people had a cavalier attitude toward the open buying of votes, was probably much more conducive to fraud than modern elections are. Some observers, however, claim that the potential for voting fraud remains high in many states, particularly through the use of phony voter registrations and absentee ballots. Other observers claim that errors leading to voting fraud are trivial in number and that a few mistakes are inevitable in a system involving millions of voters. These people argue that an excessive concern with voting fraud makes it harder for minorities and poor people to vote.

Strict Voter ID Requirements. In recent years, many states have adopted laws requiring enhanced proof of identity before voters can cast their ballots. Indiana imposed the nation's toughest voter identification (ID) law in 2005. Indiana legislators claimed that they were motivated by a desire to prevent voting fraud, but critics argued that they were really trying to suppress voter turnout among minority group

◀ Reporters in
Lexington, Kentucky, question U.S. Attorney Gregory F. Van Tatenhove about the indictments his office made against a state senator and others. The issues involved vote rigging. How frequently do you think such illegal schemes are used in U.S. elections?
(AP Photo/Hobie Hiler)

members and the poor—the individuals least likely to possess adequate identification. In 2008, the United States Supreme Court upheld the Indiana voter ID law.[13]

Reforming the Voting Process. In Florida in 2000, serious problems with the punch-card voting system may have determined the outcome of the presidential election. In response, Congress enacted the Help America Vote Act (HAVA) of 2002. The act provided funds to the states to help them implement a number of reforms. Among other things, the states were asked to replace outdated voting equipment with newer electronic voting systems. Critics of HAVA pointed out that by urging the adoption of electronic voting equipment, the act may have traded old problems for newer, more complicated ones.

These problems became particularly apparent during the 2006 midterm elections, when more than twenty-five states reported trouble at the polls on Election Day. Many of the problems involved failures in the new voting machines. In one Florida county, it was estimated that nearly 18,000 votes may have gone unrecorded by electronic voting machines, thus changing the outcome of a congressional election.

In 2008, therefore, many localities—including almost the entire state of California—retreated to using old-fashioned paper ballots. These ballots slowed the vote count, but they largely eliminated the problems with voting system errors that had plagued recent elections.

TURNING OUT TO VOTE

In 2008, the number of Americans eligible to vote was about 212.7 million people. Of that number, about 132.6 million, or 62.3 percent of the eligible population, actually cast a ballot. When voter turnout is this low, it means, among other things, that the winner of a close presidential election may be voted in by barely a quarter of those eligible to vote. (See Table 8–1 on the following page.)

Figure 8–1 on page 191 shows **voter turnout** for presidential and congressional elections from 1908 to 2008. Each of the peaks in the figure represents voter turnout in a presidential election. Thus, we can also see that turnout for congressional elections is influenced greatly by whether there is a presidential election in the same year. Whereas voter turnout during the presidential elections of 2008 was 62.3 percent, it was only 40.3 percent in the midterm elections of 2006.

The same is true at the state level. When there is a race for governor, more voters participate in the elections. Voter participation rates in gubernatorial elections are also greater in presidential election years. The average turnout in state elections is about 14 percentage points higher when a presidential election is held.

Now consider local elections. In races for mayor, city council, county auditor, and the like, it is fairly common for only 25 percent or less of the electorate to vote. Is something amiss here? It would seem that people should be more likely to vote in elections that directly affect them. At the local level, each person's vote counts more (because there are fewer voters). Furthermore, the issues—crime control, school bonds, sewer bonds, and the like—touch the immediate interests of the voters. In reality, however, potential voters are most interested in national elections, when a presidential choice is involved. Otherwise, voter participation in our representative government is very low (and, as we have seen, it is not overwhelmingly great even in presidential elections).

Voter Turnout
The percentage of citizens taking part in the election process; the number of eligible voters who actually "turn out" on Election Day to cast their ballots.

13. *Crawford v. Marion County Election Board*, 128 S.Ct. 1610 (2008).

TABLE 8–1 : **Elected by a Majority?**

Most presidents have won a majority of the votes cast in their election. We generally judge the extent of their victory by whether they have won more than 51 percent of the votes. Some presidential elections have been proclaimed *landslides,* meaning that the candidates won by an extraordinary majority of votes cast. As indicated below, however, no modern president has been elected by more than 38 percent of the population eligible to vote. The best showing was by Johnson in 1964.

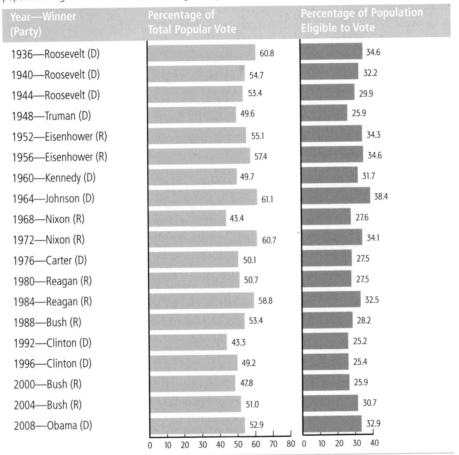

Year—Winner (Party)	Percentage of Total Popular Vote	Percentage of Population Eligible to Vote
1936—Roosevelt (D)	60.8	34.6
1940—Roosevelt (D)	54.7	32.2
1944—Roosevelt (D)	53.4	29.9
1948—Truman (D)	49.6	25.9
1952—Eisenhower (R)	55.1	34.3
1956—Eisenhower (R)	57.4	34.6
1960—Kennedy (D)	49.7	31.7
1964—Johnson (D)	61.1	38.4
1968—Nixon (R)	43.4	27.6
1972—Nixon (R)	60.7	34.1
1976—Carter (D)	50.1	27.5
1980—Reagan (R)	50.7	27.5
1984—Reagan (R)	58.8	32.5
1988—Bush (R)	53.4	28.2
1992—Clinton (D)	43.3	25.2
1996—Clinton (D)	49.2	25.4
2000—Bush (R)	47.8	25.9
2004—Bush (R)	51.0	30.7
2008—Obama (D)	52.9	32.9

Sources: Historical Data Archive, Inter-university Consortium for Political and Social Research; Michael P. McDonald and Samuel L. Popkin, "The Myth of the Vanishing Voter," *American Political Science Review,* Vol. 95, No. 4 (December 2001), p. 966; and the United States Elections Project.

The Effect of Low Voter Turnout

There are two schools of thought concerning low voter turnout. Some view low voter participation as a threat to our representative democratic government. Too few individuals are deciding who wields political power in our society. In addition, low voter participation presumably signals apathy about our political system in general. It also may signal that potential voters simply do not want to take the time to learn about the issues.

Others are less concerned. They contend that low voter participation simply indicates more satisfaction with the status quo. Also, they believe that representative

FIGURE 8–1: Voter Turnout for Presidential and Congressional Elections, 1908–2008

The peaks represent voter turnout in presidential election years; the troughs represent voter turnout in off years with no presidential elections.

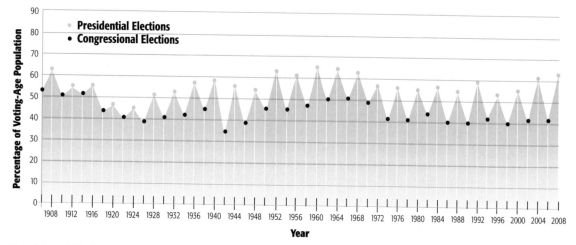

Note: Prior to 1948, the voting-age population is used as a proxy for the population eligible to vote.

Sources: Historical Data Archive, Inter-university Consortium for Political and Social Research; Michael P. McDonald and Samuel L. Popkin, "The Myth of the Vanishing Voter," *American Political Science Review,* Vol. 95, No. 4 (December 2001), p. 966; and the United States Elections Project.

democracy is a reality even if a very small percentage of eligible voters vote. If everyone who does not vote thinks that the outcome of the election will accord with his or her own desires, then representative democracy is working. The nonvoters are obtaining the type of government—with the type of people running it—that they want to have anyway.

The Voting-Age Population and the Vote-Eligible Population

In the past, the press and even many political scientists calculated voter turnout by taking the number of people who vote as a percentage of the nation's **voting-age population.** Until about 1972, this was a reasonable way to obtain an approximate figure for turnout. In recent decades, however, turnout figures based on the voting-age population have become less and less reliable. The problem is that the voting-age population is not the same as the population of eligible voters, the **vote-eligible population.** The figure for the voting-age population includes felons and ex-felons who have lost the right to vote. Above all, it includes the large number of new immigrants who are not yet citizens. Finally, it does not include Americans living abroad, who can cast absentee ballots.

In 2008, the voting-age population included 3.4 million ineligible felons and ex-felons and an estimated 19.9 million noncitizens. It did not include 5.0 million Americans abroad. The voting-age population in 2008 was 230.9 million people. The number of eligible voters, however, was only 212.7 million. If we calculated 2008 voter turnout based on the larger voting-age population, turnout would appear to be 56.8 percent, not 62.3 percent—a substantial error.

Voting-Age Population
The number of people of voting age living in the country at a given time, regardless of whether they have the right to vote.

Vote-Eligible Population
The number of people who, at a given time, enjoy the right to vote in national elections.

Franchise
The right to vote.

Registration
The entry of a person's name onto the list of registered voters for elections. To register, a person must meet certain legal requirements of age, citizenship, and residency.

LEGAL RESTRICTIONS ON VOTING

Legal restrictions on voter registration have existed since the founding of our nation. Most groups in the United States have been concerned with the suffrage issue at one time or another.

Historical Restrictions

In colonial times, only white males who owned property with a certain minimum value were eligible to vote, leaving a greater number of Americans ineligible than eligible to take part in the elections.

Property Requirements. Many government functions concern property rights and the distribution of income and wealth, and some of the founders of our nation believed it was appropriate that only people who had an interest in property should vote on these issues. The logic behind the restriction of voting rights to property owners was questioned by Thomas Paine in his pamphlet *Common Sense:*

> Here is a man who today owns a jackass, and the jackass is worth $60. Today the man is a voter and goes to the polls and deposits his vote. Tomorrow the jackass dies. The next day the man comes to vote without his jackass and cannot vote at all. Now tell me, which was the voter, the man or the jackass?[14]

The writers of the Constitution allowed the states to decide who should vote. Thus, women were allowed to vote in Wyoming in 1870 but not in the entire nation until the Nineteenth Amendment was ratified in 1920. By about 1850, most white adult males in virtually all the states could vote without any property qualification.

Further Extensions of the Franchise. Extension of the **franchise** to black males occurred with the passage of the Fifteenth Amendment in 1870. This enfranchisement was short lived, however, as the "redemption" of the South by white racists had rolled back those gains by the end of the century. As discussed in Chapter 5, it was not until the 1960s that African Americans, both male and female, were able to participate in the electoral process in all states. Women received full national voting rights with the Nineteenth Amendment in 1920. The most recent extension of the franchise occurred when the voting age was reduced to eighteen by the Twenty-sixth Amendment in 1971. One result of lowering the voting age was to depress voter turnout for several decades beginning in 1972, as you can see in Figure 8–1 on page 191. Young people are less likely to vote than older citizens. Recently, voter turnout has risen again.

Current Eligibility and Registration Requirements

Voting generally requires **registration,** and to register, a person must meet the following voter qualifications, or legal requirements: (1) citizenship, (2) age (eighteen or older), and (3) residency—the duration varies widely from state to state and with types of elections. Since 1972, states cannot impose residency requirements of more than thirty days.

Each state has different qualifications for voting and registration. In 1993, Congress passed the "motor voter" bill, which requires that states provide voter-

---

14. Thomas Paine, *Common Sense* (London: H. D. Symonds, 1792), p. 28.

registration materials when people receive or renew driver's licenses, that all states allow voters to register by mail, and that voter-registration forms be made available at a wider variety of public places and agencies. In general, a person must register well in advance of an election, although voters in Idaho, Maine, Minnesota, Wisconsin, and Wyoming are allowed to register up to, or even on, Election Day. North Dakota has no voter registration at all.

Some argue that registration requirements are responsible for much of the non-participation in our political process. There also is a partisan dimension to the debate over registration and nonvoting. Republicans generally fear that an expanded electorate would help to elect more Democrats because the kinds of persons who have trouble registering may be more likely to favor the Democrats.

Socioeconomic Status

The value assigned to a person due to occupation or income. An upper-class person, for example, has high socioeconomic status.

HOW DO VOTERS DECIDE?

Various socioeconomic and demographic factors appear to influence political preferences. We began our examination of these factors on page 120 in Chapter 6, as part of the discussion of political socialization. We go into further detail here.

Characteristics that influence political preferences include party identification, education, income and **socioeconomic status,** religion, race, and similar traits. People who share the same religion or any other demographic trait are likely to influence one another and may also have common political concerns that follow from the common characteristic. Other factors, such as perception of the candidates and issue preferences, are closely connected to the electoral process itself. Table 8–2 on the next page illustrates the impact of some of these variables on voting behavior.

Party Identification

With the possible exception of race, party identification is the most important determinant of voting behavior in national elections. Party affiliation is influenced by family and peer groups, by generational effects, by the media, and by the voter's assessment of candidates and issues.

As we have observed on more than one occasion, the number of independent voters has grown over the years. While party identification may have little effect on the voting behavior of independents, it remains a crucial determinant for the majority of the voters, who have established party identifications.

Demographic Influences

Demographic influences reflect the individual's personal background and place in society. Some factors have to do with the family into

◀ **Entertainer Sean (P. Diddy) Combs** encourages young people to vote. Historically, why have young people participated less than other age groups in our elections? (Chip East/Reuters/Corbis)

TABLE 8-2: **Votes by Groups in Presidential Elections, 1992–2008 (in Percentages)**

	1992			1996		2000		2004		2008	
	Clinton (Dem.)	Bush (Rep.)	Perot (Ref.)	Clinton (Dem.)	Dole (Rep.)	Gore (Dem.)	Bush (Rep.)	Kerry (Dem.)	Bush (Rep.)	Obama (Dem.)	McCain (Rep.)
Total Vote	43	38	19	49	41	48	48	48	51	53	46
Gender											
Men	41	38	21	43	44	42	53	44	55	49	48
Women	46	37	17	54	38	54	43	51	48	56	43
Race											
White	39	41	20	43	46	42	54	41	58	43	55
Black	82	11	7	84	12	90	8	88	11	95	4
Hispanic	62	25	14	72	21	67	31	58	40	67	31
Educational Attainment											
Not a high school graduate	55	28	17	59	28	59	39	50	50	63	35
High school graduate	43	36	20	51	35	48	49	47	52	52	46
College graduate	40	41	19	44	46	45	51	46	52	50	48
Postgraduate education	49	36	15	52	40	52	44	54	45	58	40
Religion											
White Protestant	33	46	21	36	53	34	63	32	68	34	65
Catholic	44	36	20	53	37	49	47	47	52	54	45
Jewish	78	12	10	78	16	79	19	75	24	78	21
White evangelical	23	61	15	NA	NA	NA	NA	21	79	24	74
Union Status											
Union household	55	24	21	59	30	59	37	59	40	59	39
Family Income											
Under $15,000	59	23	18	59	28	57	37	63	37	73	25
$15,000–29,000	45	35	20	53	36	54	41	57	41	60	37
$30,000–49,000	41	38	21	48	40	49	48	50	49	55	43
Over $50,000	40	42	18	44	48	45	52	43	56	49	49
Size of Place of Residence											
Population over 500,000	58	28	13	68	25	71	26	60	40	70	28
Population 50,000 to 500,000	50	33	16	50	39	57	40	50	50	59	39
Population 10,000 to 50,000	39	42	20	48	41	38	59	48	51	45	53
Rural	39	40	20	44	46	37	59	39	60	45	53

NA = Not asked.

Sources: *The New York Times;* Voter News Service; CBS News; and the National Election Pool.

which a person was born: race and (for most people) religion. Others may be the result of choices made throughout an individual's life: place of residence, educational achievement, and profession.

It is also clear that many of these factors are interrelated. People who have more education are likely to have higher incomes and to hold professional jobs. Similarly, children born into wealthier families are far more likely to complete college than children from poor families. A number of other interrelationships are not so immediately obvious; for example, many people might not realize that 88 percent of African Americans report that religion is very important in their lives, compared with only 57 percent of whites.[15]

Education. In the past, having a college education tended to be associated with voting for Republicans. In recent years, however, this correlation has become weaker. In particular, individuals with a postgraduate education—more than a bachelor's degree—have become predominantly Democratic. Also, a higher percentage of voters with only a high school education voted Republican in the last three presidential elections, compared with the pattern in previous elections, in which that group of voters tended to favor Democrats more strongly.

Economic Status. Normally, the higher a person's income, the more likely the person will be to vote Republican. Manual laborers, factory workers, and especially union members are more likely to vote Democratic. There are no hard-and-fast rules, however. Indeed, recent research indicates that a realignment is occurring among those of higher economic status: professionals such as physicians, attorneys, and college instructors now tend to vote Democratic, while small-business owners, managers, and corporate executives tend to vote Republican.

Religion. As noted in Chapter 6, voters who are more devout, regardless of their church affiliation, tend to vote Republican, while voters who are less devout are more often Democrats. In 2008, for example, Protestants who regularly attended church gave 67 percent of their votes to Republican candidate John McCain, compared with 54 percent of those who attended church less often. Among Catholics, there was a similar pattern: 50 percent of Catholics who attended church regularly voted Republican, while 58 percent of Catholics who were not regular churchgoers voted for Democratic candidate Barack Obama. There is an exception to this trend: African Americans of all religions have been strongly supportive of Democrats. As discussed in Chapter 6, Jewish voters are notably more liberal than other groups and tend to support Democrats as well.

Muslim American immigrants and their descendants are an interesting category.[16] In 2000, a majority of Muslim Americans of Middle Eastern ancestry voted for Republican George W. Bush because they shared his cultural conservatism and believed that he would do a better job of defending their civil liberties than Democrat Al Gore. Beginning with the 2004 election campaign, however, the civil liberties issue drove many of these voters toward the Democrats.

Race. African Americans voted principally for Republicans until Democrat Franklin Roosevelt's New Deal in the 1930s. Since then, they have largely identified with the Democratic Party. Indeed, Democratic presidential candidates have received, on average, more than 80 percent of the African American vote since 1956. Most Asian American groups lean toward the Democrats, although often by narrow margins.

---

15. The Gallup Poll, "A Look at Americans and Religion Today," March 23, 2004.
16. About one-third of U.S. Muslims actually are African Americans whose ancestors have been in this country for a long time. In terms of political preferences, African American Muslims are more likely to resemble other African Americans than Muslim immigrants from the Middle East.

The Hispanic Vote. The diversity among Hispanic Americans has resulted in differing political behavior. The majority of Hispanics vote Democratic. Cuban Americans, however, are usually Republican. Most Cuban Americans left Cuba because of Fidel Castro's Communist regime, and their strong anticommunism translates into conservative politics.

Since his days as Texas governor, George W. Bush had envisioned creating a stronger long-term Republican coalition by adding Hispanics, and in 2004, Bush's Latino support may have approached 40 percent.[17] In 2006, however, Hispanics favored Democratic candidates over Republicans by 73 percent to 26 percent. Why did Latino support for the Republicans fall so greatly? In a word: immigration. Bush favored immigration reform that would have granted unauthorized immigrants a path to citizenship. Most Republicans in Congress instead called for a hard line against illegal immigration. The harsh rhetoric of some Republicans convinced many Hispanics that the Republicans were hostile to Latino interests.

Directly Political Factors

Factors such as perception of the candidates and issue preferences also affect how people vote. While most people do not change their party identification from year to year, candidates and issues can change greatly, and voting behavior can therefore change as well.

Perception of the Candidates. The image of the candidate seems to be important in a voter's choice, especially of a president. To some extent, voter attitudes toward candidates are based on emotions (such as trust) rather than on any judgment about experience or policy. In some years, voters have been attracted to a candidate who appeared to share their concerns and worries. In other years, voters have sought a candidate who appeared to have high integrity and honesty.

Issue Preferences. Issues make a difference in presidential and congressional elections. Although personality or image factors may be very persuasive, most voters have some notion of how the candidates differ on basic issues or at least know which candidates want a change in the direction of government policy.

Historically, economic concerns have been among the most powerful influences on public opinion. When the economy is doing well, it is very difficult for a challenger, especially at the presidential level, to defeat the incumbent. In contrast, inflation, unemployment, or high interest rates are likely to work to the disadvantage of the incumbent.

The 2008 Presidential Elections. Economic issues, in particular the collapse of the financial markets in September and the full onset of the "Great Recession," guaranteed Barack Obama the presidency in 2008. Obama's personality also helped. Obama's steady temperament seemed well suited to chaotic times—his own staff members frequently referred to him as "no-drama Obama." John McCain's more volatile character, expressed in his frequent changes to his campaign, was not as reassuring to many voters.

---

17. A widely quoted survey put Bush's support at 44 percent, but that figure was almost certainly erroneous.

making a difference

REGISTERING AND VOTING

Very close elections, such as the 2008 Minnesota Senate race, demonstrate that your vote can make a difference. In local races, elections have sometimes been decided by one or two votes. In nearly every state, before you are allowed to cast a vote in an election, you must first register. Registration laws vary considerably from state to state.

Residency and Age Requirements   What do you have to do to register and cast a vote? In general, you must be a citizen of the United States, at least eighteen years old on or before Election Day, and a resident of the state in which you intend to register. Most states require that you meet a minimum-residency requirement. The minimum-residency requirement is very short in some states—for example, one day in Alabama and ten days in New Hampshire and Wisconsin. No state requires more than thirty days. Twenty states do not have any minimum-residency requirement at all.

Time Limits   Nearly every state also specifies a closing date by which you must be registered before an election. You may not be able to vote if you register too close to the day of the election. The closing date for registration varies from Election Day itself (Maine, Minnesota, and Wisconsin) to thirty days before the election (Arizona). In North Dakota, no registration is necessary.

In most states, your registration can be revoked if you do not vote within a certain number of years. This process of automatically "purging" the voter-registration lists of nonactive voters varies in frequency from every two years to every ten years. Ten states do not require this purging.

An Example   Let us look at voter registration in Iowa as an example. Iowa voters normally register through the local county auditor or when they obtain a driver's license (under the "motor voter" law of 1993). A voter who moves to a new address within the state must change registration by contacting the auditor. Postcard registrations must be postmarked or delivered to the county auditor no later than the twenty-fifth day before an election. Postcard registration forms in Iowa are available at many public buildings, at the county auditors' offices, or from campus groups.

For more information on voter registration, contact your county or state officials, party headquarters, labor union, or local chapter of the League of Women Voters. The Web site for the League of Women Voters is:

www.lwv.org

◀ **Disputed ballots** always have and always will be part of the election process. Here is an example of a disputed ballot that had to be inspected by a member of the State Canvassing Board in St. Paul, Minnesota. Because the contest between Norm Coleman and Al Franken for U.S. senator became exceedingly tight, such ballots were hotly disputed. Did this voter mean to vote for Norm Coleman? Coleman supporters argued that he or she did, whereas supporters of Al Franken (the eventual winner) argued that this was an invalid ballot. What do you think? (AP Photo/Dawn Villella)

key terms

Australian ballot 187

"beauty contest" 182

caucus 183

closed primary 184

coattail effect 188

corrupt practices
   acts 178

credentials
   committee 186

direct primary 183

elector 186

focus group 177

franchise 192

front-loading 185

front-runner 185

general election 175

Hatch Act 178

independent
   expenditures 181

indirect primary 183

issue advocacy
   advertising 182

office-block, or
   Massachusetts,
   ballot 187

open primary 184

party-column, or
   Indiana, ballot 187

political action
   committee (PAC) 180

political consultant 176

presidential
   primary 173

primary election 175

registration 192

socioeconomic
   status 193

soft money 180

superdelegate 183

tracking poll 177

vote-eligible
   population 191

voter turnout 189

voting-age
   population 191

chapter summary

1 The legal qualifications for holding political office are minimal at both the state and local levels, but holders of political office still are predominantly white and male and are likely to be from the professional class.

2 American political campaigns are lengthy and extremely expensive. In recent decades, they have become more candidate centered rather than party centered in response to technological innovations and decreasing party identification. Candidates have begun to rely less on the party and more on paid professional consultants to perform the various tasks necessary to wage a political campaign. The crucial task of professional political consultants is image building. The campaign organization devises a campaign strategy to maximize the candidate's chances of winning. Candidates use public opinion polls and focus groups to gauge their popularity and to test the mood of the country.

3 Interest groups are major sources of campaign funds. The contributions are often made through political action committees, or PACs. Other methods of contributing include issue advocacy advertising and setting up independent 527 organizations to register voters and run ads.

4 The amount of money spent in financing campaigns has been increasing steadily. A variety of corrupt practices acts have been passed to regulate campaign finance. New techniques, including independent expenditures, were later developed. The Bipartisan Campaign Reform Act of 2002 limited advertising by interest groups, and increased the limits on individual contributions.

5 After the Democratic convention of 1968, the McGovern-Fraser Commission formulated new rules for primaries, which were adopted by all Democrats and by Republicans in most states. These reforms opened up the nomination process for the presidency to all voters.

6 A presidential primary is a statewide election to help a political party determine its presidential nominee at the national convention. Some states use the caucus method of choosing convention delegates. The primary campaign recently has been shortened to the first few months of the election year.

7 The voter technically does not vote directly for president but chooses between slates of presidential electors. In most states, the slate that wins the most popular votes throughout the state gets to cast all the electoral votes for the state. The candidate receiving a majority (270) of the electoral votes wins. Both the mechanics and the politics of the electoral college have been criticized sharply.

8 The United States uses the Australian ballot, a secret ballot that is prepared, distributed, and counted by government officials. The office-block ballot groups candidates according to office. The party-column ballot groups candidates according to their party labels and symbols.

9 Voter participation in the United States is often considered to be low, especially in elections that do not feature a presidential contest. Turnout is lower when measured as a percentage of the voting-age population than it is when measured as a percentage of the population actually eligible to vote.

10 In colonial times, only white males who owned property were eligible to vote. The suffrage issue has concerned, at one time or another, most groups in the United States. Today, to be eligible to vote, a person must satisfy registration, citizenship, age, and residency requirements. Each state has different qualifications.

QUESTIONS FOR
discussionandanalysis

1 Some have argued that limits on campaign contributions violate First Amendment guarantees of freedom of speech. How strong is this argument? Can contributions be seen as a form of protected expression? Under what circumstances can contributions be seen instead as a method of bribing elected officials?

2 Many observers believe that holding so many presidential primary elections at such an early point is a serious problem. How might the problem be resolved? Also, is it fair and appropriate that New Hampshire always holds the first presidential primary and Iowa always conducts the first caucuses? Why or why not?

3 What changes might result if all states required voting by mail? What benefits might result? Are there any dangers? How would such a system change the nature of political campaigns?

4 Some people are more likely to vote than others. Older persons vote more frequently than younger ones. Wealthy voters make it to the polls more often than poor voters. What might cause older and wealthier individuals to exhibit greater turnout?

5 Years ago, persons with postgraduate degrees were more likely to vote for Republican than Democratic candidates, but in recent years, highly educated voters have been trending Democratic. Why might physicians and lawyers be more likely to vote Democratic than in the past? For what reasons might college professors tilt to the Democrats?

helpfulonline**Resources**

CONNECTING TO AMERICAN GOVERNMENT AND POLITICS

For excellent reports on where campaign finance comes from and how it is spent, view the site of the Center for Responsive Politics at:

www.opensecrets.org

Dave Leip's Atlas of U.S. Presidential Elections has a large collection of data and maps describing elections. Find them at:

uselectionatlas.org

Michael McDonald was one of the first political scientists to calculate voter turnout based on the number of people actually eligible to vote, as opposed to the number of people of voting age. He sponsors the United States Elections Project, which provides state-by-state data on turnout. Check it out at:

elections.gmu.edu

aspecialWebSite

FOR YOUR TEXT

Go to this book's special Web site at academic.cengage.com/polisci/Schmidt/ Brief6e. Choose "For Students." Then click on Chapter 8, where you will find an online quiz and other helpful study aids. If your professor is using CengageNOW: *American Government and Politics Today, Brief Edition,* log in and go to Chapter 8 for additional online study aids.

9

The Congress

Americans gather to celebrate Earth Day in front of the Capitol building in Washington, D.C. For many, the building itself evokes the U.S. Congress. (Todd Gipstein/Corbis)

Constituent
One of the persons represented by a legislator or other elected or appointed official.

Most Americans view Congress in a less than flattering light. In recent years, Congress has appeared to be deeply split, highly partisan in its conduct, and not very responsive to public needs. Polls show that less than 40 percent of the public have favorable opinions about Congress as a whole. Yet individual members of Congress often receive much higher approval ratings from the voters in their districts. This is one of the paradoxes of the relationship between the people and Congress. Members of the public hold the institution in relatively low regard compared with the satisfaction they express with their individual representatives.

Part of the explanation for these seemingly contradictory appraisals is that members of Congress spend considerable time and effort serving their **constituents.** If the federal bureaucracy makes a mistake, the senator's or representative's office tries to resolve the issue. What most Americans see of their own representatives, therefore, is the work of these representatives in their home states. Congress, however, was created to work not just for local constituents but also for the nation as a whole. Understanding the nature of the institution and the process of lawmaking is an important part of understanding how the policies that shape our lives are made.

In this chapter, we describe the functions of Congress, including constituent service, representation, lawmaking, and oversight of the government. We review how the members of Congress are elected and how Congress organizes itself when it meets. We also examine how bills pass through the legislative process.

THE NATURE AND FUNCTIONS OF CONGRESS

The founders of the American republic believed that the bulk of the power that would be exercised by a national government should be in the hands of the legislature. The leading role envisioned for Congress in the new government is apparent from its primacy in the Constitution. Article I deals with the structure, the powers, and the operation of Congress.

Bicameralism

The **bicameralism** of Congress—its division into two legislative houses—was in part the result of the Connecticut Compromise, which tried to balance the large-state population advantage, reflected in the House, and the small-state demand for equality in policymaking, which was satisfied in the Senate. Beyond that, the two chambers of Congress also reflected the social class biases of the founders. They wished to balance the interests and the numerical superiority of the common citizens with the property interests of the less numerous landowners, bankers, and merchants. They achieved this goal by providing that members of the House of Representatives should be elected directly by "the People," whereas members of the Senate were to be chosen by the elected representatives sitting in state legislatures, who were more likely to be members of the elite. (The latter provision was changed in 1913 by the passage of the Seventeenth Amendment, which provides that senators are also to be elected directly by the people.)

The logic of the bicameral Congress was reinforced by differences in length of tenure. Members of the House are required to face the electorate every two years, whereas senators can serve for a much more secure term of six years—even longer than the four-year term provided for the president. Furthermore, the senators' terms are staggered so that only one-third of the senators face the electorate every two years, along with all of the House members.

The bicameral Congress was designed to perform certain functions for the political system. These functions include lawmaking, representation, service to constituents, oversight (regulatory supervision), public education, and conflict resolution. Of these, the two most important and the ones that are most often in conflict are lawmaking and representation.

The Lawmaking Function

The principal and most obvious function of any legislature is **lawmaking.** Congress is the highest elected body in the country, charged with making binding rules for all Americans. This does not mean, however, that Congress initiates most of the ideas for legislation that it eventually considers. A majority of the bills that Congress acts on originate in the executive branch, and many other bills are traceable to interest groups and political party organizations. Through the processes of compromise and **logrolling** (offering to support a fellow member's bill in exchange for that member's promise to support your bill in the future), as well as debate and discussion, backers of legislation attempt to fashion a winning majority coalition. Logrolling often involves agreements to support another member's legislative **earmarks,** also known as *pork.* Earmarks are special provisions in legislation to set aside funds for projects that have not passed an

Bicameralism
The division of a legislature into two separate assemblies.

Lawmaking
The process of establishing the legal rules that govern society.

Logrolling
An arrangement in which two or more members of Congress agree in advance to support each other's bills.

Earmarks
Special provisions in legislation to set aside funds for projects that have not passed an impartial evaluation by agencies of the executive branch. Also known as *pork.*

Representation
The function of members of Congress as elected officials representing the views of their constituents.

Trustee
A legislator who acts according to her or his conscience and the broad interests of the entire society.

Instructed Delegate
A legislator who is an agent of the voters who elected him or her and who votes according to the views of constituents regardless of personal beliefs.

impartial evaluation by agencies of the executive branch. (As you will learn at the end of this chapter, normal spending projects pass through such evaluations.)

The Representation Function

Representation includes both representing the desires and demands of the constituents in the member's home district or state and representing larger national interests, such as the nation's security or the environment. Because the interests of constituents in a specific district may be at odds with the demands of national policy, the representation function is often in conflict with the lawmaking function for individual lawmakers—and sometimes for Congress as a whole. For example, although it may be in the interest of the nation to reduce defense spending by closing military bases, such closures are not in the interest of the states and districts that will lose jobs and local spending. Every legislator faces votes that set representational issues against lawmaking realities.

How should the legislators fulfill the representation function? There are several views on how this task should be accomplished.

The Trustee View of Representation. One approach to the question of how representation should be achieved is that legislators should act as **trustees** of the broad interests of the entire society. They should vote against the narrow interests of their constituents if their conscience and their perception of national needs so dictate. For example, in 2008 many legislators supported a bank bailout bill in spite of the views of the majority of their constituents.

The Instructed-Delegate View of Representation. Directly opposed to the trustee view of representation is the notion that the members of Congress should behave as **instructed delegates**—that is, they should mirror the views of the majority of the constituents who elected them in the first place. On the surface, this approach is plausible and rewarding. For it to work, however, we must assume that constituents actually have well-formed views on the issues that are decided in Congress and, further, that they have clear-cut preferences about these issues. Neither condition is likely to be satisfied very often.

Generally, most legislators hold neither a pure trustee view nor a pure instructed-delegate view. Typically, they combine both perspectives in a pragmatic mix that is often called the "politico" style.

◀ **Senator Arlen Specter** from Pennsylvania used to be a Republican but changed parties in 2009. He claimed that his views were more consistent with those of the Democrats. Was he acting as a trustee or an instructed delegate? (AP Photo/Susan Walsh)

Service to Constituents

Individual members of Congress are expected by their constituents to act as brokers between private citizens and the imposing, often faceless federal government. This function of providing service to constituents usually takes the form of **casework.** The legislator and her or his staff spend a considerable portion of their time in casework activities, such as tracking down a missing Social Security check, explaining the meaning of particular bills to people who may be affected by them, promoting a local business interest, or interceding with a regulatory agency on behalf of constituents who disagree with proposed agency regulations.

Legislators and many analysts of congressional behavior regard this **ombudsperson** role as an activity that strongly benefits the members of Congress. A government characterized by a large, confusing bureaucracy and complex public programs offers innumerable opportunities for legislators to come to the assistance of (usually) grateful constituents. Morris P. Fiorina once suggested, somewhat mischievously, that senators and representatives prefer to maintain bureaucratic confusion to maximize their opportunities for performing good deeds on behalf of their constituents:

> Some poor, aggrieved constituent becomes enmeshed in the tentacles of an evil bureaucracy and calls upon Congressman St. George to do battle with the dragon. . . . In dealing with the bureaucracy, the congressman is not merely one vote of 435. Rather, he is a nonpartisan power, someone whose phone call snaps an office to attention. He is not kept on hold. The constituent who receives aid believes that his congressman and his congressman alone got results.[1]

The Oversight Function

Oversight of the bureaucracy is essential if the decisions made by Congress are to have any force. **Oversight** is the process by which Congress follows up on the laws it has enacted to ensure that they are being enforced and administered in the way Congress intended. This is done by holding committee hearings and investigations, changing the size of an agency's budget, and cross-examining high-level presidential nominees to head major agencies.

Senators and representatives increasingly see their oversight function as a critically important part of their legislative activities. In part, oversight is related to the concept of constituency service, particularly when Congress investigates alleged arbitrariness or wrongdoing by bureaucratic agencies.

When the Republicans controlled both the executive and legislative branches of government from 2001 to 2007, many claimed that Congress failed to fulfill its oversight function. Serious allegations of wrongdoing by government officials, including some members of Congress, often went uninvestigated. Henry Waxman, the senior Democrat on the House Oversight and Government Reform Committee, identified fifteen areas in which the Republicans had refused either to permit hearings or to subpoena documents. These ranged from national security through the letting of contracts to the politicization of scientific decisions. After taking control of Congress in 2007, the Democrats launched a series of investigations into alleged wrongdoing by government officials.

Casework
Personal work for constituents by members of Congress.

Ombudsperson
A person who hears and investigates complaints by private individuals against public officials or agencies.

Oversight
The process by which Congress follows up on laws it has enacted to ensure that they are being enforced and administered in the way Congress intended.

---

1. Morris P. Fiorina, *Congress: Keystone of the Washington Establishment,* 2d ed. (New Haven, Conn.: Yale University Press, 1989), pp. 44, 47.

Agenda Setting
Determining which public-policy questions will be debated or considered.

Enumerated Power
A power specifically granted to the national government by the Constitution. The first seventeen clauses of Article I, Section 8, specify most of the enumerated powers of Congress.

The Public-Education Function

Educating the public is a function that Congress performs whenever it holds public hearings, exercises oversight over the bureaucracy, or engages in committee and floor debate on such major issues and topics as immigration, global warming, illegal drugs, and the concerns of small businesses. In so doing, Congress presents a range of viewpoints on pressing national questions. Congress also decides what issues will come up for discussion and decision; this **agenda setting** is a major facet of its public-education function.

The Conflict-Resolution Function

Congress is commonly seen as an institution for resolving conflicts within American society. Organized interest groups and spokespersons for different racial, religious, economic, and ideological interests look on Congress as an access point for airing their grievances and seeking help. This puts Congress in the position of trying to resolve the differences among competing points of view by passing laws to accommodate as many interested parties as possible. To the extent that Congress meets pluralist expectations in accommodating competing interests, it tends to build support for the entire political process.

THE POWERS OF CONGRESS

The Constitution is both highly specific and extremely vague about the powers that Congress may exercise. The first seventeen clauses of Article I, Section 8, specify most of the **enumerated powers** of Congress—that is, powers expressly given to that body.

Enumerated Powers

The enumerated, or expressed, powers of Congress include the rights to impose a variety of taxes, including tariffs on imports; borrow funds; regulate interstate commerce and international trade; establish procedures for naturalizing citizens; make laws regulating bankruptcies; coin (and print) money and regulate its value; establish standards of weights and measures; punish counterfeiters; establish post offices and postal routes; regulate copyrights and patents; establish the federal court system; punish illegal acts on the high seas; declare war; raise and regulate an army and a navy; call up and regulate the state militias to enforce laws, to suppress insurrections, and to repel invasions; and govern the District of Columbia.

The most important of the domestic powers of Congress, listed in Article I, Section 8, are the rights to collect taxes, to spend, and to regulate commerce. The most important foreign policy power is the power to declare war. Other sections of the Constitution allow Congress to establish rules for its own members, to regulate the electoral college, and to override a presidential veto. Congress may also regulate the extent of the Supreme Court's authority to review cases decided by the lower courts, regulate relations among states, and propose amendments to the Constitution.

Powers of the Senate. Some functions are restricted to one chamber. The Senate must advise on, and consent to, the ratification of treaties and must accept or reject presidential nominations of ambassadors, Supreme Court justices, other federal judges, and "all other Officers of the United States." But the Senate may delegate to the president or lesser officials the power to make lower-level appointments.

Constitutional Amendments. Amendments to the Constitution provide for other congressional powers. Congress must certify the election of a president and a vice president or itself choose those officers if no candidate has a majority of the electoral vote (Twelfth Amendment). It may levy an income tax (Sixteenth Amendment) and determine who will be acting president in case of the death or incapacity of the president or vice president (Twentieth Amendment and Twenty-fifth Amendment). In addition, Congress explicitly is given the power to enforce, by appropriate legislation, the provisions of several other amendments.

▲ **Taxpayers in line** at the post office. One of the expressed powers of Congress is the power to impose and collect taxes. Every year on April 15 (if it falls on a weekday), U.S. residents line up in front of almost every post office building in America to file their tax returns before the midnight deadline. These New Yorkers have waited until the last minute and are standing in line inside the James A. Farley Post Office building. (Mario Tama/Getty Images)

The Necessary and Proper Clause

Beyond these numerous specific powers, Congress enjoys the right under Article I, Section 8 (the elastic, or necessary and proper, clause), "[t]o make all Laws which shall be necessary and proper for carrying into Execution the foregoing Powers [of Article I], and all other Powers vested by this Constitution in the Government of the United States, or in any Department or Officer thereof." As discussed in Chapter 3, this vague statement of congressional responsibilities has provided, over time, the basis for a greatly expanded national government. It also has constituted, at least in theory, a check on the expansion of presidential powers.

HOUSE-SENATE DIFFERENCES

Congress is composed of two markedly different—but co-equal—chambers. Although the Senate and the House of Representatives exist within the same legislative institution, each has developed certain distinctive features that clearly distinguish one from the other.

Size and Rules

The central difference between the House and the Senate is simply that the House is much larger than the Senate. The House has 435 representatives, plus delegates from the District of Columbia, Puerto Rico, Guam, American Samoa, and the Virgin Islands, compared with just 100 senators. This size difference means that a greater number of formal rules are needed to govern activity in the House, whereas correspondingly looser procedures can be followed in the less crowded Senate. This difference is most obvious in the rules governing debate on the floors of the two chambers.

Rules Committee
A standing committee of the House of Representatives that provides special rules under which specific bills can be debated, amended, and considered by the House.

Filibuster
The use of the Senate's tradition of unlimited debate as a delaying tactic to block a bill.

The Senate normally permits extended debate on all issues that arise before it. In contrast, the House generally operates with an elaborate system in which its **Rules Committee** proposes time limitations on debate for any bill, and a majority of the entire body accepts or modifies those suggested time limits. As a consequence of its stricter time limits on debate, the House, despite its greater size, often is able to act on legislation more quickly than the Senate.

Debate and Filibustering

The Senate tradition of the **filibuster**, or the use of unlimited debate as a blocking tactic, dates back to 1790.[2] In that year, a proposal to move the U.S. capital from New York to Philadelphia was stalled by such time-wasting maneuvers. This unlimited-debate tradition—which also existed in the House until 1811—is not absolute, however.

Cloture. Under Senate Rule 22, debate may be ended by invoking *cloture*. Cloture shuts off discussion on a bill. Amended in 1975 and 1979, Rule 22 states that debate may be closed off on a bill if sixteen senators sign a petition requesting it and if, after two days have elapsed, three-fifths of the entire membership (sixty votes, assuming no vacancies) vote for cloture. After cloture is invoked, each senator may speak on a bill for a maximum of one hour before a vote is taken.

Increased Use of the Filibuster. Traditionally, filibusters were rare, and the tactic was employed only on issues of principle. Filibustering senators spoke for many hours, sometimes reading names from a telephone book. By the twenty-first century, however, filibusters could be invoked without such speeches, and senators were threatening to filibuster almost every significant piece of legislation to come before the body. The threats were sufficient to create a new, ad hoc rule that important legislation needed the support of sixty senators.

The Filibuster after the 2008 Elections. A major issue in the 2008 elections was whether the Democrats could elect enough senators to reach the magic number of sixty without any Republican votes. In fact, the Senate convened in 2009 with fifty-eight Democratic members, which was set to rise to fifty-nine when the Minnesota Senate race was finally resolved.

Initially, it seemed that no legislation could pass the Senate without at least a few Republican votes, and indeed, the $787 billion stimulus bill passed in February only after it was altered to win the votes of three Republican senators. In April, the Democrats came up with an antifilibuster tactic. Budget bills are governed under special *reconciliation* rules that do not permit filibusters. The Democrats therefore threatened to adopt major health-care legislation as part of a budget bill. Republicans protested, even though they had used the reconciliation tactic themselves in recent years.

On April 28, Pennsylvania senator Arlen Specter left the Republican Party to join the Democrats. That switch, plus the seating of Minnesota's Al Franken, gave the Democrats their sixty votes. It now seemed less likely that the majority party would need to use the reconciliation tactic.

---

2. *Filibuster* comes from a Spanish word for pirate, which in turn came from the Dutch term *vrijbuiter*, or freebooter. The word was first used in 1851 to accuse senators of pirating or hijacking debate.

Prestige

As a consequence of the greater size of the House, representatives generally cannot achieve as much individual recognition and public prestige as can members of the Senate. Senators are better able to gain media exposure and to establish careers as spokespersons for large national constituencies.

CONGRESSPERSONS AND THE CITIZENRY: A COMPARISON

Members of the U.S. Senate and the U.S. House of Representatives are not typical American citizens. Members of Congress are older than most Americans, partly because of constitutional age requirements and partly because a good deal of political experience normally is an advantage in running for national office. Members of Congress are also disproportionately white, male, and trained in high-status occupations. Lawyers are by far the largest occupational group among congresspersons, although the proportion of lawyers in the House is lower now than it was in the past. Compared with the average American citizen, members of Congress are well paid. In 2009, annual congressional salaries were $174,000. Increasingly, members of Congress are also much wealthier than the average citizen. Whereas about 3 percent of Americans have assets exceeding $1 million (not including their homes), almost half of the members of Congress are millionaires. Table 9–1 summarizes selected characteristics of the members of Congress.

TABLE 9–1: Characteristics of the 111th Congress, 2009–2011

Characteristic	U.S. Population (2000)*	House	Senate
Age (median)	36.7	57.0	63.1
Percentage minority	33.6	16.8	5
Religion			
Percentage church members	61.0	89.9	95
Percentage Roman Catholic	23.9	30.3	25
Percentage Protestant	51.3	53.3	50
Percentage Jewish	1.7	7.1	14
Percentage female	51.5	17.2	17
Percentage with advanced degrees	9.7	66.9	76
Occupation			
Percentage lawyers	0.4	41.4	57
Percentage blue-collar workers	10.2	3.0	2
Family income			
Percentage of families earning over $50,000 annually	34.9	100.0	100
Personal wealth			
Percentage with assets over $1 million	3.0	44.0	58

*Estimates based on 2000 census.

Sources: *CIA Factbook,* 2008; Census Bureau; and authors' updates.

Direct Primary
An intraparty election in which the voters select the candidates who will run on a party's ticket in the subsequent general election.

Party Identifier
A person who identifies with a political party.

CONGRESSIONAL ELECTIONS

The process of electing members of Congress is decentralized. Congressional elections are conducted by the individual state governments. The states, however, must conform to the rules established by the U.S. Constitution and national statutes. The Constitution states that representatives are to be elected every second year by popular ballot, and the number of seats awarded to each state is to be determined every ten years by the results of the census. Each state has at least one representative, with most congressional districts having about half a million residents. Senators are elected by popular vote (since the passage of the Seventeenth Amendment) every six years; approximately one-third of the seats are chosen every two years. Each state has two senators. Under Article I, Section 4, of the Constitution, state legislatures are given control over "[t]he Times, Places and Manner of holding Elections for Senators and Representatives"; however, "the Congress may at any time by Law make or alter such Regulations."

Candidates for Congressional Elections

Candidates for congressional seats may be self-selected. In districts where one party is very strong, however, there may be a shortage of candidates willing to represent the weaker party. In such circumstances, leaders of the weaker party must often actively recruit candidates. Candidates may resemble the voters of the district in ethnicity or religion, but they are also likely to be very successful individuals who have been active in politics before. House candidates are especially likely to have local ties to their districts.

Congressional Campaigns and Elections. Congressional campaigns have changed considerably in the past two decades. Like all other campaigns, they are much more expensive, with the average cost of a winning Senate campaign now $6.5 million and a winning House campaign more than $1.1 million. Campaign funds include direct contributions by individuals and contributions by political action committees (PACs). All of these contributions are regulated by laws, including the Federal Election Campaign Act of 1971, as amended, and most recently the Bipartisan Campaign Reform Act of 2002. Once in office, legislators spend time almost every day raising funds for their next campaign.

Most candidates for Congress must win the nomination through a **direct primary,** in which **party identifiers** vote for the candidate who will be on the party ticket in the general election. To win the primary, candidates may take more liberal or more conservative positions to get the votes of party identifiers. In the general election, they may moderate their views to attract the votes of independents and voters from the other party.

Presidential Effects. Congressional candidates are always hopeful that a strong presidential candidate on their ticket will have "coattails" that will sweep in senators and representatives of the same party. In fact, coattail effects have been quite limited, and in many recent presidential elections they have not materialized at all. One way to measure the coattail effect is to look at the subsequent midterm elections, held in the even-numbered years following the presidential contests. In these years, voter turnout falls sharply. In the past, the party controlling the White House normally lost seats in Congress in the midterm elections, in part because the coattail effect ceased to apply. In recent elections, this "midterm effect" has been less common. Table 9–2 shows the pattern for midterm elections since 1942.

The Power of Incumbency

The power of incumbency in the outcome of congressional elections cannot be overemphasized. Table 9–3 shows that a sizable majority of representatives and a slightly smaller proportion of senators who decide to run for reelection are successful. This conclusion holds for both presidential-year and midterm elections. Even in 2006, when the Democrats made sizable gains, most incumbents were safe.

A number of scholars contend that the pursuit of reelection is the strongest motivation behind the activities of members of Congress. They pursue reelection in several ways. Incumbents can use the mass media, make personal appearances with constituents, and send newsletters—all to produce a favorable image and to make the incumbent's name a household word.

Members of Congress generally try to present themselves as informed, experienced, and responsive to people's needs. Legislators also can point to things that they have done to benefit their constituents by fulfilling the congressional casework function or bringing federal government funding for highways or mass transit to the district, for example. Finally, incumbents can demonstrate the positions that they have taken on key issues by referring to their voting records in Congress.

TABLE 9–2: Midterm Gains and Losses by the Party of the President, 1942–2006

	Seats Gained or Lost by the Party of the President in the House of Representatives
1942	−45 (D.)
1946	−55 (D.)
1950	−29 (D.)
1954	−18 (R.)
1958	−47 (R.)
1962	−4 (D.)
1966	−47 (D.)
1970	−12 (R.)
1974	−48 (R.)
1978	−15 (D.)
1982	−26 (R.)
1986	−5 (R.)
1990	−8 (R.)
1994	−52 (D.)
1998	+5 (D.)
2002	+5 (R.)
2006	−30 (R.)

TABLE 9–3: The Power of Incumbency

	Election Year													
	1982	1984	1986	1988	1990	1992	1994	1996	1998	2000	2002	2004	2006	2008
House														
Number of incumbent candidates	393	411	394	409	406	368	387	384	402	403	393	404	405	404
Reelected	354	392	385	402	390	325	349	361	395	394	383	397	382	381
Percentage of total	90.1	95.4	97.7	98.3	96.0	88.3	90.2	94.0	98.3	97.8	97.5	98.3	94.3	94.3
Defeated	39	19	9	7	16	43	38	23	7	9	10	7	23	23
In primary	10	3	3	1	1	19	4	2	1	3	3	1	2	5
In general election	29	16	6	6	15	24	34	21	6	6	7	6	21	18
Senate														
Number of incumbent candidates	30	29	28	27	32	28	26	21	29	29	28	26	29	30
Reelected	28	26	21	23	31	23	24	19	26	23	24	25	23	26
Percentage of total	93.3	89.6	75.0	85.2	96.9	82.1	92.3	90.5	89.7	79.3	85.7	96.2	79.3	86.7
Defeated	2	3	7	4	1	5	2	2	3	6	4	1	6	4
In primary	0	0	0	0	0	1	0	1	0	0	1	0	1*	0
In general election	2	3	7	4	1	4	2	1	3	6	3	1	6	3

*Joe Lieberman of Connecticut lost the Democratic primary but won the general election as an independent. He aligned himself with the Senate Democrats for organizational purposes.

Sources: Norman Ornstein, Thomas E. Mann, and Michael J. Malbin, *Vital Statistics on Congress, 2001–2002* (Washington, D.C.: The AEI Press, 2002); and authors' updates.

Reapportionment
The allocation of seats in the House of Representatives to each state after each census.

Redistricting
The redrawing of the boundaries of the congressional districts within each state.

Justiciable Question
A question that may be raised and reviewed in court.

Gerrymandering
The drawing of legislative district boundary lines for the purpose of obtaining partisan or factional advantage. A district is said to be gerrymandered when its shape is manipulated by the dominant party to maximize electoral strength at the expense of the minority party.

APPORTIONMENT OF THE HOUSE

Two of the most complicated aspects of congressional elections are apportionment issues—**reapportionment** (the allocation of seats in the House to each state after each census) and **redistricting** (the redrawing of the boundaries of the districts within each state). In a landmark six-to-two vote in 1962, the United States Supreme Court made the apportionment of state legislative districts a **justiciable** (that is, a reviewable) **question.**[3] The Court did so by invoking the Fourteenth Amendment principle that no state can deny to any person "the equal protection of the laws." In 1964, the Court held that *both* chambers of a state legislature must be apportioned so that all districts are equal in population.[4] Later that year, the Court applied this "one person, one vote" principle to U.S. congressional districts on the basis of Article I, Section 2, of the Constitution, which requires that members of the House be chosen "by the People of the several States."[5]

As a result of severe malapportionment of congressional districts before 1964, some districts contained two or three times the populations of other districts in the same state, thereby diluting the effect of a vote cast in the more populous districts. This system generally benefited the conservative populations of rural areas and small towns and harmed the interests of the more heavily populated and liberal cities. In fact, suburban areas have benefited the most from the Court's rulings, as suburbs account for an increasingly larger proportion of the nation's population, while cities include a correspondingly smaller segment of the population.

Gerrymandering

Although the general issue of apportionment has been dealt with fairly successfully by the one person, one vote principle, the **gerrymandering** issue has not yet been resolved. This term refers to the tactics that were used under Elbridge Gerry, the governor of Massachusetts, in the 1812 elections to draw legislative boundaries (see Figure 9–1 on the facing page). A district is said to have been gerrymandered when its shape is altered substantially by the dominant party to maximize its electoral strength at the expense of the minority party.

In 1986, the Supreme Court heard a case that challenged gerrymandered congressional districts in Indiana. The Court ruled for the first time that redistricting for the political benefit of one group could be challenged on constitutional grounds. In this specific case, *Davis v. Bandemer,*[6] however, the Court did not agree that the districts had been drawn unfairly, because it could not be proved that a group of voters would consistently be deprived of influence at the polls as a result of the new districts.

Redistricting after the 2000 Census

In the meantime, political gerrymandering continues. Redistricting decisions are often made by a small group of political leaders within a state legislature. Typically, their goal is to shape voting districts in such a way as to maximize their party's chances of

---

3. *Baker v. Carr,* 369 U.S. 186 (1962). The term *justiciable* is pronounced juhs-*tish*-a-buhl.
4. *Reynolds v. Sims,* 377 U.S. 533 (1964).
5. *Wesberry v. Sanders,* 376 U.S. 1 (1964).
6. 478 U.S. 109 (1986).

FIGURE 9–1: The Original Gerrymander

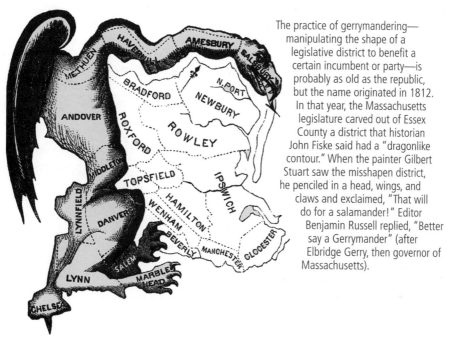

The practice of gerrymandering—manipulating the shape of a legislative district to benefit a certain incumbent or party—is probably as old as the republic, but the name originated in 1812. In that year, the Massachusetts legislature carved out of Essex County a district that historian John Fiske said had a "dragonlike contour." When the painter Gilbert Stuart saw the misshapen district, he penciled in a head, wings, and claws and exclaimed, "That will do for a salamander!" Editor Benjamin Russell replied, "Better say a Gerrymander" (after Elbridge Gerry, then governor of Massachusetts).

Source: *Congressional Quarterly's Guide to Congress,* 3d ed. (Washington, D.C.: Congressional Quarterly Press, 1982), p. 695.

winning state legislative seats, as well as seats in Congress. Two of the techniques in use are called "packing" and "cracking." By employing powerful computers and software, voters supporting the opposing party are packed into as few districts as possible or the opposing party's supporters are cracked into different districts. Consider that in Michigan, the Republicans who dominated redistricting efforts succeeded in packing six Democratic incumbents into only three congressional seats.

Clearly, partisan redistricting usually aids incumbents. After all, the party that dominates a state's legislature will make the redistricting decisions. Through gerrymandering tactics such as packing and cracking, districts can be redrawn in such a way as to ensure that party's continued strength in the state legislature or Congress. The *New York Times* estimated that only 26 of the 435 seats in the House of Representatives were open for any real competition in the 2008 elections.

"Minority-Majority" Districts

Under the mandate of the Voting Rights Act of 1965, the Justice Department issued directives to states after the 1990 census instructing them to create congressional districts that would maximize the voting power of minority groups—that is, create districts in which minority voters were the majority. The result was a number of creatively drawn congressional districts—see, for example, the depiction of Illinois's

FIGURE 9-2: The Fourth Congressional District of Illinois

This district, which is mostly within Chicago's city limits, was drawn to connect two Hispanic neighborhoods separated by an African American majority district.

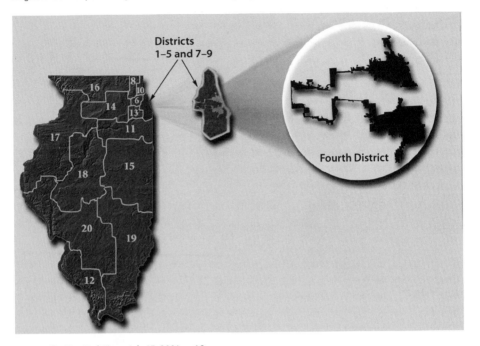

Source: *The New York Times,* July 15, 2001, p. 16.

Fourth Congressional District in Figure 9–2, which is commonly described as "a pair of earmuffs."

Many of these "minority-majority" districts were challenged in court by citizens who claimed that creating districts based on race or ethnicity alone violates the equal protection clause of the Constitution. In 2001, for example, the Supreme Court reviewed, for a second time, a case involving North Carolina's Twelfth District. The district was 165 miles long, following Interstate 85 for the most part. According to a local joke, the district was so narrow that a car traveling down the interstate highway with both doors open would kill most of the voters in the district. In 1996, the Supreme Court had held that the district was unconstitutional because race had been the dominant factor in drawing the district's boundaries. Shortly thereafter, the boundaries were redrawn, but the district was again challenged as a racial gerrymander. A federal district court agreed and invalidated the new boundaries as unconstitutional. In 2001, however, the Supreme Court held that there was insufficient evidence for the lower court's conclusion that race had been the dominant factor when the boundaries were redrawn.[7] The Twelfth District's boundaries remained as drawn.

---

7. *Easley v. Cromartie,* 532 U.S. 234 (2001).

PERKS AND PRIVILEGES

Legislators have many benefits that are not available to most people. For example, members of Congress are granted generous **franking** privileges that permit them to mail newsletters, surveys, and other correspondence to their constituents for free.[8] The annual cost of congressional mail has risen from $11 million in 1971 to more than $70 million today. Typically, the costs for these mailings rise substantially during election years.

Franking
A policy that enables members of Congress to send material through the mail by substituting their facsimile signature (frank) for postage.

Permanent Professional Staffs

More than thirty thousand people are employed in the Capitol Hill bureaucracy. About half of them are personal and committee staff members. The personal staff includes office clerks and assistants; professionals who deal with media relations, draft legislation, and satisfy constituency requests for service; and staffers who maintain local offices in the member's home district or state.

The average Senate office on Capitol Hill employs about thirty staff members, and twice that number work on the personal staffs of senators from the most populous states. House office staffs typically are about half as large as those of the Senate. The number of staff members has increased dramatically since 1960.

Privileges and Immunities under the Law

Members of Congress also benefit from a number of special constitutional protections. Under Article I, Section 6, of the Constitution, for example, "for any Speech or Debate in either House, they shall not be questioned in any other Place." The "speech or debate" clause means that a member may make any allegations or other statements he or she wishes in connection with official duties and normally not be sued for defamation (libel or slander) or otherwise be subject to legal action.

THE COMMITTEE STRUCTURE

Most of the actual work of legislating is performed by the committees and subcommittees within Congress. Thousands of bills are introduced in every session of Congress, and no single member can possibly be adequately informed on all the issues that arise. The committee system is a way to provide for specialization, or a division of the legislative labor. Members of a committee can concentrate on just one area or topic—such as taxation or energy—and develop sufficient expertise to draft appropriate legislation when needed. The flow of legislation through both the House and the Senate is determined largely by the speed with which the members of these committees act on bills and resolutions.

The Power of Committees

Sometimes called "little legislatures," committees usually have the final say on pieces of legislation.[9] Committee actions may be overturned on the floor by the House or Senate, but this rarely happens. Legislators normally defer to the expertise of the chairperson and other members of the committee who speak on the floor in defense of

---

8. The word *franking* derives from the Latin *francus*, which means "free."
9. The term *little legislatures* is from Woodrow Wilson, *Congressional Government* (New York: Meridian Books, 1956 [first published in 1885]).

Discharge Petition
A procedure by which a bill in the House of Representatives may be forced (discharged) out of a committee that has refused to report it for consideration by the House. The petition must be signed by an absolute majority (218) of representatives and is used only on rare occasions.

Standing Committee
A permanent committee in the House or Senate that considers bills within a certain subject area.

a committee decision. Chairpersons of committees exercise control over the scheduling of hearings and formal actions on bills. They also decide which subcommittee will act on legislation falling within their committee's jurisdiction. Committees normally have the power to kill proposed legislation by refusing to act on it—by never sending it to the entire chamber for a vote.

Committees only very rarely are deprived of control over bills—although this kind of action is provided for in the rules of each chamber. In the House, if a bill has been considered by a standing committee for thirty days, the signatures of a majority (218) of the House membership on a **discharge petition** can pry a bill out of an uncooperative committee's hands. From 1909 to 2010, however, although over nine hundred such petitions were initiated, only slightly more than two dozen resulted in successful discharge efforts. Of those, twenty resulted in bills that passed the House.[10]

Types of Congressional Committees

Over the past two centuries, Congress has created several different types of committees, each of which serves particular needs of the institution.

Standing Committees. By far the most important committees in Congress are the **standing committees**—permanent bodies that are established by the rules of each chamber and that continue from session to session. A list of the standing committees of the 111th Congress is presented in Table 9–4. In addition, most of the standing committees have created subcommittees to carry out their work. For example, the 111th Congress has 73 subcommittees in the Senate and 104 in the House. Each standing committee is given a specific area of legislative policy jurisdiction, and almost all legislative measures are considered by the appropriate standing committees.

Because of the importance of their work and the traditional influence of their members in Congress, certain committees are considered to be more prestigious than others. Seats on standing committees that handle spending issues are especially sought after because members can use these positions to benefit their constituents.

10. *Congressional Quarterly's Guide to Congress,* 5th ed. (Washington, D.C.: Congressional Quarterly Press, 2000); and authors' update.

▼ **In these troubled times,** the House Financial Services Committee frequently has hearings about financial markets. Here, President Bush's Treasury secretary Henry Paulson (left) explains the banking bailout bill while the head of the Federal Reserve System, Ben Bernanke, listens. Why do administration officials attend congressional hearings? (AP Photo/Manuel Balce Ceneta)

TABLE 9–4: **Standing Committees of the 111th Congress, 2009–2011**

House Committees	Senate Committees
Agriculture	Agriculture, Nutrition, and Forestry
Appropriations	Appropriations
Armed Services	Armed Services
Budget	Banking, Housing, and Urban Affairs
Education and Labor	Budget
Energy and Commerce	Commerce, Science, and Transportation
Financial Services	Energy and Natural Resources
Foreign Affairs	Environment and Public Works
Homeland Security	Finance
House Administration	Foreign Relations
Judiciary	Health, Education, Labor, and Pensions
Natural Resources	Homeland Security and Governmental Affairs
Oversight and Government Reform	Judiciary
Rules	Rules and Administration
Science and Technology	Small Business and Entrepreneurship
Small Business	Veterans' Affairs
Standards of Official Conduct	
Transportation and Infrastructure	
Veterans' Affairs	
Ways and Means	

Committees that control spending include the Appropriations Committee in either chamber and the Ways and Means Committee in the House. Members also normally seek seats on committees that handle matters of special interest to their constituents. A member of the House from an agricultural district, for example, will have an interest in joining the House Agriculture Committee.

Select Committees. In principle, a **select committee** is created for a limited time and for a specific legislative purpose. For example, a select committee may be formed to investigate a public problem, such as child nutrition or aging. In practice, a select committee, such as the Select Committee on Intelligence in each chamber, may continue indefinitely. Select committees rarely create original legislation.

Joint Committees. A **joint committee** is formed by the concurrent action of both chambers of Congress and consists of members from each chamber. Joint committees, which may be permanent or temporary, have dealt with the economy, taxation, and the Library of Congress.

Conference Committees. Special joint committees—**conference committees**— are formed for the purpose of achieving agreement between the House and the Senate on the exact wording of legislative acts when the two chambers pass legislative

Select Committee
A temporary legislative committee established for a limited time period and for a special purpose.

Joint Committee
A legislative committee composed of members from both chambers of Congress.

Conference Committee
A special joint committee appointed to reconcile differences when bills pass the two chambers of Congress in different forms.

▲ **Representative Barney Frank** (D., Mass.) chairs the House Financial Services Committee. How did he become so powerful? (AP Photo/Manuel Balce Ceneta)

proposals in different forms. No bill can be sent to the White House to be signed into law unless it first passes both chambers in identical form. Sometimes called the "third house" of Congress, conference committees are in a position to make significant alterations to legislation and frequently become the focal point of policy debates.

The House Rules Committee. Due to its special "gatekeeping" power over the terms on which legislation will reach the floor of the House of Representatives, the House Rules Committee holds a uniquely powerful position. A special committee rule sets the time limit on debate and determines whether and how a bill may be amended. This practice dates back to 1883. The Rules Committee has the unusual power to meet while the full House is in session, to have its resolutions considered immediately on the floor, and to initiate legislation on its own.

The Selection of Committee Members

In both chambers, members are appointed to standing committees by the steering committee of their party. The majority-party member with the longest term of continuous service on a standing committee is given preference when the committee selects its chairperson. The most senior member of the minority party is called the *ranking* committee member for that party. This **seniority system** is not required by law but is an informal, traditional process, and it applies to other significant posts in Congress as well. The system, although it deliberately treats members unequally, provides a predictable means of assigning positions of power within Congress.

The general pattern until the 1970s was that members of the House or Senate who represented **safe seats** would be reelected continually and eventually could accumulate enough years of continuous committee service to enable them to become the chairpersons of their committees. In the 1970s, reforms in the chairperson selection process somewhat modified the seniority system in the House. The reforms introduced the use of a secret ballot in electing House committee chairpersons and allowed for the possibility of choosing a chairperson on a basis other than seniority. The Democrats immediately replaced three senior chairpersons who were out of step with the rest of their party. In 1995, under Speaker Newt Gingrich, the Republicans chose relatively junior House members as chairpersons of several key committees, thus ensuring conservative control of the committees. The Republicans also passed a rule limiting the term of a chairperson to six years.

Seniority System
A custom followed in both chambers of Congress specifying that the member of the majority party with the longest term of continuous service will be given preference when a committee chairperson (or a holder of some other significant post) is selected.

Safe Seat
A district that returns a legislator with 55 percent of the vote or more.

THE FORMAL LEADERSHIP

The limited amount of centralized power that exists in Congress is exercised through party-based mechanisms. Congress is organized by party. When the Democratic Party, for example, wins a majority of seats in either the House or the Senate, Democrats control the official positions of power in that chamber, and every important committee has a Democratic chairperson and a majority of Democratic members. The same process holds when Republicans are in the majority.

We consider the formal leadership positions in the House and Senate separately, but you will note some broad similarities in the way leaders are selected and in the ways they exercise power in the two chambers.

Leadership in the House

The House leadership is made up of the Speaker, the majority and minority leaders, and the party whips.

The Speaker. The foremost power holder in the House of Representatives is the **Speaker of the House.** The Speaker's position is technically a nonpartisan one, but in fact, for the better part of two centuries, the Speaker has been the official leader of the majority party in the House. When a new Congress convenes in January of odd-numbered years, each party nominates a candidate for Speaker. All Republican members of the House are expected to vote for their party's nominee, and all Democrats are expected to support their candidate. The vote to organize the House is the one vote in which representatives *must* vote with their party. In a sense, this vote defines a member's partisan status.

The influence of modern-day Speakers is based primarily on their personal prestige, persuasive ability, and knowledge of the legislative process—plus the acquiescence or active support of other representatives. The major formal powers of the Speaker include the following:

1. Presiding over meetings of the House.
2. Appointing members of joint committees and conference committees.
3. Scheduling legislation for floor action.
4. Deciding points of order and interpreting the rules with the advice of the House parliamentarian.
5. Referring bills and resolutions to the appropriate standing committees of the House.

▲ **Nancy Pelosi** (D., Calif.), became Speaker of the House of Representatives in 2007, after the Democrats won control of the House in the 2006 elections. What benefits could a state receive when one of its representatives wins a leadership post? (Photo Courtesy of the U.S. Congress)

A Speaker may take part in floor debate and vote, as can any other member of Congress, but recent Speakers usually have voted only to break a tie.

The Majority Leader. The **majority leader of the House** is elected by a caucus of the majority party to foster cohesion among party members and to act as a spokesperson for the party. The majority leader influences the scheduling of debate and acts as the chief supporter of the Speaker. The majority leader cooperates with the Speaker and other party leaders, both inside and outside Congress, to formulate the party's legislative program and to guide that program through the legislative process in the House. The Democrats have often recruited future Speakers from Democratic majority leaders.

The Minority Leader. The **minority leader of the House** is the candidate nominated for Speaker by a caucus of the minority party. Like the majority leader, the leader of the minority party has as her or his primary responsibility the maintaining of cohesion within the party's ranks. The minority leader works for cooperation among the party's members and speaks on behalf of the president if the minority party controls the White House. In relations with the majority party, the minority leader consults with both the Speaker and the majority leader on recognizing members who

Speaker of the House
The presiding officer in the House of Representatives. The Speaker is chosen by the majority party and is the most powerful and influential member of the House.

Majority Leader of the House
Elected by members of the majority party to foster cohesion and to act as a spokesperson for the majority party.

Minority Leader of the House
The party leader elected by members of the minority party in the House.

Whip
A member of Congress who aids the majority or minority leader of the House or the Senate.

President Pro Tempore
The senator who presides over the Senate in the absence of the vice president.

Senate Majority Leader
The chief spokesperson of the majority party in the Senate, who directs the legislative program and party strategy.

Senate Minority Leader
The party officer in the Senate who commands the minority party's opposition to the policies of the majority party and directs the legislative program and strategy of his or her party.

wish to speak on the floor, on House rules and procedures, and on the scheduling of legislation. Minority leaders have no actual power in these areas, however.

Whips. The leadership of each party includes assistants to the majority and minority leaders known as **whips.**[11] The whips are members of Congress who assist the party leaders by passing information down from the leadership to party members and by ensuring that members show up for floor debate and cast their votes on important issues. Whips conduct polls among party members about the members' views on legislation, inform the leaders about whose vote is doubtful and whose is certain, and may exert pressure on members to support the leaders' positions. In the House, serving as a whip is the first step toward positions of higher leadership.

Leadership in the Senate

The Senate is less than one-fourth the size of the House. This fact alone probably explains why a formal, complex, and centralized leadership structure is not as necessary in the Senate as it is in the House.

The two highest-ranking formal leadership positions in the Senate are essentially ceremonial in nature. Under the Constitution, the vice president of the United States is the president (that is, the presiding officer) of the Senate and may vote to break a tie. The vice president, however, is only rarely present for a meeting of the Senate. The Senate elects instead a **president pro tempore** ("pro tem") to preside over the Senate in the vice president's absence. Ordinarily, the president pro tem is the member of the majority party with the longest continuous term of service in the Senate. As mentioned, the president pro tem is mostly a ceremonial position. More junior senators take turns actually presiding over the sessions of the Senate.

The real leadership power in the Senate rests in the hands of the **Senate majority leader,** the **Senate minority leader,** and their respective whips. The Senate majority and minority leaders have the right to be recognized first in debate on the floor

11. *Whip* comes from "whipper-in," a fox-hunting term for someone who keeps the hunting dogs from straying.

◀ **After the Democrats** took control of the U.S. Senate in the 2006 elections, Republican senator Mitch McConnell of Kentucky, left, was elected Senate minority leader for the 110th Congress. Democratic senator Harry Reid, right, who had been elected Senate minority leader at the beginning of the 109th Congress, became the Senate majority leader. It is very rare for a congressional leader to become president. How might a congressional leadership position interfere with presidential aspirations? (Photos Courtesy of Senator McConnell and Senator Reid)

and generally exercise the same powers available to the House majority and minority leaders. They control the scheduling of debate on the floor in conjunction with the majority party's policy committee, influence the allocation of committee assignments for new members or for senators attempting to transfer to a new committee, influence the selection of other party officials, and participate in selecting members of conference committees. The leaders are expected to mobilize support for partisan legislative or presidential initiatives. The leaders act as liaisons with the White House when the president is of their party, try to obtain the cooperation of committee chairpersons, and seek to facilitate the smooth functioning of the Senate through the senators' unanimous consent. The majority and minority leaders are elected by their respective party caucuses.

Senate party whips, like their House counterparts, maintain communication within the party on platform positions and try to ensure that party colleagues are present for floor debate and important votes. The Senate whip system is far less elaborate than its counterpart in the House, simply because there are fewer members to track.

HOW A BILL BECOMES LAW

Each year, Congress and the president propose and approve many laws. Some are budget and appropriation laws that require extensive bargaining but must be passed for the government to continue to function. Other laws are relatively free of controversy and are passed with little dissension. Still other proposed legislation is extremely controversial and reaches to the roots of differences between Republicans and Democrats and between the executive and legislative branches.

Figure 9–3 on the next page shows that each law begins as a bill, which must be introduced in either the House or the Senate. Often, similar bills are introduced in both chambers. A "money bill," however, must start in the House. In each chamber, the bill follows similar steps. It is referred to a committee and its subcommittees for study, discussion, hearings, and markup (rewriting). When the bill is reported out to the full chamber, it must be scheduled for debate (by the Rules Committee in the House and by the leadership in the Senate). After the bill has been passed in each chamber, if it contains different provisions, a conference committee is formed to write a compromise bill, which must be approved by both chambers before it is sent to the president to sign or veto.

HOW MUCH WILL THE GOVERNMENT SPEND?

The Constitution is very clear about where the power of the purse lies in the national government: all taxing or spending bills must originate in the House of Representatives. Today, much of the business of Congress is concerned with approving government expenditures through the budget process and with raising the revenues to pay for government programs.

From 1922, when Congress required the president to prepare and present to the legislature an **executive budget,** until 1974, the congressional budget process was so disjointed that it was difficult to visualize the total picture of government finances. The president presented the executive budget to Congress in January. It was broken down into thirteen or more appropriations bills. Some time later, after all of the bills had been debated, amended, and passed, it was more or less possible to estimate total government spending for the next year.

Executive Budget
The budget prepared and submitted by the president to Congress.

FIGURE 9–3: How a Bill Becomes Law

This illustration shows the most typical way in which proposed legislation is enacted into law. Most legislation begins as similar bills introduced into the House and the Senate. The process is illustrated here with two hypothetical bills, House Bill No. 100 (HR 100) and Senate Bill No. 200 (S 200). The path of HR 100 is shown on the left, and that of S 200, on the right.

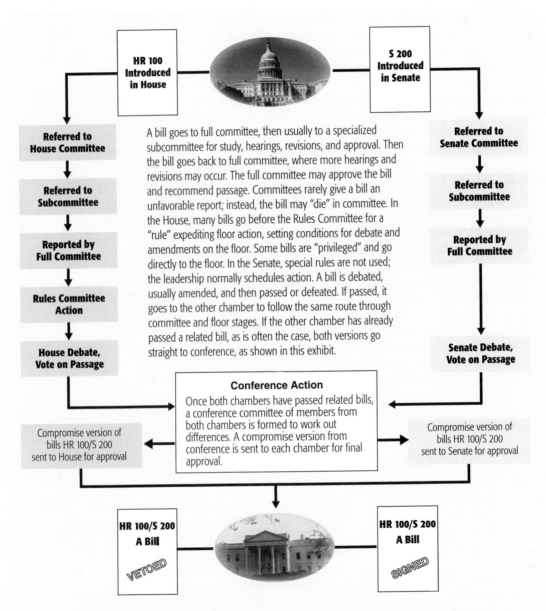

HR 100
Introduced
in House

S 200
Introduced
in Senate

Referred to
House Committee

Referred to
Senate Committee

Referred to
Subcommittee

Referred to
Subcommittee

Reported by
Full Committee

Reported by
Full Committee

Rules Committee
Action

House Debate,
Vote on Passage

Senate Debate,
Vote on Passage

A bill goes to full committee, then usually to a specialized subcommittee for study, hearings, revisions, and approval. Then the bill goes back to full committee, where more hearings and revisions may occur. The full committee may approve the bill and recommend passage. Committees rarely give a bill an unfavorable report; instead, the bill may "die" in committee. In the House, many bills go before the Rules Committee for a "rule" expediting floor action, setting conditions for debate and amendments on the floor. Some bills are "privileged" and go directly to the floor. In the Senate, special rules are not used; the leadership normally schedules action. A bill is debated, usually amended, and then passed or defeated. If passed, it goes to the other chamber to follow the same route through committee and floor stages. If the other chamber has already passed a related bill, as is often the case, both versions go straight to conference, as shown in this exhibit.

Conference Action

Once both chambers have passed related bills, a conference committee of members from both chambers is formed to work out differences. A compromise version from conference is sent to each chamber for final approval.

Compromise version of bills HR 100/S 200 sent to House for approval

Compromise version of bills HR 100/S 200 sent to Senate for approval

HR 100/S 200
A Bill
VETOED

HR 100/S 200
A Bill
SIGNED

If a compromise bill is approved by both chambers, is sent to the president, who can sign it into law or veto it and return it to Congress. Congress may override a veto by a two-thirds majority vote in both chambers; the bill then becomes law without the president's signature.

Frustrated by the president's ability to impound, or withhold, funds and dissatisfied with the entire budget process, Congress passed the Budget and Impoundment Control Act of 1974 to regain some control over the nation's spending. The act required the president to spend the funds that Congress had appropriated, ending the president's ability to kill programs by withholding funds. The other major accomplishment of the act was to force Congress to examine total national taxing and spending at least twice in each budget cycle.

The budget cycle of the federal government is described in the rest of this section. (See Figure 9–4 for a graphic illustration of the budget cycle.)

Preparing the Budget

The federal government operates on a **fiscal year (FY)** cycle. The fiscal year runs from October through September, so that fiscal 2011, or FY11, runs from October 1, 2010, through September 30, 2011. Eighteen months before a fiscal year starts, the executive branch begins preparing the budget. The Office of Management and Budget (OMB) receives advice from the Council of Economic Advisers and the Treasury Department. The OMB outlines the budget and then sends it to the various departments and agencies. Bargaining follows, in which—to use only two of many examples—the Department of Health and Human Services argues for more welfare spending, and the armed forces argue for more defense spending.

Even though the OMB has fewer than 550 employees, it is one of the most powerful agencies in Washington. It assembles the budget documents and monitors federal agencies throughout each year. Every year, it begins the budget process with a **spring review,** in which it requires all of the agencies to review their programs, activities, and goals. At the beginning of each summer, the OMB sends out a letter instructing agencies to submit their requests for funding for the next fiscal year. By the end of the summer, each agency must submit a formal request to the OMB.

Fiscal Year (FY)
A twelve-month period that is used for bookkeeping, or accounting, purposes. Usually, the fiscal year does not coincide with the calendar year. For example, the federal government's fiscal year runs from October 1 through September 30.

Spring Review
The annual process in which the Office of Management and Budget requires federal agencies to review their programs, activities, and goals and submit their requests for funding for the next fiscal year.

FIGURE 9–4: The Budget Cycle

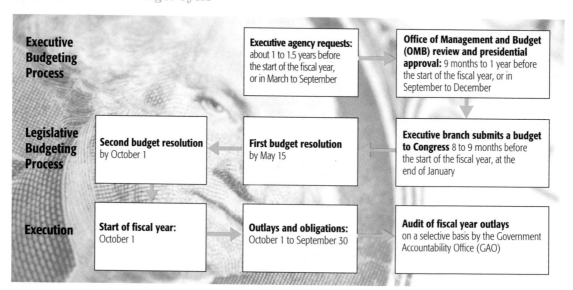

Executive Budgeting Process	**Executive agency requests:** about 1 to 1.5 years before the start of the fiscal year, or in March to September	**Office of Management and Budget (OMB) review and presidential approval:** 9 months to 1 year before the start of the fiscal year, or in September to December
Legislative Budgeting Process	**Second budget resolution** by October 1	**First budget resolution** by May 15	**Executive branch submits a budget to Congress** 8 to 9 months before the start of the fiscal year, at the end of January
Execution	**Start of fiscal year:** October 1	**Outlays and obligations:** October 1 to September 30	**Audit of fiscal year outlays** on a selective basis by the Government Accountability Office (GAO)

Fall Review
The annual process in which the Office of Management and Budget, after receiving formal federal agency requests for funding for the next fiscal year, reviews the requests, makes changes, and submits its recommendations to the president.

Authorization
A formal declaration by a legislative committee that a certain amount of funding may be available to an agency. Some authorizations terminate in a year; others are renewable automatically without further congressional action.

Appropriation
The passage, by Congress, of a spending bill specifying the amount of authorized funds that actually will be allocated for an agency's use.

First Budget Resolution
A resolution passed by Congress in May that sets overall revenue and spending goals for the following fiscal year.

Second Budget Resolution
A resolution passed by Congress in September that sets "binding" limits on taxes and spending for the following fiscal year.

Continuing Resolution
A temporary funding law that Congress passes when an appropriations bill has not been passed by the beginning of the new fiscal year on October 1.

In actuality, the "budget season" begins with the **fall review.** At this time, the OMB looks at budget requests and, in almost all cases, routinely cuts them back. Although the OMB works within guidelines established by the president, specific decisions often are left to the OMB director and the director's associates. By the beginning of November, the director's review begins. The director meets with cabinet secretaries and budget officers. Time becomes crucial. The budget must be completed by January so that it can be included in the *Economic Report of the President.*

The schedule just described cannot apply to a year in which the voters elect a new president or to a year in which a new president is inaugurated. In 2008, George W. Bush did not engage in a fall review of the FY 2010 budget, because he would no longer be in office when the budget went into effect in October 2009. Barack Obama could hardly have undertaken the fall review either, given that he was still campaigning for the presidency. Following the election of a new president, the budget process is compressed into the first months of the new administration. Indeed, Barack Obama released a budget document for FY 2010 on February 26, 2009, barely a month after he was inaugurated. Obama's budget predicted substantial deficits even after the end of the recession. Is that a problem? We discuss that issue in this chapter's feature *The Politics of Boom and Bust: Endless Federal Budget Deficits?*

Congress Faces the Budget

In January, nine months before the fiscal year starts, the president takes the OMB's proposed budget, approves it, and submits it to Congress. Then the congressional budgeting process takes over. The budgeting process involves two steps. First, Congress must authorize funds to be spent. The **authorization** is a formal declaration by the appropriate congressional committee that a certain amount of funding may be available to an agency. Congressional committees and subcommittees look at the proposals from the executive branch and the Congressional Budget Office in making the decision to authorize funds.

After the funds are authorized, they must be appropriated by Congress. The appropriations committees of both the House and the Senate forward spending bills to their respective bodies. The **appropriation** of funds occurs when the final bill is passed. In this process, large sums are in play. Representatives and senators, especially those who chair key committees, find it easy to slip earmarks, or pork, into a variety of bills. These proposals may have nothing to do with the explicitly stated purpose of the bill.

Budget Resolutions

The **first budget resolution** by Congress is due in May. It sets overall revenue goals and spending targets. Spending and tax laws that are drawn up over the summer are supposed to be guided by the first budget resolution. By September, Congress is scheduled to pass its **second budget resolution,** one that will set binding limits on taxes and spending for the fiscal year beginning October 1.

In actuality, Congress has finished the budget on time in only three years since 1977. The budget is usually broken up into a series of appropriations bills. If Congress has not passed one of these bills by October 1, it normally passes a **continuing resolution** that allows the affected agencies to keep on doing whatever they were doing the previous year with the same amount of funding. By the 1980s, continuing resolutions had ballooned into massive measures. Budget delays reached a climax in 1995 and 1996, when, in a spending dispute with Democratic president Bill Clinton,

the politics of Boom and Bust:
Endless Federal Budget Deficits?

Unless you've been vacationing on Mars, you know that the federal government has recently created the largest budget deficits in U.S. history. A deficit occurs each time the government spends more than it receives. To cover the deficit, the federal government borrows at home and abroad.

Fighting Recessions (Busts) with Deficit Spending

Many economists and government officials believe that we can help the economy out of a recession if the federal government runs a deficit—by increasing spending or lowering taxes (or both). In a recession, not enough people are borrowing and spending, so the government should be the one to borrow and spend, jump-starting the economy. When the recession is over, the government should reverse course—reduce government spending or increase taxes (or both). Under this theory, we can smooth the busts and booms in the national economy with "countercyclical" budgets.

Congress and the president, however, have never been eager to increase taxes or reduce spending during a boom. In modern times, Bill Clinton (1993–2001) has been the only president willing to raise taxes and constrain spending in a boom by enough to balance the budget. In his last four budgets, Clinton (with the help of Congress) actually ran a surplus—the government spent less than what it received in revenues. In contrast, George W. Bush (backed by a Republican Congress during his first six years) created deficits with every budget he proposed. To be sure, there was a recession during 2001 after the "dot-com bubble" burst, but the Bush administration kept running deficits right through the subsequent good years.

Enter Obama and the Democratic Congress

By the time Barack Obama was elected in 2008, the American economy was experiencing its worst recession in over sixty years. The response of Obama and the Democratic Congress was swift and monumental. At Obama's request, Congress passed the largest single stimulus spending package in the history of the United States.

Nominally set at $787 billion over two years, the eventual cost, by some calculations, will exceed $1 trillion.

The Congressional Budget Office (CBO), which reports to the Democrats in Congress, has estimated that Obama's policies will have resulted in a federal budget deficit of $1.6 trillion in 2009. That's more than 11 percent of the entire economy—the gross domestic product, or GDP. The estimated deficit is $1.5 trillion for 2010, or 10 percent of GDP. Ominously, the deficit would stay at about 5 percent of GDP all the way through 2019. That means large budget deficits even when the Great Recession is over.

Can We Run Federal Budget Deficits Forever?

If we run the deficits that the CBO predicts, the total debt of the federal government as a percentage of GDP will double by 2019. Can we do this? True, after the collapse of the financial markets in September 2008, the federal government had no trouble borrowing very large sums. Panicked investors saw the U.S. government as the world's safest borrower. But even Obama's budget chief, Peter Orszag, admitted that indefinite deficits that amount to 5 percent of GDP are "ultimately not sustainable." Investors—such as the government of China, which already owns $1 trillion of the federal government's debt—might be reluctant to lend more to Uncle Sam. Higher taxes would be inevitable.

Of course, according to theory, the government is supposed to collect higher taxes in future good years. Opinions about taxes differ. For liberal economist Paul Krugman, "it's really a political question: are we willing, ultimately, to pay the modest costs of a better society?" The conservative editorial page of the *Wall Street Journal* fumes: "Republicans will spend the next two or three generations doing little more than collecting higher taxes from the middle class to finance the Obama revolution."

FOR CRITICAL ANALYSIS

One U.S. senator has said that increases in the federal deficit are the equivalent of mortgaging our grandchildren's future without their agreement. Is this a fair criticism? Why or why not?

the Republican Congress refused to pass any continuing resolutions. As a result, some nonessential functions of the federal government were shut down for twenty-seven days. Since then, Congress has generally managed to limit continuing resolutions to their original purpose.

making a difference

LEARNING ABOUT YOUR REPRESENTATIVES

Do you know the names of your senators and your representative in Congress? A surprising number of Americans do not. Even if you know the names and parties of your elected delegates, there is still much more you could learn about them that would be useful.

Why Should You Care?
The legislation that Congress passes can directly affect your life. Consider, for example, the Medicare prescription drug benefit passed in November 2003. Some might think that such a benefit, which helps only persons over the age of sixty-five, would be of no interest to college students. Actually, legislation such as this could affect you long before you reach retirement age. Funding the benefit may mean that you will have to pay higher taxes when you join the workforce. Also, some students may be affected even sooner than that. Most students are part of a family, and family finances are often important in determining whether the family will help pay for the student's tuition. For some families, the cost of medicine for the oldest members is a substantial burden.

You can make a difference in our democracy simply by going to the polls on Election Day and voting for the candidates you would like to represent you in Congress. It goes without saying, though, that to cast an informed vote, you need to know how your congressional representatives stand on the issues and, if they are incumbents, how they have voted on bills that are important to you.

What Can You Do?
To contact a member of Congress, start by going to the Web sites of the U.S. House of Representatives (at www.house.gov) and the U.S. Senate (at www.senate.gov).

Although you can communicate easily with your representatives by e-mail, using e-mail has some drawbacks. Representatives and senators are now receiving large volumes of e-mail from constituents, and they rarely read it themselves. They have staff members who read and respond to e-mail instead. Many interest groups argue that U.S. mail, or even express mail or a phone call, is more likely to capture the attention of the representative than e-mail. You can contact your representatives using one of the following addresses or phone numbers:

United States House of Representatives
Washington, DC 20515
202-224-3121

United States Senate
Washington, DC 20510
202-224-3121

Performance Evaluations
Interest groups also track the voting records of members of Congress and rate the members on the issues. Project Vote Smart tracks the performance of thousands of political leaders, including their campaign finances, issue positions, and voting records. You can contact Project Vote Smart at:

Project Vote Smart
One Common Ground
Philipsburg, MT 59858
Voter Hotline toll-free 1-888-VOTE-SMART
(1-888-868-3762)
www.vote-smart.org

Finally, if you want to know how your representatives funded their campaigns, contact the Center for Responsive Politics (CRP), a research group that tracks money in politics, campaign fund-raising, and similar issues. You can contact the CRP at:

The Center for Responsive Politics
1101 14th St. N.W., Suite 1030
Washington, DC 20005
202-857-0044
www.opensecrets.org

▼ The OpenSecrets.org homepage
(www.opensecrets.org)

key terms

chapter summary

1   The authors of the Constitution believed that the bulk of national power should be in the legislature. The Constitution states that Congress will consist of two chambers. A result of the Connecticut Compromise, this bicameral structure established a balanced legislature, with the membership in the House of Representatives based on population and the membership in the Senate based on the equality of states.

2   The functions of Congress include (a) lawmaking, (b) representation, (c) service to constituents, (d) oversight, (e) public education, and (f) conflict resolution.

3   The Constitution specifies the enumerated, or expressed, powers of Congress, including the rights to impose taxes, to borrow funds, to regulate commerce, and to declare war. In addition, Congress enjoys the right, under the elastic, or necessary and proper, clause, to "make all Laws which shall be necessary and proper for carrying into Execution the foregoing Powers, and all other Powers vested by this Constitution in the Government of the United States, or in any Department or Officer thereof."

4   There are 435 members in the House of Representatives and 100 members in the Senate. Owing to its larger size, the House has a greater number of formal rules. The Senate tradition of unlimited debate dates back to 1790 and has been used over the years to frustrate the passage of bills. Under Senate Rule 22, cloture can be used to shut off debate on a bill.

5   Members of Congress are not typical American citizens. They are older and wealthier than most Americans, disproportionately white and male, and more likely to be trained in professional occupations.

6   Congressional elections are operated by the individual state governments, which must abide by rules established by the Constitution and national statutes. Most candidates for Congress must win nomination through a direct primary. The overwhelming majority of incumbent representatives and a slightly smaller proportion of senators who run for reelection are successful. A complicated aspect of congressional elections is apportionment—the allocation of legislative seats to constituencies. The Supreme Court's "one person, one vote" rule has been applied to equalize the populations of congressional and state legislative districts.

7   Most of the actual work of legislating is performed by committees and subcommittees within Congress. Legislation introduced into the House

or Senate is assigned to the appropriate standing committees for review. Select committees are created for a limited time for a specific purpose. Joint committees are formed by the concurrent action of both chambers and consist of members from each chamber. Conference committees are special joint committees set up to achieve agreement between the House and the Senate on the exact wording of legislative acts that were passed by both chambers in different forms. The seniority rule, which is usually followed, specifies that the longest-serving member of the majority party will be the chairperson of a committee.

8 The foremost power holder in the House of Representatives is the Speaker of the House. Other leaders are the House majority leader, the House minority leader, and the majority and minority whips. Formally, the vice president is the presiding officer of the Senate, with the most senior member of the majority party serving as the president pro tempore to preside when the vice president is absent. Actual leadership in the Senate rests with the majority leader, the minority leader, and their whips.

9 A bill becomes law by progressing through both chambers of Congress and their appropriate standing and joint committees to the president.

10 The budget process for a fiscal year begins with the preparation of an executive budget by the president. This is reviewed by the Office of Management and Budget and then sent to Congress, which is supposed to pass a final budget by the end of September. Since 1977, Congress generally has not followed its own time rules.

QUESTIONS FOR

discussionandanalysis

1 In public opinion polls, Congress is typically ranked as one of our least trusted institutions. Yet individual members of Congress usually get reasonably good marks from their constituents. Why do you think this discrepancy exists?

2 Some observers have proposed that nonpartisan panels draw congressional district boundaries in an attempt to curb gerrymandering. Who do you think would make good members of such panels? What types of people might be both knowledgeable and fair?

3 The District of Columbia is not represented in the Senate and has a single nonvoting delegate to the House. Should the District of Columbia be represented in Congress by voting legislators? Why or why not? If it should be represented, how? Would it make sense to admit it as a state? Give it back to Maryland? Explain your answer.

4 Identify some advantages to the nation that might follow when one party controls the House, the Senate, and the presidency. Identify some disadvantages that might follow from this state of affairs.

5 When the Senate was first created, Americans were often more loyal to their individual states than they are today. Confederate general Robert E. Lee, for example, believed that his native land was Virginia, not the United States. Given the strong sense of national identity that exists in the country today, is it fair that the Senate gives equal representation to all states regardless of how many people live in each? Why or why not? If not, what (if anything) could be done to address the issue?

helpful online Resources

CONNECTING TO AMERICAN GOVERNMENT AND POLITICS

You can find a considerable body of information about what Congress is doing at the Web sites of the two chambers:

www.house.gov **and** www.senate.gov

Roll Call and *The Hill* are two publications that specialize in reporting on Congress. You can see their sites at:

www.rollcall.com **and** www.thehill.com

Taxpayers for Common Sense maintains a database of earmark requests by members of Congress. Go to the organization's site at:

www.taxpayers.org

and locate the link to the earmark database.

a special WebSite

FOR YOUR TEXT

Go to this book's special Web site at academic.cengage.com/polisci/Schmidt/ Brief6e. Choose "For Students." Then click on Chapter 9, where you will find an online quiz and other helpful study aids. If your professor is using CengageNOW: *American Government and Politics Today, Brief Edition,* log in and go to Chapter 9 for additional online study aids.

10

The Presidency

The writers of the Constitution had no models to follow when they created the presidency of the United States. Nowhere else in the world was there an elected head of state. What the founders did not want was a king. In fact, given their previous experience with royal governors in the colonies, many of the delegates to the Constitutional Convention wanted to create a very weak executive who could not veto legislation. Other delegates, especially those who had witnessed the need for a strong leader in the Revolutionary Army, believed a powerful executive would be necessary for the new republic. The delegates, after much debate, created a chief executive who had enough powers granted in the Constitution to balance those of Congress. In this chapter, after looking at who can become president and at the process involved, we examine closely the nature and extent of the constitutional powers held by the president.

WHO CAN BECOME PRESIDENT?

The requirements for becoming president, as outlined in Article II, Section 1, of the Constitution, are not overwhelmingly stringent:

> No person except a natural born Citizen, or a Citizen of the United States, at the time of the Adoption of this Constitution, shall be eligible to the Office of President; neither shall any Person be eligible to that Office who shall not have attained to the Age of thirty-five Years, and been fourteen Years a Resident within the United States.

The only question that arises about these qualifications relates to the term *natural born Citizen*. Does that mean only citizens born in the United States and its territories? What about a child born to a U.S. citizen visiting or living in another country? Although the question has not been dealt with directly by the Supreme Court, it is reasonable to expect that someone would be eligible if her or his parents were Americans. The first presidents, after all, were not American citizens at birth, and other presidents were born in areas that did not become part of the United States until later. These questions were debated when George Romney, who was born in Chihuahua, Mexico, made a serious bid for the Republican presidential nomination in the 1960s.[1]

Although the Constitution states that the minimum-age requirement for the presidency is thirty-five years, most presidents have been much older than that when they assumed office. John F. Kennedy, at the age of forty-three, was the youngest elected president, and the oldest was Ronald Reagan, at age sixty-nine. The average age at inauguration has been fifty-four. There has clearly been a demographic bias in the selection of presidents. All have been male, white, and from the Protestant tradition, except for John F. Kennedy, a Roman Catholic, and Barack Obama, an African American.

> **Twelfth Amendment**
> An amendment to the Constitution, adopted in 1804, that specifies the separate election of the president and vice president by the electoral college.

THE PROCESS OF BECOMING PRESIDENT

Major and minor political parties nominate candidates for president and vice president at national conventions every four years. The nation's voters do not elect a president and vice president directly but rather cast ballots for presidential electors, who then vote for president and vice president in the electoral college.

Because victory goes to the candidate with a majority in the electoral college, it is conceivable that someone could be elected to the office of the presidency without having a plurality of the popular vote cast. Indeed, on four occasions, candidates won elections even though their major opponents received more popular votes. One of those elections occurred in 2000, when George W. Bush won the electoral college vote and became president even though his opponent, Al Gore, won the popular vote. In elections in which more than two candidates were running for office, many presidential candidates have won with less than 50 percent of the total popular votes cast for all candidates—including Abraham Lincoln, Woodrow Wilson, Harry Truman, John F. Kennedy, Richard Nixon, and in 1992, Bill Clinton.

Thus far, the electoral college has twice failed to give any candidate a majority. At that point, the election is thrown into the House of Representatives. The president is then chosen from among the three candidates having the most electoral college votes, as noted in Chapter 8. Thomas Jefferson and Aaron Burr tied in the electoral college in 1800. This happened because the Constitution had not been explicit in indicating which of the two electoral votes was for president and which was for vice president. In 1804, the **Twelfth Amendment** clarified the matter by requiring that the president and vice president be chosen separately. In 1824, the House again had to make a choice, this time among William H. Crawford, Andrew Jackson, and John Quincy Adams. It chose Adams, even though Jackson had more electoral and popular votes.

---

1. George Romney was governor of Michigan from 1963 to 1969. Romney was not nominated, and the issue remains unresolved.

THE MANY ROLES OF THE PRESIDENT

The Constitution speaks briefly about the duties and obligations of the president. Based on this brief list of powers and on the precedents of history, the presidency has grown into a very complicated job that requires balancing at least five constitutional roles. These are (1) head of state, (2) chief executive, (3) commander in chief of the armed forces, (4) chief diplomat, and (5) chief legislator of the United States. Here we examine each of these significant presidential functions, or roles. It is worth noting that one person plays all these roles simultaneously and that the needs of the roles may at times come into conflict.

Head of State

Every nation has at least one person who is the ceremonial head of state. In most democratic governments, the role of **head of state** is given to someone other than the chief executive, who leads the executive branch of government. In Britain, for example, the head of state is the queen. In much of Europe, the prime minister is the chief executive, and the head of state is a relatively powerless president. But in the United States, the president is both chief executive and head of state. According to William Howard Taft, as head of state the president symbolizes the "dignity and majesty" of the American people.

Some students of the American political system believe that having the president serve as both the chief executive and the head of state drastically limits the time available to do "real" work. Not all presidents have agreed with this conclusion, however—particularly those presidents who have skillfully blended these two roles with their role as politician. Being head of state gives the president tremendous public exposure, which can be an important asset in a campaign for reelection. When that exposure is positive, it helps the president deal with Congress over proposed legislation and increases the chances of being reelected—or getting the candidates of the president's party elected.

Chief Executive

According to the Constitution, "The executive Power shall be vested in a President of the United States of America. . . . [H]e may require the Opinion, in writing, of the principal Officer in each of the executive Departments, upon any Subject relating to the Duties of their respective Offices . . . and he shall nominate, and by and with the Advice and Consent of the Senate, shall appoint . . . Officers of the United States. . . . [H]e shall take Care that the Laws be faithfully executed."

As **chief executive,** the president is constitutionally bound to enforce the acts of Congress, the judgments of federal courts, and treaties signed by the United States. The duty to "faithfully execute" the laws has been a source of constitutional power for presidents. To assist in the various tasks of the chief executive, the president has a federal bureaucracy, which currently consists of more than 2.7 million federal civilian employees.

The Powers of Appointment and Removal. You might think that the president, as head of the largest bureaucracy in the United States, wields enormous power. The president, however, only nominally runs the executive bureaucracy. Most government positions are filled by **civil service** employees, who generally gain government employment through a merit system rather than presidential appointment.[2] Therefore, even though the president has important **appointment power,** it is limited to cabinet and subcabinet jobs, federal judgeships, agency heads, and about two thousand lesser jobs. This means that most of the 2.7 million federal employees owe no political allegiance to the president. They are more likely to owe loyalty to congressional committees or to interest groups representing the sector of society that they serve.

The president's power to remove from office those officials who are not doing a good job or who do not agree with the president is not explicitly granted by the Constitution and has been limited. In 1926, however, a Supreme Court decision prevented Congress from interfering with the president's ability to fire those executive-branch officials whom the president had appointed with Senate approval.[3]

Harry Truman spoke candidly of the difficulties a president faces in trying to control the executive bureaucracy. On leaving office, he referred to the problems that Dwight Eisenhower, as a former general of the army, was going to have: "He'll sit here and he'll say do this! do that! and nothing will happen. Poor Ike—it won't be a bit like the Army. He'll find it very frustrating."[4]

The Power to Grant Reprieves and Pardons. Section 2 of Article II of the Constitution gives the president the power to grant **reprieves** and **pardons** for offenses against the United States except in cases of impeachment. All pardons are administered by the Office of the Pardon Attorney in the Department of Justice.

The Supreme Court upheld the president's power to grant reprieves and pardons in a 1925 case concerning a pardon granted by the president to an individual convicted of contempt of court. The judiciary had contended that only judges had the authority to convict individuals for contempt of court when court orders were violated and that the courts should be free from interference by the executive branch. The Supreme Court simply stated that the president could grant reprieves or pardons for all offenses "either before trial, during trial, or after trial, by individuals, or by classes, conditionally or absolutely, and this without modification or regulation by Congress."[5]

Commander in Chief

The president, according to the Constitution, "shall be Commander in Chief of the Army and Navy of the United States, and of the Militia of the several States, when called into the actual Service of the United States." In other words, the armed forces are under civilian, rather than military, control.

Appointment Power
The authority vested in the president to fill a government office or position.

Reprieve
A formal postponement of the execution of a sentence imposed by a court of law.

Pardon
A release from the punishment for, or legal consequences of, a crime; a pardon can be granted by the president before or after a conviction.

▼ **President Harry Truman**
(1945–1953), stands with General Dwight Eisenhower in 1951. A year later, Eisenhower successfully ran for president. (Photo by George Skadding/Time Life Pictures/Getty Images)

2. See Chapter 11 for a discussion of the Civil Service Reform Act.
3. *Meyers v. United States,* 272 U.S. 52 (1926).
4. Quoted in Richard E. Neustadt, *Presidential Power: The Politics of Leadership* (New York: Wiley, 1960), p. 9. Truman may not have considered the amount of politics involved in decision making in the upper reaches of the army.
5. *Ex parte Grossman,* 267 U.S. 87 (1925).

Commander in Chief
The role of the president as supreme commander of the military forces of the United States and of the state National Guard units when they are called into federal service.

Wartime Powers. Those who wrote the Constitution had George Washington in mind when they made the president the **commander in chief.** Although we do not expect our president to lead the troops into battle, presidents as commanders in chief have wielded dramatic power. Harry Truman made the awesome decision to drop atomic bombs on Hiroshima and Nagasaki in 1945 to force Japan to surrender and thus bring World War II to an end. Lyndon Johnson ordered bombing missions against North Vietnam in the 1960s, and he personally selected some of the targets. Richard Nixon decided to invade Cambodia in 1970. Ronald Reagan sent troops to Lebanon and Grenada in 1983 and ordered U.S. fighter planes to attack Libya in 1986. George H. W. Bush sent troops to Panama in 1989 and to the Middle East in 1990. Bill Clinton sent troops to Haiti in 1994 and to Bosnia in 1995, ordered missile attacks on alleged terrorist bases in 1998, and sent American planes to bomb Serbia in 1999. George W. Bush ordered the invasion of Afghanistan in 2002 and of Iraq in 2003, and most recently, Barack Obama ordered more troops into Afghanistan shortly after taking office.

The president is the ultimate decision maker in military matters. Everywhere the president goes, so too goes the "football"—a briefcase filled with all of the codes necessary to order a nuclear attack. Only the president has the power to order the use of nuclear force.

As commander in chief, the president has probably exercised more authority than in any other role. Constitutionally, Congress has the sole power to declare war, but the president can send the armed forces into situations that are certainly the equivalent of war. Harry Truman dispatched troops to Korea in 1950. Kennedy, Johnson, and Nixon waged an undeclared war in Southeast Asia, where more than 58,000 Americans were killed and 300,000 were wounded. In neither of these situations had Congress declared war.

▶ **These military men** are in charge of how the Army, Navy, Air Force, and Marines operate. The overall decision maker is Admiral Mike Mullen (on the left), who is Chairman of the Joint Chiefs of Staff. While the leaders of the various branches of our armed forces confer with each other from time to time, they are also fiercely proud of their own branches and prefer to remain independent. Ultimately, who controls the admirals and generals of the various branches of our armed services? (Paul J. Richards/AFP/Getty Images)

The War Powers Resolution. In an attempt to gain more control over such military activities, in 1973 Congress passed the **War Powers Resolution**—over President Nixon's veto—requiring that the president consult with Congress when sending American forces into action. Once they are sent, the president must report to Congress within forty-eight hours. Unless Congress approves the use of troops within sixty days or extends the sixty-day time limit, the forces must be withdrawn.

Whether Congress had the constitutional power to set conditions on the continuation of the Iraq war was at issue in 2007. President Bush threatened to veto any emergency war-funding legislation that conditioned the funds on a timeline for the withdrawal or redeployment of the troops in Iraq.

In spite of the War Powers Resolution, the powers of the president as commander in chief are more extensive today than they were in the past. These powers are linked closely to the president's powers as chief diplomat, or chief crafter of foreign policy.

Chief Diplomat

The Constitution gives the president the power to recognize foreign governments; to make treaties, with the **advice and consent** of the Senate; and to make special agreements with other heads of state that do not require congressional approval. In addition, the president nominates ambassadors. As **chief diplomat,** the president dominates American foreign policy, a role that has been supported many times by the Supreme Court.

Diplomatic Recognition. An important power of the president as chief diplomat is that of **diplomatic recognition,** or the power to recognize—or refuse to recognize— foreign governments. In the role of ceremonial head of state, the president has always received foreign diplomats. In modern times, the simple act of receiving a foreign diplomat has been equivalent to accrediting the diplomat and officially recognizing his or her government. Such recognition of the legitimacy of another country's government is a prerequisite to diplomatic relations or treaties between that country and the United States.

Deciding when to recognize a foreign power is not always simple. The United States, for example, did not recognize the Soviet Union until 1933—sixteen years after the Russian Revolution of 1917. It was only after all attempts to reverse the effects of that revolution—including military invasion of Russia and diplomatic isolation—had proved futile that Franklin Roosevelt extended recognition to the Soviet government. In December 1978, long after the Communist victory in China in 1949, Jimmy Carter granted official recognition to the People's Republic of China.[6]

Proposal and Ratification of Treaties. The president has the sole power to negotiate treaties with other nations. These treaties must be presented to the Senate, where they may be modified. A two-thirds vote in the Senate is required for approval, or ratification. After ratification, the president can approve the senatorial version of the treaty if any changes have been made. Approval poses a problem when the Senate has added substantive amendments or reservations to a treaty, particularly when such changes may require reopening negotiations with the other signatory governments. Sometimes a president may decide to withdraw a treaty if the senatorial changes

---

War Powers Resolution
A law passed in 1973 spelling out the conditions under which the president can commit troops without congressional approval.

Advice and Consent
Terms in the Constitution describing the U.S. Senate's power to review and approve treaties and presidential appointments.

Chief Diplomat
The role of the president in recognizing foreign governments, making treaties, and effecting executive agreements.

Diplomatic Recognition
The formal acknowledgment of a foreign government as legitimate.

---

6. The Nixon administration first encouraged new relations with the People's Republic of China by allowing a cultural exchange of table tennis teams. Nixon subsequently traveled to China.

▲ **President George H. W. Bush** (1989–1993) meets with the foreign minister of Saudi Arabia, in 1990. George H. W. Bush is the father of George W. Bush, making the Bush family a true political dynasty. It is not uncommon for the children of elected officials to go into politics. (AP Photo/Barry Thumma)

are too extensive—as Woodrow Wilson did with the Versailles Treaty in 1919. Wilson believed that the senatorial reservations would weaken the treaty so much that it would be ineffective. His refusal to accept the senatorial version of the treaty led to the eventual refusal of the United States to join the League of Nations.

Before September 11, 2001, President George W. Bush indicated his intention to steer the United States in a unilateral direction on foreign policy. He rejected the Kyoto Agreement on global warming and proposed ending the 1972 Anti-Ballistic Missile (ABM) Treaty, which was part of the first Strategic Arms Limitation Treaty (SALT I). After the terrorist attacks of 9/11, however, President Bush sought cooperation from U.S. allies in the war on terrorism. Bush's return to multilateralism was exemplified in the signing of a nuclear weapons reduction treaty with Russia in 2002. Nonetheless, his attempts to gain international support for a war against Iraq to overthrow that country's government were not as successful as he had hoped. During the continuing occupation of Iraq, the Bush administration saw more erosion of other countries' support of its actions.

Executive Agreements. Presidential power in foreign affairs is enhanced greatly by the use of **executive agreements** made between the president and other heads of state. Such agreements do not require Senate approval, although the House and Senate may refuse to appropriate the funds necessary to implement them. Whereas treaties are binding on all succeeding administrations, executive agreements require each new president's consent to remain in effect.

Among the advantages of executive agreements are speed and secrecy. The former is essential during a crisis; the latter is important when the administration fears that open senatorial debate may be detrimental to the best interests of the United States or to the interests of the president.[7] There have been far more executive agreements (about 9,000) than treaties (about 1,300). Many executive agreements contain secret provisions calling for American military assistance or other support.

Executive Agreement
An international agreement made by the president, without senatorial ratification, with the head of a foreign state.

---

7. The Case Act of 1972 requires that all executive agreements be transmitted to Congress within sixty days after taking effect. Secret agreements are transmitted to the foreign relations committees as classified information.

Chief Legislator

Constitutionally, presidents must recommend to Congress legislation that they judge necessary and expedient. Not all presidents have wielded their power as **chief legislator** in the same manner. Some presidents have been almost completely unsuccessful in getting their legislative programs implemented by Congress. Presidents Franklin Roosevelt and Lyndon Johnson, however, saw much of their proposed legislation put into effect.

Creating the Congressional Agenda. In modern times, the president has played a dominant role in creating the congressional agenda. In the president's annual **State of the Union message,** which is required by the Constitution (Article II, Section 3) and is usually given in late January shortly after Congress reconvenes, the president presents a legislative program. The message gives a broad, comprehensive view of what the president wishes the legislature to accomplish during its

▲ **President George W. Bush** gives a State of the Union Address while Vice President Dick Cheney and Speaker of the House Nancy Pelosi listen. Where is that address given? (AP Photo/Charles Dharapak)

session. It is as much a message to the American people and to the world as it is to Congress. Its impact on public opinion can determine the way in which Congress responds to the president's agenda.

Since 1913, the president has delivered the State of the Union message in a formal address to Congress. Today, this address is one of the great ceremonies of American governance, and many customs have grown up around it. For example, one cabinet member, the "designated survivor," stays away to ensure that the country will always have a president even if someone manages to blow up the Capitol building. Everyone gives the president an initial standing ovation out of respect for the office, but this applause does not necessarily represent support for the individual who holds the office. During the speech, senators and House members either applaud or remain silent to indicate their opinion of the policies that the president announces.

Getting Legislation Passed. The president can propose legislation. Congress, however, is not required to pass—or even introduce—any of the administration's bills. How, then, does the president get those proposals made into law? One way is by exercising the power of persuasion. The president writes to, telephones, and meets with various congressional leaders; makes public announcements to influence public opinion; and,

Chief Legislator
The role of the president in influencing the making of laws.

State of the Union Message
An annual message to Congress in which the president proposes a legislative program. The message is addressed not only to Congress but also to the American people and to the world.

Veto Message
The president's formal explanation of a veto, which accompanies the vetoed legislation when it is returned to Congress.

Pocket Veto
A special veto exercised by the chief executive after a legislative body has adjourned. Bills not signed by the chief executive die after a specified period of time.

Line-Item Veto
The power of an executive to veto individual lines or items within a piece of legislation without vetoing the entire bill.

as head of the party, exercises legislative leadership through the congresspersons of that party.

A president whose party holds a majority in both chambers of Congress may have an easier time getting legislation passed than does a president who faces a hostile Congress. But one of the ways in which a president who faces a hostile Congress still can wield power is through the ability to veto legislation.

Saying No to Legislation. The president has the power to say no to legislation through use of the veto,[8] by which the White House returns a bill unsigned to Congress with a **veto message** attached. Because the Constitution requires that every bill passed by the House and the Senate be sent to the president before it becomes law, the president must act on each bill:

1. If the bill is signed, it becomes law.
2. If the bill is not sent back to Congress after ten congressional working days, it becomes law without the president's signature.
3. The president can reject the bill and send it back to Congress with a veto message setting forth objections. Congress then can change the bill, hoping to secure presidential approval and repass it. Or Congress can simply reject the president's objections by overriding the veto with a two-thirds roll-call vote of the members present in both the House and the Senate.
4. If the president refuses to sign the bill and Congress adjourns within ten working days after the bill has been submitted to the president, the bill is killed for that session of Congress. This is called a **pocket veto.** If Congress wishes the bill to be reconsidered, the bill must be reintroduced during the following session.

Presidents employed the veto power infrequently until after the Civil War, but it has been used with increasing vigor since then (although George W. Bush used the veto infrequently).

The Line-Item Veto. Ronald Reagan lobbied strenuously for Congress to give another tool to the president—the **line-item veto,** which would allow the president to veto *specific* spending provisions of legislation that was passed by Congress. Reagan saw the line-item veto as the only way that he could control overall congressional spending. In 1996, Congress passed the Line Item Veto Act, which provided for the line-item veto. President Clinton used the line-item veto on several occasions, but the act was challenged in court. In 1998, by a six-to-three vote, the United States Supreme Court agreed with the veto's opponents and overturned the Line Item Veto Act. The Court stated that "there is no provision in the Constitution that authorizes the president to enact, to amend, or to repeal statutes."[9]

Congress's Power to Override Presidential Vetoes. A veto is a clear-cut indication of the president's dissatisfaction with congressional legislation. Congress, however,

8. *Veto* in Latin means "I forbid."
9. *Clinton v. City of New York,* 524 U.S. 417 (1998).

◀ **President Ronald Reagan**
(1981–1989) fought hard for the line-item veto. Why did the Supreme Court overturn the Line Item Veto Act? (AP Photo)

can override a presidential veto, although it rarely exercises this power. Consider that two-thirds of the members of each chamber who are present must vote to override the president's veto in a roll-call vote. This means that if only one-third plus one of the members voting in one of the chambers of Congress do not agree to override the veto, the veto holds. In American history, only about 7 percent of all vetoes have been overridden.

Signing Statements. While President George W. Bush issued remarkably few vetoes, he made extensive use of signing statements. A **signing statement** is a written declaration that a president may make when signing a bill into law regarding the law's enforcement. Presidents have been using such statements for decades, normally to instruct agencies on how to execute the laws or for similar purposes. President Bush issued more than eight hundred statements—more than all of the previous presidents combined. Bush also tended to use the statements to serve notice that he believed parts of bills that he signed were unconstitutional or contrary to national security interests. Some contend that Bush's use of signing statements violated his duty to enforce the laws, but to date, this issue has not come before any court.

Other Presidential Powers

The powers of the president just discussed are called **constitutional powers,** because their basis lies in the Constitution. In addition, Congress has established by law, or statute, numerous other presidential powers—such as the ability to declare national emergencies. These are called **statutory powers.** Both constitutional and statutory powers have been labeled the **expressed powers** of the president, because they are expressly written into the Constitution or into law.

Presidents also have what have come to be known as **inherent powers.** These depend on the statements in the Constitution that "the executive Power shall be vested in a President" and that the president should "take Care that the Laws be faithfully executed." The most common example of inherent powers are those emergency powers invoked by the president during wartime. Franklin Roosevelt, for example, used his inherent powers to move the Japanese and Japanese Americans living in the United States into internment camps for the duration of World War II. President George W. Bush often justified expanding the powers of the presidency by saying that such powers were necessary to fight the war on terrorism.

THE PRESIDENT AS PARTY CHIEF AND SUPERPOLITICIAN

Presidents are by no means above political partisanship, and one of their many roles is that of chief of party. Although the Constitution says nothing about the function of the president within a political party (the mere concept of political parties was abhorrent to most of the authors of the Constitution), today presidents are the actual leaders of their parties.

The President as Chief of Party

As party leader, the president chooses the national committee chairperson and can try to discipline party members who fail to support presidential policies. One way of exerting political power within the party is through **patronage**—appointing individuals to government or public jobs. This power was more extensive in the past, before

Signing Statement
A written declaration that the president may make when signing a bill into law. It may contain instructions to the bureaucracy on how to administer the law or point to sections of the law that the president considers unconstitutional or contrary to national security interests.

Constitutional Power
A power vested in the president by Article II of the Constitution.

Statutory Power
A power created for the president through laws enacted by Congress.

Expressed Power
A power of the president that is expressly written into the Constitution or into statutory law.

Inherent Power
A power of the president derived from the statements in the Constitution that "the executive Power shall be vested in a President" and that the president should "take Care that the Laws be faithfully executed."

Patronage
The practice of rewarding faithful party workers and followers with government employment and contracts.

Washington
Community
Individuals regularly
involved with politics in
Washington, D.C.

the establishment of the civil service in 1883, but the president still retains important patronage power. As we noted earlier, the president can appoint several thousand individuals to jobs in the cabinet, the White House, and the federal regulatory agencies.

Perhaps the most important partisan role that the president has played in the late 1900s and early 2000s has been that of fund-raiser. The president is able to raise large amounts for the party through appearances at dinners, speaking engagements, and other social occasions. President Clinton may have raised more than half a billion dollars for the Democratic Party during his two terms. President Bush was even more successful than Clinton—until his popularity ratings dropped during his last years in office. Barack Obama's spectacular success in raising funds for his presidential campaign suggests that he will carry on this tradition.

Presidents have a number of other ways of exerting influence as party chief. The president may make it known that a particular congressperson's choice for federal judge will not be appointed unless that member of Congress is more supportive of the president's legislative program.[10] The president may agree to campaign for a particular program or for a particular candidate. Presidents also reward loyal members of Congress with support for the funding of local projects, tax breaks for regional industries, and other forms of "pork" (government funds, jobs, or favors distributed by politicians to gain political advantage).

Constituencies and Public Approval

All politicians worry about their constituencies, and presidents are no exception. Presidents are also concerned with public approval ratings.

Presidential Constituencies. Presidents have many constituencies. In principle, they are beholden to the entire electorate—the public of the United States—even those who did not vote. Presidents are certainly beholden to their party, because its members helped to put them in office. The president's constituencies also include members of the opposing party whose cooperation the president needs. Finally, the president must take into consideration a constituency that has come to be called the **Washington community,** also known as those "inside the beltway." This community consists of individuals who—whether in or out of political office—are intimately familiar with the workings of government, thrive on gossip, and measure on a daily basis the political power of the president.

Public Approval. All of these constituencies are impressed by presidents who maintain a high level of public approval, partly because doing so is very difficult to accomplish. Presidential popularity, as measured by national polls, gives the president an extra political resource to use in persuading legislators or bureaucrats to pass legislation.

Recent Presidents and the Public Opinion Polls. The impact of popular approval on a president's prospects was placed in sharp relief by the experiences of President George W. Bush. Immediately after 9/11, Bush had the highest approval ratings ever recorded. By the time he left office, only 25 percent of the public approved of his performance as president. As a result of his declining popularity, Bush accomplished very little in his second term—he was able to strengthen the American presence in Iraq and

---

10. "Senatorial courtesy" (see Chapter 12) often puts the judicial appointment in the hands of the Senate, however.

pass a huge bank bailout bill, but domestically he was unable to attain any long-term Republican goals.

Barack Obama's popularity ratings were quite high during the first half of 2009, with 60 or even 65 percent of the public approving of his performance. Thereafter, his ratings began to slip, and by the fall, they were close to the margins by which he had won office. The honeymoon, in other words, was over. Some voters were apparently concerned about Obama's ambitious policy initiatives—the most far-reaching legislative program seen in many years. Is Obama too ambitious? We discuss that issue in this chapter's *The Politics of Boom and Bust* feature on the next page.

"Going Public." Since the early 1900s, presidents have spoken more to the public and less to Congress. In the 1800s, only 7 percent of presidential speeches were addressed to the public; since 1900, 50 percent have been addressed to the public. One scholar, Samuel Kernell, has proposed that the style of presidential leadership has changed since World War II, owing partly to the influence of television, with a resulting change in the balance of national politics.[11] Presidents frequently go over the heads of Congress and the political elites, taking their cases directly to the people. This strategy, which Kernell dubbed "going public," gives the president additional power through the ability to persuade and manipulate public opinion. By identifying their own positions so clearly, presidents make compromises with Congress much more difficult and weaken the legislators' positions. Given the increasing importance of the media as the major source of political information for citizens and elites, presidents will undoubtedly continue to use public opinion as part of their arsenal of weapons to gain support from Congress and to achieve their policy goals.

SPECIAL USES OF PRESIDENTIAL POWER

Presidents have at their disposal a variety of special powers and privileges not available in the other branches of the U.S. government. These include (1) emergency powers, (2) executive orders, and (3) executive privilege.

Emergency Powers

If you were to read the Constitution, you would find no mention of the additional powers that the executive office may exercise during national emergencies. Indeed, the Supreme Court has indicated that an "emergency does not create power."[12] But it is clear that presidents have made strong use of their inherent powers during times of emergency, particularly in the realm of foreign affairs. The **emergency powers** of the president were first enunciated in the Supreme Court's decision in *United States v. Curtiss-Wright Export Corp.*[13] In that case, President Franklin Roosevelt, without authorization by Congress, ordered an embargo on the shipment of weapons to two warring South American countries. The Court recognized that the president may exercise inherent powers in foreign affairs and that the national government has primacy in these affairs.

Emergency Power
An inherent power exercised by the president during a period of national crisis.

---

11. Samuel Kernell, *Going Public: New Strategies of Presidential Leadership,* 3d ed. (Washington, D.C.: Congressional Quarterly Press, 1997).
12. *Home Building and Loan Association v. Blaisdell,* 290 U.S. 398 (1934).
13. 299 U.S. 304 (1936).

the politics of Boom and Bust:
The Audacity of Barack Obama

On the eve of the Super Tuesday presidential primaries in 2008, the *National Journal,* a conservative magazine, claimed that Barack Obama was the most liberal member of the U.S. Senate. Skeptics recalled that the *Journal* had named John Kerry the most liberal senator in 2004, when Kerry was the Democratic presidential candidate. More reliable sources have identified Obama as a typical Senate Democrat.* As a candidate, Obama championed standard liberal causes, including health-care insurance for every adult, alternative energy, shifting the tax burden onto the rich, more federal support for education, and an early withdrawal from Iraq. This agenda was similar to that of the other Democratic candidates, such as Hillary Clinton.

Obama also called for a new tone in Washington, which many people interpreted as an appeal for bipartisanship. As president-elect, Obama appointed a series of moderate figures to his cabinet, and some Republicans began to believe they had nothing to fear. They soon learned otherwise. Obama had the will and the votes to implement an ambitious agenda, something no Democrat had been able to do since Lyndon Johnson's Great Society of the 1960s. Obama was not the most liberal Democrat. He was merely the most audacious.

Hit the Ground Running

In his first hundred days, Obama undertook a dazzling series of initiatives. Every day brought a new announcement, and we can list only a few of them. Obama directed the military to prepare a plan to leave Iraq even as he ordered 17,000 new troops into Afghanistan. He banned interrogation techniques widely considered to be torture and announced the closing of the Guantánamo Bay prison that housed terrorist suspects. At his urging, Congress passed a long-stalled plan to fund children's health care. Secretary of State Hillary Clinton toured the world seeking better relationships, and Obama himself traveled to Europe and the Middle East in April.

Combating the Recession

None of these steps addressed the major problem Obama faced on taking office—the economy. The economic scene on Inauguration Day was not pretty, and Obama's reactions were characteristically bold. His first step was a $787 billion stimulus bill to jump-start the economy, passed without any Republican support in the House.

Never in history had the Congress appropriated more new funding more quickly. Treasury secretary Timothy Geithner announced a plan to raise billions in federally subsidized private funds to support the nation's battered banks by buying up their "toxic assets." On April 30, Congress approved Obama's $3.6 trillion budget for 2010 without any Republican support.

Even while Bush was still president, a collapsing automobile industry had fallen into the federal lap. Thereafter, the responsibility was Obama's. A bankrupt Chrysler was forced to become a part of Fiat, the Italian automobile maker, and General Motors became a majority-owned subsidiary of the U.S. government. These steps represented unprecedented levels of federal involvement in private industry. Republicans were appalled.

The Audacity of Hope

Was Obama's call for a new spirit in Washington only a hoax? Not quite. Charles Kesler of the Claremont Institute adopted the unusual strategy of reading Obama's own writings—especially his policy work, *The Audacity of Hope*—and assuming that Obama meant what he said.[†] Kesler was therefore able to predict Obama's behavior in office. If there is a "villain" in *The Audacity of Hope,* it is former Democratic president Bill Clinton. According to Obama, Clinton wasted his enormous political talents and failed to advance a progressive agenda. Obama meant to do better. Obama indeed envisioned a new spirit in Washington based on resolving the conflict between conservatives and liberals. But the fight ends *when the liberals win.*

Obama spoke often in the campaign of Abraham Lincoln, also from Illinois. Obama later downplayed the connection, but the affinity with Lincoln was real. Today, Americans continue to venerate Lincoln an ambitious politician for his time. Obama may be the most determined president of our times.

FOR CRITICAL ANALYSIS

What are the benefits of having the federal government more involved in banking, automobile manufacturing, health care, and other areas of the economy? What are the downsides?

---

*These include DW-Nominate, a political science project at the University of California, San Diego led by Professor Keith Poole.
†Charles Kesler, "The Audacity of Barack Obama," *Claremont Review of Books,* Fall 2008.

Examples of emergency powers are abundant, coinciding with crises in domestic and foreign affairs. Abraham Lincoln suspended civil liberties at the beginning of the Civil War (1861–1865) and called the state militias into national service. These actions and his subsequent governance of conquered areas—and even of areas of northern states—were justified by claims that they were essential to preserve the Union. Franklin Roosevelt declared an "unlimited national emergency" following the fall of France in World War II (1939–1945) and readied the federal budget and the economy for war.

President Harry Truman authorized the federal seizure of steel plants and their operation by the national government in 1952 during the Korean War. Truman claimed that he was using his inherent emergency power as chief executive and commander in chief to safeguard the nation's security, as an ongoing steel mill strike threatened the supply of weapons to the armed forces. The Supreme Court did not agree, holding that the president had no authority under the Constitution to seize private property or to legislate such action.[14] According to legal scholars, this was the first time a limit had been placed on the exercise of the president's emergency powers.

Executive Orders

Congress allows the president (as well as administrative agencies) to issue **executive orders** that have the force of law. These executive orders can do the following: (1) enforce legislative statutes, (2) enforce the Constitution or treaties with foreign nations, and (3) establish or modify rules and practices of executive administrative agencies.

An executive order, then, represents the president's legislative power. The only apparent requirement is that under the Administrative Procedure Act of 1946, all executive orders must be published in the ***Federal Register;*** a daily publication of the U.S. government. Executive orders have been used to establish procedures to appoint noncareer administrators, to implement national affirmative action regulations, to restructure the White House bureaucracy, to ration consumer goods and to administer wage and price controls under emergency conditions, to classify government information as secret, to regulate the export of restricted items, and to establish military tribunals for suspected terrorists.

Executive Privilege

Another inherent executive power that has been claimed by presidents concerns the right of the president and the president's executive officials to withhold information from, or refuse to appear before, Congress or the courts. This is called **executive privilege,** and it relies on the constitutional separation of powers for its basis.

Presidents have frequently invoked executive privilege to avoid having to disclose information to Congress on actions of the executive branch. For example, President George W. Bush claimed executive privilege to keep the head of the newly established Office of Homeland Security, Tom Ridge, from testifying before Congress. The Bush administration also resisted attempts by the congressional Government Accountability Office to obtain information about meetings and documents related to Vice President Dick Cheney's actions as chair of the administration's energy policy task force. Bush, like presidents before him, claimed that a certain degree of secrecy is essential to national security. Critics of executive privilege believe that it can be used to shield

Executive Order
A rule or regulation issued by the president that has the effect of law.

Federal Register
A publication of the U.S. government that prints executive orders, rules, and regulations.

Executive Privilege
The right of executive officials to withhold information from, or to refuse to appear before, a legislative committee.

---

14. *Youngstown Sheet and Tube Co. v. Sawyer,* 343 U.S. 579 (1952).

Impeachment
An action by the House of Representatives to accuse the president, vice president, or other civil officers of the United States of committing "Treason, Bribery, or other high Crimes and Misdemeanors."

from public scrutiny actions of the executive branch that should be open to Congress and to the American citizenry.

Limiting Executive Privilege. Limits to executive privilege went untested until the Watergate affair in the early 1970s. Five men had broken into the headquarters of the Democratic National Committee and were caught searching for documents that would damage the candidacy of the Democratic nominee, George McGovern. Later investigation showed that the break-in had been planned by members of Richard Nixon's campaign committee and that Nixon and his closest advisers had devised a strategy for impeding the investigation of the crime. After it became known that all of the conversations held in the Oval Office had been tape-recorded on a secret system, Nixon was ordered to turn over the tapes to the special prosecutor in charge of the investigation.

Nixon refused to do so, claiming executive privilege. He argued that "no president could function if the private papers of his office, prepared by his personal staff, were open to public scrutiny." In 1974, in one of the Supreme Court's most famous cases, *United States v. Nixon,*[15] the justices unanimously ruled that Nixon had to hand over the tapes. The Court held that executive privilege could not be used to prevent evidence from being heard in criminal proceedings.

▼ President Bill Clinton

speaks to Democratic members of Congress after receiving news of his impeachment in 1998. Standing behind him are Rep. Richard Gephardt (D., Mo.), Vice President Al Gore, and First Lady Hillary Rodham Clinton. What has to happen after an impeachment for a president to be removed from office? (AP Photo/Doug Mills)

ABUSES OF EXECUTIVE POWER AND IMPEACHMENT

Presidents normally leave office either because their first term has expired and they have not sought (or won) reelection or because, having served two full terms, they are not allowed to be elected for a third term (owing to the Twenty-second Amendment, passed in 1951). Eight presidents have died in office. But there is still another way for a president to leave office—by **impeachment** and conviction. Articles I and II of the Constitution authorize the House and Senate to remove the president, the vice president, or other civil officers of the United States for committing "Treason, Bribery, or other high Crimes and Misdemeanors." According to the Constitution, the impeachment process begins in the House, which impeaches (accuses) the federal officer involved. If the House votes to impeach the officer, it draws up articles of impeachment and submits them to the Senate, which conducts the actual trial.

In the history of the United States, no president has ever actually been impeached and also convicted—and thus removed from office—by means of this process. President Andrew Johnson (1865–1869), who succeeded to the

15. 318 U.S. 683 (1974).

office after the assassination of Abraham Lincoln, was impeached by the House but acquitted by the Senate. More than a century later, the House Judiciary Committee approved articles of impeachment against President Richard Nixon for his involvement in the cover-up of the Watergate break-in of 1972. Informed by members of his own party that he had no hope of surviving the trial in the Senate, Nixon resigned on August 9, 1974, before the full House voted on the articles. Nixon is the only president to have resigned from office.

The second president to be impeached by the House but not convicted by the Senate was President Bill Clinton. In September 1998, independent counsel Kenneth Starr sent to Congress the findings of his investigation of the president on the charges of perjury and obstruction of justice. The House approved two charges against Clinton: lying to the grand jury about his affair with Monica Lewinsky and obstruction of justice. The articles of impeachment were then sent to the Senate, which acquitted Clinton.

Cabinet
An advisory group selected by the president to aid in making decisions. The cabinet includes the heads of fifteen executive departments and others named by the president.

Kitchen Cabinet
The informal advisers to the president.

THE EXECUTIVE ORGANIZATION

Gone are the days when presidents answered their own mail, as George Washington did. It was not until 1857 that Congress authorized a private secretary for the president, to be paid by the federal government. Woodrow Wilson typed most of his correspondence, even though he did have several secretaries. At the beginning of Franklin Roosevelt's long tenure in the White House, the entire staff consisted of thirty-seven employees. With the New Deal and World War II, however, the presidential staff became a sizable organization.

The Cabinet

Although the Constitution does not include the word *cabinet,* it does state that the president "may require the Opinion, in writing, of the principal Officer in each of the executive Departments." Since the time of George Washington, these officers have formed an advisory group, or **cabinet,** to which the president turns for counsel.

Members of the Cabinet. Originally, the cabinet consisted of only four officials—the secretaries of state, treasury, and war and the attorney general. Today, the cabinet numbers fourteen department secretaries and the attorney general. The cabinet may include others as well. The president at his or her discretion can, for example, ascribe cabinet rank to the vice president, the head of the Office of Management and Budget, the national security adviser, or additional officials. Under President Barack Obama, the additional members of the cabinet are the following:

- The vice president
- The chair of the Council of Economic Advisers
- The administrator of the Environmental Protection Agency
- The director of the Office of Management and Budget
- The United States trade representative
- The United States ambassador to the United Nations
- The White House chief of staff

Often, a president will use a **kitchen cabinet** to replace the formal cabinet as a major source of advice. The term *kitchen cabinet* originated during the presidency of Andrew Jackson, who relied on the counsel of close friends who allegedly met with him

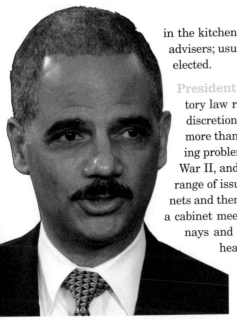

in the kitchen of the White House. A kitchen cabinet is a very informal group of advisers; usually, they are friends with whom the president worked before being elected.

Presidential Use of Cabinets. Because neither the Constitution nor statutory law requires the president to consult with the cabinet, its use is purely discretionary. Some presidents have relied on the counsel of their cabinets more than others. Dwight Eisenhower was used to the team approach to solving problems from his experience as supreme allied commander during World War II, and therefore he frequently turned to his cabinet for advice on a wide range of issues. More often, presidents have solicited the opinions of their cabinets and then have done what they wanted to do. Lincoln supposedly said—after a cabinet meeting in which a vote was seven nays against his one aye—"Seven nays and one aye; the ayes have it." In general, few presidents have relied heavily on the advice of their cabinet members.

It is not surprising that presidents tend to disregard their cabinet members' advice. Often, the departmental heads are more responsive to the wishes of their own staffs or to their own political ambitions than they are to the president. They may be more concerned with obtaining resources for their departments than with achieving the president's goals. So there is often a strong conflict of interest between presidents and their cabinet members.

▲ **Eric Holder** became President Barack Obama's attorney general. He was the first African American to fill that position. (AP Photo/Charles Dharapak)

The Executive Office of the President

When President Franklin Roosevelt appointed a special committee on administrative management, he knew that the committee would conclude that the president needed help. Indeed, the committee proposed a major reorganization of the executive branch. Congress did not approve the entire reorganization, but it did create the **Executive Office of the President (EOP)** to provide staff assistance for the chief executive and to help coordinate the executive bureaucracy. Since that time, a number of agencies have been created within the EOP to supply the president with advice and staff help. Under President Barack Obama, these agencies were the following:

- Council of Economic Advisers
- Council on Environmental Quality
- Domestic Policy Council
- National Economic Council
- National Security Council
- Office of Administration
- Office of Management and Budget
- Office of National Drug Control Policy
- Office of Science and Technology Policy
- Office of the United States Trade Representative
- President's Intelligence Advisory Board and Intelligence Oversight Board
- White House Military Office
- White House Office

Executive Office of the President (EOP)
An organization established by President Franklin D. Roosevelt to assist the president in carrying out major duties.

Several of the offices within the EOP are especially important, including the White House Office and the Office of Management and Budget.

The White House Office. The **White House Office** includes most of the key personal and political advisers to the president. Among the jobs held by these aides are those of secretary, press secretary, appointments secretary, and legal counsel to the president. Often, the individuals who hold these positions are recruited from the president's campaign staff. Their duties—mainly protecting the president's political interests—are similar to campaign functions. Under President Barack Obama, the White House Office was made up of twenty-three units, including the following:

- Chief of Staff's Office
- Council on Women and Girls
- Homeland Security Council
- Office of Cabinet Affairs
- Office of Energy and Climate Change Policy
- Office of Health Reform
- Office of Legislative Affairs
- Office of National AIDS Policy

- Office of Political Affairs
- Office of Public Engagement and Intergovernmental Affairs
- Office of Social Innovation
- Office of the First Lady
- Office of the Press Secretary
- Office of the White House Counsel
- Office of Urban Affairs Policy
- Oval Office Operations

In all recent administrations, one member of the White House Office has been named **chief of staff.** This person, who is responsible for coordinating the office, is also one of the president's chief advisers. President Obama's chief of staff is Rahm Emanuel.

In addition to civilian advisers, the president is supported by a large number of military personnel, who are organized under the White House Military Office. These members of the military provide communications, transportation, medical care, and food services to the president and the White House staff.

White House staff members are closest to the president and may have considerable influence over the administration's decisions. Often, when presidents are under fire for their decisions, the staff is accused of keeping the chief executive too isolated from criticism or help. Presidents insist that they will not allow the staff to become too powerful, but given the difficulty of the office, each president eventually turns to staff members for loyal assistance and protection.

The Office of Management and Budget. The **Office of Management and Budget (OMB)** was originally the Bureau of the Budget, which was created in 1921 within the Department of the Treasury. Recognizing the importance of this agency, Franklin Roosevelt moved it into the White House Office in 1939. Richard Nixon reorganized the Bureau of the Budget in 1970 and changed its name to reflect its new managerial function. It is headed by a director, who makes up the annual federal budget that the president presents to Congress each January for approval. In principle,

White House Office
The personal office of the president, which tends to presidential political needs and manages the media.

Chief of Staff
The person who is named to direct the White House Office and advise the president.

Office of Management and Budget (OMB)
A division of the Executive Office of the President. The OMB assists the president in preparing the annual budget, clearing and coordinating departmental agency budgets, and supervising the administration of the federal budget.

▶ **Treasury secretary** Timothy Geithner spends much of his time testifying in front of congressional committees. Why is Congress so interested in what he does? (AP Photo/Manuel Balce Ceneta)

National Security
Council (NSC)
An agency in the
Executive Office of the
President that advises
the president on national
security.

the director of the OMB has broad fiscal powers in planning and estimating various parts of the federal budget, because all agencies must submit their proposed budget to the OMB for approval. In reality, it is not so clear that the OMB truly can affect the greater scope of the federal budget. The OMB may be more important as a clearinghouse for legislative proposals initiated in the executive agencies. President Obama's OMB director is Peter Orszag.

The National Security Council. The **National Security Council (NSC)** is a link between the president's key foreign and military advisers and the president. Its members consist of the president, the vice president, and the secretaries of state and defense, plus other informal members. Included in the NSC is the president's assistant for national security affairs, also known as the national security adviser. Under President Obama, the adviser is James L. Jones, a former Marine Corps general.

▼ **U.S. Vice President**
Joseph Biden speaks at the White House Recovery and Reinvestment Act Implementation Conference at the White House in Washington, D.C., in March 2009. What is the vice president's formal role in our government? (Chris Kleponis/AFP/ Getty Images)

THE VICE PRESIDENCY

The Constitution does not give much power to the vice president. The only formal duty is to preside over the Senate—which is rarely necessary. This obligation is fulfilled when the Senate organizes and adopts its rules and when the vice president is needed to decide a tie vote. In all other cases, the president pro tem manages parliamentary procedures in the Senate. The vice president is expected to participate only informally in senatorial deliberations, if at all.

The Vice President's Job

Vice presidents have traditionally been chosen by presidential nominees to balance the ticket by attracting groups of voters or appeasing party factions. If a presidential nominee is from the North, it is not a bad idea to have a vice-presidential nominee who is from the South. If the presidential nominee is from a rural state, perhaps someone with an urban background would be most suitable as a running mate. Presidential nominees who are strongly conservative or strongly liberal would do well to have vice-presidential nominees who are more in the middle of the political road.

In recent presidential elections, vice-presidential candidates have often been selected for other reasons. Republican George W. Bush, who was subject to criticism for his lack of government experience and his "lightweight" personality, chose Dick Cheney, a former member of Congress who had also served as secretary of defense. Likewise, Barack Obama picked Joe Biden to be his running mate in 2008 to add gravitas and foreign policy experience to the ticket. Republican presidential candidate John McCain's choice of Alaska governor Sarah Palin not only balanced the ticket by gender, but also politically. Social conservatives, many of whom were suspicious of McCain, gave enthusiastic support to Palin.

Traditionally, the job of the vice president has not been very demanding. In recent years, however, presidents have granted their running mates increased responsibilities and power. President Jimmy Carter (1977–1980) was the first modern president to rely on his vice president—Walter Mondale—as a major adviser. Under

President Bush, Dick Cheney became the most powerful vice president in history. Cheney was able to place his supporters throughout the bureaucracy and exert influence on a wide range of issues. He could exercise this degree of power, however, only because he had the support of the president. In contrast, Vice President Biden's relationship to President Obama has been more conventional.

Presidential Succession

Eight vice presidents have become president because of the death of the president. John Tyler, the first to do so, took over William Henry Harrison's position after only one month. No one knew whether Tyler should simply be a caretaker until a new president could be elected three and a half years later or whether he actually should be president. Tyler assumed that he was supposed to be the chief executive, and he acted as such—although he was commonly referred to as "His Accidency." Since then, vice presidents taking over the position of the presidency because of the incumbent's death have assumed the presidential powers.

But what should a vice president do if a president becomes incapable of carrying out necessary duties while in office? When James Garfield was shot in 1881, he remained alive for two and a half months. What was Vice President Chester Arthur's role?

This question was not addressed in the original Constitution. Article II, Section 1, says only that "[i]n Case of the Removal of the President from Office, or of his Death, Resignation, or Inability to discharge the Powers and Duties of the said Office, the same shall devolve on [the same powers shall be exercised by] the Vice President." There have been many instances of presidential disability. When Dwight Eisenhower became ill for the second time in 1958, he entered into a pact with Richard Nixon specifying that the vice president could determine whether the president was incapable of carrying out his duties if the president could not communicate. John Kennedy and Lyndon Johnson entered into similar agreements with their vice presidents. Finally, in 1967, the **Twenty-fifth Amendment** was passed, establishing procedures in the event of presidential incapacity.

Twenty-fifth Amendment
A 1967 amendment to the Constitution that establishes procedures for filling presidential and vice-presidential vacancies and makes provisions for presidential incapacity.

The Twenty-fifth Amendment

According to the Twenty-fifth Amendment, when a president believes that he or she is incapable of performing the duties of office, the president must inform Congress in writing. Then the vice president serves as acting president until the president can resume normal duties. When the president is unable to communicate, a majority of the cabinet, including the vice president, can declare that fact to Congress. Then the vice president serves as acting president until the president resumes normal duties. If a dispute arises over the return of the president's ability, a two-thirds vote of Congress is required to allow the vice president to remain acting president. Otherwise, the president resumes normal duties.

When the Vice Presidency Becomes Vacant

The Twenty-fifth Amendment also addresses the issue of how the president should fill a vacant vice presidency. Section 2 of the amendment simply states, "Whenever there is a vacancy in the office of the Vice President, the President shall nominate a Vice President who shall take office upon confirmation by a majority vote of both Houses of Congress."

The question of who shall be president if both the president and vice president die is answered by the Succession Act of 1947. If the president and vice president die, resign, or are disabled, the Speaker of the House will become president, after resigning from Congress. Next in line is the president pro tem of the Senate, followed by the cabinet officers in the order of the creation of their departments (see Table 10–1).

TABLE 10–1: Line of Succession to the Presidency of the United States

1. Vice president
2. Speaker of the House of Representatives
3. Senate president pro tempore
4. Secretary of state
5. Secretary of the treasury
6. Secretary of defense
7. Attorney general (head of the Justice Department)
8. Secretary of the interior
9. Secretary of agriculture
10. Secretary of commerce
11. Secretary of labor
12. Secretary of health and human services
13. Secretary of housing and urban development
14. Secretary of transportation
15. Secretary of energy
16. Secretary of education
17. Secretary of veterans affairs
18. Secretary of homeland security

making a difference

COMMUNICATING WITH THE WHITE HOUSE

When it comes to caring about the presidency, most people do not need much encouragement. The president is our most important official. The president serves as the public face of the government and, indeed, of the nation as a whole. Many people, however, believe the president is such a remote figure that nothing they can do will affect what he or she does. That is not always true. On many issues, your voice—combined, of course, with the voices of many others—can have an impact. Writing to the president is a traditional way for citizens to express their opinions. Every day, the White House receives several thousand letters and other communications.

Why Should You Care?

The president makes many decisions that directly influence your life. A major example is the health-care legislation that Congress took up in 2009, in great part because it was one of President Obama's top priorities. Obama made it clear that while he was completely committed to passing a plan, many details of health-care policy were open to debate. Should every adult be required to obtain health-care insurance? Should a government-run insurance program be an option, in addition to private plans? What level of support should the government offer to citizens who cannot afford insurance? Your future medical care—and your taxes—were at stake.

What Can You Do?

The most traditional form of communication with the White House is, of course, by letter. Letters to the president should be addressed to:

> The President of the United States
> The White House
> 1600 Pennsylvania Avenue N.W.
> Washington, DC 20500

Letters may be sent to the First Lady at the same address. Will you get an answer? Almost certainly. The White House mail room is staffed by volunteers and paid employees who sort the mail for the president and tally the public's concerns. You may receive a standard response to your comments or a more personal, detailed response.

You can also call the White House on the telephone and leave a message for the president or First Lady. The White House has a round-the-clock comment line, which you can reach at 202-456-1111. When you call that number, an operator will take down your comments and forward them to the president's office.

The home page for the White House is:

> www.whitehouse.gov

It is designed to be entertaining and to convey information about the president. You can also send your comments and ideas to the White House using e-mail. Send comments to the president at:

> comments@whitehouse.gov

Address e-mail to the vice president at:

> vice_president@whitehouse.gov

◀ The White House

has an active Web presence. Here you see its home page. You can find information on just about all aspects of the federal government through this particular portal. Additionally, you can go to the "contact" section to e-mail your comments to the president and to the vice president. Even though both of those top officials are unlikely to personally read your e-mails, why is it still important to communicate with them? (www.whitehouse.gov)

key**terms**

advice and consent 233
appointment power 231
cabinet 243
chief diplomat 233
chief executive 230
chief legislator 235
chief of staff 245
civil service 230
commander in chief 232
constitutional
    power 237
diplomatic
    recognition 233

emergency power 239
executive
    agreement 234
Executive Office of the
    President (EOP) 244
executive order 241
executive privilege 241
expressed power 237
Federal Register 241
head of state 230
impeachment 242
inherent power 237

kitchen cabinet 243
line-item veto 236
National Security
    Council (NSC) 246
Office of Management
    and Budget
    (OMB) 245
pardon 231
patronage 237
pocket veto 236
reprieve 231
signing statement 237

State of the Union
    message 235
statutory power 237
Twelfth Amendment 229
Twenty-fifth
    Amendment 247
veto message 236
War Powers
    Resolution 233
Washington
    community 238
White House Office 245

chapter**summary**

1   The office of the presidency in the United States, combining as it does the functions of chief of state and chief executive into a single elected official, was, when created, unique. The framers of the Constitution were divided over whether the president should be a weak or a strong executive.

2   The requirements for the office of the presidency are outlined in Article II, Section 1, of the Constitution. The president's roles include both formal and informal duties. The roles of the president include head of state, chief executive, commander in chief, chief diplomat, chief legislator, and party chief.

3   As head of state, the president is ceremonial leader of the government. As chief executive, the president is bound to enforce the acts of Congress, the judgments of the federal courts, and treaties. The chief executive has the power of appointment and the power to grant reprieves and pardons.

4   As commander in chief, the president is the ultimate decision maker in military matters. As chief diplomat, the president recognizes foreign governments, negotiates treaties, signs agreements, and nominates and receives ambassadors.

5   The role of chief legislator includes recommending legislation to Congress, lobbying for the legislation, approving laws, and exercising the veto

power. In addition to constitutional and inherent powers, the president has statutory powers written into law by Congress. Presidents are also leaders of their political parties. Presidents rely on their personal popularity to help them fulfill these functions.

6   Presidents have a variety of special powers not available to other branches of the government. These include emergency power and the power to issue executive orders and invoke executive privilege.

7   Abuses of executive power are dealt with by Articles I and II of the Constitution, which authorize the House and Senate to impeach and remove the president, vice president, or other officers of the federal government for committing "Treason, Bribery, or other high Crimes and Misdemeanors."

8   The president receives assistance from the cabinet and from the Executive Office of the President (including the White House Office).

9   The vice president is the constitutional officer assigned to preside over the Senate and to assume the presidency in case of the death, resignation, removal, or disability of the president. The Twenty-fifth Amendment, passed in 1967, established procedures to be followed in case of presidential incapacity and when filling a vacant vice presidency.

QUESTIONS FOR

discussionandanalysis

1 What characteristics do you think voters look for when choosing a president? Might these characteristics change as a result of changes in the political environment and the specific problems facing the nation? If you believe voters almost always look for the same characteristics when selecting a president, why do you think this is so? If you believe voters' choices may vary depending on circumstances, which circumstances favor which kinds of leaders?

2 Many presidents have been lawyers by profession, but George W. Bush was a businessman, Ronald Reagan was an actor, and Jimmy Carter was a naval officer and peanut farmer. What advantages might these three presidents have gained from their career backgrounds? In particular, what benefits might Ronald Reagan have derived from his experience as an actor?

3 Is executive privilege really necessary? Why or why not? What would happen if executive privilege ceased to exist?

4 With a single exception, every eight years since 1953 the presidency has been taken over by the other party. The only exception is Reagan's first term—had Carter been reelected instead, the pattern would have been perfect: eight years of Republican Eisenhower, eight of Democrats Kennedy and Johnson, eight of Republicans Nixon and Ford, eight of Democrat Carter, eight of Republicans Reagan and G. H. W. Bush, eight of Democrat Clinton, eight of Republican G. W. Bush, and finally a Democrat again, Barack Obama. Why might the voters prefer to pick a president from the other party every few years?

helpfulonlineResources

CONNECTING TO AMERICAN GOVERNMENT AND POLITICS

The president's Web site, www.whitehouse.gov, contains a wealth of information on the administration.

Nate Silver became famous as an opinion poll expert during the 2008 presidential elections. Silver's continuing commentary on the president and Congress is mostly based on data and research. Check out the site at: www.fivethirtyeight.com

C-SPAN provides a companion Web site for its television series *American Presidents: Life Portraits* at: www.americanpresidents.org

The site provides extensive video resources on all of the presidents.

aspecialWebSite

FOR YOUR TEXT

Go to this book's special Web site at academic.cengage.com/polisci/Schmidt/Brief6e. Choose "For Students." Then click on Chapter 10, where you will find an online quiz and other helpful study aids. If your professor is using CengageNOW: *American Government and Politics Today, Brief Edition,* log in and go to Chapter 10 for additional online study aids.

11

The Bureaucracy

Faceless bureaucrats—this image provokes a negative reaction from many, if not most, Americans. Polls consistently report that the majority of Americans support "less government." The same polls, however, report that the majority of Americans support almost every specific program that the government undertakes. The conflict between the desire for small government and the desire for the benefits that only a large government can provide has been a constant feature of American politics. For example, the goal of preserving endangered species has widespread support. At the same time, many people believe that restrictions imposed under the Endangered Species Act violate the rights of landowners. Helping the elderly pay their medical bills is a popular objective, but hardly anyone enjoys paying the Medicare tax that supports this effort.

In this chapter, we describe the size, organization, and staffing of the federal bureaucracy. We review modern attempts at bureaucratic reform and the process by which Congress exerts ultimate control over the bureaucracy. We also discuss the bureaucracy's role in making rules and setting policy.

THE NATURE OF BUREAUCRACY

Every modern president, at one time or another, has proclaimed that his administration was going to "fix government." All modern presidents also have put forth plans to end government waste and inefficiency (see Table 11–1). Their success has been, in a

TABLE 11–1: Selected Presidential Plans to End Government Inefficiency

President	Name of Plan
Lyndon Johnson (1963–1969)	Programming, planning, and budgeting systems
Richard Nixon (1969–1974)	Management by Objectives
Jimmy Carter (1977–1981)	Zero-Based Budgeting
Ronald Reagan (1981–1989)	President's Private Sector Survey on Cost Control (the Grace Commission)
George H. W. Bush (1989–1993)	Right-Sizing Government
Bill Clinton (1993–2001)	Reinventing Government
George W. Bush (2001–2009)	Performance-Based Budgeting
Barack Obama (2009–)	Appointment of a chief performance officer

Bureaucracy
A large organization that is structured hierarchically to carry out specific functions.

word, underwhelming. Presidents generally have been powerless to significantly affect the structure and operation of the federal bureaucracy.

A **bureaucracy** is the name given to a large organization that is structured hierarchically to carry out specific functions. Generally, bureaucracies are characterized by an organization chart. The units of the organization are divided according to the specialization and expertise of the employees.

Public and Private Bureaucracies

We should not think of bureaucracy as unique to government. Any large corporation or university can be considered a bureaucratic organization. The fact is that the handling of complex problems requires a division of labor. Individuals must concentrate their skills on specific, well-defined aspects of a problem and depend on others to solve the rest of it.

Public or government bureaucracies differ from private organizations in some important ways, however. A private corporation, such as Microsoft, has a single set of leaders—its board of directors. Public bureaucracies, in contrast, do not have a single set of leaders. Although the president is the chief administrator of the federal system, all bureaucratic agencies are subject to the dictates of Congress for their funding, staffing, and, indeed, their continued existence. Furthermore, public bureaucracies supposedly serve the citizenry.

One other important difference between private corporations and government bureaucracies is that government bureaucracies are not organized to make a profit. Rather, they are supposed to perform their functions as efficiently as possible to conserve taxpayers' dollars. Perhaps it is this ideal that makes citizens hostile toward government bureaucracy when they experience inefficiency and red tape.

▼ **These microbiologists** are well-protected as they handle samples while testing for swine flu at the Department of Health and Human Services in Houston, Texas. Why do we rely on public institutions for such testing? (AP Photo/David J. Phillip)

The Size of the Bureaucracy

In 1789, the new government's bureaucracy was minuscule. There were three departments—State (with nine employees), War (with two employees), and Treasury (with thirty-nine employees)—and the Office of the Attorney General (which later became the Department of Justice). The bureaucracy was still small in 1798. At that time, the secretary of state had seven clerks and spent a total of $500 (about $9,430 in 2010 dollars) on stationery and printing. In that same year, the Appropriations Act allocated $1.4 million, or $26.4 million in 2010 dollars, to the War Department.

Times have changed. Excluding military service members, the federal bureaucracy includes approximately 2.8 million government employees. That number has remained relatively stable for the last several decades. It is somewhat deceiving, however, because many other individuals work directly or indirectly for the federal government as subcontractors or consultants and in other capacities, as you will read later in this chapter. In fact, according to some studies, the federal workforce greatly exceeds the number of official federal workers.

The figures for federal government employment are only part of the story. Figure 11–1 shows the growth in government employment at the federal, state, and local levels. Since 1982, this growth has been mainly at the state and local levels. If all government employees are included, more than 15 percent of all civilian employment is accounted for by government. Costs are commensurately high. The share of the gross domestic product accounted for by all government spending was only about 11 percent in 1929. Today, it exceeds 40 percent. One factor driving up the amount of government spending has been legislation to combat the Great Recession that began in December 2007. Is the nation getting its money's worth from such policies? We address that question in this chapter's *At Issue* feature on the facing page.

THE ORGANIZATION OF THE FEDERAL BUREAUCRACY

Within the federal bureaucracy are a number of different types of government agencies and organizations. Figure 11–2 on page 256 outlines the several bodies within the executive branch, as well as the separate organizations that provide services to Congress, to the courts, and directly to the president. The executive branch, which employs most of the government's staff, has four major types of structures. They are (1) cabinet departments, (2) independent executive agencies, (3) independent regulatory agencies, and (4) government corporations. Each has a distinctive relationship to the president, and some have unusual internal structures, overall goals, and grants of power.

FIGURE 11–1: Government Employment at the Federal, State, and Local Levels

There are more local government employees than federal and state employees combined.

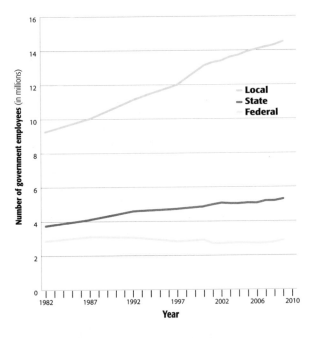

Sources: U.S. Census Bureau and the Bureau of Labor Statistics.

atIssue: Did the Stimulus Legislation Contain Too Much Pork?

In February 2009, President Obama signed an economic stimulus package nominally valued at $787 billion. Of that sum, $284 billion consisted of tax breaks. A huge share of the actual spending was distributed to state and local governments in response to grant requests. The stimulus bill soon became a centerpiece in the Republican campaign against the Obama administration, a campaign based largely on the accusation that the Democrats were spending dangerously excessive sums.

Pork, Anyone?

Due to the way the bill was written, members of Congress had little scope for inserting pork, that is, specific requests for their constituents. With such a large part of the bill spent in response to state and local requests, however, much of the spending did resemble traditional pork. The Republicans also denounced specific items that were spelled out in the bill, such as:

- $8 billion for high-speed rail, possibly including a line between Disneyland and Las Vegas.
- $2 billion for the domestic lithium ion battery industry.
- $200 million for Filipino veterans, most of whom live abroad, for service in World War II.
- $100 million for small shipyards in places such as Ketchikan, Alaska, and Bayou La Batre, Alabama.
- $2 billion for the FutureGen Alliance project, a demonstration clean-coal plant in Illinois.
- $600 million for new fuel-efficient cars for government employees.

Republicans claimed that in the end, the stimulus package was little more than a collection of items from longtime Democratic wish lists.

The Stimulus Defended

What, defenders responded, is wrong with wish lists? If you come into a small inheritance and decide to spend it all, will you spend it on things you long wanted but couldn't afford—or on things you'd never thought of before? Of course, you'll consult your wish list.

A more sweeping defense of the stimulus depends on an explanation of why the spending is helpful. The famous British economist John Maynard Keynes sought to determine how governments could combat the Great Depression of the 1930s. Keynes pointed out that in the Depression everyone was simultaneously trying to reduce both their spending and their borrowing. (Indeed, the same circumstances existed after September 2008.)

Keynes argued that at such times, the government should step in to borrow—running up the deficit—and spend on projects that would rehire the unemployed and put idle resources back to work. Ideally, the government should spend the borrowed sums on useful projects, but the economy would be stimulated *even if the projects were pointless*. Keynes gave as an example hiring one huge team of workers to dig holes in the ground and a second huge team to fill them up.

This line of thought may sound absurd. Yet according to the traditional narrative (lately disputed by some economists), it was World War II that ended the Depression. From the Keynesian point of view, President Roosevelt's rather modest New Deal budget deficits just weren't large enough. Rather, the tremendous deficits incurred to finance World War II did the trick. From a purely economic standpoint, of course, the war was worse than pointless. It was a vast exercise in destruction. Tens of millions of people died. Much of Japan and continental Europe burned to the ground.

Indeed, in 2009 some economists thought that as large as Obama's stimulus package was, it needed to be much larger to fix the economy. These economists didn't see the bill as pork—they saw it as too small.

But Was Keynes Even Right?

Certain other economists believe that deficit-based spending and temporary tax reductions cannot actually stimulate the economy, even in the middle of a serious recession with much unemployment and idle resources. These economists believe that Keynes was wrong and that government spending can only move resources from one part of the economy to another. Such theories have significant support in university economics departments but are perhaps a minority view in the broader economic policy community. Still, they have gained considerable traction among Republicans in Congress and the conservative movement in general. After all, they appear to confirm what conservatives have long suspected. Naturally, if these theories are correct, much of the stimulus bill could be called pork.

FOR CRITICAL ANALYSIS

Large-scale initiatives, including government programs, often have consequences that their advocates did not anticipate. What unanticipated consequences could follow from the government's attempts to fight the recession?

FIGURE 11–2: Organization Chart of the Federal Government, 2010

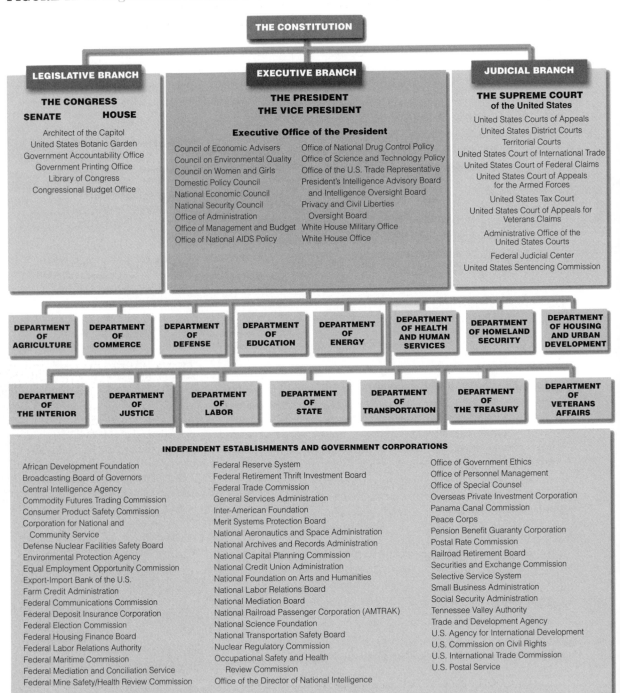

THE CONSTITUTION

LEGISLATIVE BRANCH

THE CONGRESS
SENATE   HOUSE

Architect of the Capitol
United States Botanic Garden
Government Accountability Office
Government Printing Office
Library of Congress
Congressional Budget Office

EXECUTIVE BRANCH

THE PRESIDENT
THE VICE PRESIDENT

Executive Office of the President

Council of Economic Advisers
Council on Environmental Quality
Council on Women and Girls
Domestic Policy Council
National Economic Council
National Security Council
Office of Administration
Office of Management and Budget
Office of National AIDS Policy

Office of National Drug Control Policy
Office of Science and Technology Policy
Office of the U.S. Trade Representative
President's Intelligence Advisory Board
   and Intelligence Oversight Board
Privacy and Civil Liberties
   Oversight Board
White House Military Office
White House Office

JUDICIAL BRANCH

THE SUPREME COURT
of the United States

United States Courts of Appeals
United States District Courts
Territorial Courts
United States Court of International Trade
United States Court of Federal Claims
United States Court of Appeals
   for the Armed Forces
United States Tax Court
United States Court of Appeals for
   Veterans Claims
Administrative Office of the
   United States Courts
Federal Judicial Center
United States Sentencing Commission

| DEPARTMENT OF AGRICULTURE | DEPARTMENT OF COMMERCE | DEPARTMENT OF DEFENSE | DEPARTMENT OF EDUCATION | DEPARTMENT OF ENERGY | DEPARTMENT OF HEALTH AND HUMAN SERVICES | DEPARTMENT OF HOMELAND SECURITY | DEPARTMENT OF HOUSING AND URBAN DEVELOPMENT |

| DEPARTMENT OF THE INTERIOR | DEPARTMENT OF JUSTICE | DEPARTMENT OF LABOR | DEPARTMENT OF STATE | DEPARTMENT OF TRANSPORTATION | DEPARTMENT OF THE TREASURY | DEPARTMENT OF VETERANS AFFAIRS |

INDEPENDENT ESTABLISHMENTS AND GOVERNMENT CORPORATIONS

African Development Foundation
Broadcasting Board of Governors
Central Intelligence Agency
Commodity Futures Trading Commission
Consumer Product Safety Commission
Corporation for National and
   Community Service
Defense Nuclear Facilities Safety Board
Environmental Protection Agency
Equal Employment Opportunity Commission
Export-Import Bank of the U.S.
Farm Credit Administration
Federal Communications Commission
Federal Deposit Insurance Corporation
Federal Election Commission
Federal Housing Finance Board
Federal Labor Relations Authority
Federal Maritime Commission
Federal Mediation and Conciliation Service
Federal Mine Safety/Health Review Commission

Federal Reserve System
Federal Retirement Thrift Investment Board
Federal Trade Commission
General Services Administration
Inter-American Foundation
Merit Systems Protection Board
National Aeronautics and Space Administration
National Archives and Records Administration
National Capital Planning Commission
National Credit Union Administration
National Foundation on Arts and Humanities
National Labor Relations Board
National Mediation Board
National Railroad Passenger Corporation (AMTRAK)
National Science Foundation
National Transportation Safety Board
Nuclear Regulatory Commission
Occupational Safety and Health
   Review Commission
Office of the Director of National Intelligence

Office of Government Ethics
Office of Personnel Management
Office of Special Counsel
Overseas Private Investment Corporation
Panama Canal Commission
Peace Corps
Pension Benefit Guaranty Corporation
Postal Rate Commission
Railroad Retirement Board
Securities and Exchange Commission
Selective Service System
Small Business Administration
Social Security Administration
Tennessee Valley Authority
Trade and Development Agency
U.S. Agency for International Development
U.S. Commission on Civil Rights
U.S. International Trade Commission
U.S. Postal Service

Source: *United States Government Manual, 2008–2009* (Washington, D.C.: U.S. Government Printing Office, 2009), and authors' updates.

Cabinet Departments

The fifteen **cabinet departments** are the major service organizations of the federal government. They can also be described in management terms as **line organizations.** This means that they are directly accountable to the president and are responsible for performing government functions, such as printing money or training troops. These departments were created by Congress when the need for each department arose. The first department to be created was State, and the most recent one was Homeland Security, established in 2003. A president might ask that a new department be created or an old one abolished, but the president has no power to do so without legislative approval from Congress.

Each department is headed by a secretary (except for the Justice Department, which is headed by the attorney general). Each department also has several levels of undersecretaries, assistant secretaries, and other personnel.

Presidents theoretically have considerable control over the cabinet departments, because presidents are able to appoint or fire all of the top officials. Even cabinet departments do not always respond to the president's wishes, though. One reason why presidents are frequently unhappy with their departments is that the entire bureaucratic structure below the top political levels is staffed by permanent employees. Many of these employees are committed to established programs or procedures and resist change. As we can see from Table 11–2 on the following two pages, each cabinet (executive) department employs thousands of individuals, only a handful of whom are under the control of the president. The table also describes some of the functions of each of the departments.

Cabinet Department
One of the fifteen major departments of the executive branch.

Line Organization
In the federal government, an administrative unit that is directly accountable to the president.

Independent Executive Agency
A federal agency that is not part of a cabinet department but reports directly to the president.

Independent Regulatory Agency
An agency outside the major executive departments charged with making and implementing rules and regulations.

Independent Executive Agencies

Independent executive agencies are bureaucratic organizations that are not located within a department but report directly to the president, who appoints their chief officials. When a new federal agency is created—the Environmental Protection Agency, for example—Congress decides where it will be located in the bureaucracy. In recent decades, presidents often have asked that a new organization be kept separate or independent rather than added to an existing department, particularly if a department may be hostile to the agency's creation.

Independent Regulatory Agencies

Typically, an **independent regulatory agency** is responsible for a specific type of public policy. Its function is to make and implement rules and regulations in a particular sphere of action to protect the public interest. The earliest such agency was the Interstate Commerce Commission (ICC), which was established in 1887 when Americans began to seek some form of government control over the rapidly growing business and

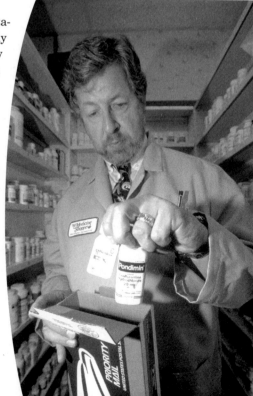

▶ **The Food and Drug Administration** can force pharmacists to remove diet drugs from their shelves if those drugs have dangerous side effects. What type of agency is the FDA? (Photo by Allan Tannenbaum//Time Life Pictures/ Getty Images)

TABLE 11–2: **Executive Departments**

Department and Year Established	Principal Functions	Selected Subagencies
State (1789) (11,368 employees)	Negotiates treaties; develops foreign policy; protects citizens abroad.	Passport Services Office; Bureau of Diplomatic Security; Foreign Service; Bureau of Human Rights and Humanitarian Affairs; Bureau of Consular Affairs.
Treasury (1789) (105,163 employees)	Pays all federal bills; borrows money; collects federal taxes; mints coins and prints paper currency; supervises national banks.	Internal Revenue Service; U.S. Mint.
Interior (1849) (68,609 employees)	Supervises federally owned lands and parks; supervises Native American affairs.	U.S. Fish and Wildlife Service; National Park Service; Bureau of Indian Affairs; Bureau of Land Management.
Justice (1870)* (109,348 employees)	Furnishes legal advice to the president; enforces federal criminal laws; supervises federal prisons.	Federal Bureau of Investigation; Drug Enforcement Administration; Bureau of Prisons.
Agriculture (1889) (96,013 employees)	Provides assistance to farmers and ranchers; conducts agricultural research; works to protect forests.	Soil Conservation Service; Agricultural Research Service; Food Safety and Inspection Service; Federal Crop Insurance Corporation; Commodity Credit Corporation; Forest Service.
Commerce (1913)† (44,302 employees)	Grants patents and trademarks; conducts a national census; monitors the weather; protects the interests of businesses.	Bureau of the Census; Bureau of Economic Analysis; Patent and Trademark Office; National Oceanic and Atmospheric Administration.
Labor (1913)† (15,385 employees)	Administers federal labor laws; promotes the interests of workers.	Occupational Safety and Health Administration; Bureau of Labor Statistics; Employment Standards Administration; Employment and Training Administration.
Defense (1947)‡ (694,456 employees)	Manages the armed forces (army, navy, air force, and marines); operates military bases; is responsible for civil defense.	National Security Agency; Joint Chiefs of Staff; Departments of the Air Force, Navy, Army; Defense Advanced Research Projects Agency; Defense Intelligence Agency; the service academies.

*Formed from the Office of the Attorney General (created in 1789).
†Formed from the Department of Commerce and Labor (created in 1903).
‡Formed from the Department of War (created in 1789) and the Department of the Navy (created in 1798).

industrial sector. This new form of organization, the independent regulatory agency, was supposed to make technical, nonpolitical decisions about rates, profits, and rules that would be for the benefit of all and that did not require congressional legislation. In the years that followed the creation of the ICC, other agencies were formed to regulate communication (the Federal Communications Commission), nuclear power (the Nuclear Regulatory Commission), and other areas. (The ICC was abolished on December 30, 1995.)

The Purpose and Nature of Regulatory Agencies. In practice, regulatory agencies are administered independently of all three branches of government. They were set up because Congress felt it was unable to handle the complexities and technicalities required to carry out specific laws in the public interest. Regulatory agencies and

TABLE 11–2: **Executive Departments (continued)**

Department and Year Established	Principal Functions	Selected Subagencies
Housing and Urban Development (1965) (9,786 employees)	Deals with the nation's housing needs; develops and rehabilitates urban communities; oversees resale of mortgages.	Government National Mortgage Association; Office of Community Planning and Development; Office of Fair Housing and Equal Opportunity.
Transportation (1967) (55,889 employees)	Finances improvements in mass transit; develops and administers programs for highways, railroads, and aviation.	Federal Aviation Administration; Federal Highway Administration; National Highway Traffic Safety Administration; Federal Transit Administration.
Energy (1977) (15,597 employees)	Promotes the conservation of energy and resources; analyzes energy data; conducts research and development.	Federal Energy Regulatory Commission; National Nuclear Security Administration.
Health and Human Services (1979)§ (76,802 employees)	Promotes public health; enforces pure food and drug laws; conducts and sponsors health-related research.	Food and Drug Administration; Public Health Service; Centers for Disease Control and Prevention; National Institutes of Health; Centers for Medicare and Medicaid Services.
Education (1979)§ (4,295 employees)	Coordinates federal programs and policies for education; administers aid to education; promotes educational research.	Office of Special Education and Rehabilitation Service; Office of Elementary and Secondary Education; Office of Postsecondary Education; Office of Vocational and Adult Education; Office of Federal Student Aid.
Veterans Affairs (1988) (284,748 employees)	Promotes the welfare of veterans of the U.S. armed forces.	Veterans Health Administration; Veterans Benefits Administration; National Cemetery Systems.
Homeland Security (2003) (180,244 employees)	Attempts to prevent terrorist attacks within the United States, control America's borders, and minimize the damage from natural disasters.	U.S. Customs and Border Protection; U.S. Coast Guard; Secret Service; Federal Emergency Management Agency; U.S. Citizenship and Immigration Services; U.S. Immigration and Customs Enforcement.

§Formed from the Department of Health, Education, and Welfare (created in 1953).

commissions actually combine some functions of all three branches of government—legislative, executive, and judicial. They are legislative in that they make rules that have the force of law. They are executive in that they provide for the enforcement of those rules. They are judicial in that they decide disputes involving the rules they have made.

Heads of regulatory agencies and members of agency boards or commissions are appointed by the president with the consent of the Senate, although they do not report to the president. When an agency is headed by a board, not an individual, the members of the board cannot, by law, all be from the same political party. Presidents can influence regulatory agency behavior by appointing people of their own parties or individuals who share their political views when vacancies occur, in particular when the chair is vacant. Members may be removed by the president only for causes specified in the law creating the agency.

Capture
The act by which an industry being regulated by a government agency gains direct or indirect control over agency personnel and decision makers.

Government Corporation
An agency of government that administers a quasi-business enterprise. These corporations are used when the activities to be performed are primarily commercial.

Agency Capture. Over the last several decades, some observers have concluded that regulatory agencies, although nominally independent, may in fact not always be so. They contend that many agencies have been **captured** by the very industries and firms that they were supposed to regulate and therefore make decisions based on the interests of the industry, not the general public. The results have been less competition rather than more competition, higher prices rather than lower prices, and less choice rather than more choice for consumers.

Deregulation and Reregulation. During the presidency of Ronald Reagan (1981–1989), some significant deregulation (the removal of regulatory restraints—the opposite of regulation) occurred. Much of it had started under President Jimmy Carter (1977–1981). For example, President Carter appointed a chairperson of the Civil Aeronautics Board (CAB) who gradually eliminated regulation of airline fares and routes. Then, under Reagan, the CAB was eliminated on January 1, 1985.

During the administration of George H. W. Bush (1989–1993), calls for reregulation of many businesses increased. Indeed, during that administration, the Americans with Disabilities Act of 1990, the Civil Rights Act of 1991, and the Clean Air Act Amendments of 1991, all of which increased or changed the regulation of many businesses, were passed. Additionally, the Cable Reregulation Act of 1992 was passed.

Under President Bill Clinton (1993–2001), the Interstate Commerce Commission was eliminated, and the banking and telecommunications industries, along with many other sectors of the economy, were deregulated. At the same time, there was extensive regulation to protect the environment, a trend somewhat attenuated by the George W. Bush administration. After the financial crisis of September 2008, many people saw inadequate regulation of the financial industry as a major cause of the nation's economic difficulties. During President Obama's administration, therefore, reregulation of that industry became a major objective.

Government Corporations

Another form of bureaucratic organization in the United States is the **government corporation.** Although the concept is borrowed from the world of business, there are important differences between public and private corporations.

A private corporation has shareholders (stockholders) who elect a board of directors, who in turn choose the corporate officers, such as president and vice president. When a private corporation makes a profit, it must pay taxes (unless it avoids them through various legal loopholes). It distributes the after-tax profits to shareholders as dividends, plows the profits back into the corporation to make new investments, or both.

A government corporation has a board of directors and managers, but it does not have any stockholders. We cannot buy shares of stock in a government corporation, and if the entity makes a profit, it does not distribute the profit as dividends. Nor does it have to pay taxes on profits; the profits remain in the corporation. The largest and most famous such government corporation is the U.S. Postal Service, with 735,000 employees. Another well-known example is AMTRAK, the passenger railway service, with a staff of close to 19,000.

Bankruptcy. The federal government can also take effective control of a private corporation in a number of different circumstances. One is bankruptcy. When a company files for bankruptcy, it asks a federal judge for relief from its creditors. The judge, operating under bankruptcy laws established by Congress, is ultimately responsible for the fate of the enterprise. When a bank fails, the government has a special interest in protecting customers who have deposited funds with the bank. The failing institution is therefore taken over by the Federal Deposit Insurance Corporation (FDIC), which ensures continuity of service to bank customers.

▲ **When the Federal National Mortgage Association** (Fannie Mae) started to fail, the federal government took over. Who ultimately paid for its losses? (Karen Bleier/AFP/Getty Images)

Government Ownership of Private Enterprises. The federal government can also obtain partial or complete ownership of a private corporation by purchasing its stock. Before 2008, such takeovers were rare, although they occasionally happened. When Continental Illinois, then the nation's seventh-largest bank, failed in 1984, the FDIC wound up in control of the institution for ten years before it could find a buyer. Significantly, the FDIC took over Continental Illinois by purchasing *preferred stock* newly issued by the bank. **Preferred stock** is a special type of investment that typically pays interest but does not let the holders vote for the corporation's board of directors. By purchasing the stock, the FDIC pumped $4.5 billion of new capital—provided by the taxpayers—into the bank, ensuring its solvency.

The Continental Illinois rescue provided a blueprint for the massive bank bailout initiated by Henry Paulson, President Bush's Treasury secretary, in October 2008. Through the end of the year, the Treasury, via the Troubled Asset Relief Program (TARP), bought $178 billion in preferred stock and similar instruments from 214 U.S. financial institutions. The largest businesses received tens of billions of dollars in new capital. For more details on the great bank bailout, see this chapter's *The Politics of Boom and Bust* feature on the following two pages.

An additional type of corporation is the government-sponsored enterprise, a business created by the federal government itself, which then sells part or all of the corporation's stock to private investors. Up until 2008, the leading examples of this kind of company were the Federal Home Loan Mortgage Corporation, known as Freddie Mac, and the Federal National Mortgage Association, commonly known as Fannie Mae. Both of these firms buy mortgages from banks and bundle them into securities that can be sold to investors. When the housing market collapsed, so—eventually—did Freddie Mac and Fannie Mae. Investors had always assumed that the federal government backed up the obligations of the two enterprises, even though the government had never issued an explicit guarantee. On September 7, 2008, the implicit guarantee

Preferred Stock
A special share of ownership in a corporation that typically confers no right to vote for the company's board of directors, but does pay interest.

the politics of Boom and Bust:
What Should the Government Do about Troubled Banks?

To a much greater extent than in earlier recessions, the Great Recession that began in December 2007 had its origins in the financial industry. A "bubble" in housing prices was accompanied by a dramatic relaxation in mortgage lending practices. In the end, banks were apparently willing to write a mortgage for anyone who walked through the door, whether the borrower had the wherewithal to pay back the loan or not. As loans went sour and losses by the financial industry mounted, it became clear that the American mortgage system was by no means the only financial market with a problem. All over the world, far too many institutions had borrowed way too much to make loans that were far too risky. Exactly what would the U.S. government—and other governments around the world—do about this problem?

The Crisis of 2008

By mid-2008, enough bad loans had piled up around the world to raise questions about the solvency of the entire banking system. When panic set in after September 15, banks were no longer certain that the loans they made to other banks would be repaid, and they stopped making such loans. The system began to grind to a halt (see Figure 11–3).

In response, the federal government created the Troubled Asset Relief Program (TARP). This legislation allowed the U.S. Treasury to purchase or insure up to $700 billion of so-called toxic assets, such as nonperforming mortgages and investments based on mortgages. Almost as soon as TARP was passed, Henry Paulson, President Bush's Treasury secretary, concluded that buying up toxic assets would not save the banks. Instead, he used most of the TARP funds to buy preferred stock in banks, thus supplying them with new capital (from the taxpayers) that they could use to cover their losses.

By the time President Obama's Treasury secretary, Timothy Geithner, was in place, only a fraction of the TARP funds remained. Geithner used much of what was left to create a new Public-Private Investment Program (PPIP) that would match private and government funds to buy up toxic assets. A serious problem with PPIP was that even with federal funds involved, there was no guarantee that investors and the banks would agree on what the toxic assets were really worth.

Zombie Banks and Nationalization

Some people thought that the steps taken by Paulson and Geithner were inadequate. These critics feared that instead of making new loans, banks would hoard the capital they received from the government, protecting themselves from future losses. The banks would be "among the living dead," still barely in business but unable to adequately

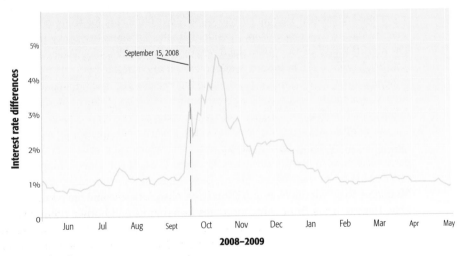

FIGURE 11–3: The Banking Crisis: September 15, 2008, and After
This chart depicts the differences between interbank interest rates and the interest rates on federal government debt. It shows that at the height of the financial crisis following September 15, 2008, banks were charging each other interest rates for three-month loans that were more than 4.5 percentage points above the rate that the U.S. government had to pay for its three-month borrowing. At these rates, few interbank loans actually took place.

September 15, 2008

Interest rate differences

2008–2009

Jun Jul Aug Sept Oct Nov Dec Jan Feb Mar Apr May

Source: Bloomberg.com.

perform the essential function of making new loans. They would be "zombie banks."

The critics argued that to prevent zombie banks, the government should take over troubled institutions completely, that is, **nationalize** them. The government would then settle the bad debts, wipe out the stockholders, and eventually sell the purified institutions back to private investors. Indeed, the government of Sweden nationalized many troubled banks during a difficult period in the 1990s and then successfully put them back into private hands after they recovered.

Nationalization was once a dirty word in American politics, because it referred to socialist plans for permanent government ownership of enterprises. By 2009, nationalization no longer seemed to be out of the question. In essence, the Obama administration effectively nationalized General Motors in the spring of 2009. Federal bureaucrats started issuing instructions to many large banks as soon as they received TARP funds. Although the current nationalizations were supposed to be temporary, matters could work out otherwise. After all, it took the FDIC ten years to find a buyer for Continental Illinois after that bank collapsed. Also, the ability of government bureaucrats to run complex institutions such as banks is certainly open to question.

An even more pertinent question is whether zombie banks were even likely to be a problem. In May 2009, Secretary Geithner announced the results of a "stress test" of the nation's nineteen largest banks. The test suggested that these banks were in better condition than many people had feared. Bankers argued that they were making plenty of loans, although statistics indicated that loan volumes were down. The Great Recession was still on, but the banking crisis was largely over (again, see Figure 11–3 on the next page).

An additional problem was that during the boom years, a large number of nonbank institutions had begun making loans based on borrowed funds. By 2007, nonbanks had about as much outstanding in loans as the entire banking industry. In 2008, this new industry vanished almost completely, and the banks were not large enough to take up the slack.

FOR CRITICAL ANALYSIS

Considering what has happened with the banks since 2009, do Secretary Geithner's steps appear to have been adequate? Would nationalization of troubled banks have been a better solution? Explain your reasoning.

---

became real when Treasury Secretary Paulson placed the two mortgage giants under a federal "conservatorship" and pumped billions in fresh capital—also provided by the taxpayers—into them through purchases of preferred and common stock.

STAFFING THE BUREAUCRACY

There are two categories of bureaucrats: political appointees and civil servants. As noted earlier, the president can make political appointments to most of the top jobs in the federal bureaucracy. The president also can appoint ambassadors to foreign posts. All of the jobs that are considered "political plums" (roughly 1,200) and that usually go to the politically well connected are listed in *Policy and Supporting Positions*, a book published by the Government Printing Office after each presidential election. Informally (and appropriately), this has been called the "Plum Book." The rest of the national government's employees belong to the civil service and obtain their jobs through a much more formal process.

Political Appointees

To fill the positions listed in the Plum Book, the president and the president's advisers solicit suggestions from politicians, businesspersons, and other prominent individuals. Appointments to these positions offer the president a way to pay off outstanding political debts. But the president must also take into consideration such things as the candidate's work experience, intelligence, political affiliations, and personal

Nationalization
The takeover of a business enterprise by the national government. Recently, the word has been used to describe temporary takeovers that are similar to bankruptcy proceedings.

characteristics. Presidents have differed in the importance they attach to appointing women and minorities to plum positions. Presidents often use ambassadorships to reward individuals for their campaign contributions.

The Aristocracy of the Federal Government. Political appointees are in some sense the aristocracy of the federal government. But their powers, although they appear formidable on paper, are often exaggerated. Like the president, a political appointee will occupy her or his position for a comparatively brief time. Political appointees often leave office before the president's term actually ends. In fact, the average term of service for political appointees is less than two years. As a result, most appointees have little background for their positions and may be mere figureheads. Often, they only respond to the paperwork that flows up from below. Additionally, the professional civil servants who make up the permanent civil service may not feel compelled to carry out their current chief's directives quickly, because they know that he or she will not be around for very long.

The Difficulty of Firing Civil Servants. This inertia is compounded by the fact that it is very difficult to discharge civil servants. In recent years, fewer than 0.1 percent of federal employees have been fired for incompetence. Because discharged employees may appeal their dismissals, many months or even years can pass before the issue is resolved conclusively. This occupational rigidity helps to ensure that most political appointees, no matter how competent or driven, will not be able to exert much meaningful influence over their subordinates, let alone implement dramatic changes in the bureaucracy itself.

▼ **A mail clerk** unloads mail from a "sweeper" at the main post office in St. Louis during the Christmas rush. The U.S. Postal Service is a government corporation. The United States enjoys one of the lowest rates for domestic letter postage in the industrialized world—$0.44. The equivalent rate in U.S. dollars is $0.57 in Britain, $0.78 in France, and $0.82 in Japan. (UPI Photo/Bill Greenblatt/Landov)

History of the Federal Civil Service

When the federal government was formed in 1789, it had no career public servants but rather consisted of amateurs who were almost all Federalists. When Thomas Jefferson took over as president, few federal administrative jobs were held by members of his party, so he fired more than one hundred officials and replaced them with his own supporters. Then, for the next twenty-five years, a growing body of federal administrators gained experience and expertise, becoming in the process professional public servants. These administrators stayed in office regardless of who was elected president. The bureaucracy had become a self-maintaining, long-term element within government.

To the Victor Belong the Spoils. When Andrew Jackson took over the White House in 1828, he could not believe how many appointed officials (appointed before he became president, that is) were overtly hostile toward him and his Democratic Party. Because the bureaucracy was reluctant to carry out his programs, Jackson did the obvious: he fired federal officials—more than all his predecessors combined. The **spoils system**—an application of the principle that to the victor belong the spoils—became the standard method of filling federal positions. Whenever a new president was elected from a party different from the party of the previous president, there would be an almost complete turnover in the staffing of the federal government.

The Civil Service Reform Act of 1883. Jackson's spoils system survived for a number of years, but it became increasingly corrupt. In addition, the size of the bureaucracy increased by 300 percent between 1851 and 1881. As the bureaucracy grew larger, the cry for civil service reform became louder. Reformers began to look to the example of several European countries—in particular, Germany, which had established a professional civil service that operated under a **merit system** in which job appointments were based on competitive examinations.

In 1883, the **Pendleton Act**—or **Civil Service Reform Act**—was passed, placing the first limits on the spoils system. The act established the principle of employment on the basis of open, competitive examinations and created the **Civil Service Commission** to administer the personnel service. Only 10 percent of federal employees were covered by the merit system initially. Later laws, amendments, and executive orders, however, increased the coverage to more than 90 percent of federal employees. The effects of these reforms were felt at all levels of government.

The Supreme Court strengthened the civil service system in *Elrod v. Burns*[1] in 1976 and *Branti v. Finkel*[2] in 1980. In those two cases, the Court used the First Amendment to forbid government officials from discharging or threatening to discharge public employees solely for not being supporters of the political party in power unless party affiliation is an appropriate requirement for the position. Additional enhancements to the civil service system were added in *Rutan v. Republican Party of Illinois*[3] in 1990. The Court's ruling effectively prevented the use of partisan political considerations as the basis for hiring, promoting, or transferring most public employees. An exception was permitted, however, for senior policymaking positions, which usually go to officials who will support the programs of the elected leaders.

1. 427 U.S. 347 (1976).
2. 445 U.S. 507 (1980).
3. 497 U.S. 62 (1990).

Spoils System
The awarding of government jobs to political supporters and friends.

Merit System
The selection, retention, and promotion of government employees on the basis of competitive examinations.

Pendleton Act (Civil Service Reform Act)
An act that established the principle of federal government employment based on merit and created the Civil Service Commission to administer the personnel service.

Civil Service Commission
The initial central personnel agency of the national government; created in 1883.

▼ **On September 19, 1881,** President James A. Garfield was assassinated by a disappointed office seeker, Charles J. Guiteau. The long-term effect of this event was to replace the spoils system with a permanent career civil service. This process began with the passage of the Pendleton Act in 1883, which established the Civil Service Commission. (Library of Congress)

"Who do I see to get big government off my back?"

The Civil Service Reform Act of 1978. In 1978, the Civil Service Reform Act abolished the Civil Service Commission and created two new federal agencies to perform its duties. To administer the civil service laws, rules, and regulations, the act created the Office of Personnel Management (OPM). The OPM is empowered to recruit, interview, and test potential government workers and determine who should be hired. The OPM makes recommendations to the individual agencies as to which persons meet the standards (typically, the top three applicants for a position), and the agencies then decide whom to hire. To oversee promotions, employees' rights, and other employment matters, the act created the Merit Systems Protection Board (MSPB). The MSPB evaluates charges of wrongdoing, hears employee appeals from agency decisions, and can order corrective action against agencies and employees.

Federal Employees and Political Campaigns. In 1933, when President Franklin D. Roosevelt set up his New Deal, a virtual army of civil servants was hired to staff the many new agencies that were created. Because the individuals who worked in these agencies owed their jobs to the Democratic Party, it seemed natural for them to campaign for Democratic candidates. The Democrats controlling Congress in the mid-1930s did not object. But in 1938, a coalition of conservative Democrats and Republicans took control of Congress and forced through the Hatch Act—or Political Activities Act—of 1939. The act prohibited federal employees from actively participating in the political management of campaigns. It also forbade the use of federal authority to influence nominations and elections, and outlawed the use of bureaucratic rank to pressure federal employees to make political contributions.

The Hatch Act created a controversy that lasted for decades. Many contended that the act deprived federal employees of their First Amendment freedoms of speech and association. In 1972, a federal district court declared the act unconstitutional. The United States Supreme Court, however, reaffirmed the challenged portion of the act in 1973, stating that the government's interest in preserving a nonpartisan civil service was so great that the prohibitions should remain.[4] Twenty years later, Congress addressed the criticisms of the Hatch Act by passing the Federal Employees Political Activities Act of 1993. This act, which amended the Hatch Act, lessened the harshness of the 1939 act in several ways. Among other things, the 1993 act allowed federal employees to run for office in nonpartisan elections, participate in voter-registration drives, make campaign contributions to political organizations, and campaign for candidates in partisan elections.

---

4. *United States Civil Service Commission v. National Association of Letter Carriers,* 413 U.S. 548 (1973).

MODERN ATTEMPTS AT BUREAUCRATIC REFORM

Government in the Sunshine Act
A law that requires all committee-directed federal agencies to conduct their business regularly in public session.

As long as the federal bureaucracy exists, attempts to make it more open, efficient, and responsive to the needs of U.S. citizens will continue. The most important actual and proposed reforms in the last several decades include sunshine and sunset laws, privatization, incentives for efficiency, and more protection for so-called whistleblowers.

Sunshine Laws before and after 9/11

In 1976, Congress enacted the **Government in the Sunshine Act.** It required for the first time that all multiheaded federal agencies—agencies headed by a committee instead of an individual—hold their meetings regularly in public session. The bill defined *meeting* as almost any gathering, formal or informal, of agency members, including a conference telephone call. The only exceptions to this rule of openness are discussions of matters such as court proceedings or personnel problems, and these exceptions are specifically listed in the bill. Sunshine laws now exist at all levels of government.

Information Disclosure. In 1966, the federal government passed the Freedom of Information Act (FOIA), which required federal government agencies, with certain exceptions, to disclose to individuals information contained in government files. FOIA requests are helpful not just to individuals. Indeed, the major beneficiaries of the act have been news organizations, which have used it to uncover government waste, scandals, and incompetence. For example, reporters learned that much of the $5 billion allocated to help small businesses recover from the effects of the 9/11 terrorist attacks went to companies that did not need such relief, including a South Dakota country radio station, a dog boutique in Utah, an Oregon winery, and a variety of Dunkin' Donuts and Subway franchises.

Curbs on Information Disclosure. Since the terrorist attacks of September 11, 2001, the trend toward government in the sunshine and information disclosure has been reversed at both the federal and state levels. Within weeks after September 11, 2001, federal agencies removed hundreds, if not thousands, of documents from Internet sites, public libraries, and the reading rooms found in various federal government departments. Information contained in some of the documents included diagrams of power plants and pipelines, structural details on dams, and safety plans for chemical plants. The military also immediately began restricting information about its current and planned activities, as did the Federal Bureau

▼ **These members of North Dakota's** Air and Army National Guard helped with anti-flooding efforts in North Dakota. Under what circumstances might National Guard units undertake military activities within the United States? (*The Forum*/Dave Wallis/AP Photo)

Sunset Legislation
Laws requiring that existing programs be reviewed regularly for their effectiveness and be terminated unless specifically extended as a result of these reviews.

Privatization
The replacement of government services with services provided by private firms.

of Investigation. These agencies were concerned that terrorists could make use of this information to plan attacks. It is possible, however, that as soon as the public starts to believe that the threat has lessened, some groups will take state and local governments to court in an effort to increase public access to state and local records by reimposing the sunshine laws that were in effect before 9/11.

Sunset Laws

Potentially, the size and scope of the federal bureaucracy can be controlled through **sunset legislation,** which places government programs on a definite schedule for congressional consideration. Unless Congress specifically reauthorizes a particular federally operated program at the end of a designated period, the program will be terminated automatically—that is, its sun will set.

The idea of sunset legislation was initially suggested by Franklin D. Roosevelt when he created the host of New Deal agencies in the 1930s. His assistant, William O. Douglas, recommended that each agency's charter should include a provision allowing for its termination in ten years. Only an act of Congress could revitalize it. The proposal was never adopted. It was not until 1976 that a state legislature—Colorado's—adopted sunset legislation for state regulatory commissions, giving them a life of six years before their suns set. Today, most states have some type of sunset law.

Privatization or Contracting Out

Another approach to bureaucratic reform is **privatization,** which occurs when government services are replaced by services from the private sector. For example, the government has contracted with private firms to operate prisons. Supporters of privatization argue that some services can be provided more efficiently by the private sector. A similar scheme involves furnishing vouchers to government "clients" in lieu of services. For example, instead of supplying housing, the government could offer vouchers that recipients could use to "pay" for housing in privately owned buildings.

The privatization, or contracting-out, strategy has been most successful on the local level. Some municipalities, for example, have contracted with private companies for such services as trash collection. This approach is not a cure-all, however, because many functions, particularly on the national level, cannot be contracted out in any meaningful way. For example, the federal government could not contract out many of the Defense Department's functions to private firms.

The increase in the amount of government work being contracted out to the private sector has led to significant controversy in recent years. Some have criticized the lack of competitive bidding for many contracts that the government has awarded. Another concern is the perceived lack of federal government oversight over the work done by private contractors. In an attempt to exercise more oversight, in 2007 the government decided to have a study done to evaluate the performance of private contractors. Some media reporters noted the irony of the government's decision to have a private contractor undertake this study.

Incentives for Efficiency and Productivity

An increasing number of state governments are beginning to experiment with schemes to run their operations more efficiently and capably. These schemes focus on maximizing the efficiency and productivity of government workers by providing incentives for improved performance. For example, many governors, mayors, and city administrators are considering ways in which government can be made more entrepreneurial. Some of the most promising measures have included permitting agencies that do not spend their entire budgets to keep some of the difference and rewarding employees with performance-based bonuses.

At the federal level, the Government Performance and Results Act of 1997 was designed to improve efficiency in the federal workforce. The act required all government agencies (except the Central Intelligence Agency) to describe their new goals and establish methods for determining whether those goals have been met. Goals may be broadly crafted (for example, reducing the time it takes to test a new drug before allowing it to be marketed) or narrowly crafted (for example, reducing the number of times a telephone rings before it is answered).

Helping Out the Whistleblowers

The term **whistleblower** as applied to the federal bureaucracy has a special meaning: it is someone who blows the whistle on gross governmental inefficiency or illegal action. Whistleblowers may be clerical workers, managers, or even specialists, such as scientists.

Laws Protecting Whistleblowers. The 1978 Civil Service Reform Act prohibits reprisals against whistleblowers by their superiors, and it set up the Merit Systems Protection Board as part of this protection. Many federal agencies also have toll-free hotlines that employees can use anonymously to report bureaucratic waste and inappropriate behavior. About 35 percent of all calls result in agency action or follow-up.

Further protection for whistleblowers was provided in 1989, when Congress passed the Whistle-Blower Protection Act. That act established an independent agency, the Office of Special Counsel (OSC), to investigate complaints brought by government employees who have been demoted, fired, or otherwise sanctioned for reporting government fraud or waste.

Some state and federal laws encourage employees to blow the whistle on their employers' wrongful actions by providing monetary incentives to the whistleblowers. At the federal level, the False Claims Act of 1986 allows a whistleblower who has disclosed information about a fraud against the U.S. government to receive a monetary award. If the government chooses to prosecute the case and wins, the whistleblower receives between 15 and 25 percent of the proceeds. If the government declines to intervene, the whistleblower can bring a suit on behalf of the government and, if the suit is successful, will receive between 25 and 30 percent of the proceeds.

The Problem Continues. Despite these efforts to help whistleblowers, there is little evidence that potential whistleblowers truly receive much protection. More than 41 percent of the employees who turned to the OSC for assistance in a recent three-year period stated that they were no longer employees of the government agencies on which they had blown the whistle. The government's difficulty in dismissing employees seems to magically disappear when the employee is a whistleblower.

Additionally, in 2006, the United States Supreme Court placed restrictions on lawsuits brought by public workers. *Garcetti v. Ceballos*[5] involved an assistant district attorney, Richard Ceballos, who wrote a memo asking if a county sheriff's deputy had

Whistleblower
In the context of government, someone who brings gross governmental inefficiency or an illegal action to the public's attention.

---

5. 541 U.S. 410 (2006).

Enabling Legislation
A statute enacted by
Congress that authorizes
the creation of an
administrative agency
and specifies the name,
purpose, composition,
functions, and powers of
the agency being created.

lied in a search warrant affidavit. Ceballos claimed that he was subsequently demoted and denied a promotion. The outcome of the case turned on whether an employee has a First Amendment right to criticize an employment-related action. In a close (five-to-four) and controversial decision, the Supreme Court held that when public employees make statements relating to their official duties, they are not speaking as citizens for First Amendment purposes. The Court deemed that when he wrote his memo, Ceballos was speaking as an employee, not a citizen, and was thus subject to his employer's disciplinary actions. The ruling will affect millions of governmental employees. In 2007, the U.S. House of Representatives passed a new whistleblower protection act that would overturn *Garcetti v. Ceballos.* The measure failed to clear the Senate. Protecting whistleblowers was an Obama campaign promise, but his administration has not yet acted on this issue.

BUREAUCRATS AS POLITICIANS AND POLICYMAKERS

Because Congress is unable to oversee the day-to-day administration of its programs, it must delegate certain powers to administrative agencies. Congress delegates power to agencies through **enabling legislation.** For example, the Federal Trade Commission was created by the Federal Trade Commission Act of 1914, the Equal Employment Opportunity Commission was created by the Civil Rights Act of 1964, and the Occupational Safety and Health Administration was created by the Occupational Safety and Health Act of 1970. The enabling legislation generally specifies the name, purpose, composition, functions, and powers of the agency.

In theory, the agencies should put into effect laws passed by Congress. Laws are often drafted in such vague and general terms, however, that they provide relatively little guidance to agency administrators as to how the laws should be implemented. This means that the agencies themselves must decide how best to carry out the wishes of Congress.

The discretion given to administrative agencies is not accidental. Congress has long realized that it lacks the technical expertise and the resources to monitor the implementation of its laws. Hence, the administrative agency is created to fill the gaps. This gap-filling role requires the agency to formulate administrative rules (regulations) to put flesh on the bones of the law. But it also forces the agency itself to become an unelected policymaker.

The Rulemaking Environment

Rulemaking does not occur in a vacuum. Suppose that Congress passes a new air-pollution law. The Environmental Protection Agency (EPA) might decide to implement the new law through a technical regulation on factory emissions. This proposed regulation would be published in the *Federal Register,* a daily government publication, so that interested parties would have an opportunity to comment on it. Individuals and companies that opposed parts or all of the rule might then try to convince the EPA to revise or redraft the regulation. Some parties might try to persuade the agency to withdraw the proposed regulation altogether. In any event, the EPA would consider these comments in drafting the final version of the regulation.

Waiting Periods and Court Challenges. Once the final regulation has been published in the *Federal Register,* there is a sixty-day waiting period before the rule can be enforced. During that period, businesses, individuals, and state and local governments can ask Congress to overturn the regulation. After the sixty-day period has lapsed, the regulation can still be challenged in court by a party having a direct interest in the rule, such as a company that expects to incur significant costs in complying with it. The company could argue that the rule misinterprets the applicable law or goes beyond the agency's statutory purview. An allegation by the company that the EPA made a mistake in judgment probably would not be enough to convince the court to throw out the rule. The company instead would have to demonstrate that the rule itself was "arbitrary and capricious." To meet this standard, the company would have to show that the rule reflected a serious flaw in the EPA's judgment.

Controversies. How agencies implement, administer, and enforce legislation has resulted in controversy. Decisions made by agencies charged with administering the Endangered Species Act have led to protests from farmers, ranchers, and others whose economic interests have been harmed. For example, the government decided to cut off the flow of irrigation water from Klamath Lake in Oregon in the summer of 2001. That action, which affected irrigation water for more than one thousand farmers in Southern Oregon and Northern California, was undertaken to save endangered suckerfish and salmon. It was believed that the lake's water level was so low that further use of the water for irrigation would harm these fish. The results of this decision were devastating for many farmers.

Negotiated Rulemaking

Since the end of World War II (1939–1945), companies, environmentalists, and other special interest groups have challenged government regulations in court. In the 1980s, however, the sheer wastefulness of attempting to regulate through litigation became more and more apparent. Today, a growing number of federal agencies encourage businesses and public-interest groups to become directly involved in drafting regulations. Agencies hope that such participation may help to prevent later courtroom battles over the meaning, applicability, and legal effect of the regulations.

▲ **A northern spotted owl** sits in a tree in a national forest in Oregon. Environmentalists filed a lawsuit in 2003 seeking to stop logging on federal lands in southwestern Oregon, claiming that the U.S. Fish and Wildlife Service had ignored the need to protect critical habitat for the owl, a threatened species. How should we balance the desire to protect rare species with our need for natural resources? (AP Photo/Don Ryan)

Congress formally approved such a process, which is called *negotiated rulemaking,* in the Negotiated Rulemaking Act of 1990. The act authorizes agencies to allow those who will be affected by a new rule to participate in the rule-drafting process. If an agency chooses to engage in negotiated rulemaking, it must publish in the *Federal Register* the subject and scope of the rule to be developed, the names of parties that will be affected significantly by the rule, and other information. Representatives of the affected groups and other interested parties then may apply to be members of the negotiating committee. The agency is represented on the committee, but a neutral

Iron Triangle
A three-way alliance
among legislators,
bureaucrats, and interest
groups to make or
preserve policies that
benefit their respective
interests.

third party (not the agency) presides over the proceedings. Once the committee members have reached agreement on the terms of the proposed rule, a notice is published in the *Federal Register,* followed by a period for comments by any person or organization interested in the proposed rule. Negotiated rulemaking often is conducted under the condition that the participants promise not to challenge in court the outcome of any agreement to which they were a party.

Bureaucrats as Policymakers

Theories of public administration once assumed that bureaucrats do not make policy decisions but only implement the laws and policies promulgated by the president and legislative bodies. Many people continue to make this assumption. A more realistic view, which is now held by most bureaucrats and elected officials, is that the agencies and departments of government play important roles in policymaking. As we have seen, many government rules, regulations, and programs are in fact initiated by the bureaucracy, based on its expertise and scientific studies. How a law passed by Congress eventually is translated into concrete action—from the forms to be filled out to decisions about who gets the benefits—usually is determined within each agency or department. Even the evaluation of whether a policy has achieved its purpose usually is based on studies that are commissioned and interpreted by the agency administering the program.

The bureaucracy's policymaking role often has been depicted by what traditionally has been called the "iron triangle." Recently, the concept of an "issue network" has been viewed as a more accurate description of the policymaking process.

Iron Triangles. In the past, scholars often described the bureaucracy's role in the policymaking process by using the concept of an **iron triangle**—a three-way alliance among legislators in Congress, bureaucrats, and interest groups. Consider as an example the development of agricultural policy. Congress, as one component of the triangle, includes two major committees concerned with agricultural policy, the House Committee on Agriculture and the Senate Committee on Agriculture, Nutrition, and Forestry. The Department of Agriculture, the second component of the triangle, has almost 100,000 employees, plus thousands of contractors and consultants. Agricultural interest groups, the third component of the triangle, include many large and powerful associations, such as the American Farm Bureau Federation, the National Cattlemen's Beef Association, and the Corn Growers Association. These three components of the iron triangle work together, formally or informally, to create policy.

For example, the various agricultural interest groups lobby Congress to develop policies that benefit their groups' interests. Members of Congress cannot afford to ignore the wishes of interest groups because those groups are potential sources of voter support and campaign contributions. The legislators in Congress also work closely with the Department of Agriculture, which, in implementing a policy, can develop rules that benefit—or at least do not hurt—certain industries or groups. The Department of Agriculture, in turn, supports policies that enhance the department's budget and powers. In this way, according to theory, agricultural policy is created that benefits all three components of the iron triangle.

Issue Networks. To be sure, the preceding discussion presents a much simplified picture of how the iron triangle works. With the growth in the complexity of government, policymaking also has become more complicated. The bureaucracy is larger, Congress has more committees and subcommittees, and interest groups are more powerful than ever. Although iron triangles still exist, often they are inadequate as descriptions of how policy is actually made. Frequently, different interest groups concerned about a certain area of policy have conflicting demands, which makes agency decision making difficult. Additionally, during periods of divided government, departments are pressured by the president to take one approach and by Congress to take another.

Many scholars now use the term *issue network* to describe the policymaking process. An **issue network** consists of individuals or organizations that support a particular policy position on the environment, taxation, consumer safety, or some other issue. Typically, an issue network includes legislators and/or their staff members, interest group leaders, bureaucrats, scholars and other experts, and representatives from the media. Members of a particular issue network work together to influence the president, members of Congress, administrative agencies, and the courts to affect public policy on a specific issue. Each policy issue may involve conflicting positions taken by two or more issue networks.

Issue Network
A group of individuals or organizations—which may consist of legislators and legislative staff members, interest group leaders, bureaucrats, scholars and other experts, and media representatives—that supports a particular policy position on a given issue.

CONGRESSIONAL CONTROL OF THE BUREAUCRACY

Many political pundits doubt whether Congress can meaningfully control the federal bureaucracy. These commentators forget that Congress specifies in an agency's enabling legislation the powers of the agency and the parameters within which it can operate. Additionally, Congress has "the power of the purse" and theoretically could refuse to authorize or appropriate funds for a particular agency (see the discussion of the budgeting process in Chapter 9). Whether Congress would actually take such a drastic measure would depend on the circumstances. It is clear, however, that Congress does have the legal authority to decide whether or not to fund administrative agencies.

Congress also can exercise oversight over agencies through investigations and hearings. Congressional committees conduct investigations and hold hearings to oversee an agency's actions, reviewing them to ensure compliance with congressional intentions. The agency's officers and employees can be ordered to testify before a committee about the details of an action. Through these oversight activities, especially in the questions and comments of members of the House or Senate during the hearings, Congress indicates its positions on specific programs and issues.

Congress can ask the Government Accountability Office (GAO) to investigate particular agency actions as well. The Congressional Budget Office (CBO) also conducts oversight studies. The results of a GAO or CBO study may encourage Congress to hold further hearings or make changes in the law. Even if a law is not changed explicitly by Congress, however, the views expressed in any investigations and hearings are taken seriously by agency officials, who often act on those views.

In 1996, Congress passed the Congressional Review Act. The act created special procedures that can be employed to express congressional disapproval of particular agency actions. These procedures have rarely been used, however. Since the act's passage, the executive branch has issued more than fifteen thousand regulations. Yet only eight resolutions of disapproval have been introduced, and none of them were passed by either chamber.

making a difference

WHAT THE GOVERNMENT KNOWS ABOUT YOU

The federal government collects billions of pieces of information on tens of millions of Americans each year. These data are stored in files and sometimes are exchanged among agencies. You are probably the subject of several federal records (for example, in the Social Security Administration; the Internal Revenue Service; and, if you are a male, the Selective Service).

Why Should You Care? Verifying the information that the government has about you can be important. On several occasions, the records of two people with similar names have become confused. Sometimes innocent persons have had the criminal records of other persons erroneously inserted into their files. Such disasters are not always caused by bureaucratic error. One of the most common crimes in today's world is "identity theft," in which one person makes use of another individual's personal identifiers (such as a Social Security number) to commit fraud. In some instances, identity thieves have been arrested or even jailed under someone else's name.

What Can You Do? The 1966 Freedom of Information Act requires that the federal government release, at your request, any identifiable information it has about you or about any other subject. Ten categories of material are exempted, however (classified material, confidential material on trade secrets, internal personnel rules, personal medical files, and the like). To request material, write directly to the Freedom of Information Act officer at the agency in question (say, the Department of Education). You must have a relatively specific idea about the document or information you want to obtain.

A second law, the Privacy Act of 1974, gives you access specifically to information the government may have collected about you. This law allows you to review records on file with federal agencies and to check those records for possible inaccuracies.

If you want to look at any records or find out if an agency has a record on you, write to the agency head or Privacy Act officer, and address your letter to the specific agency. State that "under the provisions of the Privacy Act of 1974, 5 U.S.C. 522a, I hereby request a copy of (or access to) _____." Then describe the record that you wish to investigate.

The American Civil Liberties Union (ACLU) has published a manual, called *Your Right to Government Information,* that guides you through the steps of obtaining information from the federal government. You can order it online at the following Web site:

www.aclufl.org

▲ **The home page** of the American Civil Liberties Union provides access to its analysis of many court decisions. (Screen capture from www.aclu.org)

key terms

chapter summary

1 Bureaucracies are hierarchical organizations characterized by division of labor and extensive procedural rules. Bureaucracy is the primary form of organization of most major corporations and universities, as well as governments.

2 Since the founding of the United States, the federal bureaucracy has grown from a few employees to about 2.8 million (excluding the military). Federal, state, and local employees together make up more than 15 percent of the nation's civilian labor force. The federal bureaucracy consists of fifteen cabinet departments, as well as a large number of independent executive agencies, independent regulatory agencies, and government corporations. These entities enjoy varying degrees of autonomy, visibility, and political support.

3 A federal bureaucracy of career civil servants was formed during Thomas Jefferson's presidency. Andrew Jackson implemented a spoils system through which he appointed his own political supporters. A civil service based on professionalism and merit was the goal of the Civil Service Reform Act of 1883. Concerns that the civil service be freed from the pressures of politics prompted the passage of the Hatch Act in 1939. The Civil Service Reform Act of 1978 made significant changes in the administration of the civil service.

4 There have been many attempts to make the federal bureaucracy more open, efficient, and responsive to the needs of U.S. citizens. The most important reforms have included sunshine and sunset laws, privatization, strategies to provide incentives for increased productivity and efficiency, and protection for whistleblowers.

5 Congress delegates much of its authority to federal agencies when it creates new laws. The bureaucrats who run these agencies may become important policymakers, because Congress has neither the time nor the technical expertise to oversee the administration of its laws. The agency rulemaking process begins when a proposed regulation is published. A comment period follows, during which interested parties may offer suggestions for changes. Because companies and other organizations have challenged many regulations in court, federal agencies now are authorized to allow parties that will be affected by new regulations to participate in the rule-drafting process.

6 Congress exerts ultimate control over all federal agencies, because it controls the federal government's purse strings. It also establishes the general guidelines by which regulatory agencies must abide. The appropriations process may provide a way to send messages of approval or disapproval to particular agencies, as do congressional hearings and investigations of agency actions.

QUESTIONS FOR

discussion**and**analysis

1 Consider the paradox described at the beginning of this chapter: the public believes strongly in small government but endorses almost all the activities that government actually performs. Why do you think Americans hold such contradictory beliefs?

2 Some people have proposed that the public ought to be allowed to grade federal bureaucracies. How could such a grading system be organized? How could we avoid the danger that the process would be dominated by special interests?

3 If Congress tried to make civil servants easier to fire, what political forces might stand in the way?

4 The government's response to the disaster caused by Hurricane Katrina in 2005 was widely criticized. Why might the various levels of government have failed in this crisis? What could they have done instead?

5 The U.S. attorney general, head of the Justice Department, is appointed by the president and is frequently the president's close political ally. Should the attorney general and other U.S. attorneys be appointed on a partisan basis? Why or why not?

helpful online **Resources**

CONNECTING TO AMERICAN GOVERNMENT AND POLITICS

For detailed information on where the federal budget goes, see:

www.usgovernmentspending.com

The *United States Government Manual* describes the origins, purposes, and administrators of every federal department and agency. It is available at:

www.gpoaccess.gov/gmanual

The "Plum Book," which lists the bureaucratic positions that can be filled by presidential appointment, is online at:

www.gpoaccess.gov/plumbook

a**special**WebSite

FOR YOUR TEXT

Go to this book's special Web site at academic.cengage.com/polisci/Schmidt/Brief6e. Choose "For Students." Then click on Chapter 11, where you will find an online quiz and other helpful study aids. If your professor is using CengageNOW: *American Government and Politics Today, Brief Edition*, log in and go to Chapter 11 for additional online study aids.

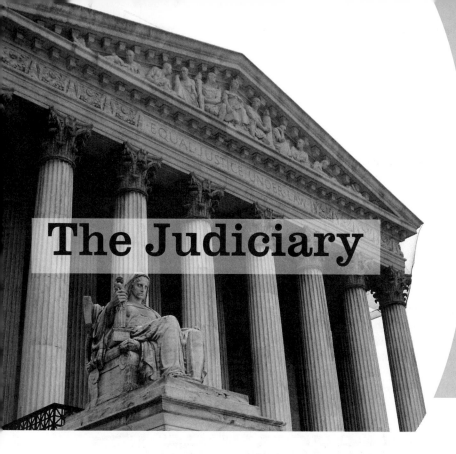

12

The Judiciary

As Alexis de Tocqueville, a French commentator on American society in the 1800s, noted, "scarcely any political question arises in the United States that is not resolved, sooner or later, into a judicial question."[1] Our judiciary forms part of our political process. The instant that judges interpret the law, they become actors in the political arena—policymakers working within a political institution. The most important political force within our judiciary is the United States Supreme Court. Yet the justices of the Supreme Court are not elected. Rather, they are appointed by the president and confirmed by the Senate, as are all other federal court judges.

How do courts make policy? Why do the federal courts play such an important role in American government? The answers to these questions lie, in part, in our colonial heritage. Most of American law is based on the English system, particularly the English *common law tradition.* In that tradition, the decisions made by judges constitute an important source of law. We open this chapter with an examination of this tradition and of the various sources of American law. We then look at the federal court system—its organization, how its judges are selected, how these judges affect policy, and how they are restrained by our system of checks and balances.

---

1. Alexis de Tocqueville, *Democracy in America* (New York: Harper & Row, 1966), p. 248.

Common Law
Judge-made law that originated in England from decisions shaped according to prevailing custom. Decisions were applied to similar situations and gradually became common to the nation.

Precedent
A court rule bearing on subsequent legal decisions in similar cases. Judges rely on precedents in deciding cases.

Stare Decisis
To stand on decided cases; the judicial policy of following precedents established by past decisions.

THE COMMON LAW TRADITION

In 1066, the Normans conquered England, and William the Conqueror and his successors began the process of unifying the country under their rule. One of the ways in which they did this was to establish king's courts. Before the conquest, disputes had been settled according to local custom. The king's courts sought to establish a common, or uniform, set of rules for the whole country. As the number of courts and cases increased, portions of the most important decisions of each year were gathered together and recorded in Year Books. Judges settling disputes similar to ones that had been decided before used the Year Books as the basis for their decisions. If a case was unique, judges had to create new rules, but they based their decisions on the general principles suggested by earlier cases. The body of judge-made law that developed under this system is still used today and is known as the **common law.**

The practice of deciding new cases with reference to former decisions—that is, according to **precedent**—became a cornerstone of the English and American judicial systems and is embodied in the doctrine of ***stare decisis*** (pronounced *ster*-ay dih-*si*-ses), a Latin phrase that means "to stand on decided cases." The doctrine of *stare decisis* obligates judges to follow the precedents set previously by their own courts or by higher courts that have authority over them.

For example, a lower state court in California would be obligated to follow a precedent set by the California Supreme Court. That lower court, however, would not be obligated to follow a precedent set by the supreme court of another state, because each state court system is independent. Of course, when the United States Supreme Court decides an issue, all of the nation's other courts are obligated to abide by the Court's decision—because the Supreme Court is the highest court in the land.

The doctrine of *stare decisis* provides a basis for judicial decision making in all countries that have common law systems. Today, the United States, Britain, and several dozen other countries have common law systems. Generally, those countries that were once colonies of Britain, including Australia, Canada, India, New Zealand, and others, have retained their English common law heritage.

SOURCES OF AMERICAN LAW

The body of American law includes the federal and state constitutions, statutes passed by legislative bodies, administrative law, and case law—the legal principles expressed in court decisions.

Constitutions

The constitutions of the federal government and the states set forth the general organization, powers, and limits of government. The U.S. Constitution is the supreme law of the land. A law in violation of the Constitution, no matter what its source, may be declared unconstitutional and thereafter cannot be enforced. Similarly, the state constitutions are supreme within their respective borders (unless they conflict with the U.S. Constitution or federal laws and treaties made in accordance with it). The Constitution thus defines the political playing field on which state and federal powers are reconciled.

Statutes and Administrative Regulations

Although the English common law provides the basis for both our civil and criminal legal systems, statutes (laws enacted by legislatures) have become increasingly important in defining the rights and obligations of individuals. Federal statutes may relate to any subject that is a concern of the federal government and may apply to areas ranging from hazardous waste to federal taxation. State statutes include criminal codes, commercial laws, and laws covering a variety of other matters. Cities, counties, and other local political bodies also pass statutes, which are called *ordinances.* These ordinances may deal with such issues as property zoning proposals and public safety. Rules and regulations issued by administrative agencies are another source of law. Today, much of the work of the courts consists of interpreting these laws and regulations and applying them to the specific circumstances of the cases that come before the courts.

Case Law

Because we have a common law tradition, in which the doctrine of *stare decisis* plays an important role, the decisions rendered by the courts also form an important body of law, collectively referred to as **case law.** Case law includes judicial interpretations of common law principles and doctrines, as well as interpretations of constitutional provisions, statutes, and administrative agency regulations. As you learned in previous chapters, it is up to the courts—and ultimately, if necessary, the Supreme Court—to decide what a constitutional provision or a statutory phrase means. In doing so, the courts, in effect, establish law. (We will discuss this policymaking function of the courts in more detail later in the chapter.)

THE FEDERAL COURT SYSTEM

The United States has a dual court system. There are state courts and federal courts. Each of the fifty states, as well as the District of Columbia, has its own independent system of courts. This means that there are fifty-two court systems in total. Here we focus on the federal courts.

Basic Judicial Requirements

In any court system, state or federal, certain requirements must be met before a case can be brought before a court. Two important requirements are *jurisdiction* and *standing to sue.*

Jurisdiction. A state court can exercise **jurisdiction** (the authority of the court to hear and decide a case) over the residents of a particular geographic area, such as a county or district. A state's highest court, or supreme court, has jurisdictional authority over all residents within the state. Because the Constitution established a federal government with limited powers, federal jurisdiction is also limited.

Article III, Section 1, of the U.S. Constitution limits the jurisdiction of the federal courts to cases that involve either a federal question or diversity of citizenship. A **federal question** arises when a case is based, at least in part, on the U.S. Constitution, a treaty, or a federal law. A person who claims that her or his rights

Case Law
Judicial interpretations of common law principles and doctrines, as well as interpretations of constitutional law, statutory law, and administrative law.

Jurisdiction
The authority of a court to decide certain cases. Not all courts have the authority to decide all cases. Where a case arises and what its subject matter is are two jurisdictional issues.

Federal Question
A question that has to do with the U.S. Constitution, acts of Congress, or treaties. A federal question provides a basis for federal jurisdiction.

Diversity of Citizenship
The condition that exists when the parties to a lawsuit are from different states or when the suit involves a U.S. citizen and a government or citizen of a foreign country. Diversity of citizenship can provide a basis for federal jurisdiction.

Justiciable Controversy
A controversy that is real and substantial, as opposed to hypothetical or academic.

Litigate
To engage in a legal proceeding or seek relief in a court of law; to carry on a lawsuit.

Amicus Curiae Brief
A brief (a document containing a legal argument supporting a desired outcome in a particular case) filed by a third party, or *amicus curiae* (Latin for "friend of the court"), who is not directly involved in the litigation but who has an interest in the outcome of the case.

Class-Action Suit
A lawsuit filed by an individual seeking damages for "all persons similarly situated."

under the Constitution, such as the right to free speech, have been violated could bring a case in a federal court. **Diversity of citizenship** exists when the parties to a lawsuit are from different states or (more rarely) when the suit involves a U.S. citizen and a government or citizen of a foreign country. The amount in controversy must be at least $75,000 before a federal court can take jurisdiction in a diversity case, however.

Standing to Sue. Another basic judicial requirement is *standing to sue,* or a sufficient "stake" in a matter to justify bringing suit. The party bringing a lawsuit must have suffered a harm, or have been threatened by a harm, as a result of the action that led to the dispute in question. Standing to sue also requires that the controversy at issue be a justiciable controversy. A **justiciable controversy** is a controversy that is real and substantial, as opposed to hypothetical or academic. In other words, a court will not give advisory opinions on hypothetical questions.

Parties to Lawsuits

In most lawsuits, the parties are the *plaintiff* (the person or organization that initiates the lawsuit) and the *defendant* (the person or organization against whom the lawsuit is brought). There may be a number of plaintiffs and defendants in a single lawsuit. In the last several decades, many lawsuits have been brought by interest groups (see Chapter 7). Interest groups play an important role in our judicial system, because they **litigate**—bring to trial—or assist in litigating most cases of racial or gender-based discrimination, virtually all civil liberties cases, and more than one-third of the cases involving business matters. Interest groups also file *amicus curiae* (pronounced ah-*mee*-kous *kur*-ee-eye) **briefs,** or "friend of the court" briefs, in more than 50 percent of these kinds of cases.

Sometimes interest groups or other plaintiffs will bring a **class-action suit,** in which whatever the court decides will affect all members of a class similarly situated (such as users of a particular product manufactured by the defendant in the lawsuit). The strategy of class-action lawsuits was pioneered by such groups as the National Association for the Advancement of Colored People (NAACP), the Legal Defense Fund, and the Sierra Club, whose leaders believed that the courts would offer a more sympathetic forum for their views than would Congress.

Procedural Rules

Both the federal and the state courts have established procedural rules that shape the litigation process. These rules are designed to protect the rights and interests of the parties, to ensure that the litigation proceeds in a fair and orderly manner, and to identify the issues that must be decided by the court—thus saving court time and expense. Court decisions may also apply to trial procedures. For example, the Supreme Court has held that the parties' attorneys cannot discriminate against prospective jurors on the basis of race or gender. Some lower courts have also held that people cannot be excluded from juries because of their sexual orientation or religion.

The parties must comply with procedural rules and with any orders given by the judge during the course of the litigation. When a party does not follow a court's order, the court can cite that person for contempt. A party who commits civil contempt (failing to comply with a court's order for the benefit of another party to the proceeding) can be taken into custody, fined, or both, until the party complies with the court's order. A party who commits *criminal* contempt (obstructing the administration of justice or bringing the court into disrespect) also can be taken into custody and fined but cannot avoid punishment by complying with a previous order.

Types of Federal Courts

As you can see in Figure 12–1, the federal court system is basically a three-tiered model consisting of (1) U.S. district courts and various specialized courts of limited jurisdiction (not all of the latter are shown in the figure), (2) intermediate U.S. courts of appeals, and (3) the United States Supreme Court.

U.S. District Courts. The U.S. district courts are trial courts. **Trial courts** are what their name implies—courts in which trials are held and testimony is taken. The U.S. district courts are courts of **general jurisdiction,** meaning that they can hear cases involving a broad array of issues. Federal cases involving most matters typically are heard in district courts. The other courts on the lower tier of the model shown in Figure 12–1 are courts of **limited jurisdiction,** meaning that they can try cases involving only certain types of claims, such as tax claims or bankruptcy petitions.

There is at least one federal district court in every state. The number of judicial districts can vary over time owing to population changes and corresponding caseloads. Today, there are ninety-four federal judicial districts. A party who is dissatisfied with the decision of a district court can appeal the case to the appropriate U.S. court of appeals, or federal **appellate court.** Figure 12–2 on the next page shows the jurisdictional boundaries of the district courts (which are state boundaries, unless otherwise indicated by dotted lines within a state) and of the U.S. courts of appeals.

U.S. Courts of Appeals. There are thirteen U.S. courts of appeals—also referred to as U.S. circuit courts of appeals. Twelve of these courts, including the U.S. Court of Appeals for the District of Columbia, hear appeals from the federal district courts located within their respective judicial circuits (geographic areas over which they

Trial Court
The court in which most cases begin.

General Jurisdiction
Exists when a court's authority to hear cases is not significantly restricted. A court of general jurisdiction normally can hear a broad range of cases.

Limited Jurisdiction
Exists when a court's authority to hear cases is restricted to certain types of claims, such as tax claims or bankruptcy petitions.

Appellate Court
A court having jurisdiction to review cases and issues that were originally tried in lower courts.

FIGURE 12–1: The Federal Court System

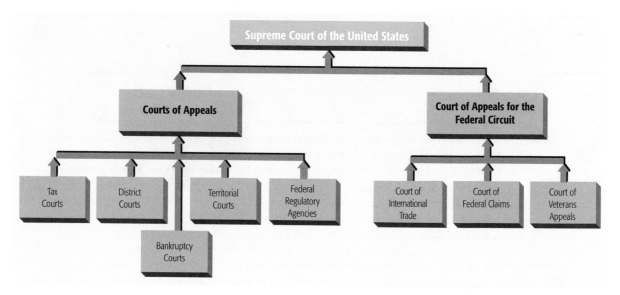

exercise jurisdiction). The Court of Appeals for the Thirteenth Circuit, called the Federal Circuit, has national appellate jurisdiction over certain types of cases, such as cases involving patent law and those in which the U.S. government is a defendant.

Note that when an appellate court reviews a case decided in a district court, the appellate court does not conduct another trial. Rather, a panel of three or more judges reviews the record of the case on appeal, which includes a transcript of the trial proceedings, and determines whether the trial court committed an error. Usually, appellate courts look not at questions of *fact* (such as whether a party did commit a certain action, such as burning a flag) but at questions of *law* (such as whether the act of flag-burning is a form of speech protected by the First Amendment to the Constitution). An appellate court will challenge a trial court's finding of fact only when the finding is clearly contrary to the evidence presented at trial or when there is no evidence to support the finding.

A party can petition the United States Supreme Court to review an appellate court's decision. The likelihood that the Supreme Court will grant the petition is slim, however, because the Court reviews only a very few of the cases decided by the appellate courts. This means that decisions made by appellate courts usually are final.

FIGURE 12–2: Geographic Boundaries of Federal District Courts and Circuit Courts of Appeals

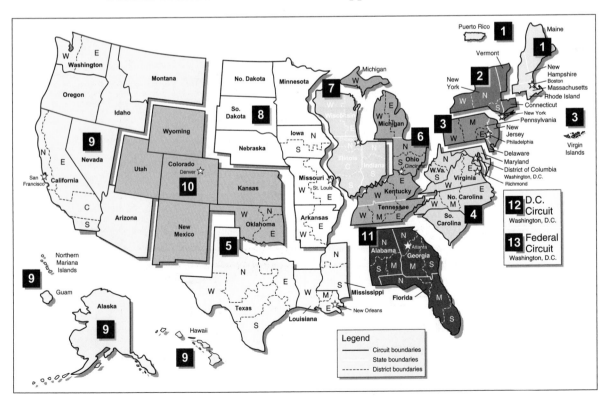

Source: Administrative Office of the United States Courts.

The United States Supreme Court. The highest level of the three-tiered model of the federal court system is the United States Supreme Court. Although the Supreme Court can exercise original jurisdiction (that is, act as a trial court) in certain cases, such as those affecting foreign diplomats and those in which a state is a party, most of its work is as an appellate court. The Court hears appeals not only from the federal appellate courts but also from the highest state courts. Note, though, that the United States Supreme Court can review a state supreme court decision only if a federal question is involved. Because of its importance in the federal court system, we look more closely at the Supreme Court later in this chapter.

Federal Courts and the War on Terrorism

As noted, the federal court system includes a variety of trial courts of limited jurisdiction, dealing with matters such as tax claims or international trade. The government's attempts to combat terrorism have drawn attention to certain specialized courts that meet in secret. We look next at these courts, as well as at the role of the federal courts with respect to the detainees held at the U.S. naval base in Guantánamo Bay, Cuba.

The FISA Court. The federal government created the first secret court in 1978. In that year, Congress passed the Foreign Intelligence Surveillance Act (FISA), which established a court to hear requests for warrants for the surveillance of suspected spies. Officials can request a warrant without having to reveal to the suspect or to the public the information used to justify the warrant. The FISA court has approved almost all of the thousands of requests for warrants that officials have submitted. There is no public access to the court's proceedings or records.

"Do you ever have one of those days when everything seems un-Constitutional?"

In the aftermath of the terrorist attacks on September 11, 2001, the Bush administration expanded the powers of the FISA court. Previously, the FISA had allowed secret domestic surveillance only if the purpose was to combat foreign intelligence gathering by foreign powers. Amendments to the FISA enacted after 9/11 changed this wording to "a significant purpose"—meaning that warrants may now be requested to obtain evidence that can be used in criminal trials. Additionally, the court has the authority to approve physical as well as electronic searches, which means that officials may search a suspect's property without obtaining a warrant in open court and without notifying the subject.

Alien "Removal Courts." Suspects' rights have been reduced in some other courts as well. In the wake of the Oklahoma City bombing in 1995 (in which 168 people died), Congress passed the Anti-Terrorism and Effective Death Penalty Act of 1996. The act included a provision creating an alien "removal court" to hear evidence against suspected "alien terrorists." The judges in this court rule on whether there is probable cause for deportation. If so, a public deportation proceeding is held in a U.S. district court. The prosecution does not need to follow procedures that normally apply in criminal cases. In addition, the defendant cannot see the evidence that the prosecution used to secure the hearing.

The Federal Courts and Enemy Combatants. After the 9/11 attacks, the U.S. military took custody of hundreds of suspected terrorists and held them at Guantánamo Bay, Cuba. The detainees were classified as *enemy combatants,* and, according to the Bush administration, they could be held indefinitely. The administration also claimed that because the detainees were not prisoners of war, they were not protected under international laws governing the treatment of prisoners of war.

Since that time, the treatment of the prisoners at Guantánamo has been a source of ongoing controversy. The United States Supreme Court held, first in 2004 and then in 2006, that the Bush administration's treatment of these detainees violated the U.S. Constitution.[2]

In response to the Court's 2006 decision, Congress passed the Military Commissions Act of 2006. The act eliminated federal court jurisdiction over challenges by noncitizens held as enemy combatants based on *habeas corpus,* the right of a detained person to challenge the legality of his or her detention before a judge. Prisoners' challenges to their detention would be reviewed by military commissions, with a limited right of appeal to the federal courts. A federal appellate court held that the act was constitutional, and the case was then

▼ **Justice Clarence Thomas with his clerks.** Where does the United States Supreme Court fit in terms of the hierarchy of the federal court system in this country?
(David Hume Kennerly/Getty Images)

2. *Hamdi v. Rumsfeld,* 542 U.S. 507 (2004); *Hamdan v. Rumsfeld,* 548 U.S. 557 (2006).

appealed to the United States Supreme Court. In June 2008, the Court ruled that the act's provisions restricting the federal courts' jurisdictional authority over detainees' *habeas corpus* challenges were illegal.[3] The decision gives Guantánamo detainees the right to challenge their detention in federal civil courts. The close (five-to-four) decision dealt a decisive blow to the Bush administration's detention policies.

In 2009, the Obama administration abolished the category of *enemy combatant* and promised to close the Guantánamo prison. President Obama did not, however, move to try all of the detainees in U.S. civilian courts. Some of the prisoners are to be tried in a revived system of military commissions, which this time should have better legal protections for the accused than were available under the Bush program.

THE SUPREME COURT AT WORK

The Supreme Court begins its regular annual term on the first Monday in October and usually adjourns in late June or early July of the next year. Special sessions may be held after the regular term ends, but only a few cases are decided in this way. More commonly, cases are carried over until the next regular session.

Of the total number of cases that are decided each year in U.S. courts, those reviewed by the Supreme Court represent less than one in four thousand. Included in these, however, are decisions that profoundly affect our lives. In recent years, the United States Supreme Court has decided issues involving capital punishment, the rights of criminal suspects, affirmative action programs, religious freedom, assisted suicide, abortion, busing, term limits for congresspersons, sexual harassment, pornography, states' rights, limits on federal jurisdiction, and many other matters with significant consequences for the nation.

Because the Supreme Court exercises a great deal of discretion over the types of cases it hears, it can influence the nation's policies by issuing decisions in some types of cases and refusing to hear appeals in others, thereby allowing lower court decisions to stand. Indeed, the fact that George W. Bush assumed the presidency in 2001 instead of Al Gore, his Democratic opponent, was largely due to a Supreme Court decision to review a Florida court's ruling. The Supreme Court reversed the Florida court's order to recount manually the votes in selected Florida counties—a decision that effectively handed the presidency to Bush.[4]

Which Cases Reach the Supreme Court?

Many people are surprised to learn that in a typical case, there is no absolute right of appeal to the United States Supreme Court. The Court's appellate jurisdiction is almost entirely discretionary—the Court chooses which cases it will decide. The justices never explain their reasons for hearing certain cases and not others, so it is difficult to predict which case or type of case the Court might select.

Factors That Bear on the Decision. A number of factors bear on the decision to accept a case. If a legal question has been decided differently by various lower courts, it may need resolution by the highest court. A ruling may be necessary if a lower court's decision conflicts with an existing Supreme Court ruling. In general, the Court

3. *Boumediene v. Bush,* 128 S.Ct. 2229 (2008).
4. *Bush v. Gore,* 531 U.S. 98 (2000).

Writ of *Certiorari*

An order issued by a higher court to a lower court to send up the record of a case for review.

Rule of Four

A United States Supreme Court procedure by which four justices must vote to grant a petition for review if a case is to come before the full court.

Oral Arguments

The arguments presented in person by attorneys to an appellate court. Each attorney presents reasons to the court why the court should rule in her or his client's favor.

Opinion

The statement by a judge or a court of the decision reached in a case. The opinion sets forth the applicable law and details the reasoning on which the ruling was based.

Affirm

To declare that a court ruling is valid and must stand.

Reverse

To annul or make void a court ruling on account of some error or irregularity.

Remand

To send a case back to the court that originally heard it.

considers whether the issue could have significance beyond the parties to the dispute. Another factor is whether the solicitor general is pressuring the Court to take a case. The solicitor general, a high-ranking presidential appointee within the Justice Department, represents the national government before the Supreme Court and promotes presidential policies in the federal courts. He or she decides what cases the government should request the Supreme Court to review and what position the government should take in cases before the Court.

Granting Petitions for Review. If the Court decides to grant a petition for review, it will issue a **writ of *certiorari*** (pronounced sur-shee-uh-*rah*-ree). The writ orders a lower court to send the Supreme Court a record of the case for review. The vast majority of the petitions for review are denied. A denial is not a decision on the merits of a case, nor does it indicate agreement with the lower court's opinion. (The judgment of the lower court remains in force, however.) Therefore, denial of the writ has no value as a precedent. The Court will not issue a writ unless at least four justices approve of it. This is called the **rule of four.**[5]

Court Procedures

Once the Supreme Court grants *certiorari* in a particular case, the justices do extensive research on the legal issues and facts involved in the case. (Of course, some preliminary research is necessary before deciding to grant the petition for review.) Each justice is entitled to four law clerks, who undertake much of the research and preliminary drafting necessary for the justice to form an opinion.

The Court normally does not hear any evidence, as is true with all appeals courts. The Court's consideration of a case is based on the abstracts, the record, and the briefs. The attorneys are permitted to present **oral arguments.** Unlike the practice in most courts, lawyers addressing the Supreme Court can be (and often are) questioned by the justices at any time during oral arguments. All statements and the justices' questions during oral arguments are recorded.

The justices meet to discuss and vote on cases in conferences held throughout the term. In these conferences, in addition to deciding cases already before the Court, the justices determine which new petitions for *certiorari* to grant. These conferences take place in the Court's oak-paneled chamber and are strictly private—no stenographers, audio recorders, or video cameras are allowed.

Decisions and Opinions

When the Court has reached a decision, its opinion is written. The **opinion** contains the Court's ruling on the issue or issues presented, the reasons for its decision, the rules of law that apply, and other information. In many cases, the decision of the lower court is **affirmed,** resulting in the enforcement of that court's judgment or decree. If the Supreme Court believes that a reversible error was committed during the trial or that the jury was instructed improperly, however, the decision will be **reversed.** Sometimes the case will be **remanded** (sent back to the court that originally heard the case) for a new trial or other proceeding. For example, a lower court might have held that a party was not entitled to bring a lawsuit under a particular law. If the Supreme Court holds

---

5. The "rule of four" is modified when seven or fewer justices participate, which occurs from time to time. When that happens, as few as three justices can grant *certiorari*.

to the contrary, it will remand (send back) the case to the trial court with instructions that the trial go forward.

The Court's written opinion sometimes is unsigned; this is called an opinion *per curiam* ("by the court"). Typically, the Court's opinion is signed by all the justices who agree with it. When in the majority, the chief justice decides who writes the opinion and often writes it personally. When the chief justice is in the minority, the senior justice on the majority side assigns the opinion.

Types of Opinions. When all justices unanimously agree on an opinion, the opinion is written for the entire Court (all the justices) and can be deemed a **unanimous opinion.** When there is not a unanimous opinion, a **majority opinion** is written, outlining the views of the majority of the justices involved in the case. Often, one or more justices who feel strongly about making or emphasizing a particular point that is not made or emphasized in the unanimous or majority written opinion will write a **concurring opinion.** That means the justice writing the concurring opinion agrees (concurs) with the conclusion given in the majority written opinion but wants to make or clarify a particular point or to voice disapproval of the grounds on which the decision was made. Finally, in other than unanimous opinions, one or more dissenting opinions are usually written by those justices who do not agree with the majority. The **dissenting opinion** is important because it often forms the basis of the arguments used years later if the Court reverses the previous decision and establishes a new precedent.

Publishing Opinions. Shortly after the opinion is written, the Supreme Court announces its decision from the bench. At that time, the opinion is made available to the public at the office of the clerk of the Court. The clerk also releases the opinion for online publication. Ultimately, the opinion is published in the *United States Reports,* which is the official printed record of the Court's decisions.

The Court's Dwindling Caseload. Some have complained that the Court reviews too few cases each term, thus giving the lower courts less guidance on important issues. Indeed, the number of signed opinions issued by the Court has dwindled notably since the 1980s. For example, in its 1982–1983 term, the Court issued signed opinions in 151 cases. By the early 2000s, this number had dropped to between 70 and 80 per term. In the term ending in June 2009, the number was 82.

THE SELECTION OF FEDERAL JUDGES

All federal judges are appointed. The Constitution, in Article II, Section 2, states that the president is to appoint the justices of the Supreme Court with the advice and consent of the Senate. Congress has established the same procedure for staffing other federal courts. This means that the Senate and the president jointly decide who shall fill every vacant judicial position, no matter what the level.

There are more than 840 federal judgeships in the United States. Once appointed to such a judgeship, a person holds that job for life. Judges serve until they resign, retire voluntarily, or die. Federal judges who engage in blatantly illegal conduct may be removed through impeachment, although such action is rare. In contrast to federal judges, many state judges—including the judges who sit on state supreme courts—are chosen by the voters in elections. Inevitably, judicial candidates must raise campaign funds, a practice that raises serious questions about judicial impartiality.

Unanimous Opinion
A court opinion or determination on which all judges agree.

Majority Opinion
A court opinion reflecting the views of the majority of the judges.

Concurring Opinion
A separate opinion prepared by a judge who supports the decision of the majority of the court but for different reasons.

Dissenting Opinion
A separate opinion in which a judge dissents from (disagrees with) the conclusion reached by the majority on the court and expounds his or her own views about the case.

Judicial Appointments

Candidates for federal judgeships are suggested to the president by the Department of Justice, senators, other judges, the candidates themselves, and lawyers' associations and other interest groups. In selecting a candidate to nominate for a judgeship, the president considers not only the person's competence but also other factors, including the person's political philosophy (as will be discussed shortly), ethnicity, and gender.

The nomination process—no matter how the nominees are obtained—always works the same way. The president makes the actual nomination, transmitting the name to the Senate. The Senate then either confirms or rejects the nomination. To reach a conclusion, the Senate Judiciary Committee (operating through subcommittees) invites testimony, both written and oral, at its various hearings.

Federal District Court Judgeship Nominations. Although the president officially nominates federal judges, in the past the nomination of federal district court judges actually originated with a senator or senators of the president's party from the state in which there was a vacancy. In effect, judicial appointments were a form of political patronage. President Jimmy Carter (1977–1981) ended this tradition by establishing independent commissions to oversee the initial nomination process. President Ronald Reagan (1981–1989) abolished Carter's nominating commissions and established complete presidential control of nominations.

A practice used in the Senate, called **senatorial courtesy,** is a constraint on the president's freedom to appoint federal district judges. Senatorial courtesy allows a senator of the president's political party to veto a judicial appointment in her or his state. During much of American history, senators from the "opposition" party (the party to which the president does not belong) have also enjoyed the right of senatorial courtesy, although their veto power has varied over time.

In 2000, Orrin Hatch, Republican chair of the Senate Judiciary Committee, announced that the opposition party (at that point, the Democrats) would no longer be allowed to invoke senatorial courtesy. The implementation of the new policy was delayed when Republican senator James Jeffords of Vermont left the Republican Party. Jeffords's departure turned control of the Senate over to the Democrats. After the 2002 elections, however, when the Republicans regained control of the Senate, they put the new policy into effect.

When the Democrats took over the Senate following the elections of 2006, Senator Patrick J. Leahy (D., Vt.), chair of the Judiciary Committee, let it be known that the old bipartisan system of senatorial courtesy would return. Of course, the Republicans, who were now in the minority, were unlikely to object to a nomination submitted by Republican president George W. Bush, and the old practices did not become truly effective until Democratic president Barack Obama took office.

Federal Courts of Appeals Appointments. There are many fewer federal courts of appeals appointments than federal district court appointments, but they are more influential. This is because federal appellate judges handle more important matters, at least from the point of view of the president, and therefore presidents take a

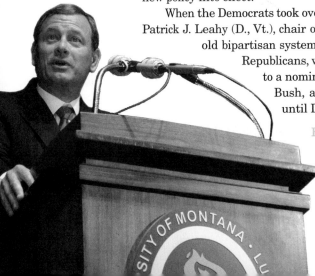

▼ The current chief justice of the United States Supreme Court is John Roberts. Because of his relative youth, he will remain chief justice for many years. How does someone become chief justice? (AP Photo/ Todd Goodrich)

keener interest in the nomination process for such judgeships. Also, the U.S. courts of appeals have become "stepping-stones" to the Supreme Court.

Supreme Court Appointments. As we have described, the president nominates Supreme Court justices. As you can see in Table 12–1, which summarizes the background of all Supreme Court justices to 2010, the most common occupational background of the justices at the time of their appointment has been private legal practice or state or federal judgeship. Those nine justices who were in federal executive posts at the time of their appointment held the high offices of secretary of state, comptroller of the treasury, secretary of the navy, postmaster general, secretary of the interior, chairman of the Securities and Exchange Commission, and secretary of labor. In the "Other" category under "Occupational Position before Appointment" in Table 12–1 are two justices who were professors of law (including William H. Taft, a former president) and one justice who was a North Carolina state employee with responsibility for organizing and revising the state's statutes.

Partisanship and Judicial Appointments

In most circumstances, the president appoints judges or justices who belong to the president's own political party. Presidents see their federal judiciary appointments as the one sure way to institutionalize their political views long after they have left office. By 1993, for example, Presidents Ronald Reagan and George H. W. Bush together

TABLE 12–1: **Background of Supreme Court Justices to 2010**

	Number of Justices (111 = Total)		Number of Justices (111 = Total)
Occupational Position before Appointment		**Political Party Affiliation**	
Private legal practice	25	Federalist (to 1835)	13
State judgeship	21	Jeffersonian Republican (to 1828)	7
Federal judgeship	31	Whig (to 1861)	1
U.S. attorney general	7	Democrat	45
Deputy or assistant U.S. attorney general	2	Republican	44
U.S. solicitor general	2	Independent	1
U.S. senator	6	**Age on Appointment**	
U.S. representative	2	Under 40	5
State governor	3	41–50	32
Federal executive post	9	51–60	60
Other	3	61–70	14
Religious Background		**Gender**	
Protestant	83	Male	108
Roman Catholic	14	Female	3
Jewish	6	**Race**	
Unitarian	7	White (non-Hispanic)	108
No religious affiliation	1	African American	2
Educational Background		Hispanic	1
College graduate	95		
Not a college graduate	16		

Sources: Congressional Quarterly, *Congressional Quarterly's Guide to the U.S. Supreme Court* (Washington, D.C.: Congressional Quarterly Press, 1996); and authors' updates.

had appointed nearly three-quarters of all federal court judges. This preponderance of Republican-appointed federal judges strengthened the legal moorings of the conservative social agenda on a variety of issues, ranging from abortion to civil rights. President Bill Clinton, a Democrat, had the opportunity to appoint about 200 federal judges, thereby shifting the ideological makeup of the federal judiciary. Then, during the first six years of his presidency, George W. Bush appointed more than 250 federal judges, again ensuring a majority of Republican-appointed judges in the federal courts.

During the first two years of his second term, President Bush also had the opportunity to fill two Supreme Court vacancies, those left by the death of Chief Justice William Rehnquist and by the retirement of Justice Sandra Day O'Connor. Bush appointed two conservatives to these positions—John G. Roberts, Jr., who became chief justice, and Samuel Alito, Jr., who replaced O'Connor. As you will read shortly, these appointments strengthened the rightward movement of the Court that had begun years before, with the appointment of Rehnquist as chief justice.

In April 2009, Justice David Souter stated that he would retire from the Supreme Court in June, at the end of the current term. In May, President Obama announced that he would nominate Judge Sonia Sotomayor to replace Justice Souter on the Court. Sotomayor, who refers to herself as Latina, was the first Hispanic to serve on the Court, and only the third woman of any background. She was expected to align with the Court's more liberal wing, as Souter had done. For that reason, conservative political activists attempted to mount a campaign against her nomination, but in the end she was confirmed easily. Because several members of the Court are either advanced in age or in poor health, the chances are high that Obama will make one or more additional appointments during his first term in office.

The Senate's Role

Ideology also plays a large role in the Senate's confirmation hearings, and presidential nominees to the Supreme Court have not always been confirmed. In fact, almost 20 percent of presidential nominations to the Supreme Court have been either rejected or not acted on by the Senate. There have been many acrimonious battles over Supreme Court appointments when the Senate and the president have not seen eye to eye about political matters.

The U.S. Senate had a long record of refusing to confirm the president's judicial nominations from the beginning of Andrew Jackson's presidency in 1829 to the end of Ulysses Grant's presidency in 1877. From 1894 until 1968, however, only three nominees were not confirmed. Then, from 1968 through 1987, four presidential nominees to the highest court were rejected. One of the most controversial Supreme Court nominations was that of Clarence Thomas, who underwent an extremely volatile and acrimonious confirmation hearing in 1991, replete with charges against him of sexual harassment. He was ultimately confirmed by the Senate, nonetheless.

President Bill Clinton had little trouble gaining approval for both of his nominees to the Supreme Court: Ruth Bader Ginsburg and Stephen G. Breyer. Clinton found it more difficult, however, to secure Senate approval for his judicial nominations to the lower courts, as did President George W. Bush. During the first term of the Bush administration, the Senate confirmed more than two hundred of President Bush's nominees. Senate Democrats, however, blocked the confirmation of some of Bush's nominees to the federal appellate courts (through the use of the filibuster, or extended debate—see Chapter 9), arguing that the nominees were conservative ideologues. In 2005, President Bush reappointed several of these nominees. When Senate Democrats threatened to block their confirmation again through the use of filibusters, a number of Republicans in the Senate said that they would change the Senate rules to prevent the use of filibusters for judicial nominations. A group of fourteen Senate Republicans and Democrats, however, reached a compromise that preserved the Senate's rules.

Judicial Activism
A doctrine holding that the federal judiciary should take an active role by using its powers to check the activities of governmental bodies when those bodies exceed their authority.

POLICYMAKING AND THE COURTS

The partisan battles over judicial appointments reflect an important reality in today's American government: the importance of the judiciary in national politics. Because appointments to the federal bench are for life, the ideology of judicial appointees can affect national policy for years to come. Although the primary function of judges in our system of government is to interpret and apply the laws, inevitably judges make policy when carrying out this task. One of the major policymaking tools of the federal courts is their power of judicial review.

Judicial Review

Remember from Chapter 2 that the power of the courts to determine whether a law or action by the other branches of government is constitutional is known as the power of *judicial review*. This power enables the judicial branch to act as a check on the other two branches of government, in line with the system of checks and balances established by the U.S. Constitution.

The power of judicial review is not mentioned in the Constitution, however. Rather, it was established by the United States Supreme Court's decision in *Marbury v. Madison*.[6] In that case, in which the Court declared that a law passed by Congress violated the Constitution, the Court claimed such a power for the judiciary:

> It is emphatically the province and duty of the Judicial Department to say what the law is. Those who apply the rule to a particular case must of necessity expound and interpret that rule. If two laws conflict with each other, the courts must decide on the operation of each.

If a federal court declares that a federal or state law or policy is unconstitutional, the court's decision affects the application of the law or policy only within that court's jurisdiction. For this reason, the higher the level of the court, the greater the impact of the decision on society. Because of the Supreme Court's national jurisdiction, its decisions have the greatest impact. For example, when the Supreme Court held that an Arkansas state constitutional amendment limiting the terms of congresspersons was unconstitutional, laws establishing term limits in twenty-three other states also were invalidated.[7]

Judicial Activism and Judicial Restraint

Judicial scholars like to characterize judges and justices as being either "activist" or "restraintist." The doctrine of **judicial activism** rests on the conviction that the federal judiciary should take an active role by using its powers to check the activities of

---

6. 5 U.S. 137 (1803).
7. *U.S. Term Limits v. Thornton*, 514 U.S. 779 (1995).

Judicial Restraint
A doctrine holding that courts should defer to the decisions made by the elected representatives of the people in the legislative and executive branches.

Congress, state legislatures, and administrative agencies when those governmental bodies exceed their authority. One of the Supreme Court's most activist eras was the period from 1953 to 1969, when the Court was headed by Chief Justice Earl Warren. The Warren Court propelled the civil rights movement forward by holding, among other things, that laws permitting racial segregation violated the equal protection clause.

In contrast, the doctrine of **judicial restraint** rests on the assumption that the courts should defer to the decisions made by the legislative and executive branches, because members of Congress and the president are elected by the people whereas members of the federal judiciary are not. Because administrative agency personnel normally have more expertise than the courts do in the areas regulated by the agencies, the courts likewise should defer to agency rules and decisions. In other words, under the doctrine of judicial restraint, the courts should not thwart the implementation of legislative acts and agency rules unless they are clearly unconstitutional.

Judicial activism sometimes is linked with liberalism, and judicial restraint with conservatism. In fact, though, a conservative judge can be activist, just as a liberal judge can be restraintist. In the 1950s and 1960s, the Supreme Court was activist and liberal. Some observers believe that the Rehnquist Court, with its conservative majority, became increasingly activist over time. The most conservative members on today's Roberts Court (John Roberts, Antonin Scalia, Clarence Thomas, and Samuel Alito) are regarded by some scholars as restraintist justices because of their deference to laws and regulations that reflected some of the policies of the Bush administration. With Democrat Barack Obama as president, some suggest that these justices may become more activist in their approach to judicial interpretation.

Other terms that are often used to describe a justice's philosophy are *strict construction* and *broad construction*. Justices who believe in strict construction look to the "letter of the law" when they attempt to interpret the Constitution or a particular statute. Those who favor broad construction try to determine the context and purpose of the law.

Ideology and the Rehnquist Court

William H. Rehnquist, who died in 2005, became the sixteenth chief justice of the Supreme Court in 1986. He was known as a strong anchor of the Court's conservative wing. The rightward movement that began shortly after Rehnquist became chief justice continued as other conservative appointments to the Court were made during the Reagan and George H. W. Bush administrations.

Interestingly, some previously conservative justices showed a tendency to migrate to a more liberal view of the law. Sandra Day O'Connor, the first female justice, gradually shifted to the left on a number of issues, including abortion. Generally, O'Connor and Justice Anthony Kennedy provided the "swing votes" on the Rehnquist Court.

Although the Court moved to the right during the Rehnquist era, it was closely divided in many cases. Consider the Court's rulings on states' rights. In 1995, the Court held, for the first time in sixty years, that Congress had overreached its powers under the commerce clause when it attempted to regulate the possession of guns in school zones. According to the Court, the possession of guns in school zones had nothing to do with the commerce clause.[8] Yet in a 2005 case, the Court ruled that

---

8. *United States v. Lopez,* 514 U.S. 549 (1995).

Congress's power to regulate commerce allowed it to ban marijuana use even when a state's law permitted such use and the growing and use of the drug were strictly local in nature.[9] What these two rulings had in common was that they supported policies generally considered to be conservative—the right to possess firearms on the one hand, and a strong line against marijuana on the other.

The Roberts Court

During its first term, which ended in 2006, the Roberts Court accepted few controversial cases for review. Some of the cases it did accept, however, revealed a continued rightward drift. In the second term of the Roberts Court (2006–2007), the addition of Justice Alito made it easier for Justices Roberts, Scalia, and Thomas to move the Court further to the right ideologically. In a 2007 case, for example, the Court upheld a 2003 federal law banning partial-birth abortion, again by a close (five-to-four) vote.[10] Justice Kennedy sided with the conservatives on the Court, giving them a majority.

9. *Gonzales v. Raich,* 545 U.S. 1 (2005).
10. *Gonzales v. Carhart,* 550 U.S. 124 (2007).

Stephen Breyer   **Ruth Bader Ginsburg**

Samuel Alito   **Anthony Kennedy**

Chief Justice John Roberts

Antonin Scalia   **Clarence Thomas**

Sonia Sotomayor   **John Paul Stevens**

◀ **Supreme Court Justices (as of late 2009)** Sonia Sotomayor is the most recent addition to the United States Supreme Court. (U.S Supreme Court)

Judicial
Implementation
The way in which court
decisions are translated
into action.

The Supreme Court's conservative drift continued in the following years. In 2008, for example, the Court established the right of individuals to own guns for private use,[11] and it upheld lethal injection as an execution method.[12] In 2009, the Court came close to overturning long-established civil rights precedents, but did not step over the line. For example, in a case concerning the Voting Rights Act of 1965, the Court released a Texas utility district from coverage under the act, but avoided a decision on the act's constitutionality.[13] (The Court did issue a warning to Congress to modernize the statute.) The Court also found that white firefighters in New Haven, Connecticut, were victims of reverse discrimination, but it did not invalidate federal employment discrimination law.[14] In these and other key cases, Justice Kennedy continued to cast the deciding vote.

WHAT CHECKS OUR COURTS?

Our judicial system is one of the most independent in the world. But the courts do not have absolute independence, for they are part of the political process. Political checks limit the extent to which courts can exercise judicial review and engage in an activist policy. These checks are exercised by the executive branch, the legislature, the public, and, finally, the judiciary itself.

Executive Checks

President Andrew Jackson was once supposed to have said, after Chief Justice John Marshall made an unpopular decision, "John Marshall has made his decision; now let him enforce it."[15] This purported remark goes to the heart of **judicial implementation**—the enforcement of judicial decisions in such a way that those decisions are translated into policy. The Supreme Court simply does not have any enforcement powers, and whether a decision will be implemented depends on the cooperation of the other two branches of government. Rarely, though, will a president refuse to enforce a Supreme Court decision, as President Jackson did. To take such an action could mean a significant loss of public support because of the Supreme Court's stature in the eyes of the nation. More commonly, presidents exercise influence over the judiciary by appointing new judges and justices as federal judicial seats become vacant.

Executives at the state level also may refuse to implement court decisions with which they disagree. A notable example of such a refusal occurred in Arkansas after the Supreme Court ordered schools to desegregate "with all deliberate speed" in 1955.[16] Arkansas governor Orval Faubus refused to cooperate with the decision and used the state's National Guard to block the integration of Central High School in Little Rock. Ultimately, President Dwight Eisenhower had to federalize the Arkansas National Guard and send federal troops to Little Rock to quell the violence that had erupted.

---

11. *District of Columbia v. Heller,* 128 S.Ct. 2783 (2008).
12. *Baze v. Rees,* 128 S.Ct. 152 (2008).
13. *Northwest Austin Municipal Utility District No. 1 v. Holder,* ___ S.Ct. ___ (2009).
14. *Ricci v. DeStefano,* ___ S.Ct. ___ (2009).
15. The decision referred to was *Cherokee Nation v. Georgia,* 30 U.S. 1 (1831).
16. *Brown v. Board of Education,* 349 U.S. 294 (1955)—referred to as the second *Brown* decision.

Legislative Checks

Courts may make rulings, but often the legislatures at local, state, and federal levels are required to appropriate funds to carry out the courts' rulings. A court, for example, may decide that prison conditions must be improved, but it is up to the legislature to authorize the funds necessary to carry out the ruling. When such funds are not appropriated, the court that made the ruling, in effect, has been checked.

Constitutional Amendments. Courts' rulings can be overturned by constitutional amendments at both the federal and state levels. Many of the amendments to the U.S. Constitution (such as the Fourteenth, Fifteenth, and Twenty-sixth Amendments) check the state courts' ability to allow discrimination, for example. Proposed constitutional amendments that were created in an effort to reverse courts' decisions on school prayer, abortion, and same-sex marriage have failed.

Rewriting Laws. Finally, Congress or a state legislature can rewrite (amend) old laws or enact new ones to overturn a court's rulings if the legislature concludes that the court is interpreting laws or legislative intentions erroneously. For example, Congress passed the Civil Rights Act of 1991 in part to overturn a series of conservative rulings in employment-discrimination cases. In 2009, Congress passed (and President Obama signed) the Lilly Ledbetter Fair Pay Act, which resets the statute of limitations for filing an equal-pay lawsuit each time an employer issues a discriminatory paycheck. The law was a direct answer to *Ledbetter v. Goodyear*, in which the United States Supreme Court held that the statute of limitations begins at the date the pay was agreed upon, not at the date of the most recent paycheck.[17] The new legislation made it much easier for employees to win pay discrimination lawsuits.

Public Opinion

Public opinion plays a significant role in shaping government policy, and certainly the judiciary is not excepted from this rule. For one thing, persons affected by a Supreme Court decision that is contrary to their views may simply ignore it. Officially sponsored prayers were banned in public schools in 1962, yet it was widely known that the ban was (and still is) ignored in many southern and rural districts. What can the courts do in this situation? Unless someone complains about the prayers and initiates a lawsuit, the courts can do nothing.

▼ **President Barack Obama** is surrounded by members of Congress as he signs the Lilly Ledbetter Fair Pay Act, which resets the statute of limitations for filing an equal-pay lawsuit. In so doing, the president and Congress in effect overturned a Supreme Court ruling on this issue. How could the Court counter this new legislation? (AP Photo/Ron Edmonds)

17. 550 U.S. 618 (2007).

Political Question
An issue that a court believes should be decided by the executive or legislative branch.

The public also can pressure state and local government officials to refuse to enforce a certain decision. As already mentioned, judicial implementation requires the cooperation of government officials at all levels, and public opinion in various regions of the country will influence whether such cooperation is forthcoming.

Additionally, the courts themselves necessarily are influenced by public opinion to some extent. After all, judges are not "islands" in our society; their attitudes are influenced by social trends, just as the attitudes and beliefs of all persons are. Courts generally tend to avoid issuing decisions that they know will be noticeably at odds with public opinion. In part, this is because the judiciary, as a branch of the government, prefers to avoid creating divisiveness among the public. Also, a court—particularly the Supreme Court—may lose stature if it decides a case in a way that markedly diverges from public opinion. For example, in 2005 the Supreme Court ruled that the execution of persons who were under the age of eighteen when they committed their crimes violates the Eighth Amendment's ban on cruel and unusual punishment. In its ruling, the Court indicated that the standards of what constitutes cruel and unusual punishment are influenced by public opinion and that today our society views juveniles as "categorically less culpable than the average criminal."[18]

Judicial Traditions and Doctrines

Supreme Court justices (and other federal judges) typically exercise self-restraint in fashioning their decisions. In part, this restraint stems from their knowledge that the other two branches of government and the public can exercise checks on the judiciary, as previously discussed. To a large extent, however, this restraint is mandated by various judicially established traditions and doctrines. For example, in exercising its discretion to hear appeals, the Supreme Court will not hear a meritless appeal just so it can rule on the issue. Also, when reviewing a case, the Supreme Court typically narrows its focus to just one issue or one aspect of an issue involved in the case. The Court rarely makes broad, sweeping decisions on issues. Furthermore, the doctrine of *stare decisis* acts as a restraint because it obligates the courts, including the Supreme Court, to follow established precedents when deciding cases. Only rarely will courts overrule a precedent.

Hypothetical and Political Questions. Other judicial doctrines and practices also act as restraints. As already mentioned, the courts will hear only what are called justiciable disputes—disputes that arise out of actual cases. In other words, a court will not hear a case that involves a merely hypothetical issue. Additionally, if a political question is involved, the Supreme Court often will exercise judicial restraint and refuse to rule on the matter. A **political question** is one that the Supreme Court declares should be decided by the elected branches of government—the executive branch, the legislative branch, or those two branches acting together. For example, the Supreme Court has refused to rule on the controversy regarding the rights of gay men and lesbians in the military, preferring instead to defer to the executive branch's decisions on the matter. Generally, though, fewer questions are deemed political questions by the Supreme Court today than in the past.

---

18. *Roper v. Simons,* 543 U.S. 551 (2005).

▲ **A defense attorney confers** with a federal district court judge in Cambridge, Massachusetts. How can the lower courts act as a check on higher courts? (AP Photo/Zara Tzanev/Pool)

The Impact of the Lower Courts. Higher courts can reverse the decisions of lower courts. Lower courts can act as a check on higher courts, too. Lower courts can ignore—and have ignored—Supreme Court decisions. Usually, this is done indirectly. A lower court might conclude, for example, that the precedent set by the Supreme Court does not apply to the exact circumstances in the case before the court; or the lower court may decide that the Supreme Court's decision was ambiguous with respect to the issue before the lower court. The fact that the Supreme Court rarely makes broad and clear-cut statements on any issue makes it easier for the lower courts to interpret the Supreme Court's decisions in different ways.

making a difference
CHANGING THE LEGAL SYSTEM

The U.S. legal system may seem too complex to be influenced by one individual, but its power nonetheless depends on the support of individuals. The public has many ways of resisting, modifying, or overturning statutes and rulings of the courts.

Why Should You Care? You may find it worth your while to attend one or more court sessions to see how the law works in practice. Legislative bodies may make laws and ordinances, but legislation is given its practical form by court rulings. Therefore, if you care about the effects of a particular law, you may have to pay attention to how the courts are interpreting it. For example, do you believe that sentences handed down for certain crimes are too lenient—or too strict? Legislative bodies can attempt to establish sentences for various offenses, but the courts inevitably retain considerable flexibility in determining what happens in any particular case.

What Can You Do? Public opinion can have an effect on judicial policies. Whichever cause may interest you, there is probably an organization that pursues lawsuits to benefit that cause, and that can use your support. A prime example is the modern women's movement, which undertook long series of lawsuits to change the way women are treated in American life. The courts only rule on cases that are brought before them, and the women's movement changed American law by filing—and winning—case after case.

In 1965, a federal circuit court opened a wide range of jobs for women by overturning laws that kept women out of work that was "too hard" for them. In 1971, the United States Supreme Court ruled that states could not prefer men when assigning the administrators of estates. (This case was brought by Ruth Bader Ginsburg, who was later to sit on the Court herself.) In 1974, the Court ruled that employers could not use the "going market rate" to justify lower wages for women. In 1975, it ruled that women could not be excluded from juries. In 1978, an Oregon court became the first of many to find that a man could be prosecuted for raping his wife. In 1996, the Virginia Military Institute was forced to admit women as cadets. Today, groups such as the National Organization for Women continue to support lawsuits to advance women's rights.

If you want information about the Supreme Court, contact the following by telephone or letter:

Clerk of the Court
The Supreme Court of the United States
1 First St. N.E.
Washington, DC 20543
202-479-3011

You can access online information about the Supreme Court at the following site:

www.oyez.org

▲ **Former president** of NOW (National Organization for Women) Kim Gandy expresses her strong opinions at a press conference at one of that group's national conventions. (AP Photo/John Russell)

key terms

affirm 286

amicus curiae brief 280

appellate court 281

case law 279

class-action suit 280

common law 278

concurring opinion 287

dissenting opinion 287

diversity of
    citizenship 280

federal question 279

general jurisdiction 281

judicial activism 291

judicial
    implementation 294

judicial restraint 292

jurisdiction 279

justiciable
    controversy 280

limited jurisdiction 281

litigate 280

majority opinion 287

opinion 286

oral arguments 286

political question 296

precedent 278

remand 286

reverse 286

rule of four 286

senatorial courtesy 288

stare decisis 278

trial court 281

unanimous opinion 287

writ of *certiorari* 286

chapter summary

1 American law is rooted in the common law tradition, which is part of our heritage from England. The common law doctrine of *stare decisis* (which means "to stand on decided cases") obligates judges to follow precedents established previously by their own courts or by higher courts that have authority over them. Precedents established by the United States Supreme Court, the highest court in the land, are binding on all lower courts. Fundamental sources of American law include the U.S. Constitution and state constitutions, statutes enacted by legislative bodies, regulations issued by administrative agencies, and case law.

2 Article III, Section 1, of the U.S. Constitution limits the jurisdiction of the federal courts to cases involving (a) a federal question, which is a question based, at least in part, on the U.S. Constitution, a treaty, or a federal law, or (b) diversity of citizenship, which arises when parties to a lawsuit are from different states or when the lawsuit involves a foreign citizen or government. The federal court system is a three-tiered model consisting of (a) U.S. district (trial) courts and various lower courts of limited jurisdiction, (b) U.S. courts of appeals, and (c) the United States Supreme Court. Cases may be appealed from the district courts to the appellate courts. In most cases, the decisions of the federal appellate courts are final because the Supreme Court hears relatively few cases.

3 The Supreme Court's decision to review a case is influenced by many factors, including the significance of the issues involved and whether the solicitor general is pressing the Court to take

the case. After a case is accepted, the justices undertake research (with the help of their law clerks) on the issues involved in the case, hear oral arguments from the parties, meet in conference to discuss and vote on the issue, and announce the opinion, which is then released for publication.

4 Federal judges are nominated by the president and confirmed by the Senate. Once appointed, they hold office for life, barring gross misconduct. The nomination and confirmation process, particularly for Supreme Court justices, is often extremely politicized. Democrats and Republicans alike realize that justices may occupy seats on the Court for decades and want to have persons appointed who share their views. In recent decades, nearly 20 percent of all Supreme Court appointments have been either rejected or not acted on by the Senate.

5 In interpreting and applying the law, judges inevitably become policymakers. The most important policymaking tool of the federal courts is the power of judicial review. This power was not mentioned specifically in the Constitution, but John Marshall claimed the power for the Court in his 1803 decision in *Marbury v. Madison*.

6 Judges who take an active role in checking the activities of the other branches of government sometimes are characterized as "activist" judges, and judges who defer to the other branches' decisions sometimes are regarded as "restraintist" judges. The Warren Court of the 1950s and 1960s was activist in a liberal direction, whereas the Rehnquist Court seemed to become increasingly activist in a conservative direction. The Roberts Court appears to be continuing the rightward movement of the Rehnquist Court, especially since the appointment of Justice Alito to replace Justice O'Connor.

7 Checks on the powers of the federal courts include executive checks, legislative checks, public opinion, and judicial traditions and doctrines.

QUESTIONS FOR
discussion**and**analysis

1 What are the benefits of having lifetime appointments to the United States Supreme Court? What problems might such appointments cause? What would be the likely result if Supreme Court justices faced term limits?

2 In many states, judges—including the judges who sit on the state supreme court—are chosen by the voters in elections. Inevitably, judicial candidates must raise campaign funds. What arguments favor electing judges? What problems can such a system create?

3 Under both President Bill Clinton and President George W. Bush, members of the opposition party in the Senate often blocked the president's nominations to district and circuit courts. Under what circumstances are such blocking actions a legitimate exercise of the Senate's power? Under

what circumstances can they rightly be described as inappropriate political maneuvers?

4 On pages 292–293, we described how the Rehnquist Court ruled in favor of states' rights in a gun control case and against states' rights on a matter concerning marijuana. Why do you think the justices might have come to different conclusions in these two cases?

5 Should Congress ever limit the jurisdiction of the federal courts for political reasons? After the Civil War, the Congress barred the Supreme Court from ruling on the constitutionality of the Reconstruction measures by which Confederate states rejoined the Union. Was this appropriate? Why or why not? Should Congress block the Court's ability to rule on issues raised by the prisoners at Guantánamo Bay? Why or why not?

helpful online **Resources**

CONNECTING TO AMERICAN GOVERNMENT AND POLITICS

For a gateway to information on all U.S. federal courts, visit:
www.uscourts.gov

The Supreme Court's official Web site,
supremecourtus.gov,
makes Court decisions available within hours of their release.

FindLaw offers searchable databases of Supreme Court decisions since 1970, plus an enormous amount of other information about the law. See it at:
www.findlaw.com

a special WebSite

FOR YOUR TEXT

Go to this book's special Web site at academic.cengage.com/polisci/Schmidt/ Brief6e. Choose "For Students." Then click on Chapter 12, where you will find an online quiz and other helpful study aids. If your professor is using CengageNOW: *American Government and Politics Today, Brief Edition,* log in and go to Chapter 12 for additional online study aids.

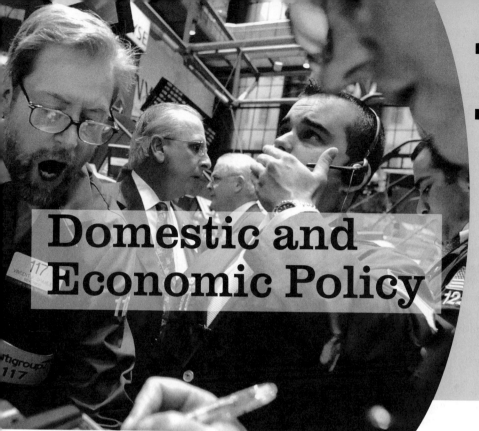

Domestic and Economic Policy

These traders on the floor of the New York Stock Exchange react to falling prices at one point during the recent economic crisis. Wall Street often reflects actions by federal policymakers.
(AP Photo/Richard Drew)

13

Typically, whenever a policy decision is made, some groups will be better off and some groups will be hurt. All policymaking generally involves such a dilemma.

Part of the public-policy debate in our nation involves domestic problems. **Domestic policy** can be defined as all laws, government planning, and government actions that concern internal issues of national importance. Consequently, the span of such policies is enormous. Domestic policies range from relatively simple issues, such as what the speed limit should be on interstate highways, to more complex ones, such as how best to protect our environment. Many of our domestic policies are formulated and implemented by the federal government, but a number of others are the result of the combined efforts of federal, state, and local governments.

We can define several types of domestic policy. *Regulatory policy* seeks to define what is and is not legal. Setting speed limits is obviously regulatory policy. *Redistributive policy* transfers income from certain individuals or groups to others, often based on the belief that these transfers enhance fairness. Social Security is an example. *Promotional policy* seeks to foster or discourage various economic or social activities, typically through subsidies and tax breaks. A tax credit for buying a fuel-efficient car would qualify as promotional.

In this chapter, we look at domestic policy issues involving health care, immigration, and energy and the environment. We also examine national economic policies

Domestic Policy
All government laws, planning, and actions that concern internal issues of national importance, such as health care, the environment, and the economy.

301

undertaken by the federal government. Before we start our analysis, though, we must look at how public policies are made.

THE POLICYMAKING PROCESS

How does any issue get resolved? First, of course, the issue must be identified as a problem. Often, policymakers have only to open their local newspapers—or letters from their constituents—to discover that a problem is brewing. On rare occasions, a crisis, such as that brought about by the terrorist attacks of September 11, 2001, creates the need to formulate policy. Like most Americans, however, policymakers receive much of their information from the national media. Finally, various lobbying groups provide information to members of Congress.

As an example of policymaking, consider the Emergency Economic Stabilization Act of 2008, commonly known as the bank bailout bill. Enacted in response to the global financial crisis of 2008, the act granted the U.S. treasury secretary, Henry Paulson, the power to spend up to $700 billion to support financial institutions. Although the bill was initially meant to fund the federal government's purchase of distressed mortgage-backed securities ("toxic assets") from banks, the language of the bill actually gave Paulson the ability to spend the funds on almost anything that could be considered support for the financial system.

No matter how simple or how complex the problem, those who make policy follow a number of steps. We can divide the process of policymaking into at least five steps: (1) agenda building, (2) policy formulation, (3) policy adoption, (4) policy implementation, and (5) policy evaluation.

Agenda Building

First of all, the issue must get on the agenda. In other words, Congress must become aware that a problem requires congressional action. Agenda building may occur as the result of a crisis, technological change, or mass media campaigns, as well as through the efforts of strong political personalities and effective lobbying groups.

Paulson proposed the bank bailout bill to Congress, with President Bush's backing, in response to a set of potentially catastrophic circumstances. On September 15, Lehman Brothers, a giant investment bank, failed. Lehman held more than $600 billion in assets and debts, making its bankruptcy the largest in U.S. history.

Earlier in 2008, the federal government had intervened when a series of major financial institutions failed. These included Bear Stearns, an investment bank, and AIG, a giant insurance firm. By September, however, members of the Bush administration were increasingly reluctant to bail out such institutions. They feared that they were creating a dangerous degree of **moral hazard,** in which individuals and institutions take excessive risks, confident that they will be rescued if something goes wrong. The government therefore allowed Lehman to fail, wiping out not only the bank's owners (the stockholders) but also almost everyone who had lent or entrusted funds to the bank.[1] We discuss other examples of moral hazard in this chapter's *The Politics of Boom and Bust* feature.

Moral Hazard
The danger that protecting an individual or institution from the consequences of failure will encourage excessively risky behavior.

---

1. Investment banks such as Lehman Brothers do not have depositors as such and are not covered by the Federal Deposit Insurance Corporation.

the politics of Boom and Bust:
Bailouts and the Danger of Moral Hazard

During every "bust" period in the U.S. economy, those who are hurt the most seek help, often in the form of a government bailout. Banks were bailed out in the latest recession, as were automobile manufacturers, a giant insurance company, mortgage lenders, home borrowers, and others. All government actions have consequences, though, and bailouts are no different. Consumers, borrowers, investors, savers, and managers all react to changes in incentives. A serious problem that can result if incentives are badly designed is moral hazard, in which those who are protected against danger respond by taking greater risks. The term *moral hazard* comes from the insurance industry, which has recognized the problem for centuries.

The Boom in Mortgage Lending and the Subsequent Bust

Members of Congress decided long ago that home ownership should be promoted. In the 1990s, Congress and several lending regulatory agencies devised programs to increase homeownership among low-income Americans. Such programs increased the likelihood that borrowers would not be able to pay back their mortgages, resulting in default. Still, problems with such mortgages remained manageable for several years.

In time, however, lending to "subprime" borrowers began to get completely out of hand. A major reason was the securitization of mortgages, in which the mortgages of many different borrowers were piled together in large pools of debt. Shares in each pool were sold to investors. The semipublic institutions Freddie Mac and Fannie Mae were established many years ago to create such bundles, but in the twenty-first century a large number of private firms entered this market.

The housing boom started in earnest in 2002. Mortgage originators increasingly approved mortgage loan applications from individuals who had unstable incomes, low incomes, or no incomes at all. Why? Because the originators knew that they could sell the risky mortgages to someone else. All the risk that the mortgage would fail would be passed on to the next group down the line. No one was responsible for verifying that the loans were sound, that the borrower responsible for making payments understood the papers that he or she had signed, or even that the paperwork existed and was in good order. Later investigations revealed that for a great number of securities, it was not. At institutions such as Washington Mutual Bank—which collapsed on September 25, 2008—loan officers who attempted to verify the bona fides of mortgage applicants could be fired. The lending environment, in short, was rife with moral hazard.

When the housing bubble popped, low-income persons who put no money down on a mortgage could walk away from the deal without loss (except to their credit rating). Likewise, mortgage originators had no investments to lose. Fannie Mae and Freddie Mac, however, were ruined. Banks and investment companies with large volumes of mortgage-backed securities on their books were in serious trouble. When taxpayers ultimately bailed out these institutions, the potential liability for American taxpayers was in the trillions of dollars.

Other Examples of Moral Hazard in Finance

Bankers, especially investment bankers, were affected by moral hazard in other ways. Often, they would receive huge bonuses if a risky investment succeeded, but would lose little if it failed. If the risky bet failed, at most the banker might have to seek employment elsewhere—while collecting a large severance package. If bad bets crippled the bank, the taxpayer might again be on the hook.

Economists have argued that moral hazard is even an issue when it comes to deposit insurance. The Federal Deposit Insurance Corporation (FDIC) now insures bank deposits up to $250,000. (Before the financial crisis, the limit was $100,000.) As a result of such insurance, depositors have no incentive to check the long-run viability of the banks in which they place their deposits. A bank that is making risky investments may be able to pay higher rates of interest on deposits than a bank that is engaging in sounder practices. Others argue, however, that ordinary citizens are in no position to judge the soundness of banks and should not be penalized for failing to do so. In part, the government has accepted this argument. Presumably, individuals and corporations capable of making deposits in excess of $250,000 should have enough financial expertise to judge the safety of the banks with which they deal.

FOR CRITICAL ANALYSIS

Is moral hazard a problem in health care? Would consumers reduce their use of medical services without harming their health if they had to help pay for medical care, or would the savings likely be limited to minor matters, rather than truly expensive procedures? Explain your answer.

The government misjudged the situation. By September, banks were no longer taking excessive risks. The danger instead was that they would avoid taking any risks at all. After Lehman's collapse, banks became fearful that other banks might go under and fail to pay their debts. Banks therefore stopped making loans to each other. (See Figure 11–3 on page 262.) The money market, which provides short-term corporate finance, froze up as well. Lending threatened to stop altogether. The resulting prospect was ominous: access to credit is essential for a vast share of the nation's firms, and a lending freeze could shut down much of the economy. Panicked financiers pleaded for the government to "do something."

Policy Formulation

During the next step in the policymaking process, various policy proposals are discussed among government officials and the public. Such discussions may take place in the printed media, on television, and in the halls of Congress. Congress holds hearings, the president voices the administration's views, and the topic may even become a campaign issue.

In the example of the bank bailout, Paulson and other officials concluded that the underlying cause of the crisis was bank losses due to the collapse in the value of the "toxic assets." The Treasury Department proposed to restore confidence by buying up these assets. To obtain congressional funding, Treasury drafted a three-page bill that granted Paulson the right to spend $700 billion on mortgage-related assets. The $700 billion figure was pulled out of a hat—the only consideration was that the sum be large enough to impress the financial markets. On September 20, five days after Lehman collapsed, Treasury sent the bill to the House.

Members of Congress were shocked by the onset of the crisis, but they were flabbergasted by Paulson's bill. Never in the history of the republic had Congress ever granted such uncontrolled spending power to an executive department, nor had it ever allocated hundreds of billions of dollars based on what was effectively a three-page memo. Still, the House set to work, adding desirable oversight mechanisms and a large dose of pork. The resulting 110-page bill was put to a vote on September 29. Members of both parties proceeded to vote it down. The next day, the Dow Jones Industrial Average, an index of stock market prices, sustained its biggest point drop in history.

Policy Adoption

The third step in the policymaking process involves choosing a specific policy from among the proposals that have been discussed.

After the House refused to pass the bank bailout bill, the Senate sought to rescue it. Senate leaders decided to amend an existing bill already passed by the House—this step circumvented the clause in the Constitution requiring that revenue bills originate in the House. By the time the Senate was done with the bill, it was 451 pages long and bursting with earmarks designed to win necessary votes. The Senate passed the measure on October 1, the House accepted it on October 3, and President Bush signed it into law within hours.

Policy Implementation

The fourth step in the policymaking process involves the implementation of the policy alternative chosen by Congress. Government action must be implemented by bureaucrats, the courts, the police, and individual citizens.

The bank bailout, now known as the Troubled Assets Relief Program (TARP), actually expanded one grant of authority beyond what Treasury had included in the initial draft—it did not require that TARP funds be spent on mortgage-related assets. In the first weeks of October, Paulson and other officials began to realize that buying up toxic assets would not resolve the financial crisis. If Treasury paid market prices for the assets, banks would gain nothing of value. If Treasury overpaid, banks would gain financial stability, but taxpayers would be granting a huge subsidy to the banking industry that would never be returned.

On October 14, therefore, President Bush and Secretary Paulson announced that instead of buying toxic assets, TARP would buy preferred stock in banks, thereby adding to their capital. From the taxpayers' point of view, this step had two virtues: the preferred stock would pay interest, and the banks could eventually buy back the preferred stock, returning TARP funds to the government.

Policy Evaluation

After a policy has been implemented, it is evaluated. Groups inside and outside the government conduct studies to determine what actually happens after a policy has been in place for a given period of time. Based on this feedback and the perceived success or failure of the policy, a new round of policymaking initiatives may be undertaken to improve on the effort.

In the example of TARP, Congress developed a series of bodies to review Treasury's actions. These included a Financial Stability Oversight Board in the executive branch and a Congressional Oversight Panel. Congress also created a special inspector general for the program. Given its size and importance, TARP was also a focus of intense interest by the media. Surprisingly, relatively few people objected to the complete transformation in the use of TARP funds. Many Americans were greatly interested, however, in whether the government's investments would promote lending and in how much bankers would be paid.

HEALTH CARE

Spending for health care is estimated to account for about 17 percent of the total U.S. economy. In 1965, about 6 percent of our income was spent on health care, but that percentage has been increasing ever since. Per capita spending on health care is greater in the United States than almost anywhere else in the world. Measured by the percentage of the **gross domestic product (GDP)** devoted to health care, America spends more than twice as much as Britain or Japan. (The GDP is the dollar value of all final goods and services produced in a one-year period.)

The Rising Cost of Health Care

There are many explanations of why health-care costs have risen so much. One is that the U.S. population is getting older. Life expectancy has gone up. Not surprisingly, elderly people make up most of the top users of health-care services. Nursing home expenditures generally are made by people older than seventy, and the use of hospitals is also dominated by the aged.

Another reason that health-care costs have risen so dramatically is advancing technology. An MRI (magnetic resonance imaging) scanner can cost more than $2 million. A PET (positron-emission tomography) scanner can cost up to $4 million. These

Gross Domestic Product (GDP)
The value of all final goods and services produced in a country in a one-year period.

Medicare
A federal health-insurance program that covers U.S. residents over the age of sixty-five. The costs are met by a tax on wages and salaries.

Medicaid
A joint state-federal program that provides medical care to the poor (including indigent elderly persons in nursing homes). The program is funded out of general government revenues.

and other machines are in increased demand around the country. Typical fees for procedures using them are high—$2,000 or more for a PET scan, for example. New procedures that involve even greater costs can be expected in the future.

The Government's Role in Financing Health Care

Today, government spending on health care constitutes more than 45 percent of total health-care spending. Private insurance accounts for just under 35 percent of payments for health care. The remainder—less than 20 percent—is paid directly by individuals or by philanthropy. The federal programs Medicare and Medicaid are the main sources of hospital and other medical benefits for 40 million U.S. residents, most of whom are over the age of sixty-five. The government also buys health insurance for its own employees, provides medical services to veterans, and offers a number of additional health-care programs.

Medicare and Medicaid. **Medicare** is specifically designed to support the elderly, regardless of income. **Medicaid,** a joint state-federal program, is in principle a program to subsidize health care for the poor. In practice, it often provides long-term health care to persons living in nursing homes. (To become eligible for Medicaid, these individuals must first exhaust their financial assets.) Medicare, Medicaid, and private insurance companies are called third parties. Caregivers and patients are the two primary parties. When third parties pay for medical care, the demand for such services increases; health-care recipients have reduced incentives to restrain their use of health care. One result is some degree of wasted resources.

Medicare Costs. The Medicare program, which was created in 1965 under President Lyndon Johnson (1963–1969), pays hospital and physicians' bills for U.S. residents over the age of sixty-five. Since 2006, Medicare has also paid for at least part of the prescription drug expenses of the elderly. In return for paying a tax on their earnings (currently set at 2.9 percent of wages and salaries) while in the workforce, retirees are assured that the majority of their hospital and physicians' bills will be paid with public funds.

Medicare is now the second-largest domestic spending program, after Social Security. Government expenditures on Medicare have routinely exceeded forecasts. The government has responded in part by imposing arbitrary reimbursement caps

on specific procedures. The government has also cut rates of reimbursement to individual physicians and physician groups, such as health maintenance organizations (HMOs). As a result, several of the nation's largest HMOs have withdrawn from certain Medicare programs, and a growing number of physicians now refuse to treat Medicare patients.

The Cost of Medicaid. Within a few years, the joint federal-state taxpayer-funded Medicaid program for low-income persons has generated one of the biggest expansions of government entitlements ever. In 1997, total Medicaid spending was around $150 billion. Ten years later, it easily exceeded $300 billion.

In recent years, the federal government has paid about 55 percent of Medicaid's total cost—the states pay the rest. President Barack Obama's 2009 stimulus package included an extra $87 billion in federal spending for Medicaid, which substantially increased the federal share of the total. The stimulus allowed the states to reduce their Medicaid budgets. It also funded an expansion in the number of individuals covered—because of the recession, newly unemployed people joined the eligible population.

At the end of the last decade, 34 million people were enrolled in the program. Today, there are more than 59 million recipients. When you add Medicaid coverage to Medicare and the military and federal employee health plans, the government has clearly become the nation's primary health insurer. More than 100 million people—one in three—in the United States have government coverage.

The Issue of Universal Coverage

More than 45 million Americans—about 16 percent of the population—do not have health insurance. Hispanic Americans are the most likely to be uninsured, with only 33 percent covered. Although many Americans receive health-insurance benefits from their employers, not all do, and individual health-insurance policies (those not obtained through an employer) are extremely costly and may be impossible to obtain at any price.

According to surveys, being uninsured has negative health consequences. People without coverage are less likely to get basic preventive care, such as mammograms; less likely to have a personal physician; and more likely to rate their own health as only poor or fair. A further problem faced by the uninsured is that when they do seek medical care, they must usually pay much higher fees than would be paid on their behalf if they had insurance coverage. One benefit of insurance coverage is that it protects the insured against catastrophic costs resulting from unusual events. Medical care for life-threatening accidents or diseases can run into thousands or even hundreds of thousands of dollars. An uninsured person who requires this kind of medical care may be forced into bankruptcy.

▼ **Childhood inoculations** are routine in this country. Should the government pay for all health-care costs for children? Why or why not? (AP Photo/J. Scott Applewhite)

National Health Insurance
A plan under which the government provides basic health insurance to all citizens. In most such plans, the program is funded by taxes on wages or salaries.

The International Experience. The United States is the only advanced industrial country with a large pool of citizens who lack health insurance. Australia, Canada, Japan, and Western Europe all provide systems of universal coverage. Such coverage is typically provided through **national health insurance.** In effect, the government takes over the economic function of providing basic health-care coverage. Private insurers are excluded from this market (though they may be able to offer supplementary plans). The government collects premiums from employers and employees on the basis of their ability to pay and then provides basic services to the entire population.

The Clinton Health-Care Proposal. Since the time of President Harry Truman (1945–1953), some liberals have sought to establish a national health-insurance system in this country. During his first two years in office, President Bill Clinton (1993–2001) attempted to steer such a proposal through Congress. Clinton's plan, developed by a panel chaired by his wife, Hillary, was dauntingly complex, and the Clintons failed to build the political groundwork necessary for such a major change. Private insurance companies knew the Clinton program would deprive them of a major line of business and naturally did everything in their power to stop the bill. In the end, the proposal was defeated. Indeed, the proposal may have been an important reason why the Republicans gained control of Congress in the 1994 elections.

Recent Proposals. In the first decade of the twenty-first century, universal health insurance began to reappear as a political issue. Unlike previous proposals, current ones do not provide for a federal monopoly on basic health insurance. Instead, universal coverage results from a *mandate* that all citizens must obtain health insurance from some source—an employer, Medicare or Medicaid, or a new plan sponsored by the federal government or a state government. Low-income families would receive a subsidy to help them pay their insurance premiums. Insurers could not reject applicants. A program of this nature was adopted by the state of Massachusetts in 2006 in response to a proposal by Republican governor Mitt Romney. The plan actually adopted was more generous than Romney's initial proposal.

The Issue of Mandated Coverage. During the 2008 Democratic presidential primary campaigns, all the major candidates advocated universal coverage programs that included a major role for private insurance. Obama's plan differed from the others in that it did not require adults to obtain coverage, although coverage was required for children. Obama's plan, in other words, had no mandated coverage. Democratic candidate Hillary Clinton criticized Obama for leaving it out. Obama may have been politically astute, however—the Republicans could not accuse him of "forcing" people to do something, never a popular position in America.

As president, Obama largely delegated the drafting of a health-care plan to Congress, a tactic he employed with other measures such as the 2009 stimulus package and energy legislation. Obama's willingness to let Congress take the lead was a notable change—recent presidents such as George W. Bush and Bill Clinton had sought to push presidential proposals through the legislative process without significant alteration. Obama's tactics eliminated much of the tug-of-war between Congress and the president that was commonplace in past decades, and it helped unify the Democrats in Congress behind proposed legislation.

The Democrats quickly adopted mandated coverage in all of their draft proposals. While some of the uninsured were indeed too poor to afford coverage, many others were well-off, healthy young adults who were gambling—most of the time success-fully—that they would stay healthy. The insurance industry wanted the premiums that these people could pay. So did the Democrats, who were concerned about how to fund universal coverage.

A Government-Backed Insurance Program? The real battle in Congress took place over the idea of a government-supported insurance program, or *public option,* that would compete with private insurance firms. President Obama and a majority of the Democrats supported a public option, arguing that competition from such a plan would hold down the cost of private insurance and also guarantee that no one would go without coverage. The insurance industry and the Republicans were in vehement opposition. Their fear was that private companies could not compete with a program backed by the vast resources of the federal government. One consulting firm estimated that if a government program reimbursed hospitals and physicians at the same low rate as Medicare, it could set its premiums 32 percent below those charged by private insurers. In this scenario, 119 million people might drop existing private coverage to switch to the government-backed plan. Democrats responded to these concerns by pro-posing that the public program should resemble the private insurers: it should be self-supporting and be managed at arm's length from the rest of the federal government. In a speech to Congress and the nation on health care in September 2009, President Obama retreated further, stating that the public option would be available only to those who did not already have insurance, either through their employers, Medicare, or some other source. By October, however, it appeared unlikely that the public option would be included in the final package.

The Issue of Funding. In its initial work on heath care, Congress assumed that extending insurance coverage to everyone would cost an extra $120 billion per year, a figure in line with estimates by the Congressional Budget Office. (This compares with fiscal year 2010 estimates of $458 billion for Medicare and $262 for the federal share of Medicaid.) President Obama's budget, however, allocated only $60 billion for universal coverage. Where would Congress get the rest of the funding? Members were unwilling to merely add onto the federal budget deficit.

One way to handle spending was to reduce the cost of the package, and indeed the several versions of a health-care bill eventually reported out by House and Senate committees had price tags closer to $80 or $100 billion per year. House bills called for funding new coverage with heavier taxes on the rich. The Senate proposed a more complicated funding arrangement that included taxes on insurance companies. One method advanced by the Democrats to bridge the funding gap was to trim the predicted increase in the cost of the Medicare program over the next decade. The Republicans seized on this last proposal as a tool to be used against the Democratic proposals. It was a potent weapon. Surveys showed that Medicare recipients were opposed to changes in the health-care system, though younger voters supported reform.

The Cost of Health Care in the Twenty-First Century

From 1975 to 2005, per capita spending on health care in the United States grew at an average rate of 4.2 percent. The main driver of the growth in health-care spending was new medical technologies and services. The increased number of elderly persons had a much smaller effect on costs. Such rates of growth cannot continue indefinitely—at these rates, health-care spending would exceed the size of the GDP by the year 2083. Using more realistic assumptions, the Congressional Budget Office (CBO) calculated that if nothing were done, health-care spending would reach 31 percent of GDP by 2035.

Those over the age of 65 run up health-care bills that are far larger than those incurred by the rest of the population. As a federal problem, therefore, health-care spending growth is largely a Medicare issue. In 2009, the government's Medicare trustees reported that the Medicare trust fund was projected to run out of funds in 2017.

Cost Containment. Such prospects explain why in 2009, health-care cost containment was as important an issue as universal coverage, and why Democrats wanted a government-run insurance plan to hold down costs. President Obama proposed a variety of other measures designed to reduce expenses. These included requiring electronic medical records, studying which treatments work best, and reducing the number of unnecessary procedures. The CBO expressed doubts that these policies would save much. In May, however, Obama appeared with a group of health-care industry representatives who agreed that the rate of growth in health-care spending could be substantially reduced.

The Downside of Cost Containment. Republicans who opposed the Democrats' health-care proposals argued that a government-run plan would lead to "rationing," presumably by reining in expenditures. Indeed, the nations with government-run national health systems spend much less per person on health care than the United States. But life expectancy is also higher in most of these countries than in the United States, possibly because of universal coverage.

Despite the apparent positive outcomes, some people believe that these government-run systems retard medical progress. As an example, if pharmaceutical companies had to rely entirely on the low payments negotiated by European governments, they might not have enough resources to develop new drugs. Cost containment in the United States is unlikely to force spending down to European levels. Still, there must be some upper limit on how much Americans are willing to spend on health care, and in coming years, we may discover where that limit lies.

IMMIGRATION

In recent years, immigration rates in the United States have been among the highest they have been since their peak in the early twentieth century. Every year, more than 1 million people immigrate to this country legally, a figure that does not include the large number of unauthorized immigrants. Those who were born on foreign soil now constitute about 13 percent of the U.S. population—more than twice the percentage of thirty years ago.

Since 1977, four out of five immigrants have come from Latin America or Asia. Hispanics have overtaken African Americans as the nation's largest minority. As you learned in Chapter 5, if current immigration rates continue, by 2050 minority groups collectively will constitute the "majority" of Americans. If such groups were to form coalitions, they could increase their political power dramatically. The "old guard" white majority would no longer dominate American politics.

The Issue of Unauthorized Immigration

Illegal immigration—or unauthorized immigration, to use the terminology of the Department of Homeland Security—has become a major national issue. Latin Americans, especially those migrating from Mexico, constitute the majority of individuals entering the United States without permission. In addition, many unauthorized immigrants enter the country legally, often as tourists or students, and then fail to return home when their visa status expires. Naturally, the unauthorized population is hard to count, but recent estimates have put the number of such persons at about 12 million.

A major complication in addressing the issue of unauthorized immigrants is that they frequently live in mixed households, in which one or more members of a family have lawful resident status, but others do not. A woman from Guatemala with permanent resident status, for example, might be married to a Guatemalan man who is in the country illegally. Often, the parents in a family are unauthorized, whereas the children, who were born in the United States, possess American citizenship. Mixed families mean that deporting the unauthorized immigrant will either break up a family or force one or more American citizens into exile.

Attempts at Immigration Reform

Some people regard the high rate of immigration as a plus for America because it offsets the low birthrate and aging population. Immigrants expand the workforce and help to support, through their taxes, government programs that benefit older Americans, such as Medicare and Social Security. Critics, though, fear that immigrants may take jobs away from American workers and alter the nature of American culture.

The split in the public's attitudes has been reflected in differences among the nation's leaders over how to handle the issue of illegal immigration. While most Republicans in Congress have favored a harder line toward illegal immigrants than most Democrats, partisan divisions were blurred by the adherence of President George W. Bush and a number of Republican senators to the pro-immigration side of the debate.

Attempted Reforms during the Bush Administration. In January 2004, President Bush proposed a new temporary worker program. Illegal immigrants would be allowed to sign up for the program, thus regularizing their status. The plan included no provisions to ease the temporary workers' path toward citizenship, however. Criticism of Bush's plan was widespread. Immigration opponents objected to normalizing the status of illegal immigrants and feared that the guest worker program would increase rates of immigration from Mexico and elsewhere. Pro-immigrant voices claimed that the program would mostly provide a source of cheap labor to employers and would do little for the immigrants themselves.

▲ **These Hispanics** are participating in a demonstration in favor of immigration reform. (AP Photo/Rogelio Solis)

The following year, Republicans in the House of Representatives united to pass a radically different proposal, the Border Protection, Anti-Terrorism, and Illegal Immigration Control Act of 2005. The bill sought to tighten border security, increase the penalties for illegal immigration and for employing undocumented workers, and make aiding illegal immigrants a crime. The bill sparked a series of immigrant rights protests and did not pass the Senate.

In 2006 and 2007, with the active participation of the Bush administration, a bipartisan group of senators that included presidential candidate John McCain (R., Ariz.) prepared immigration legislation that was far different from the House's 2005 proposal. The hugely complicated Comprehensive Immigration Reform Act of 2007 would have provided a legalization program for undocumented immigrants with an eventual path to citizenship, a guest worker program, border enforcement measures, and much more. The bill's sponsors, however, could not gather the sixty votes needed for passage. Later in the year, Congress did pass legislation authorizing the construction of a seven-hundred-mile-long fence between the United States and Mexico.

During his campaign, Obama supported immigration reform that would give illegal immigrants a path toward citizenship and also called for a crackdown on the employers who hire them. On taking office, Obama ended the Bush-era policy of raids on workplaces to round up undocumented workers. Instead, the administration tried to persuade employers to fire them. Many employers discovered that, at least for the moment, they did not actually need undocumented workers to take low-paying jobs. With high unemployment, citizens were willing to fill these positions. Due to the health-care debate, the administration deferred immigration reform until 2010 at least, leaving its short-term policy as all stick and no carrot.

ENERGY AND THE ENVIRONMENT

A major part of President Obama's legislative agenda was directed at energy and environmental issues. Energy policy addresses two major problems: (1) America's reliance on foreign oil, much of which is produced by unfriendly regimes, and (2) global warming caused by increased emissions of carbon dioxide (CO_2) and other greenhouse gases.

Oil—A Strategic Issue

The United States now imports about three-fifths of the petroleum it consumes. Fortunately, about half of all U.S. imports come from two friendly neighbors, Canada and Mexico, and only about 16 percent from Middle Eastern countries, primarily Saudi Arabia. The world's largest oil exporters, however, include a number of nations that are not friends of the United States. Russia is the world's second-largest oil exporter, after Saudi Arabia. Other major exporters include Venezuela and Iran. Both are openly hostile to American interests, and Venezuela is a major source of U.S. imports. Of course, reducing dependence on imported oil not only provides national security benefits, but also curbs CO_2 emissions.

The Government's Response. Although reducing America's dependence on foreign oil is widely considered to be desirable, in recent years the U.S. government has done little to reach that goal. President Obama's actions have been more sweeping. In 2009, Obama issued higher fuel efficiency standards for vehicles. By 2016, the new requirement will be 39 miles per gallon for cars and 30 miles per gallon for light trucks.

The standards, which begin to take effect with 2011 models, will force major changes to vehicles and will inevitably add to their price. Obama plans to open up additional territory for domestic oil drilling, although not nearly as much as the Republicans have demanded. At Obama's request, Congress has supported research into alternative fuels. Ambitious as they may be, these measures are unlikely to eliminate U.S. dependence on petroleum imports altogether.

The Price of Oil. Commentators have suggested that Americans are unlikely to prefer fuel-efficient vehicles unless gasoline costs four or more dollars per gallon, a price reached temporarily in mid-2008. Some have also argued that the United States will never conserve oil unless the federal government imposes a large tax on gasoline. Others suggest that such a step is unnecessary. With the end of the most recent recession, people will drive more and gasoline prices will rise again.

Indeed, gasoline prices may rise more than many people expect. From January 2005 to July 2008, the price of oil rose from $40 a barrel to more than $140 before falling back, but oil production remained essentially flat. Some petroleum engineers have begun to ask whether increases in oil production are even possible at prices that people are willing to pay. It is generally agreed that at some point, the world will experience *peak oil,* a time when even very high oil prices will not produce an increase in production. Thereafter, world oil production will decline. The U.S. Department of Energy (DOE) predicts that the world's conventional oil production will rise 23 percent above current levels by 2030. In other words, the DOE believes that we are many years away from peak oil. Some critics, however, believe that we may have reached peak oil already. Regardless of whether these critics are correct, oil prices are likely to rise in future years. Higher prices may be more effective than any government program in persuading Americans to conserve.

Global Warming

In the 1990s, scientists working on climate change began to conclude that average world temperatures would rise significantly in the twenty-first century. Gases released by human activity, principally CO_2, are producing a "greenhouse effect," trapping the sun's heat and slowing its release into outer space.

The Kyoto Protocol. In 1997, delegates from around the world gathered in Kyoto, Japan, for a global climate conference sponsored by the United Nations. The conference issued a proposed treaty aimed at reducing emissions of greenhouse gases to 5.2 percent below 1990 levels by 2012. Just thirty-five developed nations were mandated to reduce their emissions, however—developing nations faced only voluntary limits. The U.S. Senate voted unanimously in 1997 that it would not accept a treaty that exempted developing countries, and in 2001

▼ **These polar bears** find themselves on a moving ice float. Some contend that global warming is responsible for Arctic ice breakup and is therefore jeopardizing these animals. What can be done to reduce global warming? (Johnny Johnson/Getty Images)

President George W. Bush announced that he would not submit the Kyoto protocol to the Senate for ratification. By 2009, 183 nations had ratified the protocol. Its rejection by the United States, however, raised the question of whether it could ever be effective.

The Global Warming Debate.

Almost all scientists who perform research on the world's climate believe that global warming will be significant, but there is considerable disagreement as to how much warming will actually occur. It is generally accepted that world temperatures have already increased by about 0.74 degrees Celsius over the last century. The United Nations' Intergovernmental Panel on Climate Change predicts increases ranging from 1.1 to 6.4 degrees Celsius by 2100. This range of estimates is rather wide and reflects the uncertainties involved in predicting the world's climate.

▲ CO_2 **is a naturally occurring by-product** of human and animal respiration. It is also blamed as a factor in increasing the chances of global warming. How much should the nation spend to reduce CO_2 output? (Theo Heimann/AFP/Getty Images)

Global warming has become a major political football to be kicked back and forth by conservatives and liberals. Former vice president Al Gore's Oscar-winning and widely viewed documentary on global warming, released in 2006, further fueled the debate. (Gore received the Nobel Peace Prize in 2007 for his work.) Titled *An Inconvenient Truth,* the film stressed that actions to mitigate global warming must be taken now if we are to avert a planet-threatening crisis. Environmental groups and others have been pressing the federal government to do just that.

Some conservatives have seized on the work of scientists who believe that global warming does not exist at all. (Some of these researchers work for oil companies.) If this were true, there would be no reason to limit emissions of CO_2 and other greenhouse gases. A more sophisticated argument by conservatives is that major steps to limit emissions in the near future would not be cost-effective. Bjørn Lomborg, a critic of the environmental movement, believes that it would be more practical to take action against global warming later in the century, when the world is (presumably) richer and when renewable energy sources have become more competitive in price.[2]

The Cap-and-Trade Program

The centerpiece of the Obama administration's legislative program on energy and the environment was a cap-and-trade bill designed to limit greenhouse gas emissions. Under this plan, the federal government would establish a national target or "cap" for emissions of CO_2 and other greenhouse gases. Major emitters would need permits, which they could buy and sell on the open market—hence the "trade." Over time, the

2. Bjørn Lomborg, *Cool It: The Skeptical Environmentalist's Guide to Global Warming* (New York: Knopf, 2008).

cap would decline, thus forcing a reduction in emissions. The goal adopted by the legislation was a 17 percent cut in emissions by the year 2020.

Initially, a major share of the permits would be distributed free to utility companies, heavy manufacturers, petroleum refiners, and others. The rest of the permits would be auctioned off, potentially raising tens of billions of dollars in new federal revenues. The free permits would be phased out over ten to fifteen years. The initial distribution of free permits allowed the Democratic leadership to win the support of energy industry leaders and Democrats representing states heavily reliant on coal-burning power plants.

The Origins of Cap-and-Trade. The cap-and-trade plan for greenhouse gases is based in part on an earlier program adopted in 1990 under President George H. W. Bush. Amendments to the Clean Air Act in that year established a cap-and-trade system for sulfur dioxide emissions from coal-burning power plants in the Midwest. These emissions were creating an "acid rain" problem in eastern states. The sulfur dioxide program is widely considered to be a great success. Some observers doubt, however, that the cap-and-trade legislation for greenhouse gases will be equally successful. This is partly due to the complexity of the system, and also because the costs imposed on society by cutting back on CO_2 emissions will be much larger than the costs of curbing sulfur dioxide.

Opposition to the Program. Republican opponents of the legislation objected to the auctioning of permits on the grounds that the income raised by the federal government was a major tax increase—in effect, a tax on carbon. In addition to the cost of the permits, cap-and-trade would force energy-intensive companies to rely on more expensive energy sources, and the cost of using more expensive technologies would be a major drag on the economy. Defenders of the program, however, argued that in emitting CO_2 and other pollutants, corporations were imposing serious costs on the rest of society, costs that could only be countered by federal action.

Other conservatives pointed out that China and India were making no attempt to curb CO_2 emissions. Today, China is the world's number-one emitter of greenhouse gases, and a reduction in U.S. emissions will do little to solve the problem of global warming unless the Chinese join the effort. Defenders of cap-and-trade, however, argue that it would be impossible for the United States to ask China to reduce its emissions if we ourselves were doing nothing.

For the Obama administration, a cap-and-trade program was a priority second only to health-care reform. The House, in response, reported a 932-page proposal out of committee in May. As you might guess from its size, the measure was replete with special allowances and other provisions designed to win votes. In September, Senate Democrats proposed an alternative to the House measure.

THE POLITICS OF ECONOMIC DECISION MAKING

Nowhere are the principles of public policymaking more obvious than in the economic decisions made by the federal government. The president and Congress (and to a growing extent, the judiciary) are constantly faced with questions of economic policy. Economic policy becomes especially important when the nation enters a recession.

Recession
An economic downturn, usually characterized by a fall in the GDP and rising unemployment.

Unemployment
The inability of those who are in the labor force to find a job; the number of those in the labor force actively looking for a job, but unable to find one.

Inflation
A sustained rise in the general price level of goods and services.

Fiscal Policy
The federal government's use of taxation and spending policies to affect overall business activity.

Keynesian Economics
A school of economic thought that tends to favor active federal government policymaking to stabilize economy-wide fluctuations, usually by implementing discretionary fiscal policy.

Good Times, Bad Times

Like any economy that is fundamentally capitalist, the U.S. economy experiences ups and downs. Good times—booms—are followed by lean years. If a slowdown is severe enough, it is called a **recession.** Recessions are characterized by increased **unemployment,** the inability of those who are in the workforce to find a job. The government tries to moderate the effects of such downturns. In contrast, booms are historically associated with another economic problem that the government must address—rising prices, or **inflation.**

Measuring Unemployment. Estimates of the number of unemployed are prepared by the U.S. Department of Labor. The Bureau of the Census also generates estimates using survey research data. Critics of the published unemployment rate calculated by the federal government believe that it fails to reflect the true numbers of discouraged workers and "hidden unemployed." Though there is no exact definition or way to measure discouraged workers, the Department of Labor defines them as people who have dropped out of the labor force and are no longer looking for a job because they believe that the job market has little to offer them.

Inflation. Rising prices, or inflation, can also be a serious economic and political problem. Inflation is a sustained upward movement in the average level of prices. Another way of defining inflation is as a decline in the purchasing power of money over time. The government measures inflation using the *consumer price index,* or CPI. The Bureau of Labor Statistics identifies a market basket of goods and services purchased by the typical consumer, and regularly checks the price of that basket. Over a period of many years, inflation can add up. For example, today's dollar is worth (very roughly) about a twentieth of what it was worth a century ago. In effect, today's dollar is a 1910 nickel.

The Business Cycle. Economists refer to the regular succession of economic expansions and contractions as *the business cycle.* An extremely severe recession is called a *depression,* as in the example of the Great Depression. By 1933, actual output was 35 percent below the nation's productive capacity. Unemployment reached 25 percent. Compared with this catastrophe, recessions since 1945 have usually been mild. Nevertheless, the United States has experienced recessions with some regularity. Recession years since 1960 have included 1970, 1974, 1980, 1982, 1990, 2001, and 2008.

To try to control the ups and downs of the national economy, the government has several policy options. One is to change the level of taxes or government spending. The other possibility involves influencing interest rates and the money side of the economy. We will examine taxing and spending, or fiscal policy, first.

Fiscal Policy

Fiscal policy is the domain of Congress. A fiscal policy approach to stabilizing the economy is often associated with a twentieth-century economist named John Maynard Keynes (1883–1946). This British economist originated the school of thought that today is called **Keynesian economics,** which supports the use of government spending and taxing to help stabilize the economy. (*Keynesian* is pronounced *kayn-zee-*un.) Keynes believed that there was a need for government intervention in the economy, in part, because after falling into a recession or depression, a modern economy may become trapped in an ongoing state of less-than-full employment.

Government Spending and Borrowing. Keynes developed his fiscal policy theories during the Great Depression of the 1930s. He believed that the forces of supply and demand operated too slowly on their own in such a serious recession. Unemployment meant people had less to spend, and because they could not buy things, more businesses failed, creating additional unemployment. It was a vicious cycle. Keynes's idea was simple: in such circumstances, the government should step in and engineer the spending that is needed to return the economy to a more normal state.[3]

The spending promoted by the government could take either of two forms. The government could increase its own spending, or it could cut taxes, allowing the taxpayer to undertake the spending instead. To have the effect Keynes wanted, however, it was essential that the spending be financed by borrowing. In other words, the government should run a **budget deficit**—it should spend more than it receives.

Criticisms of Keynes. Following World War II (1939–1945), Keynes's theories were integrated into the mainstream of economic thinking. There have always been economic schools of thought, however, that consider Keynesian economics to be fatally flawed. These schools argue either that fiscal policy has no effect or that it has negative side effects that outweigh any benefits. Some opponents of fiscal policy believe that the federal government should limit itself to monetary policy, which we will discuss shortly. Others even believe that it is best for the government to do nothing at all. For a further discussion of Keynesian economics, see Chapter 11's *At Issue* feature on page 255.

▲ **John Maynard Keynes** (1883–1946) argued in favor of government intervention to smooth out economic booms and busts. (Walter Stoneman/Samuel Bourne/Getty Images)

Discretionary Fiscal Policy. Keynes originally developed his fiscal theories as a way of lifting an economy out of a major disaster such as the Great Depression. Beginning with the presidency of John F. Kennedy (1961–1963), however, policymakers have attempted to use Keynesian methods to "fine-tune" the economy. This is discretionary fiscal policy—*discretionary* meaning left to the judgment, or discretion, of a policymaker. For example, President George W. Bush advertised his tax cuts of 2001 and 2003 as a method of stimulating the economy to halt the economic slowdown of those years.

The Timing Problem. Attempts to fine-tune the economy encounter a timing problem. It takes a while to collect and assimilate economic data. Months or a year may go by before an economic difficulty can be identified. After an economic problem is recognized, a solution must be formulated. There will be an action time lag between the recognition of a problem and the implementation of policy to solve it. Getting Congress to act can easily take a year or two. Finally, after fiscal policy is enacted, it takes time for it to have an effect on the economy. Because the fiscal policy time lags are long and variable, a policy designed to combat a recession may not produce results until the economy is already out of the recession.

Budget Deficit Government expenditures that exceed receipts.

---

3. Robert Skidelsky, *John Maynard Keynes: The Economist as Savior 1920–1937: A Biography* (New York: Penguin USA, 1994).

U.S. Treasury
Securities
Debt issued by the federal
government.

Public Debt, or
National Debt
The total amount of debt
carried by the federal
government.

Because of the timing problem, attempts by the government to employ fiscal policy in the last fifty years have typically taken the form of tax cuts or increases. Tax changes can take effect more quickly than government spending. In 2009, therefore, the Obama administration was employing a novel approach with its dramatic increase in government spending. Because the recession was worldwide and associated with a financial crisis, however, economists expected it to last for several years. That meant that there should be enough time for government spending to take effect.

Another issue with tax cuts is that taxpayers may use the income to pay down their debts, instead of spending it. According to Keynesian theory, this failure to spend reduces the stimulative effect of the tax cut—and in 2009, an unusually large number of people were trying to pay off their debts.

TABLE 13–1: Net Public Debt of the Federal Government

Year	Total (Billions of Current Dollars)
1940	$ 42.7
1945	235.2
1950	219.0
1960	237.2
1970	284.9
1980	709.3
1990	2,410.1
1992	2,998.6
1993	3,247.5
1994	3,432.1
1995	3,603.4
1996	3,747.1
1997	3,900.0
1998	3,870.0
1999	3,632.9
2000	3,448.6
2001	3,200.3
2002	3,528.7
2003	3,878.4
2004	4,420.8
2005	4,592.0
2006	4,829.0
2007	5,035.1
2008	5,802.7
2009	8,531.4*
2010	9,881.9*

*Estimate.
Source: U.S. Office of Management and Budget.

Deficit Spending and the Public Debt

The government typically borrows by selling **U.S. Treasury securities.** The sale of these securities to corporations, private individuals, pension plans, foreign governments, foreign businesses, and foreign individuals adds to this nation's **public debt, or national debt.** In the last few years, foreign governments, especially those of China and Japan, have come to own about 50 percent of the U.S. public debt. Thirty years ago, the share of the U.S. public debt held by foreigners was only 15 percent. Table 13–1 shows the net public debt of the federal government since 1940.

Table 13–1 does not take into account two very important variables: inflation and increases in population. A better way to examine the relative importance of the public debt is to compare it with the gross domestic product (GDP), as is done in Figure 13–1 on the facing page. (As noted earlier in this chapter, the gross domestic product is the dollar value of all final goods and services produced in a one-year period.) In the figure, you see that the public debt reached its peak during World War II and fell until 1975. From about 1960 to 2008, the net public debt as a percentage of GDP has ranged between 30 and 62 percent.

The Public Debt in Perspective. From 1960 until the last few years of the twentieth century, the federal government spent more than it received in all but two years. Some observers considered those ongoing budget deficits to be the negative result of Keynesian policies. Others argued that the deficits actually resulted from the abuse of Keynesianism. Politicians have been more than happy to run budget deficits in recessions, but they have often refused to implement the other side of Keynes's recommendations—to run a *budget surplus* during boom times.

In 1993, however, President Bill Clinton (1993–2001) obtained a tax increase as the nation emerged from a mild recession. Between the tax increase and the "dot-com boom," the United States had a budget surplus each year from 1998 to 2002. Some commentators predicted that we would be running federal government surpluses for years to come.

FIGURE 13–1: Net Public Debt as a
Percentage of the Gross Domestic Product

During World War II, the net public debt grew dramatically. It fell thereafter but rose again from 1975 to 1995. The percentage fell after 1995, only to rise dramatically after 2008.

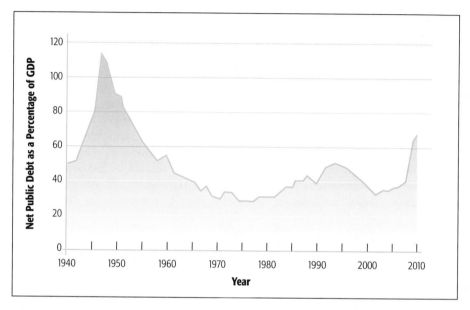

Source: U.S. Department of the Treasury.

Back to Deficit Spending. All of those projections went by the wayside because of several events. One event was the "dot-com bust" followed by the 2001–2002 recession, which lowered the rate of growth of not only the economy but also federal government tax receipts. Another event was a series of tax cuts passed by Congress in 2001 and 2003 at the urging of President George W. Bush. A third event took place on September 11, 2001. Basically, as a result of the terrorist attacks, the federal government spent much more than it had planned to spend on security against terrorism. The government also had to pay for the war in Iraq in 2003 and the occupation of that country thereafter. Finally, Congress authorized major increases in spending on discretionary programs.

Immediately upon taking office, President Obama obtained legislation from Congress that pushed the public debt to levels not seen since World War II. Such high levels of debt became a major political issue. For more details on Obama's approach to federal budget deficits, see Chapter 9's *The Politics of Boom and Bust* feature on page 223.

Monetary Policy

Controlling the rate of growth of the money supply is called *monetary policy*. This policy is the domain of the **Federal Reserve System,** also known simply as **the Fed.** The Fed is the most important regulatory agency in the U.S. monetary system.

The Fed performs a number of important functions. Perhaps the Fed's most important task is regulating the amount of money in circulation, which can be defined

Federal Reserve System (the Fed)
The system created by Congress in 1913 to serve as the nation's central banking organization.

Federal Open Market Committee
The most important body within the Federal Reserve System. The Federal Open Market Committee decides how monetary policy should be carried out.

Monetary Policy
The utilization of changes in the amount of money in circulation to alter credit markets, employment, and the rate of inflation.

loosely as checking account balances and currency. The Fed also provides a system for transferring checks from one bank to another. In addition, it holds reserves deposited by most of the nation's banks, savings and loan associations, savings banks, and credit unions. Finally, it plays a role in supervising the banking industry.

Organization of the Federal Reserve System. A board of governors manages the Fed. This board consists of seven full-time members appointed by the president with the approval of the Senate. There are twelve Federal Reserve district banks. The most important unit within the Fed is the **Federal Open Market Committee.** This is the body that actually determines the future growth of the money supply and other important economy-wide financial variables. This committee is composed of the members of the Board of Governors, the president of the New York Federal Reserve Bank, and presidents of four other Federal Reserve banks, rotated periodically.

The Board of Governors of the Federal Reserve System is independent. The president can attempt to influence the board, and Congress can threaten to merge the Fed into the Treasury Department, but as long as the Fed retains its independence, its chairperson and governors can do what they please. Hence, any talk about "the president's monetary policy" or "Congress's monetary policy" is inaccurate. The Fed remains a relatively independent source.

Loose and Tight Monetary Policies. The Federal Reserve System seeks to stabilize nationwide economic activity by controlling the amount of money in circulation. Changing the amount of money in circulation is a major aspect of **monetary policy.** You may have read a news report in which a business executive complained that money is "too tight." You may have run across a story about an economist who has warned that money is "too loose." In these instances, the terms *tight* and *loose* refer to the monetary policy of the Fed.

Credit, like any good or service, has a cost. The cost of borrowing—the interest rate—is similar to the cost of any other aspect of doing business. When the cost of borrowing falls, businesspersons can undertake more investment projects. When it rises, businesspersons undertake fewer projects. Consumers also react to interest rates when deciding whether to borrow funds to buy houses, cars, or other "big-ticket" items.

If the Fed implements a *loose monetary policy* (often called an "expansionary" policy), the supply of credit increases and its cost falls. If the Fed implements a *tight monetary policy* (often called a "contractionary" policy), the supply of credit falls and its cost increases. A loose money policy is often implemented as an attempt to encourage economic growth. You may be wondering why any nation would want a tight monetary policy. The answer is to control inflation. If money becomes too plentiful too quickly, prices increase, and the purchasing power of the dollar decreases.

Time Lags for Monetary Policy. You learned earlier that policymakers

◀ **Benjamin S. Bernanke** is the chair of the Board of Governors of the Federal Reserve System, which means he is the head of the central bank in the United States. Some commentators contend that the chair of the Fed is the most powerful person on earth, at least in terms of economics. The Fed controls the rate of growth of the amount of money in circulation and, by implication, the "tightness" or "looseness" of credit markets. Since the start of the current economic crisis, Bernanke has become increasingly powerful, and therefore more controversial. The Federal Reserve System has engaged in activities aimed at fighting the recession that it has never engaged in before. (Photo by the Federal Reserve Board)

who implement fiscal policy—the manipulation of budget deficits and the tax system—experience problems with time lags. Similar problems face the Fed when it implements monetary policy.

Sometimes accurate information about the economy is not available for months. Once the state of the economy is known, time may elapse before any policy can be put into effect. Still, the time lag in implementing monetary policy is usually much shorter than the lag in implementing fiscal policy. The Federal Open Market Committee meets eight times a year and can put a policy into effect relatively quickly. A change in the money supply may not have an effect for several months, however.

Monetary Policy during Recessions. A tight monetary policy is effective as a way of taming inflation. (Some would argue that it is the *only* way that inflation can be stopped.) If interest rates go high enough, people *will* stop borrowing. How effective, though, is a loose monetary policy at ending a recession? Under normal conditions, it is very effective. A loose monetary policy will spur an expansion in economic activity.

To combat the Great Recession, however, the Fed reduced its interest rate effectively to zero. It could not go any lower. Yet banks, seeking to rebuild their capital, did not lower their rates in response. Moreover, many businesses discovered that they could not obtain credit even to support obviously profitable investments. When consumers had credit, they were still reluctant to make major purchases. Monetary policy had run out of steam; using it was like "pushing on a string." The government has little power to force banks to lend, and it certainly has no power to make people borrow and spend. As a result, the Obama administration placed its bets on fiscal policy.

During 2008 and 2009, the Fed developed a new way to respond to the failure of banks to lend. Relying on its ability to create money, it began to make loans itself, without turning to Congress for appropriations. The Fed bought debt issued by corporations. It bought securities that were based on student loans and credit-card debt. By 2009, the Fed had loaned out close to $2 trillion in fresh credit.

THE POLITICS OF TAXATION

Congress enacts tax laws at the federal level. The Internal Revenue Code, which is the federal tax code, encompasses thousands of pages, thousands of sections, and thousands of subsections—our tax system is not very simple.

Americans pay a variety of different taxes. At the federal level, the income tax is levied on most sources of income. Social Security and Medicare taxes are assessed on wages and salaries. There is an income tax for corporations, which has an indirect effect on many individuals. The estate tax is collected from property left behind by those who have died. State and local governments also assess taxes on income, sales, and land. Altogether, the value of all taxes collected by the federal government and by state and local governments is well over 30 percent of the gross domestic product.

Federal Income Tax Rates

Individuals and businesses pay income taxes based on tax rates. Not all of your income is taxed at the same rate. The first few dollars you make are not taxed at all. The highest rate is imposed on the "last" dollar you make. This highest rate is the *marginal* tax rate. Table 13–2 on page 322 shows the 2009 marginal tax rates for individuals and married couples. The higher the tax rate—the action on the part of the

TABLE 13–2: **Marginal Tax Rates for Single Persons and Married Couples (2009)**

Single Persons		Married Filing Jointly	
Marginal Tax Bracket	Marginal Tax Rate	Marginal Tax Bracket	Marginal Tax Rate
$ 0–$ 8,350	10%	$ 0–$ 16,700	10%
$ 8,350–$ 33,950	15%	$ 16,700–$ 67,900	15%
$ 33,950–$ 82,250	25%	$ 67,900–$137,050	25%
$ 82,250–$171,550	28%	$137,050–$208,850	28%
$171,550–$372,950	33%	$208,850–$372,950	33%
$372,950 and higher	35%	$372,950 and higher	35%

government—the greater the public's reaction to that tax rate. If the highest tax rate you pay on the income you make is 15 percent, then any method you can use to reduce your taxable income by one dollar saves you fifteen cents in tax liabilities that you owe the federal government. Individuals paying a 15 percent rate have a relatively small incentive to avoid paying taxes, but consider individuals who were faced with a tax rate of 94 percent in the 1940s during World War II. They had a tremendous incentive to find legal ways to reduce their taxable incomes. For every dollar of income that was somehow deemed nontaxable, these taxpayers would reduce tax liabilities by ninety-four cents.

Loopholes and Lowered Taxes

Individuals and corporations facing high tax rates will adjust their earning and spending behavior to reduce their taxes. They will also make concerted attempts to get Congress to add **loopholes** to the tax law that allow them to reduce their taxable incomes. When Congress imposed very high tax rates on high incomes, it also provided for more loopholes than it does today. For example, special provisions enabled investors in oil and gas wells to reduce their taxable incomes.

Progressive and Regressive Taxation. As Table 13–2 shows, the greater your income, the higher the marginal tax rate. Persons with large incomes pay a larger share of their income in income tax. A tax system in which rates go up with income is called a **progressive tax** system. The federal income tax is clearly progressive.

The income tax is not the only tax you must pay. For example, the federal Social Security tax is levied on all wage and salary income at a flat rate of 6.2 percent. (Employers pay another 6.2 percent, making the total effective rate 12.4 percent.) In 2009, however, there was no Social Security tax on wages and salaries in excess of $106,800. (This "cap" changes from year to year.) Persons with very high salaries therefore pay no Social Security tax on much of their wages. In addition, the tax is not levied on investment income (including capital gains, rents, royalties, interest, dividends, or profits from a business). The wealthy receive a much greater share of their income from these sources than others do. As a result, the wealthy pay a much smaller portion of their income in Social Security taxes than do the working poor. The Social

Loophole
A legal method by which individuals and businesses are allowed to reduce the tax liabilities they owe to the government.

Progressive Tax
A tax that rises in percentage terms as incomes rise.

Security tax is therefore a **regressive tax.** To fund Medicare, a combined employer/employee 2.9 percent tax is also assessed on all wage income, with no upper limit.

Regressive Tax
A tax that falls in percentage terms as incomes rise.

What Kind of Tax System Do We Have? The various taxes Americans pay pull in different directions. The Medicare tax, as applied to wages and salaries, is entirely flat—that is, neither progressive nor regressive. Because it is not levied on investment income, however, it is regressive overall. The federal estate tax is extremely progressive, because it is not imposed at all on smaller estates. Sales taxes are regressive because the wealthy spend a relatively smaller portion of their income on items subject to the sales tax. Add everything up, and the tax system as a whole is progressive. Should the system be more progressive, as President Obama has advocated? We discuss that issue in this chapter's *At Issue* feature on the following two pages.

Social Security

Because Social Security is funded by its own special tax, the future of Social Security is in large part a tax question. Social Security was established as a means of guaranteeing a minimum level of pension benefits to all persons. Today, many people regard Social Security as a kind of "social compact"—a national promise to successive generations that they will receive support in their old age.

One complication with the Social Security system is that many people who pay into Social Security think that they are actually paying into a fund, perhaps with their name on it. This is what you do when you pay into a private pension plan. It is not true of Social Security, which is basically a pay-as-you-go transfer system in which those who are working are paying benefits to those who are retired.

The Social Security Problem. Today, the number of people who are working relative to the number of people who have retired is declining. In 1960, ten workers paid into Social Security for every one retiree. Today, the ratio is a little more than three workers per retiree. By 2030, only two workers will be available to support each retiree. In 2009, the Social Security trustees estimated that the Social Security Trust Fund would be exhausted by the year 2037.

In fact, the need to fund Social Security will put serious pressure on the federal budget long before 2037. Today, the Social Security tax brings in more revenue than the program pays out. Social Security loans the extra funds to the rest of the federal government. As Social Security costs rise, there will be fewer surplus funds for the rest of the government to borrow. In 2016, program costs will exceed tax revenues, and the rest of the government will have to start paying back what it borrowed in earlier years. These repayments will create greater and greater problems for the federal budget. The year 2037 merely represents the time when Social Security may no longer be able to fund itself completely with a combination of tax revenues and repayments from the rest of the government.

Social Security Solutions. The problem of paying for Social Security in the future is similar to the problem of funding Medicare, which we discussed earlier in this chapter. Fortunately, fixing Social Security should be much less expensive than addressing the health-care issue. Social Security could achieve long-term solvency in several

atIssue: Should the Rich Pay Even More in Taxes?

The rich have gotten richer over the last few decades, of that we are certain. Go back to 1979—in that year, the top 1 percent of income earners made 9.3 percent of the nation's total income. Thirty years later, the top 1 percent of income earners made almost 19 percent of the nation's income.

▲ **Barack Obama** campaigns in New Hampshire.
(Darren McCollester/Getty Images)

If the Rich Are Richer, Why Shouldn't They Pay More Taxes?

Not only have the rich increased their share of the nation's income, they have become wealthier (notwithstanding the recent declines in the stock market). The gap between the rich and poor has increased so much in the last few decades that some say the American dream is over. It used to be said that "a rising tide raises all boats." Many boats today are simply being swamped.

We are increasingly becoming a society divided by class. A small minority lives in opulence while the majority struggles. In the last ten years, the salaries of average workers, corrected for inflation, have barely risen. The number of millionaires and billionaires has skyrocketed. In this context it seems perfectly appropriate to raise taxes on the

rich. After all, they are now paying much lower marginal tax rates than during much of the postwar history of the United States. There have been periods when marginal federal income tax rates on the very rich exceeded 90 percent, and other periods when the rates were around 70 percent. Today, they are less than 40 percent. In addition, the tax on capital gains, which make up a much larger share of the income of the rich than of other people, is at 15 percent today for those with large incomes. This rate is lower than that assessed on wages or interest from savings accounts.

It seems appropriate that those who have benefited the most from America's economic system should pay more, particularly when many social needs are unmet and must be paid for by increased government expenditures. The rich will argue that they are the "engines of economic growth" and therefore should be encouraged to continue their hard work, but higher taxes are not going to keep the wealthy from striving.

Don't Kill the Geese That Lay the Golden Eggs

It is true that the top 1 percent of income earners now receive 19 percent of the national income, whereas thirty years ago they made less than 10 percent. The part of the story that is less often told is that in those thirty years, even as marginal federal personal income tax rates fell, the share of total income taxes paid by the top 1 percent of income earners increased from 18.3 percent to 37 percent. The top 1 percent of income-earning U.S. residents paid more than one-third of all federal income taxes in the United States on the eve of the recent economic crisis.

The top 40 percent of all income earners pay 99.1 percent of federal income taxes. That means that the lower 60 percent of income earners pay less than 1 percent of these taxes. Over the past few years, the richest 1.3 million tax filers paid more in federal income taxes than all of the 66 million U.S. tax filers below the median income in the United States—ten times more.

A shrinking number of Americans already bear a larger and larger share of the nation's income tax burden. The flip side is that a growing share of Americans pays little or no income tax. The number of those who pay nothing to support the federal government through the income tax continues to rise every year. Indeed, an increasingly large number of Americans actually receive more through the federal income tax than they pay. Twenty-five million families and individuals with incomes of less than about

$40,000 receive payments as part of the Earned Income Tax Program that substantially reduce their Social Security and Medicare taxes.

It is true that the rich have benefited most from cuts in marginal federal income tax rates. After all, they are the individuals who pay the most federal income taxes. Indeed, if you eliminated all the federal income taxes assessed on the bottom 50 percent of income earners, the U.S. Treasury would see almost no change in tax revenues received.

If we use taxes to "soak the rich," we will tax the most productive individuals in the country. Higher marginal tax rates discourage effort, and the higher the tax rate, the greater the discouragement. Every government policy action has a cost. The cost of increasing the federal marginal income tax rate on the richest Americans will be a lower rate of economic growth. More income will be redistributed, but is that the ultimate goal of society?

FOR CRITICAL ANALYSIS

How is it possible for the rich to pay more in taxes if their marginal tax rates are lower?

different ways. Benefits could be reduced for those who will retire a decade or more from now. The retirement age could be raised. Taxes could increase—for example, the cap on income subject to the Social Security tax could be raised or even eliminated, thus bringing in more taxes from individuals with high salaries. Some combination of these measures could be adopted.

In 2005, President Bush called for partially privatizing Social Security in the hope of increasing the rate of return on individuals' retirement contributions by investing them in stocks. Such a solution appears to be politically impossible in the near future, given the enormous losses sustained by the stock market in 2008 and early 2009. President Obama has stated that he intends to push for Social Security reform at some point in the next few years. He is also on record as opposing benefit cuts and supporting modifications to the cap on income.

▼ **During his presidency, George W. Bush** pushed for at least a partial privatization of our Social Security system. Why do you think he eventually dropped this request to Congress? (J. Scott Applewhite/AP Photo)

making a difference

LEARNING ABOUT ENTITLEMENT REFORM

Collectively, programs such as Medicare, Medicaid, Social Security, unemployment compensation, and several others are known as *entitlement programs*. They are called entitlements because if you meet certain qualifications—of age or income, for example—you are entitled to specified benefits. The federal government can estimate how much it will have to pay out in entitlements but cannot set an exact figure in advance. In this way, entitlement spending differs from other government spending. When Congress decides what it will give to the national park system, for example, it allocates an exact sum, and the park system cannot exceed that budget. Along with national defense, entitlements make up by far the greatest share of the federal budget. This fact led a Bush administration staff member to joke: "It helps to think of the government as an insurance company with an army."

Why Should You Care? What happens to entitlements will affect your life in two major ways. Entitlement spending will largely determine how much you pay in taxes throughout your working lifetime. Entitlement policy will also determine how much support you receive from the federal government when you grow old. Because entitlements make up such a large share of the federal budget, it is not possible to address the issue of budget deficits without considering entitlement spending. Further, as you learned in this chapter, under current policies, spending on Medicare and Social Security will rise in future years, placing ever-greater pressure on the federal budget. Sooner or later, entitlement reform will be impossible to avoid. However these programs are changed, you will feel the effects in your pocketbook throughout your life.

What Can You Do? Should Medicare and Social Security benefits be high, with the understanding that taxes must therefore go up? Should these programs be cut back in the hope of avoiding deficits and tax increases? Do entitlements mean that the old are fleecing the young—or is that argument irrelevant because we will all grow old someday? Progressives and conservatives disagree

strongly about these questions. You can develop your own opinions by learning more about entitlement reform. The following organizations take a conservative position on entitlements:

National Center for Policy Analysis
www.retirementreform.ncpa.org

The Heritage Foundation
www.heritage.org/LeadershipForAmerica/entitlements.cfm

The following organizations take a liberal stand on entitlements:

National Committee
to Preserve Social Security and Medicare
www.ncpssm.org

AARP
(formerly the American Association of Retired Persons)
www.aarp.org

▶ **The AARP lobbies** for more federal expenditures on senior citizens. Who ultimately ends up paying for many of these additional benefits? (Screen capture from www.aarp.org)

keyterms

budget deficit 317	inflation 316	moral hazard 302	regressive tax 323
domestic policy 301	Keynesian	national health	unemployment 316
Federal Open Market	economics 316	insurance 308	U.S. Treasury
Committee 320	loophole 322	progressive tax 322	securities 318
Federal Reserve System	Medicaid 306	public debt, or national	
(the Fed) 319	Medicare 306	debt 318	
fiscal policy 316	monetary policy 320	recession 316	
gross domestic product			
(GDP) 305			

chaptersummary

1 Domestic policy consists of laws, government planning, and government actions that concern internal issues of national importance. Policies are created in response to public problems or public demand for government action. Major policy problems discussed in this chapter include health care, immigration, and energy and the environment.

2 The policymaking process is initiated when policymakers become aware—through the media or from their constituents—of a problem that needs to be addressed by the legislature and the president. The process of policymaking includes five steps: agenda building, policy formulation, policy adoption, policy implementation, and policy evaluation. Policy actions typically result in both costs and benefits for society.

3 Health-care spending accounts for about 17 percent of the U.S. economy and is growing. Reasons for this growth include the increasing number of elderly persons and advancing technology. Costs are also higher because payments are picked up by third-party insurers. A major third party is Medicare, the federal program that pays health-care expenses of U.S. residents over the age of sixty-five. The federal government has tried to restrain the growth in Medicare spending.

4 About 16 percent of the population does not have health insurance—a major political issue. Individual health-insurance policies (not obtained through an employer) are expensive and may be unobtainable at any price. In most wealthy countries, this problem is addressed by a national health-insurance system under which the government provides basic coverage to all citizens. Recent proposals for universal

coverage in the United States would require residents not already covered to purchase coverage, which would be subsidized for low-income persons.

5 America has always been a land of immigrants and continues to be so. Today, more than 1 million immigrants enter the United States each year, and foreign-born persons make up more than 13 percent of the U.S. population. The status of illegal immigrants, who may number 12 million, is a major political issue. Some people wish to give such persons a legally recognized status and allow someday to become citizens. Others call for tougher laws against illegal immigration and against hiring illegal entrants.

6 Issues concerning energy and the environment are on the nation's agenda today. One problem is our reliance on petroleum imports, given that many petroleum exporters are hostile to American interests. Raising the average fuel efficiency of cars sold in the United States is one method of reducing imports. Global warming, caused by the emission of CO_2 and other greenhouse gases, is a second major problem, although some dispute how serious it is. The federal cap-and-trade program addresses global warming by requiring major emitters to obtain permits that can be bought and sold on the open market. Over time, the number of permits will drop, as will the number of permits distributed free to industry. Permits that are not free will be auctioned off, a source of revenue for the federal government.

7 Fiscal policy is the use of taxes and spending to affect the overall economy. Time lags in implementing fiscal policy can create serious difficulties. The federal government has run a deficit in most years since the 1930s. The deficit is met by U.S. Treasury borrowing. This adds to the public debt of the U.S. government. Although the budget was temporarily in surplus from 1998 to 2002, deficits now seem likely for many years to come.

8   Monetary policy is controlled by the Federal Reserve System, or the Fed. Monetary policy consists of changing the rate of growth of the money supply in an attempt to either stimulate or cool the economy. A loose monetary policy, in which more money is created, encourages economic growth. A tight monetary policy, in which less money is created, may be the only effective way of ending an inflationary spiral.

9   U.S. taxes amount to about 30 percent of the gross domestic product. Individuals and corporations that pay taxes at the highest rates will try to pressure Congress into creating exemptions and tax loopholes. Loopholes allow high-income earners to reduce their taxable incomes.

10   Closely related to the question of taxes is the viability of the Social Security and Medicare systems. As the number of people who are retired increases relative to the number of people who are working, those who are working may have to pay more for the benefits of those who retire. Proposed solutions to the problem include raising taxes, reducing benefits, or both.

QUESTIONS FOR
discussionandanalysis

1   Until recently, Congress has always opposed the establishment of a universal health-insurance system for the United States. What could be the reasons for this stance? Are the reasons compelling? What political interests might oppose a universal system, and why?

2   Under a universal health-insurance system, we would face the question of whether illegal immigrants would be covered. (They do, after all, make up a major part of the uninsured population.) What complications could arise as a result?

3   Just how serious an offense should illegal immigration be? Construct arguments in favor of considering it a felony and arguments for viewing it as a mere civil infraction.

4   Should the problem of illegal immigration be addressed by making legal immigration easier? Why or why not?

5   Are Bjørn Lomborg's arguments against taking immediate action on global warming good sense or dangerous nonsense? In either case, why? What about the requirements spelled out in the Kyoto treaty: good sense or dangerous nonsense? Again, explain your reasoning.

6   The federal income tax system collects a greater percentage of the income of wealthier persons than of poorer ones. The Social Security tax, in contrast, imposes a flat rate on all incomes—and is not collected at all on income above a certain threshold. Are the higher income tax rates for wealthy people fair? Why or why not? Is the method of calculating the Social Security tax fair? Why or why not?

helpful online **Resources**

CONNECTING TO AMERICAN GOVERNMENT AND POLITICS

Washington, D.C., is home to a variety of "think tanks" that provide detailed policy analysis. For a moderately conservative examination of domestic policy issues, visit the Web site of the American Enterprise Institute for Public Policy at:

www.aei.org

To see policy studies at a moderately liberal think tank, visit the Brookings Institution at:

www.brookings.edu

To learn more about economics from a free market point of view, see the Web site of the Library of Economics and Liberty at:

www.econlib.org

Paul Krugman, Princeton professor and *New York Times* columnist, is the dean of liberal economics columnists. You can find his blog, titled *The Conscience of a Liberal,* at:

krugman.blogs.nytimes.com

a special WebSite

FOR YOUR TEXT

Go to this book's special Web site at academic.cengage.com/polisci/Schmidt/ Brief6e. Choose "For Students." Then click on Chapter 13, where you will find an online quiz and other helpful study aids. If your professor is using CengageNOW: *American Government and Politics Today, Brief Edition,* log in and go to Chapter 13 for additional online study aids.

14

Foreign Policy

These members of the New York City Fire Department are removing the body of someone who perished in the September 11, 2001, terrorist attacks on the World Trade Centers. Those attacks changed American foreign policy forever. (AP Photo/Beth A. Keiser)

On September 11, 2001, Americans were forced to change their view of national security and of our relations with the rest of the world—literally overnight. No longer could citizens of the United States believe that national security issues involved only threats overseas or that the American homeland could not be attacked. No longer could Americans believe that regional conflicts in other parts of the world had no direct impact on the United States.

Within a few days, it became known that the 9/11 attacks on the World Trade Centers and on the Pentagon had been planned and carried out by a terrorist network named al Qaeda, which was funded and directed by the radical Islamist leader Osama bin Laden. The network was closely linked to the Taliban government of Afghanistan, which had ruled that nation since 1996.

Americans were shocked by the complexity and the success of the attacks. They wondered how our airport security systems could have failed so drastically. How could the Pentagon, the heart of the nation's defense, have been successfully attacked? Shouldn't our intelligence community have known about, and defended against, this terrorist network? And, finally, how could our foreign policy have been so blind to the anger of Islamist groups throughout the world?

In this chapter, we examine the tools of foreign policy and national security policy in the light of the many challenges facing the United States today. One such challenge for U.S. foreign policymakers today is how best to respond to the threat of terrorism. We also review the history of American foreign policy.

FACING THE WORLD: FOREIGN AND DEFENSE POLICY

The United States is only one nation in a world with almost two hundred independent countries, many located in regions where armed conflict is ongoing. What tools does our nation have to deal with the many challenges to its peace and prosperity? One tool is **foreign policy.** By this term, we mean both the goals the government wants to achieve in the world and the techniques and strategies used to achieve them. These techniques and strategies include **diplomacy, economic aid, technical assistance,** and military intervention. Sometimes foreign policies are restricted to statements of goals or ideas, such as the goal of helping to end world poverty, whereas at other times foreign policies involve comprehensive efforts to achieve particular objectives, such as preventing Iran from obtaining nuclear weapons.

As you will read later in this chapter, in the United States, the **foreign policy process** usually originates with the president and those agencies that provide advice on foreign policy matters. Congressional action and national public debate often affect foreign policy formulation as well.

National Security and Defense Policy

As one aspect of overall foreign policy, **national security policy** is designed primarily to protect the independence and the political integrity of the United States. It concerns itself with the defense of the United States against actual or potential (real or possible future) enemies.

U.S. national security policy is based on determinations made by the Department of Defense, the Department of State, and a number of other federal agencies, including the National Security Council (NSC). The NSC acts as an advisory body to the president, but it has increasingly become a rival to the State Department in influencing the foreign policy process.

Defense policy is a subset of national security policy. Generally, defense policy refers to the set of policies that direct the nature and activities of the U.S. armed forces. Defense policies are proposed by the leaders of the nation's military forces and the secretary of defense and are greatly influenced by congressional decision makers.

Diplomacy

Diplomacy is another aspect of foreign policy. Diplomacy includes all of a nation's external relationships, from routine diplomatic communications to summit meetings among heads of state. More specifically, diplomacy refers to the settling of disputes and conflicts among nations by peaceful methods. Diplomacy is also the set of negotiating techniques by which a nation attempts to carry out its foreign policy.

Of course, diplomacy can be successful only if the parties are willing to negotiate. The question of whether to negotiate with leaders such as Mahmoud Ahmadinejad, the president of Iran, became an issue in the 2008 U.S. presidential campaigns. Illinois senator Barack Obama, the Democrat, favored negotiating with Ahmadinejad without preconditions. Arizona senator John McCain, the Republican, denounced the idea of negotiating with him at all.

Foreign Policy
A nation's external goals and the techniques and strategies used to achieve them.

Diplomacy
The process by which states carry on political relations with each other; the process of settling conflicts among nations by peaceful means.

Economic Aid
Assistance to other nations in the form of grants, loans, or credits to buy the assisting nation's products.

Technical Assistance
The practice of sending experts in such areas as agriculture, engineering, or business to aid other nations.

Foreign Policy Process
The steps by which foreign policy goals are decided and acted on.

National Security Policy
Foreign and domestic policy designed to protect the nation's independence and political and economic integrity; policy that is concerned with the safety and defense of the nation.

Defense Policy
A subset of national security policy concerning the U.S. armed forces.

MORALITY VERSUS REALITY IN FOREIGN POLICY

Moral Idealism
A philosophy that views nations as normally willing to cooperate and to agree on moral standards for conduct.

Political Realism
A philosophy that views each nation as acting principally in its own interest.

From the earliest years of the republic, Americans have felt that their nation had a special destiny. The American experiment in democratic government and capitalism, it was thought, would provide the best possible life for its citizens and be a model for other nations. As the United States assumed greater status as a power in world politics, Americans came to believe that the nation's actions on the world stage should be guided by American political and moral principles.

Moral Idealism

This view of America's mission has led to the adoption of many foreign policy initiatives that are rooted in **moral idealism.** This philosophy views the world as fundamentally benign and assumes that most nations can be persuaded to take moral considerations into account when setting their policies.[1] In this perspective, nations should come together and agree to keep the peace, as President Woodrow Wilson (1913–1921) proposed for the League of Nations. Many foreign policy initiatives taken by the United States have been based on this idealistic view of the world. The Peace Corps, which was created by President John Kennedy in 1961, is one example of an effort to spread American goodwill and technology.

▲ **This Peace Corps volunteer** is helping Ghanaian farmers develop a tourist business. Her work is an example of the moral idealism that is an important component of U.S. foreign policy. What assumption is used to justify moral idealism? (Photo Courtesy of Peace Corps)

Political Realism

In opposition to the moral perspective is **political realism.** Realists see the world as a dangerous place in which each nation strives for its own survival and interests regardless of moral considerations. The United States must therefore base its foreign policy decisions on cold calculations without regard to morality. Realists believe that the United States must be prepared to defend itself militarily, because other nations are, by definition, dangerous. A strong defense will show the world that the United States is willing to protect its interests. The practice of political realism in foreign policy allows the United States to sell weapons to military dictators who will support its policies, to support American business around the globe, and to repel terrorism through the use of force.

American Foreign Policy—A Mixture of Both

It is important to note that the United States never has been guided by only one of these principles. Instead, both moral idealism and political realism affect foreign policymaking. President George W. Bush drew on the tradition of morality in foreign policy when he declared that the al Qaeda network of Osama bin Laden was "evil" and that fighting terrorism was fighting evil. The war against the Taliban government in Afghanistan, which had sheltered al Qaeda terrorists, was dubbed "Operation Enduring Freedom," a title that reflected the moral ideal of spreading democracy.

To actually wage war on the Taliban in Afghanistan, however, U.S. forces needed the right to use the airspace of India and Pakistan, neighbors of Afghanistan. The

---

1. Eugene R. Wittkopf, Charles W. Kegley, and James M. Scott, *American Foreign Policy and Process,* 7th ed. (Belmont, Calif.: Wadsworth Publishing, 2009).

United States had previously criticized both of these nations because they had developed and tested nuclear weapons. In addition, the United States had taken the moral stand that it would not deliver certain fighter aircraft to Pakistan so long as that nation continued its weapons program. When it became absolutely necessary to work with India and Pakistan, the United States switched to a realist policy, promising aid and support to both regimes in return for their assistance in the war on terrorism.

The Iraq War that began in 2003 also revealed a mixture of idealism and realism. While the primary motive for invading Iraq was realistic (the interests of U.S. security), another goal of the war reflected idealism—the liberation of the Iraqi people from an oppressive regime and the establishment of a democratic model in the Middle East. The reference to the war effort as "Operation Iraqi Freedom" emphasized this idealistic goal.

CHALLENGES IN WORLD POLITICS

The foreign policy of the United States, whether moralist, realist, or both, must be formulated to deal with world conditions. Early in its history, the United States was a weak, new nation facing older nations well equipped for war. In the twenty-first century, the United States confronts different challenges. Now it must devise foreign and defense policies that will enhance its security in a world in which it is the global superpower and has no equal.

The Emergence of Terrorism

In years past, terrorism was a strategy typically employed by radicals who wanted to change the status of a particular nation or province. For example, over many years the Irish Republican Army undertook terrorist attacks in the British province of Northern Ireland with the aim of driving out the British and uniting the province with the Republic of Ireland. In Spain, the ETA organization continues to employ terrorism. Its goal is to create an independent Basque state in Spain's Basque region. In the twenty-first century, however, the United States has confronted a new form of terrorism that is not associated with such clear-cut aims.

September 11. In 2001, terrorism came home to the United States in ways that few Americans could have imagined. In a well-coordinated attack, nineteen terrorists hijacked four airplanes and crashed three of them into buildings—two into the World Trade Center towers in New York City and one into the Pentagon in Washington, D.C. The fourth airplane crashed in a field in Pennsylvania, after the passengers fought the hijackers.

Why did the al Qaeda network plan and launch attacks on the United States? One reason was that the leaders of the network, including Osama bin Laden, were angered by the presence of U.S. troops on the soil of Saudi Arabia, which they regard as sacred. They also saw the United States as the primary defender of Israel against the Palestinians and as the defender of the royal family that governs Saudi Arabia. The attacks were intended to frighten and demoralize the American people, thus convincing their leaders to withdraw American troops from the Middle East. Al Qaeda's ultimate goals, however, were not limited to forcing the United States to withdraw from specific countries or even the entire Middle East. Al Qaeda envisioned worldwide revolutionary change, with all nations brought under the theocratic rule of an Islamist empire.

Osama bin Laden still speaks for the terrorist group al Qaeda. Here he is shown presenting a message in which he urged Iraqi militants as well as other "believers" around the world to continue the fight against the United States and its allies. Osama bin Laden is believed to be hiding in the mountainous region between Afghanistan and Pakistan. Why has it been so difficult for the United States to track him down and bring him to justice? (AP Photo)

Governments have successfully negotiated with terrorists who profess limited aims—today, radicals associated with the Irish Republican Army are part of a coalition government in Northern Ireland. There is no way to negotiate with an organization such as al Qaeda.

Bombings in Madrid and London. Since September 11, 2001, al Qaeda has not undertaken another act of terrorism on American soil. Terrorists influenced by al Qaeda have committed serious crimes in other countries, however. On March 11, 2004, ten coordinated train bombings in Madrid, Spain, killed 191 people and wounded more than 2,000 others. The subsequent investigation revealed that the attacks had been carried out by Islamist extremists.

On July 7, 2005, terrorists carried out synchronized bombings of the London Underground (subway) and bus network. Four suicide bombers, British citizens of Middle Eastern descent, claimed the lives of fifty-six people and wounded hundreds more in the attacks. It was later determined that the leader of this group had links to al Qaeda.

The War on Terrorism

After 9/11, President George W. Bush implemented stronger security measures to help ensure homeland security and protect U.S. facilities and personnel abroad. The president sought and received congressional support for heightened airport security, new laws allowing greater domestic surveillance of potential terrorists, and increased funding for the military.

A New Kind of War. In September 2002, President Bush enunciated what has since become known as the "Bush Doctrine," or the doctrine of preemption:

> We will . . . [defend] the United States, the American people, and our interests at home and abroad by identifying and destroying the threat before it reaches our borders. While the United States will constantly strive to enlist the support of the international community, we will not hesitate to act alone, if necessary, to exercise our right of self-defense by acting preemptively against such terrorists, to prevent them from doing harm against our people and our country.[2]

The concept of "preemptive war" as a defense strategy was a new element in U.S. foreign policy. The concept is based on the assumption that in the war on terrorism, self-defense must be *anticipatory*. President Bush stated on March 17, 2003, just before launching the invasion of Iraq, "Responding to such enemies only after they have struck first is not self-defense, it is suicide."

2. George W. Bush, September 17, 2002. The full text of the document from which this statement is taken can be accessed at **georgewbush-whitehouse.archives.gov/nsc/nss/2002/nss3.html**.

Opposition to the Bush Doctrine. The Bush Doctrine had many critics. Some pointed out that preemptive wars against other nations have traditionally been waged by dictators and rogue states—not democratic nations. By employing such a strategy, the United States would seem to be contradicting its basic values. Others claimed that launching preemptive wars would make it difficult for the United States to pursue world peace in the future. By endorsing such a policy itself, the United States could hardly argue against the decisions of other nations to do likewise when they felt potentially threatened. While campaigning for the Democratic presidential nomination, Barack Obama rejected the Bush Doctrine with these words:

> And part of the reason that we neglected Afghanistan, part of the reason that we didn't go after bin Laden as aggressively as we should have is we were distracted by a war of choice [in Iraq]. And that's the flaw of the Bush Doctrine. It wasn't that he went after those who attacked America. It was that he went after those who didn't.

▲ **General David Petraeus,** commander of the U.S. Central Command, is shown testifying before a congressional subcommittee. What are the types of questions members of Congress might ask him? (Photo by Alex Wong/ Getty Images)

Wars in Iraq

On August 2, 1990, the Persian Gulf became the setting for a major challenge to the international system set up after World War II (1939–1945). President Saddam Hussein of Iraq sent troops into the neighboring oil sheikdom of Kuwait, occupying that country. This was the most clear-cut case of aggression against an independent nation in half a century.

The First Gulf War. At the formal request of the king of Saudi Arabia, American troops were dispatched to set up a defensive line at the Kuwaiti border. After the United Nations (UN) approved a resolution authorizing the use of force if Saddam Hussein did not respond to sanctions, the U.S. Congress also granted such an authorization. On January 17, 1991, two days after a deadline for President Hussein to withdraw, U.S.-led coalition forces launched a massive air attack on Iraq. After several weeks, the ground offensive began. Iraqi troops retreated from Kuwait a few days later, and the First Gulf War ended. Many Americans, however, criticized President George H. W. Bush for not sending troops to Baghdad to depose Saddam Hussein.

As part of the cease-fire that ended the First Gulf War, Iraq agreed to abide by all UN resolutions and to allow UN weapons inspectors to oversee the destruction of its medium-range missiles and all chemical and nuclear weapons research facilities. Economic sanctions would be imposed on Iraq until the weapons inspectors finished their jobs. In 1999, however, Iraq placed such obstacles in the path of the UN inspectors that the inspectors withdrew from the country.

The Second Gulf War—The Iraq War. After the terrorist attacks on the United States on September 11, 2001, President George W. Bush called Iraq and Saddam

Hussein part of an "axis of evil" that threatened world peace. In 2002 and early 2003, Bush called for a "regime change" in Iraq and began assembling an international coalition that might support further military action in Iraq.

Bush was unable to convince the UN Security Council that military force was necessary in Iraq, so the United States took the initiative. In March 2003, U.S. and British forces invaded Iraq and within a month had ended Hussein's decades-old dictatorship. The process of establishing order and creating a new government in Iraq turned out to be extraordinarily difficult. In the course of the fighting, the Iraqi army, rather than surrendering, simply disintegrated. Soldiers took off their uniforms and made their way home. As a result, the task of maintaining law and order fell on the shoulders of a remarkably small coalition expeditionary force. Coalition troops were unable to immediately halt the wave of looting and disorder that spread across Iraq in the wake of the invasion.

Occupied Iraq. The people of Iraq are divided into three principal ethnic groups. The Kurdish-speaking people of the north, who had in practice been functioning as an American-sponsored independent state since the First Gulf War, were overjoyed by the invasion. The Arabs adhering to the Shiite branch of Islam live principally in the south and constitute a majority of the population. The Shiites were glad that Saddam Hussein, who had murdered many thousands of Shiites, was gone. They were deeply skeptical of U.S. intentions, however. The Arabs belonging to the Sunni branch of Islam live mainly in the center of the country, west of Baghdad. Although the Sunnis constituted only a minority of the population, they had controlled the government under Hussein. Many of them considered the occupation to be a disaster.

The Insurgency. An American-led Coalition Provisional Authority (CPA) governed Iraq until the establishment of an Iraqi interim government in 2004. One of the first acts of the CPA was formally to disband the Iraqi army. In retrospect, this decision has been viewed as a disaster. It released hundreds of thousands of well-armed young men, largely Sunnis, who no longer had jobs but did possess a great resentment toward the American invaders. In short order, a guerrilla insurgency arose and launched attacks against the coalition forces. Occupation forces also came under attack by Shiite forces loyal to Muqtada al Sadr, a radical cleric who was the son of a famous Shiite martyr. While coalition forces were able to maintain control of the country, they were now suffering monthly casualties comparable to those experienced during the initial invasion. Iraq had begun to be a serious political problem for President Bush. By May 2004, a majority of Americans no longer believed that going to war had been the right thing to do, and Bush's overall job-approval rating had fallen significantly.

The Threat of Civil War. In justifying its decision to invade Iraq, the Bush administration had claimed—incorrectly, as it turns out—that links existed between the Hussein regime and al Qaeda. Ironically, the occupation of Iraq soon led to the establishment of an al Qaeda operation in that country, which sponsored suicide bombings and other attacks against coalition troops and the forces of the newly established Iraqi government. Al Qaeda did not limit its hostility to the Americans but issued vitriolic denunciations of the Iraqi Shiites, calling them apostates and traitors to the Arab cause.

In February 2006, a bomb, believed to have been set by al Qaeda, destroyed much of the al Askari mosque, one of the holiest Shiite sites in Iraq. This attack marked a major turning point in the Iraq conflict. While Sunni and Shiite insurgents continued to launch attacks on U.S. and other coalition forces, the major bloodletting in the country now took place between Sunnis and Shiites. Shiite militias sought to force Sunni civilians out of Iraqi towns and Baghdad neighborhoods through a campaign of ethnic cleansing that included acts of indiscriminate murder. Sunni insurgents responded in kind. The Shiite-dominated Iraqi government displayed little interest in protecting Sunni civilians, and such protection increasingly fell onto the shoulders of U.S. forces—even as Sunni insurgents continued to attack the Americans.

Opposition to the War. By 2008, the war in Iraq was in its fifth year. No weapons of mass destruction—the ostensible reason for the war—were ever found. Scholars, journalists, and even intelligence reports leaked to the press began to paint a harsh picture both of the way in which the Bush administration decided to go to war and how it handled the aftermath of the initial military victory. Members of the CPA that initially governed Iraq were selected on the basis of their conservative ideology rather than their experience or ability. The CPA seemed more interested in dismantling Iraq's existing institutions than in protecting the security of the public.

By late 2006, polls indicated that about two-thirds of Americans wanted to see an end to the Iraq War—a sentiment expressed in the 2006 elections, which were seen largely as a referendum on the Iraq War policy of President Bush and the Republican-led Congress. One immediate result of the elections was that Bush dismissed his secretary of defense, Donald Rumsfeld, who was closely associated with Iraq policy failures.

Signs of Progress. In January 2007, Bush announced a major increase, or "surge," in U.S. troop strength. Bush placed General David Petraeus, the U.S. Army's leading counterinsurgency expert, in charge of all forces in Iraq. Many observers thought that Petraeus was the first leader of the American war effort to truly understand the nature of the conflict. Nevertheless, skeptics doubted that either Petraeus or the new troop levels would have much effect on the outcome.

In April 2007, however, a new development transformed the situation in Iraq once again. Beginning in the western Sunni heartland of Anbar Province, tribal leaders rose up against al Qaeda in Iraq and called in U.S. troops to help them. The new movement, called the Awakening, spread rapidly through Sunni districts and Baghdad neighborhoods. Al Qaeda, it seems, had badly overplayed its hand by terrorizing the Sunni population. Anbar Province, once the most dangerous part of Iraq, was soon one of the safest. The Shiite-dominated central government, however, resisted cooperation with the Awakening, fearing that the new movement might turn its U.S.-supplied weapons against the government.

Also in 2007, the radical Shiite cleric Muqtada al Sadr announced that his militia, the Mahdi Army, would begin observing a cease-fire. A number of Mahdi Army units had degenerated into criminal organizations, however, which continued to spread violence in Baghdad and elsewhere. In March 2008, al Sadr suspended the cease-fire. On March 25, the Iraqi government launched an operation to drive the Mahdi Army out of the southern city of Basra. The government forces were forced to call on the Americans for support, but ultimately they prevailed.

Iraqi Endgame. The reconquest of Basra by the central government marked a final turning point in the war. During subsequent months, the Iraqi government gained substantial control over its own territory (leaving aside Kurdistan, which remained autonomous). This positive development seemed to have little impact on American attitudes toward the war, which remained negative. The steep decline in terrorist and insurgent activities did push Iraq out of the headlines. During 2007, pundits had expected that the war would be a top issue in the 2008 presidential elections. As it turned out, the war was almost completely eclipsed as an issue by the economy.

Democratic candidate Barack Obama had opposed the Iraq War from the start, and he called for setting a deadline for the withdrawal of U.S. forces. Republican candidate John McCain argued that setting a deadline would only encourage the enemy. McCain's position was seriously undercut in the summer and fall of 2008, when President Bush and Iraqi Prime Minister Nouri al Maliki proceeded to negotiate a deadline for the withdrawal of all U.S. forces. This meant that the difference between Obama's position and that of Bush was now merely a matter of months. In February 2009, President Obama announced that U.S. combat forces would leave Iraq by August 31, 2010, and the rest of the American troops would be out by the end of 2011.

Afghanistan

The Iraq War was not the only military effort launched by the Bush administration as part of the war on terrorism. The first military effort was directed against al Qaeda camps in Afghanistan and the Taliban regime, which had ruled most of Afghanistan since 1996. In late 2001, after building a coalition of international allies and anti-Taliban rebels within Afghanistan, the United States began an air campaign against the Taliban regime. The anti-Taliban rebels, known as the Northern Alliance, were able to take Kabul, the capital, and oust the Taliban from power. The United States and other members of the international community then fostered the creation of an elected Afghan government.

▼ **These Taliban militants** were photographed in the late summer of 2008 in an undisclosed location in Ghazni Province in Afghanistan. Many political analysts believe that the Taliban are regaining a foothold in Afghanistan and that additional troops will be needed to keep that country free of their radical influence. Is the United States capable of pursuing antiterrorist "wars" in several countries simultaneously? (AP Photo/Rahmatullah Naikzad)

The Taliban were defeated, but not destroyed. U.S. forces were unable to locate Osama bin Laden and other top al Qaeda leaders. The Taliban and al Qaeda both retreated to the rugged mountains between Afghanistan and Pakistan, where they were able to establish bases on the Pakistani side of the border. In 2003, the Taliban began to launch attacks against Afghan soldiers, foreign aid workers, and even American troops. Afghanistan's opium poppy crop served as a major source of Taliban revenue—Afghanistan was now supplying 95 percent of the world's opium, the raw material for morphine and heroin. Despite increases in coalition forces, the Taliban continued to gain strength.

Through 2008 and 2009, the Taliban were able to take over a number of Pakistani districts, even as the United States began attacking suspected Taliban and al Qaeda targets in Pakistan using small unmanned aircraft. In 2009, the government of Pakistan initiated military action in an attempt to retake Taliban-controlled districts. In his presidential campaign, Barack Obama called for increased American troop levels to deal with the emergency, and in February 2009 he dispatched 17,000 additional soldiers to Afghanistan.

Nuclear Weapons

In 1945, the United States was the only nation to possess nuclear weapons. Several nations quickly joined the "nuclear club," however, including the Soviet Union in 1949, Britain in 1952, France in 1960, and China in 1964. Few nations have made public their nuclear weapons programs since China's successful test of nuclear weapons in 1964. India and Pakistan were among the most recent nations to do so, detonating nuclear devices within a few weeks of each other in 1998. North Korea conducted an underground nuclear explosive test in October 2006. Several other nations are suspected of possessing nuclear weapons or the capability to produce them in a short time.

With nuclear weapons, materials, and technology available worldwide, it is conceivable that terrorists could obtain a nuclear device and use it in a terrorist act. In fact, a U.S. federal indictment filed in 1998, after the attack on the American embassies in Kenya and Tanzania, charged Osama bin Laden and his associates with trying to buy nuclear bomb–making components "at various times" since 1992.

Nuclear Stockpiles. More than 32,000 nuclear warheads are known to be stocked worldwide, although the exact number is uncertain because some countries do not reveal the extent of their holdings. Although the United States and Russia have dismantled some of their nuclear weapons systems since the end of the **Cold War** and the dissolution of the Soviet Union in 1991 (discussed later in this chapter), both still retain sizable nuclear arsenals. More alarming is the fact that since the dissolution of the Soviet Union, the security of its nuclear arsenal has declined. There have been reported thefts, smugglings, and illicit sales of nuclear material from the former Soviet Union in the past two decades.

Attempts to Curb Nuclear Proliferation. For years, the United States, the European Union, and the UN have tried to prevent Iran from becoming a nuclear power. In spite of these efforts, many observers believe that Iran is now in the process of developing nuclear weapons—although Iran maintains that it is interested in developing nuclear power only for peaceful purposes. Continued diplomatic attempts to at least slow down Iran's quest for a nuclear bomb have so far proved ineffectual. Because President Bush was unwilling to engage in direct negotiations with Iran, these diplomatic efforts were undertaken by European nations, including Britain, France, and Germany. Upon taking office, President Obama attempted to carry out his campaign promises through talks with Iran that included the Europeans plus China and Russia. In May 2009, Obama observed: "By the end of the year we should have some sense whether or not these discussions are starting to yield significant benefits." This statement was close to—but not quite—a diplomatic deadline.

In contrast to its position on Iran, the Bush administration participated in multilateral negotiations with North Korea, which had tested a nuclear device in 2006.

Cold War
The ideological, political, and economic confrontation between the United States and the Soviet Union following World War II.

An agreement was reached in February 2007 that provided that North Korea would start disabling its nuclear facilities and allow UN inspectors into the country. In return, China, Japan, Russia, South Korea, and the United States—members of the six-party negotiations—would provide various kinds of aid to North Korea. North Korea, however, was allowed to keep its nuclear arsenal, which American intelligence officials believe may include as many as six nuclear bombs or the fuel to make them. In July 2007, North Korea dismantled one of its nuclear reactors and admitted UN inspectors into the country. In October 2008, the United States removed North Korea from its list of states that sponsor terrorism.

By 2009, however, North Korea was pulling back from its treaty obligations. In April, the country tested a long-range missile capable of delivering a nuclear warhead, in violation of a UN Security Council demand that it halt such tests. After the Security Council issued a statement condemning the test, North Korea ordered UN inspectors out of the country, broke off negotiations with the other members of the six-party talks, and conducted a second nuclear test.

▲ **North Korea tests** yet another medium-range missile. It has also tested a long-range missile as well as a ground-to-air missile. In the late spring of 2009, it publicly declared that it had successfully carried out its second underground nuclear test. Such public declaration was considered a rebuke to President Obama's attempt to engage North Korea in diplomatic discussions. Who is most threatened by North Korea's nuclear program? (AP Photo/KRT TV)

The New Power: China

Since Richard Nixon's visit to China in 1972, American policy has been to gradually engage the Chinese in diplomatic and economic relationships in the hope of turning the nation in a more pro-Western direction. In 1989, however, when Chinese students engaged in extraordinary demonstrations against the government, the Chinese government crushed the demonstrations, killing a number of students and protesters and imprisoning others. The result was a distinct chill in Chinese-American relations.

Chinese-American Trade Ties. An important factor in U.S.-Chinese relations has been the large and growing trade ties between the two countries. In 1980, China was granted most-favored-nation status for tariffs and trade policy on a year-to-year basis. To prevent confusion, in 1998 the status was renamed **normal trade relations (NTR) status.** In 2000, over objections from organized labor and human rights groups, Congress approved a permanent grant of NTR status to China. In 2001, Congress endorsed China's application to join the World Trade Organization (WTO), thereby effectively guaranteeing China's admission to that body.

Normal Trade Relations (NTR) Status

A status granted through an international treaty by which each member nation must treat other members as well as it treats the country that receives its most favorable treatment. This status was formerly known as *most-favored-nation status.*

While officially Communist, China today permits a striking degree of free enterprise. China has become substantially integrated into the world economic system, as evidenced by its imports and exports. In 2008, China exported $1,429 billion worth of goods to the rest of the world and imported $1,133 billion. As a result, China had a positive trade balance of $296 billion, most of which ended up as foreign reserves held by China's central bank. A full $266 billion of this balance was with the United States. In effect, China was lending the United States large sums so that American consumers could purchase Chinese goods.

China's Explosive Economic Growth. The growth of the Chinese economy during the last thirty-five years is one of the most important developments in world history. For the past several decades, the Chinese economy has grown at a rate of about 10 percent annually, a long-term growth rate previously unknown in human history. Never have so many escaped poverty so quickly.

China now produces more steel than America and Japan combined. It generates more than 40 percent of the world's output of cement. The new electrical generating capacity that China has recently added each year exceeds the entire installed capacity of Britain. (The new plants, which are usually coal fired, promote global warming and also generate some of the world's worst air pollution.) Skyscrapers fill the skyline of every major Chinese city.

In 2007, for the first time, China actually manufactured more passenger automobiles than the United States. China is building a limited-access highway system that, when complete, will be longer than the U.S. interstate highway system. Chinese demand for raw materials, notably petroleum, has led, at times, to dramatic increases in the price of oil and other commodities. Its people have begun to eat large quantities of meat, which adds to the strain on world food production. By 2050, if not before, the economy of China is expected to be larger than that of the United States. China, in short, will become the world's second superpower.

The Issue of Taiwan. Inevitably, economic power translates into military potential. Is this a problem? It could be if China had territorial ambitions. At this time, China does not appear to have an appetite for non-Chinese territory, and it does not seem likely to develop one. But China has always considered the island of Taiwan to be Chinese territory. In principle, Taiwan agrees. Taiwan calls itself the "Republic of China" and officially considers its government to be the legitimate ruler of the entire country. This diplomatic fiction has remained in effect since 1949, when the Chinese Communist Party won a civil war and drove the anti-Communist forces off the mainland.

China's position is that sooner or later, Taiwan must rejoin the rest of China. The position of the United States is that this reunification must not come about by force. Is peaceful reunification possible? China holds up Hong Kong as an example. Hong Kong came under Chinese sovereignty peacefully in 1997. The people of Taiwan, however, are far from considering Hong Kong to be an acceptable precedent.

Israel and the Palestinians

As a longtime supporter of Israel, the United States has undertaken to persuade the Israelis to negotiate with the Palestinian Arabs who live in the territories occupied by the state of Israel. The conflict, which began in 1948, has been extremely hard to resolve. The internationally recognized solution is for Israel to yield the West Bank and the Gaza Strip to the Palestinians in return for effective security commitments and abandonment by the Palestinians of any right of return to Israel proper. Unfortunately, the Palestinians have been unwilling to stop terrorist attacks on Israel, and Israel has been unwilling to dismantle its settlements in the occupied territories. Further, the two parties have been unable to come to an agreement on how much of the West Bank should go to the Palestinians and what compensation (if any) the Palestinians should receive for abandoning all claims to settlement in Israel proper.

Talks with the PLO. In December 1988, the United States began talking directly to the Palestine Liberation Organization (PLO), and in 1991, under great pressure from

▲ **This section of the Israeli** separation barrier is viewed from a West Bank suburb of Jerusalem. Israel started building the barrier in 2002, arguing that it was necessary to prevent attackers from entering Israel. Who governs the West Bank? (AP Photo/Emilio Morenatti)

the United States, the Israelis opened talks with representatives of the Palestinians and other Arab states. In 1993, both parties agreed to set up Palestinian self-government in the West Bank and the Gaza Strip. The historic agreement, signed in Cairo, Egypt, on May 4, 1994, put in place a process by which the Palestinians would assume self-rule in the Gaza Strip and in the town of Jericho. In the months that followed, Israeli troops withdrew from much of the occupied territory, the new Palestinian Authority assumed police duties, and many Palestinian prisoners were freed by the Israelis.

The Collapse of the Israeli-Palestinian Peace Process. Although negotiations between the Israelis and the Palestinians resulted in more agreements in Oslo, Norway, in 2000, the agreements were rejected by Palestinian radicals, who began a campaign of suicide bombings in Israeli cities. In 2002, the Israeli government responded by moving tanks and troops into Palestinian towns to kill or capture the terrorists. One result of the Israeli reoccupation was an almost complete collapse of the Palestinian Authority. Groups such as Hamas (the Islamic Resistance Movement), which did not accept the concept of peace with Israel even in principle, moved into the power vacuum. In 2003, President Bush attempted to renew Israeli-Palestinian negotiations by sponsoring a "road map" for peace. In its weakened condition, however, the Palestinian Authority was unable to make any commitments, and the "road map" process ground to a halt.

Israel's Unilateral Withdrawal Policy. In February 2004, Israeli Prime Minister Ariel Sharon announced a plan under which Israel would withdraw from the Gaza Strip regardless of whether a deal could be reached with the Palestinians. Israel's government voted to disengage from Gaza beginning in August 2005. Within a month, settlements had been dismantled, and all Israeli settlers and military bases were removed from the strip. Israel remained in control of Gaza's borders, airspace, and territorial waters.

Hamas and Hezbollah. In January 2006, the Islamist organization Hamas won a majority of the seats in the Palestinian Legislative Council, pushing the PLO into second place. Public statements by Hamas, as well as its charter, called for the destruction of the state of Israel. Neither Israel nor most Western governments were willing to meet with the organization.

In July, militants of the Shiite radical group Hezbollah, based in Lebanon, crossed the Israeli border, killed several Israeli soldiers, and kidnapped two others. The result was the 2006 Lebanon War, which lasted five weeks. The war consisted largely of Israeli air strikes on Lebanon and Hezbollah rocket attacks on Israel, though Israeli troops did enter southern Lebanon briefly. The war ended with a UN-brokered cease-fire.

In June 2007, the uneasy balance between the Palestinians' Hamas-dominated legislature and their president, the PLO's Mahmoud Abbas, broke down. After open fighting between the two parties, Hamas wound up in complete control of the Gaza Strip, and the PLO retained exclusive power in the West Bank. Western leaders speculated that it might be possible to negotiate exclusively with the PLO government on the West Bank, freezing out Hamas and the Gaza Strip.

For its part, Israel sought to pressure the Hamas regime in the Gaza Strip to relinquish power through an economic

▲ **President Obama and Israeli Prime Minister Netanyahu** are shown outside the Oval Office of the White House in 2009. Obama has attempted to push Netanyahu to accept a diplomatic solution to the Palestinian problem. Why would a U.S. president have influence with the head of the Israeli government? (Amos Moshe Milner/GPO via Getty Images)

blockade. Hamas retaliated by firing a series of rockets into Israel. On December 27, 2008, in the final weeks of the Bush administration, Israel responded to these attacks with a series of heavy air strikes. On January 3, 2009, Israeli ground forces entered the Strip. Israel declared a cease-fire on January 18, just days before Obama's inauguration. This declaration, however, did not entirely end the violence. Hamas and Israel continued to trade rocket attacks and air strikes during subsequent months.

On February 10, Israelis elected a new, more conservative government under Prime Minister Benjamin Netanyahu. The tough positions advocated by the new government threatened to create a fresh obstacle to the peace process. President Obama, however, remained optimistic that he could encourage negotiations between Israel and the Palestinians.

Africa

During the early 2000s, the disease AIDS (acquired immune deficiency syndrome) continued to spread throughout southern Africa. This disease infects one-fourth of the populations of Botswana and Zimbabwe and is endemic in most other nations in the southernmost part of the continent. Millions of adults are dying from AIDS, leaving orphaned children. The epidemic is taking a huge economic toll on the affected countries because of the cost of caring for patients and the loss of skilled workers. The disease may be the greatest single threat to world stability emanating from Africa. The Bush administration put in place a special aid package directed at this problem amounting to $15 billion over five years.

▲ **These displaced Sudanese women** and children seek medical treatment at an Egyptian military field hospital in a refugee camp outside of a town in Darfur, Sudan. Who was responsible for driving these residents from their homes into refugee camps? (AP Photo/Nasser Nasser)

In 2004, the world woke up to a growing disaster in Darfur, a western province of Sudan. In the spring of 2004, Sudan had reached a tenuous agreement with rebels in the southern part of the country, but the agreement did not cover a separate rebellion in Darfur. Government-sponsored militias drove more than a million inhabitants of Darfur from their homes and into refugee camps, where they faced starvation. In July 2004, the U.S. Congress labeled the situation "genocide." By 2008, at least 200,000 had died and more than 2.5 million had been made homeless as a result of militia attacks.

Until 2007, the Sudanese government had repeatedly denied UN requests to intervene in Darfur. In April 2007, however, the Sudanese president finally agreed to accept large-scale UN assistance. Many observers believed that Chinese support for the agreement was key to its acceptance by Sudan. To give the UN more time to pursue its goals diplomatically, President Bush delayed proposed U.S. sanctions against Sudan.

During 2008 and 2009, the world began to wake up to a new problem emanating from Africa—increasingly effective attacks on shipping by pirates based in Somalia. (We discussed the collapse of the Somali government in Chapter 1.) For a discussion of this problem, see this chapter's feature *The Politics of Boom and Bust: Twenty-First-Century Pirates.*

WHO MAKES FOREIGN POLICY?

Given the vast array of challenges in the world, developing a comprehensive U.S. foreign policy is a demanding task. Does this responsibility fall to the president, to Congress, or to both acting jointly? There is no easy answer to this question, because, as constitutional authority Edwin S. Corwin once observed, the U.S. Constitution created an "invitation to struggle" between the president and Congress for control over the foreign policy process. Let us look first at the powers given to the president by the Constitution.

Constitutional Powers of the President

The Constitution confers on the president broad powers that are either explicit or implied in key constitutional provisions. Article II vests the executive power of the government in the president. The presidential oath of office, given in Article II, Section 1, requires that the president "solemnly swear" to "preserve, protect and defend the Constitution of the United States."

the politics of Boom and Bust:
Twenty-First-Century Pirates

When Somali pirates seized the U.S.-flagged container ship MV *Maersk Alabama* in April 2009, they made history. This capture represented the first seizure of a U.S.-flagged ship by pirates operating from Somalia. Pirate attacks on U.S. vessels have been rare events since the wars with the Barbary States in the early nineteenth century, although in recent years piracy has been an ongoing problem in Indonesian and Malaysian territorial waters. Somali pirates, however, have taken the game to a whole new level, seizing merchant vessels from countries around the world.

Somalia's "Bust" Government

To be sure, the worldwide economic bust affected the nations of Africa, just as it affected other countries. Yet the real "bust" in Somalia was the collapse of all governmental authority since 1999. The pirates, who operate without interference by a weak local government in the Somali region of Puntland, claim that piracy is their only chance to make a decent living.

While a sure cure for piracy would be to restore governmental order inside Somalia, no nation (nor the United Nations) is prepared to do so. What remains in that desperately poor country is a large group of unemployed young Somalis who have grown up in an atmosphere of violent anarchy. Local warlords dispatch them to bring back "treasure" for their coffers in the form of ransom for seized merchant ships and their crews. The Indian Ocean has a surface area of a million square miles, and the pirates can roam just about anywhere. The *Maersk Alabama* was 240 nautical miles (440 kilometers) off the coast of Somalia when it was attacked.

Could Terrorists Turn to Piracy?

While it is bothersome, to be sure, to have merchant ships taken by pirates who then demand multimillion-dollar ransoms, there is another problem. Piracy potentially could serve as a platform for terrorists. Terrorists could imitate pirate techniques. They could hijack vessels and blow them up in crowded shipping lanes. Or they could hijack cruise ships and throw overboard passengers with the "wrong" nationalities. Or they could simply copy existing pirates and hijack ships for ransom.

Another concern is the waste of our military resources when ships must be diverted to handle pirates. In the example of the *Maersk Alabama*, the USS *Bainbridge*, an American destroyer with enough Tomahawk missiles to destroy a city, patiently faced off a few Somali pirates in a lifeboat in which they were holding the ship's captain. Navy SEAL sharpshooters eventually killed the pirates in the lifeboat and rescued Captain Richard Phillips. This was a satisfying victory, but an expensive one.

The International Response to Piracy

Naval vessels from China, France, India, Russia, and the United States, to name only a few, are now patrolling the waters of the Indian Ocean. These nations have had some success in thwarting additional seizures of merchant ships, but piracy continues. In particular, China and India have sent additional ships with helicopters and specialized navy commando units.

Observers note that the threat of piracy has resulted in more international cooperation than the world has seen in quite a while. Significantly, China and India have demonstrated their desire to take a leadership role in addressing this issue. For both nations, the Somali pirates have created the opportunity to exercise their newly strengthened navies. This comes at a time when U.S. naval power is shrinking due to budget cuts. Critics of these cuts predict that the power of America's navy will gradually decline because of the falling number of ships.

FOR CRITICAL ANALYSIS

Some believe that merchant crews should be armed to ward off pirates. Pirates have also attempted to seize cruise ships. Should the crews on those ships be armed, too? Why or why not?

War Powers. In addition, and perhaps more important, Article II, Section 2, designates the president as "Commander in Chief of the Army and Navy of the United States." Starting with Abraham Lincoln, all presidents have interpreted this authority dynamically and broadly. Indeed, since George Washington's administration, the

United States has been involved in at least 125 undeclared wars that were conducted under presidential authority. For example, in 1950 Harry Truman ordered U.S. armed forces in the Pacific to counter North Korea's invasion of South Korea. Bill Clinton sent troops to Haiti and Bosnia. In 2001, George W. Bush authorized an attack against the al Qaeda terrorist network and the Taliban government in Afghanistan. As described earlier, in 2003, Bush sent military forces to Iraq to destroy Saddam Hussein's government.

Treaties and Executive Agreements. Article II, Section 2, of the Constitution also gives the president the power to make treaties, provided that the Senate concurs. Presidents usually have been successful in getting treaties through the Senate. In addition to this formal treaty-making power, the president makes use of executive agreements (discussed in Chapter 10). Since World War II (1939–1945), executive agreements have accounted for almost 95 percent of the understandings reached between the United States and other nations.

Executive agreements have a long and important history. During World War II, Franklin Roosevelt reached several agreements with Britain, the Soviet Union, and other countries. In other important agreements, Presidents Eisenhower, Kennedy, and Johnson all promised support to the government of South Vietnam. In all, since 1946 more than eight thousand executive agreements with foreign countries have been made. There is no way to obtain an accurate count, because perhaps as many as several hundred of these agreements have been secret.

Other Constitutional Powers. An additional power conferred on the president in Article II, Section 2, is the right to appoint ambassadors, other public ministers, and consuls. In Section 3 of that article, the president is given the power to recognize foreign governments by receiving their ambassadors.

Other Sources of Foreign Policymaking

There are at least four foreign policymaking sources within the executive branch, in addition to the president. These are (1) the Department of State, (2) the National Security Council, (3) the intelligence community, and (4) the Department of Defense.

The Department of State. In principle, the State Department is the executive agency that has primary authority over foreign affairs. It supervises U.S. relations with the nearly two hundred independent nations around the world and with the United Nations and other multinational groups, such as the Organization of American States. It staffs embassies and consulates throughout the world. It does this with one of the smallest budgets of the cabinet departments.

Newly elected presidents usually tell the American public that the new secretary of state is the nation's chief foreign policy adviser. Nonetheless, the State Department's preeminence in foreign policy has declined since World War II. The State Department's image within the White House Executive Office and Congress (and even with foreign governments) is poor—it is seen as a slow, plodding, bureaucratic maze of inefficient, indecisive individuals. There is a story about how Premier Nikita Khrushchev of the Soviet Union urged President John Kennedy to formulate his own views rather than to rely on State Department officials, who, according to Khrushchev, "specialized in why something had not worked forty years ago."[3] In any event, since the days of Franklin

3. Theodore C. Sorensen, *Kennedy* (New York: Harper & Row, 1965), pp. 554–555.

Roosevelt, the State Department has often been bypassed or ignored when crucial decisions are made.

It is not surprising that the State Department has been overshadowed in foreign policy. It has no natural domestic constituency as does, for example, the Department of Defense, which can call on defense contractors for support. Instead, the State Department has what might be called **negative constituents**—U.S. citizens who openly oppose the government's policies.

The National Security Council. The job of the National Security Council (NSC), created by the National Security Act of 1947, is to advise the president on the integration of "domestic, foreign, and military policies relating to the national security." Its larger purpose is to provide policy continuity from one administration to the next. As it has turned out, the NSC—consisting of the president, the vice president, the secretaries of state and defense, the director of emergency planning, and often the chairperson of the joint chiefs of staff and the director of the Central Intelligence Agency (CIA)—is used in just about any way the president wants to use it.

The role of national security adviser to the president seems to adjust to fit the player. Some advisers have come into conflict with heads of the State Department. Henry A. Kissinger, Nixon's flamboyant and aggressive national security adviser, rapidly gained ascendancy over William Rogers, the secretary of state. More recently, Condoleezza Rice played an important role as national security adviser during George W. Bush's first term. Like Kissinger, Rice eventually became secretary of state. President Obama's national security adviser is General James L. Jones, Jr., a former commandant of the U.S. Marine Corps.

The Intelligence Community. No discussion of foreign policy would be complete without some mention of the **intelligence community.** This consists of the forty or more government agencies and bureaus that are involved in intelligence activities. The CIA, created as part of the National Security Act of 1947, is the key official member of the intelligence community.

Intelligence activities consist mostly of overt information

Negative Constituents
Citizens who openly oppose the government's policies.

Intelligence Community
The government agencies that gather information about the capabilities and intentions of foreign governments or that engage in covert actions.

▼ **President Bush is shown with his** National Security Council (NSC) the day after the terrorist attacks on September 11, 2001. At that time, the NSC consisted of the director of the Central Intelligence Agency, the secretary of defense, the secretary of state, the vice president, the chairman of the joint chiefs of staff, and, of course, the national security adviser. How important is the NSC's role in determining U.S. foreign policy? (AP Photo/Doug Mills)

gathering, but covert actions also are undertaken. Covert actions, as the name implies, are carried out in secret, and the American public rarely finds out about them. The CIA covertly aided in the overthrow of the Mossadegh regime in Iran in 1953 and was instrumental in destabilizing the Allende government in Chile from 1970 to 1973.

During the mid-1970s, the "dark side" of the CIA was partly uncovered when the Senate undertook an investigation of its activities. One of the major findings of the Senate Select Committee on Intelligence was that the CIA had routinely spied on American citizens domestically—supposedly a prohibited activity. Consequently, the CIA came under the scrutiny of oversight committees within Congress.

By 2001, the agency had again come under fire. Problems included the discovery that one of its agents was spying on behalf of a foreign power, the inability of the agency to detect the nuclear arsenals of India and Pakistan, and, above all, the agency's failure to obtain advance knowledge about the 9/11 terrorist attacks.

The Intelligence Community and the War on Terrorism. With the rise of terrorism as a threat, the intelligence agencies have received more funding and enhanced surveillance powers, but these moves have also provoked fears of civil liberties violations. In 2004, the bipartisan 9/11 commission called for a new intelligence "czar" to oversee the entire intelligence community, with full control of all agency budgets. After initially balking at this recommendation, President Bush eventually decided to create a new position—a national intelligence director—to oversee and coordinate the "foreign and domestic intelligence community."

A simmering controversy that came to a head in 2009 concerned the CIA's use of a technique called *waterboarding* while interrogating several prisoners in the years immediately following 9/11. Before 9/11, the government had defined waterboarding as a form of torture, but former vice president Dick Cheney, a public advocate of the practice, denied that it was. One concern was whether Bush administration officials would face legal action as a result of the practice. In May, President Obama, even as he denounced waterboarding, assured CIA employees that no member of the agency would be penalized for following Justice Department rulings that had legitimized harsh interrogation methods. The Obama administration initially declined to pursue cases against the Justice Department officials in question. In August 2009, however, Attorney General Eric Holder appointed a prosecutor to make a preliminary investigation of the alleged abuses.

An additional controversy arose over whether the CIA had adequately briefed Speaker of the House Nancy Pelosi concerning its interrogation practices. CIA officials claimed that they had; Pelosi claimed that they had not and were lying. Republicans seized upon the issue to demand that Pelosi herself be investigated.

The Department of Defense. The Department of Defense (DOD) was created in 1947 to bring all of the various activities of the American military establishment under the jurisdiction of a single department headed by a civilian secretary of defense. At the same time, the joint chiefs of staff, consisting of the commanders of the various military branches and a chairperson, was created to formulate a unified military strategy.

Although the Department of Defense is larger than any other federal department, it declined in size after the fall of the Soviet Union in 1991. In the subsequent ten years, the total number of civilian employees was reduced by about 400,000, to approximately 665,000. Military personnel were also reduced in number. The defense budget remained relatively flat for several years, but with the advent of the war on terrorism and the use of military forces in Afghanistan and Iraq, funding has again been increased.

CONGRESS BALANCES THE PRESIDENCY

A new interest in the balance of power between Congress and the president on foreign policy questions developed during the Vietnam War (1964–1975). Sensitive to public frustration over the long and costly war and angry at Richard Nixon for some of his

▲ **The Pentagon** takes its name from its unusual shape. When the media refer to "The Pentagon," they are making reference to the Department of Defense. (Hisham Ibrahim/Photodisc/Getty Images)

other actions as president, Congress attempted to establish limits on the power of the president in setting foreign and defense policy.

In 1973, Congress passed the War Powers Resolution over President Nixon's veto. The act limited the president's use of troops in military action without congressional approval. Most presidents, however, have not interpreted the "consultation" provisions of the act as meaning that Congress should be consulted before military action is taken. Instead, Presidents Ford, Carter, Reagan, George H. W. Bush, and Clinton ordered troop movements and then informed congressional leaders.

One of Congress's most significant constitutional powers is the so-called power of the purse. The president may order that a certain action be taken, but that order cannot be executed unless Congress funds it. When the Democrats took control of Congress in January 2007, many asked whether the new Congress would use its power of the purse to bring an end to the Iraq War, in view of strong public opposition to the war. Congress's decision was to add conditions to an emergency war-funding request submitted by the president. The conditions required the president to establish a series of timelines for the redeployment of American troops in Iraq by September 2008. President Bush immediately threatened to veto any bill that imposed such conditions on the funding. His threat carried the day.

In this circumstance, the power of Congress was limited by political considerations. Congress did not even consider the option of refusing to fund the war altogether. For one thing, there was not enough support in Congress for such an approach. For another, the Democrats did not want to be accused of placing the troops in Iraq in danger. Additionally, the threat of a presidential veto significantly limited Congress's power. To override a presidential veto requires a two-thirds majority vote in each chamber, and the Democrats simply did not have that large of a majority.

THE MAJOR FOREIGN POLICY THEMES

Although some observers might suggest that U.S. foreign policy is inconsistent and changes with the current occupant of the White House, the long view of American diplomatic ventures reveals some major themes underlying foreign policy. In the early years of the nation, presidents and the people generally agreed that the United States should avoid foreign entanglements and concentrate instead on its own development. From the beginning of the twentieth century until the present, however, a major theme has been increasing global involvement. The theme of the post–World War II years was the containment of communism. The theme for at least the first part of the twenty-first century may be the containment of terrorism.

The Formative Years: Avoiding Entanglements

Foreign policy was largely nonexistent during the formative years of the United States. Remember that the new nation was operating under the Articles of Confederation. The national government had no right to levy or collect taxes, no control over commerce, no right to make commercial treaties, and no power to raise an army (the Revolutionary army was disbanded in 1783). The government's lack of international power was made clear when Barbary pirates seized American hostages in the Mediterranean. The United States was unable to rescue the hostages and ignominiously had to purchase them in a treaty with Morocco.

The founders of the United States had a basic mistrust of European governments. This was a logical position at a time when the United States was so weak militarily that it could not influence European developments directly. Moreover, being protected by oceans that took weeks to traverse certainly allowed the nation to avoid entangling alliances. During the 1800s, therefore, the United States generally stayed out of European conflicts and politics. In this hemisphere, however, the United States pursued an actively expansionist policy. The nation purchased Louisiana in 1803, annexed Texas in 1845, gained substantial territory from Mexico in 1848, purchased Alaska in 1867, and annexed Hawaii in 1898.

Monroe Doctrine

A policy statement made by President James Monroe in 1823, which set out three principles: (1) European nations should not establish new colonies in the Western Hemisphere, (2) European nations should not intervene in the affairs of independent nations of the Western Hemisphere, and (3) the United States would not interfere in the affairs of European nations.

Isolationist Foreign Policy

A policy of abstaining from an active role in international affairs or alliances, which characterized U.S. foreign policy toward Europe during most of the 1800s.

The Monroe Doctrine. President James Monroe, in his message to Congress on December 2, 1823, stated that this country would not accept foreign intervention in the Western Hemisphere. In return, the United States would not meddle in European affairs. The **Monroe Doctrine** was the underpinning of the U.S. **isolationist foreign policy** toward Europe, which continued throughout the 1800s.

The Spanish-American War and World War I. The end of the isolationist policy started with the Spanish-American War in 1898. Winning the war gave the United States possession of Guam, Puerto Rico, and the Philippines (which gained independence in 1946). On the heels of that war came World War I (1914–1918). The United States declared war on Germany on April 6, 1917, because that country refused to give up its campaign of sinking all ships headed for Britain, including passenger ships from America. (Large passenger ships of that time commonly held over a thousand people, so the sinking of such a ship was a disaster comparable to the attack on the World Trade Center.)

In the 1920s, the United States went "back to normalcy," as President Warren G. Harding urged it to do. U.S. military forces were largely disbanded, defense spending dropped to about 1 percent of total annual national income, and the nation returned to a period of isolationism.

The Era of Internationalism

Isolationism was permanently shattered by the bombing of the U.S. naval base at Pearl Harbor, Hawaii, on December 7, 1941. The surprise attack by the Japanese caused the deaths of 2,403 American servicemen and wounded 1,143 others. Eighteen warships were sunk or seriously damaged, and 188 planes were destroyed at the airfields. President Franklin Roosevelt asked Congress to declare war on Japan immediately, and the United States entered World War II.

The United States was the only major participating country to emerge from World War II with its economy intact, and even strengthened. The United States was also the only country to have control over operational nuclear weapons. President Harry Truman had made the decision to use two atomic bombs, on August 6 and August 9, 1945, to end the war with Japan. (Historians still argue over the necessity of this action, which ultimately killed more than 100,000 Japanese and left an equal number permanently injured.) The United States truly had become the world's superpower.

The Cold War. The United States had become an uncomfortable ally of the Soviet Union after Adolf Hitler's invasion of that country. Soon after World War II ended, relations between the Soviet Union and the West deteriorated. The Soviet Union wanted a weakened Germany, and to achieve this, it insisted that Germany be divided in two, with East Germany becoming a buffer against the West. Little by little, the Soviet Union helped to install Communist governments in Eastern European countries, which began to be referred to collectively as the **Soviet bloc.** In response, the United States encouraged the rearming of Western Europe. The Cold War had begun.[4]

Containment Policy. In 1947, a remarkable article was published in *Foreign Affairs*. The article was signed by "X." The actual author was George F. Kennan, chief of the policy-planning staff for the State Department. The doctrine of **containment** set forth in the article became—according to many—the bible of Western foreign policy. "X" argued that whenever and wherever the Soviet Union could successfully challenge the West, it would do so. He recommended that our policy toward the Soviet Union be "firm and vigilant containment of Russian expansive tendencies."[5]

The containment theory was expressed clearly in the **Truman Doctrine,** which was enunciated by President Harry Truman in 1947. Truman held that the United States must help countries in which a Communist takeover seemed likely. Later that year, he backed the Marshall Plan, an economic assistance plan for Europe that was intended to prevent the expansion of Communist influence there. In 1949, the United States entered into a military alliance with a number of European nations called the North Atlantic Treaty Organization, or NATO, to maintain a credible response to any Soviet military attack.

▲ **The atomic bomb** explodes over Nagasaki, Japan, on August 9, 1945. (Photo Courtesy of U.S. Air Force)

Soviet Bloc
The Soviet Union and the Eastern European countries that installed Communist regimes after World War II and that were dominated by the Soviet Union.

Containment
A U.S. diplomatic policy adopted by the Truman administration to contain Communist power within its existing boundaries.

Truman Doctrine
The policy adopted by President Harry Truman in 1947 to halt Communist expansion in southeastern Europe.

4. See John Lewis Gaddis, *The United Nations and the Origins of the Cold War* (New York: Columbia University Press, 1972).
5. X, "The Sources of Soviet Conduct," *Foreign Affairs,* July 1947, p. 575.

Superpower Relations

During the Cold War, there was never any direct military conflict between the United States and the Soviet Union. Only on occasion did the United States enter a conflict with any Communist country in a significant way. Two such occasions were in Korea and in Vietnam.

After the end of World War II, northern Korea was occupied by the Soviet Union, and southern Korea was occupied by the United States. The result was two rival Korean governments. In 1950, North Korea invaded South Korea. Under UN authority, the United States entered the war, which prevented an almost certain South Korean defeat. When U.S. forces were on the brink of conquering North Korea, however, China joined the war on the side of the North, resulting in a stalemate. An armistice signed in 1953 led to the two Koreas that exist today. U.S. forces have remained in South Korea since that time.

▲ **In a famous meeting in Yalta** in February 1945, British prime minister Winston Churchill (left), U.S. president Franklin Roosevelt (center), and Soviet leader Joseph Stalin (right) decided the fate of several nations in Europe, including Germany. What happened to Germany immediately after World War II? (Library of Congress)

The Vietnam War (1964–1975) also involved the United States in a civil war between a Communist North and pro-Western South. When the French army in Indochina was defeated by the Communist forces of Ho Chi Minh and the two Vietnams were created in 1954, the United States assumed the role of supporting the South Vietnamese government against North Vietnam. President John Kennedy sent 16,000 "advisers" to help South Vietnam, and after Kennedy's death in 1963, President Lyndon Johnson greatly increased the scope of that support. American forces in Vietnam at the height of the U.S. involvement totaled more than 500,000 troops. More than 58,000 Americans were killed and 300,000 were wounded in the conflict. A peace agreement in 1973 allowed U.S. troops to leave the country, and in 1975 North Vietnam easily occupied Saigon (the South Vietnamese capital) and unified the nation.

Over the course of the Vietnam War, the debate concerning U.S. involvement became extremely heated and, as mentioned previously, spurred congressional efforts to limit the ability of the president to commit forces to armed combat. The military draft was also a major source of contention during the Vietnam War.

The Cuban Missile Crisis. Perhaps the closest the two superpowers came to a nuclear confrontation was the Cuban missile crisis in 1962. The Soviets placed missiles in Cuba, ninety miles off the U.S. coast, in response to Cuban fears of an American invasion and to try to balance an American nuclear advantage. President Kennedy and his advisers rejected the option of invading Cuba, setting up a naval blockade around the island instead. When Soviet vessels appeared near Cuban waters, the tension reached its height. After intense negotiations between Washington and Moscow, the Soviet ships turned around on October 25, and on October 28 the Soviet Union announced the withdrawal of its missile operations from Cuba. In exchange, the United States agreed not to invade Cuba in the future. It also agreed to remove some of its own missiles that were located near the Soviet border in Turkey.

A Period of Détente. The French word **détente** means a relaxation of tensions. By the end of the 1960s, it was clear that some efforts had to be made to reduce the threat of nuclear war between the United States and the Soviet Union. The Soviet Union had gradually begun to catch up in the building of strategic nuclear delivery vehicles in the form of bombers and missiles, thus balancing the nuclear scales between the two countries. Each nation had acquired the military capacity to destroy the other with nuclear weapons.

As the result of lengthy negotiations under Secretary of State Henry Kissinger and President Nixon, the United States and the Soviet Union signed the **Strategic Arms Limitation Treaty (SALT I)** in May 1972. That treaty "permanently" limited the development and deployment of antiballistic missiles (ABMs) and limited the number of offensive missiles each country could deploy.

The policy of détente was not limited to the U.S. relationship with the Soviet Union. Seeing an opportunity to capitalize on increasing friction between the Soviet Union and the People's Republic of China, Kissinger secretly began negotiations to establish a new relationship with China. President Nixon eventually visited that nation in 1972. The visit set the stage for the formal diplomatic recognition of that country, which occurred during the Carter administration (1977–1981).

The Reagan-Bush Years. President Ronald Reagan took a hard line against the Soviet Union during his first term, proposing the strategic defense initiative (SDI), or "Star Wars," in 1983. The SDI was designed to serve as a space-based defense against enemy missiles. Reagan and others in his administration argued that the program would deter nuclear war by shifting the emphasis of defense strategy from offensive to defensive weapons systems.

In November 1985, however, President Reagan and Mikhail Gorbachev, the Soviet leader, began to work on an arms reduction compact. In 1987, the negotiations resulted in the Intermediate-Range Nuclear Force (INF) Treaty, which required the superpowers to dismantle a total of four thousand intermediate-range missiles within the first three years of the agreement.

Beginning in 1989, President George H. W. Bush continued the negotiations with the Soviet Union to reduce the number of nuclear weapons and the number of armed troops in Europe. Subsequent events, including the dissolution of the Soviet Union (in December 1991), made the process much more complex. American strategists worried as much about who now controlled the Soviet nuclear arsenal as about completing the treaty process. In 1992, the United States signed the Strategic Arms Reduction Treaty (START) with four former Soviet republics—Russia, Ukraine, Belarus, and Kazakhstan—to reduce the number of long-range nuclear weapons.

President George W. Bush changed directions in 2001, announcing that the United States was withdrawing from the 1972 ABM treaty (SALT I). Six months later, however, Bush and Russian president Vladimir Putin signed an agreement greatly reducing the number of nuclear weapons on each side over the next few years.

Détente
A French word meaning a relaxation of tensions. The term characterized U.S.-Soviet relations as they developed under President Richard Nixon and Secretary of State Henry Kissinger.

Strategic Arms Limitation Treaty (SALT I)
A treaty between the United States and the Soviet Union to stabilize the nuclear arms competition between the two countries. SALT I talks began in 1969, and agreements were signed on May 26, 1972.

The Dissolution of the Soviet Union. After the fall of the Berlin Wall in 1989, it was clear that the Soviet Union had relinquished much of its political and military control over the states of Eastern Europe that formerly had been part of the Soviet bloc. No one expected the Soviet Union to dissolve into separate states as quickly as it did, however. Although Gorbachev tried to adjust the Soviet constitution and political system to allow greater autonomy for the republics within the union, demands for political, ethnic, and religious autonomy grew. In August 1991, antireformist conspirators launched an attempt to overthrow the Soviet government and to depose Gorbachev. These efforts were thwarted by the Russian people and Parliament under the leadership of Boris Yeltsin, then president of Russia.

Instead of restoring the Soviet state, the attempted *coup d'état* hastened the process of creating an independent Russian state led by Yeltsin. On the day after Christmas in 1991, the Soviet Union was officially dissolved. Another uprising in Russia, this time led by anti-Yeltsin members of the new Parliament who wanted to restore the Soviet Union immediately, failed in 1993.

In 2000, Yeltsin resigned because of poor health. He named Vladimir Putin, architect of the Russian military effort against an independence movement in the province of Chechnya, as acting president. A few months later, Putin won the presidency in a national election.

Russia after the Soviet Union. During Putin's presidency (2000–2008), Russia experienced a dramatic economic recovery, in part due to rises in the price of oil. At the same time, Putin chipped away at Russia's democratic institutions, slowly turning the country into what was, in essence, an elected autocracy. Putin's second term as president came to an end in 2008, and he could not immediately run for reelection. He therefore engineered the election of one of his supporters, Dmitry Medvedev, as president. Medvedev promptly appointed Putin as prime minister. It was clear that Putin retained real power in Russia.

In recent years, the United States has become concerned over Russia's aggressive attitude toward its neighbors. In 2007, Estonia was subjected to massive cyberattacks originating in Russia, apparently because Estonia had taken down a statue honoring fallen Soviet soldiers. In 2008, Russian troops entered Georgia to prevent that nation from retaking an autonomous region that was under Russian protection. The Georgian army was quickly defeated. On several occasions since 2005, Russia has cut off the transmission of natural gas to Ukraine as a result of disputes. The cutoffs have caused serious natural-gas shortages in several central European nations that rely on gas routed through Ukraine. Russia also reacted angrily to U.S. plans for antimissile defenses in eastern Europe, aimed at protecting Europe from a possible future Iranian attack. Russia appeared to believe that the defenses were directed against it.

By the end of 2008, relations between Russia and the Bush administration had grown chilly. Still, the United States needed Russian assistance in matters such as curbing Iran's nuclear program. In 2009, Vice President Joe Biden spoke of "pressing the reset button" in Russian-American relations, a slogan that was taken up by other U.S. and Russian officials.

Even as Russia reasserts itself as a great power, its future is in doubt. Its population is dropping and may fall as low as 108 million by 2050, down from 150 million. Russia not only has a low birthrate, but a very high death rate—Russian life expectancy is below that of India, despite the widespread poverty in that country. If Russia's population continues to fall, its ability to project power will decline as well.

making a difference
WORKING FOR HUMAN RIGHTS

In many countries throughout the world, human rights are not protected. In some nations, people are imprisoned, tortured, or killed because they oppose the current regime. In other nations, certain ethnic or racial groups are oppressed by the majority population.

Why Should You Care? The defense of human rights is unlikely to put a single dollar in your pocket, so why get involved? The strongest reason for involving yourself with human rights issues in other countries is simple moral altruism—unselfish regard for the welfare of others.

A broader consideration, however, is that human rights abuses are often associated with the kind of dictatorial regimes that are likely to provoke wars. To the extent that the people of the world can create a climate in which human rights abuses are unacceptable, they may also create an atmosphere in which national leaders believe that they must display peaceful conduct generally. This, in turn, might reduce the frequency of wars, some of which could involve the United States. And wars always have costs—in the form of dollars, and in the form of American lives.

What Can You Do? How can you work for the improvement of human rights in other nations? One way is to join an organization that attempts to keep watch over human rights violations. (Two such organizations are listed at the end of this feature.) By publicizing human rights violations, such groups try to pressure nations into changing their practices. Sometimes, these organizations are able to apply enough pressure and cause enough embarrassment that victims may be freed from prison or allowed to emigrate.

Another way to work for human rights is to keep informed about the state of affairs in other nations and to write personally to governments that violate human rights or to their embassies, asking them to cease these violations.

If you want to receive general information about the position of the United States on human rights violations, you can contact the State Department:

▲ **These Amnesty International activists** are protesting alleged human rights abuses during the Bush administration. What do you think they want President Barack Obama to do? (Win McNamee/Getty Images)

U.S. Department of State Bureau of Democracy, Human Rights, and Labor
2201 C St. N.W.
Washington, DC 20520
202-647-4000
www.state.gov/g/drl/hr

The following organizations are well known for their watchdog efforts in countries that violate human rights for political reasons:

Amnesty International U.S.A.
5 Penn Plaza
New York, NY 10001
212-807-8400
www.amnestyusa.org

American Friends Service Committee
1501 Cherry St.
Philadelphia, PA 19102
215-241-7000
www.afsc.org

keyterms

Cold War 339
containment 351
defense policy 331
détente 353
diplomacy 331
economic aid 331
foreign policy 331

foreign policy
    process 331
intelligence
    community 347
isolationist foreign
    policy 350
Monroe Doctrine 350

moral idealism 332
national security
    policy 331
negative
    constituents 347
normal trade relations
    (NTR) status 340

political realism 332
Soviet bloc 351
Strategic Arms
    Limitation Treaty
    (SALT I) 353
technical assistance 331
Truman Doctrine 351

chaptersummary

1 Foreign policy includes the nation's external goals and the techniques used to achieve them. National security policy, which is one aspect of foreign policy, is designed to protect the independence and the political and economic integrity of the United States. Diplomacy involves the nation's external relationships and is an attempt to resolve conflict without resort to arms. U.S. foreign policy is sometimes based on moral idealism and sometimes based on political realism—and often on a mixture of both.

2 Terrorism has become a major challenge facing the United States and other nations. The United States waged war on terrorism after the September 11 attacks. U.S. armed forces occupied Afghanistan in 2001 and Iraq in 2003.

3 In 1991 and again in 2003, the United States sent combat troops to Iraq. The second war in Iraq, begun in 2003, succeeded in toppling the decades-long dictatorship of Saddam Hussein. The Bush administration was heavily criticized for going to war with inadequate intelligence and for mismanaging the occupation. Attacks on U.S. forces and those of the new Iraqi government finally declined in 2007 and 2008, and in 2009, President Barack Obama set the end of 2011 as a date for the withdrawal of all U.S. forces.

4 Nuclear proliferation continues to be an issue due to the breakup of the Soviet Union and loss of control over its nuclear arsenal, along with the continued efforts of other nations to gain nuclear warheads. The number of warheads is known to be more than 32,000. The attempts of North Korea and Iran to gain nuclear capabilities have posed special concerns. The Middle East continues to be a hotbed of conflict despite efforts to continue the peace process between Israel and the Palestinians.

5 The formal power of the president to make foreign policy derives from the U.S. Constitution, which designates the president as commander in chief of the army and navy. Presidents have interpreted this authority broadly. They also have the power to make treaties and executive agreements. In principle, the State Department is the executive agency with primary authority over foreign affairs. The National Security Council also plays a major role. The intelligence community consists of government agencies engaged in activities varying from information gathering to covert operations. In response to presidential actions in the Vietnam War, Congress attempted to establish some limits on the power of the president to intervene abroad by passing the War Powers Resolution in 1973.

6 Three major themes have guided U.S. foreign policy. In the early years of the nation, isolationism was the primary strategy. With the start of the twentieth century, isolationism gave way to global involvement. From the end of World War II

through the 1980s, the major goal was to contain communism and the influence of the Soviet Union.

7   During the 1800s, the United States had little international power and generally stayed out of European conflicts and politics, so these years have been called the period of isolationism. The Monroe Doctrine of 1823 stated that the United States would not accept foreign intervention in the Western Hemisphere and would not meddle in European affairs. The United States pursued an actively expansionist policy in the Americas and the Pacific area, however.

8   The end of the policy of isolationism toward Europe started with the Spanish-American War of 1898. U.S. involvement in European politics became more extensive when the United States entered World War I on April 6, 1917. World War II marked a lasting change in American foreign policy. The United States was the only major country to emerge from the war with its economy intact and the only country with operating nuclear weapons.

9   Soon after the close of World War II, the uncomfortable alliance between the United States and the Soviet Union ended, and the Cold War began. A policy of containment, which assumed an expansionist Soviet Union, was enunciated in the Truman Doctrine. Following the frustrations of the Vietnam War and the apparent arms equality of the United States and the Soviet Union, the United States adopted a policy of détente. Although President Reagan took a tough stance toward the Soviet Union during his first term, his second term saw serious negotiations toward arms reduction, culminating in the signing of the Intermediate-Range Nuclear Force Treaty in 1987. After the fall of the Soviet Union, Russia emerged as a less threatening state and signed the Strategic Arms Reduction Treaty with the United States in 1992. Since 2000, Russia under Vladimir Putin has reemerged as a great power and has exhibited aggressive attitudes toward its immediate neighbors.

QUESTIONS FOR
discussionandanalysis

1   Some people believe that if no U.S. military personnel were stationed abroad, terrorists would have less desire to harm the United States and its citizens. Do you agree? Why or why not?

2   As of mid-2009, no terrorist act remotely comparable to the attacks of 9/11 had taken place on U.S. soil. Why do you think that is so? How much credit can the government take? To what extent

might terrorists experience practical difficulties in accomplishing anything like the damage inflicted on 9/11?

3   Why do you think that North Korea and Iran might want to possess nuclear weapons, even though they cannot hope to match the nuclear arsenals of the original five nuclear powers?

helpfulonline**Resources**

CONNECTING TO AMERICAN GOVERNMENT AND POLITICS

In addition to materials on international crises, the United Nations Web site contains a treasure trove of international statistics. Go to:

www.un.org/english

The Organisation for Economic Co-operation and Development (OECD) provides another major source of international statistics and economic analysis. Access its Web site at:

www.oecd.org

Finally, the *World Factbook* of the CIA is an excellent resource. Visit it at:

www.cia.gov/library/publications/the-world-factbook

aspecialWebSite

FOR YOUR TEXT

Go to this book's special Web site at academic.cengage.com/polisci/Schmidt/Brief6e. Choose "For Students." Then click on Chapter 14, where you will find an online quiz and other helpful study aids. If your professor is using CengageNOW: *American Government and Politics Today, Brief Edition*, log in and go to Chapter 14 for additional online study aids.

Appendix A

The Declaration of Independence

In Congress, July 4, 1776

A Declaration by the Representatives of the United States of America, in General Congress assembled. When in the Course of human Events, it becomes necessary for one People to dissolve the Political Bands which have connected them with another, and to assume among the Powers of the Earth, the separate and equal Station to which the Laws of Nature and of Nature's God entitle them, a decent Respect to the Opinions of Mankind requires that they should declare the causes which impel them to the Separation.

We hold these Truths to be self-evident, that all Men are created equal, that they are endowed by their Creator with certain unalienable Rights, that among these are Life, Liberty, and the Pursuit of Happiness— That to secure these Rights, Governments are instituted among Men, deriving their just Powers from the Consent of the Governed, that whenever any Form of Government becomes destructive of these Ends, it is the Right of the People to alter or to abolish it, and to institute new Government, laying its Foundation on such Principles, and organizing its Powers in such Forms, as to them shall seem most likely to effect their Safety and Happiness. Prudence, indeed, will dictate that Governments long established should not be changed for light and transient Causes; and accordingly all Experience hath shewn, that Mankind are more disposed to suffer, while Evils are sufferable, than to right themselves by abolishing the Forms to which they are accustomed. But when a long Train of Abuses and Usurpations, pursuing invariably the same Object, evinces a Design to reduce them under absolute Despotism, it is their Right, it is their Duty, to throw off such Government, and to provide new Guards for their future Security. Such has been the patient Sufferance of these Colonies; and such is now the Necessity which constrains them to alter their former Systems of Government. The History of the present King of Great-Britain is a History of repeated Injuries and Usurpations, all having in direct Object the Establishment of an absolute Tyranny over these States. To prove this, let Facts be submitted to a candid World.

He has refused his Assent to Laws, the most wholesome and necessary for the public Good.

He has forbidden his Governors to pass Laws of immediate and pressing Importance, unless suspended in their Operation till his Assent should be obtained; and when so suspended, he has utterly neglected to attend to them.

He has refused to pass other Laws for the Accommodation of large Districts of People, unless those People would relinquish the Right of Representation in the Legislature, a Right inestimable to them, and formidable to Tyrants only.

He has called together Legislative Bodies at Places unusual, uncomfortable, and distant from the Depository of their Public Records, for the sole Purpose of fatiguing them into Compliance with his Measures.

He has dissolved Representative Houses repeatedly, for opposing with manly Firmness his Invasions on the Rights of the People.

He has refused for a long Time, after such Dissolutions, to cause others to be elected; whereby the Legislative Powers, incapable of Annihilation, have returned to the People at large for their exercise; the State remaining in the mean time exposed to all the Dangers of Invasion from without, and Convulsions within.

He has endeavoured to prevent the Population of these States; for that Purpose obstructing the Laws for Naturalization of Foreigners; refusing to pass others to encourage their Migrations hither, and raising the Conditions of new Appropriations of Lands.

He has obstructed the Administration of Justice, by refusing his Assent to Laws for establishing Judiciary Powers.

He has made Judges dependent on his Will alone, for the Tenure of their offices, and the Amount and payment of their Salaries.

He has erected a Multitude of new Offices, and sent hither Swarms of Officers to harrass our People, and eat out their Substance.

He has kept among us, in Times of Peace, Standing Armies, without the consent of our Legislatures.

He has affected to render the Military independent of, and superior to the Civil Power.

He has combined with others to subject us to a Jurisdiction foreign to our Constitution, and unacknowledged by our Laws; giving his Assent to their Acts of pretended Legislation:

For quartering large Bodies of Armed Troops among us:

For protecting them, by a mock Trial, from Punishment for any Murders which they should commit on the Inhabitants of these States:

For cutting off our Trade with all Parts of the World:

For imposing Taxes on us without our Consent:

For depriving us, in many cases, of the Benefits of Trial by Jury:

For transporting us beyond Seas to be tried for pretended Offences:

For abolishing the free System of English Laws in a neighbouring Province, establishing therein an arbitrary Government, and enlarging its Boundaries, so as to render it at once an Example and fit Instrument for introducing the same absolute Rule into these Colonies:

For taking away our Charters, abolishing our most valuable Laws, and altering fundamentally the Forms of our Governments:

For suspending our own Legislatures, and declaring themselves invested with Power to legislate for us in all Cases whatsoever.

He has abdicated Government here, by declaring us out of his Protection and waging War against us.

He has plundered our Seas, ravaged our Coasts, burnt our towns, and destroyed the Lives of our People.

He is, at this Time, transporting large Armies of foreign Mercenaries to compleat the works of Death, Desolation, and Tyranny, already begun with circumstances of Cruelty and Perfidy, scarcely paralleled in the most barbarous Ages, and totally unworthy the Head of a civilized Nation.

He has constrained our fellow Citizens taken Captive on the high Seas to bear Arms against their Country, to become the Executioners of their Friends and Brethren, or to fall themselves by their Hands.

He has excited domestic Insurrections amongst us, and has endeavoured to bring on the Inhabitants of our Frontiers, the merciless Indian Savages, whose known Rule of Warfare, is an undistinguished Destruction, of all Ages, Sexes and Conditions.

In every state of these Oppressions we have Petitioned for Redress in the most humble Terms: Our repeated Petitions have been answered only by repeated Injury. A Prince, whose Character is thus marked by every act which may define a Tyrant, is unfit to be the Ruler of a free People.

Nor have we been wanting in Attentions to our British Brethren. We have warned them from Time to Time of Attempts by their Legislature to extend an unwarrantable Jurisdiction over us. We have reminded them of the Circumstances of our Emigration and Settlement here. We have appealed to their native Justice and Magnanimity, and we have conjured them by the Ties of our common Kindred to disavow these Usurpations, which, would inevitably interrupt our Connections and Correspondence. They too have been deaf to the Voice of Justice and of Consanguinity. We must, therefore, acquiesce in the Necessity, which denounces our Separation, and hold them, as we hold the rest of Mankind, Enemies in War, in Peace, Friends.

We, therefore, the Representatives of the UNITED STATES OF AMERICA, in General Congress Assembled, appealing to the Supreme Judge of the World for the Rectitude of our Intentions, do, in the Name, and by the Authority of the good People of these Colonies, solemnly Publish and Declare, That these United Colonies are, and of Right ought to be, Free and Independent States; that they are absolved from all Allegiance to the British Crown, and that all political Connection between them and the State of Great-Britain, is and ought to be totally dissolved; and that as Free and Independent States, they have full Power to levy War, conclude Peace, contract Alliances, establish Commerce, and to do all other Acts and Things which Independent States may of right do. And for the support of this declaration, with a firm Reliance on the Protection of divine Providence, we mutually pledge to each other our lives, our Fortunes, and our sacred Honor.

Appendix B

The Constitution of the United States*

The Preamble

We the People of the United States, in Order to form a more perfect Union, establish Justice, insure domestic Tranquility, provide for the common defence, promote the general Welfare, and secure the Blessings of Liberty to ourselves and our Posterity, do ordain and establish this Constitution for the United States of America.

The Preamble declares that "We the People" are the authority for the Constitution (unlike the Articles of Confederation, which derived their authority from the states). The Preamble also sets out the purposes of the Constitution.

Article I. (Legislative Branch)

The first part of the Constitution, Article 1, deals with the organization and powers of the lawmaking branch of the national government, the Congress.

Section 1. Legislative Powers

All legislative Powers herein granted shall be vested in a Congress of the United States, which shall consist of a Senate and House of Representatives.

Section 2. House of Representatives

Clause 1: Composition and Election of Members. The House of Representatives shall be composed of Members chosen every second Year by the People of the several States, and the Electors in each State shall have the Qualifications requisite for Electors of the most numerous Branch of the State Legislature.

Each state has the power to decide who may vote for members of Congress. Within each state, those who may vote for state legislators may also vote for members of the House of Representatives (and, under the Seventeenth Amendment, for U.S. senators). When the Constitution was written, nearly all states limited voting rights to white male property owners or taxpayers at least twenty-one years old. Subsequent amendments granted voting power to African American men, all women, and eighteen-year-olds.

Clause 2: Qualifications. No Person shall be a Representative who shall not have attained to the Age of twenty five Years, and been seven Years a Citizen of the United States, and who shall not, when elected, be an Inhabitant of that State in which he shall be chosen.

Each member of the House must be at least twenty-five years old, a citizen of the United States for at least seven years, and a resident of the state in which she or he is elected.

Clause 3: Apportionment of Representatives and Direct Taxes. Representatives [and direct Taxes][1] shall be apportioned among the several States which may be included within this Union, according to their respective Numbers [which shall be determined by adding to the whole Number of free Persons, including those bound to Service for a Term of Years, and excluding Indians not taxed, three fifths of all other Persons].[2] The actual Enumeration shall be made within three Years after the first Meeting of the Congress of the United States, and within every subsequent Term of ten Years, in such Manner as they shall by Law direct. The Number of Representatives shall not exceed one for every thirty Thousand, but each State shall have at Least one Representative; and until such enumeration shall be made, the State of New Hampshire shall be entitled to chuse three, Massachusetts eight, Rhode Island and Providence Plantations one, Connecticut five, New York six, New Jersey four, Pennsylvania eight, Delaware one, Maryland six, Virginia ten, North Carolina five, South Carolina five, and Georgia three.

A state's representation in the House is based on the size of its population. Population is counted in each decade's census, after which Congress reapportions House seats. Since early in the twentieth century, the number of seats has been limited to 435.

Clause 4: Vacancies. When vacancies happen in the Representation from any State, the Executive Authority thereof shall issue Writs of Election to fill such Vacancies.

The "Executive Authority" is the state's governor. When a vacancy occurs in the House, the governor calls a special election to fill it.

---

* The spelling, capitalization, and punctuation of the original have been retained here. Brackets indicate passages that have been altered by amendments to the Constitution. We have added article titles (in parentheses), section titles, and clause designations. We have also inserted annotations in blue italic type.

1. Modified by the Sixteenth Amendment.
2. Modified by the Fourteenth Amendment.

Clause 5: Officers and Impeachment. The House of Representatives shall chuse their Speaker and other Officers; and shall have the sole Power of Impeachment.

The power to impeach is the power to accuse. In this case, it is the power to accuse members of the executive or judicial branch of wrongdoing or abuse of power. Once a bill of impeachment is issued, the Senate holds the trial.

Section 3. The Senate

Clause 1: Term and Number of Members. The Senate of the United States shall be composed of two Senators from each State [chosen by the Legislature thereof],[3] for six Years; and each Senator shall have one Vote.

Every state has two senators, each of whom serves for six years and has one vote in the upper chamber. Since the Seventeenth Amendment in 1913, all senators have been elected directly by voters of the state during the regular election.

Clause 2: Classification of Senators. Immediately after they shall be assembled in Consequence of the first Election, they shall be divided as equally as may be into three Classes. The Seats of the Senators of the first Class shall be vacated at the Expiration of the second Year, of the second Class at the Expiration of the fourth Year, and of the third Class at the Expiration of the sixth Year, so that one third may be chosen every second Year; [and if Vacancies happen by Resignation, or otherwise, during the Recess of the Legislature of any State, the Executive thereof may make temporary Appointments until the next Meeting of the Legislature, which shall then fill such Vacancies].[4]

One-third of the Senate's seats are open to election every two years (in contrast, all members of the House are elected simultaneously).

Clause 3: Qualifications. No Person shall be a Senator who shall not have attained to the Age of thirty Years, and been nine Years a Citizen of the United States, and who shall not, when elected, be an Inhabitant of that State for which he shall be chosen.

Every senator must be at least thirty years old, a citizen of the United States for a minimum of nine years, and a resident of the state in which he or she is elected.

Clause 4: The Role of the Vice President. The Vice President of the United States shall be President of the Senate, but shall have no Vote, unless they be equally divided.

The vice president presides over meetings of the Senate but cannot vote unless there is a tie. The Constitution gives no other official duties to the vice president.

Clause 5: Other Officers. The Senate shall chuse their other Officers, and also a President pro tempore, in the Absence of the Vice President, or when he shall exercise the Office of President of the United States.

The Senate votes for one of its members to preside when the vice president is absent. This person is usually called the president pro tempore because of the temporary nature of the position.

Clause 6: Impeachment Trials. The Senate shall have the sole Power to try all Impeachments. When sitting for that Purpose, they shall be on Oath or Affirmation. When the President of the United States is tried, the Chief Justice shall preside: And no Person shall be convicted without the Concurrence of two thirds of the Members present.

The Senate conducts trials of officials that the House impeaches. The Senate sits as a jury, with the vice president presiding if the president is not on trial.

Clause 7: Penalties for Conviction. Judgment in Cases of Impeachment shall not extend further than to removal from Office, and disqualification to hold and enjoy any Office of honor, Trust, or Profit under the United States: but the Party convicted shall nevertheless be liable and subject to Indictment, Trial, Judgment, and Punishment, according to Law.

On conviction of impeachment charges, the Senate can only force an official to leave office and prevent him or her from holding another office in the federal government. The individual, however, can still be tried in a regular court.

Section 4. Congressional Elections: Times, Manner, and Places

Clause 1: Elections. The Times, Places and Manner of holding Elections for Senators and Representatives, shall be prescribed in each State by the Legislature thereof; but the Congress may at any time by Law make or alter such Regulations, except as to the Places of chusing Senators.

Congress set the Tuesday after the first Monday in November in even-numbered years as the date for congressional elections. In states with more than one seat in the House, Congress requires that representatives be elected from districts within each state. Under the Seventeenth Amendment, senators are elected at the same places as other officials.

Clause 2: Sessions of Congress. [The Congress shall assemble at least once in every Year, and such Meeting shall be on the first Monday in December,[5] unless they shall by Law appoint a different Day.][5]

Congress has to meet every year at least once. The regular session now begins at noon on January 3 of each year, subsequent to the Twentieth Amendment, unless Congress passes a law to fix a different date. Congress stays in session until its members vote to adjourn. Additionally, the president may call a special session.

Section 5. Powers and Duties of the Houses

Clause 1: Admitting Members and Quorum. Each House shall be the Judge of the Elections, Returns, and

---

3. Repealed by the Seventeenth Amendment.
4. Modified by the Seventeenth Amendment.

5. Changed by the Twentieth Amendment.

Qualifications of its own Members, and a Majority of each shall constitute a Quorum to do Business; but a smaller Number may adjourn from day to day, and may be authorized to compel the Attendance of absent Members, in such Manner, and under such Penalties as each House may provide.

Each chamber may exclude or refuse to seat a member-elect.

The quorum rule requires that 218 members of the House and 51 members of the Senate be present to conduct business. This rule normally is not enforced in the handling of routine matters.

Clause 2: Rules and Discipline of Members. Each House may determine the Rules of its Proceedings, punish its Members for disorderly Behaviour, and, with the Concurrence of two thirds, expel a Member.

The House and the Senate may adopt their own rules to guide their proceedings. Each may also discipline its members for conduct that is deemed unacceptable. No member may be expelled without a two-thirds majority vote in favor of expulsion.

Clause 3: Keeping a Record. Each House shall keep a Journal of its Proceedings, and from time to time publish the same, excepting such Parts as may in their Judgment require Secrecy; and the Yeas and Nays of the Members of either House on any question shall, at the Desire of one fifth of those Present, be entered on the Journal.

The journals of the two chambers are published at the end of each session of Congress.

Clause 4: Adjournment. Neither House, during the Session of Congress, shall, without the Consent of the other, adjourn for more than three days, nor to any other Place than that in which the two Houses shall be sitting.

Congress has the power to determine when and where to meet, provided, however, that both chambers meet in the same city. Neither chamber may recess for more than three days without the consent of the other.

Section 6. Rights of Members

Clause 1: Compensation and Privileges. The Senators and Representatives shall receive a Compensation for their services, to be ascertained by Law, and paid out of the Treasury of the United States. They shall in all Cases, except Treason, Felony and Breach of the Peace, be privileged from Arrest during their Attendance at the Session of their respective Houses, and in going to and returning from the same; and for any Speech or Debate in either House, they shall not be questioned in any other Place.

Congressional salaries are to be paid by the U.S. Treasury rather than by the members' respective states. The original salaries were $6 per day; in 1857 they were $3,000 per year. Both representatives and senators were paid $165,200 in 2007.

Treason is defined in Article III, Section 3. A felony is any serious crime. A breach of the peace is any indictable offense less than treason or a felony. Members cannot be

arrested for things they say during speeches and debates in Congress. This immunity applies to the Capitol Building itself and not to their private lives.

Clause 2: Restrictions. No Senator or Representative shall, during the Time for which he was elected, be appointed to any civil Office under the Authority of the United States, which shall have been created, or the Emoluments whereof shall have been encreased during such time; and no Person holding any Office under the United States, shall be a Member of either House during his Continuance in Office.

During the term for which a member was elected, he or she cannot concurrently accept another federal government position.

Section 7. Legislative Powers: Bills and Resolutions

Clause 1: Revenue Bills. All Bills for raising Revenue shall originate in the House of Representatives; but the Senate may propose or concur with Amendments as on other Bills.

All tax and appropriation bills for raising money have to originate in the House of Representatives. The Senate, though, often amends such bills and may even substitute an entirely different bill.

Clause 2: The Presidential Veto. Every Bill which shall have passed the House of Representatives and the Senate, shall, before it becomes a Law, be presented to the President of the United States; If he approve he shall sign it, but if not he shall return it, with his Objections to the House in which it shall have originated, who shall enter the Objections at large on their Journal, and proceed to reconsider it. If after such Reconsideration two thirds of that House shall agree to pass the Bill, it shall be sent together with the Objections, to the other House, by which it shall likewise be reconsidered, and if approved by two thirds of that House, it shall become a Law. But in all such Cases the Votes of both Houses shall be determined by Yeas and Nays, and the Names of the Persons voting for and against the Bill shall be entered on the Journal of each House respectively. If any Bill shall not be returned by the President within ten Days (Sundays excepted) after it shall have been presented to him, the Same shall be a Law, in like Manner as if he had signed it, unless the Congress by their Adjournment prevent its Return in which Case it shall not be a Law.

When Congress sends the president a bill, he or she can sign it (in which case it becomes law) or send it back to the chamber in which it originated. If it is sent back, a two-thirds majority of each chamber must pass it again for it to become law. If the president neither signs it nor sends it back within ten days, it becomes law anyway, unless Congress adjourns in the meantime.

Clause 3: Actions on Other Matters. Every Order, Resolution, or Vote to which the Concurrence of the Senate and House of Representatives may be necessary (except on a question of Adjournment) shall be presented to the President of the United States; and before the Same shall take Effect, shall be approved by him, or being dis-approved by him, shall be repassed by two thirds of the Senate and House of Representatives, according to the Rules and Limitations prescribed in the Case of a Bill.

The president must have the opportunity to either sign or veto everything that Congress passes, except votes to adjourn and resolutions not having the force of law.

Section 8. The Powers of Congress

Clause 1: Taxing. The Congress shall have Power To lay and collect Taxes, Duties, Imposts and Excises, to pay the Debts and provide for the common Defence and general Welfare of the United States; but all Duties, Imposts and Excises shall be uniform throughout the United States;

Duties are taxes on imports and exports. Impost is a generic term for tax. Excises are taxes on the manufacture, sale, or use of goods.

Clause 2: Borrowing. To borrow Money on the credit of the United States;

Congress has the power to borrow money, which is normally carried out through the sale of U.S. treasury bonds on which interest is paid. Note that the Constitution places no limit on the amount of government borrowing.

Clause 3: Regulation of Commerce. To regulate Commerce with foreign Nations, and among the several States, and with the Indian Tribes;

This is the commerce clause, which gives to Congress the power to regulate interstate and foreign trade. Much of the activity of Congress is based on this clause.

Clause 4: Naturalization and Bankruptcy. To establish an uniform Rule of Naturalization, and uniform Laws on the subject of Bankruptcies throughout the United States;

Only Congress may determine how aliens can become citizens of the United States. Congress may make laws with respect to bankruptcy.

Clause 5: Money and Standards. To coin Money, regu-late the Value thereof, and of foreign Coin, and fix the Standard of Weights and Measures;

Congress mints coins and prints and circulates paper money. Congress can establish uniform measures of time, distance, weight, and so on. In 1838, Congress adopted the English system of weights and measurements as our national standard.

Clause 6: Punishing Counterfeiters. To provide for the Punishment of counterfeiting the Securities and current Coin of the United States;

Congress has the power to punish those who copy American money and pass it off as real. Currently, the punishment is a fine up to $5,000 and/or imprisonment for up to fifteen years.

Clause 7: Roads and Post Offices. To establish Post Offices and post Roads;

Post roads include all routes over which mail is carried—highways, railways, waterways, and airways.

Clause 8: Patents and Copyrights. To promote the Progress of Science and useful Arts, by securing for limited Times to Authors and Inventors the exclusive Right to their respective Writings and Discoveries;

Authors' and composers' works are protected by copy-rights established by copyright law, which currently is the Copyright Act of 1976, as amended. Copyrights are valid for the life of the author or composer plus seventy years. Inventors' works are protected by patents, which vary in length of protection from fourteen to twenty years. A patent gives a person the exclusive right to control the manufac-ture or sale of her or his invention.

Clause 9: Lower Courts. To constitute Tribunals inferior to the supreme Court;

Congress has the authority to set up all federal courts, except the Supreme Court, and to decide what cases those courts will hear.

Clause 10: Punishment for Piracy. To define and punish Piracies and Felonies committed on the high Seas, and Offences against the Law of Nations;

Congress has the authority to prohibit the commission of certain acts outside U.S. territory and to punish certain vio-lations of international law.

Clause 11: Declaration of War. To declare War, grant Letters of Marque and Reprisal, and make Rules con-cerning Captures on Land and Water;

Only Congress can declare war, although the president, as commander in chief, can make war without Congress's formal declaration. Letters of marque and reprisal autho-rized private parties to capture and destroy enemy ships in wartime. Since the middle of the nineteenth century, inter-national law has prohibited letters of marque and reprisal, and the United States has honored the ban.

Clause 12: The Army. To raise and support Armies, but no Appropriation of Money to that Use shall be for a longer Term than two Years;

Congress has the power to create an army; the money used to pay for it must be appropriated for no more than two-year intervals. This latter restriction gives ultimate control of the army to civilians.

Clause 13: Creation of a Navy. To provide and maintain a Navy;

This clause allows for the maintenance of a navy. In 1947, Congress created the U.S. Air Force.

Clause 14: Regulation of the Armed Forces. To make Rules for the Government and Regulation of the land and naval Forces;

Congress sets the rules for the military mainly by way of the Uniform Code of Military Justice, which was enacted in 1950 by Congress.

Clause 15: The Militia. To provide for calling forth the Militia to execute the Laws of the Union, suppress Insurrections and repel Invasions;

The militia is known today as the National Guard. Both Congress and the president have the authority to call the National Guard into federal service.

Clause 16: How the Militia Is Organized. To provide for organizing, arming, and disciplining the Militia, and for governing such Part of them as may be employed in the Service of the United States, reserving to the States respectively, the Appointment of the Officers, and the Authority of training the Militia according to the discipline prescribed by Congress;

This clause gives Congress the power to "federalize" state militia (National Guard). When called into such service, the National Guard is subject to the same rules that Congress has set forth for the regular armed services.

Clause 17: Creation of the District of Columbia. To exercise exclusive Legislation in all Cases whatsoever, over such District (not exceeding ten Miles square) as may, by Cession of particular States, and the Acceptance of Congress, become the Seat of the Government of the United States, and to exercise like Authority over all Places purchased by the Consent of the Legislature of the State in which the Same shall be, for the Erection of Forts, Magazines, Arsenals, dock-Yards, and other needful Buildings;—And

Congress established the District of Columbia as the national capital in 1791. Virginia and Maryland had granted land for the District, but Virginia's grant was returned because it was believed it would not be needed. Today, the District covers sixty-nine square miles.

Clause 18: The Elastic Clause. To make all Laws which shall be necessary and proper for carrying into Execution the foregoing Powers, and all other Powers vested by this Constitution in the Government of the United States, or in any Department or Officer thereof.

This clause—the necessary and proper clause, or the elastic clause—grants no specific powers, and thus it can be stretched to fit different circumstances. It has allowed Congress to adapt the government to changing needs and times.

Section 9. The Powers Denied to Congress

Clause 1: Question of Slavery. The Migration or Importation of such Persons as any of the States now existing shall think proper to admit, shall not be prohibited by the Congress prior to the Year one thousand eight hundred and eight, but a Tax or duty may be imposed on such Importation, not exceeding ten dollars for each Person.

"Persons" referred to slaves. Congress outlawed the slave trade in 1808.

Clause 2: Habeas Corpus. The privilege of the Writ of Habeas Corpus shall not be suspended, unless when in Cases of Rebellion or Invasion the public Safety may require it.

A writ of habeas corpus is a court order directing a sheriff or other public officer who is detaining another person to "produce the body" of the detainee so the court can assess the legality of the detention.

Clause 3: Special Bills. No Bill of Attainder or ex post facto Law shall be passed.

A bill of attainder is a law that inflicts punishment without a trial. An ex post facto law is a law that inflicts punishment for an act that was not illegal when it was committed.

Clause 4: Direct Taxes. [No Capitation, or other direct, Tax shall be laid, unless in Proportion to the Census or Enumeration herein before directed to be taken.][6]

A capitation is a tax on a person. A direct tax is a tax paid directly to the government, such as a property tax. This clause was intended to prevent Congress from levying a tax on slaves per person and thereby taxing slavery out of existence.

Clause 5: Export Taxes. No Tax or Duty shall be laid on Articles exported from any State.

Congress may not tax any goods sold from one state to another or from one state to a foreign country. (Congress does have the power to tax goods that are bought from other countries, however.)

Clause 6: Interstate Commerce. No Preference shall be given by any Regulation of Commerce or Revenue to the Ports of one State over those of another: nor shall Vessels bound to, or from, one State, be obliged to enter, clear, or pay Duties in another.

Congress may not treat different ports within the United States differently in terms of taxing and commerce powers. Congress may not give one state's port a legal advantage over the ports of another state.

Clause 7: Treasury Withdrawals. No Money shall be drawn from the Treasury, but in Consequence of Appropriations made by Law; and a regular Statement and Account of the Receipts and Expenditures of all public Money shall be published from time to time.

Federal funds can be spent only as Congress authorizes. This is a significant check on the president's power.

Clause 8: Titles of Nobility. No Title of Nobility shall be granted by the United States: And no Person holding any Office of Profit or Trust under them, shall, without the Consent of the Congress, accept of any present, Emolument, Office, or Title, of any kind whatever, from any King, Prince, or foreign State.

No person in the United States may hold a title of nobility, such as duke or duchess. This clause also discourages bribery of American officials by foreign governments.

Section 10. Those Powers Denied to the States

Clause 1: Treaties and Coinage. No State shall enter into any Treaty, Alliance, or Confederation; grant Letters of

---

6. Modified by the Sixteenth Amendment.

Marque and Reprisal; coin Money; emit Bills of Credit; make any Thing but gold and silver Coin a Tender in Payment of Debts; pass any Bill of Attainder, ex post facto Law, or Law impairing the Obligation of Contracts, or grant any Title of Nobility.

Prohibiting state laws "impairing the Obligation of Contracts" was intended to protect creditors. (Shays' Rebellion—an attempt to prevent courts from giving effect to creditors' legal actions against debtors—occurred only one year before the Constitution was written.)

Clause 2: Duties and Imposts. No State shall, without the Consent of the Congress, lay any Imports or Duties on Imports or Exports, except what may be absolutely necessary for executing its inspection Laws; and the net Produce of all Duties and Imposts, laid by any State on Imports or Exports, shall be for the Use of the Treasury of the United States; and all such Laws shall be subject to the Revision and Controul of the Congress.

Only Congress can tax imports. Further, the states cannot tax exports.

Clause 3: War. No State shall, without the Consent of Congress, lay any Duty of Tonnage, keep Troops, or Ships of War in time of Peace, enter into any Agreement or Compact with another State, or with a foreign Power or engage in War, unless actually invaded, or in such imminent Danger as will not admit of delay.

A duty of tonnage is a tax on ships according to their cargo capacity. No states may tax ships according to their cargo unless Congress agrees. Additionally, this clause forbids any state to keep troops or warships during peacetime or to make a compact with another state or foreign nation unless Congress so agrees. A state, in contrast, can maintain a militia, but its use has to be limited to disorders that occur within the state—unless, of course, the militia is called into federal service.

Article II. (Executive Branch)

Section 1. The Nature and Scope of Presidential Power

Clause 1: Four-Year Term. The executive Power shall be vested in a President of the United States of America. He shall hold his Office during the Term of four Years, and, together with the Vice President, chosen for the same Term, be elected, as follows.

The president has the power to carry out laws made by Congress, called the executive power. He or she serves in office for a four-year term after election. The Twenty-second Amendment limits the number of times a person may be elected president.

Clause 2: Choosing Electors from Each State. Each State shall appoint, in such Manner as the Legislature thereof may direct, a Number of Electors, equal to the whole Number of Senators and Representatives to which the State may be entitled in the Congress; but no Senator or Representative, or Person holding an Office of Trust or Profit under the United States, shall be appointed an Elector.

The "Electors" are known more commonly as the "electoral college." The president is elected by electors—that is, representatives chosen by the people—rather than by the people directly.

Clause 3: The Former System of Elections. [The Electors shall meet in their respective States, and vote by Ballot for two Persons, of whom one at least shall not be an Inhabitant of the same State with themselves. And they shall make a List of all the Persons voted for, and of the Number of Votes for each; which List they shall sign and certify, and transmit sealed to the Seat of the Government of the United States, directed to the President of the Senate. The President of the Senate shall, in the Presence of the Senate and House of Representatives, open all the Certificates, and the Votes shall then be counted. The Person having the greatest Number of Votes shall be the President, if such Number be a Majority of the whole Number of Electors appointed; and if there be more than one who have such Majority, and have an equal Number of Votes, then the House of Representatives shall immediately chuse by Ballot one of them for President; and if no Person have a Majority, then from the five highest on the List the said House shall in like Manner chuse the President. But in chusing the President, the Votes shall be taken by States, the Representation from each State having one Vote; A quorum for this Purpose shall consist of a Member or Members from two thirds of the States, and a Majority of all the States shall be necessary to a Choice. In every Case, after the Choice of the President, the Person having the greater Number of Votes of the Electors shall be the Vice President. But if there should remain two or more who have equal Votes, the Senate shall chuse from them by Ballot the Vice President.][7]

The original method of selecting the president and vice president was replaced by the Twelfth Amendment. Apparently, the framers did not anticipate the rise of political parties and the development of primaries and conventions.

Clause 4: The Time of Elections. The Congress may determine the Time of chusing the Electors, and the Day on which they shall give their Votes; which Day shall be the same throughout the United States.

Congress set the Tuesday after the first Monday in November every fourth year as the date for choosing electors. The electors cast their votes on the Monday after the second Wednesday in December of that year.

Clause 5: Qualifications for President. No person except a natural born Citizen, or a Citizen of the United States, at the time of the Adoption of this Constitution, shall be eligible to the Office of President; neither shall any Person be eligible to that Office who shall not have attained to the Age of thirty five Years, and been fourteen Years a Resident within the United States.

---

7. Changed by the Twelfth Amendment.

The president must be a natural-born citizen, be at least thirty-five years of age when taking office, and have been a resident within the United States for at least fourteen years.

Clause 6: Succession of the Vice President. [In Case of the Removal of the President from Office, or of his Death, Resignation or Inability to discharge the Powers and Duties of the said Office, the same shall devolve on the Vice President, and the Congress may by Law provide for the Case of Removal, Death, Resignation or Inability, both of the President and Vice President, declaring what Officer shall then act as President, and such Officer shall act accordingly, until the Disability be removed, or a President shall be elected.][8]

This section provided for the method by which the vice president was to succeed to the presidency, but its wording is ambiguous. It was replaced by the Twenty-fifth Amendment.

Clause 7: The President's Salary. The President shall, at stated Times, receive for his Services, a Compensation, which shall neither be encreased nor diminished during the Period for which he shall have been elected, and he shall not receive within that Period any other Emolument from the United States, or any of them.

The president maintains the same salary during each four-year term. Moreover, she or he may not receive additional cash payments from the government. Originally set at $25,000 per year, the salary is currently $400,000 a year plus a $50,000 nontaxable expense account.

Clause 8: The Oath of Office. Before he enter on the Execution of his Office, he shall take the following Oath or Affirmation: "I do solemnly swear (or affirm) that I will faithfully execute the Office of President of the United States, and will to the best of my Ability, preserve, protect and defend the Constitution of the United States."

The president is "sworn in" prior to beginning the duties of the office. Currently, the taking of the oath of office occurs on January 20, following the November election. The ceremony is called the inauguration. The oath of office is administered by the chief justice of the United States Supreme Court.

Section 2. Powers of the President
Clause 1: Commander in Chief. The President shall be Commander in Chief of the Army and Navy of the United States, and of the Militia of the several States, when called into the actual Service of the United States; he may require the Opinion, in writing, of the principal Officer in each of the executive Departments, upon any Subject relating to the Duties of their respective Offices, and he shall have Power to grant Reprieves and Pardons for Offences against the United States, except in Cases of Impeachment.

The armed forces are placed under civilian control because the president is a civilian but still commander in chief of

the military. The president may ask for the help of the head of each of the executive departments (thereby creating the cabinet). The cabinet members are chosen by the president with the consent of the Senate, but they can be removed without Senate approval.

The president's clemency powers extend only to federal cases. In those cases, he or she may grant a full or conditional pardon, or reduce a prison term or fine.

Clause 2: Treaties and Appointment. He shall have Power, by and with the Advice and Consent of the Senate, to make Treaties, provided two thirds of the Senators present concur; and he shall nominate, and by and with the Advice and Consent of the Senate, shall appoint Ambassadors, other public Ministers and Consuls, Judges of the supreme Court, and all other Officers of the United States, whose Appointments are not herein otherwise provided for, and which shall be established by Law; but the Congress may by Law vest the Appointment of such inferior Officers, as they think proper, in the President alone, in the Courts of Law, or in the Heads of Departments.

Many of the major powers of the president are identified in this clause, including the power to make treaties with foreign governments (with the approval of the Senate by a two-thirds vote) and the power to appoint ambassadors, Supreme Court justices, and other government officials. Most such appointments require Senate approval.

Clause 3: Vacancies. The President shall have Power to fill up all Vacancies that may happen during the Recess of the Senate, by granting Commissions which shall expire at the end of their next Session.

The president has the power to appoint temporary officials to fill vacant federal offices without Senate approval if the Congress is not in session. Such appointments expire automatically at the end of Congress's next term.

Section 3. Duties of the President
He shall from time to time give to the Congress Information of the State of the Union, and recommend to their Consideration such Measures as he shall judge necessary and expedient; he may, on extraordinary Occasions, convene both Houses, or either of them, and in Case of Disagreement between them, with Respect to the Time of Adjournment, he may adjourn them to such Time as he shall think proper; he shall receive Ambassadors and other public Ministers; he shall take Care that the Laws be faithfully executed, and shall Commission all the Officers of the United States.

Annually, the president reports on the state of the union to Congress, recommends legislative measures, and proposes a federal budget. The State of the Union speech is a statement not only to Congress but also to the American people. After it is given, the president proposes a federal budget and presents an economic report. At any time, the president may send special messages to Congress while it is in session. The president has the power to call special sessions,

---

8. Modified by the Twenty-fifth Amendment.

to adjourn Congress when its two chambers do not agree on when to adjourn, to receive diplomatic representatives of other governments, and to ensure the proper execution of all federal laws. The president further has the ability to empower federal officers to hold their positions and to perform their duties.

Section 4. Impeachment

The President, Vice President and all civil Officers of the United States, shall be removed from Office on Impeachment for, and Conviction of, Treason, Bribery, or other high Crimes and Misdemeanors.

Treason denotes giving aid to the nation's enemies. The definition of high crimes and misdemeanors is usually given as serious abuses of political power. In either case, the president or vice president may be accused by the House (called an impeachment) and then removed from office if convicted by the Senate. (Note that impeachment does not mean removal but rather refers to an accusation of treason or high crimes and misdemeanors.)

Article III. (Judicial Branch)

Section 1. Judicial Powers, Courts, and Judges

The judicial Power of the United States, shall be vested in one supreme Court, and in such inferior Courts as the Congress may from time to time ordain and establish. The Judges, both of the supreme and inferior Courts, shall hold their Offices during good Behaviour, and shall, at stated Times, receive for their Services a Compensation, which shall not be diminished during their Continuance in Office.

The Supreme Court is vested with judicial power, as are the lower federal courts that Congress creates. Federal judges serve in their offices for life unless they are impeached and convicted by Congress. The payment of federal judges may not be reduced during their time in office.

Section 2. Jurisdiction

Clause 1: Cases under Federal Jurisdiction. The judicial Power shall extend to all Cases, in Law and Equity, arising under this Constitution, the Laws of the United States, and Treaties made, or which shall be made, under their Authority;—to all Cases affecting Ambassadors, other public Ministers and Consuls;—to all Cases of admiralty and maritime Jurisdiction;—to Controversies to which the United States shall be a Party;—to Controversies between two or more States; [—between a State and Citizens of another State;—][9] between Citizens of different States;—between Citizens of the same State claiming Lands under Grants of different States, [and between a State, or the Citizens thereof, and foreign States, Citizens or Subjects.][10]

The federal courts take on cases that concern the meaning of the U.S. Constitution, all federal laws, and treaties. They

9. Modified by the Eleventh Amendment.
10. Modified by the Eleventh Amendment.

also can take on cases involving citizens of different states and citizens of foreign nations.

Clause 2: Cases for the Supreme Court. In all Cases affecting Ambassadors, other public Ministers and Consuls, and those in which a State shall be a Party, the supreme Court shall have original Jurisdiction. In all the other Cases before mentioned, the supreme Court shall have appellate Jurisdiction, both as to Law and Fact, with such Exceptions, and under such Regulations as the Congress shall make.

In a limited number of situations, the Supreme Court acts as a trial court and has original jurisdiction. These cases involve a representative from another country or involve a state. In all other situations, the cases must first be tried in the lower courts and then can be appealed to the Supreme Court. Congress may, however, make exceptions. Today, the Supreme Court acts as a trial court of first instance on rare occasions.

Clause 3: The Conduct of Trials. The Trial of all Crimes, except in Cases of Impeachment, shall be by Jury; and such Trial shall be held in the State where the said Crimes shall have been committed; but when not committed within any State, the Trial shall be at such Place or Places as the Congress may by Law have directed.

Any person accused of a federal crime is granted the right to a trial by jury in a federal court in that state in which the crime was committed. Trials of impeachment are an exception.

Section 3. Treason

Clause 1: The Definition of Treason. Treason against the United States, shall consist only in levying War against them, or, in adhering to their Enemies, giving them Aid and Comfort. No Person shall be convicted of Treason unless on the Testimony of two Witnesses to the same overt Act, or on Confession in open Court.

Treason is the making of war against the United States or giving aid to its enemies.

Clause 2: Punishment. The Congress shall have Power to declare the Punishment of Treason, but no Attainder of Treason shall work Corruption of Blood, or Forfeiture except during the Life of the Person attainted.

Congress has provided that the punishment for treason ranges from a minimum of five years in prison and/or a $10,000 fine to a maximum of death. "No Attainder of Treason shall work Corruption of Blood" prohibits punishment of the traitor's heirs.

Article IV. (Relations among the States)

Section 1. Full Faith and Credit

Full Faith and Credit shall be given in each State to the public Acts, Records, and judicial Proceedings of every other State. And the Congress may by general Laws prescribe the Manner in which such Acts, Records and Proceedings shall be proved, and the Effect thereof.

All states are required to respect one another's laws, records, and lawful decisions. There are exceptions, however. A state does not have to enforce another state's criminal code. Nor does it have to recognize another state's grant of a divorce if the person obtaining the divorce did not establish legal residence in the state in which it was given.

Section 2. Treatment of Citizens

Clause 1: Privileges and Immunities. The Citizens of each State shall be entitled to all Privileges and Immunities of Citizens in the several States.

A citizen of a state has the same rights and privileges as the citizens of another state in which he or she happens to be.

Clause 2: Extradition. A Person charged in any State with Treason, Felony, or other Crime, who shall flee from Justice, and be found in another State, shall on Demand of the executive Authority of the State from which he fled, be delivered up, to be removed to the State having Jurisdiction of the Crime.

Any person accused of a crime who flees to another state must be returned to the state in which the crime occurred.

Clause 3: Fugitive Slaves. [No Person held to Service or Labour in one State, under the Laws thereof, escaping into another, shall, in Consequence of any Law or Regulation therein, be discharged from such Service or Labour, but shall be delivered up on Claim of the Party to whom such Service or Labour may be due.][11]

This clause was struck down by the Thirteenth Amendment, which abolished slavery in 1865.

Section 3. Admission of States

Clause 1: The Process. New States may be admitted by the Congress into this Union; but no new State shall be formed or erected within the Jurisdiction of any other State; nor any State be formed by the Junction of two or more States, or Parts of States, without the Consent of the Legislatures of the States concerned as well as of the Congress.

Only Congress has the power to admit new states to the union. No state may be created by taking territory from an existing state unless the state's legislature so consents.

Clause 2: Public Land. The Congress shall have Power to dispose of and make all needful Rules and Regulations respecting the Territory or other Property belonging to the United States; and nothing in this Constitution shall be so construed as to Prejudice any Claims of the United States, or of any particular State.

The federal government has the exclusive right to administer federal government public lands.

Section 4. Republican Form of Government

The United States shall guarantee to every State in this Union a Republican Form of Government, and shall protect each of them against Invasion; and on Application of the Legislature, or of the Executive (when the Legislature cannot be convened) against domestic Violence.

Each state is promised a republican form of government—that is, one in which the people elect their representatives. The federal government is bound to protect states against any attack by foreigners or during times of trouble within a state.

Article V. (Methods of Amendment)

The Congress, whenever two thirds of both Houses shall deem it necessary, shall propose Amendments to this Constitution, or on the Application of the Legislatures of two thirds of the several States, shall call a Convention for proposing Amendments, which, in either Case, shall be valid to all Intents and Purposes, as Part of this Constitution, when ratified by the Legislatures of three fourths of the several States, or by Conventions in three fourths thereof, as the one or the other Mode of Ratification may be proposed by the Congress; Provided that no Amendment which may be made prior to the Year One thousand eight hundred and eight shall in any Manner affect the first and fourth Clauses in the Ninth Section of the First Article; and that no State, without its Consent, shall be deprived of its equal Suffrage in the Senate.

Amendments may be proposed in either of two ways: a two-thirds vote of each chamber (Congress) or at the request of two-thirds of the states. Ratification of amendments may be carried out in two ways: by the legislatures of three-fourths of the states or by the voters in three-fourths of the states. No state may be denied equal representation in the Senate.

Article VI. (National Supremacy)

Clause 1: Existing Obligations. All Debts contracted and Engagements entered into, before the Adoption of this Constitution shall be as valid against the United States under this Constitution, as under the Confederation.

During the Revolutionary War and the years of the Confederation, Congress borrowed large sums. This clause pledged that the new federal government would assume those financial obligations.

Clause 2: Supreme Law of the Land. This Constitution, and the Laws of the United States which shall be made in Pursuance thereof; and all Treaties made, or which shall be made, under the Authority of the United States, shall be the supreme Law of the Land; and the Judges in every State shall be bound thereby, any Thing in the Constitution or Laws of any State to the Contrary notwithstanding.

This is typically called the supremacy clause; it declares that federal law takes precedence over all forms of state law. No government at the local or state level may make or enforce any law that conflicts with any provision of the Constitution, acts of Congress, treaties, or other rules and regulations issued by the president and his or her subordinates in the executive branch of the federal government.

---

11. Repealed by the Thirteenth Amendment.

Clause 3: Oath of Office. The Senators and Representatives before mentioned, and the Members of the several State Legislatures, and all executive and judicial Officers, both of the United States and of the several States, shall be bound by Oath or Affirmation, to support this Constitution; but no religious Test shall ever be required as a Qualification to any Office or public Trust under the United States.

Every federal and state official must take an oath of office promising to support the U.S. Constitution. Religion may not be used as a qualification to serve in any federal office.

Attest William Jackson Secretary

DELAWARE	Geo. Read Gunning Bedford jun John Dickinson Richard Bassett Jaco. Broom
MARYLAND	James McHenry Dan of St. Thos. Jenifer Danl. Carroll
VIRGINIA	John Blair James Madison Jr.
NORTH CAROLINA	Wm. Blount Richd. Dobbs Spaight Hu. Williamson
SOUTH CAROLINA	J. Rutledge Charles Cotesworth Pinckney Charles Pinckney Pierce Butler
GEORGIA	William Few Abr. Baldwin

Article VII. (Ratification)

The Ratification of the Conventions of nine States shall be sufficient for the Establishment of this Constitution between the States so ratifying the Same.

Nine states were required to ratify the Constitution. Delaware was the first and New Hampshire the ninth.

Done in Convention by the Unanimous Consent of the States present the Seventeenth Day of September in the Year of our Lord one thousand seven hundred and Eighty seven and of the Independence of the United States of America the Twelfth. In witness whereof we have hereunto subscribed our Names,

Go. WASHINGTON
Presid't. and deputy from Virginia

NEW HAMPSHIRE	John Langdon Nicholas Gilman
MASSACHUSETTS	Nathaniel Gorham Rufus King
CONNECTICUT	Wm. Saml. Johnson Roger Sherman
NEW YORK	Alexander Hamilton
NEW JERSEY	Wh. Livingston David Brearley Wm. Paterson Jona. Dayton
PENNSYLVANIA	B. Franklin Thomas Mifflin Robt. Morris Geo. Clymer Thos. FitzSimons Jared Ingersoll James Wilson Gouv. Morris

Articles in addition to, and amendment of, the Constitution of the United States of America, proposed by Congress and ratified by the Legislatures of the several states, pursuant to the Fifth Article of the original Constitution.

Amendments to the Constitution of the United States

(The Bill of Rights)[12]

Amendment I.
(Religion, Speech, Assembly, and Petition)

Congress shall make no law respecting an establishment of religion, or prohibiting the free exercise thereof; or abridging the freedom of speech, or of the press; or the right of the people peaceably to assemble, and to petition the Government for a redress of grievances.

Congress may not create an official church or enact laws limiting the freedom of religion, speech, the press, assembly, and petition. These guarantees, like the others in the Bill of Rights (the first ten amendments), are not absolute—each may be exercised only with regard to the rights of other persons.

Amendment II.
(Militia and the Right to Bear Arms)

A well regulated Militia, being necessary to the security of a free State, the right of the people to keep and bear Arms, shall not be infringed.

To protect itself, each state has the right to maintain a volunteer armed force. States and the federal government regulate the possession and use of firearms by individuals.

Amendment III.
(The Quartering of Soldiers)

No Soldier shall, in time of peace be quartered in any house, without the consent of the Owner, nor in time of war, but in a manner to be prescribed by law.

Before the Revolutionary War, it had been common British practice to quarter soldiers in colonists' homes. Military troops do not have the power to take over private houses during peacetime.

Amendment IV.
(Searches and Seizures)

The right of the people to be secure in their persons, houses, papers, and effects, against unreasonable searches and seizures, shall not be violated, and no Warrants shall

issue, but upon probable cause, supported by Oath or affirmation, and particularly describing the place to be searched, and the persons or things to be seized.

Here the word warrant means "justification" and refers to a document issued by a magistrate or judge indicating the name, address, and possible offense committed. Anyone asking for the warrant, such as a police officer, must be able to convince the magistrate or judge that an offense probably has been committed.

Amendment V.
(Grand Juries, Self-Incrimination, Double Jeopardy, Due Process, and Eminent Domain)

No person shall be held to answer for a capital, or otherwise infamous crime, unless on a presentment or indictment of a Grand Jury, except in cases arising in the land or naval forces, or in the Militia, when in actual service in time of War or public danger; nor shall any person be subject for the same offence to be twice put in jeopardy of life or limb; nor shall be compelled in any criminal case to be a witness against himself, nor be deprived of life, liberty, or property, without due process of law; nor shall private property be taken for public use, without just compensation.

There are two types of juries. A grand jury considers physical evidence and the testimony of witnesses and decides whether there is sufficient reason to bring a case to trial. A petit jury hears the case at trial and decides it. "For the same offence to be twice put in jeopardy of life or limb" means to be tried twice for the same crime. A person may not be tried for the same crime twice or forced to give evidence against herself or himself. No person's right to life, liberty, or property may be taken away except by lawful means, called the due process of law. Private property taken for use in public purposes must be paid for by the government.

Amendment VI.
(Criminal Court Procedures)

In all criminal prosecutions, the accused shall enjoy the right to a speedy and public trial, by an impartial jury of the State and district wherein the crime shall have been committed, which district shall have been previously ascertained by law, and to be informed of the nature and cause of the accusation; to be confronted with the witnesses against him; to have compulsory process for obtaining witnesses in his favor, and to have the Assistance of Counsel for his defence.

Any person accused of a crime has the right to a fair and public trial by a jury in the state in which the crime took place. The charges against that person must be indicated. Any accused person has the right to a lawyer to defend him or her and to question those who testify against him or her, as well as the right to call people to speak in his or her favor at trial.

---

12. On September 25, 1789, Congress transmitted to the state legislatures twelve proposed amendments, two of which, having to do with congressional representation and congressional pay, were not adopted. The remaining ten amendments became the Bill of Rights. In 1992, the amendment concerning congressional pay was adopted as the Twenty-seventh Amendment.

Amendment VII.
(Trial by Jury in Civil Cases)

In Suits at common law, where the value in controversy shall exceed twenty dollars, the right of trial by jury shall be preserved, and no fact tried by jury, shall be otherwise re-examined in any Court of the United States, than according to the rules of the common law.

A jury trial may be requested by either party in a dispute in any case involving more than $20. If both parties agree to a trial by a judge without a jury, the right to a jury trial may be put aside.

Amendment VIII.
(Bail, Cruel and Unusual Punishment)

Excessive bail shall not be required, nor excessive fines imposed, nor cruel and unusual punishments inflicted.

Bail is that amount of money that a person accused of a crime may be required to deposit with the court as a guarantee that she or he will appear in court when requested. The amount of bail required or the fine imposed as punishment for a crime must be reasonable compared with the seriousness of the crime involved. Any punishment judged to be too harsh or too severe for a crime shall be prohibited.

Amendment IX.
(The Rights Retained by the People)

The enumeration in the Constitution, of certain rights, shall not be construed to deny or disparage others retained by the people.

Many civil rights that are not explicitly enumerated in the Constitution are still held by the people.

Amendment X.
(Reserved Powers of the States)

The powers not delegated to the United States by the Constitution, nor prohibited by it to the States, are reserved to the States respectively, or to the people.

Those powers not delegated by the Constitution to the federal government or expressly denied to the states belong to the states and to the people. This amendment in essence allows the states to pass laws under their "police powers."

Amendment XI.
(Ratified on February 7, 1795— Suits against States)

The Judicial power of the United States shall not be construed to extend to any suit in law or equity, commenced or prosecuted against one of the United States by Citizens of another State, or by Citizens or Subjects of any Foreign State.

This amendment has been interpreted to mean that a state cannot be sued in federal court by one of its own citizens, by a citizen of another state, or by a foreign country.

Amendment XII.
(Ratified on June 15, 1804— Election of the President)

The Electors shall meet in their respective states, and vote by ballot for President and Vice-President, one of whom, at least, shall not be an inhabitant of the same State with themselves; they shall name in their ballots the person voted for as President, and in distinct ballots the person voted for as Vice-President, and they shall make distinct lists of all persons voted for as President, and of all persons voted for as Vice-President, and of the number of votes for each, which lists they shall sign and certify, and transmit sealed to the seat of the government of the United States, directed to the President of the Senate;—The President of the Senate shall, in the presence of the Senate and House of Representatives, open all the certificates and the votes shall then be counted;—The person having the greatest number of votes for President, shall be the President, if such number be a majority of the whole number of Electors appointed; and if no person have such majority, then from the persons having the highest numbers not exceeding three on the list of those voted for as President, the House of Representatives shall choose immediately, by ballot, the President. But in choosing the President, the votes shall be taken by States, the representation from each State having one vote; a quorum for this purpose shall consist of a member or members from two-thirds of the States, and a majority of all States shall be necessary to a choice. [And if the House of Representatives shall not choose a President whenever the right of choice shall devolve upon them, before the fourth day of March next following, then the Vice-President shall act as President, as in the case of the death or other constitutional disability of the President.][13]—The person having the greatest number of votes as Vice-President, shall be the Vice-President, if such number be a majority of the whole number of Electors appointed, and if no person have a majority, then from the two highest numbers on the list, the Senate shall choose the Vice-President; a quorum for the purpose shall consist of two-thirds of the whole number of Senators, and a majority of the whole number shall be necessary to a choice. But no person constitutionally ineligible to the office of President shall be eligible to that of Vice-President of the United States.

The original procedure set out for the election of president and vice president in Article II, Section 1, resulted in a tie in 1800 between Thomas Jefferson and Aaron Burr. It was not until the next year that the House of Representatives chose Jefferson to be president. This amendment changed the procedure by providing for separate ballots for president and vice president.

---

13. Changed by the Twentieth Amendment.

Amendment XIII.
(Ratified on December 6, 1865—
Prohibition of Slavery)

Section 1.

Neither slavery nor involuntary servitude, except as a punishment for crime whereof the party shall have been duly convicted, shall exist within the United States, or any place subject to their jurisdiction.

Some slaves had been freed during the Civil War. This amendment freed the others and abolished slavery.

Section 2.

Congress shall have power to enforce this article by appropriate legislation.

Amendment XIV.
(Ratified on July 9, 1868—
Citizenship, Due Process, and
Equal Protection of the Laws)

Section 1.

All persons born or naturalized in the United States, and subject to the jurisdiction thereof, are citizens of the United States and of the State wherein they reside. No State shall make or enforce any law which shall abridge the privileges or immunities of citizens of the United States; nor shall any State deprive any person of life, liberty, or property, without due process of law; nor deny to any person within its jurisdiction the equal protection of the laws.

Under this provision, states cannot make or enforce laws that take away rights given to all citizens by the federal government. States cannot act unfairly or arbitrarily toward, or discriminate against, any person.

Section 2.

Representatives shall be apportioned among the several States according to their respective numbers, counting the whole number of persons in each State, excluding Indians not taxed. But when the right to vote at any election for the choice of electors for President and Vice President of the United States, Representatives in Congress, the Executive and Judicial officers of a State, or the members of the Legislature thereof, is denied to any of the male inhabitants of such State, being [twenty-one][14] years of age, and citizens of the United States, or in any way abridged, except for participation in rebellion, or other crime, the basis of representation therein shall be reduced in the proportion which the number of such male citizens shall bear to the whole number of male citizens twenty-one years of age in such State.

Section 3.

No person shall be a Senator or Representative in Congress, or elector of President and Vice President, or hold any office, civil or military, under the United States, or under any State, who having previously taken an oath, as a member of Congress, or as an officer of the United States, or as a member of any State legislature, or as an executive or judicial officer of any State, to support the Constitution of the United States, shall have engaged in insurrection or rebellion against the same, or given aid or comfort to the enemies thereof. But Congress may by a vote of two-thirds of each House, remove such disability.

This provision forbade former state or federal government officials who had acted in support of the Confederacy during the Civil War to hold office again. It limited the president's power to pardon those persons. Congress removed this "disability" in 1898.

Section 4.

The validity of the public debt of the United States, authorized by law, including debts incurred for payment of pensions and bounties for services in suppressing insurrection or rebellion, shall not be questioned. But neither the United States nor any State shall assume or pay any debt or obligation incurred in aid of insurrection or rebellion against the United States, or any claim for the loss or emancipation of any slave, but all such debts, obligations and claims shall be held illegal and void.

Section 5.

The Congress shall have power to enforce, by appropriate legislation, the provisions of this article.

Amendment XV.
(Ratified on February 3, 1870—
The Right to Vote)

Section 1.

The right of citizens of the United States to vote shall not be denied or abridged by the United States or by any State on account of race, color, or previous condition of servitude.

No citizen can be refused the right to vote simply because of race or color or because that person was once a slave.

Section 2.

The Congress shall have power to enforce this article by appropriate legislation.

Amendment XVI.
(Ratified on February 3, 1913—
Income Taxes)

The Congress shall have power to lay and collect taxes on incomes, from whatever source derived, without apportionment among the several States, and without regard to any census or enumeration.

This amendment allows Congress to tax income without sharing the revenue so obtained with the states according to their population.

---

14. Changed by the Twenty-sixth Amendment.

Amendment XVII.
(Ratified on April 8, 1913— The Popular Election of Senators)

Section 1.

The Senate of the United States shall be composed of two Senators from each State, elected by the people thereof, for six years; and each Senator shall have one vote. The electors in each State shall have the qualifications requisite for electors of the most numerous branch of the State legislatures.

Section 2.

When vacancies happen in the representation of any State in the Senate, the executive authority of such State shall issue writs of election to fill such vacancies: Provided, That the legislature of any State may empower the executive thereof to make temporary appointments until the people fill the vacancies by election as the legislature may direct.

Section 3.

This amendment shall not be so construed as to affect the election or term of any Senator chosen before it becomes valid as part of the Constitution.

This amendment modified portions of Article I, Section 3, that related to election of senators. Senators are now elected by the voters in each state directly. When a vacancy occurs, either the state may fill the vacancy by a special election, or the governor of the state involved may appoint someone to fill the seat until the next election.

Amendment XVIII.
(Ratified on January 16, 1919— Prohibition)

Section 1.

After one year from the ratification of this article the manufacture, sale, or transportation of intoxicating liquors within, the importation thereof into, or the exportation thereof from the United States and all territory subject to the jurisdiction thereof for beverage purposes is hereby prohibited.

Section 2.

The Congress and the several States shall have concurrent power to enforce this article by appropriate legislation.

Section 3.

This article shall be inoperative unless it shall have been ratified as an amendment to the Constitution by the legislatures of the several States, as provided in the Constitution, within seven years from the date of the submission hereof to the States by the Congress.[15]

This amendment made it illegal to manufacture, sell, and transport alcoholic beverages in the United States.

---

15. The Eighteenth Amendment was repealed by the Twenty-first Amendment.

Amendment XIX.
(Ratified on August 18, 1920— Women's Right to Vote)

Section 1.

The right of citizens of the United States to vote shall not be denied or abridged by the United States or by any State on account of sex.

Section 2.

Congress shall have power to enforce this article by appropriate legislation.

Women were given the right to vote by this amendment, and Congress was given the power to enforce this right.

Amendment XX.
(Ratified on January 23, 1933— The Lame Duck Amendment)

Section 1.

The terms of the President and Vice President shall end at noon on the 20th day of January, and the terms of Senators and Representatives at noon on the 3d day of January, of the years in which such terms would have ended if this article had not been ratified; and the terms of their successors shall then begin.

This amendment modified Article I, Section 4, Clause 2, and other provisions relating to the president in the Twelfth Amendment. The taking of the oath of office was moved from March 4 to January 20.

Section 2.

The Congress shall assemble at least once in every year, and such meeting shall begin at noon on the 3d day of January, unless they shall by law appoint a different day.

Congress changed the beginning of its term to January 3. The reason the Twentieth Amendment is called the Lame Duck Amendment is because it shortens the time between when a member of Congress is defeated for reelection and when he or she leaves office.

Section 3.

If, at the time fixed for the beginning of the term of the President, the President elect shall have died, the Vice President elect shall become President. If a President shall not have been chosen before the time fixed for the beginning of his term, or if the President elect shall have failed to qualify, then the Vice President elect shall act as President until a President shall have qualified; and the Congress may by law provide for the case wherein neither a President elect nor a Vice President elect shall have qualified, declaring who shall then act as President, or the manner in which one who is to act shall be selected, and such person shall act accordingly until a President or Vice President shall have qualified.

This part of the amendment deals with problem areas left ambiguous by Article II and the Twelfth Amendment. If the president dies before January 20 or fails to qualify for office, the presidency is to be filled as described in this section.

Section 4.

The Congress may by law provide for the case of the death of any of the persons from whom the House of Representatives may choose a President whenever the rights of choice shall have devolved upon them, and for the case of the death of any of the persons from whom the Senate may choose a Vice President whenever the right of choice shall have devolved upon them.

Congress has never created legislation pursuant to this section.

Section 5.

Sections 1 and 2 shall take effect on the 15th day of October following the ratification of this article.

Section 6.

This article shall be inoperative unless it shall have been ratified as an amendment to the Constitution by the legislatures of three-fourths of the several States within seven years from the date of its submission.

Amendment XXI.
(Ratified on December 5, 1933— The Repeal of Prohibition)

Section 1.

The eighteenth article of amendment to the Constitution of the United States is hereby repealed.

Section 2.

The transportation or importation into any State, Territory, or possession of the United States for delivery or use therein of intoxicating liquors, in violation of the laws thereof, is hereby prohibited.

Section 3.

This article shall be inoperative unless it shall have been ratified as an amendment to the Constitution by conventions in the several States, as provided in the Constitution, within seven years from the date of the submission hereof to the States by the Congress.

The amendment repealed the Eighteenth Amendment but did not make alcoholic beverages legal everywhere. Rather, they remained illegal in any state that so designated them. Many such "dry" states existed for a number of years after 1933. Today, there are still "dry" counties within the United States, in which the sale of alcoholic beverages is illegal.

Amendment XXII.
(Ratified on February 27, 1951— Limitation of Presidential Terms)

Section 1.

No person shall be elected to the office of the President more than twice, and no person who has held the office of President, or acted as President, for more than two years of a term to which some other person was elected President shall be elected to the office of President more than once. But this Article shall not apply to any person

holding the office of President when this Article was proposed by the Congress, and shall not prevent any person who may be holding the office of President, or acting as President, during the term within which this Article becomes operative from holding the office of President or acting as President during the remainder of such term.

Section 2.

This article shall be inoperative unless it shall have been ratified as an amendment to the Constitution by the legislatures of three-fourths of the several States within seven years from the date of its submission to the States by the Congress.

No president may serve more than two elected terms. If, however, a president has succeeded to the office after the halfway point of a term in which another president was originally elected, then that president may serve for more than eight years, but not to exceed ten years.

Amendment XXIII.
(Ratified on March 29, 1961— Presidential Electors for the District of Columbia)

Section 1.

The District constituting the seat of Government of the United States shall appoint in such manner as the Congress may direct:

A number of electors of President and Vice President equal to the whole number of Senators and Representatives in Congress to which the District would be entitled if it were a State, but in no event more than the least populous State; they shall be in addition to those appointed by the States, but they shall be considered, for the purposes of the election of President and Vice President, to be electors appointed by a State; and they shall meet in the District and perform such duties as provided by the twelfth article of amendment.

Section 2.

The Congress shall have power to enforce this article by appropriate legislation.

Citizens living in the District of Columbia have the right to vote in elections for president and vice president. The District of Columbia has three presidential electors, whereas before this amendment it had none.

Amendment XXIV.
(Ratified on January 23, 1964— The Anti–Poll Tax Amendment)

Section 1.

The right of citizens of the United States to vote in any primary or other election for President or Vice President, for electors for President or Vice President, or for Senator or Representative in Congress, shall not be denied or abridged by the United States, or any State by reason of failure to pay any poll tax or other tax.

Section 2.

The Congress shall have power to enforce this article by appropriate legislation.

No government shall require a person to pay a poll tax to vote in any federal election.

Amendment XXV.
(Ratified on February 10, 1967—
Presidential Disability and
Vice Presidential Vacancies)

Section 1.

In case of the removal of the President from office or of his death or resignation, the Vice President shall become President.

Whenever a president dies or resigns from office, the vice president becomes president.

Section 2.

Whenever there is a vacancy in the office of the Vice President, the President shall nominate a Vice President who shall take office upon confirmation by a majority vote of both Houses of Congress.

Whenever the office of the vice presidency becomes vacant, the president may appoint someone to fill this office, provided Congress consents.

Section 3.

Whenever the President transmits to the President pro tempore of the Senate and the Speaker of the House of Representatives his written declaration that he is unable to discharge the powers and duties of his office, and until he transmits to them a written declaration to the contrary, such powers and duties shall be discharged by the Vice President as Acting President.

Whenever the president believes she or he is unable to carry out the duties of the office, she or he shall so indicate to Congress in writing. The vice president then acts as president until the president declares that she or he is again able to carry out the duties of the office.

Section 4.

Whenever the Vice President and a majority of either the principal officers of the executive departments or of such other body as Congress may by law provide, transmit to the President pro tempore of the Senate and the Speaker of the House of Representatives their written declaration that the President is unable to discharge the powers and duties of his office, the Vice President shall immediately assume the powers and duties of the office as Acting President.

Thereafter, when the President transmits to the President pro tempore of the Senate and the Speaker of the House of Representatives his written declaration that no inability exists, he shall resume the powers and duties of his office unless the Vice President and a majority of either the principal officers of the executive department or of such other body as Congress may by law provide, transmit within four days to the President pro tempore of the Senate and the Speaker of the House of Representatives their written declaration that the President is unable to discharge the powers and duties of his office. Thereupon Congress shall decide the issue, assembling within forty-eight hours for that purpose if not in session. If the Congress, within twenty-one days after receipt of the latter written declaration, or, if Congress is not in session, within twenty-one days after Congress is required to assemble, determines by two-thirds vote of both Houses that the President is unable to discharge the powers and duties of his office, the Vice President shall continue to discharge the same as Acting President; otherwise, the President shall resume the powers and duties of his office.

Whenever the vice president and a majority of the members of the cabinet believe that the president cannot carry out her or his duties, they shall so indicate in writing to Congress. The vice president shall then act as president. When the president believes that she or he is able to carry out her or his duties again, she or he shall so indicate to the Congress. However, if the vice president and a majority of the cabinet do not agree, Congress must decide by a two-thirds vote within three weeks who shall act as president.

Amendment XXVI.
(Ratified on July 1, 1971—
Voting Rights for Eighteen-Year-Olds)

Section 1.

The right of citizens of the United States, who are eighteen years of age or older, to vote shall not be denied or abridged by the United States or by any State on account of age.

No one eighteen years of age or older can be denied the right to vote in federal or state elections by virtue of age.

Section 2.

The Congress shall have power to enforce this article by appropriate legislation.

Amendment XXVII.
(Ratified on May 7, 1992—
Congressional Pay)

No law, varying the compensation for the services of the Senators and Representatives, shall take effect, until an election of representatives shall have intervened.

This amendment allows the voters to have some control over increases in salaries for congressional members. Originally submitted to the states for ratification in 1789, it was not ratified until 203 years later, in 1992.

Federalist Papers No. 10 and No. 51

In 1787, after the newly drafted U.S. Constitution was submitted to the thirteen states for ratification, a major political debate ensued between the Federalists (who favored ratification) and the Anti-Federalists (who opposed ratification). Anti-Federalists in New York were particularly critical of the Constitution, and in response to their objections, Federalists Alexander Hamilton, James Madison, and John Jay wrote a series of eighty-five essays in defense of the Constitution. The essays were published in New York newspapers and reprinted in other newspapers throughout the country.

For students of American government, the essays, collectively known as the Federalist Papers, *are particularly important because they provide a glimpse of the founders' political philosophy and intentions in designing the Constitution—and, consequently, in shaping the American philosophy of government.*

We have included in this appendix two of these essays: Federalist Papers No. 10 *and* No. 51. *Each essay has been annotated by the authors to indicate its importance in American political thought and to clarify the meaning of particular passages.*

Federalist Paper No. 10

Federalist Paper No. 10, penned by James Madison, has often been singled out as a key document in American political thought. In this essay, Madison attacks the Anti-Federalists' fear that a republican form of government will inevitably give rise to "factions"—small political parties or groups united by a common interest—that will control the government. Factions will be harmful to the country because they implement policies beneficial to their own interests but adverse to other people's rights and to the public good. In this essay, Madison attempts to lay to rest this fear by explaining how, in a large republic such as the United States, there will be so many different factions, held together by regional or local interests, that no single one of them will dominate national politics.

Madison opens his essay with a paragraph discussing how important it is to devise a plan of government that can control the "instability, injustice, and confusion" brought about by factions.

Among the numerous advantages promised by a well-constructed Union, none deserves to be more accurately

developed than its tendency to break and control the violence of faction. The friend of popular governments never finds himself so much alarmed for their character and fate as when he contemplates their propensity to this dangerous vice. He will not fail, therefore, to set a due value on any plan which, without violating the principles to which he is attached, provides a proper cure for it. The instability, injustice, and confusion introduced into the public councils have, in truth, been the mortal diseases under which popular governments have everywhere perished, as they continue to be the favorite and fruitful topics from which the adversaries to liberty derive their most specious declamations. The valuable improvements made by the American constitutions on the popular models, both ancient and modern, cannot certainly be too much admired; but it would be an unwarrantable partiality to contend that they have as effectually obviated the danger on this side, as was wished and expected. Complaints are everywhere heard from our most considerate and virtuous citizens, equally the friends of public and private faith and of public and personal liberty, that our governments are too unstable, that the public good is disregarded in the conflicts of rival parties, and that measures are too often decided, not according to the rules of justice and the rights of the minor party, but by the superior force of an interested and overbearing majority. However anxiously we may wish that these complaints had no foundation, the evidence of known facts will not permit us to deny that they are in some degree true. It will be found, indeed, on a candid review of our situation, that some of the distresses under which we labor have been erroneously charged on the operation of our governments; but it will be found, at the same time, that other causes will not alone account for many of our heaviest misfortunes; and, particularly, for that prevailing and increasing distrust of public engagements and alarm for private rights which are echoed from one end of the continent to the other. These must be chiefly, if not wholly, effects of the unsteadiness and injustice with which a factious spirit has tainted our public administration.

Madison now defines what he means by the term faction.

By a faction I understand a number of citizens, whether amounting to a majority or minority of the whole, who are united and actuated by some common impulse of passion, or of interest, adverse to the rights of other citizens, or the permanent and aggregate interests of the community.

Madison next contends that there are two methods by which the "mischiefs of faction" can be cured: by removing the causes of faction or by controlling their effects. In the following paragraphs, Madison explains how liberty itself nourishes factions. Therefore, to abolish factions would involve abolishing liberty—a cure "worse than the disease."

There are two methods of curing the mischiefs of faction: the one, by removing its causes; the other, by controlling its effects.

There are again two methods of removing the causes of faction: the one, by destroying the liberty which is essential to its existence; the other, by giving to every citizen the same opinions, the same passions, and the same interests.

It could never be more truly said than of the first remedy that it was worse than the disease. Liberty is to faction what air is to fire, an aliment without which it instantly expires. But it could not be a less folly to abolish liberty, which is essential to political life, because it nourishes faction than it would be to wish the annihilation of air, which is essential to animal life, because it imparts to fire its destructive agency.

The second expedient is as impracticable as the first would be unwise. As long as the reason of man continues fallible, and he is at liberty to exercise it, different opinions will be formed. As long as the connection subsists between his reason and his self-love, his opinions and his passions will have a reciprocal influence on each other; and the former will be objects to which the latter will attach themselves. The diversity in the faculties of men, from which the rights of property originate, is not less an insuperable obstacle to a uniformity of interests. The protection of these faculties is the first object of government. From the protection of different and unequal faculties of acquiring property, the possession of different degrees and kinds of property immediately results; and from the influence of these on the sentiments and views of the respective proprietors ensues a division of the society into different interests and parties.

The latent causes of faction are thus sown in the nature of man; and we see them everywhere brought into different degrees of activity, according to the different circumstances of civil society. A zeal for different opinions concerning religion, concerning government, and many other points, as well of speculation as of practice; an attachment to different leaders ambitiously contending for pre-eminence and power; or to persons of other descriptions whose fortunes have been interesting to the human passions, have, in turn, divided mankind into parties, inflamed them with mutual animosity, and rendered them much more disposed to vex and oppress each other than to co-operate for their common good. So strong is this propensity of mankind to fall into mutual animosities that where no substantial occasion presents

itself the most frivolous and fanciful distinctions have been sufficient to kindle their unfriendly passions and excite their most violent conflicts. But the most common and durable source of factions has been the various and unequal distribution of property. Those who hold and those who are without property have ever formed distinct interests in society. Those who are creditors, and those who are debtors, fall under a like discrimination. A landed interest, a manufacturing interest, a mercantile interest, a moneyed interest, with many lesser interests, grow up of necessity in civilized nations, and divide them into different classes, actuated by different sentiments and views. The regulation of these various and interfering interests forms the principal task of modern legislation and involves the spirit of party and faction in the necessary and ordinary operations of government.

No man is allowed to be a judge in his own cause, because his interest would certainly bias his judgment, and, not improbably, corrupt his integrity. With equal, nay with greater reason, a body of men are unfit to be both judges and parties at the same time; yet what are many of the most important acts of legislation but so many judicial determinations, not indeed concerning the rights of single persons, but concerning the rights of large bodies of citizens? And what are the different classes of legislators but advocates and parties to the causes which they determine? Is a law proposed concerning private debts? It is a question to which the creditors are parties on one side and the debtors on the other. Justice ought to hold the balance between them. Yet the parties are, and must be, themselves the judges; and the most numerous party, or in other words, the most powerful faction must be expected to prevail. Shall domestic manufacturers be encouraged, and in what degree, by restrictions on foreign manufacturers? [These] are questions which would be differently decided by the landed and the manufacturing classes, and probably by neither with a sole regard to justice and the public good. The apportionment of taxes on the various descriptions of property is an act which seems to require the most exact impartiality; yet there is, perhaps, no legislative act in which greater opportunity and temptation are given to a predominant party to trample on the rules of justice. Every shilling with which they overburden the inferior number is a shilling saved to their own pockets.

It is in vain to say that enlightened statesmen will be able to adjust these clashing interests and render them all subservient to the public good. Enlightened statesmen will not always be at the helm. Nor, in many cases, can such an adjustment be made at all without taking into view indirect and remote considerations, which will rarely prevail over the immediate interest which one party may find in disregarding the rights of another or the good of the whole.

The inference to which we are brought is that the causes of faction cannot be removed and that relief is only to be sought in the means of controlling its *effects*.

Having concluded that "the causes of faction cannot be removed," Madison now looks in some detail at the other method by which factions can be cured—by controlling their effects. This is the heart of his essay. He begins by positing a significant question: How can you have self-government without risking the possibility that a ruling faction, particularly a majority faction, might tyrannize over the rights of others?

If a faction consists of less than a majority, relief is supplied by the republican principle, which enables the majority to defeat its sinister views by regular vote. It may clog the administration, it may convulse the society; but it will be unable to execute and mask its violence under the forms of the Constitution. When a majority is included in a faction, the form of popular government, on the other hand, enables it to sacrifice to its ruling passion or interest both the public good and the rights of other citizens. To secure the public good and private rights against the danger of such a faction, and at the same time to preserve the spirit and the form of popular government, is then the great object to which our inquiries are directed. Let me add that it is the great desideratum by which alone this form of government can be rescued from the opprobrium under which it has so long labored and be recommended to the esteem and adoption of mankind.

Madison now sets forth the idea that one way to control the effects of factions is to ensure that the majority is rendered incapable of acting in concert in order to "carry into effect schemes of oppression." He goes on to state that in a democracy, in which all citizens participate personally in government decision making, there is no way to prevent the majority from communicating with one another and, as a result, acting in concert.

By what means is this object attainable? Evidently by one of two only. Either the existence of the same passion or interest in a majority at the same time must be prevented, or the majority, having such coexistent passion or interest, must be rendered, by their number and local situation, unable to concert and carry into effect schemes of oppression. If the impulse and the opportunity be suffered to coincide, we well know that neither moral nor religious motives can be relied on as an adequate control. They are not found to be such on the injustice and violence of individuals, and lose their efficacy in proportion to the number combined together, that is, in proportion as their efficacy becomes needful.

From this view of the subject it may be concluded that a pure democracy, by which I mean a society consisting of a small number of citizens, who assemble and administer the government in person, can admit of no cure for the mischiefs of faction. A common passion or interest will, in almost every case, be felt by a majority of the whole; a communication and concert results from the form of government itself; and there is nothing to check the inducements to sacrifice the weaker party or an obnoxious individual. Hence it is that such democracies have

ever been spectacles of turbulence and contention; have ever been found incompatible with personal security or the rights of property; and have in general been as short in their lives as they have been violent in their deaths. Theoretic politicians, who have patronized this species of government, have erroneously supposed that by reducing mankind to a perfect equality in their political rights, they would at the same time be perfectly equalized and assimilated in their possessions, their opinions, and their passions.

Madison now moves on to discuss the benefits of a republic with respect to controlling the effects of factions. He begins by defining a republic and then pointing out the "two great points of difference" between a republic and a democracy: a republic is governed by a small body of elected representatives, not by the people directly; and a republic can extend over a much larger territory and embrace more citizens than a democracy can.

A republic, by which I mean a government in which the scheme of representation takes place, opens a different prospect and promises the cure for which we are seeking. Let us examine the points in which it varies from pure democracy, and we shall comprehend both the nature of the cure and the efficacy which it must derive from the Union.

The two great points of difference between a democracy and a republic are: first, the delegation of the government, in the latter, to a small number of citizens elected by the rest; secondly, the greater number of citizens and greater sphere of country over which the latter may be extended.

In the following four paragraphs, Madison explains how in a republic, particularly a large republic, the delegation of authority to elected representatives will increase the likelihood that those who govern will be "fit" for their positions and that a proper balance will be achieved between local (factional) interests and national interests. Note how he stresses that the new federal Constitution, by dividing powers between state governments and the national government, provides a "happy combination in this respect."

The effect of the first difference is, on the one hand, to refine and enlarge the public views by passing them through the medium of a chosen body of citizens, whose wisdom may best discern the true interest of their country and whose patriotism and love of justice will be least likely to sacrifice it to temporary or partial considerations. Under such a regulation it may well happen that the public voice, pronounced by the representatives of the people, will be more consonant to the public good than if pronounced by the people themselves, convened for the purpose. On the other hand, the effect may be inverted. Men of factious tempers, of local prejudices, or of sinister designs, may, by intrigue, by corruption, or by other means, first obtain the suffrages, and then betray the interests of the people. The question resulting is, whether small or extensive republics are most favorable to the election of proper guardians of the public weal; and it is clearly decided in favor of the latter by two obvious considerations.

In the first place it is to be remarked that however small the republic may be the representatives must be raised to a certain number in order to guard against the cabals of a few; and that however large it may be they must be limited to a certain number in order to guard against the confusion of a multitude. Hence, the number of representatives in the two cases not being in proportion to that of the constituents, and being proportionally greatest in the small republic, it follows that if the proportion of fit characters be not less in the large than in the small republic, the former will present a greater option, and consequently a greater probability of a fit choice.

In the next place, as each representative will be chosen by a greater number of citizens in the large than in the small republic, it will be more difficult for unworthy candidates to practice with success the vicious arts by which elections are too often carried; and the suffrages of the people being more free, will be more likely to center on men who possess the most attractive merit and the most diffusive and established characters.

It must be confessed that in this, as in most other cases, there is a mean, on both sides of which inconveniencies will be found to lie. By enlarging too much the number of electors, you render the representative too little acquainted with all their local circumstances and lesser interests; as by reducing it too much, you render him unduly attached to these, and too little fit to comprehend and pursue great and national objects. The federal Constitution forms a happy combination in this respect; the great and aggregate interests being referred to the national, the local and particular to the State legislatures.

Madison now looks more closely at the other difference between a republic and a democracy—namely, that a republic can encompass a larger territory and more citizens than a democracy can. In the remaining paragraphs of his essay, Madison concludes that in a large republic, it will be difficult for factions to act in concert. Although a factious group—religious, political, economic, or otherwise—may control a local or regional government, it will have little chance of gathering a national following. This is because in a large republic, there will be numerous factions whose work will offset the work of any one particular faction ("sect"). As Madison phrases it, these numerous factions will "secure the national councils against any danger from that source."

The other point of difference is the greater number of citizens and extent of territory which may be brought within the compass of republican than of democratic government; and it is this circumstance principally which renders factious combinations less to be dreaded in the former than in the latter. The smaller the society, the fewer probably will be the distinct parties and interests composing it; the fewer the distinct parties and interests, the more frequently will a majority be found of the same party; and the smaller the number of individuals composing a majority, and the smaller the compass within which they are placed, the more easily will they concert and execute their plans of oppression. Extend the sphere and you take in a greater variety of parties and interests; you make it less probable that a majority of the whole will have a common motive to invade the rights of other citizens; or if such a common motive exists, it will be more difficult for all who feel it to discover their own strength and to act in unison with each other. Besides other impediments, it may be remarked that, where there is a consciousness of unjust or dishonorable purposes, communication is always checked by distrust in proportion to the number whose concurrence is necessary.

Hence, it clearly appears that the same advantage which a republic has over a democracy in controlling the effects of faction is enjoyed by a large over a small republic—is enjoyed by the Union over the States composing it. Does this advantage consist in the substitution of representatives whose enlightened views and virtuous sentiments render them superior to local prejudices and to schemes of injustice? It will not be denied that the representation of the Union will be most likely to possess these requisite endowments. Does it consist in the greater security afforded by a greater variety of parties, against the event of any one party being able to outnumber and oppress the rest? In an equal degree does the increased variety of parties comprised within the Union increase this security. Does it, in fine, consist in the greater obstacles opposed to the concert and accomplishment of the secret wishes of an unjust and interested majority? Here again the extent of the Union gives it the most palpable advantage.

The influence of factious leaders may kindle a flame within their particular States but will be unable to spread a general conflagration through the other States. A religious sect may degenerate into a political faction in a part of the Confederacy; but the variety of sects dispersed over the entire face of it must secure the national councils against any danger from that source. A rage for paper money, for an abolition of debts, for an equal division of property, or for any other improper or wicked project, will be less apt to pervade the whole body of the Union than a particular member of it, in the same proportion as such a malady is more likely to taint a particular county or district than an entire State.

In the extent and proper structure of the Union, therefore, we behold a republican remedy for the diseases most incident to republican government. And according to the degree of pleasure and pride we feel in being republicans ought to be our zeal in cherishing the spirit and supporting the character of federalists.

Publius
(James Madison)

Federalist Paper No. 51

Federalist Paper No. 51, also authored by James Madison, is another classic in American political theory. Although the Federalists wanted a strong national government, they had not abandoned the traditional American view, particularly notable during the revolutionary era, that those holding powerful government positions could not be trusted to put national interests and the common good above their own personal interests. In this essay, Madison explains why the separation of the national government's powers into three branches—executive, legislative, and judicial—and a federal structure of government offer the best protection against tyranny.

To what expedient, then, shall we finally resort, for maintaining in practice the necessary partition of power among the several departments as laid down in the Constitution? The only answer that can be given is that as all these exterior provisions are found to be inadequate the defect must be supplied, by so contriving the interior structure of the government as that its several constituent parts may, by their mutual relations, be the means of keeping each other in their proper places. Without presuming to undertake a full development of this important idea I will hazard a few general observations which may perhaps place it in a clearer light, and enable us to form a more correct judgment of the principles and structure of the government planned by the convention.

In the next two paragraphs, Madison stresses that for the powers of the different branches (departments) of government to be truly separated, the personnel in one branch should not be dependent on another branch for their appointment or for the "emoluments" (compensation) attached to their offices.

In order to lay a due foundation for that separate and distinct exercise of the different powers of government, which to a certain extent is admitted on all hands to be essential to the preservation of liberty, it is evident that each department should have a will of its own; and consequently should be so constituted that the members of each should have as little agency as possible in the appointment of the members of the others. Were this principle rigorously adhered to, it would require that all the appointments for the supreme executive, legislative, and judiciary magistracies should be drawn from the same fountain of authority, the people, through channels having no communication whatever with one another. Perhaps such a plan of constructing the several departments would be less difficult in practice than it may in contemplation appear. Some difficulties, however, and some additional expense would attend the execution of it. Some deviations, therefore, from the principle must be admitted. In the constitution of the judiciary department in particular, it might be inexpedient to insist rigorously on the principle: first, because peculiar qualifications

being essential in the members, the primary consideration ought to be to select that mode of choice which best secures these qualifications; second, because the permanent tenure by which the appointments are held in that department must soon destroy all sense of dependence on the authority conferring them.

It is equally evident that the members of each department should be as little dependent as possible on those of the others for the emoluments annexed to their offices. Were the executive magistrate, or the judges, not independent of the legislature in this particular, their independence in every other would be merely nominal.

In the following passages, which are among the most widely quoted of Madison's writings, he explains how the separation of the powers of government into three branches helps to counter the effects of personal ambition on government. The separation of powers allows personal motives to be linked to the constitutional rights of a branch of government. In effect, competing personal interests in each branch will help to keep the powers of the three government branches separate and, in so doing, will help to guard the public interest.

But the great security against a gradual concentration of the several powers in the same department consists in giving to those who administer each department the necessary constitutional means and personal motives to resist encroachments of the others. The provision for defense must in this, as in all other cases, be made commensurate to the danger of attack. Ambition must be made to counteract ambition. The interest of the man must be connected with the constitutional rights of the place. It may be a reflection on human nature that such devices should be necessary to control the abuses of government. But what is government itself but the greatest of all reflections on human nature? If men were angels, no government would be necessary. If angels were to govern men, neither external nor internal controls on government would be necessary. In framing a government which is to be administered by men over men, the great difficulty lies in this: you must first enable the government to control the governed; and in the next place oblige it to control itself. A dependence on the people is, no doubt, the primary control on the government; but experience has taught mankind the necessity of auxiliary precautions.

This policy of supplying, by opposite and rival interests, the defect of better motives, might be traced through the whole system of human affairs, private as well as public. We see it particularly displayed in all the subordinate distributions of power, where the constant aim is to divide and arrange the several offices in such a manner as that each may be a check on the other—that the private interest of every individual may be a sentinel over the public rights. These inventions of prudence cannot be less requisite in the distribution of the supreme powers of the State.

Madison now addresses the issue of equality among the branches of government. The legislature will necessarily predominate, but if the executive is given an "absolute negative" (absolute veto power) over legislative actions, this also could lead to an abuse of power. Madison concludes that the division of the legislature into two "branches" (parts, or chambers) will act as a check on the legislature's powers.

But it is not possible to give to each department an equal power of self-defense. In republican government, the legislative authority necessarily predominates. The remedy for this inconveniency is to divide the legislature into different branches; and to render them, by different modes of election and different principles of action, as little connected with each other as the nature of their common functions and their common dependence on the society will admit. It may even be necessary to guard against dangerous encroachments by still further precautions. As the weight of the legislative authority requires that it should be thus divided, the weakness of the executive may require, on the other hand, that it should be fortified. An absolute negative on the legislature appears, at first view, to be the natural defense with which the executive magistrate should be armed. But perhaps it would be neither altogether safe nor alone sufficient. On ordinary occasions it might not be exerted with the requisite firmness, and on extraordinary occasions it might be perfidiously abused. May not this defect of an absolute negative be supplied by some qualified connection between this weaker department and the weaker branch of the stronger department, by which the latter may be led to support the constitutional rights of the former, without being too much detached from the rights of its own department?

If the principles on which these observations are founded be just, as I persuade myself they are, and they be applied as a criterion to the several State constitutions, and to the federal Constitution, it will be found that if the latter does not perfectly correspond with them, the former are infinitely less able to bear such a test.

In the remainder of the essay, Madison discusses how a federal system of government, in which powers are divided between the states and the national government, offers "double security" against tyranny.

There are, moreover, two considerations particularly applicable to the federal system of America, which place that system in a very interesting point of view.

First. In a single republic, all the power surrendered by the people is submitted to the administration of a single government; and the usurpations are guarded against by a division of the government into distinct and separate departments. In the compound republic of America, the power surrendered by the people is first divided between two distinct governments, and then the portion allotted to each subdivided among distinct and separate departments. Hence a double security arises to the rights of the people. The different governments will control each other, at the same time that each will be controlled by itself.

Second. It is of great importance in a republic not only to guard the society against the oppression of its rulers, but to guard one part of the society against the injustice of the other part. Different interests necessarily exist in different classes of citizens. If a majority be united by a common interest, the rights of the minority will be insecure. There are but two methods of providing against this evil: the one by creating a will in the community independent of the majority—that is, of the society itself; the other, by comprehending in the society so many separate descriptions of citizens as will render an unjust combination of a majority of the whole very improbable, if not impracticable. The first method prevails in all governments possessing an hereditary or self-appointed authority. This, at best, is but a precarious security; because a power independent of the society may as well espouse the unjust views of the major as the rightful interests of the minor party, and may possibly be turned against both parties. The second method will be exemplified in the federal republic of the United States. Whilst all authority in it will be derived from and dependent on the society, the society itself will be broken into so many parts, interests and classes of citizens, that the rights of individuals, or of the minority, will be in little danger from interested combinations of the majority. In a free government the security for civil rights must be the same as that for religious rights. It consists in the one case in the multiplicity of interests, and in the other in the multiplicity of sects. The degree of security in both cases will depend on the number of interests and sects; and this may be presumed to depend on the extent of country and number of people comprehended under the same government. This view of the subject must particularly recommend a proper federal system to all the sincere and considerate friends of republican government, since it shows that in exact proportion as the territory of the Union may be formed into more circumscribed Confederacies, or States, oppressive combinations of a majority will be facilitated; the best security, under the republican forms, for the rights of every class of citizen, will be diminished; and consequently the stability and independence of some member of the government, the only other security, must be proportionally increased. Justice is the end of government. It is the end of civil society. It ever has been and ever will be pursued until it be obtained, or until liberty be lost in the pursuit. In a society under the forms of which the stronger faction can readily unite and oppress the weaker, anarchy may as truly be said to reign as in a state of nature, where the weaker individual is not secured against the violence of the stronger; and as, in the latter state, even the stronger individuals are prompted, by the uncertainty of their condition, to submit to a government which may protect the weak as well as themselves; so, in the former state, will the more powerful factions or parties be gradually induced, by a like motive, to wish for a government which will protect all parties, the weaker as well as the more powerful. It can be little doubted that if the State of Rhode Island was separated from the Confederacy and left to itself, the insecurity of rights under the popular form of government within such narrow limits would be displayed by such reiterated oppressions of factious majorities that some power altogether independent of the people would soon be called for by the voice of the very factions whose misrule had proved the necessity of it. In the extended republic of the United States, and among the great variety of interests, parties, and sects which it embraces, a coalition of a majority of the whole society could seldom take place on any other principles than those of justice and the general good; whilst there being thus less danger to a minor from the will of a major party, there must be less pretext, also, to provide for the security of the former, by introducing into the government a will not dependent on the latter, or, in other words, a will independent of the society itself. It is no less certain than it is important, notwithstanding the contrary opinions which have been entertained, that the larger the society, provided it lie within a practicable sphere, the more duly capable it will be of self-government. And happily for the republican cause, the practicable sphere may be carried to a very great extent by a judicious modification and mixture of the *federal principle*.

Publius
(James Madison)

Glossary

Actual Malice Either knowledge of a defamatory statement's falsity or a reckless disregard for the truth.

Advice and Consent Terms in the Constitution describing the U.S. Senate's power to review and approve treaties and presidential appointments.

Affirm To declare that a court ruling is valid and must stand.

Affirmative Action A policy in educational admissions or job hiring that gives special attention or compensatory treatment to traditionally disadvantaged groups in an effort to overcome present effects of past discrimination.

Agenda Setting Determining which public-policy questions will be debated or considered.

***Amicus Curiae* Brief** A brief (a document containing a legal argument supporting a desired outcome in a particular case) filed by a third party, or *amicus curiae* (Latin for "friend of the court"), who is not directly involved in the litigation but who has an interest in the outcome of the case.

Anti-Federalist An individual who opposed the ratification of the new Constitution in 1787. The Anti-Federalists were opposed to a strong central government.

Appellate Court A court having jurisdiction to review cases and issues that were originally tried in lower courts.

Appointment Power The authority vested in the president to fill a government office or position.

Appropriation The passage, by Congress, of a spending bill specifying the amount of authorized funds that actually will be allocated for an agency's use.

Aristocracy Rule by the "best"; in reality, rule by an upper class.

Arraignment The first act in a criminal proceeding, in which the defendant is brought before a court to hear the charges against him or her and enter a plea of guilty or not guilty.

Australian Ballot A secret ballot prepared, distributed, and tabulated by government officials at public expense. Since 1888, all states have used the Australian ballot rather than an open, public ballot.

Authoritarianism A type of regime in which only the government itself is fully controlled by the ruler. Social and economic institutions exist that are not under the government's control.

Authority The right and power of a government or other entity to enforce its decisions and compel obedience.

Authorization A formal declaration by a legislative committee that a certain amount of funding may be available to an agency. Some authorizations terminate in a year; others are renewable automatically without further congressional action.

"Beauty Contest" A presidential primary in which contending candidates compete for popular votes but the results do not control the selection of delegates to the national convention.

Bias An inclination or preference that interferes with impartial judgment.

Bicameral Legislature A legislature made up of two parts, called chambers. The U.S. Congress, composed of the House of Representatives and the Senate, is a bicameral legislature.

Bicameralism The division of a legislature into two separate assemblies.

Bill of Rights The first ten amendments to the U.S. Constitution.

Block Grant A federal grant that provides funds to state and local governments for general functional areas, such as criminal justice or mental-health programs.

Budget Deficit Government expenditures that exceed receipts.

Bureaucracy A large organization that is structured hierarchically to carry out specific functions.

Busing In the context of civil rights, the transportation of public school students from areas where they live to schools in other areas to eliminate school segregation based on residential patterns.

Cabinet An advisory group selected by the president to aid in making decisions. The cabinet includes the heads of fifteen executive departments and others named by the president.

Cabinet Department One of the fifteen major departments of the executive branch.

Capitalism An economic system characterized by the private ownership of wealth-creating assets, free markets, and freedom of contract.

Capture The act by which an industry being regulated by a government agency gains direct or indirect control over agency personnel and decision makers.

Case Law Judicial interpretations of common law principles and doctrines, as well as interpretations of constitutional law, statutory law, and administrative law.

Casework Personal work for constituents by members of Congress.

Categorical Grant A federal grant to states or local governments for specific programs or projects.

Caucus A meeting of party members designed to select candidates and propose policies.

Checks and Balances A major principle of the American system of government whereby each branch of the government can check the actions of the others.

Chief Diplomat The role of the president in recognizing foreign governments, making treaties, and effecting executive agreements.

Chief Executive The role of the president as head of the executive branch of the government.

Chief Legislator The role of the president in influencing the making of laws.

Chief of Staff The person who is named to direct the White House Office and advise the president.

Civil Disobedience A nonviolent, public refusal to obey allegedly unjust laws.

Civil Liberties Those personal freedoms, including freedom of religion and of speech, that are protected for all individuals in a society.

Civil Rights Generally, all rights rooted in the Fourteenth Amendment's guarantee of equal protection under the law.

Civil Service A collective term for the body of employees working for the government. Generally, civil service is understood to apply to all those who gain government employment through a merit system.

Civil Service Commission The initial central personnel agency of the national government; created in 1883.

Class-Action Suit A lawsuit filed by an individual seeking damages for "all persons similarly situated."

Clear and Present Danger Test The test proposed by Justice Oliver Wendell Holmes for determining when government may restrict free speech. Restrictions are permissible only when speech presents a "clear and present danger" to the public order.

Closed Primary A type of primary in which the voter is limited to choosing candidates of the party of which he or she is a member.

Coattail Effect The influence of a popular candidate on the electoral success of other candidates on the same party ticket. The effect is increased by the party-column ballot, which encourages straight-ticket voting.

Cold War The ideological, political, and economic confrontation between the United States and the Soviet Union following World War II.

Commander in Chief The role of the president as supreme commander of the military forces of the United States and of the state National Guard units when they are called into federal service.

Commerce Clause The section of the Constitution in which Congress is given the power to regulate trade among the states and with foreign countries.

Commercial Speech Advertising statements, which increasingly have been given First Amendment protection.

Common Law Judge-made law that originated in England from decisions shaped according to prevailing custom. Decisions were applied to similar situations and gradually became common to the nation.

Concurrent Powers Powers held jointly by the national and state governments.

Concurring Opinion A separate opinion prepared by a judge who supports the decision of the majority of the court but for different reasons.

Confederal System A system consisting of a league of independent states, each having essentially sovereign powers. The central government created by such a league has only limited powers over the states.

Confederation A political system in which states or regional governments retain ultimate authority except for those powers they expressly delegate to a central government.

Conference Committee A special joint committee appointed to reconcile differences when bills pass the two chambers of Congress in different forms.

Consensus General agreement among the citizenry on an issue.

Consent of the People The idea that governments and laws derive their legitimacy from the consent of the governed.

Conservatism A set of beliefs that includes advocacy of a limited role for the national government in helping individuals, support for traditional values and lifestyles, and a cautious response to change.

Constituent One of the persons represented by a legislator or other elected or appointed official.

Constitutional Power A power vested in the president by Article II of the Constitution.

Containment A U.S. diplomatic policy adopted by the Truman administration to contain Communist power within its existing boundaries.

Continuing Resolution A temporary funding law that Congress passes when an appropriations bill has not been passed by the beginning of the new fiscal year on October 1.

Cooperative Federalism A model of federalism in which the states and the national government cooperate in solving problems.

Corrupt Practices Acts A series of acts passed by Congress in an attempt to limit and regulate the size and sources of contributions and expenditures in political campaigns.

Credentials Committee A committee used by political parties at their national conventions to determine which delegates may participate. The committee inspects the claim of each prospective delegate to be seated as a legitimate representative of his or her state.

D

De Facto **Segregation** Racial segregation that occurs because of patterns of racial residence and similar social conditions.

De Jure **Segregation** Racial segregation that occurs because of laws or administrative decisions by public agencies.

Defamation of Character Wrongfully hurting a person's good reputation.

Defense Policy A subset of national security policy concerning the U.S. armed forces.

Democracy A system of government in which political authority is vested in the people.

Democratic Party One of the two major American political parties evolving out of the Republican Party of Thomas Jefferson.

Democratic Republic A republic in which representatives elected by the people make and enforce laws and policies.

Détente A French word meaning a relaxation of tensions. The term characterized U.S.-Soviet relations as they developed under President Richard Nixon and Secretary of State Henry Kissinger.

Devolution The transfer of powers from a national or central government to a state or local government.

Diplomacy The process by which states carry on political relations with each other; the process of settling conflicts among nations by peaceful means.

Diplomatic Recognition The formal acknowledgment of a foreign government as legitimate.

Direct Democracy A system of government in which political decisions are made by the people directly, rather than by their elected representatives.

Direct Primary A primary election in which voters decide party nominations by voting directly for candidates.

Direct Technique An interest group technique that uses direct interaction with government officials to further the group's goals.

Discharge Petition A procedure by which a bill in the House of Representatives may be forced (discharged) out of a committee that has refused to report it for consideration by the House. The petition must be signed by an absolute majority (218) of representatives and is used only on rare occasions.

Dissenting Opinion A separate opinion in which a judge dissents from (disagrees with) the conclusion reached by the majority on the court and expounds his or her own views about the case.

Diversity of Citizenship The condition that exists when the parties to a lawsuit are from different states or when the suit involves a U.S. citizen and a government or citizen of a foreign country. Diversity of citizenship can provide a basis for federal jurisdiction.

Divided Government A situation in which one major political party controls the presidency and the other controls Congress or in which one party controls a state governorship and the other controls the state legislature.

Divided Opinion Public opinion that is polarized between two quite different positions.

Domestic Policy All government laws, planning, and actions that concern internal issues of national importance, such as poverty, crime, and the environment.

Dominant Culture The values, customs, and language established by the group or groups that traditionally have controlled politics and government in a society.

Dual Federalism A model of federalism that looks on national and state governments as co-equal sovereign powers. Neither the state government nor the national government should interfere in the other's sphere.

E

Earmarks Special provisions in legislation to set aside funds for projects that have not passed an impartial evaluation by agencies of the executive branch. Also known as pork.

Economic Aid Assistance to other nations in the form of grants, loans, or credits to buy the assisting nation's products.

Elastic Clause, or Necessary and Proper Clause The clause in Article I, Section 8, that grants Congress the power to do whatever is necessary to execute its specifically delegated powers.

Elector A member of the electoral college, which selects the president and vice president. Each state's electors are chosen in each presidential election year according to state laws.

Electoral College A group of persons, called electors, who are selected by the voters in each state. This group officially elects the president and the vice president of the United States.

Elite Theory A perspective holding that society is ruled by a small number of people who exercise power to further their self-interest.

Emergency Power An inherent power exercised by the president during a period of national crisis.

Enabling Legislation A statute enacted by Congress that authorizes the creation of an administrative agency and specifies the name, purpose, composition, functions, and powers of the agency being created.

Enumerated Power A power specifically granted to the national government by the Constitution. The first seventeen clauses of Article I, Section 8, specify most of the enumerated powers of Congress.

Equality As a political value, the idea that all people are of equal worth.

Era of Good Feelings The years from 1817 to 1825, when James Monroe was president and there was, in effect, no political opposition.

Establishment Clause The part of the First Amendment prohibiting the establishment of a church officially supported by the national government.

Exclusionary Rule A judicial policy prohibiting the admission at trial of illegally seized evidence.

Executive Agreement An international agreement made by the president, without senatorial ratification, with the head of a foreign state.

Executive Budget The budget prepared and submitted by the president to Congress.

Executive Office of the President (EOP) An organization established by President Franklin D. Roosevelt to assist the president in carrying out major duties.

Executive Order A rule or regulation issued by the president that has the effect of law.

Executive Privilege The right of executive officials to withhold information from, or to refuse to appear before, a legislative committee.

Expressed Power A power of the president that is expressly written into the Constitution or into statutory law.

F

Faction A group or bloc in a legislature or political party acting in pursuit of some special interest or position.

Fall Review The annual process in which the Office of Management and Budget, after receiving formal federal agency requests for funding for the next fiscal year, reviews the requests, makes changes, and submits its recommendations to the president.

Federal Mandate A requirement in federal legislation that forces states and municipalities to comply with certain rules.

Federal Open Market Committee The most important body within the Federal Reserve System. The Federal Open Market Committee decides how monetary policy should be carried out.

Federal Question A question that has to do with the U.S. Constitution, acts of Congress, or treaties. A federal question provides a basis for federal jurisdiction.

Federal Register A publication of the U.S. government that prints executive orders, rules, and regulations.

Federal Reserve System (the Fed) The system created by Congress in 1913 to serve as the nation's central banking organization.

Federalist An individual who was in favor of the adoption of the U.S. Constitution and the creation of a federal union with a strong central government.

Feminism The movement that supports political, economic, and social equality for women.

Fertility Rate A statistic that measures the average number of children that women in a given group are expected to have over the course of a lifetime.

Filibuster The use of the Senate's tradition of unlimited debate as a delaying tactic to block a bill.

First Budget Resolution A resolution passed by Congress in May that sets overall revenue and spending goals for the following fiscal year.

Fiscal Policy The federal government's use of taxation and spending policies to affect overall business activity.

Fiscal Year (FY) A twelve-month period that is used for bookkeeping, or accounting, purposes. Usually, the fiscal year does not coincide with the calendar year. For example, the federal government's fiscal year runs from October 1 through September 30.

Focus Group A small group of individuals who are led in discussion by a professional consultant to gather opinions on, and responses to, candidates and issues.

Foreign Policy A nation's external goals and the techniques and strategies used to achieve them.

Foreign Policy Process The steps by which foreign policy goals are decided and acted on.

Franchise The right to vote.

Franking A policy that enables members of Congress to send material through the mail by substituting their facsimile signature (frank) for postage.

Free Exercise Clause The provision of the First Amendment guaranteeing the free exercise of religion.

Front-Loading The practice of moving presidential primary elections to the early part of the campaign to maximize the impact of these primaries on the nomination.

Front-Runner The presidential candidate who appears to be ahead at a given time in the primary season.

G

Gag Order An order issued by a judge restricting the publication of news about a trial or a pretrial hearing to protect the accused's right to a fair trial.

Gender Discrimination Any practice, policy, or procedure that denies equality of treatment to an individual or to a group because of gender.

Gender Gap The difference between the percentage of women who vote for a particular candidate and the percentage of men who vote for the candidate.

General Election An election, normally held on the first Tuesday in November, that determines who will fill various elected positions.

General Jurisdiction Exists when a court's authority to hear cases is not significantly restricted. A court of general jurisdiction normally can hear a broad range of cases.

Generational Effect A long-lasting effect of the events of a particular time on the political opinions of those who came of political age at that time.

Gerrymandering The drawing of legislative district boundary lines for the purpose of obtaining partisan or factional advantage. A district is said to be gerrymandered when its shape is manipulated by the dominant party to maximize electoral strength at the expense of the minority party.

Government The preeminent institution within a society. Government has the ultimate authority to decide how conflicts will be resolved and how benefits and privileges will be allocated.

Government Corporation An agency of government that administers a quasi-business enterprise. These corporations are used when the activities to be performed are primarily commercial.

Government in the Sunshine Act A law that requires all committee-directed federal agencies to conduct their business regularly in public session.

Grandfather Clause A device used by southern states to disenfranchise African Americans. It restricted voting to those whose grandfathers had voted before 1867.

Great Compromise The compromise between the New Jersey and Virginia plans that created one chamber of the Congress based on population and one chamber representing each state equally; also called the Connecticut Compromise.

Gross Domestic Product (GDP) The value of all final goods and services produced in a country in a one-year period.

H

Hatch Act An act passed in 1939 that restricted the political activities of government employees. It also prohibited a political group from spending more than $3 million in any campaign and limited individual contributions to a campaign committee to $5,000.

Head of State The role of the president as ceremonial head of the government.

Hispanic Someone who can claim a heritage from a Spanish-speaking country. Hispanics may be of any race.

I

Impeachment An action by the House of Representatives to accuse the president, vice president, or other civil officers of the United States of committing "Treason, Bribery, or other high Crimes and Misdemeanors."

Incorporation Theory The view that most of the protections of the Bill of Rights apply to state governments through the Fourteenth Amendment's due process clause.

Independent A voter or candidate who does not identify with a political party.

Independent Executive Agency A federal agency that is not part of a cabinet department but reports directly to the president.

Independent Expenditures Unregulated political expenditures by PACs, organizations, and individuals that are not coordinated with candidate campaigns or political parties.

Independent Regulatory Agency An agency outside the major executive departments charged with making and implementing rules and regulations.

Indirect Primary A primary election in which voters choose convention delegates, and the delegates determine the party's candidate in the general election.

Indirect Technique An interest group technique that uses third parties to influence government officials.

Inflation A sustained rise in the general price level of goods and services.

Inherent Power A power of the president derived from the statements in the Constitution that "the executive Power shall be vested in a President" and that the president should "take Care that the Laws be faithfully executed."

Initiative A procedure by which voters can propose a law or a constitutional amendment.

Institution An ongoing organization that performs certain functions for society.

Instructed Delegate A legislator who is an agent of the voters who elected him or her and who votes according to the views of constituents regardless of personal beliefs.

Intelligence Community The government agencies that gather information about the capabilities and intentions of foreign governments or that engage in covert actions.

Interest Group An organized group of individuals sharing common objectives who actively attempt to influence policymakers.

Iron Triangle A three-way alliance among legislators, bureaucrats, and interest groups to make or preserve policies that benefit their respective interests.

Isolationist Foreign Policy A policy of abstaining from an active role in international affairs or alliances, which characterized U.S. foreign policy toward Europe during most of the 1800s.

Issue Advocacy Advertising Advertising paid for by interest groups that support or oppose a candidate or a candidate's position on an issue without mentioning voting or elections.

Issue Network A group of individuals or organizations—which may consist of legislators and legislative staff members, interest group leaders, bureaucrats, scholars and other experts, and media representatives—that supports a particular policy position on a given issue.

J

Joint Committee A legislative committee composed of members from both chambers of Congress.

Judicial Activism A doctrine holding that the federal judiciary should take an active role by using its powers to check the activities of governmental bodies when those bodies exceed their authority.

Judicial Implementation The way in which court decisions are translated into action.

Judicial Restraint A doctrine holding that courts should defer to the decisions made by the elected representatives of the people in the legislative and executive branches.

Judicial Review The power of the Supreme Court and other courts to declare unconstitutional federal or state laws and other acts of government.

Jurisdiction The authority of a court to decide certain cases. Not all courts have the authority to decide all cases. Where a case arises and what its subject matter is are two jurisdictional issues.

Justiciable Controversy A controversy that is real and substantial, as opposed to hypothetical or academic.

Justiciable Question A question that may be raised and reviewed in court.

K

Keynesian Economics A school of economic thought that tends to favor active federal government policy-making to stabilize economy-wide fluctuations, usually by implementing discretionary fiscal policy.

Kitchen Cabinet The informal advisers to the president.

L

Labor Movement Generally, the economic and political expression of working-class interests; politically, the organization of working-class interests.

Latino An alternative to the term Hispanic that is preferred by many.

Lawmaking The process of establishing the legal rules that govern society.

Legislature A governmental body primarily responsible for the making of laws.

Legitimacy Popular acceptance of the right and power of a government or other entity to exercise authority.

Libel A written defamation of a person's character, reputation, business, or property rights.

Liberalism A set of beliefs that includes advocacy of positive government action to improve the welfare of individuals, support for civil rights, and tolerance for political and social change.

Libertarianism A political ideology based on skepticism or opposition toward most government activities.

Liberty The greatest freedom of the individual that is consistent with the freedom of other individuals in the society.

Limited Government A government with powers that are limited either through a written document or through widely shared beliefs.

Limited Jurisdiction Exists when a court's authority to hear cases is restricted to certain types of claims, such as tax claims or bankruptcy petitions.

Line Organization In the federal government, an administrative unit that is directly accountable to the president.

Line-Item Veto The power of an executive to veto individual lines or items within a piece of legislation without vetoing the entire bill.

Literacy Test A test administered as a precondition for voting, often used to prevent African Americans from exercising their right to vote.

Litigate To engage in a legal proceeding or seek relief in a court of law; to carry on a lawsuit.

Lobbyist An organization or individual that attempts to influence the passage, defeat, or content of legislation and the government's administrative decisions.

Logrolling An arrangement in which two or more members of Congress agree in advance to support each other's bills.

Loophole A legal method by which individuals and businesses are allowed to reduce the tax liabilities they owe to the government.

M

Madisonian Model A structure of government proposed by James Madison in which the powers of the government are separated into three branches: executive, legislative, and judicial.

Majoritarianism A political theory holding that in a democracy, the government ought to do what the majority of the people want.

Majority More than 50 percent.

Majority Leader of the House Elected by members of the majority party to foster cohesion and to act as a spokesperson for the majority party.

Majority Opinion A court opinion reflecting the views of the majority of the judges.

Majority Rule A basic principle of democracy asserting that the greatest number of citizens in any political unit should select officials and determine policies.

Media The channels of mass communication.

Medicaid A joint state-federal program that provides medical care to the poor (including indigent elderly persons in nursing homes). The program is funded out of general government revenues.

Medicare A federal health-insurance program that covers U.S. residents over the age of sixty-five. The costs are met by a tax on wages and salaries.

Merit System The selection, retention, and promotion of government employees on the basis of competitive examinations.

Minority Leader of the House The party leader elected by members of the minority party in the House.

Monetary Policy The utilization of changes in the amount of money in circulation to alter credit markets, employment, and the rate of inflation.

Monroe Doctrine A policy statement made by President James Monroe in 1823, which set out three principles: (1) European nations should not establish new colonies in the Western Hemisphere, (2) European nations should not intervene in the affairs of independent nations of the Western Hemisphere, and (3) the United States would not interfere in the affairs of European nations.

Moral Hazard The danger that protecting an individual or institution from the consequences of failure will encourage excessively risky behavior.

Moral Idealism A philosophy that views nations as normally willing to cooperate and to agree on moral standards for conduct.

N

National Committee A standing committee of a national political party established to direct and coordinate party activities between national party conventions.

National Convention The meeting held every four years by each major party to select presidential and vice-presidential candidates, write a platform, choose a national committee, and conduct party business.

National Health Insurance A plan under which the government provides basic health insurance to all citizens. In most such plans, the program is funded by taxes on wages or salaries.

National Security Council (NSC) An agency in the Executive Office of the President that advises the president on national security.

National Security Policy Foreign and domestic policy designed to protect the nation's independence and political and economic integrity; policy that is concerned with the safety and defense of the nation.

Nationalization The takeover of a business enterprise by the national government. Recently, the word has been used to describe temporary takeovers that are similar to bankruptcy proceedings.

Natural Rights Rights held to be inherent in natural law, not dependent on governments. John Locke stated that natural law, being superior to human law, specifies certain rights of "life, liberty, and property." These rights, altered to become "life, liberty, and the pursuit of happiness," are asserted in the Declaration of Independence.

Negative Constituents Citizens who openly oppose the government's policies.

Normal Trade Relations (NTR) Status A status granted through an international treaty by which each member nation must treat other members at least as well as it treats the country that receives its most favorable treatment. This status was formerly known as *most-favored-nation status.*

O

Obscenity Sexually offensive material. Obscenity can be illegal if it is found to violate a four-part test established by the United States Supreme Court.

Office of Management and Budget (OMB) A division of the Executive Office of the President. The OMB assists the president in preparing the annual budget, clearing and coordinating departmental agency budgets, and supervising the administration of the federal budget.

Office-Block, or Massachusetts, Ballot A form of general election ballot in which candidates for elective office are grouped together under the title of each office. It emphasizes voting for the office and the individual candidate, rather than for the party.

Oligarchy Rule by a few.

Ombudsperson A person who hears and investigates complaints by private individuals against public officials or agencies.

Open Primary A primary in which any registered voter can vote (but must vote for candidates of only one party).

Opinion The statement by a judge or a court of the decision reached in a case. The opinion sets forth the applicable law and details the reasoning on which the ruling was based.

Opinion Leader One who is able to influence the opinions of others because of position, expertise, or personality.

Opinion Poll A method of systematically questioning a small, selected sample of respondents who are deemed representative of the total population.

Oral Arguments The arguments presented in person by attorneys to an appellate court. Each attorney presents reasons to the court why the court should rule in her or his client's favor.

Order A state of peace and security. Maintaining order by protecting members of society from violence and criminal activity is the oldest purpose of government.

Oversight The process by which Congress follows up on laws it has enacted to ensure that they are being enforced and administered in the way Congress intended.

P

Pardon A release from the punishment for, or legal consequences of, a crime; a pardon can be granted by the president before or after a conviction.

Party Identification Linking oneself to a particular political party.

Party Identifier A person who identifies with a political party.

Party Organization The formal structure and leadership of a political party, including election committees; local, state, and national executives; and paid professional staff.

Party Platform A document drawn up at each national convention, outlining the policies, positions, and principles of the party.

Party-Column, or Indiana, Ballot A form of general election ballot in which all of a party's candidates for elective office are arranged in one column under the party's label and symbol. It emphasizes voting for the party, rather than for the office or individual.

Patronage The practice of rewarding faithful party workers and followers with government employment and contracts.

Peer Group A group consisting of members sharing common social characteristics. Such groups play an important part in the socialization process, helping to shape attitudes and beliefs.

Pendleton Act (Civil Service Reform Act) An act that established the principle of federal government employment based on merit and created the Civil Service Commission to administer the personnel service.

Pluralism A theory that views politics as a conflict among interest groups. Political decision making is characterized by bargaining and compromise.

Plurality A number of votes cast for a candidate that is greater than the number of votes for any other candidate but not necessarily a majority.

Pocket Veto A special veto exercised by the chief executive after a legislative body has adjourned. Bills not signed by the chief executive die after a specified period of time.

Police Power The authority to legislate for the protection of the health, morals, safety, and welfare of the people. In the United States, most police power is reserved to the states.

Political Action Committee (PAC) A committee set up by and representing a corporation, labor union, or special interest group. PACs raise campaign donations.

Political Consultant A paid professional hired to devise a campaign strategy and manage a campaign.

Political Culture The patterned set of ideas, values, and ways of thinking about government and politics that characterizes a people.

Political Ideology A comprehensive set of beliefs about the nature of people and the role of government.

Political Party A group of political activists who organize to win elections, operate the government, and determine public policy.

Political Question An issue that a court believes should be decided by the executive or legislative branch.

Political Realism A philosophy that views each nation as acting principally in its own interest.

Political Socialization The process by which people acquire political beliefs and values.

Political Trust The degree to which individuals express trust in the government and political institutions, usually measured through a specific series of survey questions.

Politics The struggle over power or influence within organizations or informal groups that can grant or withhold benefits or privileges.

Poll Tax A special tax that must be paid as a qualification for voting. The Twenty-fourth Amendment to the Constitution outlawed the poll tax in national elections, and in 1966, the Supreme Court declared it unconstitutional in state elections as well.

Popular Sovereignty The concept that ultimate political authority is based on the will of the people.

Precedent A court rule bearing on subsequent legal decisions in similar cases. Judges rely on precedents in deciding cases.

Preferred Stock A special share of ownership in a corporation that typically confers no right to vote for the company's board of directors, but does pay interest.

President Pro Tempore The senator who presides over the Senate in the absence of the vice president.

Presidential Primary A statewide primary election of delegates to a political party's national convention, held to determine a party's presidential nominee.

Primary Election An election in which political parties choose their candidates for the general election.

Prior Restraint Restraining an activity before it has actually occurred. When expression is involved, this means censorship.

Privatization The replacement of government services with services provided by private firms.

Progressive Tax A tax that rises in percentage terms as incomes rise.

Property Anything that is or may be subject to ownership. As conceived by the political philosopher John Locke, the right to property is a natural right superior to human law (laws made by government).

Public Agenda Issues that are perceived by the political community as meriting public attention and governmental action.

Public Debt, or National Debt The total amount of debt carried by the federal government.

Public Figures Public officials, movie stars, and other persons known to the public because of their positions or activities.

Public Interest The best interests of the overall community; the national good, rather than the narrow interests of a particular group.

Public Opinion The aggregate of individual attitudes or beliefs shared by some portion of the adult population.

R

Reapportionment The allocation of seats in the House of Representatives to each state after each census.

Recall A procedure allowing the people to vote to dismiss an elected official from office before his or her term has expired.

Recession An economic downturn, usually characterized by a fall in the GDP and rising unemployment.

Redistricting The redrawing of the boundaries of the congressional districts within each state.

Referendum An electoral device whereby legislative or constitutional measures are referred by the legislature to the voters for approval or disapproval.

Registration The entry of a person's name onto the list of registered voters for elections. To register, a person must meet certain legal requirements of age, citizenship, and residency.

Regressive Tax A tax that falls in percentage terms as incomes rise.

Remand To send a case back to the court that originally heard it.

Representation The function of members of Congress as elected officials representing the views of their constituents.

Representative Assembly A legislature composed of individuals who represent the population.

Representative Democracy A form of government in which representatives elected by the people make and enforce laws and policies, but in which the monarchy may be retained in a ceremonial role.

Reprieve A formal postponement of the execution of a sentence imposed by a court of law.

Republic A form of government in which sovereign power rests with the people, rather than with a king or a monarch.

Republican Party One of the two major American political parties. It emerged in the 1850s as an antislavery party and consisted of former northern Whigs and antislavery Democrats.

Reverse To annul or make void a court ruling on account of some error or irregularity.

Reverse Discrimination Discrimination against members of a majority group.

Rule of Four A United States Supreme Court procedure by which four justices must vote to grant a petition for review if a case is to come before the full court.

Rules Committee A standing committee of the House of Representatives that provides special rules under which specific bills can be debated, amended, and considered by the House.

S

Safe Seat A district that returns a legislator with 55 percent of the vote or more.

Sampling Error The difference between a sample result and the true result if the entire population had been interviewed.

Second Budget Resolution A resolution passed by Congress in September that sets "binding" limits on taxes and spending for the following fiscal year.

Select Committee A temporary legislative committee established for a limited time period and for a special purpose.

Senate Majority Leader The chief spokesperson of the majority party in the Senate, who directs the legislative program and party strategy.

Senate Minority Leader The party officer in the Senate who commands the minority party's opposition to the policies of the majority party and directs the legislative program and strategy of his or her party.

Senatorial Courtesy In federal district court judgeship nominations, a tradition allowing a senator to veto a judicial appointment in his or her state.

Seniority System A custom followed in both chambers of Congress specifying that the member of the majority party with the longest term of continuous service will be given preference when a committee chairperson (or a holder of some other significant post) is selected.

Separate-but-Equal Doctrine The doctrine holding that separate-but-equal facilities do not violate the equal protection clause of the Fourteenth Amendment to the U.S. Constitution.

Separation of Powers The principle of dividing governmental powers among different branches of government.

Service Sector The sector of the economy that provides services—such as health care, banking, and education—in contrast to the sector that produces goods.

Sexual Harassment Unwanted physical or verbal conduct or abuse of a sexual nature that interferes with a recipient's job performance, creates a hostile work environment, or carries with it an implicit or explicit threat of adverse employment consequences.

Signing Statement A written declaration that the president may make when signing a bill into law. It may contain instructions to the bureaucracy on how to administer the law or point to sections of the law that the president considers unconstitutional or contrary to national security interests.

Slander The public uttering of a false statement that harms the good reputation of another. The statement must be made to, or within the hearing of, someone other than the defamed party.

Social Contract A voluntary agreement among individuals to secure their rights and welfare by creating a government and abiding by its rules.

Social Movement A movement that represents the demands of a large segment of the public for political, economic, or social change.

Socialism A political ideology based on strong support for economic and social equality. Socialists traditionally envisioned a society in which major businesses were taken over by the government or by employee-cooperatives.

Socioeconomic Status The value assigned to a person due to occupation or income. An upper-class person, for example, has high socioeconomic status.

Soft Money Campaign contributions unregulated by federal or state law, usually given to parties and party committees to help fund general party activities.

Sound Bite A brief, memorable comment that can easily be fit into news broadcasts.

Soviet Bloc The Soviet Union and the Eastern European countries that installed Communist regimes after World War II and that were dominated by the Soviet Union.

Speaker of the House The presiding officer in the House of Representatives. The Speaker is chosen by the majority party and is the most powerful and influential member of the House.

Spin An interpretation of political events that is favorable to a candidate or officeholder.

Spin Doctor A political adviser who tries to convince journalists of the truth of a particular interpretation of events.

Splinter Party A new party formed by a dissident faction within a major political party. Often, splinter parties have emerged when a particular personality was at odds with the major party.

Spoils System The awarding of government jobs to political supporters and friends.

Spring Review The annual process in which the Office of Management and Budget requires federal agencies to review their programs, activities, and goals and submit their requests for funding for the next fiscal year.

Standing Committee A permanent committee in the House or Senate that considers bills within a certain subject area.

Stare Decisis To stand on decided cases; the judicial policy of following precedents established by past decisions.

State A group of people occupying a specific area and organized under one government; may be either a nation or a subunit of a nation.

State Central Committee The principal organized structure of each political party within each state. This committee is responsible for carrying out policy decisions of the party's state convention.

State of the Union Message An annual message to Congress in which the president proposes a legislative program. The message is addressed not only to Congress but also to the American people and to the world.

Statutory Power A power created for the president through laws enacted by Congress.

Straight-Ticket Voting Voting exclusively for the candidates of one party.

Strategic Arms Limitation Treaty (SALT I) A treaty between the United States and the Soviet Union to stabilize the nuclear arms competition between the two countries. SALT I talks began in 1969, and agreements were signed on May 26, 1972.

Suffrage The right to vote; a vote given in favor of a proposed measure, candidate, or the like.

Sunset Legislation Laws requiring that existing programs be reviewed regularly for their effectiveness and be terminated unless specifically extended as a result of these reviews.

Superdelegate A party leader or elected official who is given the right to vote at the party's national convention. Superdelegates are not elected at the state level.

Supremacy Clause The constitutional provision that makes the Constitution and federal laws superior to all conflicting state and local laws.

Supremacy Doctrine A doctrine that asserts the priority of national law over state laws. This principle is rooted in Article VI of the Constitution.

Symbolic Speech Expression made through articles of clothing, gestures, movements, and other forms of nonverbal communication.

T

Technical Assistance The practice of sending experts in such areas as agriculture, engineering, or business to aid other nations.

Theocracy Literally, rule by God or the gods; in practice, rule by religious leaders, typically self-appointed.

Third Party A political party other than the two major political parties (Republican and Democratic).

Ticket Splitting Voting for candidates of two or more parties for different offices. For example, a voter splits her ticket if she votes for a Republican presidential candidate and for a Democratic congressional candidate.

Totalitarian Regime A form of government that controls all aspects of the political and social life of a nation.

Tracking Poll A poll taken for the candidate on a nearly daily basis as Election Day approaches.

Trial Court The court in which most cases begin.

Truman Doctrine The policy adopted by President Harry Truman in 1947 to halt Communist expansion in southeastern Europe.

Trustee A legislator who acts according to her or his conscience and the broad interests of the entire society.

Twelfth Amendment An amendment to the Constitution, adopted in 1804, that specifies the separate election of the president and vice president by the electoral college.

Twenty-fifth Amendment A 1967 amendment to the Constitution that establishes procedures for filling presidential and vice-presidential vacancies and makes provisions for presidential incapacity.

Two-Party System A political system in which only two parties have a reasonable chance of winning.

U

U.S. Treasury Securities Debt issued by the federal government.

Unanimous Opinion A court opinion or determination on which all judges agree.

Unemployment The inability of those who are in the labor force to find a job; the number of those in the labor force actively looking for a job, but unable to find one.

Unicameral Legislature A legislature with only one legislative chamber, as opposed to a bicameral (two chamber) legislature, such as the U.S. Congress. Today, Nebraska is the only state in the Union with a unicameral legislature.

Unit Rule A rule by which all of a state's electoral votes are cast for the presidential candidate who receives a plurality of the votes in that state.

Unitary System A centralized governmental system in which ultimate governmental authority rests in the hands of the national, or central, government.

Universal Suffrage The right of all adults to vote for their representatives.

V

Veto Message The president's formal explanation of a veto, which accompanies the vetoed legislation when it is returned to Congress.

Vote-Eligible Population The number of people who, at a given time, enjoy the right to vote in national elections.

Voter Turnout The percentage of citizens taking part in the election process; the number of eligible voters who actually "turn out" on Election Day to cast their ballots.

Voting-Age Population   The number of people of voting age living in the country at a given time, regardless of whether they have the right to vote.

War Powers Resolution   A law passed in 1973 spelling out the conditions under which the president can commit troops without congressional approval.

Washington   Community   Individuals   regularly involved with politics in Washington, D.C.

Watergate Break-In   The 1972 illegal entry into the Democratic National Committee offices by participants in President Richard Nixon's reelection campaign.

Whig Party   A major party in the United States during the first half of the nineteenth century, formally established in 1836. The Whig Party was anti-Jackson and represented a variety of regional interests.

Whip   A member of Congress who aids the majority or minority leader of the House or the Senate.

Whistleblower   In the context of government, someone who brings gross governmental inefficiency or an illegal action to the public's attention.

White House Office   The personal office of the president, which tends to presidential political needs and manages the media.

White Primary   A state primary election that restricts voting to whites only; outlawed by the Supreme Court in 1944.

Writ of *Certiorari*   An order issued by a higher court to a lower court to send up the record of a case for review.

Writ of *Habeas Corpus*   *Habeas corpus* means, literally, "you have the body." A writ of *habeas corpus* is an order that requires jailers to bring a prisoner before a court or judge and explain why the person is being held.

Index